1 MONTH OF
FREE
READING

at

www.ForgottenBooks.com

By purchasing this book you are eligible for one month membership to ForgottenBooks.com, giving you unlimited access to our entire collection of over 1,000,000 titles via our web site and mobile apps.

To claim your free month visit:

www.forgottenbooks.com/free1122810

ISBN 978-0-331-43010-3
PIBN 11122810

United States
Circuit Court of Appeals
For the Ninth Circuit. ✓

D. W. JOHNSTON, as Trustee in Bankruptcy
of the Estate of DUPONT MILLING &
SALES CORPORATION, Bankrupt,

> Appellant,

vs.

JOHN P. McLAUGHLIN, Collector of Internal
Revenue,

> Appellee.

Transcript of Record.

Upon Appeal from the United States District Court for the
Northern District of California, Southern Division.

FILED

SEP 23 1931

PAUL P. O'BRIEN,
CLERK

Filmer Bros. Co. Print, 330 Jackson St., S. F., Cal.

United States
Circuit Court of Appeals
For the Ninth Circuit.

D. W. JOHNSTON, as Trustee in Bankruptcy of the Estate of DUPONT MILLING & SALES CORPORATION, Bankrupt,

Appellant,

vs.

JOHN P. McLAUGHLIN, Collector of Internal Revenue,

Appellee.

Transcript of Record.

Upon Appeal from the United States District Court for the Northern District of California, Southern Division.

Filmer Bros Co. Print, 330 Jackson St., S. F., Cal.

INDEX TO THE PRINTED TRANSCRIPT OF RECORD.

[Clerk's Note: When deemed likely to be of an important nature, errors or doubtful matters appearing in the original certified record are printed literally in italic; and, likewise, cancelled matter appearing in the original certified record is printed and cancelled herein accordingly. When possible, an omission from the text is indicated by printing in italic the two words between which the omission seems to occur.]

NAMES AND ADDRESSES OF ATTORNEYS OF RECORD.

CHAS. H. SOOY, Esq., Mills Bldg., San Francisco, Calif.,

NEIL E. LARKIN, Esq., 155 Montgomery St., San Francisco, Calif.,

FITZGERALD, ABBOTT & BEARDSLEY, Esq., Central Bank Bldg., Oakland, Calif.,

BROBECK, PHLEGER & HARRISON, Esqs., Crocker Bldg., San Francisco, Calif.,

MILTON NEWMARK, Esq., Crocker Bldg., San Francisco, Calif.,

Attorneys for Plaintiff and Appellant.

GEORGE J. HATFIELD, United States Attorney, 7th & Mission Sts., San Francisco, Calif.

ESTHER B. PHILLIPS, Assistant United States Attorney, 7th & Mission Sts., San Francisco, Calif.

————

District Court of the United States, Northern District of California, Southern Division.

No. 18,680–S.

CIVIL SUIT TO RECOVER TAXES PAID.

D. W. JOHNSTON, as Trustee in Bankruptcy of the Estate of DuPONT MILLING & SALES CORPORATION, a Bankrupt,

Plaintiff,

vs.

JOHN P. McLAUGHLIN, Collector of Internal Revenue,

Defendant.

COMPLAINT.

Comes now the above-named plaintiff and complains of above-named defendant, and for cause of action against said defendant alleges:

I.

That defendant is and at all times herein mentioned was the duly appointed, qualified and acting Collector of Internal Revenue of the United States for the First District of California.

II.

That DuPont Milling and Sales Corporation is and at all times herein mentioned was, a corporation organized and existing under and by virtue of the laws of the State of California.

III.

That in the month of December, 1929, the said DuPont Milling and Sales Corporation filed its voluntary petition in bankruptcy with the Clerk of the above-entitled court; that thereafter, pursuant to proceedings in said court in the cause therein entitled "In the Matter of the DuPont Milling and Sales Company, a Bankrupt, No. 18,735–K," said corporation [1*] was adjudicated a bankrupt; that thereafter, and on the 24th day of December, 1929, and in said proceedings, plaintiff was selected as trustee of said bankrupt estate, duly qualified as such, and ever since has been and now is the duly

---

*Page-number appearing at the foot of page of original certified Transcript of Record.

elected, qualified and acting trustee of the estate of said bankrupt.

IV.

That from and after the date of its incorporation, to wit, January, 1925, and until April 1, 1929, said DuPont Milling and Sales Corporation had and maintained its principal place of business at the City and County of San Francisco, State of California, and during said time was engaged in the milling of rice and other commercial pursuits in said city and state; that during all of said time one Paul A. DuPont was the President of said corporation, and as such actively managed and controlled all the business and affairs of said corporation.

V.

That on or about March 15, 1928, said Paul A. DuPont as president of said corporation, made, signed, acknowledged and filed a return of purported net income of said corporation for the preceding year; that said return set forth as said net income of said corporation the sum of $12,448.72; that pursuant to the provisions of the Revenue Act of the United States of 1926, an income tax amounting to $1410.58 was thereafter levied by the defendant upon said purported net income, and said last-named sum was thereafter paid by said corporation to said defendant upon the following dates and in the following amounts:

March 15, 1928	$352.65
June 15, 1928	352.65
September 15, 1928	352.64
December 15, 1928	352.64 [2]

VI.

That said return and the statements therein made by said Paul A. DuPont are and were at the time of the making thereof, false and fraudulent, in that the said corporation had no net income and did not make any profit whatsoever during the year 1927, but on the contrary thereof, and in truth and in fact said corporation suffered and took a net loss during said year and was not liable for any tax upon any income for said year; that if the true facts had been stated in said return no tax liability would have accrued against said corporation, and said sum of $1410.58 would not have been paid by said corporation or collected by defendant.

VII.

That after said 15th day of December, 1928, and before the commencement of this action, a claim for refund of said taxes, so as aforesaid paid to the defendant, was filed with the defendant as Collector of Internal Revenue as aforesaid, demanding a refund and repayment of said sum of $1410.-58, together with interest thereon at the rate of 6 per cent per annum from the dates and upon the amounts of said payments as aforesaid; that neither said sum nor any part thereof has been repaid; that said claim for refund has never been allowed by the defendant as Collector as aforesaid, but upon the contrary has been by him rejected and payment thereof refused.

VIII.

That at the time of the making of said return and said payments, said corporation was insolvent and was largely indebted to persons, firms and corporations who are now creditors of said bankrupt estate; that there are not sufficient funds or property in said bankrupt estate to pay the claims proved against and now a charge against said [3] bankrupt estate, including the claim of the creditors aforesaid.

IX.

That the defendant has now the said sum of $1410.58 so received by him as aforesaid, and holds the same for the use and benefit of the plaintiff.

WHEREFORE plaintiff prays judgment against said defendant in the sum of $1410.58, together with interest thereon at the rate of 6 per cent per annum from the respective dates of said payments as aforesaid.

CHARLES H. SOOY.

CHARLES H. SOOY,

NEIL LARKIN.

NEIL LARKIN,

FITZGERALD, ABBOTT & BEARDSLEY.

FITZGERALD, ABBOTT & BEARDSLEY,

BROBECK PHLEGER & HARRISON.

BROBECK PHLEGER & HARRISON, .

MILTON NEWMARK,

MILTON NEWMARK,

Attorneys for Plaintiff. [4]

United States of America,

State of California,

City and County of San Francisco,—ss.

D. W. Johnston, being first duly sworn, deposes and says:

That he is the Trustee in Bankruptcy of the Estate of DuPont Milling and Sales Corporation, a Bankrupt, and the plaintiff in the above-entitled action; that he has read the foregoing complaint and knows the contents thereof; that the same is true of his own knowledge, except as to those matters which are therein stated on information or belief, and as to those matters, that he believes it to be true.

D. W. JOHNSTON.
D. W. JOHNSTON.

Subscribed and sworn to before me this March 7th, 1930.

MARIE FORMAN.

[Seal]   MARIE FORMAN,

Notary Public in and for the City and County of San Francisco, State of California.

[Endorsed]: Filed Mar. 7, 1930.   [5]

[Title of Court and Cause.]

ANSWER.

Comes now the defendant, John P. McLaughlin, by his attorney, George J. Hatfield, United States Attorney for the Northern District of California, and for answer to the complaint in the above-entitled action, admits, denies and alleges as follows:

I.

Admits the matters and things in Paragraph I of said complaint.

II.

Admits the matters and things in Paragraph II of said complaint.

III.

Admits the matters and things in Paragraph III of said complaint.

IV.

Answering all the allegations contained in Paragraph IV of said complaint, the defendant admits that from and after the date of its incorporation, to wit, January, 1925, and until April 1, 1929, said DuPont Milling and Sales Corporation had and maintained its principal place of business at the City and County of San Francisco, State of California, and during said time was engaged in the milling of rice and other commercial pursuits in said City and State; admits that during all of said time one Paul A. DuPont was the president of said corporation, but denies, for lack of sufficient information to form a belief thereof, that said Paul A. DuPont actively managed and controlled all the business and affairs of said corporation.   [6]

V.

Answering all the allegations contained in Paragraph V of said complaint, the defendant admits same and alleges further that W. B. Thompson, who was treasurer of the said corporation during the calendar year 1927, joined with Paul A. DuPont, as president of said corporation, in the preparation, signing, acknowledgment, and filing of the said return of the DuPont Milling and Sales Corporation.

VI.

Answering the allegations contained in Paragraph VI of said complaint, the defendant denies each and every allegation contained therein for lack of sufficient information to form a belief thereof.

VII.

Answering the allegations contained in Paragraph VII of said complaint, the defendant admits all of same, and alleges further that said claim for refund was forwarded by the defendant to the Commissioner of Internal Revenue, and that said Commissioner, after due consideration of said claim, rejected same in its entirety on August 16, 1929.

VIII.

Answering the allegations contained in Paragraph VIII of said complaint, the defendant denies each and every allegation contained therein, for lack of sufficient information to form a belief thereof.

IX.

Answering the allegations contained in Paragraph IX of said complaint, the defendant denies each and every allegation contained therein. [7]

And for a further and separate defense, the defendant alleges:

1.   That on or about November 3, 1928, the Commissioner of Internal Revenue caused an examination to be made of the books and affairs of the DuPont Milling and Sales Corporation in connection with an audit of the income tax return filed by said

corporation for the calendar year 1927, and it was determined that said return was correct in all respects.

2. That on November 3, 1928, the plaintiff, Du-Pont Milling and Sales Corporation, by its then vice-president, Ralph D. Wilson, signed an "Agreement as to Final Determination of Tax liability"; that said agreement was completed on December 11, 1928, when same was signed by the then Commissioner of Internal Revenue, D. H. Blair, and approved by the Secretary of the Treasury, all in accordance with the provisions of Section 606 of the Revenue Act of 1928.

WHERE*FOR,* the defendant prays that the plaintiff take nothing by his action and that defendant have judgment for proper costs and for such other and further relief as may be just and proper in the premises.

GEO. J. HATFIELD,
United States Attorney,
Attorney for the Defendant.
By ESTHER B. PHILLIPS,
Asst. United States Attorney. [8]

United States of America,
Northern District of California,
City and County of San Francisco,—ss.

John P. McLaughlin, being first duly sworn, deposes and says:

That he is the Collector of Internal Revenue for the First District of California and the defendant in the above-entitled action; that he has read the foregoing answer and knows the contents thereof, and that the same is true of his own knowledge, except as to those matters therein stated to be alleged upon information and belief, and as to those matters he believes it to be true.

JOHN P. McLAUGHLIN.

Subscribed and sworn to before me this 2d day of April, 1930.

[Seal]   RAYMOND HASKINS,
Notary Public in and for the City and County of
San Francisco, State of California.

My commission expires Sept. 20, 1931.

Received April 4, 1930.

C. H. SOOY,
Atty. for Plaintiff.

[Endorsed]: Filed Apr. 9, 1930.   [9]

———

[Title of Court and Cause.]

AGREED STATEMENT OF FACTS.

It is hereby stipulated and agreed by and between the parties hereto, by their respective attorneys, that the following facts, together with the facts alleged in the complaint and admitted by the answer in this cause, shall be taken as true, without prejudice, however, to the right of either party to introduce other and further evidence not inconsistent with the facts herein stipulated to be true. It is further stipulated that this cause may be tried by the court sitting without a jury.

I.

That the Collector of Internal Revenue, defendant herein, accepted payment of income taxes from the DuPont Milling & Sales Corporation in the sum of $1,410.58, for the tax year 1927, as shown by said corporation's income tax return, with no knowledge of the facts reported in such return other than as they were therein stated.

II.

That said income tax return referred to in Paragraph I above, should have reflected a net loss for said year 1927 instead of a net income of $12,448.72 and upon which said net loss no income tax liability would have been due.

III.

That the books of account of the DuPont Milling & Sales Corporation had been intentionally prepared and kept under the direction of the president of said corporation, who owned and/or controlled more than majority of its corporate stock, in such manner as to conceal and for the purpose of concealing from those stockholders, directors and/or [10] creditors of the corporation, who were not acting in aid or assistance of him, the fact that the corporation had suffered a net loss for the year 1927.

IV.

That said income tax return for said year was likewise intentionally prepared in such way, and tax paid thereon, for the purpose of concealing from those stockholders, directors and creditors of the corporation, who were not acting in collusion with the president of the corporation, the fact that it had suffered a net loss for the year 1927.

V.

That after said return was filed, an Internal Revenue agent of San Francisco, acting in the usual course, made an audit of the DuPont Milling & Sales Company's books and tax return for 1927, approved the tax return and recommended that an agreement be entered into with said taxpayer for a final determination of its tax liability for the year 1927 and that he was in ignorance that the facts were other than as they appeared upon the return and in the books of the DuPont Milling & Sales Corporation.

VI.

That the Commissioner of Internal Revenue, acting upon the basis of the tax return, the audit and the report of the Internal Revenue agent at San Francisco, referred to above in Paragraph V, entered into an agreement with the taxpayer for a final determination of the tax, without knowledge that the facts were other than as they appeared in the return and upon the audit.

VII.

That a photostatic copy of the corporate income tax return of the DuPont Milling & Sales Corporation for the tax year 1927, marked Exhibit "A," [post, p. 21], being a true and correct   [11]   copy of the original as filed by said corporation with the defendant, is attached hereto and is hereby admitted in evidence is this cause by the parties.

VII.

That a photostatic copy of the agreement entered into by and between the DuPont Milling & Sales Corporation and the Commissioner of Internal Revenue, marked Exhibit "B," with a photostatic copy of the approval of the Secretary of the Treasury marked Exhibit "C," being true and correct copies of the originals of said documents now on file with the Commissioner of Internal Revenue, are attached hereto and are hereby admitted in evidence in this cause by the parties.

FITZGERALD, ABBOTT and BEARDSLEY,
BROBECK, PHLEGER & HARRISON,
            MILTON NEWMARK,
            C. H. SOOY,
            NEIL E. LARKIN,
                  Attorneys for Plaintiff.
            GEO. J. HATFIELD.
            GEO. J. HATFIELD,
                  U. S. Attorney.
            ESTHER B. PHILLIPS.
            ESTHER B. PHILLIPS,
                  Asst. U. S. Attorney,
            (Attorneys for Defendant).

Dated: Feby. 2d, 1931.

(Here follow Exhibits "A," "B" and "C.")

[Endorsed]: Filed Feb. 2, 1931.   [12]

[Title of Court and Cause.]

SUPPLEMENT TO AGREED STATEMENT OF FACTS.

It is hereby stipulated and agreed by and between the parties hereto by their respective attorneys that the following is true:

I.

That there are now in existence creditors of the DuPont Milling and Sales Corporation who were creditors of said Corporation as of March 15, 1928.

II.

That parts of the credits owing to these creditors at the present time are made up of credits owing to such creditors as of March 15, 1928.

III.

That this stipulation is made as a supplement to the agreed statement of facts heretofore filed in this case and may be deemed a part of it.

Dated Feb. 13, 1931.

   C. H. SOOY,
   NEIL E. LARKIN,
    (Attorneys for Plaintiff).
   GEO. J. HATFIELD,
   ESTHER B. PHILLIPS,
    (Attorneys for Defendant).

[Endorsed: Filed Feb. 13, 1931. [13]

In the Southern Division of the United States District Court, for the Northern District of California.

No. 18,680–S.

D. W. JOHNSTON, as Trustee in Bankruptcy of the Estate of DuPONT MILLING & SALES CORPORATION, a Bankrupt,

Plaintiff,

vs.

JOHN P. McLAUGHLIN, Collector of Internal Revenue,

Defendant.

JUDGMENT.

This cause having come on regularly for trial upon the 3d day of February, 1931, before the Court sitting without a jury, a trial by jury having been waived by oral stipulation; Neil E. Larkin, Esquire, appearing as attorney for plaintiff and Esther B. Phillips, Assistant United States Attorney, appearing as attorney for defendant, and oral and documentary evidence having been int*orudc*ed and closed, and the cause having been submitted to the Court for consideration and decision, and Court after due deliberation having rendered its decision and ordered that judgment be entered herein in favor of defendant and for costs:

Now, therefore, by virtue of the law and by reason of the premises aforesaid, it is considered by the Court that plaintiff take nothing by this action, and that defendant go hereof without day, and that said defendant do have and recover of and from said plaintiff his costs herein expended taxed at $15.00.

Judgment entered this 22d day of April, 1931.

WALTER B. MALING,

Clerk.   [14]

———

[Title of Court and Cause.]

BILL OF EXCEPTIONS.

BE IT REMEMBERED that on the 7th day of March, 1930, the above-entitled action was commenced by the filing of a complaint and the issuance of a summons; that thereafter and on or about the 4th day of April, 1930, the defendant appeared therein and filed his answer to said complaint.

AND BE IT FURTHER REMEMBERED that the above-entitled cause came on regularly for trial before the above-entitled court, sitting without a jury, a jury having been waived by both parties, on or about the 3d day of February, 1931, Honorable A. F. St. Sure, United States District Judge, presiding, Charles H. Sooy, Neil E. Larkin, Fitzgerald, Abbott & Beardsley, Brobeck, Phleger & Harrison and Milton Newmark appearing as attorneys for plaintiff and Geo. J. Hatfield, United States Attorney, and Esther B. Phillips, Assistant United States Attorney, appearing as attorneys for defendant, whereupon the following proceedings were had.

The parties thereupon made and filed the following stipulations in writing:

[Title of Court and Cause.]

AGREED STATEMENT OF FACTS.

It is hereby stipulated and agreed by and between the parties hereto by their respective attorneys, that the following facts, together with the facts alleged in the complaint and admitted by the answer in this cause, shall be taken as true, without prejudice, however, to the right of either party to introduce other and further evidence not inconsistent with the facts herein stipulated to be true. It is further stipulated that this cause may be tried by the   [15]   Court sitting without a jury.

I.

That the Collector of Internal Revenue, defendant herein, accepted payment of income taxes from the DuPont Milling & Sales Corporation in the sum of $1,410.58, for the tax year 1927, as shown by said corporation's income tax return, with no knowledge of the facts reported in such return other than as they were therein stated.

II.

That said income tax return referred to in Paragraph I above should have reflected a net loss for said year 1927 instead of a net income of $12,448.72 and upon which said net loss no income tax liability would have been due.

III.

That the books of account of the DuPont Milling

& Sales Corporation had been intentionally prepared and kept under the direction of the president
of said corporation, who owned and/or controlled
more than a majority of its corporate stock, in such
manner as to conceal and for the purpose of concealing from those stockholders, directors and/or
creditors of the corporation, who were not acting in
aid or assistance of him, the fact that the corporation had suffered a net loss for the year 1927.

IV.

That said income tax return for said year was
likewise intentionally prepared in such way, and
tax paid thereon, for the purpose of concealing from
those stockholders, directors and creditors of the
corporation, who were not acting in collusion with
the president of the corporation, the fact that it had
suffered a net loss for the year 1927.

V.

That after said return was filed, an Internal Rev-
enus [16] Agent at San Francisco, acting in the
usual course, made an audit of the DuPont Milling
& Sales Company's books and tax return for 1927,
approved the tax return and recommended that an
agreement be entered into with said taxpayer for
a final determination of its tax liability for the year
1927 and that he was in ignorance that the facts
were other than as they appeared upon the return
and in the books of the DuPont Milling & Sales Corporation.

VI.

That the Commissioner of Internal Revenue, acting upon the basis of the tax return, the audit and the report of the Internal Revenue agent at San Francisco, referred to above in Paragraph V, entered into an agreement with the taxpayer for a final determination of the tax, without knowledge that the facts were other than as they appeared in the return and upon the audit.

VII.

That a photostatic copy of the corporate income tax return of the DuPont Milling & Sales Corporation for the tax year 1927, marked Exhibit "A," being a true and correct copy of the original as filed by said corporation with the defendant, is attached hereto and is hereby admitted in evidence in this cause by the parties.

VIII.

That a photostatic copy of the agreement entered into by and between the DuPont Milling & Sales Corporation and the Commissioner of Internal Revenue, marked Exhibit "B," with a photostatic copy of the approval of the Secretary of the Treasury marked Exhibit "C," being true and correct copies of the originals of said documents now on file with the Commissioner of Internal Revenue, are attached hereto   [17]   and are hereby admitted in evidence in this cause by the parties.

CHARLES H. SOOY,

NEIL E. LARKIN,

FITZGERALD, ABBOTT & BEARDSLEY,

BROBECK, PHLEGER & HARRISON,

MILTON NEWMARK,

Attorneys for Plaintiff.

GEO. J. HATFIELD,

U. S. Attorney,

ESTHER B. PHILLIPS,

Asst. U. S. Attorney,

(Attorney for Defendant).

Dated: Feb. 2d, 1931.

[Title of Court and Cause.]

SUPPLEMENT TO AGREED STATEMENT FACTS.

It is hereby stipulated and agreed by and between the parties hereto by their respective attorneys that the following is true:

I.

That there are now in existence creditors of the Dupont Milling and Sales Corporation who were creditors of said corporation as of March 15, 1928.

II.

That part of the credits owing to these creditors at the present time are made up of credits owing to such creditors as of March 15, 1928.

III.

That this stipulation is made as a supplement to the agreed statement of facts heretofore filed in this case and   [18]   may be deemed a part of it.

A. H. SOOY,
NEIL E. LARKIN,
FITZGERALD, ABBOTT & BEARDSLEY,
BROBECK, PHLEGER & HARRISON,
MILTON NEWMARK,
Attorneys for Plaintiff.
GEO. J. HATFIELD,
U. S. Attorney,
ESTHER B. PHILLIPS.
Asst. U. S. Attorney,
(Attorneys for Defendant).

(Here follows Exhibit "A.")   [19]

EXHIBIT "A."

UNITED STATES OF AMERICA,
TREASURY DEPARTMENT,
WASHINGTON.

March 29, 1930.

PURSUANT to Section 882 of the Revised Statutes, I hereby certify that the annexed is a true copy of Corporation Income Tax Returns for 1927, (with schedules and Certificate of Inventory—(Form 1126 attached), filed by Du Pont Milling and Sales Corporation, San Francisco, California, the originals of which are on file in this Department.

IN WITNESS WHEREOF, I have hereunto set my hand, and caused the seal of the Treasury Department to be affixed, on the day and year first above written.

By direction of the Secretary:

[Seal]   F. A. BIRGFELD,
          Chief Clerk, Treasury Department.

MK   WWB   AMR   EEA   FFT   CMC

2

IN WITNESS WHEREOF, I have hereunto set my hand, and caused the seal of the Treasury Department to be affixed, on the day and year first above written.

In presence of the Secretary:

[Seal]

J. A. BIRGFELD,
Chief Clerk, Treasury Department.

BK WTD ABB EBA FFT CMC

CORPORATION INCOME TAX RETURN

1120

AU. REVENUE

ms, Oil and Gas Wells, Timber, etc. (submit analysis, see instruction 20)

s Not Reported Above. (Itemize below, or on separate sheet):

nd wages. (Not itemized in Item 3, 13, or 14 above)

for prior year. (Submit schedule)

	6 776 57		
	9 720 69		
	12 124 02		
	4 327 55		
		81 865 81	

, Deductions in Items 12 to 22

ncome (Item 11 minus Item 23) 12 448 72

COMPUTATION OF TAX

27.	12 448 72	28. Income Tax (13½% of Item 27)	1 410 58
m 24 above)		29. If the Net Income of a Domestic Corporation is Less Than	
,000 (for a domestic corporation having a	2 000 00	$25,270, Enter the Amount in Excess of $25,000	
less than $25,270)			
25 minus Item 26)	10 448 72	30. Total Tax (Item 28 plus Item 29)	1 410 58

ax Paid at Source. (This credit can only be allowed to a nonresident foreign corporation) ....

d Profits Taxes Paid to a Foreign Country or to a Possession of the United States by a domestic corporation ......

(Item 30 minus Items 31 and 32) 1 410 58

ided return must be marked "Amended" at top of return   Checks and drafts will be accepted only if payable

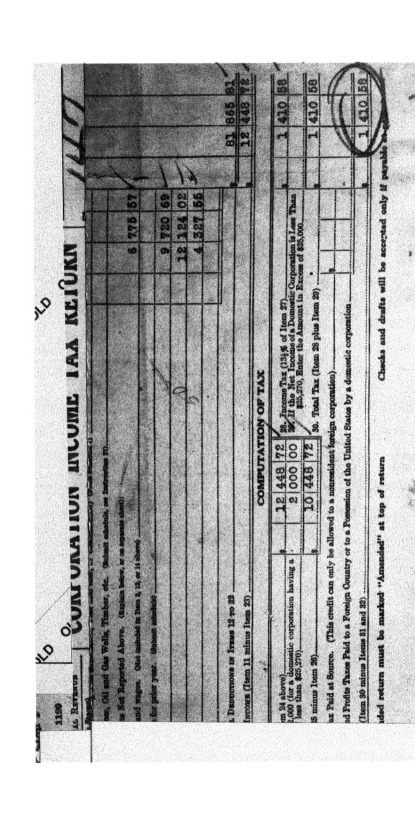

was acquired ....

ITEMS	AMOUNT	(Enter as Item 2e)
	$47672 87	$

SCHEDULE G—BAD [DEBTS]

	2. SALES ON ACCOUNT	3. BAD DEBTS
	$	$
		4534 06

SCHEDULE H—DIVIDENDS DEDUCTIBLE   (See Instruction 19)

1. NAME OF CORPORATION	AMOUNT OF DIVIDENDS	
	2. Domestic	3. Foreign
	$	$

SCHEDULE I—EXPLANATION OF DEDUCTION FOR DEPRECIATION   (See Instruction 20)

2. DATE ACQUIRED	3. AGE WHEN ACQUIRED	4. PROBABLE LIFE AFTER ACQUIREMENT	5. COST (Exclusive of Land)	6. VALUE AS OF MARCH 1, 1913 (Exclusive of Land)	AMOUNT OF DEPRECIATION CHARGED OFF	
					7. Previous years	8. This year
			$	$	$	$

Attach a separate sheet if any of the above schedules do not provide sufficient space

2—14448

ITEMS

ASSETS

1. Cash

2. Notes receivable

3. Accounts receivable

Less reserve for bad debts

4 Inventories:

Raw materials

Work in process

Finished goods

Supplies

5. Investments:

Obligations of a State, Territory, or any political subdivision thereof, or the District of Columbia

Securities issued under the Federal Farm Loan Act, or under such Act as amended

Obligations of the United St...

Items	Beginning of Taxable Year		End of Taxable Year	
(describe fully): ... for Insurance	60 00	$ 2 300 09	230 00	$ 7 195 71
		60 00		230 00
(describe fully): Acceptances	58 027 50	116 632 56	100 500 00	109 037 07
Sold	58 595 06		8 537 07	
(less stock in treasury)	182 620 00	182 620 00	185 600 00	185 600 00
(less stock in treasury)	2 017 04	2 017 04	2 715 79	2 715 79
LIABILITIES		$ 408 629 69		$ 519 590 77

1. Net income from Item 34, page 1 of the return................. $ 12,418.72

2. Nontaxable income:
   (a) Interest on obligations of a State, Territory, or any political subdivision thereof, or the District of Columbia............................
   (b) Interest on securities issued under the Federal Farm Loan Act, or under such Act as amended...................................
   (c) Interest on obligations of the United States (to possessions............
   (d) Dividends deductible under section 234(a) 6 of the Revenue Act of 1926....................................
   (e) Proceeds of life insurance policies paid upon the death of the insured............................
   (f) Other items of nontaxable income (to be detailed):
       (1)..
       (2)..
       (3)..

3. Charge against bad debts, if Item 18, page 1 of return, is not an addition to a reserve........................

4. Charge against reserves for contingencies, etc. (to be detailed):
   (a)..
   (b)..
   (c)..

5. Total of Lines 1 to 4, inclusive........................

6. Total from Line 14........................

7. Net profit for year as shown by books, before any adjustments are made therein (Line 5 minus Line 6)........................

8. Surplus and undivided profits as shown by balance sheet at close of preceding taxable year........................

9. Other credits to surplus (to be detailed):
   (a)..
   (b)..
   (c)..

10. Total of Lines 7 to 9, inclusive........................

11. Total from Line 17........................

12. Surplus and undivided profits as shown by balance sheet at close of taxable........................

13. Unallowable deductions:
    (a) Donations, gratuities, and contributions........................
    (b) Income and profits taxes paid to the United States, and so much of such taxes paid to its possessions or foreign countries as are claimed as a credit in Item 35, page 1 of the return........................
    (c) Federal taxes paid on tax-free covenant bonds........................
    (d) Special improvement taxes tending to increase the value of the property assessed........................
    (e) Furniture and fixtures, additions, or betterments treated as expense on the books........................
    (f) Replacements and renewals........................
    (g) Insurance premiums paid on the life of any officer or employee where the corporation is directly or indirectly a beneficiary........................
    (h) Interest on indebtedness incurred or continued to purchase or carry obligations or securities the interest upon which is wholly exempt from taxation........................
    (i) Additions to reserve for bad debts which are not included in Item 18, page 1 of return........................
    (j) Additions to reserves for contingencies, etc. (to be detailed):
        (1)..
        (2)..
        (3)..
    (2) Other unallowable deductions (to be detailed):
        (1)..
        (2)..
        (3)..

14. Total of Line 13........................
15. Dividends paid during the taxable year (state whether paid in cash, stock of the corporation, or other property):
    (a) Date paid 1-4-1927 Character Cash
    (b) Date paid 4-1-1927 Character "
    (c) Date paid 7-1-1927 Character "
    (d) Date paid 10-1-1927 Character "
16. Other debits to surplus (to be detailed):
    (a)..
    (b)..
    (c)..

17. Total of Lines 15 and 16........................

QUESTIONS

KIND OF BUSINESS

1. By means of the key letters given below, identify the corporation's main income-producing activity with one of the general classes, and follow this by a special description of the business sufficient to give the information called for under each general class.

A—Agriculture and related industries, including fishing, logging, ice harvesting, etc., and also the leasing of such property. State the product or products. B—Mining and quarrying, including gas and oil wells, and also the leasing of such property. State the product or products. C—Manufacturing. State the product and also the material if not implied by the name of the product. D—Construction-excavations, buildings, bridges, railroads, ships, etc., also equipping and installing same with systems, devices, or machinery, without their manufacture. State nature of structure built, materials used, or kind of installations. E1—Transportation-rail, water, local, etc. State the kind and special product transported, if any. E2—Public utilities—gas (natural, coal, or water); electric light or power (hydro or steam generated); heating (steam or hot water); telephone; waterworks or power. E3—Storage—without trading or profit from sales—(elevators, warehouses, stockyards, etc.). State product stored. E4—Leasing transportation or utilities. State kind of property. F—Trading in goods bought and not produced by the trading concern. State manner of trade, whether wholesale, retail, or commission, and product handled. Sales with storage with profit primarily from sales. G—Service—domestic, including hotels, restaurants, etc.; amusements; other professional, personal, or technical service. State the service. H—Finance, including banking, real estate, insurance. I—Concerns not falling in above classes (a) because of combining several of them with no predominant business, or (b) for other reasons.

2. Concerns whose business involves activity falling in two or more of the above general classes, where the same product is concerned, should report business as identified with but one of the above general classes; for example, concerns in A or B which also transport and market their own product exclusively or mainly, should still be identified with classes A or B; concerns in C (manufacturing) which own or control that source of material supply in A or B and which also transport, sell, or install their own product exclusively or mainly, should be identified with manufacturing; concerns in D may control or own the source of supply of materials used exclusively or mainly in their constructive work; concerns in E1 or E2 may own or control the source of their material or power; concerns in F may transport or store their own merchandise, but its production would identify them with A, B, or C.

3. Answers:
   (a) General class (use key letter designation)........................C
   (b) Main income-producing business (give specifically the information called for under each key letter, also whether acting as principal, or as agent on commission; state if inactive or in liquidation)........................
   ....
   ....
   ....

AFFILIATIONS WITH OTHER CORPORATIONS
SEE INSTRUCTION 34

4. Does the corporation own 95 per cent or more of the outstanding capital stock of another domestic corporation or of other corporations?........................No

5. Is over 95 per cent or more of your outstanding capital stock owned by another corporation?........................No

6. Is 95 per cent or more of your outstanding capital stock as well as 95 per cent or more of the outstanding capital stock of another corporation or of other corporations owned or controlled by the same individual or partnership or by the same individuals, partnerships, or corporations in substantially the same proportion?........................No

7. (a) Did the corporation file Forms 851, 852, 853, and 853A for the taxable year 1922 or subsequent taxable years?........................ If the answer to this question is "yes," these forms will not be required, except under the circumstances described in question (b). If the answer to this question is "no," and the answer to questions 4, 5, and 6, or to any of them, is "yes," procure from the Collector of Internal Revenue for your district Forms 851, 852, 853, and 853A, Affiliations Schedules 1, 2, 3, and 4, which shall be filled in and filed as a part of this return. If the answer to this question is "no," question (b) need not be answered.

(3) Did substantially the same conditions as set out in the Affiliations Schedules filed for 1926 or prior years, obtain during the entire taxable 1927? Yes. If the answer to this question is "no," a statement, setting the particulars in which the situation has changed, should be attached to and made a part of this return. If there have been substantial change in stockholdings a complete schedule of such changes should be submitted on Form 853, Affiliations Schedule 3. If there are companies other than those covered by the Affiliations Schedule for prior years which, applying the tests contained in questions 4, 5, or 6, have come into the affiliated group since 1926, Forms 851, 852, 853, and 853A, required for the entire group for the taxable year.

(e) Did the corporation file a consolidated return for the preceding year?........................

PREDECESSOR BUSINESS

8. Did the corporation file a return under the same name for the taxable year? Yes. Was the corporation in any way an outgrowth, continuation, or reorganization of a business or businesses in existence any prior year since December 31, 1917? Yes. If answer is "yes," give name and address of each predecessor business, and the date of the change:

Du Pont, Carleton & Co.

24 Bluxome St., San Francisco, Califor-

Upon such change were any asset values increased or decreased? the answer is "yes," closing balance sheets of old business and opening of new business must be furnished.

BASIS OF RETURN

9. Is this return made on the basis of actual receipts and disbursements? If not, describe fully what other basis or method was used in computing

1 Schedule covering Items 4 and 22

LIST OF ATTACHED SCHEDULES

10. Enter below a list of all schedules accompanying a brief title and the schedule number. The name and address be placed on each separate schedule accompanying the return.

....
....
....
....
....
....

LD

1. Net income from Item 24, page 1 of the return............ $ | 12,448 | 72
2. Nontaxable income:
   (a) Interest on obligations of a State, Territory, or any political sub-division thereof, or the District of Columbia....

12. Unallowable deductions:
   (a) Donations, gratuities, and contributions............
   (b) Income and profits taxes paid to the United States, and so much of such taxes paid to its possessions or foreign countries as are allowed as a credit in line 30 of the return........

AFFILIATIONS WITH OTHER CORPORATIONS

SEE INSTRUCTION 38

4. Does the corporation own 95 per cent or more of the outstanding capital stock of another domestic corporation or of other corporations? _____ NO

5. Is over 95 per cent or more of your outstanding capital stock owned by another corporation? _____ NO

6. Is 95 per cent or more of your outstanding capital stock as well as 95 per cent or more of the outstanding capital stock of another corporation or of other corporations owned or controlled by the same individual or partnership or by the same individuals, partnerships, or corporations in substantially the same proportion? NO

7. If the answer to questions 4, 5, and 6, or to any of them, is "yes," answer the following:

   (a) Did the corporation file Forms 851, 852, 853, and 853A for the taxable year 1922 or subsequent taxable year? _____ If the answer to this question is "yes," these forms will not be required, except under the circumstances described in question (b). If the answer to this question is "no," and the answer to questions 4, 5, and 6, or to any of them, is "yes," procure from the Collector of Internal Revenue for your district Forms 851, 852, 853, and 853A, Affiliations Schedules 1, 2, 3, and 4, which shall be filled in and filed as a part of this return. If the answer to this question is "no," question (b) need not be answered.

AFFIDAVIT

We, the undersigned, president and treasurer of the corporation for which this return is made, being severally duly sworn, each for himself depose and say that this return, including the accompanying schedules and statements, has been examined by him and is, 'o the best of his knowledge and belief, a true and correct return, made in good faith, for the taxable year as stated, pursuant to the Revenue Act of 1926 and the Regulations issued under authority thereof.

Sworn to and subscribed before me this _____ day of _____, 1923

NOTARIAL
SEAL

_____
(Signature of officer administering oath)

_____
(Title)

CORPORATE
SEAL

GOVERNMENT PRINTING OFFICE   2—14445

DU PONT MILLING & SALES CORPORATION
140 Front Street,
San Francisco California.

ITEM 4.

Mill Revenue $78713.08
Commissions 3834.78
Interest 1432.08
Miscellaneous 679.06
Storage 1806.35
Drayage ....×............ 8602.13
Hulls 1731.15
_____

$96798.63

* * * * * * * * * *

ITEM 22.

(c)

Insurance $3623.54
Telephone & Cables 3512.63
General 1522.00
Stationery 712.56
Legal 349.96 $9720.69
_____

(d)

Drayage $9053.77
Auto 816.20
Freight 2254.05 $12124.02
_____

(e)

Advertising $49.06
Travel 1637.89
Inspection Fees 151.50

D. W. Johnston vs.

Commissions 216.00
Miscellaneous 1207.15
Collections 1015.95
Charity 50.00 $4327.55
                                     ————

                                        A–5.

John P. McLaughlin.

—— 1126

J. S. Internal Revenue   CERTIFICATE OF INVENTORY

(To be filed with Collector of Internal Revenue with Income Tax Ret

For Calendar Year 1927

)r for fiscal year begun January 1, 1927, and ended December 31, 1927.

Jame—Du Pont Milling & Sales Corporation.

Address—140 Front Street, San Francisco, California.

Number of sh

PRINCIPAL CERTIFICATE   submitted her

I swear (or affirm) that the closing inventory of the taxpayer named abo
ng to $212369.22, was taken under my direction, and that to the best of my
.nd belief is true and complete in every respect; that the method of prici
aaterial, work in process, and finished goods was at *cost or market whiche
hat I have carefully read all of the instructions on the reverse side of
hat this inventory was taken in accordance therewith; and that the follo
iersons whose separate certificates are subscribed hereon or attached here
fficers and employees under whose personal direction the various parts of
ory were taken:

Name	Title or position	Part of inventory taken	
V. B. Thompson	Secretary	Rice & Rice Products	$1
?. C. Kearfott	Accountant	" " " "	$
ames W. Means	Supt. Feed Mill	Feed Products	$
Vm. P. Lapoint	Clerk	Misc. Mdse.	$
J. Toner	Asst. Book-keeper	" "	$
....			$
....			$

Sworn to and subscribed before me this 10 day of March, 1928.

W. B. THO

(Signat

M. Hugo   I. R. Agent   Secy-Treas

(Signature of officer administering óath)   (Title)   (Title)

*State "cost" or "cost or market, whichever is lower." If any other basi
escribe fully, state why used and date on which inventory was last reco
tock.

SUBSIDIARY CERTIFICATE

I (or we), the undersigned employees of the taxpayer named above,
ffirm) that I (or we) personally directed and observed the taking of the p
aventory set opposite my (or our) names, and, to the best of my (or our)
nd belief, is true and complete in every respect; that I (or we) have car
he instructions on the reverse side of this form and that the parts of th
or which I am (or we are) responsible was taken in accordance therewith.

Signature	Title or position	Part of invent
V. B. Thompson	Secretary	Rice & Rice Prod
?. C. Kearfott	Accountant	" " " '
ames W. Means	Supt. Feed Mill	Feed Products
Vm. P. Lapoint	Clerk	Misc. Mdse.
J. Toner	Asst. Book-keeper	" "
....		

Sworn to and subscribed before me this 10th day of March, 1928.

[Seal].

W. W. HEALEY,

(Signature of officer administerin

Notary Public in and for the City and County of San

(Title)

This certificate of inventory must be submitted by all taxpayers engaged in a trade or business in which the production, purchase, or sale of merchandise of any kind is an income-producing factor.

The principal certificate will be signed by the taxpayer or an executive officer and the subordinate certificate by officers and employees (such as department heads, superintendents, etc.) designated by the taxpayer or executive officer who fills in the principal certificate actually directs and observes the taking of the inventory, the subsidiary certificate need not be filled in.

Extracts from Regulations 69

ART. 1611. **Need of Inventories.**—In order to reflect the net income correctly, inventories at the beginning and end of each year are necessary in every case in which the production, purchase, or sale of merchandise is an income-producing factor. The inventory should include raw materials and supplies on hand that have been acquired for sale, consumption, or use in productive processes, together with all finished or partly finished goods. Only merchandise title to which is vested in the taxpayer should be included in the inventory. Accordingly, the seller should include in his inventory goods under sale contracts for which title has not yet passed and applied to the contract and goods out upon consignment, but should exclude from inventory goods sold, title to which has passed to the purchaser. A purchaser should include in inventory merchandise purchased, title to which has passed to him although such merchandise is in transit or for other reasons has not been reduced to physical possession, but should not include goods ordered for future delivery, transfer of title to which has not yet been effected. In cases where inventories are required, the taxpayer should file with his return a certificate of inventory on Form 1126.

ART. 1612. **Valuation of Inventories.**—Section 205 provides two tests to which each inventory must conform:

First. It must conform as nearly as may be to the best accounting practice in the trade or business, and

Second. It must clearly reflect the income.

It follows, therefore, that inventory rules can not be uniform but must give effect to trade customs which come within the scope of the best accounting practice in the particular trade or business.

expenses a reasonable proportion of management expense, but not including any cost of selling or return on capital, whether by way of interest or profit.

(4) In any industry in which the usual rules for computation of cost of production are inapplicable, costs may be approximated upon such basis as may be reasonable and in conformity with established trade practice in the particular industry. Among such cases are (a) farmers and raisers of livestock (see article 1616), (b) miners and manufacturers who by a single process or uniform series of processes derive a product of two or more kinds, sizes, or grades, the unit cost of which is substantially alike (see article 1617, and (c) retail merchants who use what is known as the "retail method" in ascertaining approximate cost (see article 1618).

ART. 1614. **Inventories at market.**—Under ordinary circumstances and for normal goods in an inventory, "market" means the current bid price prevailing as the date of the inventory for the particular merchandise in the volume in which usually purchased by the taxpayer, and is applicable in the case of—

(a) Of goods purchased and on hand, and

(b) Of basic elements of cost (material, labor, and burden) in goods in process of manufacture and in finished goods on hand; unless, however, of goods on hand or in process of manufacture for delivery upon firm sales contracts (i. e., those not legally subject to cancellation by either party) at fixed prices entered into before the date of the inventory, which goods must be inventoried at cost.

When no open market exists or where quotations are nominal, due to stagnant market conditions, the taxpayer must use such evidence of a fair market price at the date or dates nearest the inventory as may be available, such as specific purchases or sales by the taxpayer or others in reasonable volume and made in good faith, or compensation paid for cancellation of contracts for purchase commitments. Where the taxpayer in the regular course of business has offered for sale such merchandise at prices lower than the current price, the inventory may be valued at such prices less proper allowance for selling expense, and the correctness of such prices will be determined by reference to the actual sale of the taxpayer for a reasonable period before and after the date of the inventory. Prices which vary materially from the actual prices so ascertained will not be accepted as reflecting the market.

ART. 1615. **Inventories by dealers in securities.**—A dealer in securities, who is in the books of account regularly inventories unsold securities on hand may either—

(a) At cost,

(b) At cost or market, whichever is lower, or

(c) At market value,

may make his return upon the basis upon which his accounts are kept; provided that a description of the method employed shall be included in or attached to the return, that all the securities must be inventoried by the same method, and that such method must be adhered to in subsequent years, unless another be authorized by the Commissioner. For the purpose of this rule a dealer in securities is a merchant of securities, whether an individual, partnership, or corporation, with an established place of business, regularly engaged in the purchase of securities and their resale to customers; that is, one who as a merchant buys securities and sells them to customers with a view to the gains and profits that may be derived therefrom.

basis, provided that the use of such method is designated upon the return, that accurate accounts are kept, and that such method is consistently adhered to unless a change is authorized by the Commissioner. Under this method the goods in the inventory are ordinarily priced at the selling prices, and the total retail value of the goods in each department or of each class of goods is reduced to approximate cost by deducting the percentage which represents the difference between the retail selling value and the purchase price. This percentage is determined by departments or by classes of goods, and should represent as accurately as may be the amounts added to the cost prices of goods to cover selling and other expenses of doing business and for the margin of profit. In computing the percentage above mentioned, proper adjustment should be made for all mark-ups and mark-downs.

A taxpayer maintaining more than one department in his store or dealing in classes of goods carrying different percentages of gross profit should not use a percentage of profit based upon an average of his entire business, but should compute and use in valuing his inventory the proper percentages for the respective departments or classes of goods.

EXHIBIT "B."

UNITED STATES OF AMERICA,
TREASURY DEPARTMENT,
WASHINGTON.

March 29, 1930.

Pursuant to Section 882 of the Revised Statutes, I hereby certify that the annexed is a true copy of Agreement as to final Determination of Tax Liability for 1927, in the amount of $1,410.58, signed November 3, 1928 by the DuPont Milling and Sales Corporation, San Francisco, California, the originals of which are on file in this department.

IN WITNESS WHEREOF, I have hereunto set my hand, and caused the seal of the Treasury Department to be affixed on the day and year first above written.

By direction of the Secretary.

F. A. BIRGFELD,
Chief Clerk, Treasury Department.

WVP EA FFT CMC.

AGREEMENT AS TO FINAL DETERMINATION OF TAX LIABILITY.

This Agreement, made in duplicate under and in pursuance of Section 606 of the Revenue Act of 1928, by and between DuPont Milling and Sales Corporation a taxpayer residing at, or having its principal place of business at at 140 Front Street, San Francisco, California, and the Commissioner of Internal Revenue;

Whereas, there has been a determination of the tax liability of said taxpayer in respect of Federal Income Taxes for the year 1927 in the principal sum of One Thousand Four Hundred Ten Dollars and Fifty Eight Cents ($1,410.58); and

Whereas, said taxpayer hereby agrees to this determination and consents to the assessment and collection of any deficiency in tax included in the amount of the principal [20] tax liability so determined, together with any penalty or interest, applicable thereto as provided by law, and/or to accept any abatement, credit, or refund, made in accordance with such determination, together with any interest due thereon as provided by law;

Now, This Agreement Witnesseth, that said taxpayer and said commissioner of Internal Revenue hereby mutually agree that the principal amount of such liability so determined shall be final and conclusive if and when this agreement is approved by the Secretary of the Treasurer or the Undersecretary.

In Witness Whereof, the above parties have subscribed their names to these presents in duplicate.

Signed this 3rd day of November, 1928.

    DuPONT MILLING & SALES COR-
        PORATION,
                Taxpayer.

(Seal)   By RALPH D. WILSON, V. P.

Signed Dec. 11, 1928.

                D. H. BLAIR,
      Commissioner of Internal Revenue.

The above agreement has been approved by the

Secretary of the Treasurer in accordance with the provisions of Section 606 of the Revenue Act of 1928, the approval being specifically enumerated on Schedule 620.

Dated Dec. 11, 1928.

BF   FFL   CPS   CBA   E–1

(See Reverse Side)

INSTRUCTIONS.

The agreement should be signed by the taxpayer, if possible.   Whenever it is necessary to have the agreement executed by an attorney or agent on behalf of the taxpayer, an authenticated copy of the document, specifically   [21]   authorizing such agent or attorney to sign the agreement on behalf of the taxpayer shall accompany the agreement.

If the agreement is signed by the administrator, executor, or trustee on behalf of an estate or trust, an attested copy of the letters testamentary, or the order of the court vesting such person with authority to so act, together with a certificate to the effect that such authority remains in full force and effect must be submitted with the agreement.

Where the taxpayer is a corporation, the agreement shall be signed by the corporate name, followed by the signature and title of an officer having authority to bind the corporation, and his signature shall be attested by the secretary of the corporation over the corporate seal.   In the absence of a seal a certified copy of the resolutions of the Board of Directors specifically authorizing an officer or officers to enter into the agreement shall be filed with the agreement.

2–14698

A–1

EXHIBIT "C."

UNITED STATES OF AMERICA,
TREASURY DEPARTMENT,
WASHINGTON.

December 23, 1930.

Pursuant to the provisions of Section 661, Chapter 17, Title 28 of the United States Code (Section 882 of the Revised Statutes of the United States), I hereby certify that the annexed is a true copy of Schedule No. 620, dated December 11, 1928, approved December 13, 1928 by A. W. Mellon, Secretary of the Treasury, showing approval of agreement as to final determination of income tax liability for 1927, [22] in the amount of $1,410.58, in the case of DuPont Milling and Sales Corporation; on file in this Department.

In Witness Whereof, I have hereunto set my hand and caused the seal of the Treasury Department to be affixed on the day and year first above written.

By direction of the Secretary of the Treasury.

(Seal)   F. A. BIRGFELD,
                      Chief Clerk, Treasury Dept.

Thesaur Amer. Systent Sigii.

RES   JP   EEA   B.

TREASURY DEPARTMENT,
WASHINGTON.

December 11, 1928.

Officer of Commissioner of Internal Revenue.

The Honorable,

The Secretary of the Treasury.

Sir:

I have the honor to submit for your consideration the following schedule of cases proposed to be closed by agreement, and ask your approval of my action in entering into the agreements with the taxpayers, listed as to final determination for the years indicated of income tax.

Name of Taxpayer	Years Covered by Agreement	Tax Liability.
DuPont Milling and Sales Corporation.	1927	$1,410.58

Respectfully,

D. H. BLAIR,
Commissioner.

Schedule W 620.

TREASURY DEPARTMENT,
Office of the Secretary.

December 13, 1928.

Approved.

A. W. MELLON,
Secretary of the Treasury.

Letters mailed Dec. 14, 1928.   [23]

AND BE IT FURTHER REMEMBERED that thereafter the said Court ordered that judgment be entered for defendant, to which ruling and order of the Court the plaintiff then and there duly excepted and hereby designates as

PLAINTIFF'S EXCEPTION No. 1.

AND BE IT FURTHER REMEMBERED that thereafter and pursuant to said last-mentioned order of said Court, to wit, on or about the 22d day of April, 1931, judgment was entered in favor of the defendant and against plaintiff, to which judgment plaintiff then and there duly excepted and hereby designates as

PLAINTIFF'S EXCEPTION No. 2.

Now, within the time allowed by law, plaintiff's counsel presents the foregoing as their proposed bill of exception in the above-entitled action, and prays that the same may be settled and allowed.

Dated: this 10th day of July, 1931.

C. H. SOOY.

C. H. SOOY.

NEIL E. LARKIN.

NEIL E. LARKIN.

FITZGERALD, ABBOTT & BEARDSLEY.

FITZGERALD, ABBOTT & BEARDSLEY.

BROBECK, PHLEGER & HARRISON.

BROBECK, PHLEGER & HARRISON.

MILTON NEWMARK,

MILTON NEWMARK.

STIPULATION FOR ALLOWANCE OF BILL OF EXCEPTIONS.

IT IS HEREBY STIPULATED AND AGREED that the foregoing bill of exceptions was presented by plaintiff within the time allowed by law therefor and that the same is a true and correct copy of the proceedings had at the trial of the above-entitled action, and that the same may be certified, [24] allowed and settled as provided by law and the practice of said court by Hon. A. F. St. Sure, United States District Judge, who presided at the trial of said cause.

Dated: July 10, 1931.

C. H. SOOY.

C. H. SOOY,

NEIL E. LARKIN,

NEIL E. LARKIN,

FITZGERALD, ABBOTT & BEARDSLEY.

FITZGERALD, ABBOTT & BEARDSLEY,

BROBECK, PHLEGER & HARRISON.

BROBECK, PHLEGER & HARRISON,

MILTON NEWMARK.

MILTON NEWMARK,

Attorneys for Plaintiff.

GEO. J. HATFIELD,

U. S. Attorney,

GEO. J. HATFIELD,

By ESTHER B. PHILLIPS.

ESTHER B. PHILLIPS,

Asst. U. S. Attorney,

Attorneys for Defendant.

ORDER SETTLING AND ALLOWING BILL OF EXCEPTIONS.

I, the undersigned, Judge of the District Court of the United States, do hereby certify that the foregoing bill of exceptions having been presented within the time allowed by law therefor, is a true and correct copy of the proceedings had at the trial of said action, and do hereby settle and allow the same and order that said bill of exceptions be filed with the Clerk of this court.

Dated: Aug. 4, 1931.

A. F. ST. SURE,
United States District Judge.   [25]

Receipt of a copy of the within plaintiff's proposed bill of exceptions is hereby admitted this ——— day of June, 1931.

————————————————,
Attorney for Defendant.

Receipt of a copy of the within plaintiff's proposed bill of exceptions is hereby admitted this June 26, 1931.

GEO. J. HATFIELD,
Attorney for Defendant.

[Endorsed]: Filed Aug. 4, 1931.   [26]

[Title of Court and Cause.]

PETITION FOR APPEAL.

The above-named plaintiff D. W. Johnston, as Trustee in Bankruptcy of the Estate of DuPont Milling and Sales Corporation, considering himself aggrieved by the judgment rendered and entered in the above-entitled action on the 22d day of April, 1931, which said judgment is to the effect that plaintiff take nothing by his complaint, and that defendant have judgment against plaintiff for his costs, hereby appeals from said judgment to the United States Circuit Court of Appeals for the Ninth Circuit, and said plaintiff prays that this, his appeal to said United States Circuit Court of Appeals for the Ninth Circuit may be allowed, and that a transcript of the record, papers and pleadings upon which said judgment was made, duly authenticated, may be sent to the United States Circuit Court of Appeals for the Ninth Circuit.

Dated: San Francisco, California, this 25th day of June, 1931.

C. H. SOOY.

C. H. SOOY,

NEIL E. LARKIN.

NEIL E. LARKIN,

FITZGERALD, ABBOTT & BEARDS-
LEY.

FITZGERALD, ABBOTT & BEARDS-
LEY,

BROBECK, PHLEGER & HARRI-
SON.

BROBECK, PHLEGER & HARRI-
SON,

MILTON NEWMARK.

MILTON NEWMARK,

Attorneys for Plaintiff.

[Endorsed]: Filed Jun. 25, 1931. [27]

[Title of Court and *Costs.*]

ASSIGNMENT OF ERRORS.

Comes now the plaintiff above named and files the following assignment of errors upon which he will rely upon the prosecution of his appeal in the above-entitled action from the judgment entered therein on the 22d day of April, 1931:

1.   That the evidence was and is insufficient to justify the decision and judgment of said District Court.

2.   That said judgment of the District Court is contrary to the evidence.

3.   That said District Court erred in rendering and entering judgment for defendant in said action in that said judgment is contrary to the law and the facts.

WHEREFORE said plaintiff prays that judgment of the District Court of the United States for the Northern District of California, Southern Division, hereinabove referred to, be reversed, and for such other and further relief as may be proper in the premises.

C. H. SOOY.
C. H. SOOY,
NEIL E. LARKIN.
NEIL E. LARKIN,
FITZGERALD, ABBOTT & BEARDS-
LEY.
FITZGERALD, ABBOTT & BEARDS-
LEY,

BROBECK, PHLEGER & HARRI-
SON.

BROBECK, PHLEGER & HARRI-
SON,

MILTON NEWMARK,
MILTON NEWMARK,
Attorneys for Plaintiff.

[Endorsed]: Filed Jun. 25, 1931. [28]

[Title of Court and Cause.]

ORDER ALLOWING APPEAL AND FIXING AMOUNT OF BOND.

On motion of C. H. Sooy, one of the attorneys for the plaintiff above named,—

IT IS ORDERED that the appeal of said plaintiff to the United States Circuit Court of Appeals for the Ninth Circuit from the judgment rendered and entered in the above-entitled action on the 22d day of April, 1931, be, and the same is hereby allowed, and that a duly authenticated transcript of the record, papers and proceedings on which said judgment was made be sent to the United States Circuit Court of Appeals for the Ninth Circuit.

IT IS FURTHER ORDERED that said plaintiff file with the Clerk of this court a good and sufficient bond in the sum of $250.00 conditioned as required by law, to cover prosecution of this appeal and damages, judgment and costs, and that said bond on appeal shall operate as and constitute a supersedeas bond.

Dated: June 25, 1931.

A. F. ST. SURE,
United States District Judge.

Receipt of copy of the within order allowing appeal and fixing amount of bond is hereby admitted this 26 day of June, 1931.

GEO. J. HATFIELD,
Attorney for Defendant.

[Endorsed]: Filed Jun. 26, 1931. [29]

PREMIUM CHARGED FOR THIS BOND IS $10.00 PER ANNUM.

AMERICAN SURETY COMPANY OF NEW YORK.
Organized in 1884.

[Title of Court and Cause.]

UNDERTAKING FOR COSTS ON APPEAL.

WHEREAS, D. W. Johnston, as Trustee in Bankruptcy of the Estates of Dupont Milling & Sales Corporation, a Bankrupt, in the above-entitled action is about to appeal to the United States Circuit Court of Appeals for the Ninth Circuit from a judgment entered against him in said action in said United States District Court, in and for the Northern District of California, Southern Division, in favor of John P. McLaughlin, and for costs of suit,—

NOW, THEREFORE, in consideration of the premises, and of such appeal, the undersigned, American Surety Company of New York, a corporation duly organized and existing under the laws of the State of New York, and duly authorized to transact a general surety business in the State of California, does undertake and promise on the part of the appellant, that the said appellant will pay all costs which may be awarded against him on the appeal, or on a dismissal thereof, not exceeding the sum of Two Hundred Fifty ($250.00) Dollars, to which amount it acknowledges itself bound.

It is further stipulated as a part of the foregoing bond, that in case of the breach of any condition thereof, [30] the above-named District Court may, upon notice to the Surety above named, American Surety Company of New York, of not less than ten days, proceed summarily in the action, suit, case or proceeding in which the same was given to ascertain the amount which such sureties are bound to pay on account of such breach, and render judgment therefor against them, and award execution therefor.

Signed and Sealed at San Francisco, California, this 26th day of June, 1931.

AMERICAN SURETY COMPANY OF NEW YORK.

By K. F. WARRACK,
Resident Vice-president.

[Seal]   Attest: B. DUCRAY,
Resident Assistant Secretary.

Approved

A. F. ST. SURE,
District Judge.

State of California,

City and County of San Francisco.

On this 26th day of June, in the year one thousand nine hundred and thirty-one, before me, John McCallan, a notary public in and for said City and County, state aforesaid, residing therein, duly commissioned and sworn, personally appeared K. F. Warrack and B. Ducray, known to me to be the Resident Vice-President and Resident Assistant Secretary respectively of the American Surety Company of New York, the corporation described in and that executed the within and foregoing instrument, and known to me to be the persons who executed the said instrument on behalf of the said corporation, and they both duly acknowledge to me that such corporation executed the same.

IN WITNESS WHEREOF, I have hereunto set my hand and affixed my official seal, at my office, in the said City and County of San Francisco, the day and year in this certificate first above written.

[Seal]   JOHN McCALLAN,

Notary Public in and for the City and County of San Francisco, State of California.

My commission expires Apr. 12, 1933.

[Endorsed]: Filed Jun. 26, 1931. [31]

[Title of Court and Cause.]

PRAECIPE FOR TRANSCRIPT OF RECORD.

To the Clerk of Said Court:

Sir: Please prepare record on appeal to the Circuit Court of Appeals for the Ninth Circuit in the above-entitled matter, and include therein the following papers and documents:

Complaint.

Answer.

Stipulation of facts and waiver of jury, together with three exhibits attached to said stipulations marked Exhibits "A," "B," and "C."

Judgment.

Bill of exceptions.

Petition for appeal.

Assignment of errors.

Order allowing appeal and fixing amount of bond.

Bond on appeal.

Citation on appeal with admission of service.

This praecipe.

C. H. SOOY,

C. H. SOOY,

NEIL E. LARKIN.

NEIL E. LARKIN,

FITZGERALD, ABBOTT & BEARDSLEY,

FITZGERALD, ABBOTT & BEARDSLEY,

BROBECK, PHLEGER & HARRISON,
BROBECK, PHLEGER & HARRISON,
   MILTON NEWMARK.
   MILTON NEWMARK,
    Attorneys for Plaintiff.

Receipt of a copy of the within praecipe is hereby admitted this June 25, 1931.
    GEO. J. HATFIELD,
    Attorney for Defendant.

[Endorsed]: Filed Jun. 26, 1931. [32]

[Title of Court and Cause.]

CERTIFICATE OF CLERK U. S. DISTRICT COURT TO TRANSCRIPT OF RECORD.

I, Walter B. Maling, Clerk of the District Court of the United States, in and for the Northern District of California, do hereby certify the foregoing 32 pages, numbered from 1 to 32, inclusive, to be a full, true and correct copy of the record and proceedings as enumerated in the praecipe for record on appeal, as the same remain on file and of record in the above-entitled suit, in the office of the Clerk of said court, and that the same constitutes the record on appeal to the United States Circuit of Appeals for the Ninth Circuit.

I further certify that the cost of the foregoing transcript of record is $13.55; that the said amount was paid by the plaintiff and appellant, and that the original citation issued in said suit is hereto annexed.

IN WITNESS WHEREOF, I have hereunto set my hand and affixed the seal of said District Court this 21st day of August, A. D. 1931.

[Seal] WALTER B. MALING,

Clerk, United States District Court for the Northern District of California. [33]

CITATION ON APPEAL.

United States of America,—ss.

The President of the United States of America to John P. McLaughlin, Defendant, GREETING:

YOU ARE HEREBY CITED AND ADMONISHED to be and appear at a United States Circuit Court of Appeals for the Ninth Circuit, to be holden at the City of San Francisco, in the State of California, within thirty days from the date hereof, pursuant to an order allowing an appeal, of record in the Clerk's office of the United States District Court for the Southern Division of the Northern District of California, wherein D. W. Johnston, as Trustee in Bankruptcy, etc., is appellant, and you are appellee, to show cause, if any there be, why the decree or judgment rendered against the said appellant, as in the said order allowing appeal mentioned, should not be corrected, and why speedy justice should not be done to the parties in that behalf.

WITNESS, the Honorable A. F. ST. SURE United States District Judge for the Northern District of California, this 25th day of June, A. D. 1931.

A. F. ST. SURE,

United States District Judge.

Rec'd this 26 day of June, 1931.

GEO. J. HATFIELD.

Filed Jun. 26, 1931.   [34]

[Endorsed]: No. 6586. United States Circuit Court of Appeals for the Ninth Circuit. D. W. Johnston, as Trustee in Bankruptcy of the Estate of DuPont Milling & Sales Corporation, Bankrupt, Appellant, vs. John P. McLaughlin, Collector of Internal Revenue, Appellee. Transcript of Record. Upon Appeal from the United States District Court for the Northern District of California, Southern Division.

Filed August 21, 1931.

PAUL P. O'BRIEN,

Clerk of the United States Circuit Court of Appeals for the Ninth Circuit.

No. 6586

IN THE

United States Circuit Court of Appeals

For the Ninth Circuit

D. W. JOHNSTON, as Trustee in Bankruptcy of the Estate of Dupont Milling & Sales Corporation, Bankrupt,

Appellant,

vs.

JOHN P. McLAUGHLIN, Collector of Internal Revenue,

Appellee.

BRIEF FOR APPELLANT.

C. H. SOOY,
Mills Building, San Francisco,

NEIL E. LARKIN,
155 Montgomery Street, San Francisco,

FITZGERALD, ABBOTT & BEARDSLEY,
Central Bank Building, Oakland,

BROBECK, PHLEGER & HARRISON,
Crocker Building, San Francisco,

MILTON NEWMARK,
Crocker Building, San Francisco,

Attorneys for Appellant.

FILED

OCT 10 1931

PAUL P. O'BRIEN,
CLERK

Subject Index

Table of Authorities Cited

Subject Index

Table of Authorities Cited

United States Circuit Court of Appeals
For the Ninth Circuit

D. W. JOHNSTON, as Trustee in Bankruptcy of the Estate of Dupont Milling & Sales Corporation, Bankrupt,

Appellant,

vs.

JOHN P. McLAUGHLIN, Collector of Internal Revenue,

Appellee.

BRIEF FOR APPELLANT.

This cause, at issue upon complaint and answer (Tr. 2-6), was submitted upon agreed statements of fact. (Tr. 17-20.) Judgment was for defendant and plaintiff appeals.

The error relied on is that the judgment is contrary to the law and the facts. Under the law, upon the agreed facts, judgment should have been for plaintiff.

STATEMENT OF FACTS.

DuPont Milling and Sales Corporation, now a bankrupt, had no taxable income for the year 1927. It suffered a loss in that year. The president of the corporation, for the purpose of deceiving and defrauding its directors, stockholders and creditors, so kept the books of the corporation that they falsely indicated a profit. For the same fraudulent purpose the president made, on behalf of the corporation, a false income tax return showing taxable income that did not exist. (Tr. 22-31.) Because of this false return, money of the corporation was paid by the corporation to the defendant as an income tax, the defendant being the Collector of Internal Revenue for the district. Subsequently an agreement as to final determination of tax liability was entered into between the Commissioner of Internal Revenue and the corporation, the signature of the corporation being affixed by an officer other than the president who made the false return. (Tr. 31.) The corporation has since been adjudicated a bankrupt. Plaintiff is trustee of its estate. Creditors of the corporation, who were such at the time of the wrongful payment, are now creditors of the bankrupt estate. There are not sufficient assets in the bankrupt estate to pay claims of the creditors.

ARGUMENT AND AUTHORITIES.

In brief, the stipulated and admitted facts present a case in which an officer of a corporation, and as such a trustee for the corporation, fraudulently paid money of the corporation to one to whom the money was not due, and who parted with no consideration therefor, and this to the detriment of the then and now existing creditors. The case is therefore controlled by the following elementary rules of law:

1. **Officers of corporations are trustees of its property.** 14 C. J. 99.

2. **It is the duty of a trustee to hold and apply the corpus of the trust to and for trust purposes only.** C. C. 2229.

3. **A** violation of that duty is a fraud against the beneficiary of the trust, that is, the corporation. C. C. 2234.

4. **One** to whom property is transferred in violation of a trust holds the same as an involuntary trustee under such trust, unless he purchased in good faith and for a valuable consideration. C. C. 2243.

. 5. **Property** obtained by one through the fraudulent practices of a third person will be held under a constructive trust for the person defrauded, though the person receiving the property be innocent of collusion. *Perry on Trusts,* 7th Ed.; Sec. 211.

6. **Money** received by a third person through the fraud of another may be recovered by the person defrauded in an action for money had and received against the third person. *Clifford Banking Co. v. Donovan Commercial Co.,* 94 S. W. 527.

7. **A** complaint setting forth the particular facts and circumstances under which it is claimed that one person has received and has money he ought not in equity and good conscience to retain, but ought to return, is as much a complaint for

money had and received as though it were in the
form of the common count for money had and
received. 41 C. J. 63; *Chung Kee v. Davidson,*
102 Cal. 195.

8. The right of action for the recovery of the
fraudulently diverted money was in the corporation. It was property of the corporation, and, as
such, it is now vested in the trustee in bankruptcy. *In re Thomas,* 156 Fed. 214.

9. There is likewise vested in the trustee all
rights of action on behalf of creditors of the corporation. 7 C. J. 246; *Cottrell v. Albany Card &
Paper Mfg. Co.,* 126 N. Y. Supp. 1070.

When the president of the corporation paid out its
money for a non-existent tax upon the false return,
he violated his trust as an officer of the corporation.
The defendant, to whom the money was paid in violation of the trust, became a like trustee, since, regardless of the good faith in which the money may have
been received, it was received for no valuable or other
consideration. The defendant, having thus received
money of the corporation without consideration, is in
a position where in equity and in good conscience he
ought not to retain the money, but ought to return it
to the corporation.

The corporation being now in bankruptcy, all rights
of action in the premises, both on its behalf and on
behalf of its creditors, are vested in the trustee in
bankruptcy, the plaintiff herein.

Under the stipulated and admitted facts, plaintiff
should therefore have had judgment against the de-

fendant, as for money had and received, unless the
defense interposed by the defendant is sound.

THE DEFENSE.

Th defense was rested upon a limitation upon the
jurisdiction of the Court assumed to be imposed by
Sec. 606 of the Revenue Act of 1928, the argument
being divided into four points, as follows:

1. **That this action by the trustee in bankruptcy is precluded by the agreement as to final
determination of tax liability executed by the
vice-president of the corporation. The agreement
is generally referred to as a "closing agreement."**

2. **That the fraud in this transaction is such
as exempts the "closing agreement" from the
operation of Sec. 606 of the Revenue Act of 1928.**

3. **That an action upon the ground of fraud
will lie only against the person guilty of the
fraud.**

4. **That only an innocent person can complain
of fraud.**

The claim thus sought to be defeated is not only
so inherently just that there ought to be a refund by
the government without suit; but, by reason of its
nature, since it arises out of fraud, it is exempt from
the operation of the Act by the plain language of the
Act itself. The closing agreement provided for by the
Act is made by the Act final as well as conclusive upon
the Courts "except upon a showing of fraud." In

addition to the fact that the Act exempts cases founded upon fraud, the fact is that the Act itself has no bearing upon this case.

In this connection the defendant relied upon the cases of *Bankers Reserve Life Co. v. U. S.,* 42 Fed. (2d) 313, and *Aetna Life Ins. Co. v. Eaton,* 40 Fed. (2d) 965, 43 Fed. (2d) 711. These cases involve a similar statute (Sec. 1106(b) of the Revenue Act of 1926), but they are not determinative of the issue here. In neither of these cases was fraud involved. In each case all the facts were known, both to the taxpayer and the government. In each case the tax return reflected exactly and in full the true income upon which the tax was assessed and paid. By reason of a subsequent decision of the Supreme Court in another case it had developed that certain income reported and assessed should have been exempt, and it was sought to recover the excess thus appearing to have been paid. The closing agreements, executed after the payments, were held to bar recovery. The reason for the bar is clearly stated by the Circuit Court of Appeals, 43 Fed. (2d) at 713, where it is said:

> "No fraud, malfeasance or misrepresentation of fact, affected the assessments there claimed."

Therefore, of course, the statute was a complete bar. Fraud being the foundation of the action here, neither of these decisions can have any bearing upon the issue now before the Court.

It was argued by the defendant that the fraud exempted by the statute from its operation must be such fraud as pertains to the making of the closing agreement, and not to the causing or making of the original return. This argument involves both an error of law and a misconception of the extent and effect of the fraud in this case. The fraud that brought about the erroneous tax return, that is, the falsification of the corporation's books by the president, was a continuing fraud. It entered as effectually into the making of the closing agreement as it did into the false return. The closing agreement was, therefore, a direct result of the fraud.

But fraud as a cause of the return, as distinguished from the closing agreement, is an entirely sufficient foundation for this action. Recent as is the statute in question, that point has been fully determined, and this too by a case cited by defendant in support of his contention, and evidently not followed by the trial Court. The case is that of *Carter Music Co. v. Bass,* 20 Fed. (2d) 391. In its opinion the Court stated the facts and its conclusions as follows:

> "The case made here is simply this, as established by plaintiff and admitted by defendant: Plaintiff paid defendant, for the year 1920, $4,950.34 more than was due for that year. This payment was made to defendant **upon his assertion to plaintiff that that amount was due,** and upon his demand for payment, and plaintiff would not have paid it, except for the claim and demand. From this statement it follows, nothing else appearing, that from the standpoint of natural justice and equity defendant has taken and is withholding from plaintiff without right $4,950.34 of plaintiff's money.

Upon what theory, then, does the defendant refuse payment, and does he contest it here? Simply this: That though the defendant recognizes the injustice of the situation, that the United States should keep money which had been wrongfully exacted from plaintiff through him, and has endeavored to assist the taxpayer to obtain a refund, he is prevented from making such refund, and required to defend this suit, by a ruling from Washington that, 'while there is no doubt that the opinion works a hardship on the taxpayer,' they are of the opinion that plaintiff is not entitled to recover because of the fact that, **after plaintiff had, on December 5, 1922, paid** the money for which it sues, it did **on October 6, 1923, execute an agreement in writing,** which agreement they say was executed under the authority of, in accordance with, and has the effect ascribed to it by section 1312 of the act of 1921 (Comp. St. Sec. 6371 4/5gg) and section 1106b of the act of 1926. * * * Plaintiff meets the defense of the agreement with two propositions: (1) That there was no assessment and determination of taxes for the year 1920 made and agreed to as contemplated in the statute. (2) That, if there was such an assessment and agreement made as contemplated by the statute, it cannot constitute a defense to this cause, because, if in fact made, the payment by plaintiff **and the agreement following** were all induced by a misrepresentation of fact, which under the very terms of the statute deprives them of any effect.

Examining these contentions, I think they both must be sustained.''

It was argued by the defendant that an action upon the ground of fraud will lie only against the person guilty of the fraud, that is, where the fraud was participated in by the defendant. This is true as to actions **for damages** upon the ground of fraud. Here we have, not an action for damages, but for money had and received. It is maintainable against the defendant, not on the theory that he was guilty of or in any manner participated in the fraud, but because he is the beneficiary of the fraud. It was he who received the money fraudulently caused to be paid out of the corporation's funds. He is, therefore, chargeable in this action, not as upon a cause of action for damages, but for the money he received. The nature of the action and the basis of defendant's liability are clearly set forth in *Carter Music Co. v. Bass* (supra). The Court there said:

> "This is a suit at law, brought under the authority of and in accordance with the statutes of the United States allowing such suit, and the principles of the common law controlling same, against J. W. Bass, collector of internal revenue, to recover from him personally for sums collected by him and paid to him as taxes in excess of amounts actually due by plaintiff.
>
> That such a suit can be maintained, that it is personal, and that it is controlled by the common-law principles of a suit in assumpsit on the money counts, except as modified by statute, is well established by the authorities. Sage v. United States, 250 U. S. 37, 39 S. Ct. 415, 63 L. Ed. 828: Smietanka v. Indiana Steel Co., 257 U. S. 4, 42 S. Ct. 1, 66 L. Ed. 99; International Paper Co. v. Burrill (D. C.) 260 F. 664; New York Life Ins. Co. v. Anderson, (C. C. A.) 263 F. 527; Holmes, Federal Taxes (6th Ed.) 1547. Of such suits

Holmes, supra, says: 'Suits against collectors are brought on the theory of money had and received. In such suits the plaintiff may recover only such money as he is in equity entitled to, and as defendant is not entitled to retain.' In the Anderson case, supra, it is said: 'That a taxpayer's suit of this sort is essentially an action of assumpsit for money had and received has been too long settled to admit of doubt.' "

The defendant also argued that only a plaintiff innocent of fraud can complain of the fraud. It was said that the trustee in bankruptcy stands in the shoes of the bankrupt corporation, and has no better right than the bankrupt itself. This argument ignores two facts that defeat it: (1) the bankrupt corporation was not guilty of the fraud, and (2), while the trustee represents in a sense the bankrupt, he is also and primarily the representative of the creditors of the bankrupt, and as such is vested with all their rights. It will be observed that the complaint alleges and the supplemental stipulation admits, "that at the time of the making of said return and said payment said corporation was largely indebted to persons, firms, and corporations who are now creditors of said bankrupt estate." It is on behalf of these existing creditors who were defrauded that the trustee sues here. The argument of the defendant takes cognizance only of the law applicable to the most common action for money had and received arising out of fraudulent transactions, that is, an action by the injured person against the one who defrauded him. In such actions, and the transactions upon which they are founded, but two persons are involved. In the situation here presented five persons or groups are involved. They are: (1) the president of the corporation, who falsified the books upon which the return was based; (2) the corporation, whose money was wrongfully paid out; (3) the defendant, who received the money without consideration; (4) the existing creditors of the corporation, who were defrauded by the wrongful payment, and who are now creditors of the bankrupt estate; and (5) the plaintiff, who, as trustee, represents not only the corporation, but the defrauded creditors in whose right he sues.

With this distinction in mind, it is clear that it is not the guilty person who brings this action; nor is it brought upon his or its behalf. The guilty person was the president of the corporation. His falsification of the books was not within his authority as president. It was antagonistic to the corporation, and therefore not the act of the corporation. Nor was the tax return, founded as it was upon the falsified books, the free act of the corporation. It is not on behalf of the defrauded corporation or its stockholders that the trustee sues here, but on behalf of the existing and defrauded creditors of the corporation. The defendant is not sought to be held by reason of any participation in the fraud, but because he received the fruits of the fraud, that is, the money paid as a tax when there was in fact no income to be taxed. The injured persons are the creditors, and it is their injury and right that are the foundation of this action.

The injured persons being the creditors, no closing agreement of the corporation could destroy their rights. They have done nothing to waive their right;

nor has their representative, the trustee. A corporation cannot defeat its creditors by fraudulently paying out its funds so as to place them beyond the reach of its creditors. Nor, after such payment, can it waive any right of the creditors by any subsequent agreement with the person to whom the money was paid.

Applying the principles stated in the opening paragraphs of this brief, this is simply a case where, by reason of the fraudulent act of its president, money of the corporation which should belong to creditors of the corporation was paid to the defendant. The defendant received the money without parting with anything of value therefor. The defendant is, therefore, in the position of having received money which in equity and good conscience he ought not to retain, but ought to pay to the creditors of the corporation,— or to the plaintiff, who, as trustee in bankruptcy, represents the creditors in this action. In its last analysis it is a case in which one person has been deprived of money by the fraud of another, and the fruits have gone to a third person. The successors in law of the defrauded persons, that is, the creditors who were such at the time, bring this action through their representative, the trustee, not in the right of the defrauded corporation, but in their own right as creditors existing at the time of the fraudulent payment. The subsequent closing agreement between the corporation and the beneficiary of the fraud cannot waive the rights of these creditors.

It is submitted, therefore, that the defendant is liable as for money had and received, and that his liability is to the creditors, or the trustee who represents them as plaintiff in this action. The judgment should have been for the plaintiff as for money had and received by the defendant. The judgment rendered for the defendant should be reversed.

Dated, San Francisco,
October 10, 1931.

Respectfully submitted,
C. H. Sooy,
Neil E. Larkin,
Fitzgerald, Abbott & Beardsley,
Brobeck, Phleger & Harrison,
Milton Newmark,

Attorneys for Appellant.

IN THE

United States Circuit Court of Appeals

For the Ninth Circuit

_3_

D. W. JOHNSTON, as Trustee in Bankruptcy of the Estate of DuPont Milling & Sales Corporation, a Bankrupt,

Appellant,

vs.

JOHN P. McLAUGHLIN, Collector of Internal Revenue,

Appellee.

BRIEF FOR APPELLEE.

F I L E

NOV 2 0 1

PAUL P. O'BRI

GEO. J. HATFIELD,
United States Attorney,

ESTHER B. PHILLIPS,
Asst. United States Attorney,
Attorneys for Appellee.

Parker Printing Company, 545 Sansome Street, San Francisco

Table of Cases

No. 6586

United States Circuit Court of Appeals

For the Ninth Circuit

D. W. JOHNSTON, as Trustee in Bankruptcy of the Estate of DuPont Milling & Sales Corporation, a Bankrupt,

Appellant,

vs.

JOHN P. McLAUGHLIN, Collector of Internal Revenue,

Appellee.

BRIEF FOR APPELLEE.

STATEMENT OF THE CASE.

The amount involved in this case is small, but the principles are important, and the case is important as a precedent.

The facts appear in an Agreed Statement of Facts (Tr. p. 10), and a supplement to the Agreed Statement (Tr. p. 14). The appellant will be referred to herein as plaintiff and the appellee as defendant.

It has been stipulated that during 1927 the DuPont Milling & Sales Company suffered a loss; that under the direction of its president, who controlled the majority of the stock, its books were kept in such manner as to conceal the loss from those stockholders, directors and creditors who were not acting in aid of him. It has been stipulated that for this purpose the Company's income tax return for 1927 was made out to show a profit, and the tax shown to be due on the return was paid to defendant collector.

The books of the company were audited by an Internal Revenue Agent, and the return was approved, in ignorance of the truth. The Commissioner, also in ignorance that the facts were other than as they appeared in the company's books and its tax return, made a contract with the DuPont Milling & Sales Company, by which an agreement was made between them as to a final determination of the company's tax liability for 1927. This agreement was approved by the Secretary of the Treasury (see Exhibits "B" and "C" attached to Agreed Statement of Facts, Tr. pp. 31, 34). It is stipulated that the defendant, the Collector of the tax, accepted it with no knowledge of the facts other than as they appeared in the return. The answer pleads affirmatively as a defense the agreement made between the Commissioner and the DuPont Company. The trustee in bankruptcy for the DuPont Milling & Sales Company sues to recover the tax paid under these circumstances.

The question for the court is one of law, namely, what effect shall be given to this contract? The statute permits that the agreement be set aside by a showing of "fraud". But "fraud" in what respect? Fraud in making the return? Or fraud in making the agreement? Fraud practiced upon whom and by whom?

ARGUMENT.

(1) The statute upon closing agreements.

The affirmative defense relies on Section 606 of the Revenue Act of 1928, which reads:

"Closing Agreements.

"(a) *Authorization.* The Commissioner (or any officer or employee of the Bureau of Internal Revenue, including the field service, authorized in writing by the Commissioner) is authorized to enter into an agreement in writing with any person relating to the liability of such person (or of the person or estate for whom he acts) in respect of any internal-revenue tax for any taxable period ending prior to the date of the agreement.

"(b) *Finality of Agreements.* If such agreement is approved by the Secretary or the Undersecretary, within such time as may be stated in such agreement, or later agreed to, such agreement shall be final and conclusive, and, except upon a showing of fraud or malfeasance, or misrepresentation of a material fact—

"(1) the case shall not be reopened as to the matters agreed upon or the agreement modified, by any officer, employee, or agent of the United States, and

"(2) in any suit, action, or proceeding, such agreement, or any determination, assessment, collection, payment, abatement, refund, or credit made in accordance therewith, shall not be annulled, modified, set aside, or disregarded. (May 29, 1928, 8:00 a. m., c. 852, Sec. 606 (a-b), 45 Stat.)"

This section resembles Section 1106(b) of the Act of 1926 which reads:

"If after a determination and assessment in any case the taxpayer has paid in whole any tax or penalty, or accepted any abatement, credit, or refund based on such determination and assessment, and an agreement is made in writing between the taxpayer and the Commissioner, with the approval of the Secretary, that such determination and assessment shall be final and conclusive, then (except upon a showing of fraud or malfeasance or misrepresentation of fact materially affecting the determination or assessment thus made) (1) the case shall not be reopened or the determination and assessment modified by any officer, employee, or agent of the United States, and (2) no suit, action, or proceeding to annul, modify or set aside such determination or assessment shall be entertained by any court of the United States."

(2) Cases upon closing agreements as to tax liability.

The question has arisen several times as to the binding effect of such closing agreements.

Bankers' Reserve Life Co. v. United States, 42
Fed. (2d) 313 (Court of Claims).

Plaintiff paid income taxes for 1924 in the sum of
$27,727.71. In determining the tax, the Commissioner
assessed and the plaintiff paid it under the theory that
a certain principle of law regarding the inclusion of
tax exempt securities applied. Thereafter, and on
February 25, 1928, the taxpayer and the Commissioner,
with the approval of the Secretary, executed an agreement as to the final determination and assessment of
the correctness of the tax paid. (This agreement was
made under Section 1106 of the Act of 1926 quoted
above.) At the time this agreement was made, a case
was pending in the Supreme Court which involved the
computation of such a tax and inclusion of such interest. Thereafter the Supreme Court rendered a
decision the effect of which would (in the absence of
such an agreement) have been to entitle plaintiff to a
refund. Plaintiff filed claim, and on rejection, filed
suit. A demurrer to the complaint was sustained.

"The purpose of the statute in providing for
closing agreements was to enable the taxpayer and
the government *finally and completely* to settle all
controversies in respect of the tax liability for a
particular year or years and to protect the taxpayer against a further demand by the reopening
of a case as a result of a different view of the
matter being taken by the government officers or
as the result of subsequent court decisions prior
to the expiration of the statute of limitations, and
to prevent the filing of additional claims for refund or the institution of suit by the taxpayer for

the same reason." (Italics ours.) Certiorari was
denied. (282 U. S. 871.)

Aetna Life Insurance Co. v. Eaton, 40 Fed. (2d)
  965; 43 Fed. (2d) 711 (C. C. A. 2nd Circuit).

In this action, the lower court sustained a demurrer
for lack of jurisdiction. The Appellate Court reversed
him on the jurisdictional question, but directed dismissal of the complaint for failure to state a cause of
action. This case is like the *Bankers' Reserve Life
Co. v. United States,* supra. An agreement for final
determination of taxes was made in January, 1928.
Under the Supreme Court's decision in June, 1928, a
refund would have been due, were it not for the final
agreement. It was held that the final agreement was a
defense. Certiorari was denied (282 U. S. 887).

It has been held that the matter of interest upon
a credit for over-payment is a part of the Commissioner's "determination" of a refund within the
meaning of the term as used in Section 1106 (b) of
the Revenue Act of 1926; that a closing agreement
upon tax liability and the amount of a refund pre-
cludes the taxpayer from claiming that interest on the
refund accrues prior to the agreement; and that the
Court of Claims is without jurisdiction to modify or
annul such a closing agreement.

Parish & Bingham Corporation v. U. S., 44
  Fed. (2d) 993;
Lloyd Smith v. U. S., 44 Fed. (2d) 990.

The next case enjoys the favor of both appellant
and appellee.

Carter Music Co. v. Bass, Collector, etc., 20
Fed. (2d) 390.

In this case an agreement was made, but was shown
to have been made and procured under a misrepresentation of fact by the defendant. Held, the agreement was not a defense. Appellant appears to rely
on this case as fully determinative of the case at bar
(Appellant's Brief p. 7). Not so. There is not the
slightest suggestion in the Agreed Statement of Facts
that there was any misrepresentation by the defendant or by the Commissioner or by any agent of either
of them.

(3) **Rule of Construction**: the terms "fraud", "malfeasance" and
"misrepresentations" as used in the statute, should relate to
the subject matter of the statute, the closing agreement.

The statute uses the word "fraud" in conjunction
with "malfeasance" and "misrepresentation of a
material fact". Malfeasance is a word of very general meaning; but misrepresentation of a material
fact has a more specific meaning. We think it clear
that these three causes for setting aside the final determination provided in the statute ought to be subject
to the same basic rule of construction. If one of
these terms must be construed to relate to things done
between the parties, then all of them should be so
construed.

This is a statute of repose. If this purpose is to be
advanced, the only sensible construction of the words

"fraud", "malfeasance" or "misrepresentation of a material fact" is that there shall be fraud, misrepresentation of fact, etc., between the parties to the agreement in the making of the agreement. If they are construed to apply to some other person, not a party to the agreement, or that it might relate to a misrepresentation, fraud by one of the parties, but not in connection with the agreement, the purpose of the statute would be avoided. To illustrate: let us suppose that the taxpayer's bookkeepers grossly overstate the net income shown in the books for the purpose of getting a larger Christmas bonus. This is a misrepresentation of a material fact upon which he relies. Upon such a showing, ought the taxpayer to be allowed to set aside his final agreement with the Commissioner? Supposing in the calculation of the taxable income the taxpayer's accountant, for private reasons of his own (let us say, revenge) miscalculates the taxpayer's invested capital, and, relying upon his audit, the taxpayer makes his agreement with the Commissioner. Ought this to be sufficient cause for the taxpayer to set aside his agreement with the Commissioner? The facts were certainly misrepresented to him, though not by the Commissioner.

If the taxpayer may set the agreement aside because of misrepresentation of fact made to him by his own employees, then the Commissioner should have the same privilege. Suppose the Revenue Agent auditing the taxpayer's account, anticipates starting in business for himself, and because of such motive, and the hope of making a friend, reduces the taxpayer's tax liability, the taxpayer himself being innocent of wrong. The Commissioner relies on his audit, pays a refund and enters into an agreement as to final liability. Would the purpose of the statute be served if the Commissioner is allowed to set aside an agreement made under such circumstances? In substance, such a construction of the statute would mean that either party, after making a final determination as provided by the statute, can say: "Hold! My agent was a rascal and I was deceived by him. Let us, therefore, set aside the agreement." This means that neither can have any real reliance upon such an agreement because neither can know all the motives and circumstances which led the other to enter into the agreement.

On the other hand if the terms "fraud", "malfeasance" or "misrepresentation", as used in the statute, are limited to the subject matter of the statute, namely, the determination made between the parties, then it would follow that it is only "fraud", "malfeasance" or "misrepresentation" *between the parties* to the agreement which will be ground for rescinding the agreement. Such a construction of the statute is comparatively simple.

The meaning of fraud in this context is well defined.

"The essential element of fraud that must exist in any case properly brought within that desig-

nation *is a mistake of one party as to a material
fact induced by the other in order that it might
be acted upon,* or (in cases where there is a duty
of disclosure) at least taken advantage of with
knowledge of its falsity to secure action. Generally all of the requirements of an action of deceit will be found to exist." *Williston on Contracts,* Vol. III, Sec. 1487.

Williston then goes on to state the elements of an
action for deceit:

"(1) False representations of material facts;

(2) Knowledge of the falsity of the representations by the person making them;

(3) Ignorance of the falsity on the part of the
person to whom the representations were made;

(4) Intent or at least reason to expect that the
representations will be acted on by the person to
whom they were made;

(5) Action by such person to his damage."

If this be the legal definition of "fraud" (and we
submit that it is, by all the authorities, English and
American, and that Congress must be assumed to have
used the word in its ordinary meaning) a definite and
simple rule of construction is afforded. "Fraud",
"misrepresentation of fact" and "malfeasance",
which are grounds for setting aside the contract,
would be limited to "fraud", "misrepresentation"
and "malfeasance", which are practiced by one party
to the agreement to the detriment of the other, and

such "fraud", "misrepresentation" or malfeasance" must be connected in some wise with the subject matter of the agreement.

The contrary rule, for which plaintiff contends, is that there shall be no limitation upon the purpose of such "fraud", "misrepresentation" or "malfeasance", that is, such acts need not have been done by one of the parties to the agreement for the detriment of the other party, and that these grounds shall not be limited to the agreement, or even to the tax return, but may relate to things back of the tax return, for example, the keeping of the taxpayer's books, the auditing of his books, the return, itself, and lastly, the making of the agreement.

In enacting this statute, Congress undoubtedly had in mind the relief of the taxpayer. It will be remembered that there were no statute of limitations applicable to the tax liability under the early income tax acts and little or no limitation upon the power of the United States through its Internal Revenue Bureau to determine and re-determine the tax liability of its citizens. In thus providing that an agreement might be entered into, which would settle, once and for all, the liability of the taxpayer, Congress must have intended to give the taxpayer something he might rely on. If such an agreement can be overthrown only when "fraud", "malfeasance" and "misrepresentation" are shown to have existed between the parties to the agreement, a taxpayer whose conscience is free and clear of wrong-doing, can be satisfied that his liability has been finally determined. If these terms are given a broad and general meaning, not limited to the parties to the contract, and not even limited to the agreement itself, then he could have no such peace of mind.

This brings us to a consideration of the history of section 606 of the Revenue Act of 1928, which is quoted upon page 3 above.

(4) History of Section 606 of the Revenue Act of 1928.

Congress by Section 1312 of the Revenue Act of 1921 (42 Stat. 313) authorized, for the first time, the final and conclusive settlement of tax liability as between the Government and a taxpayer, said Section reading as follows:

"FINAL DETERMINATION AND ASSESSMENT.

Sec. 1312. That if after a determination and assessment in any case the taxpayer has without protest paid in whole any tax or penalty, or accepted any abatement, credit, or refund based on such determination and assessment, and an agreement is made in writing between the taxpayer and the Commissioner, with the approval of the Secretary, that such determination and assessment shall be final and conclusive, then (except upon a showing of fraud or malfeasance or misrepresentation of fact materially affecting the determination or assessment thus made) (1) the case shall not be reopened or the determination and assessment modified by any officer, employee, or

agent of the United States, and (2) no suit, action,
or proceeding to annul, modify, or set aside such
determination or assessment shall be entertained
by any court of the United States.''

This section, in substance, first appeared in H. R.
8235, the Revenue Bill of 1921, as Section 1001 (Committee Print, page 270).

Later it appeared as Section 1001, Title X, page 75,
in the Bill as introduced by Mr. Fordney of the House
on August 15, 1921.

In the report of the Ways and Means Committee
(Report No. 350, August 16, 1921), accompanying said
Bill, Mr. Fordney, speaking for the Committee, said:

"TITLE X, ADMINISTRATIVE PROVISIONS.

Section 1001 would permit the taxpayer and
the Commissioner to reach an agreement as to
the amount of taxes due which, except upon a
showing of fraud or malfeasance, would be conclusive and binding upon the parties. This provision would expedite the collection of taxes and
prevent much litigation.''

In the Bill as reported to the Senate the Section
appeared as Section 1312, and in the Report of the
Senate Committee on Finance, accompanying the Bill
(Senate Report 275, page 31, Sept. 26, 1921) Mr. Pen-
rose, speaking for the Committee, had this to say:

"FINAL DETERMINATION OF TAXES.

Section 1312 authorizes the Commissioner of
Internal Revenue, with the approval of the Sec-

retary of the Treasury and with the consent of the taxpayer, to reach a final settlement in tax cases which shall not be reopened or modified by any officer, employee, or agent of the United States, and which shall not be annulled or set aside by any court of the United States.

Under the present method of procedure a taxpayer never knows when he is through, as a tax case may be opened at any time because of a change in ruling by the Treasury Department. It is believed that this provision will tend to promote expedition in the handling of tax cases and certainty in tax adjustment. Your committee, therefore, recommends its adoption.''

In the Revenue Act of 1924, the Section relating to ''Final determinations and assessments'' appears as Section 1006 (43 Stat. 340). The language of this Section is substantially identical with that of Section 1312 of the Revenue Act of 1921; the only change made providing that such final agreements of settlement might be made whether or not the taxes in question were paid under protest.

This Section appears in H. R. 6715, Revenue Bill of 1924, as Section 1006, and Mr. Green of the Committee on Ways and Means in Report No. 179 accompanying the Bill, and speaking for the Committee, has this to say of said Section 1006, at page 33:

''This section reenacts the provisions of Section 1312 of the existing law, with the omission of the requirement that such final determination and assessment, in cases in which the tax or penalty

was paid in whole, shall only be made if it was
paid without protest. Since the payment of the
tax with or without protest does not necessarily
affect the desirability of making such a final agreement, it is desirable to eliminate the words 'without protest' from the section.''

Section 1106 (b) of the Revenue Act of 1926, quoted
on page 4 above, was a reenactment, without change,
of Section 1006 of the Revenue Act of 1924, and
Section 1106 (b) of the Revenue Act of 1926 was in
substance reenacted by Section 606 of the Revenue
Act of 1928 (45 Stat. 874). For convenience, we will
quote Section 606 again.

"SEC. 606. CLOSING AGREEMENTS

(a) *Authorization.*—The Commissioner (or
any officer or employee of the Bureau of Internal
Revenue, including the field service, authorized
in writing by the Commissioner) is authorized to
enter into an agreement in writing with any person relating to the liability of such person (or of
the person or estate for whom he acts) in respect
of any internal-revenue tax for any taxable period
ending prior to the date of the agreement.

(b) *Finality of agreements.*—If such agreement is approved by the Secretary, or the Undersecretary, within such time as may be stated in
such agreement, or later agreed to, such agreement shall be final and conclusive, and, except
upon a showing of fraud or malfeasance, or misrepresentation of a material fact—

(1) the case shall not be reopened as to the
matters agreed upon or the agreement modi-

fied, by any officer, employee, or agent of the United States, and

(2) in any suit, action, or proceeding, such agreement, or any determination, assessment, collection, payment, abatement, refund, or credit made in accordance therewith, shall not be annulled, modified, set aside, or disregarded.

(c) Section 1106 (b) of the Revenue Act of 1926 is repealed, effective on the expiration of 30 days after the enactment of this Act, but such repeal shall not affect any agreement made before such repeal takes effect.''

It will be noted that Section 606 is broader than Section 1106 of the Revenue Act of 1926, but that Section 606 (b) as to the finality of such agreements is substantially identical with said Section 1106 (b).

The Report of the Ways and Means Committee on the Revenue Bill of 1928, later the Revenue Act of 1928 (Report No. 2, page 32), contains the following statement by Mr. Green, Chairman of said Ways and Means Committee:

"SEC. 606. CLOSING AGREEMENTS

The closing of tax cases for the earlier years is a difficult problem. Statistics recently gathered show that an abnormally large percentage of closed cases are reopened by the taxpayer or the Government. Among the causes contributing thereto are claims by taxpayers, the effect of subsequent decisions and changes in the regulations and the law. The constant reopening of closed cases must be discouraged and one of the most effective means of preventing the reopening of cases is the execution of closing agreements. Such agreements are authorized by section 1106 (b) of the Revenue Act of 1926. There are, however, a number of restrictions in that section, the practical effect of which is to delay and often to render it impossible to secure the agreement. These restrictions have been removed in section 606 of the bill. It is believed that under this section it will be possible to execute many more closing agreements than in the past.''

From this history it is clear that Congress in enacting Section 606 and the kindred sections of the 1921, 1924, and 1926 Acts, intended that agreements executed in accordance with the provisions of these sections should be conclusive and binding upon the Courts, and intended to discourage the reopening of tax cases. The benefit was intended primarily for the taxpayer but both parties are within the scope and purpose of the statute.

(5) The trustee in bankruptcy stands in the shoes of the bankrupt.

The trustee in bankruptcy takes the bankrupt's estate subject to such claims and with such rights as the bankrupt has himself, subject, of course, to the powers and special rights conferred on the trustees by statute. It is hardly necessary to cite authorities for so elementary a rule.

Collier on Bankruptcy, 13th Ed. p. 1531.

(6) The principles of an account stated are applicable.

The making of a "final agreement" as to tax liability is statutory. The nearest analogy is an account stated which is formally agreed on by the parties to be correct. No principle of law can be better settled than the rule that when an account is stated and agreed on by the parties, it becomes a new contract between them, and if a suit is brought, it is not based upon the original items, but on the balance appearing in the account stated. For such a rule it is hardly necessary to cite authority.

See

> *Toland v. Sprague,* 12 Peters 300; 9 L. Ed. 1093;
>
> *Oil Company v. Van Etten,* 107 U. S. 325; 27 L. Ed. 319;
>
> 1 *Corpus Juris* 705.

It is well settled that the surrender of a doubtful claim or right is a good consideration for an account stated and that it is not open to one party to say that such a right or claim surrendered by the other subsequently proved to be invalid.

> *Gardner v. Watson,* 170 Cal. 570.

Similarly, there is no question but that an account stated can be impeached by a showing of fraud, duress or mistake.

> *Gardner v. Watson,* 170 Cal. 570;
>
> 1 *Corpus Juris,* 711 and 712, citing cases.

Plaintiff suggests that the defendant received this money for no valuable or other consideration (Appellant's Brief p. 11). This argument entirely overlooks the point that subsequently a contract was made respecting this money with the government *for which a valuable consideration was given*. The government at that time made a contract binding upon itself under which it could not even have opened a dispute, unless upon a showing of fraud, misrepresentation, etc. It is idle for the appellant now to say that this was not a good consideration because as the facts developed, no more taxes would have been due: the fact is that upon the facts as they then appeared, both parties surrendered a right, the government gave up all right to sue for additional taxes, and the taxpayer gave up a right to sue for a refund.

Similarly, as to the suggestion that this suit is nothing but a suit for money had and received. It is submitted that an action would not lie for money had and received where, after payment, a contract is made between the parties by which both agree that the money is due and owing, and the recipient in good faith binds himself not to ask for more. Admittedly, if fraud is practiced by one against the other, the defrauded party has a remedy against the other. But can an innocent party to such an account be subjected to suit by the guilty or by his trustee? It is contrary to all legal principles to permit it. Yet in fact, if not in form, *this is an action to set aside a contract on the ground of fraud.*

(7) The return in question was a corporate act.

Plaintiff's brief suggests that the income tax return was not a corporate act. It was signed by the President and the Treasurer of the Company, the certificate of inventory was prepared by various officers and employees of the company. Either the return was a corporate act, or no return at all was made. If no return at all was made, we are at a loss to know what standing plaintiff has to bring this suit. We think it impossible to distinguish the making of the return and the payment of the money shown to be due upon the return: either both were corporate acts, or neither was a corporate act.

CONCLUSION.

The amount involved in this case is only $1410.58. It is not in itself enough to be of great moment to either party. The principle at stake, however, is important. The statute imparting finality to agreements such as the one involved in this case was a statute of repose. It ought not to be so construed as to nullify its purpose.

Respectfully submitted,

GEO. J. HATFIELD,
United States Attorney,

ESTHER B. PHILLIPS,
Asst. United States Attorney,
Attorneys for Appellee.

United States Circuit Court of Appeals

For the Ninth Circuit

D. W. JOHNSTON, as Trustee in Bankruptcy of the Estate of DuPont
Milling & Sales Corporation, Bankrupt,

> *Appellant,*

vs.

JOHN P. MCLAUGHLIN, Collector of
Internal Revenue,

> *Appellee.*

APPELLANT'S PETITION FOR A REHEARING.

C. H. SOOY,
Mills Building, San Francisco,

NEIL E. LARKIN,
155 Montgomery Street, San Francisco,

FITZGERALD, ABBOTT & BEARDSLEY,
Central Bank Building, Oakland,

BROBECK, PHLEGER & HARRISON,
Crocker Building, San Francisco,

MILTON NEWMARK,
Crocker Building, San Francisco,

Attorneys for Appellant
and Petitioner.

FILED

FEB 25 1932

PAUL P. O'BRIEN,

PERNAU-WALSH PRINTING CO., SAN FRANCISCO

No. 6586

United States Circuit Court of Appeals
For the Ninth Circuit

D. W. JOHNSTON, as Trustee in Bankruptcy of the Estate of DuPont Milling & Sales Corporation, Bankrupt,

Appellant,

vs.

JOHN P. McLAUGHLIN, Collector of Internal Revenue,

Appellee.

APPELLANT'S PETITION FOR A REHEARING.

To the Honorable Curtis D. Wilbur, Presiding Judge, and to the Associated Judges of the United States Circuit Court of Appeals for the Ninth Circuit:

Conceiving the questions of law upon which this controversy rests to have been erroneously determined, appellant respectfully petitions the Court for a rehearing. In this behalf appellant respectfully submits the following points.

By admissions in the pleadings and stipulations of fact, these things are definitely established:

(1) The defendant, an officer of the Government, has money to which he is not entitled.

(2) There was no taxable income.

(3) There was no tax to be paid.

(4) The money was not paid as a tax, since there was no tax or taxable income.

(5) Detriment to existing creditors of the corporation resulted from the payment.

(6) One purpose of the false return and payment was to defraud these creditors.

(7) The creditors were in no wise at fault.

(8) This action is in behalf of the creditors, represented by the trustee in bankruptcy as plaintiff.

(9) Rights of the corporation or its stockholders are not involved.

The Court in its opinion says, "This is an action to recover taxes paid." Appellant respectfully submits that that is not true. This is the equitable action for money had and received, against a defendant who received money which in equity and good conscience he ought not to retain. Designating the payment as a tax does not make it so. It is elementary that equity looks through form, and to the substance. In form, there was a payment as of a tax, upon a false return, when there was in fact no taxable income, and no tax. The substance was the payment of money to one to whom there was nothing due. Certainly the Court should look through this form, just as it does through innumerable other colorable transactions in which money of an insolvent is, in fraud of creditors, paid to another, who, for lack of consideration, has no right in equity or good conscience to retain the money.

Clearly Section 606 of the Revenue Act, a statute concerning recovery of taxes paid, is inapplicable. That statute is not a general law. It is part of the revenue law, and deals only with taxes. Its purpose is to set at rest, by closing agreements, controversies concerning over- and under-payments of taxes. It was never intended to prevent recovery, for creditors of an insolvent, of money of the insolvent fraudulently paid as a tax when there was in fact no tax or income to be taxed. By every principle of law and statutory construction, the transaction here is not within the scope of the statute. Shorn of is false form, the payment was not the payment of a tax, but simply a fraudulent handing over of money of the corporation to one to whom nothing was due, and this without consideration and in fraud of existing creditors. There was here no tax controversy to be set at rest, but merely a colorable payment in fraud of creditors. As in all other cases, the beneficiary of the fraud, who received the fruits of the fraud without consideration, should be held to be a trustee of the fund received. The remedy in such cases is the equitable action for money had and received. The statute of limitations controlling that remedy is that applicable to any other action for money had and received, founded upon fraud. The jurisdiction of the Court arises from its general jurisdiction of actions at law and in equity, and is not controlled by this special statute concerning controversies over taxes. Here there was no tax, but simply a fraudulent payment in the guise of a tax.

No parallel or precedent for this action is to be found in the reported cases, for the reason that they all involve controversies concerning an over- or under-payment, where there was some tax to be paid. The singularity of this case, founded as it is upon a fraudulent use of the forms of law concerning revenue, should not deter the Court from righting the wrong merely because of use of the revenue law as an instrumentality of the fraud, there being in fact no income to be affected by the revenue law, and hence no tax to be paid. The cloak or guise under which a fraud is perpetrated should never be a determining factor protecting that fraud. Here, by the decision of the Court, a limitation found in the revenue law only, is made to protect the fraud, solely for the reason that the forms of the revenue law were used for the perpetration of the fraud. The inherent power of the Court can not be so limited. Despite the use of this or any other form, the Court should look to the substance of the transaction, and, applying the general underlying principles of law, right the wrong done by the fraud.

It is further said in the opinion that "No person can take advantage of his own wrong." That is an elementary principle, but we conceive it to have no application here. In considering this point it is necessary to keep clearly in mind who will benefit by the judgment sought here. It is also necessary to remember that there were two wrongs. First, the wrong against the Government, by the filing of the false return. That, however, was a wrong without injury, since there was in fact no income, and therefore no tax due to the Government. The second wrong, the foundation of this action, was to the creditors. It consisted of defrauding the creditors by payment of funds of the insolvent corporation to one to whom nothing was due.

The wrong complained of, the fraud upon creditors, was the act of the corporation or its officers, but the injury was to the creditors. An action by the corporation might have been successfully resisted on the ground that the corporation could not take advantage of its own wrong. But, while both wrongs were the acts of the corporation, the persons injured by the wrong complained of were the then and now existing creditors of the corporation. These creditors have been guilty of no wrong. Righting of the wrong done them will be of no advantage to the wrongdoer, the corporation. A judgment for the plaintiff will but take from the defendant money he received without consideration, and has therefore no right in equity or good conscience to retain, and give that money to creditors of the corporation, who are innocent of any wrong. This will not in any sense right the wrong, but will deprive the beneficiary of the fruits of the wrong, restoring those fruits, not to the corporation, but to creditors of the corporation, who are now and were such at the time of the wrong.

It is no answer to this position to say that the trustee in bankruptcy represents the corporation. In a sense he does represent the corporation, but also and primarily he represents the creditors. An action such as this is distinctly for the benefit of the creditors, and not the corporation. A defense available against the corporation, arising out of the fact that the wrong complained of was the act of the corporation, is not available against innocent creditors of the corporation. Had there been no bankruptcy, and had the corporation conveyed its property without consideration in violation of the bulk sales law, or any other of the numerous laws enacted for the protection of creditors, no one would assert that the beneficiary of the wrong could defend an action by the creditors on the ground that the wrong complained of was the act of the corporation.

The intervening of the bankruptcy does not change this situation. The primary purpose of bankruptcy is to distribute the bankrupt estate, including property wrongfully conveyed by the bankrupt, ratably among the bankrupt's creditors. For this purpose numerous kinds of actions are permitted to be maintained by the trustee to recover property fraudulently conveyed by the bankrupt. We conceive this to be no different from these other cases of fraudulent transfers. In none of these other cases does the fact that the corporation has been guilty of a wrong prevent the trustee in bankruptcy from recovering for creditors property wrongfully transferred by the bankrupt. In no essential respect does this fraudulent transfer from the bankrupt to the defendant here differ from any of the other fraudulent conveyances by bankrupts so frequently set aside by the Courts in actions by trustees in bankruptcy.

We think the Court has stressed too much, and perhaps been misled in its decision by, consideration of the fact that the trustee in bankruptcy also represents the bankrupt corporation. Incidentally he does represent the corporation, but only for the purpose of gathering the corporation's assets and distributing them among creditors. Bankruptcy acts, as well as all other insolvency acts, are primarily for the benefit of creditors, and to secure ratable distribution of assets among them. Incidentally, of course, the bankrupt benefits by being shielded from further claims of creditors. Actions, however, by the trustee in bankruptcy are not in furtherance of the benefit to the bankrupt, but in furtherance of the administration of the bankrupt's estate and for the benefit of creditors. So this action, prosecuted by the trustee in the course of the administration of the bankrupt's estate, is not in any sense for the benefit of the bankrupt, but rather for the benefit of the then and now existing creditors, who are innocent of wrong, and in fact defrauded by the act of the bankrupt.

We submit that the two major points touched upon by the opinion of the Court should have been resolved in favor of the appellant, that is, (1) that the Court is not deprived of jurisdiction by Section 606 of the Revenue Act, and (2) that the fact that the corporation was guilty of wrong is no defense to the action by the trustee representing creditors, they being innocent of any wrong but defrauded thereby, and being the true beneficiaries of the action.

Dated, San Francisco,
February 24, 1932.

Respectfully submitted,
C. H. Sooy,
Neil E. Larkin,
Fitzgerald, Abbott & Beardsley,
Brobeck, Phleger & Harrison,
Milton Newmark,
*Attorneys for Appellant
and Petitioner.*

CERTIFICATE OF COUNSEL.

I hereby certify that I am of counsel for appellant and petitioner in the above entitled cause and that in my judgment the foregoing petition for a rehearing is well founded in point of law as well as in fact and that said petition for a rehearing is not interposed for delay.

Dated, San Francisco,
February 24, 1932.

C. H. Sooy,
*Of Counsel for Appellant
and Petitioner.*

United States
Circuit Court of Appeals
For the Ninth Circuit.

WARREN H. PILLSBURY, Deputy Commissioner,
Thirteenth Compensation District under the Longshoremen's and Harbor-Workers' Act,

Appellant,

vs.

PACIFIC STEAMSHIP COMPANY, a corporation,
and UNION INSURANCE SOCIETY OF CAN-
TON, LTD., a corporation,

Appellees,

V. H. HAMMER,

Defendant.

Transcript of Record.

Upon Appeal from the United States District Court for the Southern
District of California, Central Division.

FILED

AUG 24 1931

PAUL P. O'BRIEN,
CLERK

Parker, Stone & Baird Co., Law Printers, Los Angeles.

United States
Circuit Court of Appeals
For the Ninth Circuit.

WARREN H. PILLSBURY, Deputy Commissioner, Thirteenth Compensation District under the Longshoremen's and Harbor-Workers' Act,

Appellant,

vs.

PACIFIC STEAMSHIP COMPANY, a corporation, and UNION INSURANCE SOCIETY OF CANTON, LTD., a corporation,

Appellees,

V. H. HAMMER,

Defendant.

Transcript of Record.

Upon Appeal from the United States District Court for the Southern District of California, Central Division.

Parker, Stone & Baird Co., Law Printers, Los Angeles.

INDEX.

[Clerk's Note: When deemed likely to be of an important nature, errors or doubtful matters appearing in the original record are printed literally in italic; and, likewise, cancelled matter appearing in the original record is printed and cancelled herein accordingly. When possible, an omission from the text is indicated by printing in italics the two words between which the omission seems to occur.]

PAGE

Names and Addresses of Attorneys.

For Defendant and Appellant:

SAMUEL W. McNABB, Esq.,
United States Attorney,

DOROTHY LENROOT BROMBERG, Esq.,
Assistant United States Attorney,

IGNATIUS F. PARKER, Esq.,
Assistant United States Attorney,
Federal Building,
Los Angeles, California.

For Complainants and Appellees:

McCUTCHEN, OLNEY,
MANNON & GREENE, Esqs.,
Roosevelt Building,
Los Angeles, California.

United States of America, ss.

To PACIFIC STEAMSHIP COMPANY, a corporation, and UNION INSURANCE SOCIETY OF CANTON, Ltd., a corporation, and

To McCutchen, Olney, Mannon & Greene, their attorneys, Roosevelt Bldg., Los Angeles, California   Greeting:

You are hereby cited and admonished to be and appear at a United States Circuit of Appeals for the Ninth Circuit, to be held at the City of San Francisco, in the State of California, on the 24th day of August, A. D. 1931, pursuant to Order allowing appeal, filed in the Clerk's Office of the District Court of the United States, in and for the Southern District of California, in that certain action entitled Pacific Steamship Company, a corporation, et al vs. Warren H. Pillsbury, Deputy Commissioner, et al, No. S-99-C, wherein the Deputy United States Commissioner for the 13th Compensation District is the defendant and appellant and you are the plaintiffs and appellees; and you are ordered to show cause, if any there be, why the decree in the said cause mentioned, should not be corrected, and speedy justice should not be done to the parties in that behalf.

WITNESS, the Honorable HARRY A. HOLLZER United States District Judge for the Southern District of California, this..........day of August, A. D. 1931, and of the Independence of the United States, the one hundred and fifty-sixth

Hollzer

U. S. District Judge for the Southern District of California.

Received copy of within citation this 8th day of August, 1931

McCutchen Olney Mannon & Greene

Attorneys for Appellees

[Endorsed]: In the United States Circuit Court of Appeals for the Ninth Circuit Pacific Steamship Company, et al vs. Warren H. Pillsbury, et al Citation Filed Aug 8 1931 R. S. Zimmerman, Clerk By B B Hansen Deputy Clerk

———

IN THE DISTRICT COURT OF THE UNITED STATES FOR THE SOUTHERN DISTRICT OF CALIFORNIA

PACIFIC STEAMSHIP COMPANY, a corporation, and UNION INSURANCE SOCIETY OF CANTON, LTD., a corporation,

Complainants,

vs.

No. S 99-C

WARREN H. PILLSBURY, Deputy Commissioner, Thirteenth Compensation District under the Longshoremen's and Harbor-workers' Act, and V. H. HAMMER,

Defendants.

BILL OF COMPLAINT

Come now the complainants and for their bill of complaint against the defendants allege:

I.

That the complainant Pacific Steamship Company is now and at all times herein mentioned was a corporation

organized and existing under and by virtue of the laws of
the State of Maine and an employer within the provisions
of the Longshoremen's and Harbor Workers' Compensation Act, hereinafter referred to as the "Act".

II.

That the complainant Union Insurance Society of Canton, Ltd., is now and at all times herein mentioned was
an insurance company organized as a corporation under
and by virtue of the laws of the Kingdom of Great
Britain, and authorized to do and doing business in the
State of California, and the insurance carrier secured
by the Pacific Steamship Company, a corporation, in accordance with the provisions of the Act.

III.

That the defendant Warren H. Pillsbury is now and
at all times herein mentioned was the Deputy Commissioner of the Thirteenth Compensation District under the
provisions of the Act.

IV.

That the defendant V. H. Hammer, hereinafter referred to as the "claimant", was, at the time of receiving
the personal injury hereinafter referred to, an employee
of the complainant Pacific Steamship Company, a corporation, within the provisions of the Act, a resident of San
Diego, California, and as defendants are informed and
believe and therefore allege, a citizen of the United States
of America and of the State of California.

V.

That on August 16, 1930, the claimant sustained personal injury while working as a longshoreman in the
employ of the complainant Pacific Steamship Company

upon the navigable waters of the United States, to-wit, on board a lighter then alongside the steamship RUTH ALEXANDER in the port of San Diego, California, within the aforesaid Thirteenth Compensation District. That the claimant made claim against complainants herein for compensation for said injury before the defendant, Warren H. Pillsbury, who, as said Deputy Commissioner, duly heard said claim and, upon evidence oral and documentary tendered by claimant and complainants, did, on November 20, 1930, make and file in his office his compensation order and award of compensation, copy of which is attached as Exhibit "A" hereto. That a copy of the record of hearing before said Deputy Commissioner, including transcript of oral testimony, and documentary evidence introduced by the parties, is filed herewith under the certificate of said Deputy Commissioner.

VI.

That said compensation order and award of compensation is not in accordance with law or with the provisions of the Act in the respects following: That it appears from the evidence adduced at said hearing that claimant did not work in the occupation of a longshoreman for substantially the whole of the year preceding his injury, his service in such employment in fact being less than five months of such immediately preceding year, earning therefrom at the maximum the sum of $25.00 per week. That during said period of less than five months that claimant was engaged in the employment of a longshoreman claimant did not work regularly every day or any certain number of days per week or any certain number of hours per day on the days when claimant did work, but claimant as all other longshoremen in the port of the City of San Diego and elsewhere worked for various employers and in various employments as a longshoreman when and if there was work in such employment for him to do. That the determination of earnings and the compensation rate to be based thereon is provided by Section 10 of said Act; that based upon the actual earnings of the claimant, to-wit, $25.00 per week, his compensation rate under said section and under subdivision c thereof, is the sum of $16.67 per week, which said sum the complainants paid to claimant from the date of said injury to the date of the termination of the disability of claimant. That the defendant Warren H. Pillsbury, as said Deputy Commissioner, erroneously failed and refused to determine said compensation rate pursuant to Section 10, subdivision c, of said Act, and determined the same under subdivision b thereof, fixing said compensation in the maximum amount allowable under said Act, to-wit, in the sum of $25.00 per week. That said subdivision b, and subdivision a, of said Section 10 cannot fairly and reasonably be applied in determining said compensation rate for said claimant.

VII.

That said Deputy Commissioner Warren H. Pillsbury arbitrarily and capriciously in applying said Section 10, subdivision b, of said Act, considered and selected for determinating the compensation which should be awarded to said claimant the annual earnings of another longshoreman who was not of the same class as claimant, but of a distinctly different and higher earnings class than said claimant, contrary to and in violation of the provisions of Section 10, subdivision b, of said Act.

VIII.

That said claimant V. H. Hammer was not at the time of his said injury nor at any time during the continuance of his disability and is not now entitled to compensation at the rate of $25.00 per week as awarded by said Deputy Commissioner Warren H. Pillsbury in his compensation order and award dated November 20, 1930, nor is said claimant entitled to compensation at any rate in excess of $16.67 per week, nor to any amount in excess of $133.36 which, prior to said award, had been paid by complainants to said claimant. That the further sum of $95.21 directed by said award to be paid, is not due or owing to said claimant under said award or at all, for the reason that in so far as it directs the payment of said further sum of $95.21, said award is contrary to law as aforesaid.

IX.

That said claimant V. H. Hammer is insolvent and if an interlocutory injunction be not issued herein staying the payment of the amounts in excess of the $16.67 per week required to be paid by the compensation order and award filed on the 20th day of November, 1930, as aforesaid, said excess payments would have to be made and if the complainants herein are successful in this action said payments in excess of $16.67 per week cannot be recovered from said claimant and said complainants will lose the benefits of any favorable decision herein and by reason thereof will suffer irreparable damage.

WHEREFORE complainants pray that said compensation order and award be suspended and set aside and that the payments of the amounts in excess of $16.67 per week required by said award be stayed pending final decision herein; and for such other, further or different relief as to the Court may seem equitable and just, together with costs of suit.

> Farnham P. Griffiths
>
> McCutchen, Olney, Mannon & Greene,
>
> Solicitors for Complainants

UNITED STATES OF AMERCA   )
)

STATE OF CALIFORNIA   ) ss.
)

CITY AND COUNTY OF SAN FRANCISCO)

J H Cooper, being first duly sworn, on oath deposes and says:

That he is an officer, to wit, Secretary of Pacific Steamship Company, a corporation, one of the complainants herein; that he makes this verification by authority for and on behalf of said complainants; that he has read the foregoing bill of complaint, knows the contents thereof, and that the same is true as he verily believes.

> J H Cooper

Subscribed and sworn to before me this 13th day of December, 1930.

> [Seal]   Frank L. Owen
>
> NOTARY PUBLIC
>
> In and for the State of California,
> City and County of San Francisco.

EXHIBIT "A"

UNITED STATES EMPLOYEES' COMPENSATION COMMISSION

13th Compensation District

In the matter of the claim for compensation under the Longshoremen's and Harbor Workers'
Compensation Act.

E. V. HAMMER,
Claimant

against

PACIFIC STEAMSHIP CO.,
Employer

UNION INSURANCE SOCIETY
OF CANTON, Ltd.,
Insurance Carrier

. COMPENSATION
ORDER

. AWARD OF
. COMPENSATION

. CASE NO. 10-526

. CLAIM NO. 383

. . . .

Such investigation in respect to the above entitled claim having been made as is considered necessary, and a hearing having been duly held in conformity with law, the Deputy Commissioner makes the following:

FINDINGS OF FACT

That on the 16th day of August, 1930, the claimant above named was in the employ of the employer above named at San Diego, in the State of California in the 13th Compensation District, established under the provisions of the Longshoremen's and Harbor Workers' Compensation Act, and that the liability of the employer for compensation under said Act was insured by the Union Insurance Society of Canton, Ltd.

That on said day claimant herein while performing service for the employer as a stevedore on board a lighter then alongside one of the defendant's ships sustained accidental injury occurring in the course of and arising out of his employment and resulting in disability as follows: while at work he slipped and fell on his wrist spraining it;

That notice of injury was not given within thirty days, but that the employer had knowledge of the injury and that the employer has not been prejudiced by failure to give notice;

That the employer furnished claimant with medical treatment, etc., in accordance with section 7 (a) of the said act:

PAGE TWO

That the claimant did not work as a stevedore for substantially the whole of the year preceding his injury, his service in such employment in fact commencing on April 4, 1930 and terminating with his injury; that during the time that claimant worked as a stevedore he was able and willing to work and sought work on each working day with the exception of two or three days during the period which are considered negligible; that another stevedore employed at the port of San Diego during the year immediately preceding claimant's injury, i. e., one Trimble, worked substantially the whole year as a stevedore and earned during said year wages in excess of $1,950.00, the maximum provided by said Act; that claimant's wages and compensation rate is therefore fixed at said maximum under section 10 (b) of said Act;

That as the result of the injury sustained the claimant was wholly disabled from the date thereof to Monday,

October 20, 1930 and is entitled to 9 and 1/7 weeks compensation, $25. a week for such disability amounting to $228.57;

Jurisdiction is reserved to determine hereafter whether said injury has caused disability subsequent to October 20, 1930;

That the employer has paid compensation for 8 weeks at $16.67 a week to and including Oct. 12, 1930, amounting to $133.36 and is entitled to credit therefore together with any further payments which may have been made subsequent to the date of the hearing:

Upon the foregoing facts the Deputy Commissioner makes the following:

AWARD

That the employer, the Pacific Steamship Company, and the insurance carrier, the Union Insurance Society of Canton, Ltd., shall pay to the claimant compensation as follows:

The sum of $95.21 to claimant forthwith

Given under my hand at San Francisco, California. this 20th day of November, 1930.

WARREN H. PILLSBURY
Deputy Commissioner
13th Compensation District

WHP:P

[Endorsed]: S 99-C In the District Court of the United States for the Southern District of California Pacific Steamship Company, a corporation, and Union Insurance Society of Canton, Ltd., a corporation, Complainants, vs. Warren H. Pillsbury, Deputy Commissioner, Thirteenth Compensation District under the Longshoremen's and Harbor Workers' Act, and V. H. Hammer,

Defendants Bill of Complaint McCutchen, Olney, Mannon & Greene Attorneys for Complainants. Balfour Building San Francisco, California   Roosevelt Building   Los Angeles, California

---

IN THE DISTRICT COURT OF THE UNITED STATES FOR THE SOUTHERN DISTRICT OF CALIFORNIA

PACIFIC STEAMSHIP COMPANY,)
a corporation, and UNION INSUR-)
ANCE SOCIETY OF CANTON,)
LTD., a corporation,)
)
Complainants,)
)
vs.   ) No. S-99-C
)
WARREN H. PILLSBURY, Deputy)
Commissioner, Thirteenth Compensa-)
tion District under the Longshore-)
men's and Harbor-workers' Act, and)
V. H. HAMMER,)
)
Defendants.)
———————————————————)

NOTICE OF MOTION FOR LEAVE TO AMEND BILL OF COMPLAINT

TO: Warren H. Pillsbury, as Deputy Commissioner, Thirteenth Compensation District, United States Employees Compensation Commission, defendants, and to Samuel W. McNabb, United States Attorney, and Ignatius F. Parker and Dorothy Lenroot Bromberg, Assistant United States Attorneys, Solicitors for said defendant.

TO: V. H. Hammer, defendant:

You and each of you will please take notice, and you are hereby notified, that on Monday, the 16th day of

March, 1931, at the hour of 10 o'clock A. M. of said day,
or as soon thereafter as counsel can be heard, complainants will move the court for an order granting them leave
to amend the bill of complaint on file in the above entitled
case in the manner and form set forth in the copy of said
amendment herewith annexed.

Dated: San Francisco, California, March 3, 1931.

McCutchen, Olney, Mannon & Greene,
Farnham P. Griffiths
Charles E. Finney
Solicitors for Complainants

IN THE DISTRICT COURT OF THE UNITED
STATES FOR THE SOUTHERN DISTRICT
OF CALIFORNIA

PACIFIC STEAMSHIP COMPANY,
a corporation, and UNION INSUR-
ANCE SOCIETY OF CANTON,
LTD., a corporation,

     Complainants,

    vs.   No. S-99-C

WARREN H. PILLSBURY, Deputy
Commissioner, Thirteenth Compensation District under the Longshoremen's and Harbor-workers' Act, and
V. H. HAMMER,

     Defendants.

AMENDMENT TO BILL OF COMPLAINT

Complainants above named, having obtained leave of
court, file this amendment to their bill of complaint as
follows:

Amend paragraph VI of said bill of complaint to read as follows:

VI.

That said compensation order and award of compensation is not in accordance with law or with the provisions of the Act in the respects following: That it appears from the evidence adduced at said hearing that claimant did not work in the occupation of a longshoreman for substantially the whole of the year preceding his injury, his service in such employment in fact being less than five months of such immediately preceding year, earning therefrom less than the sum of $25.00 per week. That during said period of less than five months that claimant was engaged in the employment of a longshoreman claimant did not work regularly every day or any certain number of days per week or any certain number of hours per day on the days when claimant did work, but claimant as all other longshoremen in the port of the City of San Diego and elsewhere worked for various employers and in various employments as a longshoreman when and if there was work in such employment for him to do. That the determination of earnings and the compensation rate to be based thereon is provided by Section 10 of said Act; that based upon the actual earnings of the claimant, his compensation rate under said section and under subdivision c thereof, is not to exceed the sum of $16.67 per week, which said sum the complainants paid to claimant from the date of said injury to the date of the termination of the disability of claimant. That the defendant Warren H. Pillsbury, as said Deputy Commissioner, erroneously failed and refused to determine said compensation rate pursuant to Section 10, subdivision c, of said Act, and determined the same under subdivision b thereof, fixing said compensation in the maximum amount allowable under said Act, to wit, in the sum of $25.00 per week. That said subdivision b, and subdivision a, of said Section 10 cannot fairly and reasonably be applied in determining said compensation rate for said claimant.

Add the following paragraph:

VIII-A

That the construction placed upon Section 10 of the Act by said defendant, Warren H. Pillsbury, results in the compensation of said claimant being computed on an arbitrary and unreasonable basis, not according to any prescribed scale gauged by the previous wages or earnings of claimant, and so construed said Act deprives complainants of their property without due process of law, and by reason thereof said Act is void and repugnant to the Fifth Amendment of the Constitution of the United States.

> McCutchen, Olney, Mannon & Greene,
> Farnham P. Griffiths,
> Charles E. Finney,
> > Solicitors for Complainants.

[Endorsed]: No. S-99-C In the District Court of the United States for the Southern District of California. Pacific Steamship Company, a corporation, and Union Insurance Society of Canton, Ltd., a corporation, complainants, vs. Warren H. Pillsbury, Deputy Commissioner, Thirteenth Compensation District under the Longshoremen's and Harbor-Workers' Act, and V. H. Hammer, Defendants. Notice of Motion for Leave to Amend Bill of Complaint. Receipt of a copy of the within motion admitted March 5/1931 Dorothy Lenroot Bromberg Ass. U. S. Attorney Filed Mar 5 - 1931 R. S. Zimmerman, Clerk By M L Gaines Deputy Clerk McCutchen, Olney, Mannon & Greene Counselors at Law Balfour Building San Francisco, California Roosevelt Building, Los Angeles, California

---

IN THE DISTRICT COURT OF THE UNITED STATES, IN AND FOR THE SOUTHERN DISTRICT OF CALIFORNIA, CENTRAL DIVISION.

PACIFIC STEAMSHIP COMPANY, a corporation, and UNION INSURANCE SOCIETY OF CANTON, LTD., a corporation,

)
)
)
) No. S-99-C
)
Complainants,) ANSWER.
)
vs.)
)
WARREN H. PILLSBURY, Deputy) Commissioner, Thirteenth Compensation District under the Longshoremen's and Harbor-workers' Act, and V. H. HAMMER,
)
)
)
)
)
Defendants.)

COMES now the defendant, Warren H. Pillsbury, Deputy Commissioner, 13th Compensation District, United States Employees' Compensation Commission, by his attorneys, SAMUEL W. McNABB, United States Attorney for the Southern District of California, and

IGNATIUS F. PARKER, and DOROTHY LENROOT BROMBERG, Assistant United States Attorneys for said district, and for Answer to the Bill of Complaint filed herein, admits, denies and alleges as follows:

I.

Admits the allegations of Paragraphs I, II, III, IV and V of the Bill of Complaint herein.

II.

Answering Paragraph VI of the Bill of Complaint herein, this defendant admits that it appears from the evidence adduced at said hearing that claimant did not work in the occupation of a longshoreman for substantially the whole of the year preceding his injury, and further admits the allegation that this defendant determined the compensation awarded to the claimant under Section 10 (b), Longshoremen's and Harbor Workers' Compensation Act, and further admits that the complainants herein paid to the claimant compensation for 8 weeks at $16.67 a week to and including October 12, 1930, amounting to $133.36, and denies each and every remaining allegation of Paragraph VI of Complainant's Bill herein.

III.

Answering Paragraphs VII and VIII of Complainants' Bill herein, this defendant denies each and every allegation therein contained.

IV.

Answering paragraph IX of the Bill of Complaint herein, this defendant alleges that he is without information or belief sufficient to enable him to answer said Paragraph IX and on that ground denies each and every allegation of said Paragraph IX.

WHEREFORE, defendant, Warren H. Pillsbury, as Deputy Commissioner, 13th Compensation District, United States Employees' Compensation Commission, prays that the complainants take nothing by their Bill of Complaint herein and that said Bill of Complaint be dismissed with costs against the complainants herein, and for such other and further relief as to the Court may seem proper in the premises.

Samuel W. McNabb

SAMUEL W. McNABB,

UNITED STATES ATTORNEY,

Ignatius F. Parker

IGNATIUS F. PARKER,

Assistant U. S. Attorney,

Dorothy Lenroot Bromberg

DOROTHY LENROOT BROMBERG,

Assistant U. S. Attorney,

Attorneys for Defendant, Warren H. Pillsbury, as Deputy Commissioner, Thirteenth Compensation District, United States Employees' Compensation Commission.

UNITED STATES OF AMERICA,
SOUTHERN DISTRICT OF CALIFORNIA)
) ss.
Central Division.   )

WARREN H. PILLSBURY, being first duly sworn, deposes and says:

That he is Deputy Commissioner of the 13th Compensation District, United States Employees' Compensation Commission, and one of the defendants in the above entitled action; that he has read the foregoing answer and knows the contents thereof; that the same is true of his own knowledge, except as to the matters which are herein stated on his information or belief, and as to those matters that he believes it to be true.

Warren H Pillsbury
WARREN H. PILLSBURY.

SUBSCRIBED AND SWORN to before me this 14 day of January, 1931.

[Seal]   Mary S. Haines

NOTARY PUBLIC
in and for the County of Los Angeles,
State of California
My Commission Expires Jan. 28, 1933

[Endorsed]: No. S-99-C In the District Court of the United States for the Southern District of California. Central Division. Pacific Steamship Company, a corporation, and Union Insurance Society of Canton, Ltd., a corporation, Complainants, vs. Warren H. Pillsbury, Deputy Commissioner, Thirteenth Compensation District under the Longshoremen's and Harbor-workers' Act, and V. H. Hammer, Defendants. Answer. Received copy of within answer this 23d day of January, 1931 McCutchen Olney, Mannon & Greene Attorney for Complainants. Filed Jan 23 1931 R. S. Zimmerman, Clerk By M L Gaines Deputy Clerk

––––––––

At a stated term, to wit: The FEBRUARY Term, A. D. 1931, of the District Court of the United States of America, within and for the CENTRAL Division of the Southern District of California, held at the Court Room thereof, in the City of LOS ANGELES on MONDAY the 9TH day of FEBRUARY in the year of our Lord one thousand nine hundred and thirty-One

Present:

The Honorable GEO. COSGRAVE, District Judge.

Pacific Steamship Company,
  a corporation, et al.,   Plaintiffs,)

        vs.   ) No. S-99-C-Eq.

Warren H. Pillsbury, etc., Defendants.)

This cause coming before the Court for hearing on Motion of Complainants for Interlocutory Injunction pursuant to Notice, etc., filed January 30th, 1931; and, for hearing on Motion of Warren H. Pillsbury for the Court to hear, consider and rule; Harold A. Black, Esq., of the firm of Messrs. McCutchen, Olney, Mannon & Greene, appearing as counsel for the plaintiffs, argues to the Court in support of said Motion for Interlocutory Injunction, whereupon, Dorothy L. Bromberg, Assistant United States Attorney, appearing as counsel for the Government, argues to the Court in opposition to said Motion, and said Attorney Black having thereupon argued further to the Court, said Motion is denied and exception noted for Complainants, and that said Motion of Warren H. Pillsbury for the Court to hear, consider and rule be submitted on briefs to be filed 15 x 15; date for oral argument to be determined later pending decision in another case in another court in another jurisdiction.

IN THE DISTRICT COURT OF THE UNITED
STATES FOR THE SOUTHERN DISTRICT
OF CALIFORNIA CENTRAL DIVISION

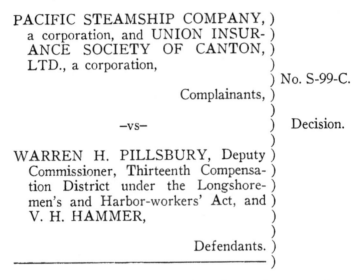

PACIFIC STEAMSHIP COMPANY,
a corporation, and UNION INSUR-
ANCE SOCIETY OF CANTON,
LTD., a corporation,

Complainants,

—vs—

WARREN H. PILLSBURY, Deputy
Commissioner, Thirteenth Compensation District under the Longshoremen's and Harbor-workers' Act, and
V. H. HAMMER,

Defendants.

No. S-99-C.

Decision.

The bill of complaint in this action seeks suspension and
setting aside of the order of Warren H. Pillsbury, Deputy
Commissioner of the Thirteenth Compensation District
under the Longshoremen's and Harbor Workers' Act,
(44 Stat. 1424; 33 USCA 901), wherein the Deputy
Commissioner awarded to V. H. Hammer compensation
for injury suffered while working as a stevedore on board
a lighter then alongside one of the plaintiff's ships at the
port of San Diego. Compensation was awarded at the
rate of $25.00 a week under Section 10 of the Act.

Claimant had been employed as teamster for San Diego
County for a number of months and began work as a
stevedore on April 6, 1930. He continued in this employment until August 16th following, a period of four
and one half months, when the accident occurred from

which he suffered the injury. It was admitted that this was in the course of his employment.

The testimony on which the award is based is so confusing and uncertain as to render a clear finding of facts by the Commissioner very difficult and a review of the evidence by the court equally so. Claimant stated that he had worked as much as five days a week and a total of 270 days during the year and estimated his wages as $35 a week. This estimate, however, was not based on any exact figures but upon his living expenses. From the time he commenced as a stevedore he lost no time on account of illness and took but a few days vacation and was on hand daily to accept any offered employment.

It fairly appears from the testimony taken at the hearing that the stevedore workers at San Diego harbor may be placed in three general classes: Those constituting a regular gang that worked on the "white boats", being the Steamships Harvard and Yale, at least four days a week, and had a preference as to all other cargo handling and had fairly regular employment. The next in order are referred to as the lumber list, whose employment was not so steady and continuous as those on the list just mentioned. The third list was known as the cargo list. When there were not enough men to supply the lumber list they were taken from the cargo list. Claimant was on the latter list. He worked on some lumber boats and occasionally on the Harvard or Yale. He was not in a regular gang. Only men in the regular gang or preferred list worked as much as 270 days or parts of days a year. The manager of the Marine Service Bureau, which seemed to be the principal agency in distributing the work at San

Diego, was called as a witness and believed that claimant was earning over $100 per month but he could not say how much. The average earnings of men in the class similar to that of claimant were estimated by him to be $130 a month. None made more than $150. The nearest approach to accuracy in the entire testimony is the amount actually earned by claimant during the four and one half months of his employment. This is conceded to be $355.38, or a weekly amount of $19.00, and of this amount $50 is estimated. Trimble, upon whose earnings the award to claimant was based, was on the regular gang working the Harvard and Yale regularly. He was described by the Pacific Coast S. S. Co. as working harder and longer hours than any other man on the waterfront and averaged $223.79 per month.

The Commissioner found that claimant did not work substantially the whole of the year preceding his injury; that he was able and willing to work and sought work on each working day; "that another stevedore employed at the port of San Diego during the year immediately preceding claimant's injury, i. e., one Trimble, worked substantially the whole of the year as a stevedore and earned during said year wages in excess of $1950; . . . . that claimant's wage and compensation rate is therefore fixed at such maximum under Section 10 (b) of said Act."

Complainant's point of attack is the action of the Commissioner in fixing the compensation of claimant under subdivision (b) of Section 10 instead of under subdivision (c), and further rating compensation of claimant according to that earned by the workman Trimble who, complainant claims, is not in a class similar to that of claimant within the contemplation of the Act.

The Act in question, Longshoremen's and Harbor Workers' Act, (44 Stat. 1424; 33 USCA 901), provides in Section 910:

"Except as otherwise provided in this chapter, the average weekly wage of the injured employee at the time of the injury shall be taken as the basis upon which to compute compensation and shall be determined as follows:

(a) If the injured employee shall have worked in the employment in which he was working at the time of the injury, whether for the same or another employer, during substantially the whole of the year immediately preceding his injury, his average annual earnings shall consist of three hundred times the average daily wage or salary which he shall have earned in such employment during the days when so employed.

(b) If the injured employee shall not have worked in such employment during substantially the whole of such year, his average annual earnings shall consist of three hundred times the average daily wage or salary which an employee of the same class working substantially the whole of such immediately preceding year in the same or in similar employment in the same or a 'neighboring place shall have earned in such employment during the days when so employed.

(c) If either of the foregoing methods of arriving at the annual average earnings of an injured employee can not reasonably and fairly be applied, such annual earnings shall be such sum as, having regard to the previous earnings of the injured employee and of other employees of the same or most similar class, working in the same or most similar employment in the same or a neighboring locality, shall reasonably represent the annual earning capacity of the injured employee in the employment in which he was working at the time of the injury.

By the provisions of the Act involved in this action (Longshoremen's and Harbor Workers' Act, 44 Stat. 1424; 33 USCA 901), two general methods of arriving at the compensation to be awarded injured employees are provided, with a third method which is to be used when neither of the first two can reasonably and fairly be applied. This may be said to result in three divisions of employees: First, those who have worked substantially the whole of the year immediately preceding the injury and whose average annual earnings are fixed at three hundred times the average daily wage earned during the time they were so employed. Second, those who have not worked the whole of such year; their average annual earnings are deeemed to be three hundred times the average daily wage of a person of the same class who works substantially the whole of such year in similar employment and neighborhood.

It is evident that both of these provisions contemplate employment that is continuous and regular to the extent of affording employment for substantially the whole of the year. By administrative construction a variation or tolerance of ten percent from the 300 day standard year is allowed so that the minimum constituting what is substantially a whole year is 270 days. In order to effect a computation under subdivision (b) the employment must be such that there are those who have worked in it or similar employment substantially the whole of the year immediately preceding the injury.

The third method is to be used when neither of the methods mentioned can fairly and reasonably be applied. This situation might arise in many cases. For instance if an employee works 365 days a year it would be an injustice to him to compensate him on the basis of only 300 days. On the other hand if an employee worked fewer than 270 days it would be unfair to the employer to fix his compensation on the assumption that he worked a full 300 days.

In the third case, i. e., if either of the methods described cannot reasonably and fairly be applied, the compensation is to be based on the annual earning capacity of the injured employee, the elements determining this being the previous earnings of the injured employee and of other employees in a situation most nearly similar.

Two questions are presented to the court: Was the Commissioner justified in fixing the compensation of claimant as provided in subdivision (b) of Section 10 of the Act, i. e., according to the wages earned by one who was employed during substantially the whole of the year in a similar employment in the same locality? If this course was proper, was the basis of comparison, i. e., the wages of Trimble, a proper one?

Admittedly there were three classes of stevedores at San Diego. Trimble was on a regular gang or preferred list, the members of which were the only ones working 270 days a year. Claimant was not on this list but was on the cargo list and did not work 270 days a year. Trimble worked harder and longer hours than any other man on the waterfront.   He was on the preferred list, the one most favorably situated.   Claimant was on the least preferred, the most unfavorably situated.   In the face of claimant's actual earnings of $355, or less than $90 per month, and his situation on a list not working 270 days a year he cannot be deemed in the same class as Trimble. Since no one in claimant's class worked substantially the whole of the year immediately preceding his injury, there is no basis of comparison by which the provisions of subdivision (b) can be applied.

Mahoney vs. Marshall, 46 Fed (2d) 539.

Luckenbach Steamship Co. vs. Marshall, Decided by Judge McNary on March 16, 1931, District Court of Oregon.   Undecided by Circuit Court to date.

Nelson Co. vs. Pillsbury, 48 Fed (2d) 883.

The Act in question is wise in its conception and beneficient in its operation.   It must be interpreted and enforced with such care that it shall not be an agency of unfairness either to the employer or to the employee.   Its careful and fair administration is the best guaranty of its permanence.

The proceedings are therefore referred back to the Commissioner with instructions to fix the compensation of claimant as under subdivision (c).

Geo. Cosgrave

U. S. District Judge.

[Endorsed]: No. S-99-C Eq. Filed Jun 26 1931
R. S. Zimmerman, Clerk By Francis E. Cross, Deputy
Clerk

––––––

At a stated term, to wit: The FEBRUARY Term,
A. D. 1931, of the District Court of the United States
of America, within and for the CENTRAL Division of
the Southern District of California, held at the Court
Room thereof, in the City of LOS ANGELES on FRI-
DAY the 26th day of JUNE in the year of our Lord one
thousand nine hundred and thirty-One

Present:

The Honorable GEO. COSGRAVE, District Judge.

Pacific Steamship Co., a corp., et al.,)
        Plaintiffs,)
    vs.)
) No. S-99-C
Warren H. Pillsbury, Deputy) Eq.
 Commissioner, et al., Defendants.)

On February 9, 1931, the cause having been ordered
submitted on briefs 15 x 15 etc. and briefs having been
filed and duly considered, upon consideration whereof the
court now files its "Decision," and, pursuant thereto, the
proceedings are referred back to the commissioner with
instructions to fix the compensation of claimant etc.

IN THE DISTRICT COURT OF THE UNITED
STATES FOR THE SOUTHERN DISTRICT OF
CALIFORNIA CENTRAL DIVISION

PACIFIC STEAMSHIP COMPANY,)
a corporation, and UNION INSUR-)
ANCE SOCIETY OF CANTON,)
LTD., a corporation,)
)
           Complainants,)
)
      –vs–   ) No. S-99-C.
)
WARREN H. PILLSBURY, Deputy)
Commissioner, Thirteenth Compensa-)
tion District under the Longshore-)
men's and Harbor-workers' Act, and)
V. H. HAMMER,)
)
           Defendants.)
—————————————————)

DECREE.

This cause came regularly on to be heard at this term
of court on March 23, 1931 upon complainants' bill of
complaint, amendment to bill of complaint, answer of
defendant Warren H. Pillsbury, Deputy Commissioner,
Thirteenth Compensation District, United States Employees Compensation Commission, and certified copy of
the transcript and record of hearings before said Deputy
Commissioner, the complainants and defendant Warren
H. Pillsbury appearing through their respective counsel,
and defendant V. H. Hammer not appearing although
duly and regularly served with process by the United
States Marshal; and said cause having been fully argued, briefed and submitted, and the court being fully

advised of the law and the facts renders herein its decree.

FINDINGS OF FACT.

The court finds that claimant V. H. Hammer had been engaged in the employment of a longshoreman for a period of 4½ months prior to the time when he sustained the injury for which he claims compensation; that during that period he earned Three hundred fifty-five dollars and thirty-eight cents ($355.38), or a weekly amount of approximately Nineteen dollars ($19.00); that said claimant did not work as much as 270 days during the year immediately preceding his injury, nor did he work at an equivalent rate during the weeks that he was engaged in the longshoring industry; that said claimant did not work at the rate of 6 days or parts of days per week during the time when he was employed in said industry; that said claimant was ready to work if he could have secured employment on all but a few days during the time that he was employed in said industry; and

The court finds that longshoremen at the port of San Diego where said claimant was employed and injured are divided in three general classes, namely: those employed in regular gangs in this employment, those who specialize in the handling of lumber, and those on the general cargo list who receive such work as is not obtained by either of the first two classes; that one Trimble, upon whose earnings the award of claimant was based, was a member of the first class and secured more work than any other longshoreman in the port of San Diego during the year immediately preceding the injury to claimant; that said claimant was a member of the third class, all of whom secured less than 270 days or parts of days work during the year.

CONCLUSIONS OF LAW.

From the foregoing facts the Court concludes as matters of law that Subdivision (b) of Section 10 of the Longshoremen's and Harborworkers' Compensation Act cannot reasonably and fairly be applied to determine the annual average earnings of said claimant; that Subdivision (c) of said Section 10 of said Longshoremen's and Harborworkers' Compensation Act should have been applied by said Deputy Commissioner to arrive at the annual average earnings of said claimant; that said claimant and said Trimble are not in the same class within the longshoring industry and that the award of said defendant Deputy Commissioner is not in accordance with law; and

BY REASON OF THE PREMISES, IT IS HEREBY ORDERED, ADJUDGED AND DECREED that said compensation order and award of compensation made by said defendant Deputy Commissioner in favor of said claimant V. H. Hammer on the 20th day of November, 1930, be and the same is hereby suspended and set aside; and the said defendant Warren H. Pillsbury, Deputy Commissioner for the Thirteenth Compensation District under the Longshoremen's and Harborworkers' Compensation Act be and he is hereby enjoined from enforcing said compensation order and award of compensation made by him on said 20th day of November, 1930; and

IT IS FURTHER ORDERED, ADJUDGED AND DECREED that said proceedings herein be and they are hereby referred back to said defendant Deputy Commissioner, and said Deputy Commissioner be and he is hereby directed to make a compensation order and award of compensation in said proceeding in accordance with this decree and in accordance with the opinion filed herein on June 26, 1931; and that no other or further or different compensation order or award of compensation be made or entered; and

IT IS FURTHER ORDERED, ADJUDGED AND DECREED that said claimant and defendant V. H. Hammer pay back to complainants herein any sums which may have been received by him in excess of the amounts which may be due him under the compensation order and award of compensation which is to be made and entered herein by said Deputy Commissioner in accordance with law and this decree and the opinion of this Court.

Dated: July 2nd, 1931.

Geo. Cosgrave
United States District Judge.

Approved as to form as provided in Rule 44.

McCutchen, Olney, Mannon & Greene

Not approved as to form because of the objections filed herewith

Received copy of within Decree this 1st day of July, 1931

Dorothy Lenroot Bromberg
Attorney for Defendant.

Decree entered and recorded 7/2/31. R. S. Zimmerman Clerk. By Francis E. Cross Deputy Clerk.

[Endorsed]: No. S-99-C. In the District Court of the United States for the Southern District of California, Central Division. Pacific Steamship Company, a corporation, and Union Insurance Society of Canton, Ltd., a corporation, Complainants, -vs- Warren H. Pillsbury, Deputy Commissioner, Thirteenth Compensation District under the Longshoremen's and Harborworkers' Act, and V. H. Hammer, Defendants. Decree. Filed Jul 2 1931 R. S. Zimmerman, Clerk By Francis E. Cross, Deputy Clerk, McCutchen, Olney, Mannon & Greene Attorneys for Complainants. Balfour Building San Francisco, California

---

IN THE DISTRICT COURT OF THE UNITED STATES IN AND FOR THE SOUTHERN DISTRICT OF CALIFORNIA CENTRAL DIVISION

PACIFIC STEAMSHIP COMPANY,)
a corporation, (
UNION INSURANCE SOCIETY OF)
CANTON, Ltd., a corporation, (
)
Complainants, (No. S-99-C
)
vs. (
) PETITION
WARREN H. PILLSBURY, Deputy (FOR
Commissioner 13th Compensation Dis-) APPEAL
trict, under the Longshoremen's and (
Harbor Workers' Compensation Act,)
and (
V. H. HAMMER,)
Defendants and (
Appellants.)

TO THE HONORABLE GEORGE COSGRAVE, DISTRICT JUDGE:

The above named defendant WARREN H. PILLS-
BURY, feeling aggrieved by the Decree and Findings of
Fact and Conclusions of Law rendered and entered in
the above entitled cause on the 2nd day of July, 1931, does
hereby appeal from said Decree to the Circuit Court of
Appeals for the Ninth Circuit for the reasons set forth
in the Assignments of Errors filed herewith, and your
Petitioner respectfully prays that the appeal be allowed
and that Citation be issued as provided by law, and that
a transcript of the record proceedings and documents
upon which said Decree was based, duly authenticated, be
sent to the United States Circuit Court of Appeals for
the Ninth Circuit under the rules of such court in such
cases made and provided.

Samuel W. McNabb

SAMUEL W. McNABB

United States Attorney

IGNATIUS F. PARKER

Assistant United States Attorney

Dorothy Lenroot Bromberg

DOROTHY LENROOT BROMBERG

Assistant United States Attorney

DATED: This 7th day of August, 1931.

IN THE DISTRICT COURT OF THE UNITED
STATES IN AND FOR THE SOUTHERN
DISTRICT OF CALIFORNIA
CENTRAL DIVISION

PACIFIC STEAMSHIP COMPANY, a corporation, UNION INSURANCE SOCIETY OF CANTON, Ltd., a corporation, Complainants, vs. WARREN H. PILLSBURY, Deputy Commissioner 13th Compensation District, under the Longshoremen's and Harbor Workers' Compensation Act, and V. H. HAMMER, Defendants and Appellants.	No. S-99-C ORDER ALLOWING APPEAL

The Petition of the Defendant in the above entitled cause for an appeal from the Final Decree is hereby granted and the appeal is allowed; and shall suspend and stay all further proceedings in this court until the termination of said appeal by the United States Circuit Court of Appeals for the Ninth Circuit.

Hollzer
United States District Judge

DATED: This 7 day of August, 1931.

[Endorsed]: No. S-99-C In the District Court of the United States for the Southern District of California Central Division Pacific Steamship Co, et al vs. Warren H. Pillsbury, et al Order and Petition on Appeal Filed Aug 8 1931 R. S. Zimmerman, Clerk By B. B. Hansen Deputy Clerk

IN THE DISTRICT COURT OF THE UNITED
STATES IN AND FOR THE SOUTHERN
DISTRICT OF CALIFORNIA
CENTRAL DIVISION

PACIFIC STEAMSHIP COMPANY,)
  a corporation, (
UNION INSURANCE SOCIETY OF)
  CANTON, Ltd., a corporation, (
)
           Complainants, (
     vs.   )
          (
WARREN H. PILLSBURY, Deputy)
  Commissioner 13th Compensation Dis- (
  trict, under the Longshoremen's and)
  harbor Workers' Compensation Act, (
  and   )
V. H. HAMMER,   (
)
      Defendants and (
      Appellants.)
	No. S-99-C
	
	ASSIGN-
	MENT OF
	ERRORS

Comes now the defendant and appellant, Warren H.
Pillsbury, Deputy Commissioner for the 13th Compensation District in the above entitled cause and files the
following Assignment of Errors upon which he will rely
in the prosecution of the appeal herein petitioned for
in said cause from the decree of this Honorable Court entered on the 2nd day of July, 1931.

I.

The Court erred in finding that the exact amount
the claimant V. H. Hammer earned during the period
he was employed as stevedore was $355.38.

II.

The Court erred in finding that said claimant did not
work at the rate of six days or parts of days per week
during the time he was employed in said industry.

III.

The Court erred in finding that longshoremen in the Port of San Diego are divided into three general classes within the meaning of the Longshoremen's and Harbor Workers' Compensation Act.

IV.

The Court erred in finding that one Trimble upon whose earnings the award of said claimant was based, belonged to a different class within the meaning of the Longshoremen's and Harbor Workers' Compensation Act, than said claimant.

V.

The Court erred in its implied finding that there was no evidence before the Deputy Commissioner which, if believed, would make the amount awarded to said claimant by the Deputy Commissioner fair and reasonable within the intent of Section 10 of the Longshoremen's and Harbor Workers' Compensation Act.

VI.

The Court erred in its conclusion of law that Subdivision (b) of Section 10 of the Longshoremen's and Harbor Workers' Compensation Act, cannot reasonably and fairly be applied to determine the annual average earnings of said claimant and that Subdivision (c) of said Section of said Act should have been applied by said Deputy Commissioner to arrive at the average annual earnings of said claimant.

VII.

The Court erred in its implied conclusion of law that wherever the result obtained by applying Subdivision (b) of Section 10 of the Longshoremen's and Harbor Workers' Compensation Act is in excess of the actual earnings of the claimant, said section cannot fairly and reasonably be applied.

VIII.

The Court erred in suspending and setting aside the Compensation order and award of compensation made by the Deputy Commissioner, defendant herein, on the 20th day of November, 1930, in favor of the claimant V. H. Hammer, and in enjoining the enforcement of such order and award.

IX.

The Court erred in ordering, adjudging and decreeing that said claimant and defendant V. H. Hammer pay back to the plaintiffs herein any sums which may have been received by him under the compensation order and award of compensation which the court has ordered said Deputy Commissioner to make in accordance with its decree, for the reasons that:

(a) The Court has only such jurisdiction under the Longshoremen's and Harbor Workers' Compensation Act as is given to it by the terms of said Act, and the Act does not provide for an order compelling the claimants of a compensation award to repay to the employer or insurance companies any amount he may have received in excess of that that the Deputy Commissioner may be required to make by order of the Court;

(b) Said decree was prematurely entered in that V. H. Hammer herein, although duly served with process, made no appearance in the case and his default was not entered.

(c) Said portion of the decree is based upon issues not made by the pleadings.

> Samuel W. McNabb
> SAMUEL W. McNABB,
> United States Attorney,
> Dorothy Lenroot Bromberg
> DOROTHY LENROOT BROMBERG
> Assistant United States Attorney,
> Ignatius F. Parker
> IGNATIUS F. PARKER,
> Assistant United States Attorney.

DATED: This 7th day of August, 1931.

[Endorsed]: No. S-99-C In the District Court of the United States for the Southern District of California, Central Division Pacific Steamship Co. et al vs. Warren H. Pillsbury, et al Assignment of Errors Filed Aug 8 1931 R. S. Zimmerman, Clerk By B B Hansen, Deputy Clerk

―――

IN THE DISTRICT COURT OF THE UNITED
STATES IN AND FOR THE SOUTHERN
DISTRICT OF CALIFORNIA
CENTRAL DIVISION

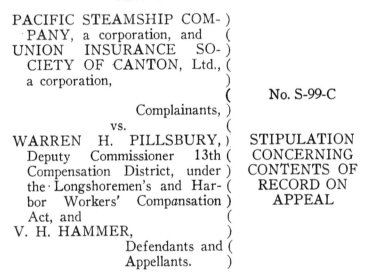

PACIFIC STEAMSHIP COM-
PANY, a corporation, and
UNION INSURANCE SO-
CIETY OF CANTON, Ltd.,
a corporation,

           Complainants,

      vs.

WARREN H. PILLSBURY,
Deputy Commissioner 13th
Compensation District, under
the Longshoremen's and Har-
bor Workers' Compansation
Act, and
V. H. HAMMER,

         Defendants and
         Appellants.

No. S-99-C

STIPULATION
CONCERNING
CONTENTS OF
RECORD ON
APPEAL

IT IS HEREBY STIPULATED by and between the parties hereto that the original copy of the record of hearing before the Deputy Commissioner, including the transcript of oral testimony and documentary evidence introduced by the parties and filed by the plaintiffs herein under the Certificate of the Deputy Commissioner and referred to in Paragraph V of plaintiffs' complaint may be transmitted to the Clerk as part of the record on appeal herein, and shall be incorporated into the transcript of record on appeal herein in addition to the portions of the record indicated by the praecipe filed herein.

Samuel W. McNabb
SAMUEL W. McNABB,
United States Attorney,
Dorothy Lenroot Bromberg
DOROTHY LENROOT BROMBERG
Assistant United States Attorney
Ignatius F. Parker
IGNATIUS F. PARKER,
Assistant United States Attorney,
Attorneys for defendant
McCutchen, Olney, Mannon & Greene
Attorneys for Complainants.

DATED: This 7th day of August, 1931.

IT IS SO ORDERED:

Hollzer
United States District Judge.

[Endorsed]: No. S-99-C In the District Court of the United States for the Southern District of California Central Division Pacific Steamship Co, et al vs. Warren H. Pillsbury, et al Stipulation Concerning Contents of Record on Appeal Filed Aug 8 1931 R. S. Zimmerman, Clerk By B B Hansen, Deputy Clerk

IN THE DISTRICT COURT OF THE UNITED
STATES IN AND FOR THE SOUTHERN
DISTRICT OF CALIFORNIA
CENTRAL DIVISION

PACIFIC STEAMSHIP COMPANY,)
a corporation, UNION INSURANCE)
SOCIETY OF CANTON, Ltd., a cor-)
poration,)
                 Complainants,)
)
      vs.   ) No. S-99-C.
)
WARREN H. PILLSBURY, Deputy)
Commissioner, 13th Compensation Dis-)
trict, under the Longshoremen's and)
Harbor Workers' Compensation Act,)
and V. H. HAMMER,)
)
   Defendants and Appellants.)

ORDER THAT ORIGINAL COPY OF THE REC-
ORD BEFORE THE DEPUTY COMMIS-
SIONER NEED NOT BE PRINTED AND MAY
BE TRANSMITTED BY THE CLERK TO THE
UNITED STATES CIRCUIT COURT OF AP-
PEALS.

ON MOTION of Samuel W. McNabb, United States
Attorney for the Southern District of California, and
Dorothy Lenroot Bromberg, Assistant United States Attorney for said District, and good cause appearing therefor;

IT IS HEREBY ORDERED that the original copy of
the Record of the Hearing before the Deputy Commissioner, including the Transcript of oral testimony and
documentary evidence introduced by the parties and filed
by the Complainants herein, and referred to in Paragraph
V of Complainants' Complaint, need not be printed and

may be transmitted by the Clerk of this Court to the United States Circuit Court of Appeals for the Ninth Circuit as part of the record on appeal herein and returned to the files of this Court upon determination of the appeal in the United States Circuit Court of Appeals for the Ninth Circuit.

DATED: August 13, 1931.

Hollzer
United States District Judge.

[Endorsed]: Filed Aug 13 1931   R. S. Zimmerman, Clerk,   By Edmund L. Smith, Deputy Clerk.

IN THE DISTRICT COURT OF THE UNITED
STATES IN AND FOR THE SOUTHERN
DISTRICT OF CALIFORNIA
CENTRAL DIVISION

PACIFIC STEAMSHIP COM-
PANY, a corporation and
UNION INSURANCE SOCIETY
OF CANTON, Ltd., a corpora-
tion,

Complainants,

vs.

WARREN H. PILLSBURY, Dep-
uty Commissioner 13th Compensation District, under the Longshoremen's and Harbor Workers'
Compensation Act, and
V. H. HAMMER,

Defendants and
Appellants.

No. S-99-C

PRAECIPE
FOR
TRANSCRIPT
OF RECORD

TO THE CLERK OF THE ABOVE ENTITLED
COURT:

Please prepare a record on appeal in the above entitled cause and include therein the following:

1. Bill of Complaint and Application for Mandatory Injunction;
2. Amendment to Bill of Complaint;
3. Answer;
4. Minute Order entered Monday the 9th day of February, 1931, denying plaintiffs' motion for an Interlocutory Injunction;
5. Decision entered June 26, 1931;
6. Minute order of June 26, 1931;
7. Petition for Appeal and Order allowing appeal;
8. Assignment of Errors;
9. Citation on Appeal;
10. Stipulation concerning contents of record on appeal;
11. This Praecipe.
12. Final Decree.

> Samuel W. McNabb
> SAMUEL W. McNABB
> > United States Attorney
>
> Dorothy Lenroot Bromberg
> DOROTHY LENROOT BROMBERG
> > Assistant United States Attorney,
>
> Ignatius F. Parker,
> IGNATIUS F. PARKER,
> > Assistant United States Attorney.

DATED: This 7th day of August, 1931.

IT IS HEREBY STIPULATED that the above material comprises the entire record on appeal.

> McCutchen, Olney, Mannon & Greene
> Solicitors for Complainants.

[Endorsed]: No. S-99-C In the District Court of the United States for the Southern District of California Central Division Pacific Steamship Co, et al, vs. Warren H. Pillsbury, et al Praecipe for Transcript of Record Filed Aug 10 1931 R. S. Zimmerman, Clerk By Edmund L. Smith Deputy Clerk

IN THE DISTRICT COURT OF THE UNITED
STATES IN AND FOR THE SOUTHERN
DISTRICT OF CALIFORNIA
CENTRAL DIVISION

PACIFIC STEAMSHIP COMPANY,)
a corporation, and UNION INSUR-)
ANCE SOCIETY OF CANTON,)
LTD., a corporation,)
)
Complainants,)
)
           –vs–) No. S-99-C.
)
WARREN H. PILLSBURY, Deputy)
Commissioner, Thirteenth Compensa-)
tion District under the Longshore-)
men's and Harbor-workers' Act, and)
V. H. HAMMER,)
)
Defendants.)

CLERK'S CERTIFICATE.

I, R. S. Zimmerman, clerk of the United States District
Court for the Southern District of California, do hereby
certify the foregoing volume containing 43 pages, numbered from 1 to 43 inclusive, to be the Transcript of
Record on Appeal in the above entitled cause, as printed
by the appellant, and presented to me for comparison and
certification, and that the same has been compared and
corrected by me and contains a full, true and correct copy
of the citation; bill of complaint; notice of motion for
leave to amend bill of complaint; amendment to bill of
complaint; answer; minute order of February 9, 1931;
decision; minute order of June 26, 1931; decree; petition
for appeal; order allowing appeal; assignment of errors;

stipulation concerning contents of record on appeal, and praecipe.

I DO FURTHER CERTIFY that the fees of the Clerk for comparing, correcting and certifying the foregoing Record on Appeal amount to..................and that said amount has been paid me by the appellant herein.

IN TESTIMONY WHEREOF, I have hereunto set my hand and affixed the Seal of the District Court of the United States of America, in and for the Southern District of California, Central Division, this..............day of August in the year of Our Lord One Thousand Nine Hundred and Thirty-one, and of our Independence the One Hundred and Fifty-sixth.

R. S. ZIMMERMAN,
Clerk of the District Court of the United States of America, in and for the Southern District of California.

By

Deputy.

ted States Circuit Court of Appeals

For the Ninth Circuit

N H. PILLSBURY, Deputy Commis-
r 13th Compensation District,
r the Longshoremen's and Harbor
kers' Compensation Act, and V.
[AMMER,

Appellants,

vs.

J STEAMSHIP COMPANY, a corpora-
UNION INSURANCE SOCIETY OF
ton LTD., a corporation,

Appellees.

No. 6587

---

rief of Amici Curiae on Behalf of Seattle Waterfront Employers and Portland Waterfront Employers.

---

ppeal from the United States District Court for the Southern
District of California, Central Division.

BOGLE, BOGLE & GATES,
LAWRENCE BOGLE,
STANLEY B. LONG,
    Central Building, Seattle.
GROSSCUP & MORROW,
W. CARR MORROW,
JOHN AMBLER,
    Republic Building, Seattle.
Solicitors for Seattle Waterfront Employers,
Amici Curiae.

WOOD, MONTAGUE & MATTHIESSEN,
ERSKINE WOOD,
GUNTHER F. KRAUSE,
    Yeon Building, Portland.
Solicitors for Portland Waterfront Employers,
Amici Curiae.

WARREN H. PILLSBURY, Deputy Commissioner 13th Compensation District, under the Longshoremen's and Harbor Workers' Compensation Act, and V. H. HAMMER,

Appellants,

vs.

PACIFIC STEAMSHIP COMPANY, a corporation; UNION INSURANCE SOCIETY OF CANTON LTD., a corporation,

Appellees.

No. 6587

Brief of Amici Curiae on Behalf of Seattle Waterfront Employers and Portland Waterfront Employers.

Upon Appeal from the United States District Court for the Southern District of California, Central Division.

STATEMENT.

The above case is the fourth case of its kind decided in the lower courts of the Pacific Coast and the second case to reach this court on appeal. These cases are as follows:

> *Mahoney v. Marshall,* 46 Fed. (2d) 359 (Winkler case, Washington). (Already before this court.)
> *Luckenbach v. Marshall,* 48 Fed. (2d) 625 (Bromberg case, Oregon). (On its way to this court.)
> *Nelson v. Pillsbury,* 48 Fed. (2d) 883 (3 Awards, California). (On its way to this court.)
> *Pacific Steamship Company v. Pillsbury* (Hammer case, California) 1931 A. M. C. 1243.

The undersigned counsel have participated in all but the *Nelson* case. Each case involves the same fundamental question of law, based, however, upon somewhat varied facts. Examinations of the decisions of the lower courts reveals the following principal facts found by the courts below.

───────

WINKLER CASE.

Winkler worked 182 days or parts of days:

Admitted earnings previous year........................$1,266.20

Average admitted earnings per week.................$ 24.34

Compensation paid and upheld by court, per week ....$ 16.23

Deputy Commissioner's award based on earnings of M. Diegnan. (Worked 284 days or parts of days)..$2,314.45

Deputy Commissioner gave Winkler theoretical annual earning capacity, ($\frac{\$2,314.45}{284}$ multiplied by 300) $2,445.00

Compensation awarded by Deputy Commissioner, per week ....$ 25.00

BROMBERG CASE

Bromberg worked 153 days or parts of days:

Admitted earnings previous year........................$1,121.38

Average admitted earnings per week

$\left(\dfrac{\$1121.38}{49 \text{ weeks actually worked}}\right)$ ....$ 22.88

Compensation paid and upheld by court, per

week ....$ 15.26

Deputy Commissioner's award based on actual

earnings Hermson (worked 271 days or parts

of days) $2,276.69

Deputy Commissioner's award based on theo-

retical earning capacity $\dfrac{\$2,276.69}{271}$ multi-

plied by 300 ....$2,520.00

Compensation awarded by Deputy Commis-

sioner, per week ....$ 25.00

———

NELSON CASE.

Lawlor actual earnings estimated,

per month $100.00

Lost 3 months account illness, worked less than 5 days a week remaining 9 months, not member of regular gang, "free lance". Compensation based by Deputy Commissioner upon actual earnings of W. Davidson working 297 days and receiving in actual wages previous year $2,138.95. Deputy awarded $25.00 per week compensation.

Peterson actual earnings previous

year $1,600.00

working about 250 days and voluntarily laying off about 3 weeks. Again W. Davidson's earnings were used as the basis for compensation and $25.00 per week awarded.

Kugland worked about 260 days with no record of lay-off, illness or injury. Actual record showed earnings $870.37. Testified to doing outside work. W. Davidson's record was again used and the maximum $25.00 per week awarded.

The court divided the men into earnings groups as shown by the testimony and held that none of the three above mentioned were anything like the earnings class of Davidson. In other words, the court held to arrive at the ultimate result sought, the "earning capacity" of the individual and those of his *same earnings class* must be examined. The court held it was error to merely take the earnings of some individual high earner and use that indiscriminately as the basis for awarding the maximum in each case.

HAMMER CASE.

Hammer employed on cargo list, lowest grade of water-front employment, actual earnings previous 4½ months $355.38; actual average weekly earnings 19 weeks, $18.68. Deputy Commissioner's award based on earnings of Trimball who averaged for 14 months before accident $223.79 per month, or over $50.00 a week. Trimble was employed on regular gang or preferred list, the highest grade of water-front work and "Trimble worked harder and longer hours than any other man on the water-front".

ARGUMENT.

Compensation under the Longshoremen's Act in common with all but two of the compensation acts of the United

States is based upon a percentage of "wages" or "earnings". In Bulletin 496 of the United States Bureau of Labor Statistics published by the United States Government Printing Office in November, 1929, we find on page 16 the following:

"In all but two States (Washington and Wyoming) the amount of compensation is based upon wages."

On the same page it refers to the percentages allowed by the compensation acts of the various states, starting at 50% in 15 states to 66-2/3% in 16 states and under the United States Employees Compensation Act and the Longshoremen's and Harbor Workers' Act. On the same page we find the following:

"It is obvious that the reduction of a workkman's income by one-half or even by one-third, the most liberal percentage provision, leaves a large proportion of his loss uncompensated."

On page 18 of the same publication we again find the following:

"Another leveling feature of most laws is the establishment of a weekly maximum and minimum. The former may prevent the higher paid employee from securing the full proportion of his earnings that the percentage provision would indicate, while the minimum named is often affected by the qualification that if the wages received are less than such minimum the amount of the actual wages shall be paid as a benefit."

These quotations and the wording of the Act itself and the fundamental theory of all compensation acts clearly demonstrate that any construction of the Act which utterly disregards earnings of the injured individual in every case is absolutely unsound and unthinkable. Such a construction giving the maximum award to every longshoreman regardless of the facts of his case completely overlooks the safeguards to employer and employee of the maximum and minimum limits fixed by the Act.

In Section 8 of the Longshoremen's Act, 33 U. S. C. A. 908, we find the various percentages allowed for disability, the basic theory being that "66 2/3 per centum of the average weekly wages shall be paid to the injured employee during the continuance of"

1. Permanent total

2. Temporary total

     or

3. Permanent partial disability.

In Section 9 of the Act, 33 U. S. C. A. 909, percentage of "average" wages allowed to widows and surviving children are enumerated, always with the proviso "that the aggregate shall in no case exceed 66 2/3 per centum of such wages."

As a further limitation upon the maximum to be received in case of injury, we find these two provisions:

In Section 6 of the Act, 33 U. S. C. A. 906,

> "Compensation for disability shall not exceed $25.00 per week, nor be less than $8.00 per week, providing, however, that if the employee's wages at the time of injury are less than $8.00 per week, he shall receive his full weekly wage."

We find the same limitation in the case of death benefits. It will be noticed that the Federal Act used the term "wages" and speaks of a percentage of "average wages". The term "wages" is a misnomer. Under the British Acts, the word used is "earnings", which is correct. *"Wages" technically means the rate of the remuneration for services performed. "Earnings" on the other hand represents the rate of remuneration multiplied by the time worked, or the result of wage rate and time worked.* Under the Act, however, "wages" means the same as "earnings". Wages are usually *fixed,* earnings are *"average"*, depending on the variable element of time worked.

In *Sloat v. Rochester Taxicab Company*, 163 N. Y. S. 904, a taxicab driver's wages were $12.00 per week and his tips average $5.10 per week. The Commissioner added the two in computing his average annual earnings. An attempt was made to distinguish between "earnings" under the British statute and "wages" under the New York Act. The employer attempted in this case to hold the compensation down to "wages" and not to "earnings". The court said:

> "We must give further attention to Section 14. In three of its five subdivisions it speaks of the 'average annual earnings' of the employee, indicating the legislature saw no broad distinction between the word 'earnings' and the word 'wages', and under the facts of this case no distinction between them is apparent."

This case was affirmed by the highest court of New York, 221 N. Y. 481, 116 N. E. 1076.

We now have the fundamental principle of this Compensation Act; namely, that an employee during compensation will receive 66 2/3 per centum of his "wages" or "earnings". Then we come to Section 10 of the Act, 33 U. S. C. A. 910, which provides the mechanics for carrying out the principle of the Act. It provides in substance three methods of arriving at the "average weekly wages" of the employee. "Wages" means "earnings" and the three methods prescribed by the statutes are the mechanics for arriving at the "*average* weekly earnings" of an injured man. Under (a) if the injured man has worked substantially the entire year preceding his injury, his average annual earnings are 300 times his average daily wage, or his daily earnings. Under (b) if an injured man has not worked substantially the whole of the preceding year, his average annual earnings consist of 300 times the average daily earnings of an employee "of the same class" who worked substantially the entire preceding year in the same locality and the same work.

Knowing that any purely mechanical method of computing "average annual earnings" will not fit all cases, Section (c) provides that if the two preceding methods cannot "reasonably or fairly" be applied that the "average annual earnings" of the injured man shall be such sum as having regard to the previous earnings of the injured man and those of someone working in the same class "shall reasonably represent the annual earning capacity" of the injured employee in his employment at the time of the injury. Of course, the "average annual earnings" divided by 52 gives the "average weekly earnings" to which the percentages are applied.

The ultimate problem is, what is the "earning capacity" of the injured employee? (a) and (b) give a mechanical "convenience" device. If it leads to an unfair or unreasonable result then (c) will be applied.

In *Gunther v. U. S.*, 41 Fed. (2d) 151, this court so held, saying:

> "* * * his ability to earn should be the primal basis of determining compensation.

> "* * * the conclusion to be arrived at is a sum 'which shall reasonably represent the earning capacity' ".

There the court held (b) could "fairly and reasonably" be applied to the facts of the case before it. In all the cases referred to above, the Commissioner made no express finding on this fundamental question which had been definitely put in issue, but the lower court has held that the application of (b) to the individual case leads to an unfair and unreasonable result and, therefore, (c) must be applied. We ask affirmance.

––––––

FINDINGS OF COMMISSIONER.

In the four cases decided to date by the lower courts, great stress has been laid by the claimant and the government upon the findings of the Commissioner, upon the well-known doctrine laid down by this and other courts that his findings are conclusive if supported by any testimony. Taking it all in all, the employers have not found fault with the findings of *fact* of the Commissioner; it is only with the *conclusions* drawn by the Commissioner that they have taken issue. It is obvious from reading the decisions of the four lower courts that the Commissioners have made no attempt to find what we believe to be the fundamental finding which they have to make; namely, what is the *average annual earning capacity* of the injured employee. The findings of the Commissioner in all the cases have merely held that the claimant was injured under circumstances entitling him to compensation under the Longshoremen's and Harbor Workers' Act. Thereupon, some longshoreman in the port of an extraordinarily high earning ability is selected. His wages are divided by the number of days he worked, then multiplied by 300 and the result is arbitrarily stated to be the *average annual earning capacity* of the injured man, when in fact the result is higher than the earnings of the high earner. In the Washington case and the Oregon case the Commissioner made a specific finding that they were of the same class, basing this obviously upon the proposition that the two men were both longshoremen. Of course, we disagree with this *conclusion,* not *finding.* In the California case now before the court and apparently in *Nelson v. Pillsbury* (above), there was not even a finding by the Deputy Commissioner that the injured man and the man by whose earning record his compensation was computed were "of the same class". We may, therefore, dismiss the argument about the sacred character of the Commissioner's findings. His findings as far as they affect these cases are merely arbitrary conclusions upon which the court must exercise its judgment. *The question involved is not a question of fact; it is solely a question of law.*

If, from the facts, the Deputy Commissioner finds that the application of (a) and (b) would lead, in a particular case, to an "unfair or unreasonable" result, then we must proceed as follows:

If the injured man's actual earnings for some time prior to the time of his accident reasonably represent his annual earning capacity in the longshoring industry, we believe that they must be used to compute his compensation. Where actual earnings are unknown, or where for some reason such as lost time, etc., an employee's actual earnings do not fairly represent his earning capacity in the industry, then so-called "class" earnings must be considered. This is very clearly illustrated in the case of *Orlando v. Snyder,* 246 N. Y. S. 224, where the court said:

> "If his past earnings for the time concerning which the proof was given appear to be indicative of what he normally earned, there would be no reason to consider the earnings of other employees, but if for any reason the proof indicates that his actual earnings for that period were not fairly representative, consideration may be given other earnings of others 'who worked in the same or a neighboring locality' ".

Consideration of class earnings eliminates another objection which has been made to actual earnings. It has been said that if a new man starts to work, his actual earnings for the past year might not reasonably represent his earning capacity during the period of his injury. If, however, class earnings are used and men of his class have increased their earning capacity, this element must be considered by the Commissioner in determining what fairly represents an injured employee's earning capacity during the period of his disability; *in other words, actual earnings are only controlling where they reasonably represent the earning capacity of an injured man during the period of his disability. If they do not fairly represent his earning capacity, then outside class earnings and other elements must be considered by the Deputy Commissioner in determining the ultimate result.*

NEW YORK ACT.

The Longshoremen's and Harbor Workers' Act was borrowed from the New York Act. Although under extraordinary circumstances jurisdictions borrowing laws in this fashion do not follow the construction placed on such laws in the earlier jurisdiction, still, we have been referred to no reason whatsoever in this case why the Federal courts should not follow the construction placed on a compensation act by the courts of New York before that act was bodily borrowed by the Congress of the United States. The courts of New York had very definitely laid down these principles of law as applicable to their Act.

Section (c) (3 under the New York Act) is applicable to piece work. *Shaw v. American Body Company,* 178 N. Y. S. 369.

Section (c) is applicable to seasonal industries. *Blatchley v. Dairymen's League,* 232 N. Y. S. 437, and cases cited.

Section (c) may be applied to other than season industries when (a) and (b) cannot "reasonably and fairly" be applied.

Prentice v. N. Y. State Railways, 168 N. Y. S. 55, where a man worked 7 days a week; here the court said:

"The number 300, used in those subdivisions, is not an arbitrary selection, but was evidently selected because it bears an approximately close relation to the number of working days in a year, Sundays and holidays excluded. Manifestly, where an employee works seven days a week for substantially an entire year, the method of determining his average annual earnings, indicated in either subdivision 1 or 2, would be an injustice to him, just as much as *it would be an injustice to the employer to apply those subdivisions to a case where the injured employee has worked less than six days a week for a substantial period of time.* The claim here falls more appropriately within subdivision 3 of the section, which provides for a case where 'either of the foregoing methods of arriving at the annual average earnings of an injured employee cannot reasonably and fairly be applied.' The commission properly determined that this claim falls within subdivision 3."

Reno v. Shenandoah Cotton Co., 179 N. Y. S. 46, where a man worked 5 nights a week.

Rooney v. Great Lakes, 180 N. Y. S. 653, where a man worked as fireman and coal passer. Here the court said:

"The true test is the average weekly earnings, regard being had to the known and recognized incidents of the employment, including the element of discontinuousness."

Roskie v. Amsterdam Yarn Mills, 181 N. Y. S. 891, where a man worked 5½ days a week.

The policy of the New York Act is to give compensation not to exceed 2/3 of earnings.

Friedenberg v. Empire, 154 N. Y. S. 351 (a very early case under the New York Act).

In *Roskie v. Amsterdam,* the court said:

"The award should not exceed 2/3 of the earning capacity."

In *Littler v. Fuller,* 233 N. Y. 369, 119 N. E. 554, the court again said:

"The award should not exceed 2/3 of the earning capacity."

GUNTHER DECISION.

In the Winkler case on pp. 33-38 of appellee's brief now before this court, the relation of the Gunther case to the situation involved in the cases referred to above is discussed at length.

The fundamental distinction is that in the Gunther case this court found the application of (b) was fair and reasonable.

In the Winkler and other cases referred to above, the Deputy Commissioner made no finding on this point, but the *court did.* The court's findings we submit are amply supported by testimony.

If there is any question in the court's mind, and if it feels that it should have the finding of the Deputy Commissioner on this point, we suggest the cases be referred back for a finding under proper instructions. We believe this unnecessary, as the testimony is substantially undisputed and the conclusion is really one of law for the court.

CONCLUSION.

The facts shown by the Winkler case (Washington), the Bromberg case (Oregon), the Nelson case (California) and the present case (Hammer) all show that as far as the facts of those cases are concerned the application of (a) and (b) would lead to an unfair and unreasonable result. This result in the Winkler case would lead to giving a man more when he is laid up on account of injury than he actually earned per week in the industry during the three years immediately preceding his accident under normal conditions. In the Bromberg case, likewise from the decision of the lower court, it appears that his total annual earnings were $1,121.38 or an average weekly earning capacity of $22.88. By the Deputy Commissioner's award he was allowed $25.00 per week compensation. The same result follows in this case.

It has been urged that the employers are asking the court for some unusual construction. We respectfully submit that the reverse is the case. The construction now sought by the employers was uniformly placed on the Act until the decision of this court in the Gunther case. In each case, the Deputy Commissioner, after deciding (a) and (b) led to an unreasonable result, determined what reasonably represented the injured man's "annual earning capacity" and then applied the percentages of the Act.

From the foregoing, we respectfully submit the following:

1. That the fundamental principle underlying the Longshoremen's and Harbor Workers' Act is to give to an injured employee 2/3 of his earnings when laid up; thus imposing upon the employer 2/3 of the economic loss sustained by the injury and upon the employee 1/3. This 1/3 acting as an incentive for the injured man to return to work.

2. Section 10 of the Longshoremen's and Harbor Workers' Act provides a mechanical formula for determining the "average annual earnings" of employees. This mechanical formula was obviously designed to eliminate the necessity in individual cases of exhaustive examinations of earnings figures.

3. Knowing that any rigid mechanical device would lead to results which would violate the fundamental principles of the Act, the framers put in a third section which stated in effect that if the rigid mechanical methods led to an unfair or unreasonable result, that the third method should be adopted.

4. The New York cases and cases from other jurisdictions illustrate the application of Section (c). There have been few American cases on the longshoring industry as such, as the Act is new. The British decisions, cited by appellees in the Winkler case, however, on longshoremen are enlightening and vigorously uphold the position for which the employers are now contending.

5. It is a proposition of law for which no authority need be cited, that a court will so construe an Act that it will carry out the intention of the legislature and that the result attained will be fair and reasonable, particularly where the Act itself so provides.

We respectfully submit that the judgment of the District Court should be affirmed on the facts presented, from strict legal construction, economic expediency, and upon sound compensation principles as illustrated by the decisions of the great state from which the Act was bodily borrowed.

Respectfully submitted,

BOGLE, BOGLE & GATES,

LAWRENCE BOGLE,

STANLEY B. LONG,

Central Building Seattle.

GROSSCUP & MORROW,

W. CARR MORROW,

JOHN AMBLER,

Republic Building, Seattle.

Solicitors for Seattle Waterfront Employers,

Amici Curiae.

WOOD, MONTAGUE & MATTHIESSEN,

ERSKINE WOOD,

GUNTHER F. KRAUSE,

Solicitors for Portland Waterfront Employers,

Yeon Building, Portland.

Amici Curiae.

United States Circuit Court of Appeals

For the Ninth Circuit

WARREN H. PILLSBURY, Deputy Commissioner 13th Compensation District, under the Longshoremen's and Harbor Workers' Compensation Act, and V. H. HAMMER,

Appellants,

vs.

PACIFIC STEAMSHIP COMPANY, a corporation; UNION INSURANCE SOCIETY OF CANTON, LTD., a corporation,

Appellees.

Supplementary Memorandum for Appellees.

Upon Appeal from the United States District Court for the Southern District of California, Central Division.

FARNHAM P. GRIFFITHS,
CHARLES E. FINNEY,
GEORGE E. DANE,
McCUTCHEN, OLNEY, MANNON & GREENE,
Balfour Building,
San Francisco, California.

Solicitors for Appellees.

Parker Printing Company, 545 Sansome Street, San Francisco

No. 6587

IN THE

United States Circuit Court of Appeals

For the Ninth Circuit

WARREN H. PILLSBURY, Deputy Commissioner 13th Compensation District,
under the Longshoremen's and Harbor
Workers' Compensation Act, and V. H.
HAMMER,

Appellants,

vs.

PACIFIC STEAMSHIP COMPANY, a corporation; UNION INSURANCE SOCIETY OF
CANTON, LTD., a corporation,

Appellees.

Supplementary Memorandum for Appellees.

Upon Appeal from the United States District Court for the
Southern District of California, Central Division.

I. *Distinctions Between the Gunther Case and the Case
at Bar.*

II. *The District Court Did Not Try the Case De Novo.*

III. *The Fact that the Deputy Commissioner Applied Subsection (b) of Section 10 of the Act Without the Essential Findings for such Conclusion Warranted Without More the Suspension of his Award.*

I.

DISTINCTIONS BETWEEN THE GUNTHER CASE AND THE CASE AT BAR.

1. Subsection (b) of Section 10 could properly be applied in the *Gunther* case because Gunther was a steady and regular worker. His wife testified that "he worked steadily". The gang boss testified that he was "a hustler" and had steady employment. A fellow worker, Witt, testified that he had known Gunther for a number of years, and that they had worked together, though not during all of the year preceding the accident, and earned practically the same money. Witt earned in excess of the maximum and worked substantially all the year. The fair inference is that Gunther worked *at the rate of,* if not actually, 300 days a year.

Furthermore Witt, who was taken as the key man for the application of Subsection (b), was a stevedore in the same class as Gunther. They worked together at the same rate of pay and "they both earned practically the same money".

We thus have in the *Gunther* case the two elements essential to the application of Subsection (b), namely, that Gunther was a regular, not an intermittent, worker employed at the rate of 300 days a year, that is 6 days a week, even though he did not in fact work the whole year; and secondly, that the model or key man was a stevedore in the same class with himself.

Hammer, on the other hand, belonged in the lowest of the three classifications of stevedores in San Diego. His position with that gang foreclosed to him the possibility of work at the rate of 6 days a week in steady employment. The Commissioner did not find and the evidence does not show that he worked at that rate, but shows on the contrary that he averaged not more than 4 days work per week. Trimble, with whom he was compared for the purpose of the application of Subsection (b) was a steady worker in the first classification of stevedores who had employment at the rate of substantially 300 days per year.

But for the fact that this court did not want to overturn the finding of the Commissioner that Gunther had not worked more than 200 days in the year, the statement that he had worked along with Witt and that they had earned practically the same money, taken with the evidence that Witt worked substantially the whole year, might even have justified the application of Subsection (a) in the *Gunther* case.

2. Even assuming the use of Subsection (c) to have been proper in the *Gunther* case, this court held it was improperly applied. Earning capacity was what was sought to be found. The Commissioner took the evidence of *certain* employers but there was no showing that these were the *only* employers. On this theory the Deputy

Commissioner found the earnings to have been only
$895. This could not have been all. The wife of Gunther
testified that their expenses were not less than $40 per
week, of which $35 per month was actually identified as
rent. She testified that they had no income other than
Gunther's earnings. Witt, his companion stevedore,
testified that the two men worked together though not
during all the year; that both earned practically the same
money and that he, Witt, had earned $2100.

This court therefore concluded that the substantial
evidence showed Gunther to have earned more than the
Commissioner found and that the Commissioner's finding
was not based upon substantial but only upon partial and
unpersuasive evidence.

In contrast, Hammer's actual earnings were shown by
the payrolls of *all* the companies for whom he worked,
with the exception of 12 jobs on lumber ships his earnings
from which were fairly estimated by other stevedores.
Hammer had all his employment through the Marine
Service Bureau with the exception of a few jobs on the
Harvard and Yale which were picked up at 6 days work
through the payrolls. Therefore in distinction to Gunther
all his earnings were accounted for. The claim of greater
earnings based on loose estimates of expenses and guesses
of witnesses was obviously speculative and properly
ignored by the District Court.

The District Court in this case and the district courts
in the Northern District of California, Oregon and Washington in similar cases have suspended awards of deputy
commissioners to stevedores under Subsection (b). They

distinguish the *Gunther* case and deem their action not inconsistent with it. We submit that these decisions may stand without disturbance of the Gunther decision, with which we think they are in harmony.

II.

THE DISTRICT COURT DID NOT TRY THE CASE DE NOVO.

It is suggested on pages 4 and 23 of the Government's brief that the District Court may not try the case *de novo* or weigh the evidence, but is bound to sustain the Commissioner's findings if supported by any evidence. The cases are to this general effect, but show the true test to be not whether there is *any*, but whether there is any *substantial* supporting evidence. The cases quite as clearly hold that the Deputy Commissioner's findings must not be arbitrary or capricious or based on mere speculative evidence.

> "The compensation order may be set aside only if it is found to be 'not in accordance with law', i. e., if it is based upon error of law, *or is not supported by any substantial evidence, or is so manifestly arbitrary and unreasonable as to transcend the authority vested in the Deputy Commissioner.*" (Italics ours.)
>
> *Wheeling Corrugating Co. v. McManigal,* 41 F. (2d) 593, 594 (C. C. A. 4th, 1930).

In

> *Wellgeng v. Marshall,* 32 F. (2d) 922, 924,

Judge Neterer suspended a compensation order because "the finding is clearly arbitrary and capricious".

In

> *Grays Harbor Stevedore Co. v. Marshall,* 36 F. (2d)
> 814, 815 (W. D. Wash., 1929),

the court said:

> "The evidence is scanty, ambiguous, indefinite, and
> uncertain in respect to the elements of effect, continu-
> ity, and time, and is not legally sufficient to warrant
> what appears to be the deputy's arbitrary finding."

Most of the cases say that evidence may not be taken
before the District Court but that the court must deal
with the case on the evidence already taken before the
Commissioner, though one Circuit Court of Appeals has
held that new evidence may actually be taken by the District Court.

> *Crowell v. Benson,* 45 F. (2d) 66, 68 (C. C. A. 5th,
> 1930); affirming, 33 F. (2d) 137. The case is now
> on certiorari in the U. S. Supreme Court, 283
> U. S. 814, 75 L. Ed. 1430.

However no new evidence was taken in this *Hammer*
case so we are not concerned about that.

As respects disturbance of the Commissioner's findings
of fact, the District Court did not do that. The findings
of fact are shown on pages 9 and 10 of the printed transcript and were all matters agreed to and conceded at
the opening of the hearing—pages 1 onward of the typewritten transcript. The *so-called* finding of fact "that
claimant's wages and compensation rate is therefore fixed
at said maximum under Section 10 (b) of said Act" is of
course no true finding of fact but a conclusion of law, and

we submit "not in accordance with law" as required by the Act. The findings necessary to this conclusion were not made by the Commissioner, namely that Hammer worked at the rate of 6 days a week and that there was another stevedore *in his same class* who worked substantially the whole year and earned the maximum compensation.

In this posture of the case there is nothing in any of the cases cited by our opponents nor in any of the cases that we have read, nor in common sense, to foreclose the District Court against examining the record before the Commissioner to see whether there is any *substantial* evidence to sustain his conclusion. The District Court here, as we have pointed out, properly found that there was no such substantial evidence.

The District Court's conclusion that the claimant's earnings were $355.38 or $19.00 a week, objected to at page 23 of the government's brief, is, as we have repeatedly pointed out, based on the only *substantial* evidence as to earnings in the record. The so-called testimony of greater earnings was purely surmise and speculation against the positive payroll records from all the companies for whom Hammer worked, supplemented by reasonable proof of what he earned for the lumber companies not included in the payrolls. On this feature then, the District Court was not weighing the evidence or overruling any finding of the Commissioner, but merely stating what the only substantial evidence showed and so finding (Printed transcript, page 30). All of the court's other findings (and it was required to make findings

under Equity Rule 70½) are on evidence which was all
one way. If this particular finding, to which exception
is taken, were omitted and the case sent back without it,
the court would again have to suspend the award if the
Commissioner came to any other conclusion on the record
before him. There would be no substantial evidence to
sustain it. The case is not intended to be tossed back
and forth in this way like a medicine ball from court to
Commissioner.

———

III.

THE FACT THAT THE DEPUTY COMMISSIONER APPLIED SUBSECTION (b) OF SECTION 10 OF THE ACT WITHOUT THE ESSENTIAL FINDINGS FOR SUCH CONCLUSION WARRANTED WITHOUT MORE THE SUSPENSION OF HIS AWARD.

An award which lacks essential findings is not "in
accordance with law".

Howard v. Monahan, 33 F. (2d) 220 (S. D. Texas,
1929).

Respectfully submitted,

FARNHAM P. GRIFFITHS,
CHARLES E. FINNEY,
GEORGE E. DANE,
McCUTCHEN, OLNEY, MANNON & GREENE,
Solicitors for Appellees.

United States
Circuit Court of Appeals
For the Ninth Circuit.

GILBERT S. JOHNSON,

Appellant,

vs.

UNITED STATES OF AMERICA,

Appellee.

Transcript of Record.

Upon Appeal from the United States District Court for the Southern District of California, Central Division.

FILED

AUG 24 1931

PAUL P. O'BRIEN,

CLERK

Parker, Stone & Baird Co., Law Printers, Los Angeles.

United States
Circuit Court of Appeals
For the Ninth Circuit.

GILBERT S. JOHNSON,

Appellant,

vs.

UNITED STATES OF AMERICA,

Appellee.

Transcript of Record.

Upon Appeal from the United States District Court for the Southern
District of California, Central Division.

Parker, Stone & Baird Co., Law Printers, Los Angeles.

INDEX.

Names and Addresses of Attorneys.

For Appellant:

DAVID H. CANNON, Esq.,
Bank of America Building,

H. L. ARTERBERRY, Esq.,
Rowan Building,
Los Angeles, California.

For Appellee:

SAMUEL W. McNABB, Esq.,
United States Attorney,

P. V. DAVIS, Esq.,
Assistant United States Attorney,
Federal Building,
Los Angeles, California.

United States of America, ss.

To UNITED STATES OF AMERICA   Greeting:

You are hereby cited and admonished to be and ap
pear at a United States Circuit Court of Appeals fo
the Ninth Circuit, to be held at the City of San Fran
cisco, in the State of California, on the 13 day o
January, A. D. 1931, pursuant to the Petition for Ap
peal and Order thereon in the Clerk's Office of the Dis
trict Court of the United States, in and for the South
ern District of California, in that certain action wherei
Gilbert S. Johnson is defendant and Appellant and you ar
Appellee to show cause, if any there be, why the judgmen
and sentence in the said cause mentioned, should not b
corrected, and speedy justice should not be done to th
parties in that behalf.

WITNESS, the Honorable Geo. Cosgrave Unite
States District Judge for the Southern District of Cali
fornia, this 15th day of December, A. D. 1930, and o
the Independence of the United States, the one hundre
and fifty fifth

Geo. Cosgrave
U. S. District Judge for the Southern District o
California.

[Endorsed]:   Filed Dec 15 1930   R. S. Zimmerman
Clerk   By W E Gridley   Deputy Clerk

Filed................................

No...........................

Viol: Section 215 Federal Penal Code—Using the United States mails for furtherance of a scheme to defraud and violation Section 215 Federal Penal Code.

IN THE DISTRICT COURT OF THE UNITED STATES IN AND FOR THE SOUTHERN DISTRICT OF CALIFORNIA SOUTHERN DIVISION.

At a stated term of said Court, begun and holden at the City of Los Angeles, County of Los Angeles, within and for the Southern Division of the Southern District of California, on the second Monday of January, in the year of our Lord one thousand nine hundred and twenty-five:

The Grand Jurors of the United States of America empaneled, sworn and charged by said Court to inquire into and true presentment make of crimes and offenses within and for said Division and District aforesaid, on their oaths present:

That Gilbert S. Johnson, hereinafter referred to as the defendant, heretofore and prior to the several acts of using the United States mails hereinafter set out in this indictment, did devise and intend to devise, a certain scheme and artifice to defraud and to obtain money and property, by means of false and fraudulent pretenses, representations and promises from F. J. Rappe, H. W. Shafer, J. W. Barbee, E. F. Youngman, E. B. Boadway, J. T. Junell, May McGrail, Owen B. Jacoby, M. T. Clark, W. H. Hemphill, Mrs. S. L. Wright and divers other persons throughout the United States of America, including the public generally, and whose names are too numerous to be set out herein and many of whom are to the grand jurors unknown, all of said persons being hereinafter referred to in this indictment as the persons to be defrauded. The said scheme and artifice, was in substance and effect as follows, to-wit:

(1) That the said defendant would acquire or contract to acquire, large blocks of oil and gas leases in what is commonly known as wild-cat territory remote from existing oil and gas production, at nominal prices or through his agreements to drill a test well or wells, for oil and gas thereon.

(2) That the said defendant would then organize and control a succession of trust estates, corporations and concerns, among them being, Lewis Oil and Gas Company, Stephens Oil Syndicate, Texas Trojan Oil Company, Fernando Oil Company, Johnson Oil Company, Unit Production Syndicate, Banner Unit Syndicate, Runnels Oil Syndicate, Mexia-Terrace Oil Company, Corsicana-Mexia Oil Fields Syndicate, Mexia-Powell Oil Syndicate, Fortuna Petroleum Syndicate, Admiral Oil Company, Powell Petroleum Company, Gilbert Johnson and Company, Texas Oil and Stock Exchange, would prepare and cause to be prepared, Declarations of Trust creating each of said trust estates and articles of incorporation creating said corporations, and giving to himself full and complete control of the assets, operations and activities of said trust estates, corporations and concerns.

(3) It was further a part of said scheme and artifice, that the said defendant, after the organization of the

respective trust estates, corporations and concerns, and after instituting a campaign for the sale of stock or units of beneficial interest therein, would assign certain oil and gas leases, previously acquired by himself as aforesaid, or portions of such leases, to such trust estates, at enormous and excessive prices and at unlawful and wrongful profit to himself, and would cause such trust estates, corporations and concerns to assume, carry out and complete the original drilling agreements through which such leases were obtained and to assume other obligations thereon, and would withhold and retain for himself, large portions of said leases, acquired as aforesaid, and would use and dispose of the same for his own benefit in fraud of the rights of the stockholders and unit-holders of said trust estates, corporations and concerns, and in fraud of the persons to be defrauded.

(4) It was a further part of said scheme and artifice that the said defendant would fix the amount of the capitalization of each of the said trust estates, corporations and concerns, in amounts ranging from One Hundred Thousand dollars to Three Million dollars respectively, without regard to the actual value of the assets of such trust estates then owned or thereafter to be acquired, and greatly in excess thereof, and through the provisions of the respective Declarations of Trust, articles of incorporation and regulations, would authorize himself to increase such capitalization at his will and pleasure, and convenience, and without regard to the actual value of the assets of such trust estates, then owned or thereafter to be acquired.

(5) It was further a part of said scheme and artifice that the defendant would sell and offer for sale, to the

persons to be defrauded, the shares, units and stock of said several trust estates, corporations and concerns, by means of false and fraudulent pretenses, representations and promises, as hereinafter set forth, and would induce the said persons to be defrauded to pay their money to him, the said defendant, which said money he would thereupon, in large part, appropriate to his own use and benefit, and would embezzle and misappropriate the same.

(6) It was further a part of said scheme and artifice, that the said defendant, prior to, and before, the actual organization of some of the said trust estates and before such trust estates had acquired any assets whatsoever, would offer for sale and sell to the persons to be defrauded, stock or units of beneficial interests in such trust estates.

(7) It was further a part of said scheme and artifice, that the said defendant would organize, own and operate so-called brokerage companies to-wit: Gilbert Johnson and Company and Texas Oil and Stock Exchange, as a medium through which to dispose of the stock or units of interest in the said trust estates and concerns, and as such brokerage concerns would fraudulently contract with himself as an officer and trustee of the respective trust estates and concerns, for the sale of the stock or units of interest of the said trust estates and concerns, and by and through such contracts appropriate to himself large portions of the money and property belonging to the said trust estates.

(8) It was further a part of said scheme and artifice, that the said defendant would, through his so-called brokerage companies, offer for sale and sell to the persons to be defrauded, stock or units of interest in the respective

trust estates at gradually ascending prices ranging from slightly less than par value to greatly in excess of par value, through false and fraudulent misrepresentations as to the value of the lease holdings of the respective trust estates and corporations and concerns, the location of such leases as to oil producing or proven oil territory, the progress of development thereon, the assurance of gusher oil production through the drilling or development of the said leases and the unusual, enormous and unlimited profits to accrue to investors in the stocks or units of interest in the respective trust estates, without regard to the actual facts or the real values of such stock or units of interest, it being intended wrongfully and fraudulently to lead the said persons to be defrauded to believe that the respective trust estates were growing financially stronger in the ratio represented by the increase in prices at which the stock or units of interest were being offered for sale.

(9) It was further a part of said scheme and artifice to defraud, that the said defendant would drill for oil, a well or wells, for many of the said trust estates, or cause the same to be drilled, upon some one or more of the leases assigned to each of the said trust estates, in a pretended search for oil or gas, and charge said trust estate such exhorbitant and excessive amounts for such drilling that the funds and assets of the said trust estate would be quickly exhausted and the trust estate become insolvent.

(10) It was further a part of said scheme and artifice to defraud, that the said defendant would use certain of the said trust estates, organized by him for that particular purpose, as merger companies, towit: The Johnson Oil Company and the Admiral Oil Company, to provide a

burying ground for the trust estates previously organized by him and which under his management and control had become insolvent and so recorded and shown on the minute book of the insolvent company, and as a means whereby the persons to be defrauded, who were unit holders or stockholders of said insolvent trust estates, could be induced to pay to him additional money and property as merger or exchange fees in exchanging their units or stock in said insolvent concerns for the units or stock of said merger companies and as a means of eliminating all such holders of units or stock of said insolvent companies as should refuse or fail to pay such merger or exchange fees.

(11)   It was further a part of said scheme and artifice, that the said defendant would arrange mergers of said insolvent trust estates and would fraudulently and unlawfully assign or transfer title of all the remaining assets of such insolvent trust estates, if any, to the so-called merger companies, and then in a further effort to obtain money and property from the stockholders in the insolvent estates, and through and by the use of the United States mails, would notify such stockholders that upon surrender of the stock or units of interest in such insolvent trust estates and the payment to them of a specified exchange or merger fee, within a certain specified time arbitrarily fixed by said defendant, stock or units of interest in the merger company would be issued to them in exchange.

(12)   It was further a part of said scheme and artifice, that in one of the trust estates, to wit: the Johnson Oil Company, the said defendant, in order to stimulate the sale of its stock or units, would declare and advertise a fraudulent quarterly dividend payable at a future date to

stockholders of record on an intervening date and after declaring such fraudulent dividend he would offer for sale and would sell to the persons to be defrauded, stock or units of interest in said Johnson Oil Company, which would participate in such dividend.

(13) It was further a part of said scheme and artifice to defraud, that the said defendant would misappropriate, embezzle and convert to his own use and benefit, a part of the money and property obtained from the persons intended to be defrauded, the exact amount so misappropriated, embezzled and converted being to these grand jurors unknown.

(14) It was further a part of said scheme and artifice to defraud, that the said defendant would make false and fraudulent representations, pretenses and promises to the said persons intended to be defrauded through and by means of divers letters, circular letters, pamphlets, newspapers, house organs, advertisements and publications, circulated and intended to be circulated by and through the United States mails, and in effect and substance as follows, to-wit:

(a) To the effect following, the said representation being made about September 4, 1920, to-wit: That the last offering of Lewis Oil and Gas stock at 85 cents was then being made; that said stock would be absolutely withdrawn from the market on September 10, 1920; that, therefore, this was the last opportunity to secure an interest in said company; that within 60 days or less it was expected that three big wells on the Sloan tract would be gushing forth big profits for the stockholders; that this was but the beginning of the tremendous certain success of the enterprise; that with the completion of these three

wells there was every probability that the earnings of
the Lewis Oil and Gas Company would be around $1,000,-
000.00 a year; whereas, in truth and in fact, as the
defendant then and there well knew and intended, it was
not intended to withdraw the stock of the Lewis Oil and
Gas Company from the market on September 10, 1920,
or on any other date, as long as the persons to be defrauded could be induced to purchase the same; that it
was not expected that the three wells on the Sloan tract
would be gushing forth big profits for the stockholders
of said company, nor would the production from said
wells be the beginning of tremendous certain success of
the enterprise, nor would there be any probability or possibility of the earnings of said company being $1,000,000.00
a year, for the reason that the said defendant then intended that he would by fraudulent devices, appropriate to
his own use and benefit, a large part of the income from
said wells and would divert to others of his promotional
concerns, the balance of said income so that the stockholders of the Lewis Oil and Gas Company would receive
little or no part of the same.

(b)   To the effect following, to-wit: That the defendant believed that the Stephens Oil Syndicate would be
fully financed without the expense of a single dollar to
the syndicate members, the entire financing cost to be
borne by himself and that every dollar that the members
had sent in would go into a drilling fund without deduction of a cent for commissions or expense to anyone;
whereas, in truth and in fact, as the defendant then and
there well knew and intended, it was at all times intended
by said defendant that he would divert to himself in
the name of Gilbert Johnson and Company, a large part

of the proceeds of money received from the sale of the stock of said Stephens Oil Syndicate under the guise of a bonus and as commissions for the sale of said stock, so that only a portion of the money received from the members of said syndicate could or would go into a drilling fund for the operations of said syndicate.

(c) To the effect that Gilbert Johnson (meaning, thereby, the defendant), of Gilbert Johnson and Company, and president of the big, successful Johnson Oil Company, is president and general manager of the Fernando Oil Company, which in itself assures a competent administration of the affairs of the enterprise (meaning the said Fernando Oil Company), fair and square treatment for the stockholders, and an equitable distribution of all accruing profits; whereas, in truth and in fact, as the said defendant then and there well knew and intended, the Johnson Oil Company was not a big and successful oil company, but was a purely promotional stock selling enterprise, and that said defendant was not a successful or honest executive of any company, but was a promotor of many fraudulent enterprises and was a confidence man and swindler, and the fact that he was president and general manager of said Fernando Oil Company did not assure a competent administration of its affairs or a fair and square treatment of its stockholders, or an equitable distribution of all accruing profits, but in fact, gave assurance that there would be no distribution of money to stockholders, but that whatever profit accrued would be misappropriated and embezzled by said defendant.

(d) To the effect that after October 7, 1920, there would be no further offerings of Texas Trojan Oil Company stock at any price; whereas, in truth and in fact, as the defendant then and there well knew and intended, the said stock would not be withdrawn from the market and there would be further offerings of said stock as long as the persons to be defrauded could be induced to purchase the same, and said representation was made by the defendant for the purpose of inducing said persons to send their money to him, the said defendant, immediately, and without delay, for the purchase of said stock, which said money would be, in large part, misappropriated and embezzled by the said defendant.

(e)　That on March 19, 1921, the defendant made the following representations to the persons to be defrauded, to-wit:

"The Unit Production Syndicate has a total authorized capitalization of only $150,000.00, consisting of 3,000 units of the par value of $50.00 per unit. This No. 1 well will be rushed to completion at the earliest possible moment, and will, I am confident, be placed on production within 75 to 90 days of this date, possibly sooner. Judging from the production of the Guaranty gusher, and the other wells that have to date been brought in in this amazingly rich pool, it may be depended to come in with production of from 1,000 to 3,000 barrels of high gravity refining oil per day. A total of four wells will be drilled on this 40-acre lease, and the entire property is so thoroughly proven that every one of these four wells is practically certain to be a great gusher. From the facts already established, I believe that I am ultra conservative when I predict that this 40-acre lease of the Unit Production Syndicate will produce from 12,500 to 25,000 barrels of oil per acre, and "the reasonable probabilities greatly exceed even the higher figures. It is upon these figures that I base my estimate that I will be able to pay back to all unit holders from $250.00 to $500.00 per unit, although it is easily possible for the profits to greatly exceed even the latter figure.

"The bringing in of the No. 1 well with a production of even 1,000 barrels of oil per day and there is every reason to believe that the well will come in with a flow of from 2,000 to 3,000 barrels of oil per day or more, will provide ample funds almost immediately for the payment of liberal dividends to all unit-holders of the Unit Production Syndicate, and also provide ample funds for the drilling of additional wells.

"Hence I am confident that within four to five months from this date the Unit Production Syndicate will begin the payment of big, regular dividends, and these units will, within a comparatively short time, pay profits of from $250.00 to $500.00 each, or in other words, from five to ten times the amount of the investment if units are bought now at the initial price of $50.00 each."

Whereas, in truth and in fact, as the said defendant then and there well knew and intended, there was no basis of fact for the prediction that any well on the property of said syndicate would come in with production of 1,000 to 3,000 barrels of high gravity refining oil per day; that it was not intended to drill four wells on said 40 acre lease; that said property was not thoroughly proven but was in fact, purely wild-cat property; that there was no basis for the prediction that said 40 acre lease would produce from 12,500 to 25,000 barrels of oil per acre or of any amount remotely approximating said figures, or that said defendant would be able to pay back to the unit holders from $250.00 to $500.00 per unit, or, in fact, any sum of money; that all the statements made by the defendant in regard to said syndicate and in regard to the prospective production and prospective profits to its unit holders, were false, fraudulent, extravagant and grossly exaggerated, and were made for the purpose of inducing the persons to be defrauded to purchase said units and with the purpose on the part of the defendant to misappropriate and embezzle a large part of the money so received from the said persons.

(f) To the effect that the organization of the Banner Unit Syndicate had been effected along remarkably conservative lines; that at the time said representation was made, towit: on April 16, 1921, preparations had been made for drilling the first well on the syndicate's 100 acres and that 8 or 10 wells would be drilled on said land; that from facts already established regarding the richness of said land, the defendant estimated that the units of said syndicate, which were being offered at $50.00 each, would ultimately return profits of from $500.00 to $1,000.00 each; whereas, in truth and in fact, as the defendant then and there well knew, the said lease and property of said syndicate was not located in proven territory, nor were any facts established indicating a likelihood of finding oil in paying quantities thereon; that the defendant did not intend to drill 8 or 10 wells on said lease, and there was no foundation for the assertion that the units of said syndicate would return profits of $500.00 to $1,000.00 each or, in fact, any profit whatever.

(g) To the effect that, on May 1, 1921, the Marine Oil Syndicate owned 520 acres of the richest oil territory in Stephens County, Texas, including 320 acres located within 1,000 feet of the great Yeaman No. 1 gusher of the Johnson Oil Company; that the management of said Syndicate pledged itself to immediately begin the drilling of two wells on the said land; whereas, in truth and in fact, as the defendant then and there well knew, the said syndicate had not been organized and owned no property at the time said representation was made; that the said Yeaman No. 1 well of the Johnson Oil Company was not a great well or a gusher well, but was only a gas well producing no oil, and that the management of said Syndicate (to-wit: the defendant), would not drill two wells but would drill but one; that the 520 acres referred to were not in the part of Stephens County, Texas, where large production of oil was found, and was not the richest oil territory in said county, but was in disproven territory so far as production of oil was concerned.

(h) To the effect that the success of the Johnson Oil Company had been one of the sensations of the oil fields of Texas; that said company had only begun to grow and that each week, each month and each year would witness said enterprise becoming stronger and stronger, greater and greater, and more and more profitable to its thousands of stockholders; that the defendant was looking forward eagerly to the day when the said company would be a complete unit in the petroleum industry—producers, refiners, transporters and marketers—and that ultimately it would duplicate the gigantic success of the Texas Company and make for every stockholder who held even a fair sized block of the stock an independent fortune; whereas in truth and in fact, as the defendant then and there well knew, the Johnson Oil Company was not then or at any time, a sensational success, but was then experiencing great difficulty in raising money through sales of stock; that it did not at that time, or at any other time, have any prospect of becoming a great oil producing or profit earning institution or of becoming an organization of similar size and commercial importance as the Texas Company; that there was no basis for the profits held out as likely to accrue to investors in the stock of the Johnson Oil Company, and that the false and fraudulent misrepresentations were made to deceive the persons to be defrauded, and to induce them to turn over money and property to the said defendant without receiving anything of value in return therefor, which said money would be, in large part, misappropriated and embezzled by said defendant.

(i) To the effect that on January 6, 1922, Runnels Oil Syndicate had property holdings of 5,000 acres in one solid block on a clearly defined oil structure; that hundreds of producing oil wells were a possibility; that stupendous profits were possible and probable for unit-holders of said Syndicate; that the defendant believed that well No. 1 of the said Syndicate would prove a gusher and that these units, then obtainable at $30.00 per unit, would sell for at least $1,000.00 each; whereas, in truth and in fact, as the defendant then and there well knew, the properties of the said syndicate were purely wild-cat properties; were entirely unproven as oil or gas producing properties; had originally been acquired without cost other than an agreement to drill a test well for oil and gas thereon; were purely speculative; were at a great distance from oil producing fields; that there were no developments in the drilling of the well up to that time, or at any time, that justified or would form a reasonable basis for the defendant's expressed belief that the said well would be brought in as a gusher oil well or would produce oil or gas in any commercial quantities; that there was no basis in fact or in reason for his expressed belief that units of said syndicate would sell for $1,000.00 each upon the completion of said well; that said defendant had held said property with an uncompleted well from October 28, 1919, until July 1921, as the property of the Lewis Oil & Gas Company, and of the Johnson Oil Company, without making any effort to complete the drilling of the well by those syndicates because of the improbability of finding oil or gas in commercial quantites therein, and that the said false and fraudulent misrepresentations were made by said defendant solely for the purpose of inducing the persons to be defrauded to purchase the units of said Syndicate, which were then and thereafter of no value.

(j)   To the effect that on April 21, 1922, all available units of the Corsicana-Mexia Oil Fields Syndicate had been subscribed, no more being offered at any price, and hence a large number of the clients of defendant and a great number of the readers of the Texas Oil Bulletin, being the advertisement and publication of defendant, had found it impossible to secure an interest in the Great Powell Structure; that, moved by an overwhelming desire to have every client of Gilbert Johnson and Company, and every reader of the Texas Oil Bulletin participate in the tremendous profits that the defendant was confident would be made by the bringing in of great gushers on the Powell Structure, he had personally selected 500 acres of leases on the great Powell structure adjacent to and surrounding the three wells being drilled thereon, and had formed for the development of these leases the Mexia-Powell Oil Syndicate with a capitalization of $150,000.00

divided into 6000 units of the par value of $25.00 per unit; that said announcement was first, last and only offering of units of Mexia-Powell Oil Syndicate units at $20.00 per unit; that the price of these units would rapidly advance and the bringing in of gusher production in the three wells then rapidly approaching the Woodbine gusher sand on the Powell structure might make them worth anywhere from $250.00 to $500.00 per unit during the few weeks then ensuing:

Thereby causing the persons intended to be defrauded to understand and believe that all the units of the Corsicana Mexia Oil Fields Syndicate had been sold; that large numbers of readers of the Texas Oil Bulletin and others who were anxious to secure an interest in properties on the so-called Powell structure were unable to do so and that in order to give these persons such a chance the said defendant had organized the said Mexia-Powell Oil Syndicate purely and solely for the purpose of providing a means whereby these persons could secure an interest in the Powell structure; that 500 acres of leases had been selected for development by the said syndicate and that development upon adjacent leases might make the units of the said syndicate worth from $250.00 to $500.00 per unit within a few weeks:

Whereas, in truth and in fact, as the defendant then and there well knew, all the units of the Corsicana-Mexia Oil Fields Syndicate had not been sold, a large quantity were then available for sale, and would be, and were later offered for sale; that the Mexia-Powell Oil Syndicate had not been organized to provide means whereby those who were unable to secure an interest in the Powell structure through stockholdings in the Corsicana-Mexia Oil Fields

Syndicate could secure such an interest, but had been organized on January 10, 1922, six days prior to the organization of the Corsicana-Mexia Oil Fields Syndicate, and efforts had continuously been made to sell its stock or units through a certain brokerage concern during all the intervening time and had proven unsuccessful, and the sale of the stock had been thrown back into the hands of the defendant; that all of the stock of the said Mexia-Powell Syndicate had been issued to the defendant for the said leases at the time the said syndicates were organized; that this was not the first, last and only offering of units in the said syndicate, and that the defendant would, and did, make further offerings of the said units at $20.00 per share on subsequent dates, and that he would not, and did not, intend to develop the properties of the said syndicate, but would, and did, divert all the money and property of said syndicate to his own use and benefit, and that these false representations, pretenses and promises were knowingly and wilfully made in an effort to induce the persons intended to be defrauded to turn over money and property to the said defendant in exchange for these worthless oil stocks and without giving anything of adequate value in return therefor.

(k)   That on September 22, 1922, the defendant made the following representation in a circular letter sent to the persons to be defrauded, to-wit:

"ABSOLUTELY LAST OFFERING OF UNITS OF FORTUNA PETROLEUM SYNDICATE AT TWENTY DOLLARS PER UNIT.

"For the purpose of providing funds to drill the No. 1 Halsell well of the Fortuna Petroleum Syndicate to the pay sand, we offer a limited allotment of these units of the par value of $25.00 per unit at the special price of $20.00 per unit, payable either all cash with order, or one half cash with order, the balance in 30 days. Notice is hereby given, however, that all orders for units of the Fortuna Petroleum Syndicate at $20.00 per unit must be mailed to us not later than Saturday, September 30, after which this offer will be absolutely withdrawn from the market.

"The Fortuna properties are located in what has already been proven to be one of the richest oil zones in the world. These properties are located on one of the best defined oil structures in this entire zone, the Fortuna properties are of such an extent, aggregating 1,090 acres, that the bringing in of production in the No. 1 Halsell well will make them worth from $1,000,000.00 to $5,000,000.00. The capitalization of the Fortuna Petroleum Syndicate was extremely low, being only 4,000 units of the par value of $25.00 per unit, and the present offering is at the special price of $20.00 per unit.

"The No. 1 Halsell well is now actually under way, and drilling at a depth of about 500 feet by one of the most successful contractors in the business. The rapid completion of this well to the pay sand is absolutely assured. We believe, therefore, that within a few weeks time every outstanding "unit of Fortuna Petroleum Syndicate will be worth anywhere from $250.00 to $500.00 per unit or more."

Whereas, in truth and in fact, as the defendant then and there well knew, the said properties were not located in one of the richest proven oil zones in the world, but in purely wild-cat territory and remote from oil production; that the properties would not be worth from $1,000,000.00 to $5,000,000.00, but would be, and were, of a purely speculative value, and that no reasonable basis existed upon which a prediction could be made that every outstanding unit would be worth from $250.00 to $500.00 or more, that such statements were made by the said defendant solely for the purpose of deceiving the persons to be defrauded.

(1) That the defendant, on December 1, 1922, made the following representations to the persons to be defrauded in a printed circular entitled "Progress Report No. 2", to-wit:

"IF YOU OWN STOCK OR UNITS OF JOHNSON OIL COMPANY, MARINE OIL SYNDICATE, MEXIA TERRACE OIL COMPANY, CORSICANA-MEXIA OIL FIELDS SYNDICATE, OR RUNNELS OIL SYNDICATE WHICH HAVE NOT YET BEEN EXCHANGED FOR STOCK OF THE ADMIRAL OIL COMPANY, THIS COMMUNICATION IS OF VITAL IMPORTANCE TO YOU.

"When the ADMIRAL OIL COMPANY was organized, every share of the stock was turned back into the treasury, with the exception of only 10,000 shares which was paid out for the lease holdings around which the Admiral Company was organized, and absolutely the only way that Admiral stock can be taken out of the treasury is through the surrender of stock or units of one of the above named enterprises which were absorbed and the payment in cash of the required consideration for such transfer, depending upon which security is surrendered.

"I know positively that the best interests of every individual stockholder have been served in bringing about the consolidation of these several companies into the Admiral Oil Company. Efficiency will be greatly increased, economies will be effected, and through the development of a large number of carefully selected properties large ultimate profits will be absolutely assured. . . . . I am going to stay on the job day and night until we make of the Admiral Oil Company one of the giant independent oil projects of the Southwest.

"The Admiral Oil Company has before it a tremendously profitable future, we are confident, and if you own any of the securities which can be exchanged for Admiral stock at this time, do so without fail while the opportunity is still available."

Thereby the said defendant caused the persons to be defrauded, to understand and believe that the entire treasury stock of the Admiral Oil Company, was outstanding and that there would not be any stock for public sale; that the best interest of every stockholder in the various merged syndicates had been served by the bringing about of the merger into the Admiral Oil Company; that the merger would provide for more efficient management and economy of operation; that the development of the large number of properties obtained by the merger would, and did, assure the ultimate earning of large profits for stockholders of the Admiral Oil Company, and that by paying the merger or transfer fees they would participate in such profits; that Gilbert Johnson as president and manager of the Admiral Oil Company, would devote his entire attention to the affairs of the Admiral Oil Company until it became one of the giant independent oil projects of the Southwest; and that said company had in prospect a tremendously profitable future:

Whereas, in truth and in fact, as the defendant then and there well knew, the said defendant had previously increased the capitalization of the said Admiral Oil Company from $1,000,000.00 to $3,000,000.00, and would, and did, thereafter offer its stock for sale to the general public; that the best interests of the stockholders in the various syndicates merged by and into the Admiral Oil Company would not be served at all by the merger, but that in truth and in fact, the merging of these various insolvent syndicates by and into the Admiral Oil Company was simply another scheme and artifice by which the defendant could and would obtain additional money and property from the persons to be defrauded by and through the payment of the transfer or merger fees; that the consolidation or merger of the several syndicates into the Admiral Oil Company would not bring efficiency in management, or economy in operation as the management and operation of the said syndicates had been a joint and interchangeable operation, and the change of names would not affect inefficiency of the defendant in the operation and management of said Admiral Oil Company or of the merged syndicates; that the development upon the merged properties had already proven them worthless as oil producing properties and that there was little, if any, prospect of ultimate profits of any sort, and in truth and in fact, there never were any profits, and the whole enterprise was a failure, and the purchasers of its stock lost their entire investment, and that Gilbert Johnson, the said defendant, would not, and did not, devote his entire time to the making of the Admiral Oil Company into a giant independent oil project, but would devote his efforts towards making it a giant stock selling enterprise, and to the promotion of other fraudulent stock selling enterprises:

(m) To the effect that any money paid to the stockholders for shares of Johnson Oil Company went into the treasury of the company and had been used for drilling operations; that, although said company had met with some reverses in drilling, nevertheless an honest and economical effort had been made to develop new production of oil, and that said company was then (July 21, 1922), continuing to make progress; whereas, in truth and in fact, as the defendant then and there well knew, all money received from the persons intended to be defrauded for stock of the Johnson Oil Company was not used for drilling operations, but large sums were appropriated by the said defendant to his own use and benefit; that no honest or economical effort had been made by the defendant to develop new production; that the company did not continue to make progress, but at that time was on the verge of bankruptcy and did make a financial failure; that these statements were made by the defendant for the purpose of deception and of inducing the persons to be defrauded to part with their money and property without receiving anything of value therefor.

(n) That on August 30, 1924, the defendant made the following representations to the persons to be defrauded, in a circular letter sent by mail to said persons, to-wit:

"FORTUNE SMILES
 THEN SMILES AGAIN
    ON THOSE WHO GRASP THEIR GREAT
    OPPORTUNITIES QUICKLY

"And before you right now is the kind of an offering that wins the smiles of fortunes.

"In the very limited offering of units of the Powell Petroleum Company are embodied the features that bring fourth large and quick profits. Large acreage, low capitalization and a rapid development campaign have many times meant fortunes won.

"BUT! REMEMBER! In addition to these features, the location for the first well of the Powell Petroleum Company on their Greer lease has been made where they have actual, tangible assurance of bringing in a real gusher well. In addition to large acreage, low capitalization and a rapid development compaign you have actual assurance of production, without which these other features would be of little value.

"Many offers are made to participate in the drilling of wells. BUT! How many of these offers have any real assurance that the drilling of those wells will result in success? And right on this point investors can be assured hinges their opportunities of gaining financial independence with a modest investment. When the details of an offering are under consideration, let your most careful attention be directed at this feature. The first question to ask yourself is: "What assurance is there of actually securing production?

"In the offering of a small number of units of the Powell Petroleum Company can plainly be seen the assurance of an investment in these units resulting in splendid profits. In profits of 1000% in sixty days and greater profits with the further development of their properties. And to the investor who has enough energy and foresight to secure some of these units before they are all taken, just such profits should quickly accrue.

"The exact structures underlying the properties of the Powell Petroleum Company have been so well defined and the existence of a great pool of oil has been so amply assured through an expenditure of more than one hundred and fifty thousand dollars in drilling operations that the outcome of the Powell Petroleum Company Greer No. 1 well can hardly be other than a great woodbine gusher. Which should mean a profit on every dollar placed into this exceptional offer of 1000% in sixty days time and greater profits to follow.

"When an offering has even a fair chance of returning a profit of 1000% in sixty days time, with additional profits to follow, that offer is worthy of careful consideration. But—when in addition real assurance of realizing those profits and realizing them in so short a time is given, as it is in the limited offering of units in the Powell Petroleum Company, then that offer should be grasped quickly—before it has moved into the past."

Whereas, in truth and in fact, as the defendant then and there well knew, he had no actual or tangible assurance that the said well would be brought in a real gusher oil well or that it would produce oil in commercial quantities or at all, but in fact and in truth, he knew that the prospects of this well finding oil in any commercial quantity, or at all, had been disproven by the wells previously drilled by him on adjacent properties and which proved to be dry holes and not oil producers; that there was no basis in reason or in fact assuring the earnings of profits by the said company, and that there were no prospects of paying 1,000 per cent in profits, or any profits, to stock-holders of the said company within sixty days or at any time, and in truth and in fact, the said well was completed as a dry hole, and no profits were ever earned by the said company; and that these false and fraudulent representations, pretenses and promises were purposely made to deceive the said persons to be defrauded and to induce them to pay their money to the said defendant without receiving anything of value in return therefor, which said money would be, by the defendant, misappropriated, embezzled and converted to his own use and benefit.

(o) And the Grand Jurors say and present that the defendant made many other false, inflammatory, exaggerated and gross misrepresentations, pretenses and promises, too numerous to mention or set forth herein, for the purpose of causing and inducing the persons to be defrauded to believe that they might make and would be safe in making safe and profitable investments in the shares, units and interests of the several corporations, trust estates and concerns hereinbefore mentioned, when in fact the said representations, pretenses and promises were and would be false and untrue and were and would be made by the defendant without any reasonable foundation to believe them to be true, and in fact were and would be known by the defendant to be false and untrue, and with the intent on the part of said defendant to appropriate to his own use and to embezzle and misappropriate a large part of the money to be paid and which was paid to him by the persons to be defrauded.

And the Grand Jurors aforesaid, upon their oaths aforesaid, do further present that the said defendant, on the 5th day of October, in the year nineteen hundred and twenty-two, at Los Angeles, California, in the Southern Division of the Southern District of California, and within the jurisdiction of this court, for the purpose of executing said scheme and artifice, unlawfully, wilfully, knowingly and feloneously caused to be delivered by mail of the United States according to the direction thereon a certain letter, to-wit: a letter directed to Mr. F. J. Rappe, Los Angeles, Calif., which the said defendant then lately before had placed in the post office of the United States at Fort Worth, Texas, for delivery by the post office establishment of the United States to the said Mr. F. J. Rappe at said address, towit: at said Los Angeles, California, and which said letter then and there was and is of the tenor following, to-wit:

"ADMIRAL OIL COMPANY

General Offices W. T. Waggoner Bldg.

P. O. Box 1720

October 2, 1922.

Mr. F. J. Rappe,
Los Angeles, Calif. FORT WORTH, TEXAS.

Dear Sir:

You are, according to the records, the owner and holder of one units of the Corsicana Mexia Oil Fields Syndicate. In accordance with the communication of the Corsicana Mexia Oil Fields Syndicate of this date, enclosed herewith, all Corsicana Mexia unit holders are privileged to subscribe for stock of the Admiral Oil Company on the basis of one Corsicana Mexia unit and $7.00 for 50 shares of stock of the Admiral Oil Company of the par value of $50.00. This allows you a credit of $43.00 per unit for your Corsicana Mexia holdings.

"The cash consideration of $7.00 per unit may be paid either all in cash at this time or one-half cash and the balance in thirty days. If all cash is paid now, your new certificate for stock of the Admiral Oil Company will be mailed to you as soon as the transfer can be made. If the cash consideration is paid in two equal monthly installments, your new certificate for Admiral Oil Company stock will be mailed to you upon receipt of the last payment.

"It is essential that all who wish to avail themselves of this offer to exchange stock of the Admiral Oil Company for units of the Corsicana Mexia Oil Fields Syndicate on the above basis accept the offer immediately. Therefore, please endorse your Corsicana Mexia certificate in blank, attach to the form of remittance blank below and forward to us in the enclosed addressed envelope with your remittance for $7.00, or for one-half this amount, in which event it will be understood that the balance is to be paid in thirty days. Make your remittance payable "to Admiral Oil Company.

Yours truly,
ADMIRAL OIL COMPANY.

"Admiral Oil Company,
P. O. Box 1720, ...
Fort Worth, Texas.   Date.

Gentlemen: I am the owner of one unit-s of Corsicana Mexia Oil Fields Syndicate which I desire to exchange for stock of the Admiral Oil Company on the basis of 50 shares of Admiral Oil Stock for one Corsicana Mexia Oil Fields Syndicate unit and $7.00. You will find enclosed my Corsicana Mexia certificate endorsed in blank together with remittance for $7.00 , (If only one-half this amount is enclosed, it will be understood that the balance is to be paid in thirty days).

Yours truly,

Name...

Address..."

That at the time of causing such letter to be delivered by mail of the United States according to the direction thereon, the said defendant then and there well knew that said letter was for the purpose of executing said scheme and artifice; contrary to the form of the statute of the United States in such case made and provided and against the peace and dignity of the United States.

SECOND COUNT.

And the Grand Jurors aforesaid, upon their oaths aforesaid, do further present:

That Gilbert S. Johnson, the identical person named in the first count of this indictment, on the fifteenth day of January, in the year nineteen hundred-twenty three, at Pasadena, Calif., in said Division and District and within the jurisdiction of this Court, so having devised the scheme and artifice to defraud and to obtain money and property by means of false and fraudulent pretenses, representations and promises described in the first count of this indictment, the allegations concerning which in said first count are incorporated by reference thereto in this count as fully as if they were here repeated, for the purpose of executing said scheme and artifice, unlawfully, wilfully and feloniously did knowingly cause to be delivered by mail of the United States, according to the direction thereon, a certain letter directed to Mrs. Evelyne B. Boadway, 1 Ford Place, Pasadena, Calif., which the said defendant then lately before had placed and caused to be placed in the post office of the United States at Fort Worth, Texas, for delivery by the post office establishment of the United States to Mrs. Evelyne B. Boadway at said address, which said letter then and there was and is of the tenor following, to-wit:

ADMIRAL OIL COMPANY
Producers of Crude Oil
P. O. Box 1720
FORT WORTH, TEXAS.

January 12, 1923.

Mrs. Evelyne B. Boadway,
   1 Ford Place,
     Pasadena, Calif.

Dear Mrs. Boadway:

Will you pardon the delay in answering your letter which has been occasioned by the fact that I have been in the fields most of the time during the past thirty days.

I am delighted now to be able to report to you a discovery of tremendous importance on the Powell structure where the Admiral Oil Company owns more than 2500 acres of leases. The importance of this discovery to the Admiral Oil Company can hardly be over-estimated. I honestly believe that within the coming six or nine months these leases will attain a value of $10,000,000 to $25,000,000.

You will find enclosed copy of a special report which we are sending out to stockholders announcing this discovery, and under separate cover I am having sent to you a copy of the current issue of the Texas Oil World which gives full details regarding this latest sensation.

With this new development I am sure that you can pay the exchange fee and secure your Admiral stock with absolute certainty that you will not only get all of your original investment back but within a few months time will realize a very large profit indeed.

As I wrote you on a previous occasion, I have surely had my trials, troubles and tribulations the past year, but this discovery on the Powell structure marks, I am sure, the beginning of a new era for all of my clients as well as myself, and I assure you, Mrs. Boadway, that it gives me quite as much pleasure on behalf of my clients as it does for myself.

With all good wishes, I am,

Sincerely yours,

GSJ-c

Encl.   Gilbert Johnson.

That at the time of causing said letter to be delivered by mail of the United States according to the direction thereon. the defendant then and there well knew that said letter was for the purpose of executing said scheme and artifice; contrary to the form of the statute of the United States in such case made and provided and against the peace and dignity of the United States.

THIRD COUNT.

And the Grand Jurors aforesaid, upon their oaths aforesaid, do further present:

That Gilbert S. Johnson, the identical person named in the first count of this indictment, on the third day of February, in the year nineteen hundred - twenty three, at

Cucamonga, Calif., in said Division and District and within the jurisdiction of this Court, so having devised the scheme and artifice to defraud and to obtain money and property by means of false and fraudulent pretenses, representations and promises described in the first count of this indictment, the allegations concerning which in said first count are incorporated by reference thereto in this count as fully as if they were here repeated, for the purpose of executing said scheme and artifice, unlawfully, wilfully and feloniously did knowingly cause to be delivered by mail of the United States, according to the direction thereon, a certain letter directed to Mr. J. T. Junell, Cucamonga, Calif., Box 124, which the said defendant then lately before had placed and caused to be placed in the post office of the United States at Fort Worth, Texas, for delivery by the post office establishment of the United States to Mr. J. T. Junell at said address, which said letter then and there was and is of the tenor following, to-wit:

ADMIRAL OIL COMPANY
Producers of Crude Oil
P. O. Box 1720
FORT WORTH, TEXAS.

January 31, 1923.

Mr. J. T. Junell,
Cucamonga, Calif.
Box 124.

Dear Sir:

We are in receipt of your letter of December 14th regarding your holdings in the Marine Oil Syndicate and the Mexia Terrace Oil Company.

It is needless for us to say that we sympathize with you and regret in the deepest manner the unfortunate condition you now find yourself facing. We wish, however, to correct the wrong impression you are harboring as the trustees of the Marine Oil Syndicate and Mexia Terrace Oil Company were acting within their rights at the time they assigned the properties, assets etc., to the Admiral Company. Both of the above companies were heavily in debt and in order to prevent the companies going into the hands of a receiver, the consolidation was made with the Admiral Oil Company. It was for the best interests of the stockholders as it afforded them an opportunity to change a security which was a loss into one that has excellent prospective value.

The instructions laid down by the board of trustees of the Admiral Oil Company absolutely prohibit the issuance of any stock unless the cash exchange fee is paid. This rule applies both to large and small stockholders, and we wish to assure you that there has not been one deviation from this rule.

We are willing to cooperate with you in every way and are willing to allow you to make payments over a long period of months, but in order to take advantage of this proposition you must surrender your old certificates and make some kind of a small cash payment at the time the certificates are forwarded to this office.

Owing to the important discovery recently made upon the south end of the Powell structure, the privilege of making the exchange will not remain open indefinitely and for that reason we advise you to give the matter your early attention.

Very truly yours,

FEB-C   ADMIRAL OIL COMPANY
                                        F. E. Browne
                                            Secretary.

That at the time of causing said letter to be delivered by mail of the United States according to the directions thereon, the defendant then and there well knew that said letter was for the purpose of executing said scheme and artifice; contrary to the form of the statute of the United States in such case made and provided and against the peace and dignity of the United States.

FOURTH COUNT.

And the Grand Jurors aforesaid, upon their oaths aforesaid, do further present:

That Gilbert S. Johnson, the identical person named in the first count of this indictment, on the first day of April, one thousand nine hundred and twenty three at Cucamonga, California, in said division and District and within the jurisdiction of this Court, so having devised the scheme and artifice to defraud and to obtain money and property by means of false and fraudulent pretenses, representations and promises described in the first count of this indictment, the allegations concerning which in said first count are incorporated by reference thereto in this count as fully as if they were here repeated, for the purpose of executing said scheme and artifice, unlawfully, wilfully and feloniously did knowingly cause to be delivered by mail of the United States, according to the direction thereon, a certain letter directed to Mr. J. T. Junell, Box 124, Cucamonga, Calif., which the said defendant then lately before had placed and caused to be placed in the post office of the United States at Fort Worth, Texas, for delivery by the post office establishment of the United States to Mr. J. T. Junell at said address, which said letter then and there was and is of the tenor following, to-wit:

"Fort Worth, Texas, March 26, 1923.

J. T. Junell,
  Box 124, Cucamonga, Calif.

IN ACCOUNT WITH
ADMIRAL OIL COMPANY
PRODUCERS OF CRUDE OIL
EXECUTIVE OFFICE
NEIL P. ANDERSON BUILDING
FORT WORTH, TEXAS.

In accordance with our records as of this date you are the owner and holder of the following securities which are subject to exchange for stock of the Admiral Oil Company upon payment of the exchange fee indicated on the statement below:

Number of Shares.	Name of Company	Exchange Fee Required.	Number of Admiral Shares to which You Will be Entitled.
418	Johnson Oil Co......................	41.80	418
3	Marine Oil Syndicate...........	45.00	300
	Corsicana Mexia Oil Fields Syndicate		
300	Mexia Terrace Oil Co.........	15.00	75
	Runnels Oil Syndicate...........		
	Total	101.80	793

Note:—Unless certificates for your holdings of the old companies are forwarded to us for exchange for stock of the Admiral Oil Company on or before Saturday, April 7, 1923, you will forfeit all future right to claim the privilege of making the exchange thereafter.

If not convenient for you to make the exchange payment all in cash at this time, it may be paid one-third cash when you send in your old certificates, one-third in thirty days, and the balance one-third in sixty days. In order to protect your interests, however, at least one-third of the amount of exchange fee required as shown on the above statement must be mailed to us with certificates for your holdings not later than April 7, 1923.

ADMIRAL OIL COMPANY.

Please return this statement with your Certificates and Remittance."

That at the time of causing said letter to be delivered by mail of the United States according to the direction thereon, the defendant then and there well knew that said letter was for the purpose of executing said scheme and artifice; contrary to the form of the statute of the United States in such cases made and provided and against the peace and dignity of the United States.

FIFTH COUNT.

And the Grand Jurors aforesaid, upon their oaths aforesaid, do further present:

That Gilbert S. Johnson, the identical person named in the first count of this indictment, on the thirteenth day of May, in the year nineteen hundred- twenty three, at Pasadena, Calif., in said Division and District and within the jurisdiction of this Court, so having devised the scheme and artifice to defraud and to obtain money and property by means of false and fraudulent pretenses, representations and promises described in the first count of this indictment, the allegations concerning which in said first count are incorporated by reference thereto in this count as fully as if they were here repeated, for the purpose of executing said scheme and artifice, unlawfully, wilfully and feloniously did knowingly cause to be delivered by mail of the United States, according to the direction thereon, a certain letter directed to Mr. H. W. Shafer, P. O. Box 397, Pasadena, Calif., which the said defendant then lately before had placed and caused to be placed in the post office of the United States at Fort Worth, Texas, for delivery by the post office establishment of the United States to Mr. H. W. Shafer at said address, which said letter then and there was and is of the tenor following, to-wit:

Fort Worth, Texas, May 10, 1923.

Mr. H. W. Shafer,
>P. O. Box 397
>>Pasadena, Calif.

IN ACCOUNT WITH
ADMIRAL OIL COMPANY
PRODUCERS OF CRUDE OIL
Executive office
NEIL P. ANDERSON BUILDING
FORT WORTH, TEXAS

You are, in accordance with our records, the owner of the following securities which are subject to exchange for stock of the Admiral Oil Company upon payment of the exchange fee indicated on the statement below:

Number of Shares or units	Name of Company	Exchange fee Required	Number of Admiral Shares to Which you will be entitled.
2486	Johnson Oil Co.........	248:60	2486
15	Marine Oil Syndicate	225:00	1500
	Corsicana-Mexia Oil Fields Syndicate....		
100	Mexia Terrace Oil Co...............	5:00	25
	Runnels Oil Syndicate...............		
	Total..............	478:60	4011
	Amount paid to date	25:00	
	Balance due	453:60	

The above statement of your account, as shown on our books, is placed in your hands in order that you may have exact knowledge of the present condition of your account, and your attention is called to the fact that all monthly payment must be made promptly when due.

ADMIRAL OIL COMPANY.

Important: This account is in arrears and unless remittance is made immediately to place it in good standing, it will be subject to cancellation without further notice. A. O. Co.

That at the time of causing said letter to be delivered by mail of the United States according to the direction thereon, the defendant then and there well knew that said letter was for the purpose of executing said scheme and artifice; contrary to the form of the statute of the United States in such case made and provided and against the peace and dignity of the United States.

SIXTH COUNT.

And the Grand Jurors aforesaid, upon their oaths aforesaid, do further present:

That Gilbert S. Johnson, the identical person named in the first count of this indictment, on the third day of February, in the year nineteen hundred-twenty four, at Los Angeles, Calif., in said Division and District and within the jurisdiction of this Court, so having devised the scheme and artifice to defraud and to obtain money and property by means of false and fraudulent pretenses, representations and promises described in the first count of this indictment, the allegations concerning which in said first count are incorporated by reference thereto in this count as fully as if they were here repeated, for the purpose of executing said scheme and artifice, unlawfully, wilfully and feloniously did knowingly cause to be delivered by mail of the United States, according to the direction thereon, a certain letter directed to Mr. O. L. Hopkins, 2808 West Avenue, 31, Los Angeles, Calif., which the said defendant then lately before had placed and caused to be placed in the post office at Fort Worth, Texas, for delivery by the post office establishment of the United States to Mr. O..L. Hopkins at said address, which said letter then and there was and is of the tenor following, to-wit:

Gilbert S. Johnson
President and General
Manager

Frederick E. Browne
Secretary and
Treasurer

Schuyler G. Tryon
Vice President and
Field Manager

ADMIRAL OIL COMPANY
Producers of Crude Oil
P. O. Box 1720
FORT WORTH, TEXAS
January 31, 1924.

Mr. O. L. Hopkins,

2908 West Avenue, 31,

Los Angeles, Calif.

Dear Sir:

It has been a long time since we have issued any reports on the Admiral Oil Company for the reason there has been nothing of importance to report and it has been necessary for us to conserve every dollar. We now have in course of preparation, however, a complete report covering the operations of the past year and the outlook for the future. This report will be off the press, we hope, within a week, and a copy of it will be promptly forwarded to you.

Meanwhile, we will tell you that some of our holdings northeast of Powell now look remarkably good and there is little doubt that another great oil pool will be opened up in that area within the coming few weeks. We are going to try to finance an oil well on our Skiles lease at the earliest possible moment and we hope it will prove to be a tremendous producer. We have leases enough northeast of Powell to pull the Admiral Oil Company out in good shape, pay back all the money ever invested in it, and leave the company in good financial condition if another pool is opened up in that territory similar to the pool south of Powell and that seems now to be almost a certainty.

We regret very much our inability to make a refund of the money which you sent us for payment of your investment with us. The unsuccessful drilling campaign launched by the Admiral Oil Company in the early part of 1923 has placed the company in such financial condition that we have been only able to exist through Mr. Johnson's liberal cash advances until he is now practically without funds. We trust that you will bear with us until you receive a copy of the report, above mentioned and now being prepared.

With all good wishes, we are

Yours very truly,
ADMIRAL OIL COMPANY,
B/LS   By W. F. Bateman.

That at the time of causing said letter to be delivered by mail of the United States according to the direction thereon, the defendant then and there well knew that said letter was for the purpose of executing said scheme and artifice; contrary to the form of the statute of the United States in such case made and provided and against the peace and dignity of the United States.

Samuel W. McNabb
United States Attorney.

J. E. Simpson
Assistant United States Attorney.

John S. Pratt
Special Assistant to the Attorney General
of the United States.

[Endorsed]: Filed Jun 19 1925 Chas. N. Williams, Clerk By Murray E. Wire Deputy Clerk

---

At a stated term, to wit: The February Term, A. D. 1925, of the District Court of the United States of America, within and for the Central Division of the Southern District of California, held at the Court Room thereof, in the City of Los Angeles, California, on Friday, the 19th day of June, in the year of our Lord one thousand nine hundred and twenty-five.

Present:

The Honorable WM. P. JAMES, District Judge.

United States of America, Plaintiff,)
)
         vs.   ) No. 7260-H-Crim.
)
Gilbert S. Johnson,   Defendant,)

An Indictment having been presented to the Court in this cause by the Foreman of the Grand Jury, and filed herein; upon motion of Albert K. Lucas, Assistant United States Attorney, appearing in behalf of the Government, it is by the Court ordered that the bail of defendant herein be fixed in the sum of $10,000.00, and that a bench warrant issue for the apprehension of said defendant.

(59/239)

IN THE DISTRICT COURT OF THE UNITED
STATES IN AND FOR THE SOUTHERN
DISTRICT OF CALIFORNIA,
CENTRAL DIVISION.

UNITED STATES OF AMERICA,)
)
                    Plaintiff,)   NO. 7260-H
         vs.   )
)   CRIMINAL
GILBERT S. JOHNSON,   )
                 Defendant.)

- - - - - - oOo - - - - - -
MOTION TO QUASH INDICTMENT.
- - - - - - - - - - - - - - -

TO THE HONORABLE JUDGE OF SAID COURT:

Comes now the defendant, GILBERT S. JOHNSON, in the above entitled cause and moves the court to quash the indictment herein because said indictment, and each and every count thereof, is fatally and fundamentally defective and void upon its face for the following reasons, to wit:

(1) Said indictment and each and every count thereof, fails to charge the crime against the laws of the United States pursuant to Section 215 of the Criminal Code.

(2) Said indictment, and each and every count thereof, fails to inform the defendant of the nature and cause of the accusation against him. in this, that said indictment charges only in general terms and this defendant will be unable to meet the charges of such a general nature.

(3) Because said indictment charges and attempts to charge other and different crimes and offenses not contemplated by Section 215 of the Criminal Code of the United States, which section contemplates only the misuse of the United States mail in furtherance of schemes to

defraud, in this, that said indictment in paragraph 5 of page 3, solemnly charges the defendant with the crime of embezzlement, which said crime is not contemplated by Section 215 of the Criminal Code. And again, in paragraph 13 of page 6 of said indictment, defendant is again charged and attempted to be charged with the crime of embezzlement.

(4) Because said indictment, and each and every count thereof, is founded upon malice, passion and prejudice, in this, that in paragraph (c) on page 8 of said indictment, the defendant is charged and attempted to be charged with being "a promoter of many fraudulent enterprises and was a confidence man and swindler", which said charges, are crimes and offense not contemplated or cognizable by the laws or statutes of the United States, and particularly, Section 215 of the United States Criminal Code, and the same paragraph further charges and attempts to charge the crime of embezzlement.

(5) Because said indictment, and each and every count thereof, further charges and attempts to charge the defendant with the crime of embezzlement, in this, that said charge or attempted charge is found in paragraph (d) of page 8 of said indictment. This same vice is found in paragraph (e) on page 9 of said indictment, and again the same charge is found in paragraph (h) on page 11 of said indictment.

(6) Because said indictment in paragraph (n) of page 19 again charges and attempts to charge the defendant with the crime of embezzlement and conversion, which said crimes and offenses, are not cognizable by Section 215 of the United States Criminal Code. The same vice is found in paragraph (o) on page 19 of said indictment.

(7) Because said other crimes charged and attempted to be charged, to wit; the crimes of embezzlement and conversion, and also denominating the defendant as being

"a promoter of many fraudulent enterprises", and further designating him as being "a confidence man and swindler", tend to degrade the defendant and are highly prejudicial, and will prevent him from having a fair and an impartial trial under Section 215 of the Criminal Code, as guaranteed to him by the Constitution and laws of the United States.

WHEREFORE, defendant prays that this motion to quash be sustained and said indictment dismissed and that he be discharged.

McLean, Scott & Sayers

H L Arterberry

Attorneys for Defendant.

IN THE DISTRICT COURT OF THE UNITED STATES IN AND FOR THE SOUTHERN DISTRICT OF CALIFORNIA, CENTRAL DIVISION.

UNITED STATES OF AMERICA,)) Plaintiff,) vs.)) GILBERT S. JOHNSON,) Defendant.)	NO. 7260-H CRIMINAL

--------oOo--------

POINTS AND AUTHORITIES IN SUPPORT OF THE MOTION TO QUASH

An indictment must be so clear and exact in its language as to advise the accused and the court beyond doubt of the offense intended to be charged, Rumley v. United States, 293 Fed. 532 (C. C. A. 2).

In an indictment for use of mails in furtherance of a scheme to defraud, the particulars of the scheme are matters of substance and must be set forth with sufficient certainty to acquaint the defendant with the charge against him. Savage v. United States, 270 Fed. 14 (C. C. A. 8).

In the case of United States v. Howard, Fed. Cas. No. 15, 403, Mr. Justice Story, in discussing the tests of surplusage and of material variance, used this language:

"The material parts which constitute the offense charged must be stated in the indictment, and that must be proved in evidence. But allegations not essential to such a purpose, which might be entirely ommitted without affecting the charge against the defendant, and without detriment to the indictment; are considered as mere surplusage, and may be disregarded in evidence. But no allegation, whether it be necessary or unnecessary, whether it be more or less particular, which is descriptive of the identity of that which is legally essential to the charge in the indictment, can ever be rejected as surplusage."

See also Mathews v. United States, 15 Fed. (2d) 139-143 (C. C. A. 8).

The case of Naftzger v. United States, 200 Fed. 494, (C. C. A. 8) holds that an unnecessary allegation which, however, was descriptive of the identity of something which was legally essential to the charge, could not be considered surplusage.

Kercheval v. United States, 12 Fed. (2d) 904-908, holds that conversion is not an element of crime under Section

215 of the Penal Code; see also <u>Nelson v. United States,</u> 16 Fed. (2d) 71-75 (C. C. A. 8).

In the very recent case of <u>Beck v. United States,</u> reported in the advance sheets of August 1st, 1929, 33 Fed. (2d) 107 (C. C. A. 8)

At page 109, among other things, the court says:

"There follows five printed pages of "representations", all of which, are alleged in the most general terms to be false and untrue. It is not alleged wherein they are false. It is true, as claimed by appellant, that there are many instances where in order to comply with the constitutional requirements of certainty in the accusation, a pleader should not only allege the falsity of the misrepresentation, but "allege affirmatively in what the falsehood consisted." 25 C. J. 628. But the particular vice of this indictment reaches farther than that; the unfair part of it is that the defendant is charged with falsely representing many things which counsel for the government assure the court are not false at all."

In connection with the Beck case, supra, it is particularly interesting to note on page 110 thereof, in discussing the indictment in said case and what was generally referred to as the "shotgun" clause, and comparing same with paragraph (o) on page 19 of the indictment in this case, wherein the same vice is found in the present indictment that was condemned by the court in the Beck case and in this connection, we shall quote a part of the language of the court in the <u>Beck</u> case:

"The quoted "shotgun" clause is in such general terms that it is unfair to the defendants. It gives them no inkling of what facts may be concealed in the underbrush of glittering generality, and no opportunity to defend against them. The courts are properly lenient with regard to the form of an indictment which substantially advises the defendant of the charge; they are likewise critical of a charge which is that in form alone, and can serve no purpose save as a foundation for evidence that will catch the defendant off his guard. In the early history of civil pleading, plaintiffs used to allege certain acts of negligence and then quietly add "on account of the aforesaid and other negligent acts". Occasionally, it is still done; but not when the court's attention is directed thereto. The constitution compels that the rule of criminal pleading should be at least as fair. A trial judge would be justified in sustaining a demurrer to an indictment with such Mother Hubbard allegations; or in treating it as surplusage. In this case, neither course was taken. The motion for a bill of particulars was asked and denied. While such a motion is generally within the sound discussion of the court, it should have been sustained."

In the case of U. S. v. Cruikshank, 91 U. S. 442, the Supreme Court laid down the following rule:

"It is an elementary principle of criminal pleading that when the definition of an offense, whether it be of common law or by statute, includes generic terms, it is not sufficient that the indictments which charge the offense be in the same generic terms as in the definition, but it must state the species; it must descend to particularities."

In the case of U. S. v. Hess, 31 L. Ed. 518, the Supreme Court said:

"The object of the indictment is: first, to furnish the accused with such a description of the charge against him

as will enable him to make his defense and avail himself
of a conviction or acquittal, for protection against a further prosecution for the same cause; and second, to inform the court of the facts alleged so that it may decide
whether they are sufficient in law to support a conviction
if one should be had, for these facts are to be stated, not
conclusions of law alone. A crime is made up of acts and
intent, and these must be set forth in the indictment with
reasonable particularity of time, place and circumstances."

In the case of Brenner v. U. S. 287 Fed. 640, opinion
by the Circuit Court of Appeals Second Circuit, Justice
Manton speaking for the Court, used this language:

"It is essential to the sufficiency of the indictment that
it set forth the facts which the pleader claims constitute
the alleged criminal breach, so distinctly as to advise the
accused of the charge which he has to meet, and to give
him a fair opportunity to prepare his defense so particularly as to avail himself of a conviction or acquittal in
advance of another prosecution for the same offense, and
so clearly that the court may be able to determine whether
or not the facts as stated are sufficient to support a conviction. Fontana v. U. S., 262 Fed. 283. The indictment
must charge the offense in more than the generic terms as
in the definition. It must descend to particularities.
U. S. v. Cruikshank, 92 U. S. 542, 23 L. Ed. 588. A
crime, unless otherwise provided by statute, is made of
acts intent, and they must be set forth in the indictment
with reasonable particularity as to time, place and circumstances. Such particularities are matters of substance
and not of form, and their omission is not aided or cured
by a verdict.

In U. S. v. Hess, 124 U. S. 483, 31 L. Ed. 516, it is said: "The essential requirements indeed or the particulars constituting the offense of devising a scheme to defraud are wanting. Such particulars are matters of substance and not of form, and their omission is not aided or cured by a verdict." "

In the case of U. S. v. Potter, 56 Fed. 89-90, the Circuit Court of Appeals, speaking through Judge Putnam, used this language:

"In order to properly inform the accused of the 'nature and cause of the accusation', within the meaning of the constitution and of the rules of the common law, a little thought will make it plain, not only to the legal, but to all other educated minds, that not only must all the elements of the offense be stated in the indictment, but that also they must be stated with clearness and certainty, and with a sufficient degree of particularity to indentify the transaction to which the indictment relates as to place, persons and things and other details. The accused must receive sufficient information to enable him to reasonably understand, not only the nature of the offense, but the particular act or acts touching which he must be prepared with his proof; and when his liberty, and perhaps his life, are at stake, he is not to be left so scantily informed as to cause him to rest his defense upon the hypothesis that he is charged with a certain act or series of acts, with the hazard of being surprised by proofs on the part of the prosecution of an entirely different act or series of acts, at least so far as such surprise can be avoided by reasonable particularity and fullness of description of the alleged offense. These rules are well expressed in U. S. v. Cruikshank, 92 U. S. 542, 557, as follows:

'In criminal cases prosecuted under the laws of the United States the accused has the constitutional right to be informed of the nature and cause of the accusation.' Amendment 6 in U. S. v. Mills, 7 Pet. 142, this was construed to mean that the indictment must set forth the offense 'with clearness and all necessary certainty to apprise the accused of the crime with which he stands charged;' and in U. S. v. Cooke, 17 Wall. 174, that 'every ingredient of which the offense is composed must be accurately and clearly alleged.' It is an elementary principal of criminal pleading that where the definition of an offense, whether it be at common law or by statute, 'including generic terms, it is not sufficient that the indictment shall charge the offense in the same generic terms as in the definition; but it must state the species—it must descend to particulars.' 1 Arch Cr. Pr. & Pl. 291. The object of the indictment is, first, to furnish the accused with such a description of the charge against him as will enable him to make his defense, and avail himself of his conviction or acquittal for protection against a further prosecution for the same cause; and second, to inform the court of the facts alleged, so that it may decide whether they are sufficient in law to support a conviction, if one should be had. For this, facts are to be stated, not conclusions of law alone. A crime is made up of acts and intent; and these must be set forth in the indictment with reasonable particularity of time, place and circumstances.' "

In the case of Anderson v. U. S., 294 Fed. 597, opinion by the Circuit Court of Appeals, Second Circuit, the court held:

"The crime must be charged with precision and certainty, and every ingredient of which it is composed, must be accurately and clearly alleged. Evans v. U. S., 153 U. S. 584, 14 Sup. Ct. 934, 38 L. ed. 830. To allege that what was done was unlawful is merely to state the conclusion of the pleader. Brenner v. U. S., supra. The facts supporting the legal conclusion must be alleged. To admit this essential fact is to render the indictment void."

In this connection see also Goldberg v. U. S., 277 Fed. 215, opinion by the Circuit Court of Appeals, Eighth Circuit; Reeder v. U. S., 262 Fed. 38, opinion by Elliott District Judge, certiorari denied by supreme court, 64 L. ed. 726.

The defect in the indictment for failure to charge the defendants with any criminal act distinctly and expressly, with precision and certainty, is not cured by the "whereas clauses" set forth in said indictment.

In the case of Dalton v. U. S., 127 Fed. 547, the Circuit Court of Appeals, Seventh Circuit, had this very question under consideration. The court, speaking through Judge Jenkins, had this to say:

"We then come to the 'whereas' clause, which is not an allegation of a scheme, but is a negation—a denial of the truth of preceding allegations. This word 'whereas' implies a recital, and in general, cannot be used in the direct and positive averment of a fact. It is thus defined:

'(1) The thing being so that; considering that things are so; implying an admission of facts, something followed by a different statement, and sometimes by inference of something consequent. (2) While on the contrary; the fact or case really being that; when in fact.' Century Dictionary.

The statement sought to be negatived by the 'whereas' clause should have been made positively in the indictment, the purpose of the 'whereas' clause being to set forth the real truth concerning the allegations supposed to have been theretofore averred. The difficulty here is that the allegations thus denied are not positively charged in the indictment to be part of the scheme to defraud. If it be a denial of anything averred, it is a denial of the allegations of the pleader with respect to the class of persons intended to be defrauded."

In the case of Foster v. U. S. 253 Fed. 482, the Circuit Court of Appeals, Ninth Circuit, speaking through Judge Gilbert, used this language:

"The plaintiffs in error had the constitutional right to be informed of the nature and cause of the accusation against them. To furnish them with that information it was necessary to set forth in the indictment the particular facts and circumstances which rendered them guilty and to make specific that which the statute states in general."

MISCONDUCT OF COUNSEL IN DRAFTING INDICTMENT.

Counsel for the government may be guilty of misconduct just as prejudicial to the right of a defendant as in making final argument to the jury in the case, by display of malice, hatred, contempt, ridicule or scorn, and making assertions and statements not based on truth or fact. Because in the latter case, defendant's counsel could make a proper objection and protect the rights of the defendant from such unwarranted abuse. While in the first instance, by heaping unwarranted abuse on a defendant under the guise of a solemn accusation by a grand jury in the form of an indictment; much greater harm and injury can result from attacks of that nature, than in the latter case. And it is these tactics to which we desire to direct the court's attention to the misconduct and evident unfairness of the drafter of this indictment, when he, knowingly and deliberately, inserted a lot of accusations which have no proper place in an indictment such as this. For instance, the indictment in the present case is literally honeycombed with charges and accusations against this defendant, charging that he <u>misappropriated,</u> <u>embezzled</u> and <u>converted</u> to his own use and benefit, large sums of money and property alleged to have been acquired by him in furtherance of the alleged scheme to defraud. This, in the face of all the courts saying that such allegations constitute no part or parcel of a mail fraud indictment. Not satisfied with these allegations, which are repeated in practically every paragraph of the alleged scheme to defraud, but the alleged scheme, and particularly paragraph (o) on page 19 of said indictment, contains what the court describes and condemns in the Beck case, as the "shotgun" clause.

Not satisfied with the wrongful allegations above referred to, but the pleader in this case so far forgets himself as to make charges against this defendant under the guise of a solemn charge of a Grand Jury of the United States, in charging this defendant with being a "confidence man and swindler", when the pleader knew, or by the slightest investigation, could have known, that this defendant has never been even as much as charged, much less, convicted of any offense against the laws of the United States, or of any state within the United States.

This, in the face of the elementary principle that every man is presumed to be innocent until proven guilty.

We submit that all these unwarranted, unjustified, malicious, and slanderous statements, have only one purpose and effect, and that is to so prejudice this defendant before a jury upon the trial of said case, that he will be denied a fair and an impartial trial, as guaranteed to him by the laws and Constitution of the United States.

We further submit that such allegations cannot be treated as mere surplusage, as they are collateral to and a part of the main charge of the indictment. We therefore, respectfully submit that the indictment in this case should be quashed and held for naught, and defendant be discharged. See:—

Beck v. United States, 33 Fed. (2d) 107-113—(C. C. A. 8)

Latham v. United States, 226 Fed. 420—(C. C. A. 5)

Miller v. United States, 287 Fed. 864—(C. C. A. 5)

De Luca v. United States, 298 Fed. 416

United States v. Gradwell, 227 Fed. 243

Agnew v. United States, 165 U. S. 36-45

United States v. American Tobacco Co., 177 Fed. 774

United States v. Nevin, 199 Fed. 833

McKinney v. United States, 199 Fed. 29—(C. C. A. 7)

Respectfully submitted,
McLean, Scott & Sayers
H L Arterberry
Attorneys for Defendant.

[Endorsed]: Filed Sep 3 1929 R. S. Zimmerman, Clerk By Murray E. Wire Deputy Clerk

————

At a stated term, to wit: The September Term, A. D. 1929, of the District Court of the United States of America, within and for the Central Division of the Southern District of California, held at the Court Room thereof, in the City of Los Angeles, California, on Tuesday, the 10th day of September, in the year of our Lord one thousand nine hundred and twenty-nine.

Present:

The Honorable EDWARD J. HENNING, District Judge.

United States of America, Plaintiff,)
)
       vs.   ) No. 7260-H-Crim.
)
Gilbert S. Johnson,   Defendant,)

This cause coming on for hearing on Motion to Quash Indictment; Herman L. Arterberry, Esq., appearing as counsel for the defendant, argues in support of said Motion, and thereupon a statement is made for the Government by P. V. Davis, Assistant United States Attorney, and counsel having argued further on Motion to Quash Indictment, it is ordered that same be submitted on authorities now on file, and to be filed within five days by both parties.

(71/804)

At a stated term, to wit: The September Term, A. D. 1929, of the District Court of the United States of America, within and for the Central Division of the Southern

District of California, held at the Court Room thereof, in the City of Los Angeles, California, on Friday, the 15th day of November, in the year of our Lord one thousand nine hundred and twenty-nine.

Present:

The Honorable EDWARD J. HENNING, District Judge.

United States of America, Plaintiff,)
　　　　　　　　　　　　　　　　　　　　)
　　　　　　　　vs.　　　　　　　　　　　) No. 7260-H-Crim.
　　　　　　　　　　　　　　　　　　　　)
Gilbert S. Johnson,　　　　Defendant,)

On September 10th, 1929, proceedings having been had on the Motion to Quash Indictment, and the said Motion having been ordered submitted on authorities on file, and to be filed, and thereafter the Court having duly considered said Motion, now hands down its "Ruling on Motion to Quash" which is filed this date, and pursuant thereto, the Motion to Quash Indictment is denied.
(72/310)

[TITLE OF COURT AND CAUSE.]

RULING ON MOTION TO QUASH.

The motion to quash the indictment has been argued orally and elaborate briefs have been submitted which I have studied with great care.

There is a great deal of force in the contention of the defendant that the indictment contains language which should not be there. There is no excuse whatever for using the phrase "a promoter of many fraudulent enterprises and was a confidence man and swindler." However, that does not charge a separate offense.

A statement of that kind in an indictment serves no useful purpose and a public officer has no right to indulge in spleen, invective and recrimination in the performance of his public duty. I believe, however, that any possible prejudice to the defendant by the use of such a phrase in the indictment can be cured by proper instructions to a jury at the proper time.

Defendant contends that the indictment should have been brought in Texas in the district where the defendant resides, where the properties alleged to have been used for the basis of a fraudulent scheme are located, and from where the letters involved in the alleged scheme were mailed, and that most of the witnesses to be called by the Government at the trial reside in Texas.

While there may be some force to that contention an examination of the indictment indicates that all the letters set up in the indictment were addressed to residents of this district.

A quashing of the indictment would result in making further prosecution impossible because of the statute of limitations. Without knowing in detail why the trial of the case has been so long delayed, (indictment filed June 19, 1925), at least a portion of the delay and possibly the greater part of it was brought about by the steps taken by the defendant to prevent removal to this district.

In view of all the circumstances, as well as the law and facts presented to the Court, the motion to quash is denied.

Dated this 15th day of November, 1929.

Edward J. Henning
Edward J. Henning,
Judge.

[Endorsed]: Filed Nov 15 1929 R. S. Zimmerman, Clerk By Francis E. Cross, Deputy Clerk

———

At a stated term, to wit: The September Term, A. D. 1930, of the District Court of the United States of America, within and for the Central Division of the Southern District of California, held at the Court Room thereof, in the City of Los Angeles, Calif., on Tuesday, the 11th day of November in the year of our Lord one thousand nine hundred and thirty-

Present:

The Honorable GEORGE COSGRAVE, District Judge.

United States of America, Plaintiff,)
)
     vs.   ) No. 7260-H-Crim.
)
Gilbert S. Johnson,   Defendant,)

This cause coming before the Court for arraignment and plea, and trial of defendant Gilbert S. Johnson; Samuel W. McNabb, United States Attorney, and Peter V. Davis, Assistant United States Attorney, appearing as counsel for the Government; John S. Pratt, Esq., Special Assistant to the Attorney General, being present, and also Edward Van Meter and Dudley Hossack being present and alternating as the official stenographic reporters of the testimony and the proceedings; said defendant being present in court with his attorney, H. L. Arterberry, Esq., who moves the Court that David H. Cannon and Wm. P. McLean, Esqs., be associated as counsel for the defendant, and the Court having thereupon so ordered, said defendant waives the reading of the Indictment, states his true name to be as given therein; and, upon being required to plead, the defendant enters his plea of not guilty; whereupon,

At the hour of 10:10 o'clock a. m., it is by the Court ordered that this trial be proceeded with, and that a jury be impanelled herein, and twelve (12) names of those so drawn, being as follows, to-wit:

Albert B. Ruddock, Henry M. Laud, Edward R. Wagner, Roydon Vosburg, Walter C. Day, Alvah Ganter, Wm. Monten, P. H. Pennington, W. J. Riley, Wm. Joseph, J. Herbert Smith and Troy V. Cox.

The names of those so drawn are now called and examined for cause by the Court; and thereafter, said jurors having been examined for cause by P. V. Davis and David H. Cannon, Esqs., respectively,

Albert Ruddock and Edward R. Wagner are excused on peremptory challenges made by counsel for the defendant and the plaintiff, respectively; whereupon, it is by the Court ordered that two more names be drawn from the jury box, and the names of Charles H. Barker and Warren A. Pike are drawn therefrom; the said jurors so drawn are called and examined for cause by the Court, and by Attorneys Davis and Cannon, respectively.

W. J. Riley is excused on peremptory challenge made by counsel for the defendant, and the Court having thereupon ordered that one more name be drawn from the jury box, the name of Noble E. Dawson is drawn therefrom; the said Noble E. Dawson is called and is examined by the Court for cause, and the said prospective juror having thereupon been challenged for cause by David H. Cannon, Esq., it is by the Court ordered that said juror be excused for cause, and challenged allowed; whereupon, it is by the Court ordered that one more name be drawn from the jury box, and the name of H. Lewis Haynes is drawn therefrom; the said H. Lewis Haynes is called and is examined for cause by the Court; and thereafter, by Attorneys Davis and Cannon, respectively, and passed for cause.

Wm. Monten is excused on peremptory challenge made by counsel for the plaintiff; whereupon, it is by the Court ordered that one more name be drawn from the jury box, and the name of Chas. E. Stimson is drawn therefrom; the said Chas. E. Stimson is called and is examined for cause by the Court and Attorney Davis, respectively; and, not having been passed for cause, is excused by the Court for cause; whereupon, it is ordered that one more name be drawn from the jury box, and the name of Gustaf Olson is drawn therefrom; the said Gustaf Olson is called and is examined for cause by the Court, and the prospective juror having thereupon been examined for cause by Attorneys Davis and Cannon, respectively, is passed for cause.

Charles H. Barker, heretofore examined for cause, is now excused on peremptory challenge by counsel for the defendant; whereupon, it is by the Court ordered that one more name be drawn from the jury box, and the name of Thos. R. Jones is drawn therefrom; the said Thos. R. Jones is called and is examined for cause by the Court, and said juror having thereupon been examined for cause by Attorneys Davis and Cannon, is passed for cause.

P. H. Pennington is excused on peremptory challenge made by counsel for the plaintiff, and the Court having thereupon ordered that one more name be drawn from the jury box, Norman W. McMillan's name is drawn therefrom, and the said Norman W. McMillan is called and is examined for cause by the Court, and Attorney Davis, respectively.

J. Herbert Smith is excused on peremptory challenge made by counsel for the defendant; whereupon, it is ordered that one more name be drawn from the jury box, and the name of Isidor Weinberger is drawn therefrom; the said Isidor Weinberger is called and is examined for cause by the Court, and said juror having thereupon been examined by Attorneys Davis and Cannon, respectively, is passed for cause.

Walter C. Day is excused on peremptory challenge made by counsel for the defendant; whereupon, it is by the Court ordered that one more name be drawn from the jury box, and the name of Ford J. Upton is drawn therefrom; the said Ford J. Upton is called and examined by the Court and Attorney Davis, respectively, and is passed for cause.

Norman W. McMillan, heretofore examined for cause, is excused on peremptory challenge made by the defendant, and the Court having thereupon ordered that one more name be drawn from the jury box, the name of Mark H. Potter is drawn therefrom; the said Mark H. Potter is called and examined for cause by the Court and Attorney Davis, respectively, and passed for cause.

Alvah Gonter is excused on peremptory challenge made by the defendant, whereupon it is by the Court ordered that one more name be drawn from the jury box, and the name of James Pirie is drawn therefrom, and the said James Pirie is called and examined for cause by the

Court, and by Attorneys Davis and Cannon, respectively, and is passed for cause.

Warren A. Pike, heretofore examined for cause, is excused on defendant's peremptory challenge; whereupon, it is by the Court ordered that one more name be drawn from the jury box, and the name of Charles McMasters is drawn therefrom; the said Charles McMasters is called and examined for cause by the Court, and by Attorneys Davis and Cannon, respectively, and is passed for cause.

The jurors, now in the jury box, are accepted and sworn in a body as the jury to try this cause, the names of those so sworn being as follows, to-wit:

THE JURY

Thos. R. Jones,	Gustaf Olson,
Henry M. Loud,	Mark H. Pottter,
Charles McMaster,	H. Lewis Haynes,
Roydon Vosburg,	Wm. Joseph,
Ford J. Upton,	Isidor Weinberger,
James Pirie,	Troy V. Cox,

At the hour of 11:31 o'clock a. m., a recess is declared for a period of five minutes.

At the hour of 11:40 o'clock a. m., court reconvenes; the jury being present, and all being present as before, it is by the Court ordered that this trial be proceeded with; whereupon, John S. Pratt, Esq., makes opening statement in behalf of the Government.

Now, at the hour of 12:00 o'clock, noon, the Court admonishes the jury that during the progress of this trial, they are not to speak to anyone about this cause, or any matter or thing therewith connected; that until said cause is finally submitted to them for their deliberation under the instruction of the Court, they are not to speak to each other about this cause, or any matter or thing therewith connected, or form or express any opinion concerning the merits of the trial until it is finally submitted to them, and declares a recess to the hour of 1:30 o'clock p. m.

At the hour of 1:35 o'clock p. m., the Court reconvenes; the jury being present, and all others being present as before, it is by the Court ordered that the trial be proceeded with; whereupon, John S. Pratt resumes his opening statement to the jury; and closes at the hour of 2:22 o'clock p. m.

David H. Cannon, Esq., reserves opening statement in behalf of defendant, and H. L. Arterberry, Esq., having thereupon objected to the introduction of evidence under this Indictment on the grounds set forth in the motion to quash, said motion is denied, and exception noted.

On motion of John S. Pratt, Esq., the following exhibits are offered and admitted in evidence for the Government, to-wit:

Government's) : Copies of following documents:
  Ex. No. 1)

   A. Declaration of Trust, Admiral Oil Co.

   B.   "   "   "   "   "   " Amendment to article, etc.

   C.   "   " Banner Unit Syndicate.

   D.   "   " Corsicana-Mexia Oil Fields Syndicate.

   E.   "   " Fortuna Petroleum Syndicate

   F.   "   " Johnson Oil Co.

3-N, two-page letter 2/9/24 to J. Jones from W. F. Bateman, and envelope postmarked 2/9/24.

3-O, letter, 3-page, 3/7/24 to Henry S. Holden from W. F. Bateman, and envelope postmarked 3/7/24 attached.

3-P, letter dated March 24, 1924 to W. F. Jungk from W. F. Bateman, and envelope attached, postmarked 3/24/24 to W. F. Jungk.

3-Q, two-page letter dated 3/29/24 to W. P. Hill from W. F. Bateman, and envelope postmarked 3/29/24 to W. P. Hill.

3-R, letter May 9, 1924, to A. W. Ringland from W. F. Bateman.

and the following exhibit is now offered and marked for identification, for the Government, to-wit:

Government's) : Letter dated 1/31/24 to O. L. Hopkins
Ex. No. 4,)   from Admiral Oil Co.
for Ident.)

At the hour of 4:12 o'clock p. m., the Court reminds the jury of the admonition heretofore given, and declares a recess until the hour of 9:30 o'clock a. m., tomorrow.

At the hour of 11:31 o'clock a. m., it is by the Court ordered that the petit jurors not impanelled as the jury to try this cause, be, and they are hereby, excused from further attendance upon this court until further notified.

———

At a stated term, to wit: The September Term, A. D. 1930, of the District Court of the United States of America, within and for the Central Division of the Southern District of California, held at the Court Room thereof, in the City of Los Angeles, California, on Wednesday, the 12th day of November, in the year of our Lord one thousand nine hundred and thirty.

Present:

The Honorable GEORGE COSGRAVE, District Judge.

United States of America, Plaintiff,)
)
        vs.   ) No. 7260-H-Crim.
)
Gilbert S. Johnson,   Defendant,)

This cause coming before the Court for further trial; John S. Pratt, Esq., Special Assistant to the Attorney General, and Peter V. Davis, Assistant United States Attorney, appearing as counsel for the Government; H. L. Arterberry and David H. Cannon, Esqs., appearing as counsel for the defendant; and, Edward Van Meter being present as official stenographic reporter of the testimony and the proceedings;

Now, at the hour of 10:15 o'clock a. m., court reconvenes in this case, the jury being present, and all others appearing as before, it is by the Court ordered that this trial be proceeded with, whereupon,

W. F. Bateman, heretofore sworn, resumes the stand and testifies further on direct examination conducted by P. V. Davis, Esq., and the following exhibit is offered and admitted in evidence for the Government, to-wit:

Government

    Ex. No. 2: Books, records, certificate stub books, etc., covering those books heretofore marked Government Exhibit No. 2 for Ident. and more besides as follows:

Government

    Ex. No. 2-A: Declaration of trust.

             -B: Minute Book Lewis Oil Co.

             -C: Mexia Powell Oil Syndicate

-D: Minute Book Texas Oil Co.

-E: Johnson Oil Company Minute Book.

-F: Minute Book Stephens Oil Syndicate.

-G: Corsicana Mexia Oil Co.

-H: Minute Book Marine Oil Co.

Government's

Ex. No. 2-I: Miss. Oil & Refining Co. Copy of Minutes.

-J: Runnels Oil Syndicate.

-K: Mexia Terrace Oil Co. Minute Book.

-L: Banner Unit Syndicate.

-M: Log of Wells Drilled.

-N: Gilbert Johnson & Co. Stock Sales Record.

-O: Admiral Oil Co. Bk. #1 Stock Sales—A-O Co.

-P: Gilbert Johnson Co. Time Payment Record Book.

-Q: "   "   "   "

-R: "   "   "   ..

-S: "   " General Ledger 1924 to May, 1929.

-T: "   "   "   .. 1922 & some acc. 1920-1928

-U: Admiral Oil Co. Cash Journal.

-V: Johnson Oil Co. Check Register & Cash Journal.

-W: Admiral Oil Co. Book #2 Stock Sales.

-X: Gilbert Johnson & Co. Check Record & Voucher Record.

-Y: General Ledger Powell Petroleum Co.

-Z: "   "   Corsicana-Mexia Oil Syndicate.

2-AA: Gilbert Johnson & Co. Gen'l. Ledger 1920.

2-BB: "   " " Stock Sales Record.

2-CC: Gilbert Johnson & Co. Cash Book.

2-DD: "   "   "   "   "   "

2-EE: "   "   "   "   "

2-FF: .   "   "   "   "   "

2-GG: Texas Oil & Stock Exchange.

2-HH: Gilbert Johnson & Co. Journal Cash Book.

2-II : Gilbert Johnson & Co. Cash Journal Yukon Oil & Gas Co.

2-JJ : Admiral Oil Co. Gen'l. Ledger.

2-KK: Texas Oil & Stock Exchange.

2-LL: Gilbert Johnson & Co. Check Register.

2-MM: Admiral Oil Co. Stock Sales Book

2-NN: Gilbert Johnson & Co. Check Register

2-OO: "   " " " Journal.

2-PP: "   " " " "

2-QQ: "   " " " Powell Petroleum.

2-RR: Admiral Oil Co. Ledger.

2-SS: Partial Pay Book.

2-TT: Certificate Ledger.

2-UU: "   "

2-VV: Partly Issed "

Government's

Ex. No. 2-WW: Consolidated Stockholders Ledger.
    2-XX: "   "   "
    2-YY:
    2-ZZ:
    2-AAA: "
    2-BBB:
    2-CCC:
    2-DDD:
    2-EEE: "   "
    2-FFF:
    2-GGG:
    2-HHH:
    2-III:
    2-JJJ: "
    2-KKK:
    2-LLL:
    2-MMM: "   "
    2-NNN: Stock Certificate Books.
    2-OOO: "   "   "
    2-PPP: "   "   "
    2-QQQ: Bank Statements and Cancelled
              Checks.

At the hour of 11:05 o'clock a. m., the jury are told to remember the admonition heretofore given and a recess is declared for a period of five minutes.

At the hour of 11:20 o'clock a. m., court reconvenes, and all being present as before, said witness Bateman resumes the stand and testifies further on direct examination conducted by P. V. Davis, Esq., and the following exhibits are offered and admitted in evidence for the Government, to-wit:

Government's Ex. No. 5:   Minute Book of Powell Petro-
                                         leum Co.
    "   " 6:   "   "   " Admiral Oil
                                         Company.
    "   " 7:   "   "   " Fortuna
                                         Petroleum
                                         Syndicate.

At the hour of 11:45 o'clock a. m., W. F. Bateman is examined by the Court, whereupon,

At the hour of 11:46 o'clock a. m., W. F. Bateman testifies on cross-examination conducted by David H. Cannon, Esq.,

At the hour of 12:05 o'clock p. m., the Court admonishes the jury and declares a recess to the hour of 1:30 o'clock p. m.

At the hour of 1:30 o'clock p. m., court reconvenes, and all being present as before, W. F. Bateman resumes the stand and testifies further on cross-examination conducted by David H. Cannon, Esq., and said witness having thereupon testified on redirect examination conducted by P. V. Davis, Esq., the following exhibits are offered and admitted in evidence for the Government, to-wit:

Government's Ex. No. 8:   Texas Oil Bulletin   1/1/21.
    "   " " 9:   "   "   "   1/22/21.

whereupon, said witness Bateman testifies on recross-examination and redirect examination conducted by David H. Cannon and Peter V. Davis, Esqs., respectively, and thereafter, said witness testifies on recross-examination conducted by the said David H. Cannon, Esq.

Dudley M. Brown is called and sworn and testifies for the Government on direct examination conducted by John

S. Pratt, Esq., and the following exhibits are offered and admitted in evidence for the Government, to-wit:

Government's Ex. No. 10: Texas Oil Bulletin of 8/25/22.
" " " 11: " " " " 8/11/22.
" " 12: " " " " 9/22/22.
" " 13: " " " " 7/14/22.
" " 14: " " " " 6/23/22.
" " 15: " " " " 6/9/22.
" " 16: " " " " 5/26/22.
" " 17: " " " " 5/12/22.
" " 18: " " " " 4/7/22.
" " 19: " " " " 4/21/22.
" " 20: " " " " 5/5/22.
" " 21: " " " " 3/31/22.

At the hour of 2:32 o'clock p. m., a recess is declared for a period of five minutes.

At the hour of 2:37 o'clock p. m., court reconvenes, and all being present as before, upon motion of John S. Pratt, Esq., the following exhibits are offered and admitted in evidence for the Government, to-wit:

Government's Ex. No. 22: Texas Oil Bulletin of 8/28/19.
" " " 23: " " " " 3/24/22.
Government's Ex. No. 24: Texas Oil Bulletin of 9/10/19.
" " " 25: " " " " 9/20/19.
" " 26: " " " " 10/1/19.
" " 27: " " " " 10/8/19.
" " 28: " " " " 10/15/19.
" " 29: " " " " 11/5/19.
" " 30: " " " " 11/12/19.
" " 31: " " " " 11/19/19.
" " 32: " " " " 11/26/19.

"	"	33:	"	"	"	" 12/27/19.
"	"	34:	"	"	"	" 1/10/20.
"	"	35:	"	"	"	" 2/5/20.
"	"	36:	"	"	"	" 3/4/20.
"	"	37:	"	"	"	" 3/17/20.
"	"	38:	"	"	"	" 4/17/20.
"	"	39:	"	"	"	" 4/24/20.
"	"	40:	"	"	"	" 3/27/20.
"	"	41:	"	"	"	" 5/1/20.
"	"	42:	"	"	"	" 5/8/20.
"	"	43:	"	"	"	" 5/15/20.
"	"	44:	"	"	"	" 5/22/20.
"	"	45:	"	"	"	" 5/29/20.
"	"	46:	"	"	"	" 6/5/20.
"	"	47:	"	"	"	" 6/16/20.
"	"	48:	"	"	"	" 6/26/20.
"	"	49:	"	"	"	" 7/3/20.
"	"	50:	"	"	"	" 7/10/20.
"	"	51:	"	"	"	" 7/17/20.
"	"	52:	"	"	"	" 7/24/20.
"	"	53:	"	"	"	" 7/31/20.
"	"	54:	"	"	"	" 8/7/20.
"	"	55:	"	"	"	" 8/28/20.
"	"	56:	"	"	"	" 9/4/20.
"	"	57:	"	"	"	" 9/18/20.
"	"	58:	"	"	"	" 9/25/20.
"	"	59:	"	"	"	" 10/9/20.

Government's Ex. No. 60: Texas Oil Bulletin of 10/23/20.
"   " " 61:   "   "   "   " 10/30/20.
"   " 62:   "   "   "   " 11/20/20.
"   " 63:   "   "   "   " 12/11/20.

" " 64: " " " " 12/25/20.

" " 65: " " " " 1/29/21.

" " 66: " " " " 2/5/21.

" " " 67: " " " " 2/12/21.

" " 68: " " " " 2/19/21.

" " 69: " " " " 2/26/21.

" " 70: " " " " 3/5/21.

" " " 71: " " " " 3/18/21

and letter attached to J. A. Grisham from A. J. Wright dated 3/16/21.

" " 72: Texas Oil Bulletin of 3/19/21.

" " 73: " " " " 4/2/21.

" " 74: " " " " 4/23/21.

" " 75: " " " " 5/7/21.

" " 76: " " " " 5/21/21.

" " 77: " " " " 6/4/21.

" " 78: " " " " 6/11/21.

" " 79: " " " " 6/25/21.

" " 80: " " " " 7/11/21.

" " " 81: " " " " 8/6/21.

" " 82: " " " " 8/13/21.

" " 83: " " " " 8/20/21.

" " 84: " " " " 9/3/21.

" " 85: " " " " 9/10/21.

" " 86: " " " " 9/24/21.

" " 87: " " " " 10/8/21.

" " 88: " " " " 10/22/21.

" " 89: " " " " 10/29/21.

" " 90: " " " " 11/5/21.

" " 91: " " " " 11/26/21.

" " 92: " " " " 12/10/21.

" " 93 : " " " " 12/17/21.

" " 94 : " " " " 12/24/21.

Government's Ex. No. 95 : Texas Oil Bulletin of 1/13/22.

" " " 96 : " " " " 1/20/22.

" " " 97 : " " " " 1/27/22.

" " 98 : Letter 9/14/20 to Ola Nelson from D. M. Brown and letter attached postmarked 9/14/20.

" " 99 : Letter 8/23/20 to T. H. Jones from D. M. Brown, 2 pages and envelope postmarked 8/24/20.

" Ex. No. 100 : Letter 12/2/21 to C. A. Sherwood from D. M. Brown.

" " " 101 : " 10/19/21 " Wm. Satta Hammersley from D. M. Brown.

" " " 102 : Letter 4/5/21 to H. T. Feidler from D. M. Brown.

" " " 103 : " 10/11/20 " E. S. Rowland from D. M. Brown.

" " " 104 : " 9/16/20 " Barbara Runge " D. M. Brown.

" " " 105 : " 8/13/20 " A. H. Schutte " D. M. Brown.

" " " 106 : 2-page letter 8/2/20 to W. N. Weinacht from D. M. Brown.

" " " 107: Letter 6/17/20 to D. H. Clark from D. M. Brown.

" " " 108: " 10/15/20 " E. A. Trombley from D. M. Brown.

" " " 109: " to E. C. Overman from D. M. Brown, 10/6/20.

" " " 110: " 10/1/20 to Henry S. Holden from D. M. Brown

" " " 111: " 9/11/20 " E. A. Trombley from D. M. Brown, and envelope postparked 9/11/20 to Mr. and Mrs. E. A. Trombley.

" " " 112: Letter 9/13/20 to Ola Nelson from D. M. Brown, and envelope postmarked 9/13/20.

At the hour of 3:55 o'clock p. m., the Court reminds the jury of the admonition hertofore given and declares a recess for a period of five minutes.

At the hour of 4:03 o'clock p. m., court reconvenes, and all being present as before, witness Brown resumes the stand and testifies further on an examination conducted by John S. Pratt, Esq.

At the hour of 4:27 o'clock p. m., said witness Brown testifies on cross-examination conducted by David H. Cannon, Esq., whereupon,

At the hour of 4:47 o'clock p. m., said witness testifies on redirect and recross-examination conducted by John S. Pratt and David H. Cannon, Esqs., respectively.

At the hour of 4:56 o'clock p. m., the Court admonishes the jury and declares a recess until the hour of 9:30 o'clock a. m., tomorrow.

At a stated term, to wit: The September Term, A. D. 1930, of the District Court of the United States of America, within and for the Central Division of the Southern District of California, held at the Court Room thereof, in the City of Los Angeles, California, on Thursday, the 13th day of November, in the year of our Lord one thousand nine hundred and thirty.

Present

The honorable GEORGE COSGRAVE, District Judge.

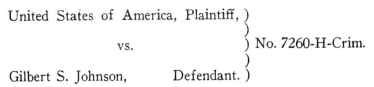

United States of America, Plaintiff,)
)
vs.) No. 7260-H-Crim.
)
Gilbert S. Johnson, Defendant.)

This cause coming before the Court for further trial; John S. Pratt, Esq., Special Assistant to the Attorney General, and Peter V. Davis, Assistant United States Attorney, appearing for the Government; defendant Gilbert S. Johnson being present in court with his attorneys, H. L. Arterberry and David H. Cannon, Esqs.; and, Edward Van Meter being present as official stenographic reporter of the testimony and the proceedings; now, at the hour of 9:32 o'clock a. m., court reconvenes and the jury being present and all others appearing as before, it is by the Court ordered that this trial be proceeded with, whereupon,

Charles E. Newmeyer is called and sworn and testifies for the Government on direct examination conducted by John S. Pratt, Esq., and the following exhibit is offered and admitted in evidence for the Government, to-wit:

Government's Ex. No. 113: Texas Oil Bulletin of 9/4/20.

      " " " " 2/3/22.

      " " " " 2/17/22.

      " " " " 2/24/22.

      " " " " 3/17/22.

      " " " " 3/3/22.

and the following exhibits are offered and marked for identification for the Government, to-wit:

Government's Ex. No.) :
  114 for Ident.)

Circular letter 9/16/22 from Gilbert Johnson & Company to Stockholders of Mexia Terrace Oil Company (later admitted in evid.)

Government's Ex. No.) :
  115 for Ident.)

Letter 11/27/22 to J. W. Barbee from Gilbert Johnson, and progress report No. 1.

Government's Ex. No.) :
  116 for Ident.)

Circular letter 12/1/22 from Admiral Oil Company (later admitted in evid.)

and thereafter, the following exhibit having been offered and admitted in evidence, for the Government, to-wit:

Government's Ex. No. 117:

29 copies of the Texas Oil Radio dated as follows:

1/15/23	5/2/23	6/21/24	11/1/24	3/1/24
5/23/23	7/5/24	11/22/24	12/23/22	6/30/23
7/26/24	12/6/24	2/10/23	3/15/24	8/13/24
1/1/25	3/10/23	4/1/24	8/30/24	2/20/25
3/26/23	4/19/24	9/13/24	11/18/22	4/10/23
5/10/24	9/27/24	6/2/24	10/4/24.	

the following exhibit is offered and marked for identification, for the Government, to-wit:

Government's Ex. No.) :
118 for Ident.   )
Proof of Texas Oil Radio.

At the hour of 10:45 o'clock a. m., the Court admonishes the jury, and declares a recess for a period of ten minutes.

At the hour of 11:03 o'clock a. m., court reconvenes, and all being present as before, said witness Charles E. Newmeyer resumes the stand and testifies further on direct examination conducted by John S. Pratt, Esq., and the following exhibit is offered and admitted in evidence, for the Government, to-wit:

Government's Ex. No. 119:

Bundle of letters, all written by Charles E. Newmeyer, and enumerated as follows:

Letter 5/3/21 to J. W. Barbee from Chas. E. Newmeyer.
"   8/5/21 " J. M. Murphy   "   "   "   "
"   8/23/21 " C. M. Fargo   "   "   "   "
Envelope postmarked 8/23/21 to C. M. Fargo.
Letter 8/31/21 to H. W. Shafer from Chas. E. Newmeyer
"   10/21/21 to C. W. Bruce   "   "   "   "
Envelope, 10/21/21 to C. W. Bruce.
Letter 11/23/21 to E. F. Youngman from Chas. E. Newmeyer.
Envelope postmarked—to E. F. Youngman.
Letter 11/29/21 to H. W. Shafer from Chas. E. Newmeyer.
Balance Sheet, 10/1/21.
Letter 12/5/21 to C. A. Sherwood from Chas. E. Newmeyer.

Envelope postmarked 12/5/21, to C. A. Sherwood.

Letter 12/6/21 to May McGrail from Chas. E. New-
     meyer.

Letter 1/17/22 to J. R. Jones from Chas. E. Newmeyer.

  "   1/28/22 to F. J. Rappe   "   "   "   "

  "   5/18/22 to James W.

                    Barbee from Chas. E. Newmeyer.

  "   5/27/22 to L. A.

                    Bayette   "   "   "   "

  "   6/9/22 to WM. Van

                    Hodge   "   "   "   "

Envelope postmarked 6/23/22.

Letter 6/19/22 to Wm. Van

                    Hodge   "   "   "   "

  "   6/27/22 to S. L. Barber   "   "   "   "

Envelope postmarked 6/21/22 to S. L. Barber.

Letter 7/21/22 to E. A. Trombley from Chas. E. New-
     meyer.

Envelope postmarked 7/21/22 to E. A. Trombley.

Letter 8/21/22 to Wm. Van Hodge

                    from Chas. E. Newmeyer.

  "   9/12/22 to W. P. Butler   "   "   "   "

  "   9/20/22 to W. P. Butler   "   "   "   "

  "   9/26/22 to C. W. Bruce from C. E. Newmeyer.

Envelope postmarked 9/26/22 to C. W. Bruce.

Letter dated 9/27/22 to C. M. Fargo from C. E. New-
     meyer.

Envelope postmarked 9/27/22 to C. M. Fargo.

Letter dated 9/27/22 to Mrs. E. Wehrhan from C. E.
                    Newmeyer.

  "   "   9/30/22 to H. W.

                    Shafer from C. E. Newmeyer.

  "   "   10/11/22 to C. W.

                    Bruce   "   "   "   "

Envelope postmarked 10/11/22 to C. W. Bruce.

Letter 10/12/22 to S. A. Robison from C. E. Newmeyer.

Envelope postmarked 10/12/22 to S. A. Robison.

Letter 10/18/22 to H. Mendenhall from C. E. Newmeyer.

   "   10/18/22 to J. Jones   "   "   "   "

   "   2/16/23 to C. J. Knapp   "   "   "

   "   2/21/23 to C. G. Steed   "   "   "

Statement dated 2/21/23 to C. G. Steed.

Letter dated 3/7/23   to Charles
                        J. Knapp from C. E. Newmeyer.

   "   "   3/15/23 " C. J. Knapp "   "   "   "

   "   "   June 8, 1923, to Jacob E. Warren from C. E. Newmeyer.

   "   "   June 13, 1923, to W. T. Dixon from C. E. Newmeyer.

   "   "   July 5, 1923 to Owen B. Jacoby from C. E. Newmeyer.

   "   "   12/15/22 to Dave Cantine from C. E. Newmeyer.

Envelope postmarked 12/15/22 to Dave Cantine.

Letter dated 11/2/22 to J. Jones from C. E. Newmeyer.

Letter dated 10/9/22 to Samuel Brockway from C. E. Newmeyer.

   "   "   10/9/22 to Geo. W. Patro from C. E. Newmeyer.

Envelope postmarked 10/9/22 to Geo. W. Patro.

Letter dated Oct. 7, 1922 to H. L. Allen from C. E. Newmeyer.

Envelope postmarked 10/7/22 to H. L. Allen.

Letter dated 10/2/22 to J. H. M. Harrison from C. E. Newmeyer.

   "   "   9/29/22 to Celia A. Green from C. E. Newmeyer.

" " 9/5/22 to J. Jones from C. E. Newmeyer.

" " Sept. 1, 1922 to Samuel Brackway from C. E. Newmeyer.

" " 8/21/22 to Ruby Patterson from C. E. Newmeyer.

" (Undated) to Gilbert Johnson & Company, P. O. Box 624, Fort Worth, Texas.

Envelope postmarked 8/21/22 to Miss Ruby Patterson.

Letter dated 8/19/22 to W. S. Coons from C. E. Newmeyer.

Envelope postmarked 8/19/22 to W. S. Coons.

Letter dated 7/22/22 to S. A. Robison from C. E. Newmeyer.

Yellow sheet—cash order blank—Johnson Oil Co. stock.

Envelope postmarked 7/2/22 to S. A. Robison.

Letter dated 7/21/22 to Edwin D. Sargent from C. E. Newmeyer.

Letter dated 7/18/22 to D. C. Willett from C. E. Newmeyer.

Envelope postmarked 7/18/22 to D. C. Willett.

Letter dated July 6, 1922 to D. C. Willett from C. E. Newmeyer.

Envelope postmarked –/6/22, to D. C. Willett.

Letter dated July 5, 1922 to C. M. Fargo from C. E. Newmeyer.

Envelope postmarked 7/5/22 to C. M. Fargo.

Letter dated July 3rd, 1922, to William Van Hodge from C. E. Newmeyer.

" " June 20, 1922 to C. M. Fargo from C. E. Newmeyer.

" " " 15, 1922 to L. A. Boyette " " "

" " 6/12/22 to C. W. Bruce " " "

Envelope dated 6/12/22 to C. W. Bruce.

Letter dated 6/7/22 to Chas. M. Armentrout from C. E. Newmeyer.

Envelope dated 6/7/22 to "   "

Letter 6/1/22 to Dr. F. M. Newman

from C. E. Newmeyer.

" 5/29/22 " S. L. Barber

"   "   "   "

Envelope postmarked 5/23/22 to S. L. Barber.

Letter 2/8/22 to L. A. Boyette from C. E. Newmeyer.

Envelope postmarked 2/8/22 to L. A. Boyette.

Letter 12/6/21 to J. Jones from C. E. Newmeyer.

whereupon the following exhibits are offered and marked for identification towit:

Government's Ex. No.) :
    120 for Ident.   )

Letter 10/2/22 to F. J. Rappe from—

Government's Ex. No.)
    121 for Ident.   )

Letter 1/12/23 to Evelyne B. Boodway from Gilbert S. Johnson.

Government's Ex. No.) :
    122 for Ident.   )

Form letter, Fort Worth, Texas, March 26, 1923, to J. T. Junell, from Admiral Oil Co., and envelope post-marked 3/29/23 to J. T. Rannell.

Government's Ex. No.) :
    123 for Ident.   )

Bundle of letters, as follows:

Circular, Gilbert Johnson & Co.

Spcl. to Stockholders, 7/22/21, from Gilbert Johnson.

Letter 7/19/21 to Mrs. C. G. Steed from   "   "

" 7/16/21 " " " " " "

" 7/1/21 " " " " " "

" 6/18/21 " " " " " "

" 5/28/21 " E. A. Trombley from "

Circular, Gilbert Johnson & Co.

"   "   "   " "

Letter 4/19/21 to Hugh W. Smith from "   " &
Co., by A. J. Wright.

Envelope 4/18/21 to C. G. Steed from "   " " Co

Circular 4/16/21 " " " " " " " " "

Letter 4/7/21 to C. W. Bruce " "

" 3/28/21 " C. G. Steed

Circular 3/12/21 to H. W. Schafer " "

Letter 3/21/21 to Hugh Leroy " " " " "

Circular 3/18/21 to E. A. Trombley from Gilbert Johnson & Co.

Letter 3/12/21 to Chas. A. Cleary from Gilbert Johnson
& Co.

Communication and Circular, 2/19/21, to R. E. L. Roberts from Gilbert Johnson Co.

Circular 12/9/20 to H. W. Shafer from Gilbert Johnson & Co.

Envelope 1/18/30 to E. A. Trombley from " ,
son & Co.

Letter 1/27/21 to Joseph Hotz from Gilbert Johnson
& Co.

Letter 2/1/21 to J. B. Rose, from Gilbert Johnson Co.

" 2/4/21 to E. A. Trombley from Gilbert Johnson
& Co.

Envelope

2/14/21 to E. A. Trombley from Gilbert Johnson & Co.

Letter 2/8/21 to E. " " " " "

Circular 2/21/21

Cash Order "   "

Envelope to Mrs. C. C. Steed

Circular 2/23/21,   "

Letter 3/8/21 to E. C. Overman "   "

" 11/28/20 " " "   "   "   "

" 11/20/20 " E. A. Trombley "   "

Spcl. communication 11/16/20,   "   "   "   " "

"   "   11/18/20, R. E. L. Roberts from Gilbert Johnson & Co.

"   "   11/12/20 from Gilbert Johnson

Letter 10/8/20 to E. C. Overman from "   "

Report to Stockholders 9/28/20—from Gilbert Johnson.

Spcl. communication 11/1/21   "   "   "

Letter 11/3/21 to C. G. Steed

Spcl. communication 11/5/21   "   "   "

Communication
         to Stockholders 12/1/21 from Gilbert Johnson.

Circular 12/9/21 to J. W. Barbee   "   "   "

Letter 12/9/21 to H. W. Shafer   "   "

Circular 1/10/22   "   "

"   "   "   "   "

Letter 1/21/22 to E. F. Youngman from   "   : Co.

" 1/27/22 " " "   "   "   "   "

" 1/27/27 " J. W. Barbee   "   "

Circular 2/8/22   "   "   "

Envelope
         & circular 2/10/22 to C. G. Steed from "

Spcl. Report 3/15/22   "   "

Communication 3/17/22

"   3/31/22

Letter circular 4/3/22,
         to E. A. Trombley   "   "   " " "

" & · "   to E. C. Overman from   ··

Circular 5/1/22 from

Circular 5/18/22 "   ··

Envelope 6/17/22 to E. C. Overman from "

Circular 6/22/22   "   "

Envelope 7/1/22 to W. P. Hill   "   "   ·· ·

Envelope 7/8/22 to E. C. Overman from Gilbert Johnson

Circular 7/15/22 from   "   " & Co.

    "   7/21/22 "   " " "

    "   7/27/22 "

    "   7/31/22 "

Telegram 8/4/22 to Hugh W. Smith from "   .

Circular 8/8/22   "   "

    "   8/19/22   "   " " "

Envelope & circular 9/6/22 to E. C. Overman from Gilbert Johnson & Co.

Circular 9/11/22 from Gilbert Johnson & Co.

Envelope 9/21/22 to Chas. O. Bedbury
                        from Gilbert Johnson & Co.

Circular 9/30/22   "   "   "   " "

    "   10/2/22 " Mrs. Cecilia G. Steed from Admiral
                                     Oil Co.

    "   10/2/22 from Gilbert Johnson Co.
        "   "   "   "   "

    "   10/6/22 to J. M. Murphy from Gilbert Johnson
                Co.

    "   10/14/22 from Gilbert Johnson Co.

 ··   "   to H. W. Shafer from Admiral Oil Co.

Letter 10/24/22 to Joseph A. Schott from Admiral Oil
Co.

Circular Paper from Admiral Oil Co.

Letter 11/1/22 to Admiral Oil Co. from Hugh W. Smith.

Envelope 12/6/22 to H. W. Shafer from Admiral Oil Co.

Letter 12/2/22 to W. L. Hammersley from Gilbert Johnson

" 12/8/22 to H. W. Shafer from Admiral Oil Co.

" 11/14/22 to H. Mendenhall from " " "

" 10/28/22 " " " " " " "

" 11/8/22 " Oswald T. Shreve from Admiral Oil Co.

" 10/25/22 " Henry S. Holden " " " "

" 5/14/20 " E. A. Trinbley from Gilbert Johnson &
Co.

Letter 8/23/20 " Special to Stockholders from Gilbert S.
Johnson

Letter 7/23/20 to Special to Stockholders from Gilbert S.
Johnson

Circular, Fernando Oil Co.

Letter 4/12/20 to W. P. Hill from Gilbert Johnson & Co.

" & Circular 4/6/20 to J. H. Carr from Gilbert Johnson & Co.

" 6/12/20 to E. A. Trombley from Gilbert S. Johnson.

Specl. Letter Report 6/15/20 to R. E. L. Roberts from
Gilbert S. Johnson.

Specl. Letter report, 6/19/20 to W. P. Hill from Gilbert
S. Johnson.

" " " 7/15/20 to R. E. L. Roberts from
Gilbert S. Johnson.

Circular, Lewis Oil & Gas Co.

Spcl. communication and circular 4/12/20 to J. H. Carr
from Gilbert S. Johnson.

Letter 1/22/20 to Theo. H. James from Gilbert S. Johnson.

" 11/1/21 " H. W. Schafer from " " "

Envelope to Mrs. C. C. Steed.

Circular.

Personal Report from Gilbert Johnson, Pres.

Letter to Stockholders, 9/22/21, from Gilbert Johnson.
Spcl. communication, 9/16/21,   "   "   "
    "   "   9/12/21   "   "   "
Envelope 12/8/22 to Wm. Von Hodge
                              from Admiral Oil Co.
    "   12/9/22 to H. W. Shafer   "   "   "   "
Circular   "   "   "   "
    "   12/7/22 from The Mississippi Oil & Refining Co.
    "   12/30/20 "   Admiral Oil Co.
    "   1/10/23 "   "   "   "
    "   1/10/23 "   "   "   "
Letter 1/12/23 to W. Latta Hammersley from Admiral
              Oil Co.
    "   1/22/23 to T. J. Speed from Gilbert Johnson.
    "   1/18/23 " Gilbert Johnson from Hugh W. Smith.
    "   2/7/23   " F. M. Newman from Admiral Oil Co.
    "   2/15/23 " J. T. Junell from   "   "   "
Circular 2/14/23 to C. J. Knapp
                      from Texas Oil & Stock Exchange.
    "   3/1/23   "   "   "   "   "   "
Envelope 3/1/23 " Hugh W. Smith from Admiral Oil Co.
Circular 3/8/23   "   "   "   "
Envelope & circular 3/22/23 to C. G. Steed
                              from Admiral Oil Co.
Circular 3/22/23   "   "   "   "
Letter & Bill 4/2/23 to C. E. Webster from F. J. Rappe.
    "   3/28/23 to Hugh W. Smith from Gilbert Johnson.
    "   4/3/23 to Admiral Oil Co. from Hugh W. Smith.
    "   3/29/23 to C. Dialler from Texas Oil & Stock Ex-
              change.
Bill 3/21/23 to Cecila G. Steed from Admiral Oil Co.
Letter 4/18/23 to F. J. Rappe from Gilbert Johnson.

Letter 4/21/23 to Hugh W. Smith from Gilbert Johnson.

Circular 4/21/23 to " " "

"   5/5/23 " Rosa Harmon " Admiral Oil Co.

Form Telegram.

Bill 5/11/23   to Cecila G. Steed from " " "

Envelope 5/12/23 to " " " " " " "

Letter 5/10/23 to Hugh W. Smith " " " "

"   5/12/23 " Joseph M. Murphy " " " "

Circular 6/1/23 " Hugh W. Smith " " " "

"   6/4/23 " " " " " " " "

Letter 6/18/23 " " " " " " " "

Circular 6/23/23 to M. E. Olson " " " "

"   7/6/23 " A. E. Nunnery " Texas Oil &
Stock Exch.

"   7/13/23 " Florence B. Livezey from Admiral
Oil Co.

Letter 9/5/23 to W. S. Coons from Texas Oil & Stock
Exch.

"   2/9/24 to O. C. Kirkwold   from Admiral Oil Co.

Circular 2/9/24 to C. G. Steed " " " "

"   " " " " "

"   2/21/24 to H. W. Shafer " " " "

"   2/23/24 " C. G. Steed " " " "

"   3/8/24 " Hugh W. Smith from " " "

"   " C. G. Steed " " " "

"   3/25/24 " J. M. Murphy " Texas " &
Stock Exch.

"   3/28/24 " C. G. Steed " Admiral Oil Co.

Letter 4/4/24 to

John C. Krusniak " Texas " & Stock Exch.

Circular 4/12/24 to J. H. Carr " " " " " "

"   4/15/24 " Hugh W. Smith " Admiral Oil Co.

"   4/17/24 " C. G. Steed   "   "   " "
"   4/18/24 " F. M. Newman from Texas Oil & Stock Exch.

Letter 4/21/24 to D. H. Gager from Admiral Oil Co.
"   4/24/24 to J. A. Boyd   "   "   " "

Circular 5/7/24 to C. G. Steed from   "   " "
"   5/10/24   " Texas Oil & Stock Exch.

Letter 5/23/24 to Hugh W. Smith from Admiral Oil Co.
"   "   " J. M. Murphy   " Texas Oil & Stock Exch.

Circular 5/30/24 to H. W. Shafer   " Admiral Oil Co.
"   6/14/24 " C. G. Steed from Texas Oil & Stock Exch.

Circular from Texas Oil & Stock Exch.
"   "   "   " "   "   "

"   6/14/24 to C. G. Steed from Admiral Oil Co.
"   6/20/24 " " "   "   "   "   " "
"   6/28/24 " J. H. Carr   " Texas Oil & Stock Exch.

"   7/9/24 " Alfred Friedman from Admiral Oil Co.

"   7/10/24 " J. H. Carr from Texas Oil & Stock Exch.

"   7/24/24 " Theo. H. James " Admiral Oil Co.
"   7/25/24 " C. G. Steed   from   "   " "
"   8/6/24 " " "   "   "   "   " "
"   8/22/24 " " "   "   "   "   " "
"   8/23/24 "
           Horace Enoch from Texas Oil & Stock Exch.
"   8/30/24   "   "   " "   "   "
"   9/6/24 to
           Geo. L. Drake "   "   " "   "   "

Letter 9/8/24 to
   A. E. Nunnery " " " " " "

Circular 9/10/24 to Joseph Friedman
       from Gilbert Johnson.

  " 9/13/24   " Texas Oil & Stock Exch.

  " 9/17/24 to
    Wm. Hardy " " " " " "

  " 9/25/24 to
    Joseph Friedman " " " " " "

  " 9/25/24 to
    C. G. Steed " Gilbert Johnson.

  " 10/4/24   " Texas Oil & Stock "

  " 10/13/24   " Admiral Oil Co.

Order Blank 10/14/24 to
   H. W. Shafer " Gilbert Johnson.

Circular 10/30/24 to
    Wm. Hardy " Texas Oil & Stock Exch.

Letter 7/6/24 to
   J. E. Baldridge " " " " " "

Circular 11/15/24   " " " " " "

Letter 11/20/24 to
   Horace Enoch " " " " " "

Circular 11/22/24   " Gilbert Johnson.

Letter 11/24/24 to Wm. C. Betts & wife from Admiral Oil Co.

Circular 12/12/24 to John R. O'Donahoe from Texas Oil & Stock Exch.

  " 1/22/25 from Gilbert Johnson

  " 3/28/25 " Admiral Oil Co.

At the hour of 11:43 o'clock a. m., said witness New-meyer testifies on cross-examination conducted by David H. Cannon, Esq.

At the hour of 12:00 o'clock, noon, the Court admonishes the jury and declares a recess until the hour of 1:30 o'clock p. m., today.

At the hour of 1:30 o'clock p. m., court reconvenes, and all being present as before, said witness C. E. Newmeyer resumes the stand and testifies on cross-examination conducted by David H. Cannon, Esq., and said witness having thereupon testified on re-direct and re-cross-examination conducted by John S. Pratt and David H. Cannon, Esqs., respectively, said witness testifies on re-direct examination conducted by John S. Pratt, Esq.

At the hour of 2:47 o'clock p. m., a recess is declared for a period of five minutes.

At the hour of 2:58 o'clock p. m., court reconvenes, and all being present as before,

James H. MacBride is called and sworn and testifies for the Government on direct examination conducted by John H. Pratt, Esq., and said witness having testified on cross-examination conducted by David H. Cannon, Esq., said witness testifies on redirect examination conducted by John H. Pratt, Esq.

Tom Popplewell is called and sworn and testifies for the Government on direct examination conducted by John S. Pratt, Esq., whereupon, Mrs. Lydian Shpack Chastain is called and sworn and testifies for the Government on direct examination conducted by John S. Pratt, Esq., and said witness having thereupon testified on cross-examination conducted by David H. Cannon, Esq.

Frederick E. Browne is called and sworn and testifies for the Government on direct examination conducted by John H. Pratt, Esq., and the following exhibits are offered and marked for identification for the Government, towit

Government's Ex. No.) :
    124 for Ident.   )

Letter sgd. F. E. Browne, to J. T. Junell, dated 1/31/23, and envelope postmarked 1/31/23 to J. T. Junell.

Government's Ex. No.) :
    125 for Ident.   )

Letter 5/10/22 to H. W. Shafer from Admiral Oil Company.

Government's Ex. No.) :
    126 for Ident.   )

Bundle of letters enumerated as follows:

Letter 4/12/23 to J. A. Boyd from F. E. Browne, envelope attached, to J. A. Boyd postmarked 4/12/23.

Letter 3/12/23 to H. W. Shafer from F. E. Browne (2 pages), envelope attached, to H. W. Shafer, postmarked 3/12/23.

Letter 3/10/23 to W. N. Weinacht from F. E. Browne.

Letter 3/3/23 to Chas. M. Armentrout from F. E. Browne, envelope attached, postmarked 3/3/23 to Charles M. Armentrout.

Letter 3/2/23 to O. C. Kirkwood from F. E. Browne, envelope postmarked 3/2/23 to O. C. Kirkwood, attached.

Letter 2/25/22 to O. C. Kirkwold from F. E. Browne (2 pages).

Letter 2/17/22 to F. E. Browne from—envelope to O. C. Kirkwood postmarked 2/25/22.

    "   12/8/21 " C. W. Bruce from F. E. Browne, envelope to

    " "   " Postmarked 12/8/21 attached.

" 1/13/21 " stockholders of Texas Trojan Oil Co. from F. E. Browne, envelope to R. E. L. Roberts, postmarked 1/13/21 attached.

" 1/14/21 " Stockholders of Stephens Oil Syndicate from F. E. Browne, envelope postmarked to D. C. Willett, 1/15/21, page attached to Johnson Oil Company.

" 12/20/22 " John Duncan from F. E. Browne.

" 12/22/22 " Chas. M. Armentrout from F. E. Browne (2 pages), envelope attached to Chas. M. Armentrout, postmarked 12/23/22.

" 10/14/22 " D. C. Willett from F. E. Browne, envelope attached to D. C. Willett, postmarked 10/14/22.

" 10/20/22 " D. C. Willett from F. E. Browne, envelope attached to D. C. Willett, postmarked 10/20/22.

" 10/28/22 " D. C. Willett from F. E. Browne, envelope attached to D. C. Willett, postmarked 10/28/22.

" 11/14/22 " D. C. Willett from F. E. Browne, (2 pages), envelope attached, postmarked 11/14/22, to D. C. Willett.

" 11/20/22 " Elsie Dorsey from F. E. Browne.

" 11/21/22 " John Duncan " " " "

" 11/23/22 " Hugh W. Smith " " " "

" 1/5/23 " Melbourne M. Martin from F. E. Browne (2 pages)

" 1/9/23 " Hugh W. Smith from F. E. Browne, envelope attached, postmarked 1/9/23 to Hugh W. Smith.

" 1/12/23 " Chas. M. Armentrout from F. E. Browne, envelope attached, postmarked 1/13/23 to Chas. M. Armentrout.

" 1/15/23 " Edwin D. Sargent from F. E. Browne.

" 1/16/23 " J. Jones from F. E. Browne.

" 1/31/23 " Hugh W. Smith from F. E. Browne.

" 2/8/23 " Fred B. Albrechts from F. E. Browne.

" 2/15/23 " W. N. Weinacht from F. E. Browne.

" 2/16/23 " Matilda Cecilia G. Steed from F. E. Browne, envelope postmarked 2/16/23, to Matilda Cecilia G. Steed.

" 2/19/23 " James W. Barbee from F. E. Browne (2 pages).

" 2/26/23 " John G. Borge from " " "

" 4/3/23 " Ina Earle Corder from F. E. Browne.

" 4/12/23 " D. C. Willett from F. E. Browne, envelope attached to D. C. Willett, postmarked 4/12/23.

Letter 4/18/23 written in ink from D. C. Willett.

" 4/13/23 to Ina Earle Corder from F. E. Browne.

" 4/14/23 " W. Latta Hammersley from F. E. Browne, envelope attached to W. Latta Hammersley, postmarked 4/14/23.

" 4/14/23 " J. B. Nolle from F. E. Browne.

" 5/1/23 " Jesse Pinner, F. E. Browne, (2 pages).

" 5/4/23 " O. L. Hopkins from F. E. Browne.

"   " " "   "   "   " "   "   "

" " W. L. Hammersley from F. E. Browne (2 pages) envelope attached, postmarked 5/4/23 to W. L. Hammersley.

" 5/7/23 " H. W. Shafer from F. E. Browne, envelope attached postmarked 5/7/23 to H. W. Shafer.

" 5/17/23 " Edwin D. Sargen from F. E. Browne.

" 6/9/23, " D. C. Willett from F. E. Browne, envelope attached, postmarked 6/9/23, to D. C. Willett.

"   " W. P. Hill from F. E. Browne (2 pages) envelope attached, postmarked 6/9/23 to W. P. Hill.

" 6/13/23 " O. L. Hopkins from F. E. Browne.

Carbon copy of letter March 28, 1923 to Gilbert S. Johnson from W. Latta Hammersley.

Government's Ex. No. 127 for Ident.: 5 pages of History of the Yeoman Survey.

"   " 128 "   " 6-page letter 3/21/22 to L. W. Morris from Gilbert S. Johnson, and answers to Interrogatories propounded by L. W. Morris, 8 pages; and statement of accounts attached (3 pgs. in addition).

"   " 129 "   " 2-page letter 7/2/24 to Wm. Hipple, from Gilbert S. Johnson, and envelope postmarked to Wm. Hipple, not postmarked.

"   " 130 "   " 3-page letter dated 5/20/24 to J. M.

					Donaldson from Gilbert S. Johnson and envelope to J. M. Donaldson, Post-office Inspector, Fort Worth, Texas.
"	"	131	"	"	3-page letter to J. M. Donaldson from Gilbert S. Johnson; envelope postmarked 6/26/24 to J. M. Donaldson, and copy of letter to Gilbert S. Johnson, 5/17/24, from Post-office Inspector.

At the hour of 4:49 o'clock p. m., the Court admonishes the jury to remember the admonition heretofore given, and takes a recess until the hour of 9:30 o'clock a. m., to-morrow.

At a stated term, to wit: The September Term, A. D. 1930, of the District Court of the United States of America, within and for the Central Division of the Southern District of California, held at the Court Room thereof, in the City of Los Angeles, California, on Friday, the 14th day of November, in the year of our Lord one thousand nine hundred and thirty.

Present:

The Honorable GEORGE COSGRAVE, District Judge.

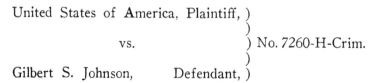

United States of America, Plaintiff,)
)
          vs.   ) No. 7260-H-Crim.
)
Gilbert S. Johnson,   Defendant,)

This cause coming before the Court for further trial; John S. Pratt, Esq., Special Assistant to the Attorney General, and Peter V. Davis, Assistant United States Attorney, appearing for the Government; H. L. Arterberry and David H. Cannon, Esqs., appearing as counsel for the defendant, Gilbert S. Johnson, who is also present, and Edward Van Meter being present as official stenographic reporter of the testimony and proceedings:

Now, at the hour of 9:32 o'clock a. m., court reconvenes, all being present, including the jury, and it is by the Court ordered that this trial be proceeded with, whereupon,

Frederick E. Browne, heretofore sworn, resumes the stand and testifies further on direct examination conducted by J. S. Pratt, Esq., and, in connection with said witness' testimony, Government Exhibit No. 126, for identification, except carbon copy of letter dated March 28, 1923, to Gilbert S. Johnson from W. Latto Hammersley, is now admitted in evidence as Government Exhibit No. 126, and thereafter, said witness testifies on cross-examination conducted by David H. Cannon, Esq.

At the hour of 9:45 o'clock a. m., Court reminds the jury of the admonition heretofore given herein, and declares a recess for a period of fifteen minutes.

At the hour of 10:01 o'clock a. m., court reconvenes, and all being present as before, witness Browne resumes the stand and testifies further on cross-examination conducted by David H. Cannon, Esq., whereupon, said witness testifies on redirect examination conducted by John S. Pratt, Esq.

At the hour of 11:02 o'clock a. m., the Court reminds the jury of the admonition heretofore given herein, and declares a recess for a period of fifteen minutes.

At the hour of 11:24 o'clock a. m., court reconvenes, and all being present as before, Samuel Ross Sloane is called and sworn and testifies for the Government on direct examination conducted by John S. Pratt, Esq., and the following exhibit is offered and marked for identification for the Government, to-wit:

Government's Ex. No. 132 for Ident.: Large diagram on cardboard, "Stephens County, Texas" (later admitted in evidence).

At the hour of 12:08 o'clock p. m., the Court reminds the jury of the admonition heretofore given herein, and declares a recess until the hour of 1:15 o'clock p. m.

Now, at the hour of 1:15 o'clock p. m., court reconvenes, and all being present as before including the jury, said witness Sloane, heretofore sworn, resumes the stand and testifies on cross-examination conducted by David H. Cannon, Esq., and the following exhibits are offered and marked for identification for the defendant, to-wit:

Defendant's Ex. A for Ident.: Map of Stephens County, Texas.

" B " " Blue print of T. E. & L. Co. Surveys, Stephens Co., Texas.

whereupon said witness Sloane testifies on redirect and re-cross-examination conducted by John S. Pratt and David H. Cannon, Esqs., respectively, and the following exhibit is offered and admitted in evidence for the defendant, to-wit:

Defendant's Ex. C: True Copy of lease, seven pages, dated 4/25/21, between Ira A. Sloane and wife, et al., and Gilbert S. Johnson.

Frederick E. Browne resumes the stand and testifies further on direct examination conducted by John S. Pratt, Esq., and the following exhibits are offered and marked for identification for the Government, to-wit

Government's Ex. No. 133 for Ident.: Marine Oil Syndicate Certificate to F. E. Brown, sgd. Gilbert Johnson, dated 6/25/21. (later admitted in evidence)

" " 134 " " Unit Production Syndicate Certificate to F. E. Browne, sgd. Gilbert Johnson, dated 4/14/21 (later admitted in evidence)

At the hour of 2:01 o'clock p. m., the Court reminds the jury of the admonition heretofore given herein, and declares a recess for a period of fifteen minutes.

At the hour of 2:50 o'clock p. m., court reconvenes, and all being present as before, witness Frederick E.

Browne resumes the stand and testifies further on re-direct examination conducted by John S. Pratt, Esq., and said witness Browne having thereupon testified on cross-examination conducted by David H. Cannon, Esq., tes-tifies on redirect examination conducted by John S. Pratt, Esq.,

At the hour of 3:45 o'clock p. m., the jury are reminded of the admonition and a recess is declared for a period of ten minutes.

At the hour of 4:25 o'clock p. m., the Court reconvenes, and all being present as before, John S. Pratt, Esq., con-tinues reading from certain exhibits to the jury.

Tom Popplewell, heretofore sworn, resumes the stand and testifies further on direct examination conducted by John S. Pratt, Esq., and on motion of said Attorney Pratt, the following exhibits are offered and admitted in evidence as part of Government Exhibit No. 2, as follows, to-wit:

Government's Ex. No. 2:

        2 -   RRR—Cash book.
        2 -   SSS—Lewis Oil & Gas Co. Journal.
        2 -   TTT—Book of Texas Trojan Oil Co.
        2 -   UUU—Looseleaf book of Johnson Oil Co.
        2 -   VVV—General Ledger of Lewis O. & Gas Co.
        2 - WWW—Journal of Johnson Oil Co.
        2 -   XXX—Cash book of Johnson Oil Co.

whereupon the witness Popplewell testifies on cross-ex-amination and redirect examination conducted by David H. Cannon and John S. Pratt, Esqs., respectively, and thereafter, said witness having testified on recross-ex-amination conducted by David H. Cannon, Esq.,

At the hour of 5:05 o'clock p. m., the Court reminds the jury of the admonition heretofore given herein, and declares a recess until the hour of 9:30 o'clock a. m., Tuesday, November 18, 1930.

————

At a stated term, to wit: The September Term, A. D. 1930, of the District Court of the United States of America, within and for the Central Division of the Southern District of California, held at the Court Room thereof, in the City of Los Angeles, California, on Tuesday, the 18th day of November, in the year of our Lord one thousand nine hundred and thirty.

Present:

The Honorable GEORGE COSGRAVE, District Judge.

United States of America, Plaintiff,)
)
      vs.   ) No. 7260-H-Crim.
)
Gilbert S. Johnson,   Defendant,)

This cause coming before the Court for further trial of defendant Gilbert S. Johnson; John S. Pratt, Esq., Special Assistant to the Attorney General, and Peter V. Davis, Assistant United States Attorney, appearing as counsel for the Government; said defendant being present in court with his attorneys, H. L. Arterberry and David H. Cannon, Esqs.; and, Edward Van Meter being present in court as official stenographic reporter of the testimony and the proceedings; now, at the hour of 9:45 o'clock a. m., court reconvenes, the jury being present, and all others appearing as before, it is by the Court ordered that this trial be proceeded with, whereupon, Attorneys Pratt and Cannon make statements relative to Government's Exhibit No. 2.

Colonel Theodore H. James is called and sworn and testifies for the Government on direct examination conducted by John S. Pratt, Esq., and the following exhibits are offered and marked for Identification for the Government, to-wit:

Government's Ex. No. 135 for Ident.: Card dated 1/14/20 to Theo. H. James from Gilbert Johnson & Co.

" " 136 " " Certificate of Johnson Oil Co. to Theo. H. James for 20 shares, No., 10,191.

" " " 137 " " Certificate of Johnson Oil Co. to Theo. H. James for two shares, No. 13,575. (Above exhibits later admitted in evidence.)

whereupon, said witness testifies on cross-examination and redirect examination conducted by David H. Cannon and John S. Pratt, Esqs., respectively.

James L. Donaldson is called and sworn and testifies for the Government on direct examination conducted by John S. Pratt, Esq., and the following exhibit is offered and marked for Identification for the Government, to-wit:

Government's Ex. No. 131 for Ident.: Letter 6/23/24 to Gilbert S. Johnson from J. M. Donaldson, Postoffice Inspector. (To be attached to previous group.)

whereupon, said witness testifies on cross-examination conducted by David H. Cannon, Esq.

L. W. Morris is called and sworn and testifies for the Government on direct examination conducted by John S. Pratt, Esq., and said witness having thereupon testified on cross-examination conducted by David H. Cannon, Esq., Government's Exhibit No. 128, for Identification, is now admitted in evidence.

At the hour of 10:54 o'clock a. m., the Court admonishes the jury and declares a recess for a period of ten minutes.

At the hour of 11:06 o'clock a. m., court reconvenes, and all being present as before,

L. W. Morris resumes the stand and testifies further on cross-examination and redirect examination conducted by David H. Cannon and John S. Pratt, Esqs., respectively.

John R. Halsell is called and sworn and testifies for the Government on direct examination conducted by John S. Pratt, Esq., and the following exhibits are offered and marked for Identification for the Government, to-wit:

Government's Ex. No. 138 for Ident.: Oil and Gas Lease dated 5/1/22 between John R. Hallsell and Gilbert S.

Johnson. (Later admitted in evidence).

" " 139 " " Chart of Jack County, Texas. (Not admitted in evidence).

" " 140 " " Plat of Johnson Subdivision of the N. W. portion of the J. R. Halsell Ranch. (Admitted in evidence).

" " 141 " " Map of Jack County. (Admitted in evidence).

" " 142 " " Release dated 11/29/24 Sgd. Gilbert S. Johnson, et al., 3 pages. (Later admitted in evidence).

" " 143 " " Release dated 4/25/24 from Empire Gas & Fuel Co. (1 sheet) (Later admitted in evidence).

whereupon, said witness testifies on cross-examination and redirect examination conducted by David H. Cannon and John S. Pratt, Esqs., respectively, and said witness having thereupon testified on recross-examination conducted by David H. Cannon, Esq.,

At the hour of 12:02 o'clock p. m., the Court admonishes the jury and declares a recess to the hour of 1:30 o'clock p. m.

At the hour of 1:33 o'clock p.m., court reconvenes, and all being present as before, including the jury, it is by the Court ordered that this trial be proceeded with, whereupon,

L. W. Morris, heretofore sworn, resumes the stand and testifies on cross-examination conducted by David H. Cannon, Esq., and the following exhibit is offered and marked for Identification for the Government, towit:

Government's Ex. No. 128-A for Ident.: Personal Report of Johnson Oil Co. dated 10/1/-21, 8 sheets; balance sheet of Johnson Oil Co; envelope postmarked 10/1/21 to Theo. H. James, Special communication to stockholder of Johnson Oil Co. 1/10/22, 4 pages; and declaration of Trust, 6 sheets.

James L. Donaldson, heretofore sworn, resumes the stand and testifies on redirect examination conducted by John S. Pratt, Esq., and the following exhibit is offered and admitted in evidence for the Government, to-wit:

Government's Ex. No. 144: Certified copy of agreement dated 5/1/22 between John R. Halsell and Gilbert S. Johnson.

and Government's Exhibit No. 128-A for Identification having thereupon been admitted in evidence and attached to Government's Exhibit No. 128, the following exhibits are offered and marked for Identification for the Government, to-wit:

Government's

    Ex. No. 131 for Identification now admitted in evidence.

    "   "   "   130 "   "   "   "   "   "

    "   "   "   123 "   "   "   "   "   "   as indicated, to-wit: Letter to Theo. H. James from Gilbert Johnson, 7/24/24, 2 pages; envelope postmarked July 24, 1924 to Theo. H. James; envelope to Admiral Oil Company; special stockholders order blank for Admiral Oil Company; special stockholders order blank for Admiral Oil Stock and "Announcement Extraordinary", dated 7/19/24, "to those stockholders", etc., from Admiral Oil Co.—4 sheets.

Erasmus Olivari is called and sworn and does not testify, at this time, whereupon,

Robert L. Holmes is called and sworn and testifies for the Government on direct examination conducted by John S. Pratt, Esq., and the following exhibits are offered and marked for Identification for the Government, to-wit:

Government's Ex. No. 145 for Ident.:   Photostat. copy of letter dated Oct. 19, 1922, to Gilbert S. Johnson from Magnolia Petroleum Company.

    "   "   146 "   "   Two photostatic copies of 2 checks to Gilbert S. Johnson for $2,000.00, 3/19/23,

No. A-20,525, and for
$2,000.00, 10/25/22,
No. A-18,238, respec-
tively.

whereupon, said witness testifies on cross-examination
conducted by David H. Cannon, Esq.

At the hour of 2:37 o'clock p. m., the Court declares a
recess for a period of ten minutes.

At the hour of 2:50 o'clock p. m., court reconvenes, and
all being present as before,

Erasmus Olivari, heretofore sworn, takes the stand and
testifies on direct examination conducted by John S.
Pratt, Esq., and the following exhibit is offered and admitted in evidence for the Government, to-wit:

Government's Ex. No. 147:   Loose-leaf folder containing
photostatic copies of division
and transfer orders, etc., of
Gulf Pipe Line Co.

whereupon, said witness testifies on cross-examination
conducted by David H. Cannon, Esq.

At the hour of 3:05 o'clock p. m., E. R. Patty is called
and sworn and testifies for the Government on direct examination conducted by John S. Pratt, Esq., and the following exhibits are offered and marked for Identification
for the Government, to-wit:

Government's Ex. No. 148 for Ident.: Photostatic copies of
Western Union Tele-
gram to Prairie Pipe
Line Co. from Lillie
B. Walker, et al.,
2/9/21; two trans-
fer orders dated

11/24/22 to Prairie Oil & Gas Co. from Admiral Oil Co. and dated 1/17/22 to Prairie Oil & Gas Co. from Johnson Oil Co. respt. and Division order to Prairie, etc., from Ira **A.** Sloan 1/14/21.

" " 149 " " Photostatic copy of Division Order and two transfer orders as follows: Division Order 6/3/21 to Prairie Oil & Gas Co. from Johnson Oil Co. Transfer Order 11/24/22 to Prairie Oil & Gas Co. from Admiral Oil Co. Transfer Order 12/9/24 to Prairie Oil & Gas Co. from L. J. Wardlow.

Government's Ex. No. 150 for Ident.: 1 sheet entitled "Summary" figures at bottom $230,-813.31. (Later admitted in evidence.)

" " 151 " " Photostatic copies of Transfer Order to Prairie Oil & Gas Co. from Gilbert Johnson & Co. 4/27/25.

Photostatic copy of Transfer Order to Prairie Oil & Gas Co. from Admiral Oil Co. 11/24/22. Photostatic copies of Division Order to Prairie Oil & Gas Co. from Ira A. Sloan, 7/26/21.

" " 152 " " Photostatic copy of Division Order dated 10/28/22 to Prairie Oil & Gas Co. from G. O. Bateman, et al.

" " 153 " " Photostatic copy of front of check to Johnson Oil Co. for $128,275.65 f r o m The Prairie Oil & Gas Co. 2/1/21; photostatic copy of endorsement on back of check; and photostatic copy of memorandum of settlement by the Prairie Oil & Gas Co. dated January 31, 1921.

whereupon, said witness testifies on cross-examination conducted by David H. Cannon, Esq.

F. J. Rappe is called and sworn and testifies for the Government on direct examination conducted by John S. Pratt, Esq., and the following exhibit offered and marked for Identification is now admitted in evidence for the Government, to-wit:

Government's Ex. No. 120 for Ident. and admitted in evidence: Letter to F. J. Rappe, dated 10/2/1923, from Admiral Oil Co.

At the hour of 4:08 o'clock p. m., said witness Rappe testifies on cross-examination conducted by David H. Cannon, Esq., and thereafter,

At the hour of 4:12 o'clock p. m., said witness Rappe having testified on redirect examination conducted by John S. Pratt, Esq.,

O. L. Hopkins is called and sworn and testifies for Gov. on direct examination conducted by John S. Pratt, the following exhibit is offered and admitted in evidence for the Government, to-wit:

Government's Ex. No. 154: Stock certificate for 200 shares of stock in Admiral Oil Co., No. 6274, dated 6/6/23.

whereupon, the following exhibit is offered and marked for Identification for the Government, to-wit:

Government's Ex. No. 155 for Ident.: 6 checks to Admiral Oil Co. sgd. by O. L. Hopkins and four receipts to O. L. Hopkins from Gilbert Johnson & Co. and stubs for money sent.

and the following exhibit having thereupon been offered and admitted in evidence for the Government, to-wit:

Government's Ex. No. 4: Letter to O. L. Hopkins from W. F. Bateman, dated 1/31/24.

said witness Hopkins testifies on cross-examination conducted by David H. Cannon, Esq., and the following exhibit is offered and admitted in evidence for the defendant, to-wit:

Defendant's Ex. D: Letter 10/18/22, to Gilbert Johnson & Co. from O. L. Hopkins (2 pages)

W. P. Butler is called and sworn and testifies for the Government on direct examination conducted by John S. Pratt, Esq., whereupon, said witness is not cross-examined at this time.

At the hour of 5 o'clock p. m., the Court reminds the jury of the admonition heretofore given herein, and declares a recess until the hour of 9:30 O'clock a. m., tomorrow.

At a stated term, to wit: The September Term, A. D. 1930, of the District Court of the United States of America, within and for the Central Division of the Southern District of California, held at the Court Room thereof, in the City of Los Angeles, California, on Wednesday, the 19th day of November, in the year of our Lord one thousand nine hundred and thirty-

Present:

The Honorable GEORGE COSGRAVE, District Judge.

United States of America, Plaintiff,)
)
         vs.   ) No. 7260-H-Crim.
)
Gilbert S. Johnson,   Defendant,)

This cause coming before the Court for further trial of defendant Gilbert S. Johnson; John S. Pratt, Esq.,

Special Assistant to the Attorney General, and Peter V. Davis, Assistant United States Attorney, appearing as counsel for the Government; the said defendant being present in court with his attorneys, H. L. Arterberry and David H. Cannon, Esqs., and Edward Van Meter being present in court as official stenographic reporter of the testimony and proceedings;

Now, at the hour of 9:32 o'clock a. m., court reconvenes; the jury being present, it is by the Court ordered that this trial be proceeded with; whereupon,

Upon motion of John S. Pratt, Esq., Government Exhibits Nos. 123 and 125, heretofore marked for Identification, are now admitted in evidence, for the Government, to-wit:

Government's Ex. No. 123 for ident., admitted in evidence: Large bundle of letters.

" " 125 for ident., admitted in evidence: Letter 5/10/23 to H. W. Shafer from Admiral Oil Company.

Otto B. Johnson is called and sworn and testifies for the Government on direct examination conducted by John S. Pratt, Esq., and the following exhibits are offered and marked for identification for the Government, to-wit:

Government's Ex. No. 156 for Ident.: Minute book of Fernando Oil Co. (Later admitted in evidence).

" " 157 " " Certified copy of articles of Incorporation of Fernando Oil Co., dated July 17, 1920. (Later admitted in evidence).

whereupon the following exhibit is offered and admitted in evidence, for the Government, to-wit:

Government's Ex. No. 158 in evidence: Permit; Fourth Amended Permit; Second Amended Permit; Amended Permit; Amendment of Permit in the matter of the Application of Fernando Oil Co.

and thereafter, the following exhibit having been offered and marked for identification, for the Government, to-wit:

Government's Ex. No. 159 for ident.:   Letter to stockholders of Fernando Oil Co., dated 7/19/22, 3 pages from Otto B. Johnson; assessment notice, 2 pages; envelope postmarked 7/21/22, to Mabel Hammersley; letter to stockholders of Fernando Oil Co., 2 pages, 8/30/22, from Otto B. Johnson; envelope postmarked 8/30/22, to Mabel Hammersley; 2-page letter to stockholders of the Fernando Oil Co., 9/20/22, from Otto B. Johnson; envelope postmarked 9/20/22, to Mrs. Mabel Hammersley; two-page letter to W. L. Hammersley from Otto B. Johnson, dated 9/15/22; envelope postmarked 9/15/22, to W. L. Hammersley; two-page letter to Fellow Stockholders, etc., 10/5/22, from Otto B. Johnson; envelope postmarked 10/5/22 to Mabel Hammersley; letter 10/13/22 to Mabel Hammersley, from Otto B. Johnson, 2-page; letter, 3 pages, dated 10/31/22 to W. Lotta Hammersley from Otto B. Johnson; and 3-page statement of Fernando Oil Co. (Later admitted in evidence).

said witness Johnson testifies on cross-examination conducted by David H. Cannon, Esq.

Evelyne B. Boadway is called and sworn and testifies for the Government on direct examination conducted by John S. Pratt, Esq., and the following exhibit is offered and marked for Identification, for the Government, to-wit:

Government's Ex. No. 160 for ident.: Statement dated 3/31/23 to Evelyne B. Boadway from Admiral Oil Company; Certificate of Admiral Oil Co. to Evelyne B. Boadway for 534 shares No. 6007 and dated 5/31/23; letter dated 12/13/23 to Evelyne B. Boadway from Admiral Oil Co. and Circular of Admiral Oil Co., 8 pages. (Later admitted in evidence)

whereupon, Government's Exhibit No. 121, heretofore marked for identification, is now admitted in evidence, for the Government, to-wit:

Government's Ex. No. 121 for Ident., admitted in evidence: Letter dated 1/12/23 to Evelyne B. Boadway from Gilbert S. Johnson.

and thereafter said witness Boadway having testified on cross-examination conducted by David H. Cannon, Esq., the following exhibits are offered and admitted in evidence for the defendant, to-wit:

Defendant's Ex. E: Copy of letter 8/31/21, to Evelyne B. Boadway from Gilbert Johnson & Company; Runnels Oil Syndicate cash order blank, and two-page letter to Gilbert Johnson & Co. from Evelyne B. Boadway, dated 8/18/21.

" F: Carbon copy of letter dated 10/4/21 to Evelyne B. Boadway from Gilbert Johnson & Company.

" G: Letter to Gilbert Johnson Company from Evelyne B. Boadway, 11/25/22. Letter to Dear Mr. Wright from Evelyne B. Boadway, May 1, 1922, 3 pages.

Letter, copy, to Evelyne B. Boadway from Gilbert Johnson & Co., May 17, 1922.

Letter to Dear Mr. Johnson from Evelyne B. Boadway, Oct. 23, 1922.

Letter to Evelyne B. Boadway (copy) from Admiral Oil Co. 11/4/22.

Letter to Evelyne B. Boadway (copy) from Gilbert Johnson & Co., May 31, 1922.

Letter to Admiral Oil Co. from Evelyne B. Boadway, Nov. 10, 1922.

Letter to Evelyne B. Boadway (copy) from Gilbert Johnson & Co., Oct. 4, 1922.

Letter to Gilbert Johnson from Evelyne B. Boadway, Aug. 2, 1923.

Letter to Evelyne B. Boadway (copy) from Admiral Oil Co., 5/31/24.

Letter to Gilbert Johnson from Evelyne B. Boadway, May 20, 1924.

Letter from Evelyne B. Boadway, dated Oct. 18, 1921.

Letter (copy) from Gilbert Johnson & Co. to Evelyne B. Boadway, Oct. 25, 1921.

Letter (copy) to Evelyne B. Boadway from Gilbert Johnson & Co., April 26, 1922.

Letter (copy) to Evelyne B. Boadway from Gilbert Johnson & Co., Feb. 20, 1922.

Letter to Gilbert Johnson & Co., from Evelyne B. Boadway, 2/14/22. Subscription to one Unit Corsicana Mexia Oil Fields Syndicate, etc., sgd. Evelyne B. Boadway, dated 2/13/22.

Envelope attached to Gilbert Johnson
& Co., postmarked 2/13/—

Letter (copy) Evelyne B. Boadway
from Gilbert Johnson & Co., dated
Aug. 29, 1922.

Letter to Gilbert Johnson & Co. from
Evelyne B. Boadway.

Letter to Gilbert Johnson from Evelyne B. Boadway, Aug. 13, 1921.

Letter to Mr. Batemen from Evelyne
B. Boadway, June 5, 1924.

Letter to Gilbert Johnson & Co. from
Evelyne B. Boadway, 5/20/22.

At the hour of 10:49 o'clock a. m., the Court reminds
the jury of the admonition heretofore given herein, and
declares a recess for a period of ten minutes.

At the hour of 11:00 o'clock a. m., court reconvenes,
the jury being present and all others appearing as before;
said witness Evelyne B. Boadway resumes the stand, and
David H. Cannon, Esq., reads further from defendant's
Exhibit G, whereupon, said witness testifies on redirect
and recross-examination conducted by John S. Pratt and
David H. Cannon, Esqs., respectively.

J. C. Reese is called and sworn and testifies for the
Government on direct examination conducted by John S.
Pratt, Esq., and the following exhibits are offered and
admitted in evidence for the Government, to-wit:

Government's Ex. No. 161: Correct copy of lease dated
2/3/20, between S. N. Shoun
and J. C. Reese.

" " 162: Lease (correct copy of) dated
6/24/20 between L. N. Shoun
and J. C. Reese.

" "   163: Correct copy of lease dated
6/24/20, between L. N. Shoun
and J. C. Reese.

and said witness having thereupon testified on cross-examination and redirect examination conducted by David H.
Cannon and John S. Pratt, Esq., respectively, the following exhibits are offered and admitted in evidence, for the
Government, to-wit:

Government's Ex. No. 164 in evid.: Correct copy of lease
dated 6/26/20 between
L. N. Shoun and J. C.
Reese.

" "   165 "   " Correct copy of lease
dated 11/1/21 between
L. N. Shoun and J. C.
Reese.

and Government's Exhibit No. 139, heretofore marked for
identification, is now admitted in evidence.

Joe L. Journell is called and sworn and testifies for the
Government on direct examination conducted by John S.
Pratt, Esq., and the following exhibit is offered and ad-
mitted in evidence for the Government, to-wit:

Government's Ex. No. 166: 1 certif. of Johnson Oil Co.
for 38 shares, to J. T. Junell, No. 13,736.

1 certif. of Johnson Oil Co. for 80 shares, to J. T.
Junell, No. 7,105.

1 certif. of Fernando Oil Co. for 50 shares, to J. T.
Junell, No. 346.

1 certif. of Mexia Terrace Oil Co. for 300 shares,
to J. T. Junell, No. 168.

1 certif. of Marine Oil Syndicate for 1 unit of
stock, to J. T. Junell, No. 1275.

1 certif. of Marine Oil Syndicate for 2 units of stock, to J. T. Junell, No. 3561.

At the hour of 12:05 o'clock p. m., the Court reminds the jury of the admonition heretofore given herein, and declares a recess until the hour of 1:30 o'clock p. m.

At the hour of 1:30 o'clock p. m., the court reconvenes, the jury being present and all others being present as before; it is by the Court ordered that this trial be proceeded with, whereupon,

Joe T. Journell, heretofore sworn, resumes the stand and testifies further on direct examination conducted by John S. Pratt, Esq., and the following exhibits, heretofore marked for identification, are now admitted in evidence, for the Government, to-wit:

Government's Ex. No. 124 for Ident., now admitted in evidence: Letter dated 1/31/23 and envelope attached.

" " 122 " " now admitted in evidence: Statement 3/26/23 and envelope attached.

whereupon, an addition to Government Exhibit No. 123 is also now admitted in evidence for the Government, to-wit:

Government's Ex. No. 123, additional: Letter to J. T. Junell from Gilbert Johnson & Company dated 1/15/21.

W. F. Bateman, heretofore sworn, resumes the stand and testifies further on direct examination conducted by P. V. Davis, Esq., and the following Government exhibits are now offered and admitted in evidence for the Government, to-wit:

Government's Ex. No. 2:

YYY: General vouchers and Journal Vouchers of Runnels Oil Syndicate.

ZZZ: Stock ledger control of stock sales in various companies.

AAAA: Work sheets of witness Bateman.

BBBB: Stock ledger of Mexia Powell Oil Syndicate.

CCCC: Marine Oil Syndicate cash vouchers.

DDDD: Cancelled checks and statements of National Bank of Commerce, Johnson Oil Co. and Bank Book of National Bank of Commerce, Fort Worth, Texas.

EEEE: Bank book of Continental National Bank of Fort Worth, Texas.

FFFF: Cancelled checks and Bank statements of Continental National Bank of Fort Worth, Texas, and bank book of the National Bank of Commerce, Fort Worth, Texas, with Johnson Oil Company.

GGGG: Bundle of Journal Vouchers of Marine Oil Syndicate.

HHHH: Bundle of cancelled checks of Marine Oil Syndicate.

IIII: 1 sheet of paper showing debit and credit item, Mexia-Terrace Oil Co., 8/24/21, etc.; debit memorandum attached dated 10/31/21, to Mexia-Terrace Oil Co.; and debit memorandum dated Oct. 31, 1921, to Mexia-Terrace Oil Co.

JJJJ: Stock control ledger of Admiral Oil Co.

KKKK: Recapitulations (book) Admiral Oil Co.

LLLL: Five books of stubs to unit certificates, and certificates, of Mexia-Terrace Oil Co.

MMMM: Book of stubs to unit certificates and also certificates of Mexia Powell Oil.

NNNN: Book of stubs to unit certificates and also certificates of Mexia Powell Oil Syndicate.

OOOO: Check book and check stubs of Runnels Oil Syndicate, as follows—

Check stub book and blank checks of Runnels Oil Syndicate.

1 book of certificates of Runnels Oil Syndicate.

1 book of certificates of Runnels Oil Syndicate (some missing).

1 book of certificates of Runnels Oil Syndicate (some missing).

1 book of certificates of Runnels Oil Syndicate (some missing).

1 book of certificates of Runnels Oil Syndicate (some missing).

1 book of certificates of Runnels Oil Syndicate (some missing).

PPPP: Book of Texas Oil & Stock Exchange.

QQQQ: Book of Johnson Oil Company Special offering J. Oil Co. stock at 50¢.

RRRR: Bundle of miscellaneous documents, to-wit: Journal vouchers, check vouchers, cancelled checks, and bank book of Continental National Bank, Fort Worth, Texas.

SSSS: 10 books of stubs and certificates of Mexia-Terrace Oil Company.

whereupon said witness Bateman testifies on cross-examination and redirect-examination conducted by David H.

Cannon and P. V. Davis, Esqs., respectively, and thereafter, said witness having testified on recross-examination conducted by David H. Cannon, Esq.,

Hugh W. Smith is called and sworn and testifies for the Government on direct examination conducted by P. V. Davis, Esq., and the following exhibit is offered and admitted in evidence for the Government, to-wit:

Government's Ex. No. 167: Record of payments made to Gilbert S. Johnson & Company, Fort Worth, Texas.

whereupon said witness Smith is not cross-examined at this time.

Henry S. Holden is called and sworn and testifies for the Government on direct examination conducted by P. V. Davis, Esq., and the following exhibits having thereupon been offered and admitted in evidence for the Government, to-wit:

Government's Ex. No. 168: 1 certif. to Henry S. Holden for 3 units, Marine Oil Syndicate.

1 certif. to Henry S. Holden for 2 units, Marine Oil Syndicate.

1 certif. to Henry S. Holden for 1 unit, Marine Oil Syndicate.

1 certif. to Henry S. Holden for 100 shares Fernando Oil Company.

1 certif. to Henry S. Holden for 50 shares Johnson Oil Company.

1 certif. to Henry S. Holden for 50 shares Johnson Oil Company.

1 certif. to Henry S. Holden for 100 shares Johnson Oil Company.

1 certif. to Henry S. Holden for 20 shares Johnson Oil Company.

1 certif. to Henry S. Holden for 120 shares Johnson Oil Company.

1 certif. to Henry S. Holden for 80 shares Johnson Oil Company.

said witness Holden is not cross-examined at this time.

At the hour of 2:43 o'clock p. m., the Court declares a recess for a period of ten minutes.

At the hour of 2:55 o'clock p. m., court reconvenes, and all being present as before,

Mrs. C. G. Steed, Mr. Joseph M. Murphy and Elsie Dorsey are called and sworn and testify, respectively, on direct examination conducted by John S. Pratt, Esq., and said witnesses having thereupon testified, respectively, on cross-examination conducted by David H. Cannon, Esq., W. H. Hemphill is called and sworn and testifies for the Government on direct examination conducted by John S. Pratt, Esq., and said defendant being hard of hearing, counsel stipulate as to what the said witness' testimony would be, and said David H. Cannon, Esq., having so stipulated, said witness is not cross-examined at this time.

George B. Pratt is called and sworn, and counsel having stipulated as to what his testimony would be, and said witness not having been cross-examined,

N. J. Sodermark is called and sworn and testifies for the Government on direct examination conducted by John S. Pratt, Esq., and said Attorney Pratt having thereupon made a statement to the Court as to what said witness' testimony would be, and David H. Cannon, Esq., having stipulated as to what the testimony of said witness would be, said witness now testifies further on direct examination, and thereafter, said witness Sodermark is questioned by David H. Cannon, Esq.

George Haken is called and sworn and testifies for the
Government on direct examination conducted by John S. .
Pratt, Esq., and said Attorney Pratt having thereupon
made a statement to the Court as to what said witness'
testimony would be if interrogated further, said witness is
questioned by David H. Cannon, Esq., and said Attorney
Cannon having so stipulated respecting further possible
interrogations, and thereafter said witness having testified
further on an examination conducted by John S. Pratt,
Esq,. said witness is not cross-examined at this time.

At the hour of 3:54 o'clock p. m., the Court reminds the
jury of the admonition heretofore given herein and declares a recess for the period of five minutes.

At the hour of 4:01 o'clock p. m., court reconvenes, and
all being present as before,

John M. Dunn is called and sworn and testifies for the
Government on direct examination conducted by John S.
Pratt, Esq., whereupon said witness testifies on cross-
examination and redirect examination conducted by David
H. Cannon and John S. Pratt, Esqs., respectively, and said
witness having thereupon testified on recross-examination
conducted by David H. Cannon, Esqs., said witness Dunn
is examined by the Court, and thereafter said witness testifies on recross-examination conducted by David H.
Cannon, Esq.

At the hour of 4:57 o'clock p. m., the Court reminds
the jury of the admonition heretofore given herein, and
declares a recess until the hour of 9:30 o'clock a. m. to- ·
morrow.

At a stated term, to wit: The September Term. A. D.
1930, of the District Court of the United States of

America, within and for the Central Division of the Southern District of California, held at the Court Room thereof, in the City of Los Angeles, California, on Thursday the 20th day of November in the year of our Lord one thousand nine hundred and thirty-

Present:

The Honorable GEORGE COSGRAVE, District Judge.

United States of America, Plaintiff,)
)
       vs.   ) No. 7260-H-Crim.
)
Gilbert S. Johnson,   Defendant,)

This cause coming before the Court for further trial of defendant Gilbert S. Johnson; John S. Pratt, Esq., Special Assistant to the Attorney General, and Peter V. Davis, Assistant United States Attorney, appearing as counsel for the Government; said defendant being present in court with his attorneys, H. L. Arterberry and David H. Cannon, Esqs.; and, Edward Van Meter being present as official stenographic reporter of the testimony and the proceedings;

Now, at the hour of 9:47 o'clock a. m., court reconvenes, the jury being present, it is by the Court ordered that this trial be proceeded with, whereupon, Attorneys Pratt, Cannon and Arterberry read certain exhibits to the jury, respectively; all as reflected by the reporter's transcript.

Upon motion of John S. Pratt, Esq., the following is introduced as a part of Government's Exhibit No. 123, to-wit:

Government's Ex. No. 123: Letter 10/4/24 to - - - from Manager E. C. Hands, Manager Texas Oil and Stock Exchange (2 pages), and subscription for shares in J. M. Dunn Oil Co. entitled "Special Clients limited offering of shares in the J. M. Dunn Oil Company".

R. E. Skiles is called and sworn and testifies for the Government on direct examination conducted by John S. Pratt, Esq., and the following exhibits are offered and admitted in evidence for the Government, towit:

Government's Ex. No. 169: Large map of Navarro County, Texas.

        "   "   170: Drawing in pencil on one sheet of paper.

whereupon, the following exhibit is offered and marked for Identification for the Government, to-wit:

Government's Ex. No. 171 for Ident.: Letter 8/20/24 to R. E. Skiles from Gilbert S. Johnson, and copy of instrument attached; letter 3/18/24, to R. E. Skiles, from Gilbert S. Johnson and copy of instrument attached.

At the hour of 11:05 o'clock a. m., the Court reminds the jury of the admonition heretofore given herein, and declares a recess for a period of five minutes.

At the hour of 11:14 o'clock p. m., court reconvenes, and all appearing as before, witness R. E. Skiles resumes the stand and testifies further on direct examination conducted by John S. Pratt, Esq., and the following exhibit is offered and marked for Identification for the Government, to-wit:

Government's Ex. No. 172 for Ident.: Letter dated 3/1/24, to First State Bank, etc., from Gilbert S. Johnson.

At the hour of 11:42 o'clock a. m., said witness Skiles testifies on an examination conducted by the Court, whereupon,

At the hour of 11:43 o'clock a. m., David H. Cannon, Esq., reads from the circular of the Texas Oil Radio dated March 15th, 1930, to the jury, and from other documents, as reflected by the reporter's transcript, and said witness Skiles having thereupon testified on cross-examination conducted by David H. Cannon, Esq., testifies on questions propounded by John S. Pratt, Esq.

At the hour of 12 o'clock, noon, the Court admonishes the jury and declares a recess until the hour of 1:30 o'clock p. m., today.

At the hour of 1:31 o'clock p. m., court reconvenes, and all appearing as before, and Dudley Hossack and Edward Van Meter being present and alternating as official stenographic reporters of the testimony and the proceedings, said witness R. E. Skiles, heretofore sworn, resumes the stand and testifies on further cross-examination conducted by David H. Cannon, Esq., whereupon, said witness testifies on redirect and recross-examination conducted by John S. Pratt and David H. Cannon, Esqs., respectively.

Henry L. Albritton is called and sworn and testifies for the Government on direct examination conducted by John S. Pratt, Esq., and the following exhibit is offered and marked for Identification for the Government, to-wit:

Government's Ex. No. 173 for Ident.: Drawing (Plat of Map) on cardboard of Navarro County, Texas.

At the hour of 2:05 o'clock p. m., said witness Albritton testifies on cross-examination and redirect examination conducted by David H. Cannon and John S. Pratt, Esqs., respectively, and the said witness having thereupon testified on recross-examination conducted by David H.

Cannon, Esq., the following exhibits are offered and admitted in evidence for the Government, to-wit:

Government's Ex. No. 174: 1 certified copy of assignment of Oil and Gas lease—Gilbert S. Johnson to Admiral Oil Co.

" " " 1 certified copy of assignment of Oil and Gas lease—Gilbert S. Johson to Corsicana Mexia Oil Fields Syndicate.

" " " 1 certified copy of assignment of Oil and Gas lease—Gilbert S. Johnson to Mexia Terrace Oil Co.

" " " 1 certified copy of assignment of Oil and Gas lease—Gilbert S. Johnson to S. G. Vidler.

" " " 2 certified copies of assignment of Oil and Gas lease—Gilbert S. Johnson to Corsicana Mexia Oil Fields Syndicate.

" " " 1 certified copy of assignment of Oil and Gas lease—J. Afton Burke to Gilbert S. Johnson.

" " 175: Certified copy of Oil and Gas lease—G. M. Westbrook to Gilbert S. Johnson.

" " " Certified copy of Oil and Gas lease—Gilbert S. Johnson to Johnson Oil Company.

" " " Certified copy of Assignment of Oil and Gas Lease—Gilbert S. Johnson to Mehia Powell Oil Syndicate.

" " "   Certified copy of assignment
of Oil and Gas Lease—Gilbert
S. Johnson to Marine Oil
Syndicate.

" " "   Certified copy of assignment
of Oil and Gas Lease—Gil-
bert S. Johnson to Corsicana
Mexia Oil Fields Syndicate.

" " "   Certified copy of Oil and Gas
Lease—G. M. Westbrook to
Gilbert S. Johnson.

" " 176:   Oil and Gas Lease—A. J. Oliver, et al., to L. W. Watson,
dated 7/6/21.

" " "   Assignment Oil and Gas
Lease—A. J. Oliver, et al., to
L. W. Watson, dated 7/6/21.

" " "   Assignment of Oil and Gas
Lease—A. J. Oliver, et al., to
L. W. Watson, dated 7/6/21.

" " "   Oil and Gas Lease—R. H.
Stricklin, et al., to L. W.
Watson, dated 7/6/21.

" " "   Assignment of Oil and Gas
Lease—R. H. Stricklin, et al.,
to L. W. Watson, dated
7/6/21.

Government's Ex. No. 177:   Copies of the following documents :

" " "   Assignment of Oil and Gas
Lease signed by Gilbert S.
Johnson 5/18/21.

" " "   Oil and Gas Lease dated Nov.
23, 1920 between Sloan, et al.,
and Gilbert Johnson.

"   "   "   Assignment of Oil and Gas Lease signed by Gilbert S. Johnson, Dec. 2/20.

"   "   "   Assignment of Oil and Gas Lease signed by W. S. Tarbell, Jan. 10, 1921.

"   "   "   Assignment of Oil and Gas Lease Mar. 4, 1921, signed by W. S. Tarvell, et al.,

"   "   "   Agreement dated March 1, 1921 between Sloan, et al., and Gilbert S. Johnson.

"   "   "   Assignment of Oil and Gas Lease, signed by Gilbert S. Johnson, Mar. 15, 1921.

"   "   "   Affidavit signed by Texas Pacific Coal & Oil Company, dated April 1, 1921.

"   "   "   "   Affidavit signed by Gilbert Johnson, dated April 20, 1921.

"   "   "   Affidavit signed by J. Burris Mitchell, dated October 31, 1919.

"   "   "   Affidavit signed by Erle C. Johnson dated January 3, 1920.

"   "   "   Affidavit signed by J. Burris Mitchell, dated April 27, 1920.

"   "   "   Affidavit signed by Homer N. Chapman, dated December 3, 1919.

"   ".   "   Memorandum of Agreement between Chapman, et al, and Gilbert Johnson 2/17/20.

" " " Assignment of Oil and Gas Lease dated May 18, 1921, signed Gilbert S. Johnson.

" " " Assignment of Oil and Gas Lease, dated Feb. 17, 1920, signed Homer N. Chapman and Jack Robert.

" " " Assignment of Oil and Gas Lease, dated March 25, 1920, signed Gilbert S. Johnson.

" " " Assignment of Oil and Gas Lease, dated Mar. 22nd, 1920, signed Gilbert S. Johnson.

" " " Assignment of Oil and Gas Lease dated July 20, 1920, sgd. Gilbert S. Johnson.

" " " Assignment of Oil and Gas Lease, dated August 11, 1920, sgd. Gilbert S. Johnson.

" " " Affidavit signed by C. E. Cooper, et al., dated March 25th, 1920.

" " " Affidavit signed by Gilbert Johnson, etc., dated December 15th, 1920.

" " 178: Certified copies of 5 following documents:

" " " Affid. of John R. Halsell, dated 7/12/22.

" " " Assignment from Gilbert S. Johnson to Empire Gas and Fuel Co. 9/14/22.

" " " Assignment from Gilbert S. Johnson to J. R. Halsell 10/6/22.

" " " Assignment from Gilbert S. Johnson to – – – – 10/20/22.

" " " Agreement between John R. Halsell and Gilbert S. Johnson, 5/1/22.

At the hour of 2:37 o'clock p. m., the Court reminds the jury of the admonition heretofore given herein, and declares a recess for a period between five and ten minutes.

At the hour of 2:50 o'clock p. m., court reconvenes, and all others appearing as before, said Attorney Pratt takes the seat in the box and reads certain documents to the jury, as reflected by the reporter's transcript, whereupon, said David H. Cannon, Esq., reads from the documents to the jury, as reflected by the reporter's transcript, whereupon, said David H. Cannon, Esq., reads from the documents to the jury.

At the hour of 3:58 o'clock p. m., the Court reminds the jury of the admonition heretofore given herein, and declares a recess for a period of five minutes.

At the hour of 4:06 o'clock p. m., court reconvenes, and all being present as before, John S. Pratt, Esq., resumes the reading from exhibits to the jury, and said H. L. Arterberry, Esq., having thereupon read from exhibits to the jury, the circular of October 2, 1922, is admitted in evidence and added to Government's Exhibit No. 123, heretofore admitted in evidence for the Government.

At the hour of 5:04 o'clock p. m., the Court reminds the jury of the admonition heretofore given herein, and declares a recess in this cause until the hour of 9:30 o'clock a. m., tomorrow.

At a stated term, to wit: The September Term, A. D. 1930, of the District Court of the United States of America, within and for the Central Division of the Southern District of California, held at the Court Room thereof, in the City of Los Angeles, California, on Friday, the 21st day of November, in the year of our Lord one thousand nine hundred and thirty-

Present:

The Honorable GEORGE COSGRAVE, District Judge.

United States of America, Plaintiff,)
)
vs.   ) No. 7260-H-Crim.
)
Gilbert S. Johnson,   Defendant,)

This cause coming on before the Court for further trial; John S. Pratt, Esq., Special Assistant to the Attorney General, and Peter V. Davis, Assistant United States Attorney, appearing as counsel for the Government; said defendant being present in court with his attorneys, H. L. Arterberry and David H. Cannon, Esqs.; and Edward Van Meter being present as official stenographic reporter of the testimony and the proceedings; now, at the hour of 9:35 o'clock a. m., the court reconvenes, and all being present as indicated, including the jury, it is by the Court ordered that this trial be proceeded with, whereupon, the following exhibit is offered and marked for Identification for the Government, to-wit:

Government's Ex. No. 179 for Ident.: Chart "Diagram of Organization and merger of defendant's companies".

James W. Thompson, Postoffice Inspector, is called and sworn and testifies for the Government on direct examination conducted by John S. Pratt, Esq., and the following exhibit is offered and marked for Identification, for the Government, to-wit:

Government's Ex. No. 180 for Ident.: Chart.

whereupon, said witness Thompson testifies on cross-examination conducted by David H. Cannon, Esq., and said witness having thereupon testified on an examination conducted by the Court, testifies on cross-examination conducted by David H. Cannon, Esq.,

At the hour of 10:03 o'clock a. m., the Court reminds the jury of the admonition heretofore given, and declares a recess for a period of five minutes.

At the hour of 10:10 o'clock a. m., court reconvenes, and all being present as before,

William Hipple, Accountant, is called and sworn and testifies for the Government on direct examination conducted by John S. Pratt, Esq., and at this point in this trial, Dudley Hossack acts and alternates with Edward Van Meter as official stenographic reporter of the testimony and the proceedings, and the following exhibit is offered and marked for Identification for the Government, to-wit:

Government's Ex. No. 181 for Ident.: 3-page document entitled "Brief statement of facts regarding leases of Marine Oil Syndicate." (Later admitted in evidence).

whereupon, said witness testifies for the Government on redirect examination conducted by John S. Pratt, Esq.

At the hour of 12:02 o'clock p. m., the Court reminds the jury of the admonition heretofore given, and declares a recess to the hour of 1:30 o'clock p. m.

At the hour of 1:30 o'clock p. m., court reconvenes, and all being present as before, William Hipple, heretofore sworn, resumes the stand and testifies further on direct examination conducted by John S. Pratt, Esq., and the following exhibits are offered and marked for Identification for the Government, to-wit:

Government's Ex. No. 182 for Ident.: Letter to Wm. Hipple from Gilbert S. Johnson, dated 9/-25/24 — 3 pages. (Later admitted in evidence).

" " 183 " " Schedule of Oil and Gasoline sales from Johnson Oil Company entitled "Johnson Oil Company Income from Crude Oil and Gasoline Sales". (Later admitted in evidence).

" " 184 " " Paper entitled "Corsicana - Mexia Oil Fields Syndicate stock sale exhibit showing sales of Treasury stock and Gilbert Johnson's Personal Stock."

At the hour of 2:45 o'clock p. m., the Court declares a recess for a period of five minutes.

At the hour of 3 o'clock p. m., court reconvenes, and all being present as before, witness Hipple, heretofore sworn, resumes the stand and testifies further on direct examination conducted by John S. Pratt, Esq., and said witness having thereupon testified on an examination conducted by David H. Cannon, Esq., cross-examination is reserved until later, and the following exhibit is offered and admitted in evidence for the Government, to-wit:

Government's Ex. No. 185:   Summary—large sheet of paper in typewriting.

Samuel C. Bennetts, Accountant, is called and sworn and testifies for the Government on direct examination conducted by John S. Pratt, Esq., and said witness having thereupon testified on an examination on voir dire, testifies further on direct examination conducted by John S. Pratt, Esq., whereupon, said witness Bennetts is cross-examined by David H. Cannon, Esq., with the privilege of continuing the cross-examination later.

At the hour of 3:54 o'clock p. m., said witness Bennetts testifies on redirect examination conducted by John S. Pratt, Esq., whereupon, said witness is questioned further by David H. Cannon, Esq., and the Court having thereupon examined said witness, David H. Cannon, Esq., reserves further cross-examination until later, and the following exhibit is offered and admitted in evidence for the Government, to-wit:

Government's Ex. No. 186:   One sheet entitled "Analysis of Condition of Admiral Oil Company", etc.

At the hour of 4:05 o'clock p. m., the Court reminds the jury of the admonition heretofore given herein, and declares a recess for a period of five minutes.

At the hour of 4:16 O'clock p. m., court reconvenes, and all being present as before, except David H. Cannon, Esq., certain documents are read to the jury by John S. Pratt, Esq., whereupon, at the hour of 5:07 o'clock p. m., David H. Cannon, Esq., comes into court.

At the hour of 5:08 o'clock p. m., the Court admonishes the jury, and continues this case until next Tuesday, November 25th, 1930, 9:30 o'clock a. m., and declares a recess generally until next Monday, November 24th, 1930.

At a stated term, to wit: The September Term, A. D. 1930, of the District Court of the United States of America, within and for the Central Division of the Southern District of California, held at the Court Room thereof, in the City of Los Angeles, California, on Tuesday, the 25th day of November, in the year of our Lord one thousand nine hundred and thirty.

Present:

The Honorable GEORGE COSGRAVE, District Judge.

United States of America, Plaintiff,)
)
vs.   ) No. 7260-H-Crim.
)
Gilbert S. Johnson,   Defendant,)

This cause coming before the Court for further trial of defendant Gilbert S. Johnson; John S. Pratt, Esq., Special Assistant to the Attorney General, and Peter V. Davis, Assistant United States Attorney, appearing as counsel for the Government; said defendant being present in court with his attorneys, H. L. Arterberry and

David H. Cannon, Esqs.; and, Dudley Hossack and Albert H. Bargion being present and alternating as official stenographic reporters of the testimony and the proceedings; now, at the hour of 9:30 o'clock a. m., court reconvenes, the jury being present, and all others appearing as indicated, it is by the Court ordered that this trial be proceeded with; whereupon,

William Hipple, heretofore sworn, resumes the stand and testifies on cross-examination conducted by David H. Cannon, Esq.

At the hour of 10:45 o'clock a. m., the Court reminds the jury of the admonition heretofore given herein, and declares a recess for a period of ten minutes.

At the hour of 11 o'clock a. m., court reconvenes, and all appearing as before, including the jury, witness Hipple resumes the stand and testifies further on cross-examination conducted by David H. Cannon, Esq.

At the hour of 12 o'clock, noon, the Court reminds the jury of the admonition, and declares a recess until the hour of 1:30 o'clock p. m., whereupon,

At the hour of 1:35 o'clock p. m., court reconvenes, and all appearing as before, including the jury, witness Hipple resumes the stand and testifies further on cross-examination conducted by David H. Cannon, Esq., and thereafter, said witness having testified on redirect examination conducted by John S. Pratt, Esq., the following exhibit, heretofore marked for Identification, is now admitted in evidence for the Government, to-wit:

Government's Ex. No. 129:   Letter dated 7/2/24, and envelope attached.

whereupon, the following exhibit is offered and marked for Identification for the Government, to-wit:

Government's Ex. No. 187: Small memorandum ."Gilbert Johnson & Company (Broker)" "The following pertains", etc.

and thereafter, said witness Hipple testifies on recross-examination conducted by David H. Cannon, Esq.

At the hour of 3:13 o'clock p. m., the Court reminds the jury of the admonition heretofore given herein, and declares a recess for a period of ten minutes.

At the hour of 3:25 o'clock p. m., court reconvenes, and all being present as before, witness Hipple testifies further on recross-examination and redirect examination conducted by David H. Cannon and John S. Pratt, Esqs.

John S. Pratt, Esq., states that he would like to have all books referred to in the testimony and used in testimony, and those here in the court admitted in evidence, and whatever other exhibits may have been identified; said motion is by the Court granted, and the Clerk is instructed to put appropriate filing mark upon them, if any.

At the hour of 3:28 o'clock p. m., the Government rests.

David H. Cannon, Esq., having a certain motion to make to the Court, the jury are excused, and in their absence, H. L. Arterberry, Esq., moves the Court for an instructed verdict, and David H. Cannon, Esq., having thereupon argued to the Court in support thereof,

At the hour of 3:50 o'clock p. m., the Court makes a statement, and thereafter, David H. Cannon, Esq., having made a further statement, the said motion of the counsel for the defendant for an instructed verdict is by the Court denied, and exception noted.

At the hour of 3:55 o'clock p. m., the Court declares a recess for a period of five minutes; and

At the hour of 4:03 o'clock p. m., court reconvenes, and all being present as before, David H. Cannon, Esq., makes opening statement to the jury, whereupon,

E. M. Westbrook is called and sworn and testifies for the defendant on direct examination conducted by David H. Cannon, Esq., and the following exhibit is offered and marked for Identification for the defendant, to-wit:

Defendant's Ex. H for Ident.: Map—Powell District, Navarro County.

At the hour of 4:08 o'clock p. m., Edward Van Meter, official court reporter, comes into court to supersede D. L. Hossack, who has been acting as the official stenographic reporter of the testimony and the proceedings.

At the hour of 4:36 o'clock p. m., witness Westbrook testifies on cross-examination conducted by John S. Pratt, Esq., whereupon, said witness testifies on redirect examination conducted by David H. Cannon, Esq.

At the hour of 4:50 o'clock p. m., the Court admonishes the jury, and declares a recess until the hour of 9:30 o'clock a. m., tomorrow.

———

At a stated term, to wit: The September Term, A. D. 1930, of the District Court of the United States of America, within and for the Central Division of the Southern District of California, held at the Court Room thereof, in the City of Los Angeles, California, on

Wednesday, the 26th day of November, in the year of our Lord one thousand nine hundred and thirty.

Present:

The Honorable GEORGE COSGRAVE, District Judge.

United States of America, Plaintiff,)
)
vs.) No. 7260-H-Crim.
)
Gilbert S. Johnson, Defendant,)

This cause coming before the Court for further trial of defendant Gilbert S. Johnson; John S. Pratt, Esq., Special Assistant to the Attorney General, and Peter V. Davis, Assistant United States Attorney, appearing as counsel for the Government; said defendant Gilbert S. Johnson being present in court with his attorneys, H. L. Arterberry and David H. Cannon, Esqs.; and, Dudley Hossack and Albert H. Bargion being present and alternating as official stenographic reporters of the testimony and the proceedings; now, at the hour of 9:35 o'clock a. m., court reconvenes, and all being present as indicated, including the jury, it is by the Court ordered that this trial be proceeded with; whereupon,

L. M. Brown is called and sworn and testifies for the defendant on direct examination conducted by David H. Cannon, Esq., and thereafter, said witness having testified on cross-examination conducted by John S. Pratt, Esq.,

H. L. Arterberry, Esq., takes the stand and reads from deposition of A. W. Dyar, and said John S. Pratt, Esq., having thereupon read the cross-examination from said deposition of A. W. Dyar, said Attorney Arterberry reads from the redirect examination from said deposition.

H. L. Arterberry, Esq., now reads from the deposition of John R. Halsell.

At the hour of 10:45 o'clock a. m., the Court reminds the jury of the admonition heretofore given herein, and declares a recess for a period of ten minutes.

At the hour of 10:55 o'clock a. m., court reconvenes, and all being present as before, H. L. Arterberry, Esq., resumes the stand and reads further from the said deposition of John R. Halsell, and the said Peter V. Davis, Esq., having thereupon read from the cross-examination from said deposition, H. L. Arterberry, Esq., reads the redirect examination from said deposition.

H. L. Arterberry, Esq., now reads from deposition of W. D. COnway, and John S. Pratt, Esq., having thereupon read from the cross-examination of said witness, H. L. Arterberry, Esq., reads from redirect examination of said witness.

H. L. Arterberry, Esq., now reads from the deposition of R. R. Weed, whereupon, P. V. Davis, Esq., reads from the cross-examination in said deposition.

At the hour of 12 o'clock, noon, the Court reminds the jury of the admonition heretofore given herein, and declares a recess to the hour of 1:30 o'clock p. m.,

At the hour of 1:30 o'clock p. m., today, court reconvenes, and all being present as before, P. V. Davis, Esq., takes the stand and reads from said deposition of R. R. Weed, whereupon, David H. Cannon, Esq., reads from the redirect examination and the recross-examination in said deposition.

David H. Cannon, Esq., now reads from the deposition of W. C. McGlothlin, whereupon, the said John S. Pratt, Esq., reads the cross-examination from said deposition, and the said David H. Cannon, Esq., having thereupon read the redirect examination in said deposition,

David H. Cannon, Esq., reads from the deposition of Carl L. Mayer, and thereafter, P. V. Davis, Esq., reads the cross-examination from said deposition, whereupon, David H. Cannon, Esq., reads the redirect examination and the recross-examination from said deposition.

David H. Cannon, Esq., now reads from the deposition of J. H. Clark, and thereafter, John S. Pratt, Esq., reads the cross-examination from said deposition.

H. L. Arterberry, Esq., reads the direct examination from the deposition of J. E. Redburn, and John S. Pratt, Esq., having thereupon read the cross-examination from said deposition,

H. L. Arterberry, Esq., reads from the deposition of G. A. Hanson, and thereafter, the said P. V. Davis, Esq., having read the cross-examination from said deposition,

H. L. Arterberry reads from the deposition of A. E. Thomas, and he having also read from the cross-examination of said witness in the said deposition,

H. L. Arterberry, Esq., reads from the deposition of George Thompson, Jr., whereupon, John S. Pratt, Esq., reads the cross-examination from the said deposition.

At the hour of 3:16 o'clock p. m., the Court reminds the jury of the admonition heretofore given herein, and declares a recess for a period of ten minutes.

At the hour of 3:33 o'clock p. m., court reconvenes, and all being present as before, H. L. Arterberry, Esq., reads from the deposition of G. O. Bateman, and thereafter, P. V. Davis, Esq., having read from cross-examination in said deposition, said Attorney Arterberry reads the redirect examination from the said deposition.

David H. Cannon, Esq., now reads from the deposition of Lee I. Dodwell, and John S. Pratt, Esq., having thereupon read the cross-examination in said deposition, said Attorney Cannon reads from the deposition of P. C. Thomas, whereupon, John S. Pratt, Esq., reads from the cross-examination in said deposition of witness Thomas.

David H. Cannon, Esq., reads from the deposition of George Sawtelle, and thereafter, P. V. Davis, Esq., having read from the cross-examination in said deposition;

Now, at the hour of 4:58 o'clock p. m., the Court· admonishes the jury and declares a recess until Friday, November 28th, 1930, 9:30 o'clock a. m.

————

At a stated term, to wit: The September Term, A. D. 1930, of the District Court of the United States of America, within and for the Central Division of the Southern District of California, held at the Court Room thereof, in the City of Los Angeles, California, on Friday the 28th day of November, in the year of our Lord one thousand nine hundred and thirty.

Present:

The Honorable GEORGE COSGRAVE, District Judge.

United States of America,   Plaintiff,)
)
vs.   ) No. 7260-H-Crim.
)
Gilbert S. Johnson,   Defendant,)

This cause coming before the Court for further trial of defendant Gilbert S. Johnson; John S. Pratt, Esq., Special Assistant to the Attorney General, and Peter V. Davis, Assistant United States Attorney, appearing as counsel for the Government; said defendant being present in court with his attorneys, H. L. Arterberry and David H. Cannon, Esqs.; and, Dudley Hossack and Albert H. Bargion being present and alternating as official stenographic reporters of the testimony and the proceedings; now, at the hour of 9:34 o'clock a. m., court reconvenes, and all being present as before, including the jury,

David H. Cannon, Esq., reads from the deposition of George Sawtelle, and P. V. Davis, Esq., having thereupon read from the recross-examination in said deposition,

David H. Cannon, Esq., reads from the deposition of W. L. Knight, and thereafter, John S. Pratt, Esq., having read from the cross-examination in said deposition, said Attorney Cannon reads from the redirect examination in said deposition.

Gilbert S. Johnson is called and sworn and testifies for himself on direct examination conducted by David H. Cannon, Esq., and the following exhibit is offered and marked for Identification, to-wit:

Defendant's Ex. I for Ident.:   Large Map of Texas.

At the hour of 11:22 o'clock a. m., the Court reminds the jury of the admonition heretofore given herein, and declares a recess for a period of ten minutes.

At the hour of 11:14 o'clock a. m., court reconvenes, and all appearing as before, including the jury, said defendant Gilbert S. Johnson resumes the stand and testifies further on direct examination conducted by Attorney Cannon.

At the hour of 12:05 o'clock p. m., the jury are reminded of the admonition herein, and the Court declares a recess until the hour of 1:30 o'clock p. m.

At the hour of 1:32 o'clock p. m., court reconvenes, and all being present as before, defendant Gilbert S. Johnson resumes the stand and testifies further on direct examination conducted by David H. Cannon, Esq., and the following exhibits are offered and marked for Identification for the defendant, to-wit:

Defendant's Ex. J for Ident.: Large Map of Mexia District, Texas.

" K "   "   "   "   " Limestone County "

At the hour of 3:10 o'clock p. m., the Court reminds the jury of the admonition heretofore given herein, and declares a recess for a period of ten minutes.

At the hour of 3:22 o'clock p. m., court reconvenes, and all being present as before, said defendant Gilbert S. Johnson resumes the stand and testifies further on direct examination conducted by David H. Cannon, Esq., and the following exhibit is offered and marked for Identification, to-wit:

Defendant's Ex. L for Ident.:

At the hour of 4 o'clock p. m., defendant Gilbert S. Johnson is cross-examined by John S. Pratt, Esq., and thereafter,

At the hour of 4:59 o'clock p. m., the Court admonishes the jury and declares a recess until the hour of 9:30 o'clock a. m., December 1st, 1930.

At a stated term, to wit: The September Term, A. D. 1930, of the District Court of the United States of America, within and for the Central Division of the Southern District of California, held at the Court Room thereof, in the City of Los Angeles, California, on Monday, the 1st day of December, in the year of our Lord one thousand nine hundred and thirty.

Present:

The Honorable GEORGE COSGRAVE, District Judge.

United States of America, Plaintiff,)
)
vs.) No. 7260-H-Crim.
)
Gilbert S. Johnson, Defendant,)

This cause coming before the Court for further trial of defendant Gilbert S. Johnson; John S. Pratt, Esq., Special Assistant to the Attorney General, and Peter V. Davis, Assistant United States Attorney, appearing as counsel for the Government; and said defendant being present in court with his attorneys, H. L. Arterberry and David H. Cannon, Esqs.; and, Dudley L. Hossack and Albert H. Bargion being present and alternating as official stenographic reporters of the testimony and the proceedings; now, at the hour of 9:35 o'clock a. m., court reconvenes, and all appearing as indicated, including the jury, it is by the Court ordered that this trial be proceeded with, whereupon,

Gilbert S. Johnson, defendant herein, heretofore sworn, resumes the stand and testifies further on cross-examination conducted by John S. Pratt, Esq.

At the hour of 10:45 o'clock a. m., the Court reminds the jury of the admonition heretofore given herein, and declares a recess for a period of ten minutes.

At the hour of 11:00 o'clock a. m., court reconvenes, and all being present as before, John S. Pratt, Esq., further cross-examines defendant Gilbert S. Johnson.

At the hour of 11:56 o'clock a. m., the Court reminds the jury of the admonition, and declares a recess in this case until the hour of 1:30 o'clock p. m., today.

At the hour of 1:35 o'clock p. m., court reconvenes, and all appearing as before, and with the permission of the Court, further cross-examination of defendant Gilbert S. Johnson is deferred temporarily; and,

Major Frederick Russell Burnham is called and sworn and testifies for the defendant on direct examination conducted by David H. Cannon, Esq., and said witness having thereupon testified on cross-examination conducted by John S. Pratt, Esq.

At the hour of 2:06 o'clock p. m., the Court reminds the jury of the admonition heretofore given herein, and declares a recess for a period of fifteen minutes.

At the hour of 2:40 o'clock p. m., court reconvenes, and all being present as before, witness Frederick Russell Burnham resumes the stand and testifies on further cross-examination conducted by John S. Pratt, Esq., and thereafter, said witness having testified on redirect examination conducted by David H. Cannon, Esq., testified on an examination conducted by the Court, whereupon, said witness testifies on recross-examination conducted by John S. Pratt, Esq., and on an examination conducted by the Court.

At the hour of 3:16 o'clock p. m., Gilbert S. Johnson, defendant herein, resumes the stand and testifies on cross-examination conducted by John S. Pratt, Esq., and said witness having thereupon testified on an examination conducted by the Court,

At the hour of 3:45 o'clock p. m., the Court reminds the jury of the admonition heretofore given herein, and declares a recess for a period of ten minutes.

At the hour of 4:03 o'clock p.m., court reconvenes, and all being present as before, defendant Gilbert S. Johnson resumes the stand and testifies further on direct examination conducted by John S. Pratt, Esq.

At the hour of 4:58 o'clock p. m., the Court reminds the jury of the admonition, and declares a recess until the hour of 9:30 o'clock a. m., tomorrow.

————

At a stated term, to wit: The September Term, A. D. 1930, of the District Court of the United States of America, within and for the Central Division of the Southern District of California, held at the Court Room thereof, in the City of Los Angeles, California, on Tuesday, the 2nd day of December, in the year of our Lord one thousand nine hundred and thirty.

Present:

The Honorable GEORGE COSGRAVE, District Judge.

United States of America, Plaintiff,)
)
          vs.   ) No. 7260-H-Crim.
)
Gilbert S. Johnson,   Defendant,)

This cause coming before the Court for further trial of defendant Gilbert S. Johnson; John S. Pratt, Esq., Special Assistant to the Attorney General, and Peter V. Davis, Esq., Assistant United States Attorney, appearing as counsel for the Government; defendant Johnson being present in court with his attorneys, H. L. Arterberry and David H. Cannon, Esqs.; and, Edward Van Meter and Dudley L. Hossack being present as official stenographic reporters of the testimony and the proceedings; now, at the hour of 9:33 o'clock a. m., court reconvenes, and all appearing as indicated, including the jury, it is by the Court ordered that this trial be proceeded with, whereupon,

Gilbert S. Johnson, heretofore sworn, resumes the stand and testifies further on cross-examination conducted by John S. Pratt, Esq.,

At the hour of 10:45 o'clock p. m., the court reminds the jury of the admonition heretofore given herein, and declares a recess for a period of ten minutes.

At the hour of 10:55 o'clock p. m., court reconvenes, and all being present as before,

Gilbert S. Johnson, defendant, resumes the stand and testifies further on cross-examination conducted by John S. Pratt, Esq.

At the hour of 12:04 o'clock p. m., the Court reminds the jury of the admonition heretofore given herein, and declares a recess until the hour of 1:30 o'clock p. m.

At the hour of 1:32 o'clock p. m., court reconvenes, and all being present as before, including the jury, defendant Gilbert S. Johnson, heretofore sworn, resumes the stand and testifies further on cross-examination conducted by John S. Pratt, Esq.,

At the hour of 2:34 o'clock p. m., counsel for the Government closes cross-examination of said witness Johnson, and David H. Cannon, Esq., having thereupon started his redirect examination of said witness Johnson, the Court declares a recess for a period of ten minutes with instruction to the jury to remember the admonition heretofore given herein.

At the hour of 2:47 o'clock p. m., court reconvenes, and all being present as before, witness Johnson resumes the stand and testifies on redirect examination conducted by David H. Cannon, Esq., and said witness having thereupon testified on recross-examination and redirect examination conducted by Attorneys Pratt and Cannon, defendant's Exhibits A to L, heretofore marked for Identification, are now admitted in evidence for the defendant, and the following exhibits are offered and admitted in evidence for the defendant, to-wit:

Defendant's Ex.M: Hendrick's Map of Stephens County, Texas.

" N: " " " East Young — West Jack and parts of adjoining counties.

At the hour of 3:20 o'clock p. m., the defendant, Gilbert S. Johnson, rests, and the Government offers no rebuttal evidence.

At the hour of 3:21 o'clock p. m., the Court declares a recess for a period of five minutes with instruction to the jury to remember the admonition heretofore given herein.

At the hour of 3:30 o'clock p. m., court reconvenes, and all being present as before, except the jury, H. L. Arterberry, Esq., moves the Court for a directed verdict, and David H. Cannon, Esq., having also moved the Court for a directed verdict, said motion is by the Court denied and exception noted; all as reflected by the reporter's transcript, and thereafter, the jury having returned into the court room, and all being present as before, Peter V. Davis, Esq., opens his opening argument to the jury at the hour of 3:33 o'clock p. m., and closes at the hour of 4:37 o'clock p. m., and

At the hour of 4:38 o'clock p. m., the defendant having waived argument to the jury,

At the hour of 4:40 o'clock p. m., the Court admonishes the jury and declares a recess in this trial until the hour of 9:30 o'clock a. m., tomorrow.

————

At a stated term, to wit: The September, Term, A. D. 1930, of the District Court of the United States of America, within and for the Central Division of the Southern District of California, held at the Court Room thereof, in the City of Los Angeles, California, on Wednesday, the 3rd day of December, in the year of our Lord one thousand nine hundred and thirty.

Present:

The Honorable GEORGE COSGRAVE, District Judge.

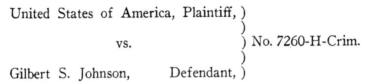

United States of America, Plaintiff,)
)
    vs.   ) No. 7260-H-Crim.
)
Gilbert S. Johnson, Defendant,)

This cause coming before the Court for further trial of defendant Gilbert S. Johnson; John S. Pratt, Special Assistant to the Attorney General, and Peter V. Davis, Assistant United States Attorney, appearing as counsel for the Government; said defendant being present in court with his attorneys, H. L. Arterberry and David H. Cannon, Esqs.; and, Albert H. Bargion being present as official stenographic reporter of the testimony and the proceedings; now, at the hour of 9:42 o'clock a. m., court reconvenes, and all being present as indicated, including the jury, the Court instructs the jury re the law involved in this case, and thereafter,

At the hour of 11 o'clock a. m., John S. Pratt, Esq., having made a statement, David H. Cannon, Esq., takes certain exceptions to the refusal of the Court to give certain instructions, and takes exception to certain instructions given, all as reflected by the reporter's transcript, whereupon, the Court instructs the jury further.

At the hour of 11:14 o'clock a. m., Olcott S. Bulkley is sworn as the bailiff to care for the jury during their deliberation upon a verdict, whereupon, the jury retire for deliberation, and the Court declares a recess until the return of the jury into the court room.

At the hour of 12:05 o'clock p. m., it is by the Court ordered that the jury be taken to lunch at the expense of the Government, in the custody of two bailiffs, also at the expense of the Government, and thereafter,

At the hour of 1:15 o'clock, p. m., the jury returned for further deliberation, and request that the following exhibits be given them:

Indictment—6 count-letters—Judge's Instructions—Issues of Bulletin with facsimile of $128,000 check.

Two big charts showing price of stock sales and also the amalgamation chart showing mergers of various companies.

and Attorneys Arterberry, Cannon, Pratt and Davis having discussed the propriety of the preceding documents to be taken into the jury, in the presence of the judge in his chambers, and the Court having ordered that all of the preceding documents be taken to the jury, and said documents having been given to the jury, and the jury having been informed that the Court will instruct them on any point of law desired, and the jury having thereupon desired the minutes of the Johnson Oil Company, it is by the Court ordered that the jury may have any and all exhibits desired that have been introduced in evidence.

At the hour of 3 o'clock p. m., the jury return into court, and all being present as before, except Attorneys Davis and Cannon,

At the hour of 3:05 o'clock p. m., court reconvenes; whereupon, the jury request further instructions, and the Court having thereupon instructed the jury further, H. L. Arterberry, Esq., takes exception to the instructions, and asks further instructions, and thereafter, the Court having instructed the jury further, the jury retire for further deliberation, and

At the hour of 3:17 o'clock p. m., the Court declares a recess until the jury report, and

At the hour of 4:48 o'clock p. m., Thomas Vick is sworn as the bailiff to care for the jury by Deputy Clerk Cross.

It is by the Court ordered that the jury be taken to dinner in charge of two bailiffs about the hour of 6 o'clock p. m., provided they have not agreed upon a verdict by that time.

At the hour of 6 o'clock p. m., the jury are taken to dinner in charge of two bailiffs at the expense of the Government, and

At the hour of 7:30 o'clock p. m., the jury return to the jury room for further deliberation.

At the hour of 9:30 o'clock p. m., it is by the Court ordered that the jury be locked up for the night in the custody of the two bailiffs, and at the expense of the Government, with the proviso that if the said jury agree upon a verdict during the interim, to present a sealed verdict to the bailiff, and thereafter, the said jury be allowed to disband to be present in open court, tomorrow, 10 o'clock a. m., at which time, the said verdict will be read in open court in the presence of said jury, and if the said jury do not agree, to be given their breakfast tomorrow morning at the expense of the Government, also breakfast for the two bailiffs at the expense of the Government, after which, the said jury may then deliberate further.

At the hour of 9:32 o'clock p. m., the Court declares a recess until tomorrow morning.

———

At a stated term, to wit: The September Term, A. D. 1930, of the District Court of the United States of America, within and for the Central Division of the

Southern District of California, held at the Court Room thereof, in the City of Los Angeles, California, on Thursday, the 4th day of December, in the year of our Lord one thousand nine hundred and thirty-

Present:

The Honorable GEORGE COSGRAVE, District Judge.

United States of America, Plaintiff,)
)
vs.   ) No. 7260-H-Crim.
)
Gilbert S. Johnson,   Defendant,)

Olcott S. Bulkley, Bailiff, informs Francis E. Cross, Clerk, that the jury were in the custody of Thomas Vick and Olcott S. Bulkley, Bailiffs, all night at the Hotel Rosslyn, and that they were taken to their breakfast at the hour of 8 o'clock a. m., this morning; and thereafter, the jury returned to the jury room at the hour of 9:30 o'clock a. m., for further deliberation.

At the hour of 11:50 o'clock a. m., it is by the Court ordered that the jury be taken to lunch at the hour of 12 o'clock, noon, at the expense of the Government in the custody of two bailiffs, also at the expense of the Government.

At the hour of 12:10 o'clock p. m., the jury are taken to lunch at the expense of the Government in the custody of Thomas Vick and Olcott S. Bulkley, Bailiffs.

At the hour of 1:30 o'clock p. m., the jury return to the jury room for further deliberation upon a verdict.

At the hour of 4:18 o'clock p. m., court reconvenes, and all being present as before, except David H. Cannon, Esq., the jury return into court, and present their verdict;

the verdict as presented, is read in open court by the Clerk of the Court, and the Court having thereupon ordered that the said verdict be filed, H. L. Arterberry, Esq., requests that the jury be polled, and each *jury* having stated that it is his verdict; the verdict, as presented and read in open court, and ordered filed and entered herein, being as follows, to-wit:

IN THE DISTRICT COURT OF THE UNITED STATES, IN AND FOR THE SOUTHERN DISTRICT OF CALIFORNIA, CENTRAL DIVISION. United States of America, Plaintiff, vs. Gilbert S. Johnson, Defendant, No. 7260-H-Criminal—VERDICT. We, the Jury in the above-entitled cause, find the defendant, Gilbert S. Johnson, Guilty as charged in the 1st count of the Indictment, and Not Guilty as charged in the 2nd count of the Indictment, and Not Guilty as charged in the 3rd count of the Indictment, and Not Guilty as charged in the 4th count of the Indictment, and Not Guilty as charged in the 5th count of the Indictment, and Not Guilty as charged in the 6th count of the Indictment. Los Angeles, California, December 4th, 1930. ROYDON VOSBURG, FOREMAN OF THE JURY. FILED DEC 4 1930, R. S. ZIMMERMAN, Clerk, By Francis E. Cross, Deputy Clerk.

The aforesaid verdict as presented by the jury having been filed and entered herein, it is by the Court ordered that the jury herein be excused from further attendance upon this court except Thomas B. Jones, until December 20th, 1930.

H. L. Arterberry, Esq., counsel for the defendant, wishes to communicate with David H. Cannon, Esq., also counsel for the defendant, as to further proceedings here-in, and thereafter, H. L. Arterberry, Esq., having requested the Court that the defendant herein be permitted to remain on bond until further order of the Court, and S. W. McNabb, United States Attorney, having made a statement for the Government, it is by the Court ordered that the said defendant remain in custody of the United States Marshal until such time as a bond is arranged to the satisfaction of the United States District Attorney, and until further order of the Court.

At the hour of 4:30 o'clock p. m., the Court declares a recess,, subject to call, until the hour of 5 o'clock p. m., today.

At the hour of 4:58 o'clock p. m., all being present except John S. Pratt, Esq., Special Assistant to the Attorney General, David H. Cannon, Esq., states to the Court that it is agreeable with Attorneys Davis and Pratt for the time for passing sentence to go over until a week from next Monday in view of the fact that the defendant has to make some arrangements with respect to his bond; whereupon, said Attorney Cannon further states Attorneys Pratt and Davis are willing for defendant Johnson to remain on the bond now in force until pronouncement of sentence, and said Attorney Davis not offering any opposition thereto, it is by the Court ordered that this cause be continued to the hour of 2 o'clock p. m., December 15th, 1930, for pronouncement of sentence upon Gilbert S. Johnson; said defendant to remain on bond now in force until said date of sentence.

At a stated term, to wit: The September Term, A. D. 1930, of the District Court of the United States of America, within and for the Central Division of the Southern District of California, held at the Court Room thereof, in the City of Los Angeles, California, on Friday, the 5th day of December, in the year of our Lord one thousand nine hundred and thirty-

Present:

The Honorable GEORGE COSGRAVE, District Judge.

United States of America, Plaintiff,)
)
vs.   ) No. 7260-H-Crim.
)
Gilbert S. Johnson,   Defendant,)

Peter V. Davis, Assistant United States Attorney, appearing as counsel for the Government, states to the Court that in the above-entitled case, the Court entered an order impounding the books and files and records of these several organizations that were involved in this case, and inasmuch as a large number of these records and books were not used, and there will be no further use of them, said Attorney Davis moves the Court to release the impounding order insofar as the records in this case are concerned which were not offered or admitted as exhibits, whereupon, it is by the Court so ordered.

At a stated term, to wit: The September Term, A. D. 1930, of the District Court of the United States of America, within and for the Central Division of the Southern District of California, held at the Court Room thereof, in the City of Los Angeles, California, on Monday, the 15th day of December, in the year of our Lord one thousand nine hundred and thirty-

Present:

The Honorable GEORGE COSGRAVE, District Judge.

United States of America, Plaintiff,)
)
vs.   ) No. 7260-H-Crim.
)
Gilbert S. Johnson,   Defendant,)

This cause coming before the Court for pronouncement of sentence upon Gilbert S. Johnson; Peter V. Davis, Assistant United States Attorney, appearing as counsel for the Government, and said defendant being present in court with his attorneys, H. L. Arterberry and David H. Cannon, Esqs., said Attorney Cannon files motion in arrest of judgment, and the Court having thereupon overruled said motion, and exception noted, Walter B. Scott, Esq., of Fort Worth, Texas, makes a statement in behalf of the defendant, whereupon, P. V. Davis, Esq., makes a statement to the Court, and does not urge any particular penalty or sentence, and the Court having thereupon made a statement, it is by the Court ordered and adjudged that the defendant, Gilbert S. Johnson, for the crime of the violation of Section 215 of the Federal Penal Code, Use of Mails in Scheme to Defraud, of which he stands convicted, be imprisoned in the Federal Penitentiary at McNeil Island for the term and period of four years on the first count of the Indictment, and thereafter, said Attorney Cannon having filed Petition for Appeal, S. W. McNabb, United States Attorney, states to the Court that he has wired to the District Attorney's office at Fort Worth, Texas, to see if they approve of Texas Sureties on bond in Texas, and if so, Attorney McNabb offers no objection to the bond; whereupon, later, in the presence

of David H. Cannon, Esq., S. W. McNabb, Esq., reads
the telegram received from United States Attorney Dodge
to the effect that "Johnson bonds just executed by sureties
who are president and vice-president of the First National
Bank and approved", and that "Bonds go forward to you
(McNabb) by mail immediately," United States Attorney
McNabb thereupon states that he understands from the
said telegram that the bonds are approved by the United
States Attorney, and Commissioner at Fort Worth, Texas,
and are sufficient, whereupon, David H. Cannon, Esq.,
moves the Court that defendant Gilbert S. Johnson be
released on bond, and it is by the Court so ordered.

[TITLE OF COURT AND CAUSE.]

VERDICT.

We, the Jury in the above-entitled cause, find the defendant, Gilbert S. Johnson,

Guilty as charged in the 1st count of the Indictment, and

Not guilty as charged in the 2nd count of the Indictment, and

Not guilty as charged in the 3rd count of the Indictment, and

Not guilty as charged in the 4th count of the Indictment, and

Not guilty as charged in the 5th count of the Indictment, and

Not guilty as charged in the 6th count of the Indictment.

Los Angeles, California, December 4th, 1930.

Roydon Vosburg
FOREMAN OF THE JURY.

Filed Dec 4 1930   R. S. Zimmerman, Clerk   By Francis E. Cross, Deputy Clerk

[TITLE OF COURT AND CAUSE.]

BILL OF EXCEPTIONS

BE IT REMEMBERED that this cause came on regularly for trial on the 11th day of November, 1930, before the Honorable George Cosgrave, Judge of said Court, and a jury therein being duly impaneled and sworn to try said cause, John S. Pratt, Esq., and P. V. Davis, Esq., appearing as attorneys for the plaintiff, and David H. Cannon, Esq., and H. L. Arterberry, Esq., appearing as attorneys for the defendant,

WHEREUPON, the trial of said cause proceeded and the following proceedings were had:

MR. ARTERBERRY: Before we proceed with the evidence, in order to protect the record, the defendant desires to object to the introduction of any evidence under this indictment.

THE COURT: Do you desire to state the grounds?

MR. ARTERBERRY: The grounds are set forth in our motion to quash.

THE COURT: Heretofore submitted and passed upon?

MR. ARTERBERRY: Yes, your Honor, before Judge Henning.

THE COURT: Overruled.

MR. ARTERBERRY: An exception.

TITLE OF THE COURT AND CAUSE

MOTION TO QUASH INDICTMENT

TO THE HONORABLE JUDGE OF SAID COURT:

Comes now the defendant, GILBERT S. JOHNSON, in the above entitled cause and moves the court to quash the indictment herein because said indictment, and each and every count thereof, is fatally and fundamentally defective and void upon its face for the following reasons, to-wit:

(1) Said indictment and each and every count thereof, fails to charge the crime against the laws of the United States pursuant to Section 215 of the Criminal Code.

(2) Said indictment, and each and every count thereof, fails to inform the defendant of the nature and cause of the accusation against him, in this, that said indictment charges only in general terms and this defendant will be unable to meet the charges of such a general nature.

(3) Because said indictment charges and attempts to charge other and different crimes and offenses not contemplated by Section 215 of the Criminal Code of the United States, which section contemplates only the misuse of the United States mail in furtherance of schemes to defraud, in this, that said indictment in paragraph 5 of page 3, solemnly charges the defendant with the crime of embezzlement, which said crime is not contemplated by Section 215 of the Criminal Code. And again, in paragraph 13 of page 6 of said indictment, defendant is again charged and attempted to be charged with the crime of embezzlement.

(4)   Because said indictment, and each and every count thereof, is founded upon malice, passion and prejudice, in this, that in paragraph (c) on page 8 of said indictment, the defendant is charged and attempted to be charged with being "a promoter of many fraudulent enterprises and was a confidence man and swindler", which said charges, are crimes and offense not contemplated or cognizable by the laws or statutes of the United States, and particularly, Section 215 of the United States Criminal Code, and the same paragraph further charges and attempts to charge the crime of embezzlement.

(5)   Because said indictment, and each and every count thereof, further charges and attempts to charge the defendant with the crime of embezzlement, in this, that said charge or attempted charge is found in paragraph (d) of page 8 of said indictment.   This same vice is found in paragraph (e) on page 9 of said indictment, and again the same charge is found in paragraph (h) on page 11 of said indictment.

(6)   Because said indictment in paragraph (n) of page 19 again charges and attempts to charge the defendant with the crime of embezzlement and conversion, which said crimes and offenses, are not cognizable by Section 215 of the United States Criminal Code.   The same vice is found in paragraph (o) on page 19 of said indictment.

(7)   Because said other crimes charged and attempted to be charged, to-wit; the crimes of embezzlement and conversion, and also denominating the defendant as being "a Promoter of many fraudulent enterprises", and further designating him as being "a confidence man and swin-

dler", tend to degrade the defendant and are highly prejudicial, and will prevent him from having a fair and an impartial trial under Section 215 of the Criminal Code, as guaranteed to him by the Constitution and laws of the United States.

WHEREFORE, defendant prays that this motion to quash be sustained and said indictment dismissed and that he be discharged.

(signed)   McLean, Scott & Sayers

(signed)   H. L. Arterberry

Attorneys for Defendant.

TITLE OF THE COURT AND CAUSE

POINTS AND AUTHORITIES IN SUPPORT OF THE MOTION TO QUASH

An indictment must be so clear and exact in its language as to advise the accused and the court beyond doubt of the offense intended to charged, Rumley v. United States, 293 Fed. 532 (CCA 2).

In an indictment for use of mails in furtherance of a scheme to defraud, the particulars of the scheme are matters of substance and must be set forth with sufficient certainty to acquaint the defendant with the charge against him. Savage v. United States, 270 Fed. 14 (CCA 8).

In the case of United States v. Howard, Fed. Cas. No. 15, 403, Mr. Justice Story, in discussing the tests of surplusage and of material variance, used this language:

"The material parts which constitute the offense charged must be stated in the indictment, and that must be proved in evidence. But allegations not essential to such a purpose, which might be entirely ommitted without affecting the charge against the defendant, and without detriment to the indictment; are considered as mere surplusage, and may be disregarded in evidence. But no allegation, whether it be necessary or unnecessary, whether it be more or less particular, which is descriptive of the identity of that which is legally essential to the charge in the indictment, can ever be rejected as surplusage."

See also Mathews v. United States, 15 Fed. (2d) 139-143 (CCA8).

The case of Naftzger v. United States, 200 Fed. 494, (CCA8) Holds that an unnecessary allegation which, however, was descriptive of the indentity of something which was legally essential to the charge, could not be considered surplusage. ·

Kercheval v. United States, 12 Fed. (2d) 904-908, holds that conversion is not an element of crime under Section 215 of the Penal Code; see also Nelson v. United States, 16 Fed. (2d) 71-75 (CCA8).

In the very recent case of Beck v. United States, reported in the advance sheets of August 1st, 1929, 33 Fed. (2d) 107 (CCA8).

At page 109, among other things, the court says:

"There follows five printed pages of "representations", all of which, are alleged in the most general terms to be false and untrue. It is not alleged wherein they are false. It is true, as claimed by appellant, that there are many instances wherein order to comply with the constitutional requirements of certainty in the accusation, a pleader should not only allege the falsity of the misrepresentation, but "allege affirmatively in what the falsehood consisted." 25 C. J. 628. But the particular vice of this indictment reaches farther than that; the unfair part of it is that the defendant is charged with falsely representing many things which counsel for the government assure the court are not false at all."

In connection with the Beck case, supra, it is particularly interesting to note on page 110 thereof, in discussing the indictment in said case and what was generally referred to as the "shotgun" clause, and comparing same with paragraph (o) on page 19 of the indictment in this case, wherein the same vice is found in the present indictment that was condemned by the court in the Beck case and in this connection, we shall quote a part of the language of the court in the Beck case:

"The quoted "shotgun" clause is in such general terms that it is unfair to the defendants. It gives them no inkling of what facts may be concealed in the underbrush of glittering generality, and no opportunity to defend against them. The courts are properly lenient with regard to the form of an indictment which substantially advises the defendant of the charge; they are likewise critical of a charge which is that in form alone, and can serve no purpose save as a foundation for evidence that will catch the defendant off his guard. In the early history of civil pleading, plaintiffs used to allege certain acts of negligence and then quietly add "on account of the aforesaid and other negligent acts". Occasionally, it is still done; but not when the court's attention is directed thereto. The constitution compels that the rule of criminal pleading should be at least as fair. A trial judge would be justified in sustaining a demurrer to an indictment with such Mother Hubbard allegations; or in treating it as surplusage. In this case, neither course was taken. The motion for a bill of particulars was asked and denied. While such a motion is generally within the sound discussion of the court, it should have been sustained."

In the case of U. S. v. Cruikshank, 91 U. S. 442, the Supreme Court laid down the following rule:

"It is an elementary principle of criminal pleading that when the definition of an offense, whether it be of common law or by statute, includes generic terms, it is not sufficient that the indictments which charge the offense be in the same generic terms as in the definition, but it must state the species; it must descend to particularities."

In the case of U. S. v. Hess, 31 L. Ed. 518, the Supreme Court said:

"The object of the indictment is: first, to furnish the accused with such a description of the charge against him as will enable him to make his defense and avail himself of a conviction or acquital, for protection against a further prosecution for the same cause; and second, to inform the court of the facts alleged so that it may decide whether they are sufficient in law to support a conviction if one should be had, for these facts are to be stated, not conclusions of law alone. A crime is made up of acts and intent, and these must be set forth in the indictment with reasonable particularity of time, place and circumstances."

In the case of Brenner v. U. S. 287 Fed. 640, opinion by the Circuit Court of Appeals Second Circuit, Justice Manton speaking for the Court, used this language:

"It is essential to the sufficiency of the indictment that it set forth the facts which the pleader claims constitute the alleged criminal breach, so distinctly as to advise the accused of the charge which he has to meet, and to give him a fair opportunity to prepare his defense so particularly as to avail himself of a conviction or acquittal in advance of another prosecution for the same offense, and so clearly that the court may be able to determine whether or not the facts as stated are sufficient to support a convition. Fontana v. U. S., 262 Fed. 283. The indictment must charge the offense in more than the generic terms as in the definition. It must descend to particularities. U. S. v. Cruikshank, 92 U. S. 542, 23 L. Ed. 588. A crime, unless otherwise provided by statute, is made of acts and intent, and they must be set forth in the indictment with reasonable particularity as to time, place and circumstances. Such particularities are matters of substance and not of form, and their omission is not aided or cured by a verdict.

In U. S. v. Hess, 124 U. S. 483, 31 L. Ed. 516, it is said: "The essential requirements indeed or the particulars constituting the offense of devising a scheme to defraud are wanting. Such particulars are matters of substance and not of form, and their omission is not aided or cured by a verdict."

In the case of U. S. v. Potter, 56 Fed 89-90, the Circuit Court of Appeals, speaking through Judge Putnam, used this language:

"In order to properly inform the accused of the 'nature and cause of the accusation', within the meaning of the constitution and of the rules of the common law, a little

thought will make it plain, not only to the legal, but to al'
other educated minds, that not only must all the elements
of the offense be stated in the indictment, but that also
they must be stated with clearness and certainty, and with
a sufficient degree of particularity to identify the transaction to which the indictment relates as to place, persons
and things and other details.   The accused must receive
sufficient information to enable him to reasonably understand, not only the nature of the offense, but the particular act or acts touching which he must be prepared with
his proof; and when his liberty, and perhaps his life, are
at stake, he is not to be left so scantily informed as to
cause him to rest his defense upon the hypothesis that he
is charged with a certain act or series of acts, with the
hazard of being surprised by proofs on the part of the
prosecution of an entirely different act or series of acts,
at least so far as such surprise can be avoided by reasonable particularity and fullness of description of the alleged
offense.   These rules are well expressed in U. S. v. Cruikshank, 92 U. S. 542, 557, as follows:

'In criminal cases prosecuted under the laws of the
United States the accused has the constitutional right to
be informed of the nature and cause of the accusation.'
Amendment 6 in U. S. v. Mills, 7 Pet. 142, this was construed to mean that the indictment must set forth the
offense 'with clearness and all necessary certainty to apprise the accused of the crime with which he stands
charged;' and in U. S. v. Cooke, 17 Wall. 174 that 'every
ingredient of which the offense is composed must be accurately and clearly alleged.'   It is an elementary principal of criminal pleading that where the definition of an

offense, whether it be at common law or by statute, 'including generic terms, it is not sufficient that the indictment shall charge the offense in the same generic terms as in the definition; but it must state the species—it must descend to particulars.' 1 Arch Cr. Pr. & Pl. 291. The object of the indictment is, first, to furnish the accused with such a description of the charge against him as will enable him to make his defense, and avail himself of his conviction or acquittal for protection against a further prosecution for the same cause; and second, to inform the court of the facts alleged, so that it may decide whether they are sufficient in law to support a conviction, if one should be had. For this, facts are to be stated, not conclusions of law alone. A crime is made up of acts and intent; and these must be set forth in the indictment with reasonable particularity of time, place and circumstances.' "

In the case of Anderson v. U. S., 294 Fed. 597, opinion by the Circuit Court of Appeals, Second Circuit, the court held:

"The crime must be charged with precision and certainty, and every ingredient of which it is composed, must be accurately and clearly alleged. Evans v. U. S., 153 U. S. 584, 14 Sup. Ct. 934, 38 L. Ed. 830. To allege that what was done was unlawful is merely to state the conclusion of the pleader. Brenner v. U. S., supra. The facts supporting the legal conclusion must be alleged. To admit this essential fact is to render the indictment void."

In this connection see also Goldberg v. U. S., 277 Fed. 215, opinion by the Circuit Court of Appeals, Eighth Circuit; <u>Reeder v. U. S.</u>, 262 Fed. 38, opinion by Elliott District Judge, certiorari denied by supreme court, 64 L. Ed. 726.

The defect in the indictment for failure to charge the defendants with any criminal act distinctly and expressly, with precision and certainty, is not cured by the "whereas clauses" set forth in said indictment.

In the case of Dalton v. U. S., 127 Fed. 547, the Circuit Court of Appeals, Seventh Circuit, had this very question under consideration. The court, speaking through Judge Jenkins, had this to say:

"We then come to the 'whereas' clause, which is not an allegation of a scheme, but is a negation—a denial of the truth of preceding allegations. This word 'whereas' implies a recital, and, in general, cannot be used in the direct and positive averment of a fact. It is thus defined:

'(1) The thing being so that; considering that things are so; implying an admission of facts, something followed by a different statement, and sometimes by inference of something consequent. (2) While on the contrary; the fact or case really being that; when in fact.' Century Dictionary.

The statement sought to be negatived by the 'whereas' clause should have been made positively in the indictment, the purpose of the 'whereas' clause being to set forth the real truth concerning the allegations supposed to have been theretofore averred. The difficulty here is that the allegations thus denied are not positively charged in the indictment to be part of the scheme to defraud. If it be a denial of anything averred, it is a denial of the allegations of the pleader with respect to the class of persons intended to be defrauded."

In the case of <u>Foster v. U. S.</u>, 253 Fed. 482, the Circuit Court of Appeals, Ninth Circuit, speaking through Judge Gilbert, used this language:

"The plaintiffs in error had the constitutional right to be informed of the nature and cause of the accusation against them. To furnish them with that information it was necessary to set forth in the indictment the particular facts and circumstances which rendered them guilty and to make specific that which the statute states in general."

MISCONDUCT OF COUNSEL IN DRAFTING INDICTMENT.

Counsel for the government may be guilty of misconduct just as prejudicial to the rights of a defendant as in making final argument to the jury in the case, by display of malice, hatred, contempt, ridicule or scorn, and making assertions and statements not based on truth or fact. Because in the latter case, defendant's counsel could make a proper objection and protect the rights of the defendant from such unwarranted abuse. While in the first instance, by heaping unwarranted abuse on a defendant under the guise of a solemn accusation by a grand jury in the form of an indictment; much greater harm and injury can result from attacks of that nature, than in the latter case. And it is these tactics to which we desire to direct the court's attention to the misconduct and evident unfairness of the drafter of this indictment, when he, knowingly and deliberately, inserted a lot of accusations which have no proper place in an indictment such as this. For instance, the indictment in the present case is literally honeycombed with charges and accusations against this defendant, charging that he misappropriated, embezzled and converted to his own use and benefit, large sums of money and property alleged to have been acquired by him in furtherance of the alleged scheme to defraud. This, in the face of all the courts saying that such allegations constitute no part or parcel of a mail fraud indictment. Not satisfied with these allegations, which are repeated in practically every paragraph of the alleged scheme to defraud, but the alleged scheme, and particularly paragraph (o) on page 19 of said indictment, contains what the court describes and condemns in the Beck case, as the "shotgun" clause.

Not satisfied with the wrongful allegations above referred to, but the pleader in this case so far forgets himself as to make charges against this defendant under the guise of a solemn charge of a Grand Jury of the United States, in charging this defendant with being "a confidence man and swindler", when the pleader knew, or by the slightest investigation, could have known, that this defendant has never been even as much as charged, much less, convicted of any offense against the laws of the United States, or of any state within the United States. This, in the face of the elementary principle that every man is presumed to be innocent until proven guilty.

We submit that all these unwarranted, unjustified, malicious, and slanderous statements, have only one purpose and effect, and that is to so prejudice this defendant before a jury upon the trial of said case, that he will be denied a fair and an impartial trial, as guaranteed to him by the laws and Constitution of the United States.

We further submit that such allegations cannot be treated as mere surplusage, as they are collateral to and a part of the main charge of the indictment. We therefore, respectfully submit that the indictment in this case should be quashed and held for naught, and defendant be discharged. See:—

> Beck v. United States, 33 Fed. (2d) 107-113— (CCA8)
>
> Latham v. United States, 226 Fed. 420—(CCA5)
>
> Miller v. United States, 287 Fed. 864—(CCA5)
>
> De Luca v. United States, 298 Fed. 416
>
> United States v. Gradwell, 227 Fed. 243
>
> Agnew v. United States, 165 U. S. 36-45
>
> United States v. American Tobacco Co., 177 Fed. 774
>
> United States v. Nevin, 199 Fed. 833
>
> McKinney v. United States, 199 Fed. 29—(CCA7)

Respectfully submitted,

(signed) McLean, Scott & Sayers,

(signed) H. L. Arterberry.

Attorneys for Defendant.

During the deliberations of the jury on the verdict, the jury called for and was given the original indictment in the case.

The defendant requested the District Court to give each of the following instructions to the jury but the said request was in each instance refused and the requested instructions were not given:

"If there was no scheme to defraud devised by the defendant, then the defendant is not guilty and should be acquitted. In order to warrant a conviction of the defendant, you must find and believe from the evidence that the defendant devised a scheme to defraud within the meaning of the law, and in this connection you are instructed that in order to establish a scheme to defraud, the Government must establish that the necessary effect of carrying the scheme mentioned in evidence into effect was to defraud the persons buying stock or units of interest out of their money or property and that the defendant knew that said alleged scheme would necessarily have that effect, and unless the Government has proved that such was the necessary effect of the things that the defendant did and the defendant had knowledge that such was the necessary effect of his activities, then the evidence is insufficient to establish a scheme to defraud and it is your duty to acquit him, without considering any other feature of the charge in the indictment or the evidence offered in the case."

"The Court charges the jury that a false promise, such as the statute describes, is a promise—not merely one that is not fulfilled—but a promise that it is known at the time that it is made that it is not going to be fulfilled, or else a promise that is impossible of performance. Merely because a promise is made and not kept would not warrant you in concluding that the party making that promise had a criminal intent, or warrant you in finding him guilty because you may believe he made a promise which was not fulfilled."

"The defendant cannot be convicted unless you believe beyond all reasonable doubt that he made false representations with the intent to defraud. An *inccorect* statement, grossly misrepresenting facts, does not amount to fraud in law, unless the false representations were knowingly and willfully made with fraudulent intent."

"It is common knowledge that most business enterprises are aided by advertisements passing through the mails, and at every hand we see claims of capacity, performance, and results which we know cannot stand cross-examination. Parties who have anything to sell have the habit of puffing their wares, and we are all familiar with the fact that it is a very prevalent thing in the course of business to exaggerate the merits of goods people have to sell, and within any proper, reasonable bounds, such a practice is not criminal. It must amount to a substantial deception."

"You are instructed that a man may be visionary in his plans and believe that they will succeed, and yet, in spite of their ultimate failure be incapable of committing a conscious fraud. If you believe that the defendant in this case really entertained the belief of the ultimate success of his projects corresponding with his representations, he did not commit the offense charged and you should return a verdict of not guilty. The significant fact is the intent and purpose. The question presented to you in this case is <u>not</u> whether the business enterprises of the defendant, Gilbert S. Johnson, were practicable or not, if you believe from the evidence that the defendant entered, in good faith, into these business enterprises, believing that out of the moneys received, he could by investment or otherwise, make enough to repay said investors according to his promise, he is not guilty, no matter how visionary might seem his plan or scheme."

"The burden is upon the Government to prove a fraudulent intent on the part of the accused. Such intent must be proved specifically, and it cannot be implied from the fact that the pretenses alleged were made, and that they were false, and that accused knew them to be false. Such intent is to be determined by the jury upon all the facts and circumstances disclosed by the evidence, but it is not an inference of law arising from the proof of the making of false statements."

"The Court instructs the Jury that the indictment in this case was returned and filed in this Court on the 19th day of June, 1925 and you are instructed that the defendant cannot be convicted on any act, whether criminal or otherwise, which you may believe he committed at any time prior to..........day of........................, 19..... Under the law the government cannot prosecute one for such a crime as is here charged unless the indictment is returned within three (3) years from and after the commission of the alleged criminal act."

"In determining whether or not the defendant did believe that he would be able to carry out and fulfill such promises and representations as you may believe and find from the testimony he made, you should take into consideration the various enterprises in which the said Gilbert S. Johnson was interested and you have a right to consider the relationships between all of said enterprises and the prospects of success of each of said enterprises as they then and that time appeared to him, and in determining whether or not he thought or believed that he could carry out the representations and promises made, you may consider the sources of income which he might expect to receive from properties and leases which he was interested in and owned in various parts of Texas, and you may also take into consideration the prospects of income from the development of oil wells as they appeared to him at the time the representations and promises were made, and if from a consideration of all these facts and circumstances you believe that the defendant honestly and in good faith believed that he would carry out the promises and representations made by him, then he is not guilty in this case and this is true, even though you believe that all the enterprises with which the said defendant was connected eventually failed, and all persons investing money failed to realize any substantial return or any return for the money invested by them."

"The Court instructs the Jury that matters of fact, if any, which are left uncertain by the evidence, cannot be made certain to the prejudice of the defendant by inference. In the absence of evidence, no inference can be drawn by the jury against the defendant; but, on the contrary, all the inferences and presumptions consistent with the facts proved are to be drawn and indulged in favor of the innocence of the defendant. No fact or circumstances upon which they may base a conclusion of guilt is sufficient, unless such fact or circumstance has been proved beyond a reasonable doubt and to the same extent as if the whole conclusion depended upon that one fact or circumstance."

"If upon a fair and impartial consideration of all the evidence in the case the jury find that there are two reasonable theories, supported by the testimony in the case and that one of such theories is consistent with the theory that the defendant is guilty, as charged in some one or more or all of the counts in the indictment and that the other of such theories is consistent with the innocence of the defendant, then it is the policy of the law, and the law makes it the duty of the jury to adopt that rule which is consistent with the innocence of the defendant and in such case to find the defendant not guilty."

"The law is that in order that the jury may be warranted in finding a person guilty upon circumstantial evidence alone, all the facts and circumstances necessary to establish the conclusion of guilt must each be proved beyond a reasonable doubt; and all such facts and circumstances must be consistent with each other and with the conclusions sought to be established, which conclusion is that the accused is guilty as charged in some one or more or all of the counts in the indictment; and all such facts and circumstances must be consistent with any reasonable theory of the innocence of the accused; and all such facts and circumstances when taken together must be of such a convincing nature as to produce in the minds of the jurors a reasonable and moral certainty that the accused is guilty in manner and form as charged in some one or more of the counts in the indictment."

"You are instructed that it is a matter of common knowledge that beginning in the year of 1921, the business of the country generally passed through a period of deflation and depression that brought loss and even ruin to business enterprises of supposed soundness and strength, and you are further instructed that from the evidence in this case it appears that the price of oil in the State of Texas fell from a price of $3.50 per barrel to $1.00 per barrel, and this is one of the reasons that the defendant ascribes to some of his misfortune in the oil business, and if you so believe you should give the defendant the benefit of such condition and take these facts into consideration with all the evidence in this case."

Mr. Cannon: I would like to take an exception to the Court's remarks as being prejudicial at this time. If the Court please, I desire at this time, without particularizing, unless your Honor requires me to do it, the refusal or failure of the Court to give each and every of the requested instructions prepared and submitted to your Honor by the defendant's counsel, and take the exceptions to each one of those particular instructions that were refused.

ALL OF THE INSTRUCTIONS GIVEN TO THE JURY

THE COURT: Gentlemen of the Jury, the evidence in the case that we have been considering is all in; the arguments made. It is now the duty of the Court to deliver its charge or instructions to you; to explain the law pertinent to the case and the matters charged in the indictment. This is the sole province of the Court, you understand, of course; and the law as laid down by the Court you are to accept unhesitatingly as the law, regardless of your own opinion, feelings or sympathies. The facts, however, are to be solely judged by you; as to the credibility of the witnesses, what witnesses you will believe or what not to believe, that is a matter solely within your own province and power and, notwithstanding an opinion might be expressed by the Court as to the value of certain evidence, the Court might express its belief or disbelief of certain evidence, that it is not true, you will understand that you are the sole judges of the evidence.

I want to commend you, gentlemen, at this time, for your very earnest attention given to the case, and what I know will be your careful consideration of it; and I want to commend counsel in this case with their lawyer-like attitude and handling of the case without dealing in any trifling matters, but in a just and proper professional attitude toward the matter before us.

The indictment in this case is very lengthy, contains a large number of matters, but I will attempt to summarize it for your benefit. It charges that the defendant devised a scheme to defraud and to obtain money by means of false pretenses from F. J. Rappe, H. W. Shafer and various other persons named in the indictment, and also other persons who are unknown.

This scheme was in substance as follows:

The defendant would acquire oil and gas leases in wild cat territory at nominal prices and would then organize a succession of concerns, some being corporations and some trust estates—and when I speak of these concerns, you will understand that they mean either one or the other. You will remember that, from the evidence in the case, there were many what were denominated common law trusts or trust estates; they were the ones where units were sold. In others, there were some corporations regularly formed, as we do in California. He would give to himself complete control of the assets of these concerns. The defendant would then assign certain oil and gas leases previously acquired by himself to such trust estates or concerns at excessive prices and unlawful profits to himself, and would cause such trust estates to assume the drilling agreements and would retain for himself large portions of said leases and dispose of the same in fraud of the rights of the unit-holders.

You will remember and note this fact, that a further instruction will be given you on the structure of these trust estates and the duty of the defendant with respect to the people who invest or did invest in them.

The defendant would fix the amount of capitalization of the trust estates in amounts without regard to the actual value and would authorize himself to increase such capitalization without regard to the actual value; that he would sell the shares by means of false and fraudulent pretenses, representations and promises, as hereinafter set forth, and would induce the persons whom he intended to defraud to pay their money to him, which he would thereupon appropriate to his own use, or a portion of it.

The defendant, before the actual organization of some of the trust estates would offer for sale and sell units of such trust estates.

That the defendant would organize, own and operate brokerage companies as a medium through which to dispose of the stock units and as such brokerage concerns would fraudulently contract with himself for the sale of the stock of the concerns and by such contracts appropriate portions of the money belonging to said trust estate.

The defendant would sell units at gradually ascending prices through false misrepresentations as to the value of the lease holdings, the location of such leases, as to oil-producing territory, the progress of development thereon, the assurance of gusher oil productions and the enormous profits to accrue to investors without regard to the actual facts or the real values, it being intended fraudulently to lead said investing persons to believe that the trust estates were growing stronger.

Defendant would drill for oil upon one of the leases in a pretended search for oil and charge such trust estates such excessive amounts for such drilling that the funds would be quickly exhausted and such trust estates become insolvent.

I will take occasion to observe right there, gentlemen, that I do not believe that the evidence supports that particular charge; that there was no pretended search for oil, so far as I can observe. The evidence shows that the defendant did actually drill for oil and did not at any time drill merely for the purpose of making a pretended search.

That defendant would use certain trust estates as merger companies to provide a burying ground for the trust estates previously organized by him and become insolvent, whereby the stockholders in the trust estates could be induced to pay exchange fees in exchanging for stock in the new companies and as a means to eliminate all who should refuse to pay.

That the defendant would arrange mergers of the insolvent companies and notify stockholders that on surrender of their stock and payment of an exchange fee, stock in the merger company would be issued to them.

That defendant would advertise a fraudulent dividend of the Johnson Oil Company to stimulate stock sales payable on a future date to stockholders of an intervening date, and then offer stock for sale participating in such dividend.

Again, that the defendant would misappropriate part of the money obtained.

As the fourteenth particular of the fraudulent scheme, it is charged that the defendant would make false representations by means of advertisements through the United States mails, as follows:

On September 4, 1920, that the last offering of Lewis Oil & Gas stock was made, and was to be withdrawn on September 10th; that this was the last chance to secure an interest; that it was not intended to withdraw the Lewis Oil & Gas stock; it was not believed that the large wells would come in; and that there was no possibility of earnings or that the earnings would be great because defendant would appropriate the returns to himself. That the Stephens Oil Syndicate, believed by defendant to be fully financed, when defendant knew that he would divert to himself a large part of the proceeds from the sale of stock of Stephens Oil Syndicate; and in the further particular that it was stated that the defendant is president of the Fernando Oil Company and this insures fair treatment of stockholders, when, as a matter of fact, the defendant was only a promoter and not a successful executive of an oil company. That no further offerings of Texas Trojan stock would be made after October 7, 1920, and defendant knew at that time that that was not the case, that the stock would not at that time be withdrawn.

That on April 21, 1922, all available units of the Corsicana-Mexia Oil Syndicate had been subscribed, no more being offered at any price, and hence a large number of the clients of defendant and a great number of the readers of the Texas Oil Bulletin had found it impossible to secure an interest in the Great Powell Structure, but, moved by an overwhelming desire to have every client of Gilbert Johnson & Company, and every reader of the

Texas Oil Bulletin participate in the tremendous profits
that the defendant was confident would be made by the
bringing in of great gushers on the Powell Structure, he
had personally selected 500 acres of leases on the Great
Powell Structure adjacent to and surrounding the three
wells being drilled thereon, and had formed for the development of these leases the Mexia-Powell Oil Syndicate
with a capitalization of $150,000 divided into 6,000 units
of the par value of $25.00 per unit; that this announce-
ment was the first, last and only offering of units of
Mexia-Powell Oil .Syndicate units at $20.00 per unit; that
the price of these units would rapidly advance and that
the bringing in of gusher production in the three wells
then rapidly approaching the Woodbine gusher sand on
the Powell structure, might make them worth anywhere
from $250.00 to $500.00 per unit during the few weeks
then ensuing, thereby causing the persons intended to be
defrauded to understand and believe that all the units of
the Corsicana-Mexia Oil Fields Syndicate had been sold,
and whereas, in truth and in fact, the defendant then and
there well knew all of the units of the Corsicana-Mexia
Oil Syndicate had not been sold, a large quantity were
then available for sale, and would be, and were later
offered for sale; that the Mexia-Powell Oil Syndicate had
not been organized to provide means whereby those who
were unable to secure an interest in the Powell structure
through stockholdings in the Corsicana-Mexia Oil Fields
Syndicate could secure such an interest, but had been
organized on January 10, 1922, six days prior to the
organization of the Corsicana-Mexia Oil Fields Syndicate,
and efforts had continuously been made to sell its stock or
units through a certain brokerage concern during all of

the intervening time and had proven unsuccessful, and the sale of the stock had been thrown back into the hands of the defendant.

That on September 22nd, defendant sent circular letters—September 22, 1922, offering the last offering of Fortuna at $20.00 a unit.

On December 1, 1922, defendant published progress report No. 2, about merging into the Admiral Oil Company.

A further particular that Johnson Oil Company, July 21, 1922, was continuing to make progress and trying to make new production; that the money paid in had been used for drilling. That, on the contrary, the defendant then and there well knew that all money received from the persons intended to be defrauded for stock of the Johnson Oil Company was not used for drilling operations, but large sums had been appropriated by the defendant to his own use and benefit; that no honest or economical effort had been made by the defendant to develop new production; that the company did not continue to make progress, but at the same time was on the verge of bankruptcy and did make a financial failure; that these statements were made by the defendant for the purpose of seduction and of inducing the persons to be defrauded to part with their money and property without receiving anything of value therefor.

The further particular that, on August 30, 1924, the defendant made the following representations in a circular letter and sent by mail, which letter begins with:

"FORTUNE SMILES—THEN SMILES AGAIN—ON THOSE WHO GRASP THEIR GREAT OPPORTUNITIES QUICKLY," and stresses an offering of a

number of units of the Powell Petroleum Company. That
was the offering of the Powell Petroleum Company,
whereas, in truth and in fact, as the defendant then and
there well knew, that he had no actual or tangible assurance that the said well would be brought in a real gusher
oil well or that it would produce oil in commercial quantities or at all, but, on the contrary, he knew that the prospects of this well finding oil in any commercial quantity,
or at all, had been disproven by the wells previously
drilled by him on adjacent properties which proved to be
dry holes and not oil producers; that there was no basis
in reason or in fact assuring the earnings of profits by
that company; that he made many other false and exaggerated and gross misrepresentations, pretenses and
promises too numerous to mention or to set forth.

That, gentlemen, is specified as the scheme to defraud.
Now, if you find that any of those things were done, it is
not necessary that you find that they were all done or
accomplished as a scheme to defraud, but if you find that
any of them were done with the intent to defraud, taken
in connection with the mailing of the letters to further
the scheme, it would be sufficient on which to base a conviction of the defendant.

That, on the 5th day of October, in the year 1922, at
Los Angeles, California, in the Southern District—that
is, within this judicial district—for the purpose of executing said scheme and artifice, the defendant caused to be
delivered by mail of the United States a certain letter to
F. J. Rappe—or Rappe, I do not recall how that was
pronounced—that was a letter on the stationery of the
Admiral Oil Company, dated October 2, 1922, directed
to F. J. Rappe, Los Angeles, California, with reference

to the Corsicana-Mexia Oil Fields Syndicate. It begins, you may remember:

"You are, according to the records, the owner and holder of one units of the Corsicana-Mexia Oil Fields Syndicate. In accordance with the communication of the Corsicana-Mexia Oil Fields Syndicate of this date, enclosed herewith, all Corsicana-Mexia unit holders are privileged to subscribe for stock of the Admiral Oil Company on the basis of one Corsicana-Mexia unit and $7.00 for 50 shares of stock of the Admiral Oil Company of the par value of $50.00," and so forth.

That is the first count of the indictment, the mailing of the Rappe letter. The second count of the indictment sets forth that on January 12, 1923, he mailed a letter to Mrs. Evelyne B. Boadway of Pasadena. You will remember that letter. It was with reference to—I will read a portion of it.

"Dear Mrs. Boadway:

"Will you pardon the delay in answering your letter which has been occasioned by the fact that I have been in the fields most of the time during the past thirty days.

"I am delighted now to be able to report to you a discovery of tremendous importance to the Powell structure where the Admiral Oil Company owns more than 2,500 acres of leases. The importance of this discovery to the Admiral Oil Company can hardly be over-estimated. I honestly believe that within the coming six or nine months these leases will attain a value of $10,000,000 to $25,-000,000."

Then, there was a special report enclosed, and references made to it.

"With this new development I am sure that you can pay the exchange fee and secure your Admiral stock with absolute certainty that you will not only get all of your original investment back, but within a few months' time will realize a very large profit indeed."

You will remember, I think—that is my recollection, and counsel of course are at liberty and I desire you to correct me if I make any inaccurate statements of the evidence, as we want to figure the thing over here so we will have a fair and a clear statement of facts—it seems to me, as I remember, that Mrs. Boadway wrote to the company, to the Admiral Company with reference to the necessity for the payment of this exchange fee, and this was a reply.

The third count sets forth the letter written under date January 31, 1923, on the stationery of the Admiral Oil Company to J. T. Junell, Cucamonga.

"We are in receipt of your letter of December 14th regarding your holdings in the Marine Oil Syndicate and the Mexia Terrace Oil Company.

"It is needless for us to say that we sympathize with you and regret in the deepest manner the unfortunate condition you no_ find yourself facing. We wish, however, to correct the wrong impression you are harboring as the trustees of the Marine Oil Syndicate and Mexia Terrace Oil Company were acting within their rights at the time they assigned the properties, assets, etc., to the Admiral Company. * * *

"We are willing to cooperate with you"—and then winds up:

"Owing to the important discovery recently made upon the south end of the Powell structure, the privilege of making the exchange will not remain open indefinitely and for that reason we advise you to give the matter your early attention."

I suppose that was in answer to a letter of inquiry written by Mr. Junell.

The fourth count charges that on March 26, 1923, a letter was mailed to Mr. Junell at Cucamonga, setting forth his account with the Admiral Oil Company, being billed, in effect, for this exchange fee.

"Unless certificates for your holdings of the old companies are forwarded to us for exchange for stock of the Admiral Oil Company on or before Saturday, April 7, 1923, you will forfeit all future rights to claim the privilege of making the exchange thereafter.

"If not convenient for you to make the exchange payment all in cash at this time, it may be paid one-third cash"—and so forth.

The fifth count sets forth a letter dated—or, rather, the statement of May 10, 1923, to H. W. Shafer of Pasadena, which is, in effect, a similar one to that sent to Mr. Junell of Cucamonga, an account asking his prompt attention, being the charge for the transfer fee.

The sixth count sets forth a letter under date of January 31, 1924, of the Admiral Oil Company to O. L. Hopkins, 2908 West Avenue 31, Los Angeles, California.

"It has been a long time since we have issued any reports on the Admiral Oil Company for the reason there has been nothing of importance to report, and it has been necessary for us to conserve every dollar. We now have in course of preparation, however, a complete report covering the operations of the past year and the outlook for the future," and so forth.

"Meanwhile, we will tell you that some of your holdings northeast of Powell now look remarkably good and there is little doubt that another great oil pool will be opened up in that area within the coming few weeks. We are going to try to finance an oil well on our Skiles lease at the earliest possible moment and we hope it will prove to be a tremendous producer. We have leases enough northeast of Powell to pull the Admiral Oil Company out in good shape, to pay back all the money ever invested in it, and leave the company in good financial condition if another pool is opened up in that territory similar to the pool south of Powell, and that seems now to be almost a certainty.

"We regret very much our inability to make a refund of the money which you sent us for payment of your investment with us. The unsuccessful drilling campaign launched by the Admiral Oil Company in the early part of 1923 has placed the company in such a financial condition that we have been only able to exist through Mr. Johnson's liberal cash advances until he is now practically without funds."

I do not know that I noticed that letter before, but I mean—well, if a fraudulent intent, if the jury are satisfied that a fraudulent intent has been proven, that letter would constitute an offense, and it might be inferred from it that its object was to seek to allay the fears of Mr. Hopkins. So far as soliciting any money, however, and asking for him to purchase, to go in deeper, it seems to be bare of anything on that kind, so that is for your consideration, however

MR. CANNON: Does your Honor want these suggestions we have as we go along, or at the conclusion of the charge?

THE COURT: As in regard to any statement of fact, not my own opinion of it, you see, but any statement of fact that I might make a mistake about in referring to I want to be corrected now.

Now, gentlemen, that in brief is the indictment in this case: that the defendant conceived and formed a plan to defraud, and the particulars of the plan are set forth at great length as I just stated to you, in fourteen different particulars. I did not number them, of course; that is not necessary. For instance, that he would organize this company and that he would secure leases at nominal value and turn them over to the syndicates or concerns at greatly enhanced values, and that he would then make these exaggerated statements for the purpose of leading the investors to invest their money, when he did not, in reality and in good faith, really believe that the chances were as he stated.

That it is not necessary that you find that all of these fourteen particulars have been supported by the evidence. Any one of them would be sufficient to, if you are satisfied that any one—that the evidence sustains any one of them, that would be sufficient on which to base a conviction with reference to that particular item. Now, the statute under which the indictment in this case is drawn provides that whoever, having devised or intending to devise any scheme or artifice to defraud, or of obtaining money or property by means of false or fraudulent representations or promises, shall, for the purpose of executing such scheme or artifice or attempting so to do, place or cause to be placed any letter, writing, circular, or advertisement, in any post office or authorized depository for mail matter, to be sent or delivered by the post office establishment of the United States, any such letter, circular or advertisement, shall be punished as provided in the statute.

The mailing of all of these letters by the defendant, the letters that are set forth in the six counts, is admitted. The responsibility of the defendant for all of the printed matter, and I think the mailing of them, some of them at least, of the Texas Oil Radio or Oil Bulletin and all of the printed advertising, that is all admitted.

By the finding of an indictment no presumption whatsoever arises to indicate that a defendant is guilty, or that he has any connection with, or responsibility for, the act charged against him. A defendant is presumed to be innocent at all stages of the proceeding until all of the evidence presented shows him to be guilty beyond a reasonable doubt. And this rule applies to every material element of the offense charged. Mere suspicion will not authorize a conviction. A reasonable doubt is such a doubt as you may have in your minds when, after fairly and impartially considering all of the evidence, you do not feel satisfied to a moral certainty of a defendant's guilt. In order that the evidence submitted shall afford proof beyond a reasonable doubt, it must be such as you would be willing to act upon in the most important and vital matters relating to your own affairs.

The misrepresentations and false claims charged against the defendant include not only such statements of present or existing facts, but also promises of large future profits. It is common knowledge that nothing is more alluring than the expectation of receiving large returns on small investments. Eagerness to take the chances of large gains lies at the foundation of many schemes to defraud, and, even when the matter of chance is eliminated, any scheme or plan which holds out the prospect of receiving more than is parted with appeals to the cupidity of all.

In the light of this, the statute must be read, and so read it includes everything designed to defraud by representations as to the past or present, or suggestions and promises as to the future. The significant fact is the intent and purpose. It was with the purpose of protecting the public against all such intentional efforts to despoil, and to prevent the post office from being used to carry them into effect, that this statute has been passed.

The offense contains two essential elements: First, that there shall be devised a scheme or artifice for the purpose of obtaining money or property by means of false pretenses; and, second, that for the purpose of executing such scheme, or attempting so to do, there shall be caused to be delivered by the United States mail, according to the direction thereon, a letter or postcard, writing or circular, which has theretofore been deposited in the United States mails, to be sent or delivered by the post office establishment. Both of these elements must be established before conviction is authorized. The words "scheme" and "artifice" as used in the statute, include any plan or course of action intentionally devised for the purpose of deceiving and tricking others, and thus fraudulently obtaining their money or property. It is not essen-

tial to the making out of the charge that the scheme or
artifice should have been successfully carried out, or that
the defendant made a profit on the venture.   Nor is it a
defense for a defendant so charged to show that the persons with whom he dealt and intended to deal received
some return for an investment of money, or that they
would have received some return for such investment.
It is essential only that it be shown that the scheme be
formed with a fraudulent intent.   It is necessary that the
government prove that the scheme or artifice employed by
the defendant was of the kind charged in the indictment.
It is not necessary that it be proved that the scheme and
artifice included the making of all of the alleged false
pretenses, representations and promises, but it is sufficient if any one or more of the same be proved to have
been made, and that the same were designed to and would
be reasonably effective in deceiving and defrauding persons with whom the defendant proposed to and did deal.

It is your duty first to determine whether there was
such a scheme as is charged in the indictment in this
case.   And in considering this case the jury are to start
with the presumption that there was no such scheme; that
the law presumes all transactions in a business are to be
fair and honorable; and if you find that there was such
a scheme, your finding must be based solely upon the evidence in the case, which must be sufficiently strong to
overcome the presumption against its existence, and convince you of its existence beyond a reasonable doubt; and
if you can account for all the facts and circumstances in
the case, which you believe to be established by the evidence in the case, upon any reasonable hypothesis consistent with the non-existence of such scheme, it will be

your duty to find that there was no such scheme, in which event it is your duty to find the defendant not guilty as charged in the indictment.

The good faith of the defendant or his bad faith in these matters is to be determined and his several acts and declarations construed and interpreted by the conditions existing at the time the statements or promises were made, as they appeared to him at the time and not by the final result of the enterprises or by their present condition or situation. The defendant is not on trial for evolving or devising an improvident or impractical scheme, even though you believe the plan to have been such. He is not on trial for errors of judgment. He is on trial for a criminal offense, an essential element of that offense is an evil or criminal intent which is incumbent upon the government to prove to your satisfaction and beyond all reasonable doubt and if under all the evidence, the government has failed to prove the existence of such evil or criminal intent in the mind of the defendant, then it is your duty to acquit him.

The law presumes that the defendant did not intend to defraud the persons who made purchases of stock or units of interest from the defendant, Gilbert S. Johnson, and this presumption of law is a matter of evidence and, has of itself sufficient force and effect to require the jury to find the defendant not guilty unless after fully and fairly considering all the evidence in the case you are convinced beyond all reasonable doubt and to a moral certainty that the defendant is guilty in a manner and form as charged in the indictment or in some one or more counts in the indictment.

It is essential that the letters and writing described in the respective counts in the indictment be shown to have been deposited in the United States mail, by the defendant or by his agents, for the purpose of being transmitted to others, and that he caused them to be delivered by mail to the persons to whom they were addressed. That, as I remarked to you before, is admitted, however, in this case. It is further essential that such letters and writings were intended by the defendant to be so transmitted and delivered in aid and furtherance of the unlawful scheme or artifice to defraud, if such you find there was. It is not necessary that it be shown that the contents of the letters or writings mailed were of a nature calculated to be effective in carrying out the fraudulent plan; it is sufficient if, having devised a scheme or artifice to defraud, the defendant deposited or caused to be deposited in the post office the letters or writings with the thought and intent that they would be delivered to the addressees to assist in carrying the scheme into effect.

If a man through no mistake or error uses written or printed matter containing statements of fact regarding the character, condition or uses of a thing he is selling, for the purpose of persuading a purchaser to buy, and where he has full opportunity to have read and known the contents of such written or printed matter, he cannot afterwards excuse his use thereof by asserting that he was ignorant of the contents of such written or printed documents.

You are the sole judges of the credibility of the witnesses who have testified upon this trial. A witness is presumed to speak the truth. This presumption, however, may be repelled by the manner in which he testified; by the character of his testimony, or by evidence affecting his character for truth, honesty and integrity or his motives; by contradictory evidence; also, by proof that he has at other times made statements inconsistent with his testimony.

In judging the credibility of the witnesses in this case, you may believe the whole or any part of the evidence of any witness, or may disbelieve the whole or any part of it, as may be dictated by your judgment as reasonable men. You should carefully scrutinize the testimony given, and in so doing consider all of the circumstances under which any witness has testified, his demeanor, his manner while on the stand, his intelligence, the relation which he bears to the government or to the defendant, the manner in which he might be affected by the verdict and the extent to which he is contradicted or corroborated by other evidence, if at all, and every matter that tends reasonably to shed light upon his credibility. If a witness is shown knowingly to have testified falsely on the trial touching any material matter, the jury should distrust his testimony in other particulars, and in that case you are at liberty to reject the whole of the witness' testimony.

The defendant has offered himself as a witness and has testified before you. Having done so, you are to estimate and determine his credibility in the same way as you would that of any other witness. It is proper to consider all of the matters that have been suggested to you in that connection, including the interest that the defendant may have in the case, his hopes and his fears, and what he has to gain or lose as a result of your verdict.

There is nothing peculiarly different in the way the jury is to consider the proof in a criminal case from that by which men give their attention to any question depending upon evidence presented to them. You are not limited in your consideration of the evidence to the bald expressions of the witnesses; you are authorized to draw such inferences from the facts and circumstances which you find have been proved as seem justified in the light of your experience as reasonable men. You are expected to use your good sense, consider the evidence for the purposes only for which it has been admitted, and in the light of your knowledge of the natural tendencies and propensities of human beings, resolve the facts according to deliberate and conscious judgment.

Any testimony as to which an objection was sustained and any testimony which was ordered stricken out must be wholly left out of your account and disregarded.

You understand that a reasonable doubt is not a mere possible or imaginary doubt or a bare conjecture, for it is difficult to prove a thing to an absolute certainty.

You are to consider the strong probabilities of the case. A conviction is justified only when such probabilities exclude all reasonable doubt as the same has been defined to you. Without it being restated or repeated, you are to understand that the requirement that a defendant's guilt be shown beyond a reasonable doubt is to be considered in connection with and as accompanying all the instructions that are given to you.

If the defendant, or his agents or employees, with the knowledge of the—if the defendant or if his agents or employees, with his knowledge, made false and fraudulent representations and assurances for the purpose of deceiving persons in respect to the true condition of the leases, assets, financial status and conditions of the trust estates and other organizations, the shares of stock of which the defendant was selling and offering for sale to the public, then in that event, you are instructed that the ultimate intent to make such representations and assurances good, or to make the business of the several organizations, whose shares of stock the defendant was selling, a success, would not furnish a legal excuse for such representations.

It is immaterial how confident the defendant may have been that oil or gas would be ultimately discovered on the leases of the various syndicates as represented and stated by the defendant, and it is immaterial if any such oil products were later discovered on the said leases, if the alleged representations were made for the purpose of getting money from persons purchasing said shares or stock of said trust estates or corporations and such representations were not true and the defendant knew, at the time that he made them, that they were not true.

No matter how seemingly fair and honest a scheme may appear, if the purpose of it is to defraud, it is within the statute.

The defendant cannot be convicted if all the testimony is as fairly consistent with his innocense as with his guilt; he cannot be convicted in the absence of an actual fraudulent intent, no matter how unsuccessful the enterprise may have been or how inconsistent it may have been with sound judgment.

If you should find that the advertising matter or statements of the defendant should contain some exaggerations, that does not constitute a scheme to defraud. The fact that one who advertises a business fails to make settlement with some of his creditors, the advertisements being substantially true, does not constitute a scheme to defraud.

The intent, you understand, is a question of fact at all times and must be found by you in the light of all of the evidence and beyond all reasonable doubt.

The intent of the defendant charged under the provisions of the law stated is a material element necessary to prove the offense, and in arriving at a decision upon that question all the facts and circumstances shown in the case as touching the conduct of the defendant should be considered. If a man shall make to another a representation as to things which do not exist, and it appears that he has no reasonable ground to believe that the fact is as he states it, such statements and conduct are to be taken into consideration in determining whether an innocent misstatement has been made in good faith, or whether the intent was that others were to be deceived and that the first person should reap a benefit and others suffer a loss. Criminal intent may be implied from the acts and conduct of the accused. His acts and his conduct, considered in their relation to the charge made, may establish satisfactorily a criminal intent, notwithstanding the declarations of a defendant that no such intent was present in his mind. If the statements alleged to have been falsely and fraudulently made by the defendant were made in good faith, and if the defendant believed at the time, or had reason to believe them to be true, they would not be evidence of a fraud. However, a reckless statement of a thing as a fact, of which the narrator is ignorant, and as to which he has no honest belief as to its truth, may be considered as a false representation within the meaning of the law applicable to this case.

You will remember that the defendant asserted that he believed, himself, every thing that was stated in the indictment—everything that was stated in all of the matters sent out; that he believed his sale of the stock to his various buyers would actually bring them profits; that the prospect of large values that the stock might make justified the investment, and though you may find from the evidence that the defendant did honestly believe that the sale of the stock he was trying to sell would result in profit to the buyers, still this honest belief of profit to the buyers is not a defense to this prosecution if you further believe from all of the evidence that the defendant, notwithstanding such belief, devised a scheme to defraud and used the mails in furtherance of such scheme, if in furtherance of this scheme he used the mails in making promises that he knew were false or that he did not have reasonable grounds to believe to be true, or made statements not warranted by the existing facts, then, notwithstanding any honest belief of profits to the buyers, he is guilty of the crime charged.

Of course, you will understand that, I think, I have stated before to you that no matter how visionary a scheme was, a man may advertise an entirely visionary scheme and that, to the ordinary mind, contains no chance of profit, still if he honestly and conscientiously believes that, then there is no intent, there is no false statement, there is no intent to deceive, but, of course, his belief is a very essential factor. His belief or lack of belief is a very essential factor in the case.

Now, with respect to these units, you will remember that some discussion was had of them. So far as I am advised, this system of selling in California is not pur-

sued. The unit system or the trust estate, or what is
known as the common law trust estate, is, in effect, a
partnership; that is, you, the defendant—not a partnership as defined in the California law, but the party offering the trust estate announces that he has a certain property and he invites others to participate with him, not in
buying stock in the corporation, but in buying units
which give to the parties buying the units actual ownership in the properties then found. That is a legitimate
system of business, in the state of Texas at least, and
there is no reflection on anybody for adopting such a
system. It, itself, does not give evidence of any dishonest motive. There are certain duties, however, which
one engages, that are important to be considered.

There is evidence in this case tending to prove that the
defendant, operating as a broker under the name of Gilbert Johnson & Company, entered into contracts with
several syndicates or companies of which he was the
promotor, organizer and dominant head, whereby Gilbert
Johnson & Company undertook to sell the units or shares
of these syndicates or companies. There is also evidence
tending to prove that in selling these units or shares to
the public a considerable proportion of the purchase price
paid by the public was absorbed by Gilbert Johnson &
Company as commissions or expenses or otherwise, so
that in many instances a comparatively small proportion
of the amount thus paid by the public actually went into
the treasury of the respective syndicates or companies
and became available for the development purposes for
which they were said to be organized. Further, it is the
contention of the government in this case that in soliciting
the public to purchase these shares or units the defendant

failed to disclose that a large proportion of the money paid for the same would not go to the syndicates or companies, but would be absorbed in commissions and other charges by the said brokerage concern of Gilbert Johnson & Company.

Now, I charge you that the payment of an exorbitant and unreasonable commission, not warranted by the financial conditions or necessities of the occasion and undisclosed to the parties interested, is fraudulent if, in your judgment, they are grossly excessive and are not so disclosed.

And I further charge you that when the shares or units of such concerns as are involved in this case are selling for much more than their par value, it should not require the payment of large commissions to dispose of them. If it does, the selling price must be altogether artificial and the inference may be made by the jury either that the company is fraudulent if the commission is not excessive, or that the commission is fraudulent if the company is what it purports to be. I further charge you that the promotor of a corporation or other similar concern, such as these syndicates, stand in a relation of trust toward those who are invited to purchase the shares or units, and he must deal fairly with them and must faithfully disclose all facts which might influence them in deciding upon the judiciousness of the purchase.

If, therefore, you find from the evidence, beyond a reasonable doubt, that the defendant knowingly so manipulated the several contracts, or any of them, whereby Gilbert Johnson & Company were to sell these units or shares with a commission so grossly excessive as to convince you that they are fraudulent, and the amount of such commissions or deductions was not disclosed to the purchasers of such units or shares, such a finding by you would make it necessary to find the defendant guilty of devising the scheme to defraud described in the indictment, if, at the same time, you find beyond a reasonable doubt that he did so with the intent to defraud, as I have already defined it to you. And having so found, if you further find that he used the mails to carry the fraudulent scheme into effect, as alleged in the indictment, it will then be your duty to find him guilty as charged.

You are instructed that a corporation or syndicate may lawfully pay a commission for selling its capital stock. The stock of an established corporation, having a ready sale on the market, may be sold at a profit on a small commission, while stock of a purely speculative character, having no standing on the market may only be sold through the greatest efforts, and upon a commission might seem excessive, so an individual or a corporation may by force of circumstances be compelled to pay what might seem an exorbitant rate of interest, or to give what might seem a large bonus in order to raise money in a particular emergency, and yet the agreement to pay the interest or give the bonus may be prompted by honest motives and by sound business judgment. For these reasons, each case must depend upon its own facts and circumstances, and the amount of the commission alone cannot be made the sole criterion of fraud.

Further with respect to this unit system: I have already charged you that it is unlawful for the promotor of a company or of a syndicate, such as those involved in this case, to make a profit by selling property to the syndicate at the time of organization without disclosing it to those who are invited to purchase its shares or units. This same rule of law applies to the president or trustee or other chief officer of the company or syndicate after its organization has been perfected. That is to say, the president or trustee or other chief officer is forbidden to make any profit by selling property to it without making the fullest disclosure not only to an independent board of trustees, but also to those who are solicited to purchase the shares. Such an officer stands in a trust relation to the company and he is bound to act faithfully in the interests of the company and of the stockholders and of the proposed stockholders. To make any undisclosed profit for himself is fraudulent and to solicit the public to purchase shares without fully informing them of such profit to himself is a fraud upon them. There is evidence in this case tending to prove that after the organization of several of these syndicates he sold them leases at a profit to himself personally without disclosing this fact to those he was inviting to buy stock. It is for you to determine, beyond a reasonable doubt, whether this is the fact and if you so find, you would be warranted in finding that he devised the scheme to defraud described in the indictment.

You are instructed, gentlemen, that the good character of a person accused of a crime, when proven, for the traits involved in the charge—in this case, for honesty and integrity—is itself a fact in the case. It must be considered in connection with all the other facts and circumstances adduced in evidence on the trial, and if, after such consideration, the jury are not satisfied beyond a reasonable doubt, of the defendant's guilt, you should acquit him. If, however, you are satisfied from all the evidence in the case, that the defendant is guilty, you are to convict him, notwithstanding proof of good character. In the Federal courts, there is no presumption that the defendant is of good character. Neither is it presumed that he is of bad character.

Respecting the evidence introduced by the defendant of what is known as "character evidence" or evidence of "good character," particularly as to his honesty and fair dealing with his fellow men, and also as to his veracity and truthfulness, you are instructed that the law is: That good character, when considered in connection with the other evidence in the case, may create a reasonable doubt. The circumstances may be such that an established reputation for good character, if it is relevant to the issue, (and *is* is of especial value in cases like the one at bar, where the element of intent to defraud is involved) such evidence would alone create a reasonable doubt, although without the other evidence would be convincing.

Such, gentlemen, is what the Court has deemed advisable to explain to you in reference to the law in this case.

There are certain other observations I desire to make in a general way and with reference to the case, and which you are to understand, even though or if any intimation as to my belief or disbelief in certain evidence is given, it does not control you, because you are the sole judges of the facts. The law itself is that which prohibits the United States Post Office system from being used in furtherance of a fraud or fraudulent schemes, but knowledge is very general that there is such a law. It is one of the wisest laws, to my mind, that is on the statute books. The Post Office Department or system by which, at a very nominal and trifling expense, information and knowledge is disseminated, newspapers are sent, books and periodicals that enlighten the human mind, is a great civilizer; it is a great factor in civilization. In fact, I have always thought it is the most important factor. The ability of people freely to communicate their thoughts and ideas—that is promoted in a singular and extremely striking way by the United States Post Office Department, and as far as that goes, by the universal Postal Union which covers all the civilized countries of the earth, and it is a thing that may well challenge the imagination of any man that any one person on the face of the earth within reasonable limits is able to communicate with any other person. Now, so zealously does the government guard that system, that it has passed this law; and, obviously, while it is a thing of great interest and of great benefit generally, it is right, and I sympathize with the law, which says that it shall not be used to promote any fraud. That is the reason, then, why such a law is passed and why we must zealously protect it. I am not intimating that this defendant has violated it, or anything of that kind.

The defendant himself comes before us here and he says he believed all of the statements made in these Bulletins or letters here admitted. He says that he believes everything—at the time, that he believed everything in all of these Bulletins. Now, that is really the vital question in this case, whether he did or not.

You will remember that the defendant—apparently, he must have been a very young man, started in the town of Goldfield, promoting, according to his own admissions, promoting enterprises similar to this, and through the course of a good many years, he says that he has been selling stocks by means of the United States mails. He even condemns the government for interfering with his scheme, in some of the circulars, in which you will remember that he criticized the government and the postal authorities for interfering. He explained, I think, to some of the investors that except for the pernicious activity of the postal officials the enterprise would have continued.

Now, no prejudice is to be entertained against one who does that, because the advertising of goods is legitimate. It is done all the time, and within certain limits a person has a right to what is known, "to puff his wares." That is very true. The fact, however, that the defendant says he believed all these things that were stated, does not necessarily control you in your judgment. You do not have to believe that if I am caught in the act of setting fire to a house and I say to the officer, "Well, I did not intend to burn that house," he does not have to believe that, and probably would not. Therefore, if you are convinced that the defendant could not have believed many of the things that he advertised, then, of course, that is enough to overcome his claim that it was innocent on his part. There is evidence here that at one time he advertised that he had a certain lease and it would be the general understanding among oil people that all leases are subject to a royalty payment; that is the general understanding—and the Court will take note of that—among oil men, so by saying that he owned a lease, that implies the owning of a lease subject to a royalty payment. That is all right. This defendant, however, did not say he owned only a one-half interest in it. Now, and, by the way, the defendant was to claim that certain explanations were made in some of his publications. So far, however, I have no recollection of any evidence of that fact, so it stands before you uncontradicted that he gave the customers to understand that he owned the leases, whereas, in fact, he owned only one-half of it. Now, that might be an oversight; it might have been unintentional. To my mind, that is not so very flagrant, but it is illustrative. They say that "straws tell which way the wind blows." Now, it might be that the defendant did not consider that extremely important, but he was used to make reckless statements. That is an element that you may consider properly in this case, that there were extravagant statements made. Of course, there is no denying that. For instance, I think it was yesterday afternoon, something was shown here where it was said that a big gusher was absolutely assured, a big gusher absolutely assured. Now, it is difficult, gentlemen of the jury, to reconcile that with honest belief in anybody. "Assured" means, as we all know, "sure," "That it was sure;" and it is significant, gentlemen, that every single one of these statements contains an invitation to buy stock; every single one without exception, so far as I remember, is an invitation to buy stock—not only an invitation, but an urgent invitation. Well, now, the defendant might have been entirely innocent; he might have honestly believed that, but his honest belief is not sufficient unless the facts warranted him in expressing such belief, unless his information and facts warranted him.

The evidence in this case shows that from the very beginning this defendant pursued a consistent line of advertising, and I will not, I think go too strong in calling it extravagant advertising. It is a little singular, gentlemen, that if he was honest in his belief, that that continued. Here is the Texas Oil Radio of December 6, 1924; and another Texas Oil Radio of February 20, 1925: "Quick Pay Off For Premier Stockholders."

Well, so far as I can see, they are along the same line. Now, all I desire to observe is, that if this defendant throughout those years from 1918—was it?

MR. CANNON: 1919.

MR. PRATT: 1919.

THE COURT: —1919 until 1925 believed, and after the repeated failures of the geologists, or mistakes of the geologists upon whom he relied, if the repeated failures— according to the evidence in this case, every investor lost everything that he put in, with the exception of those who sold at a time when there was a chance of profit, now, gentlemen, that fact is not to determine you at all because, as I explained repeatedly, the fact that people lose money in a scheme is not any necessary proof of any crookedness, of falsehood or scheme to defraud, but I spoke of it only in connection with the observation that I am about to make: that if, throughout that series of years, almost six years—at least five years—he still believed and invited the public to join him, certainly he had strong faith. His faith is strong.

The vital question, gentlemen, for you to determine is whether this defendant was honest in these various representations..

JUROR H. LEWIS HAYNES: Your Honor, may I ask a question?

THE COURT: Yes, sir.

JUROR HAYNES: If it is proper, I would like to have you clarify to me the distinction between "a particular" and "a count", which you refer to in that indictment.

THE COURT: A what?

JUROR HAYNES: A particular and a count, which you spoke of in the indictment; you refer to fourteen particulars and six counts, I believe. I do not understand the difference.

THE COURT: Well, I will go over that again. That was probably due to my confusion or inaccuracies in my statement. The indictment charges first, that he conceived and formed a plan to defraud; that Gilbert Johnson did devise a scheme to defraud, and it was, in substance, as follows:—Now, here follow fourteen particulars in which, according to the indictment and the position of the Government, are constituted and made up the scheme to defraud. The instruction was that not all of those particulars constituting the scheme to defraud need to be proven; any of them relating to the letters that were sent would be sufficient. Then, in the last or fourteenth particular, that is divided up into, I think there are twenty-six letters in the alphabet—well, this runs up to L or runs up to O. That made subdivisions of that fourteenth; that it was further a part of the scheme and artifice to defraud, that the defendant would make fraudulent, false pretenses and promises to the person intended to be defrauded, through and by means of divers circular letters, pamphlets, newspapers, and house organs, publicly circulated and intended to be circulated in effect and substance, as follows: Then they detail the various—

JUROR HAYNES: A count, then, is just a subdivision under a particular?

THE COURT: Yes.

JUROR HAYNES: Thank you.

THE COURT: I suppose I used it, although that is not particularly a legal term.

JUROR MARK H. POTTER: There is one thing that has bothered me all the way through this case, and that is: Why the Government brought this case here to California and it was not tried in Texas.

THE COURT: The law is that a case of this kind may be prosecuted anywhere that the letter is received, either where the letter is received or where it is·sent from. There is no objection to that statement, I believe?

MR. PRATT: Correct.

MR. CANNON: Both where it is mailed and received.

THE COURT: Now, the reason why this is prosecuted in California, I do not know, but, gentlemen, let me admonish you that under your oath as jurors you are not to be influenced by anything of that sort. Your oath as jurors requires you to judge this case under the instructions of the Court, and you are expressly instructed that whether the case is prosecuted in Texas or in California is no affair of the jury whatever. You are to bring in your verdict in accordance with these instructions and according to the evidence—yes, in accordance with the instructions. Now, gentlemen, I seem to have taken considerably more time than I anticipated in this charge, that I thought could be given satisfactorily in the first half hour, but it was not.

Here is a form of verdict, where you are satisfied as to whether he is guilty or not guilty, and as applying to each of the six counts, and your unanimous verdict, you understand, is required. You will choose one of your members as foreman.

Are there exceptions to the charge?

MR. PRATT: I want to make this suggestion, if the Court please.

THE COURT: Yes, sir.

MR. PRATT: I am wondering if the juror who inquired as to the difference between a particular and a count has been confused, and may I state it?

THE COURT: Yes, you may.

MR. PRATT: That in this indictment, the defendant is charged with devising a scheme to defraud, and in several counts, namely, in six different counts, he is charged with causing the delivery of a specific letter to carry that scheme into effect. The scheme itself, as described in the indictment, has numerous features which the Court mentioned as various particulars, but it is one scheme. Then he is charged with what is the gist of the offense, namely, the use of the mails, causing a letter to be delivered in furtherance of that scheme. That is the first count. And in the successive counts, the same scheme is adopted and separate letters in each count are described as having been caused to be delivered in furtherance of it. I make that suggestion to perhaps clarify it in the minds of the jury.

THE COURT: Yes, I think your suggestion is quite kindly, and I assume that the Jury understand that the indictment charges the scheme to defraud. It gives a great many particulars, as I explained to you, which constitute what the scheme was. That is all.

JUROR TROY V. COX: Your Honor, are we to designate a decision on each count?

THE COURT: Each count of the indictment, yes, one, two, three, four, five, six.

MR. CANNON: May I have an exception to that? I would like to take some exceptions, if the Court please, to the Court's charge. I will state for the benefit of the Jury and for the Court, that insofar as defendant is concerned, we are willing to admit if he is guilty on any one of the counts, he is guilty on them all.

THE COURT: Now, wait a minute. If you have any exceptions to make, you make them. Strike out the statements of the counsel, and gentlemen of the Jury, you are instructed to disregard any statements of counsel and exceptions that counsel is about to make to the charge are merely formal matters and for his own protection; and you are under no conditions to regard them for any purpose whatever. Now, proceed and take your exceptions.

MR. CANNON: I would like to take an exception to the Court's remark as being prejudicial at this time. If the Court please, I desire at this time, without particularizing, unless your Honor requires me to do it, the refusal or failure of the Court to give each and every of the requested instructions prepared and submitted to your Honor by the defendant's counsel, and take the exceptions to each one of those particular requested instructions that were refused.

I also take exception to the Court's instruction with respect to the trust estates, and particularly to the effect that the trust estates constituted a partnership, either under the law of this State or under the law of any other State.

I also take exception to the Court's instruction with respect to the duty devolving upon Mr. Johnson and upon the other trustees of these various syndicates, in the Court's holding under the instructions that there was any obligation on his part to disclose the full amount of the commission, was that he was receiving any commission or any profit from dealing with the particular syndicates themselves, in view of the fact that the declarations of trust themselves provided that he can so do.

I except to the instructions of the Court with respect to the nature of the declaration of trust, in view of the fact that it seems to me—

MR. PRATT: I object to the statement of counsel, in view of the fact that it is not the time and place for him—

THE COURT: Yes, just confine yourself to the exceptions.

MR. CANNON: I am willing to make a blanket exception to the whole thing, except—

THE COURT: All right; then, make it.

MR. CANNON: —except the fact, if the Court please, the Courts, as I understand them, require me to particularize in what respects I object to the charge; and that is all I am attempting to do.

THE COURT: No, I do not agree with you, counsel, there. I think you protect your rights fully when you note the exception to that portion of the charge specified.

MR. CANNON: All right. I except to the Court's instruction with respect to the operations of the defendant with respect to his Goldfield operations, as being similar to those charged in this indictment, it not being mentioned in the indictment.

I also object and take an exception—of course, I take an exception in the last remark I made.

I also take an exception to the Court's suggestion that it will be sufficient under the law to find any one of the elements of the alleged scheme as set out in the indictment would be sufficient; that is, if the Jury finds any one of those particulars éxist, that that would be sufficient to sustain the charge laid in the indictment, so far as the devising of the scheme is concerned.

THE COURT: Well, there may be some confusion in that. That was qualified or followed by the statement that any one was sufficient to base a conviction on the count in the indictment relating to it.

MR. CANNON: I take an exception to that modified charge.

THE COURT: Very well.

MR. CANNON: May I state what my idea of the law is on it?

THE COURT: No, no; you are absolutely prohibited from doing that, according to my understanding of the correct practice.

MR. DAVIS: Pardon me, your Honor. Under the rules of this Court, I believe that exceptions to each request offered is sufficient, but I think in relation to those matters that the Court gives of his own motion, I think the rule requires that the portion excepted to be pointed out.

THE COURT: Yes.

MR. DAVIS: And the reasons for the exception stated. That refers to the instructions given by the Court of his own motion.

THE COURT: My understanding is: That the exception is sufficient when it specifies that portion excepted to. If the Government suggests the other course, however, I will allow it.

MR. CANNON: Now, I am in a quandary. Shall I state my idea of what the law is with respect to the establishment of that scheme?

THE COURT: That would seem to involve it, if that is the position of the Government.

MR. DAVIS: Now, your Honor, I do not understand it that way.

MR. CANNON: All right.

THE COURT: The reasons must necessarily involve that.

MR. DAVIS: Yes, the reason why—I think the rule is very quickly obtained here, may be very easily obtained —but my recollection of the rule is that where exceptions are made to the instructions given by the Court of his own motion, without being requested by either the defendant or the plaintiff, in relation to that instruction counsel is entitled to state and must, in fact, state the grounds upon which he bases that exception. I do not understand that to mean that he is entitled to argue the law, on it.

MR. CANNON: I am not going to argue it.

THE COURT: Very well, if the Government takes that position, we are compelled to follow it, of course. Proceed.

MR. CANNON: Do I understand I am to state what my objection is to that particular instruction?

THE COURT: Yes, you may state what your objection is.

MR. CANNON: My objection to that particular instruction is that the finding of a scheme to exist, on only one of these particulars mentioned in the indictment, would not be sufficient, but the Jury, before passing to the consideration as to the mailing of these letters must first find there was a scheme to defraud, substantially as laid in the indictment.

I take exception to the Court's charge—

MR. PRATT: Now, may I be permitted—

THE COURT: Do not interrupt counsel. Let him go on.

MR. CANNON: I take exception to the Court's charge with respect to the collection and the payment of excessive commissions, as being a fraud as a matter of law, it being a question for the Jury to determine. And the same with respect to the Court's instruction with respect to undisclosed profits being realized by Mr. Johnson as being a matter of law a fraud, as set out in the indictment.

I take exception to the Court's comment upon the facts in the case, as being unfair and prejudicial to the defendant, and particularly to the Court's comment with respect to the owning of a certain lease and the Court's comments with respect to the failure of the defendant to show a correction of any such statement contained in the literature. And, I furthermore, take exception to the Court's comments on the facts and the analogy or the example which the Court gave with respect to the commission of arson, or the burning of a building, and particularly in that kind of a case the matter of intent of the defendant is not involved, and an example of that kind being prejudicial to the rights of the defendant, whereas, the matter of intent to defraud is the very crux of this case.

And then, I also except to the Court's remarks with respect to the course of conduct of the operations of the defendant generally, and particularly with respect to his having made these reckless or extravagant statements as designated by the Court, over a course of five years.

THE COURT: With respect to the instruction as to the scheme to defraud, before a conviction can be had, the letter described in each count of the indictment must be found by you to have been written in furtherance of the scheme to defraud. That, of necessity, will require you to find the existence of a scheme to defraud, with reference to the subject matter of that letter. You understand that, of course.

Swear the officer.

(Whereupon an officer was sworn to take charge of the Jury.)

THE COURT: You will now retire, gentlemen of the Jury.

(Whereupon the Jury retired from the Court to consider of their verdict.)

THE COURT: Is there something?

MR. PRATT: If the Court please, are the exhibits to go to the Jury?

THE COURT: The exhibits are so numerous they need not go to the Jury unless they ask for them. There is nothing further. Recess until the return of the Jury.

(Whereupon a recess was taken.)

LOS ANGELES, CALIFORNIA, WEDNESDAY, DECEMBER 3, 1930, 2 P. M.

———

(The Jury returned into the Courtroom.)

THE COURT: Gentlemen of the Jury, I have been advised that you desire further instructions.

A JUROR: Your Honor, we seem to be somewhat obscured on several points of the instructions. Is it possible for us to have a copy of your instructions regarding the defining of the weight of the evidence in the case?

THE COURT: Regarding the—

THE JUROR: Confining our deliverations to the evidence in the case—perhaps that would be a better way to put it.

THE COURT: Well, I am not quite clear on just what you want. You say, "regarding the confining of your deliberations to the evidence?"

THE JUROR: Yes, sir. At least, you could repeat it orally, I think, would be enough in that case.

THE COURT: Yes.

THE JUROR: And, furthermore, would you give us your instructions regarding the intent in the case, if you did give us any instructions as to what the intent must be, and how it must be proved.

THE COURT: Well, very well. I cannot recall any instructions specifically directed to confining or basing your verdict upon the evidence in this case. That, of course, goes without saying that it is your duty to confine your decision to the evidence before you. Now, for illustration, a question was asked about the bringing of the indictment in this State instead of somewhere else. The instruction was that that was an immaterial matter so far as you were concerned, and you should not consider it. You are not to be influenced by any of your feelings, either for or against, for instance, the system of advertising, and you are to arrive at your verdict solely, gentlemen, from the evidence adduced before you, not from any impressions, feelings, or, it might be, prejudices that you have that have not been caused by the evidence in the case. Do I make myself clear on that point, in your judgment?

A JUROR: You do to me.

THE COURT: Now, with respect to what constitutes or what will constitute intent or what will enable you or assist you in finding what the intent was, you must arrive at what you deem to be the intent from the whole evidence in the case, gentlemen, from all of the evidence. not from any one particular fact. It is not out of place to say in matters of this kind which involve fraud, and you will recall that the instructions were that fraud is very often produced or proven, rather, indirectly. In other words, no one admits or says expressly that he has committed a fraud, and if such actions were done that the necessary result of the actions were fraudulent, however, that is a fraud, as though it were expressly proven that fraud was expressly intended. The whole matter, gentlemen, revolves around the proposition of false representations. If the defendant intended to convey a false impression for the purpose of securing money, that is determinative of the case, if you find that to be the case. If the defendant in this case attempted by his letters, by his circulars to give anything other than true and correct knowledge of the situation, that would be sufficient on which to base a judgment of fraudulent intent.

A JUROR: Will your Honor repeat the instructions as to whether—as to the outcome having any bearing on the case, the outcome of the suit?

THE COURT: Yes, the outcome of the suit has no bearing on the case. gentlemen, in my judgment. In other words, even though some of these investments might have produced vast returns to the investors, if, at the time the defendant made false statements regarding them, he would still be guilty. That is the law in this matter.

If you think you are satisfied, you can again retire.

MR. ARTERBERRY: If your Honor please, I duly take exception to your Honor's instructions on the question of the false representations, and suggest that your Honor charge the Jury in lieu thereof, that false representations must be fraudulently made knowingly, and made with a fraudulent intent. A man may make a misrepresentation unintentionally and based on the information he has, and be in entirely good faith, and we desire that your Honor so instruct the Jury.

THE COURT: You are instructed, gentlemen, that these additional instructions are given you together with all the other instructions. I certainly think that you understand that intent must accompany everything. You understand that, of course; that is the general principal as to all crimes, and I am very sure the Jury understand that intent always must be proven in fact. The intent is the intentional—things having been intentionally done, are really the foundation of the case. There might be this to call to your attention, however. Certain of these Bulletins were sent out and the statements in them the defendant denied knowledge of. Defendant cannot deny knowledge of what was done under his direction. It was all done by his employees. That is about the only room or occasion I could see for any particular question on intent, Mr. Arterberry.

MR. ARTERBERRY: One point, if your Honor please: You will recall that the defendant testified that he received certain information from the driller of the well in Desdemona when your Honor asked him on cross-examination about the "well being assured." The driller told him he was then in the pay sand and he had a well, and he made his representations based on that. Now, if the defendant in good faith and honestly made that representation based on that, he is entitled to the benefit of that.

THE COURT: Well, the defendant, of course, must have been justified from his knowledge of the situation. The fact that he believed it to be true, would not exonerate him unless he believed it on a sufficient foundation or evidence.

A JUROR: Several of the jurors want to know if there is any objection to having all of your instructions in the jury room.

THE COURT: The situation with that, gentlemen, is this: The instructions are supposed to be—well, no, I will not say "are supposed to be." In charges given you, it is not always written. In this case, it is not; it was made up practically from fragments, as we went along, and it would not be possible to give you the entire charge. It seems to me, however, that your finding is, from necessity, confined to a rather narrow compass; that is, to the good faith of the defendant in making the representations that he did.

You will now retire again under the control of the bailiff and consider further of your verdict.

(Whereupon the Jury retired from the courtroom.)

THE COURT: Recess until the report of the Jury.

To John S. Pratt, Esq., Special Assistant to Attorney General, and to P. V. Davis, Esq., Assistant to United States Attorney:

SIRS: You will please take notice that the foregoing constitutes and is the proposed Bill of Exceptions of the defendant, Gilbert S. Johnson, in the above entitled action and that the defendant will ask the allowance of the same.

DATED this..............day of March, 1931.

David H. Cannon

H. L. Arterberry

Attorneys for the above named defendant.

IT IS HEREBY STIPULATED that the foregoing Bill of Exceptions is correct and that the same be settled and allowed by the Court.

David H. Cannon

H. L. Arterberry

Attorneys for said Defendant.

John S. Pratt   By P. V. Davis

Special Assistant to Attorney General

P. V. Davis

Assistant to United States Attorney

Attorneys for Plaintiff

Copy hereof received this 25 day of March, 1931.

John S. Pratt   By P V D

Special Assistant to Attorney General.

P. V. Davis

Assistant to United States Attorney

Attorneys for Plaintiff

The foregoing bill of exceptions is hereby approved and allowed.

July 31st, 1931.

Geo. Cosgrave
U. S. DISTRICT JUDGE

[Endorsed]: Lodged Mar 31 1931 R. S. Zimmerman, Clerk By F. Betz Deputy Clerk

[Endorsed]: Filed Aug 1 1931 R. S. Zimmerman, Clerk By Edmund L. Smith Deputy Clerk

———

[TITLE OF COURT AND CAUSE.]

ORDER.

On motion of counsel for defendant for an extension of time within which to file the proposed Bill of Exceptions, and good cause appearing therefor:

IT IS THEREFORE ORDERED BY THE COURT that the time be extended to and including February 15, 1931, for filing the proposed Bill of Exceptions.

DATED THIS 22nd day of January, 1931.

Geo. Cosgrave
United States District Judge.

[Endorsed]: Filed Jan 23 1931 5 P M R. S. Zimmerman, Clerk By L B Figg Deputy Clerk

———

[TITLE OF COURT AND CAUSE.]

ORDER.

On motion of counsel for defendant for an extension of time within which to file the proposed Bill of Exceptions and extending the time for filing and docketing the transcript of the record in the above styled case in the United States Circuit Court of Appeals for the Ninth Circuit, and good cause appearing therefor:

IT IS THEREFORE ORDERED BY THE COURT that the time be extended to and including January 22, 1931, for filing the proposed Bill of Exceptions, and that the time required for the defendant to file, record and docket the case in the United States Circuit Court of Appeals, be and it is hereby extended to and including February 20, 1931.

DATED this 22nd day of December, 1930.

Geo. Cosgrave
United States District Judge.

O. K.

  P. V. Davis

    Asst U. S. Atty

[Endorsed]: Filed Dec 22 1930　R. S. Zimmerman, Clerk　By W E Gridley　Deputy Clerk

---

[TITLE OF COURT AND CAUSE.]

ORDER EXTENDING TIME FOR FILING BILL OF EXCEPTIONS

For satisfactory reasons appearing and upon motion of David H. Cannon, Esq. one of the attorneys for the above named appellant

IT IS HEREBY ORDERED, that the term and time for the signing and sealing of the bill of exceptions herein, as the same may be settled and signed, be, and the same is hereby extended for thirty (30) days after date hereof, and that whenever so settled and signed, the said bill of exceptions herein shall stand as settled, signed and filed, and made a part of the record herein, as of the 4 day of December, 1930, which 4 day of December, 1930 is within the original time allowed under the rules of this Court for the presenting, signing and filing of said bill of exceptions herein; and the United States shall have thirty (30) days after service of the bill of exceptions in which to submit amendments.

Dated this 14th day of February, 1931

Geo. Cosgrave

Judge

[Endorsed]: Filed Feb 13 1931 R. S. Zimmerman, Clerk By L B Figg Deputy Clerk

---

[TITLE OF COURT AND CAUSE.]

ORDER EXTENDING TIME FOR FILING BILL OF EXCEPTIONS

For satisfactory reasons appearing and upon motion of H. L. Arterberry, Esq., one of the attorneys for the above named appellant,

IT IS HEREBY ORDERED, that the term and time for the signing and sealing of the bill of exceptions herein, as the same may be settled and signed, be, and the same is hereby extended for thirty (30) days after date hereof, and that whenever so settled and signed, the said bill of exceptions herein shall stand as settled, signed and filed, and made a part of the record herein, as of the 4th day of December, 1930, which 4th day of December, 1930, is within the original time allowed under the rules of this Court for the presenting, signing and filing of said bill of exceptions herein; and the United States shall have thirty (30) days after service of the bill of exceptions in which to submit amendments.

DATED this 10th day of March, 1931.

Geo. Cosgrave
Judge.

O. K.
P. V. Davis
Asst U. S. Atty

[Endorsed]: Filed Mar 17 1931 R. S. Zimmerman, Clerk By Edmund L. Smith Deputy Clerk

---

[TITLE OF COURT AND CAUSE.]

ORDER

ON MOTION of the appellee in the above entitled cause, and good cause appearing therefor, the said appellee is granted to and including June 20, 1931 in which to file any proposed Amendments to the Bill of Exceptions herein, which it may desire to offer and submit.

DATED this 22nd day of May, 1931.

Geo. Cosgrave
U. S. DISTRICT JUDGE.

[Endorsed]: Filed May 22 1931 R. S. Zimmerman, Clerk By Francis E Cross, Deputy Clerk

---

[TITLE OF COURT AND CAUSE.]

ORDER EXTENDING TIME FOR FILING PROPOSED AMENDMENTS TO BILL OF EXCEPTIONS.

On motion of counsel for the United States of America, and good cause appearing therefor, the said United States of America, appellee herein is granted an extension of time for the period of thirty days from and after date hereof in which to file and serve proposed amendments to the Bill of Exceptions herein.

Dated: this 23d day of April, 1931.

Geo. Cosgrave
United States District Judge.

O. K. as to form

H L Arterberry,
Atty for Deft.

Filed Apr 23 1931 R. S. Zimmerman, Clerk By Francis E. Cross. Deputy Clerk

---

[Title of Court and Cause.]

PETITION FOR APPEAL

Comes now said Gilbert S. Johnson, petitioner, the defendant in the above entitled cause, and respectfully shows that a verdict of guilty was returned against him by a jury on the indictment in said cause, and judgment and sentence were pronounced by the District Court of the United States for the Southern District of California, Central Division, on the 15th day of December, 1930, upon said verdict against your petitioner, adjudging your petitioner guilty under a violation of Section 215 of the Penal Code of the United States, as charged on Count 1 of said indictment, and sentencing him to imprisonment in the United States Penitentiary at McNeil's Island, in the State of Washington for——4 years on said Count 1, and to pay a fine of $1,000.00 on said Count, and your petitioner respectfully shows that in said judgment and the proceedings had prior thereto in the above entitled cause, certain errors were committed to the prejudice of your petitioner, all of which will more in detail appear in the assignment of errors which is filed in this court by your petitioner, together with this petition.

WHEREFORE, your petitioner, the said Gilbert S. Johnson, prays that an appeal may be allowed him from said judgment to the Circuit Court of Appeals of the United States, Ninth Judicial Circuit, and that said appeal may be made a supersedeas upon the filing of a bond to be fixed by the Court; that the petitioner may be admitted to bail pending the determination of the appeal in said court, and that all further proceedings in said District Court may be suspended and stayed, and that all further necessary orders and processes may be made or issued to the end that on appeal the errors complained of may be corrected by said Circuit Court of Appeals for the Ninth Circuit of the United States, and that said judgment and sentence may be set aside and held for naught.

Your petitioner further prays that a citation in due form of law may issue requiring the United States of America, the respondent in said appeal, to appear in said United States Circuit Court of Appeals for the Ninth Circuit, and then and there to make answer to the assignment of errors made by your petitioner upon the record in the proceedings in said cause; and the said petitioner herewith presents his assignment of errors in accordance with the rules of said United States Circuit Court of Appeals, and the course and practise in this Honorable Court.

Your petitioner further prays the Court to grant him leave to file an amended assignment of errors within thirty days after said bill of exceptions has been settled, signed and filed in said District Court.

Gilbert S. Johnson,

Defendant.

[TITLE OF COURT AND CAUSE.]

ASSIGNMENT OF ERRORS

Comes now Gilbert S. Johnson, defendant in the indictment in the above entitled cause, and in connection with his Petition for Appeal herein, says that in the record and proceedings prior to and during the trial of the above entitled cause in said District Court error has intervened to his prejudice, and makes the following assignment of errors, which he, the said defendant, avers occurred in the trial of said cause, to-wit:

I.

Said District Court erred in denying and overruling the Motion to Quash the indictment herein and in requiring the defendant to plead thereto upon each and all of the grounds set out in the said Motion to Quash on file herein.

II.

Said District Court erred in overruling the objection of the defendant to the introduction of any testimony in support of said indictment and which said Motion was based upon each and all of the grounds set out in said written Motion to Quash on file herein and which objection was made by the defendant after the jury in said cause had been sworn to try the cause and before the introduction of any testimony in said cause, and which said ruling of the Court in overruling said objection was duly and regularly excepted to.

III.

The said District Court erred in failing and refusing to give the following instruction which was requested by the defendant:

"If there was no scheme to defraud devised by the defendant, then the defendant is not guilty and should be acquitted. In order to warrant a conviction of the defendant, you must find and believe from the evidence that the defendant devised a scheme to defraud within the meaning of the law, and in this connection you are instructed that in order to establish a scheme to defraud, the Government must establish that the necessary effect of carrying the scheme mentioned in evidence into effect was to defraud the persons buying stock or units of interest out of their money or property and that the defendant knew that said alleged scheme would necessarily have that effect, and unless the Government has proved that such was the necessary effect of the things that the defendant did and the defendant had knowledge that such was the necessary effect of his activities, then the evidence is insufficient to establish a scheme to defraud and it is your duty to acquit him, without considering any other feature of the charge in the indictment or the evidence offered in the case."

IV.

The said District Court erred in failing and refusing to give the following instruction which was requested by the defendant:

"The Court charges the jury that a false promise, such as the statute describes, is a promise—not merely one that is not fulfilled—but a promise that it is known at the time that it is made that it is not going to be fulfilled, or else a promise that is impossible of performance. Merely because a promise is made and not kept would not warrant you in concluding that the party making that promise had a criminal intent, or warrant you in finding him guilty because you may believe he made a promise which was not fulfilled.

V.

The said District Court erred in failing and refusing to give the following instruction which was requested by the defendant:

"The defendant cannot be convicted unless you believe beyond all reasonable doubt that he made false representations with the intent to defraud. An incorrect statement, grossly misrepresenting facts, does not amount to fraud in law, unless the false representations were knowingly and willfully made with fraudulent intent."

VI.

The said District Court erred in failing and refusing to give the following instruction which was requested by the defendant:

"It is common knowledge that most business enterprises are aided by advertisements passing through the mails, and at every hand we see claims of capacity, performance, and results which we know cannot stand cross-examination. Parties who have anything to sell have the habit of puffing their wares, and we are all familiar with the fact that it is a very prevalent thing in the course of business to exaggerate the merits of goods people have to sell, and within any proper, reasonable bounds, such a practice is not criminal. It must amount to a substantial deception."

VII.

The said District Court erred in failing and refusing to give the following instruction which was requested by the defendant:

"You are instructed that a man may be visionary in his plans and believe that they will succeed, and yet, in spite of their ultimate failure be incapable of committing a conscious fraud. If you believe that the defendant in this case really entertained the belief of the ultimate success of his projects corresponding with his representations, he did not commit the offense charged and you should return a verdict of not guilty. The significant fact is the intent and purpose. The question presented to you in this case is not whether the business enterprises of the defendant, Gilbert S. Johnson, were practicable or not, if you believe from the evidence that the defendant entered, in good faith, into these business enterprises, believing that out of the moneys received he could by investment or otherwise, make enough to repay said investors according to his promises, he is not guilty, no matter how visionary might seem his plan or scheme."

VIII.

The said District Court erred in failing and refusing to give the following instruction which was requested by the defendant:

"The burden is upon the Government to prove a fraudulent intent on the part of the accused. Such intent must be proved specifically, and it cannot be implied from the fact that the pretenses alleged were made, and that they were false, and that accused knew them to be false. Such intent is to be determined by the jury upon all the facts and circumstances disclosed by the evidence, but it is not an inference of law arising from the proof of the making of false statements."

IX.

The said District Court erred in failing and refusing to give the following instruction which was requested by the defendant:

"The intent to defraud in this case, like the intent to defraud in any similar criminal case, is a question of fact and not a question of law, and as such question of fact must be found by the jury to be proved by all the evidence in the case beyond all reasonable doubt in order to justify the jury in finding the defendant guilty."

X.

The said District Court erred in failing and refusing to give the following instruction which was requested by the defendant:

"So that there will be no confusion in your minds regarding the question of intent, and, because this is a very important matter for the jury to consider, I want you to definitely understand the question of intent. As I have heretofore instructed you, like all other questions of fact in this case, the existence or non-existence of a fraudulent intent is solely for you to determine from the evidence in the case."

XI.

The said District Court erred in failing and refusing to give the following instruction which was requested by the defendant:

"The Court instructs the Jury that the indictment in this case was returned and filed in this Court on the 19 day of June, 1925, and you are instructed that the defendant cannot be convicted on any act, whether criminal or otherwise, which you may believe he committed at any time prior to...............day of........................, 19...., Under the law the government cannot prosecute one for such a crime as is here charged unless the indictment is returned within three (3) years from and after the commission of the alleged criminal act."

XII.

The said District Court erred in failing and refusing to give the following instruction which was requested by the defendant:

"In determining whether or not the defendant did believe that he would be able to carry out and fulfill such promises and representations as you may believe and find from the testimony he made, you should take into consideration the various enterprises in which the said Gilbert S. Johnson was interested and you have a right to consider the relationships between all of said enterprises and the prospects of success of each of said enterprises as they then and that time appeared to him, and in determining whether or not he thought or believed that he could carry out the representations and promises made, you may consider the sources of income which he might expect to receive from properties and leases which he was interested in and owned in various parts of Texas, and you may also take into consideration the prospects of income from the development of oil wells as they appeared to him at the time the representations and promises were made, and if from a consideration of all these facts and circumstances you believe that the defendant honestly and in good faith believed that he would carry out the promises and representations made by him, then he is not guilty in this case and this is true, even though you believe that all the enterprises with which the said defendant was connected eventually failed, and all persons investing money failed to realize any substantial return or any return for the money invested by them."

XIII.

The said District Court erred in failing and refusing to give the following instruction which was requested by the defendant: .

"The Court instructs the Jury that matters of fact, if any, which are left uncertain by the evidence, cannot be made certain to the prejudice of the defendant by inference. In the absence of evidence, no inference can be drawn by the jury against the defendant; but, on the contrary, all the inferences and presumptions consistent with the facts proved are to be drawn and indulged in favor of the innocence of the defendant. No fact or circumstances upon which they may base a conclusion of guilt is sufficient, unless such fact or circumstance has been proved beyond a reasonable doubt and to the same extent as if the whole conclusion depended upon that one fact or circumstance."

XIV.

The said District Court erred in failing and refusing to give the following instruction which was requested by the defendant:

"If upon a fair and impartial consideration of all the evidence in the case the jury find that there are two reasonable theories, supported by the testimony in the case and that one of such theories is consistent with the theory that the defendant is guilty, as charged in some one or more or all of the counts in the indictment and that the other of such theories is consistent with the innocence of the defendant, then it is the policy of the law, and the law makes it the duty of the jury to adopt that rule which is consistent with the innocence of the defendant and in such case to find the defendant not guilty."

XV.

The said District Court erred in failing and refusing to give the following instruction which was requested by the defendant:

"The law is that in order that the jury may be warranted in finding a person guilty upon circumstantial evidence alone, all the facts and circumstances necessary to establish the conclusion of guilt must each be proved beyond a reasonable doubt; and all such facts and circumstances must be consistent with each other and with the conclusions sought to be established, which conclusion is that the accused is guilty as charged in some one or more or all of the counts in the indictment; and all such facts and circumstances must be consistent with any reasonable theory of the innocence of the accused; and all such facts and circumstances when taken together must be of such a convincing nature as to produce in the minds of the jurors a reasonable and moral certainty that the accused is guilty in manner and form as charged in some one or more of the counts in the indictment."

XVI.

The said District Court erred in failing and refusing to give the following instruction which was requested by the defendant:

"You are instructed that it is a matter of common knowledge that beginning in the year of 1921, the business of the country generally passed through a period of deflation and depression that brought loss and even ruin to business enterprises of supposed soundness and strength, and you are further instructed that from the evidence in this case it appears that the price of oil in the State of Texas fell from a price of $3.50 per barrel to $1.00 per barrel, and this is one of the reasons that the defendant ascribes to some of his misfortunes in the oil business, and if you so believe you should give the defendant the benefit of such condition and take these facts into consideration with all the evidence in this case."

XVII.

Said District Court erred in giving the following instructions to the Trial Jury:

"You will remember that the defendant—apparently, he must have been a very young man, started in the town of Goldfield, promoting, according to his own admissions, promoting enterprises similar to this, and through the course of a good many years, he says that he has been selling stocks by means of the United States mails. He even condemns the government for interfering with his scheme, in some of the circulars, in which you will remember that he criticized the government and the postal authorities for interfering. He explained, I think, to some of the investors that except for the pernicious activity of the postal officials the enterprise would have continued.

Now, no prejudice is to be entertained against one who does that, because the advertising of goods is legitimate. It is done all the time, and within certain limits a person has a right to what is known, " 'to puff his wares.' " That is very true. The fact, however, that the defendant says he believed all these things that were stated, does not necessarily control you in your judgment. You do not have to believe that if I am caught in the act of setting fire to a house and I say to the officer, " 'Well, I did not intend to burn that house,' " he does not have to believe that, and probably would not."

XVIII.

, . Said District Court erred in giving the following instructions to the Trial Jury:

"There is evidence here that at one time he advertised that he had a certain lease and it would be the general understanding among oil people that all leases are subject to a royalty payment; that is the general understanding— and the Court will take note of that—among oil men, so by saying that he owned a lease, that implies the owning of a lease subject to a royalty payment. That is all right. This defendant, however, did not say he owned only a one-half interest in it. Now, and, by the way, the defendant was to claim that certain explanations were made in some of his publications. So far, however, I have no recollection of any evidence of that fact, so it stands before you uncontradicted that he gave the customers to understand that he owned the leases, whereas, in fact, he owned only one-half of it. Now, that might be an oversight; it might have been unintentional. To my mind, that is not so very flagrant, but it is illustrative. They say that " 'straws tell which way the wind blows.' " Now, it might be that the defendany did not consider that extremely important, but he was used to making reckless statements. That is an element that you may consider properly in this case, that there were extravagant statements made. Of course, there is no denying that. For instance, I think it was yesterday afternoon, something was shown here where it was said that a big gusher was absolutely assured, a big gusher absolutely assured. Now, it is difficult, gentlement of the jury, to reconcile that with honest belief in anybody. " 'Assured' " means, as we all know, " 'sure,' " "That it was sure;" and it is significant, gentlemen, that every single one of these statements contains an invitation to buy stock; every single one without exception, so far as I remember, is an invitation to buy stock—not only an invitation, but an urgent invitation. Well, now, the defendant might have been entirely innocent; he might have honestly believed that, but his honest belief is not sufficient unless the facts warranted him in expressing such belief, unless his information and facts warranted him.

The evidence in this case shows that from the very beginning this defendant pursued a consistent line of advertising, and I will not, I think go too strong in calling it extravagant advertising. It is a little singular, gentlemen, that if he was honest in his belief, that that continued."

XIX.

Said District Court erred in giving the following instructions to the Trial Jury:

"JUROR H. LEWIS HAYNES: Your Honor, may I ask a question?

THE COURT: Yes, sir.

JUROR HAYNES: If it is proper, I would like to have you clarify to me the distinction between " 'a particular' " and " 'a count' ", which you refer to in that indictment.

THE COURT: A what?

JUROR HAYNES: A particular and a count, which you spoke of in the indictment; you refer to fourteen particulars and six counts, I believe. I do not understand the difference.

THE COURT: Well, I will go over that again. That was probably due to my confusion or inaccuracies in my statement. The indictment charges first, that he conceived and formed a plan to defraud; that Gilbert Johnson did devise a scheme to defraud, and it was, in substance, as follows:—Now, here follow fourteen particulars in which, according to the indictment and the position of the Government, are constituted and made up the scheme to defraud. The instruction was that not all of those particulars constituting the scheme to defraud need to be proven; any of them relating to the letters that were sent would be sufficient. Then, in the last or fourteenth particular, that is divided up into, I think there are twenty-six letters in the alphabet—well, this runs up to L or runs up to O. That made subdivisions of that fourteenth; that it was further a part of the scheme and artifice to defraud, that the defendant would make fraudulent, false pretenses and promises to the person intended to be defrauded, through and by means of divers circular letters, pamphlets, newspapers, and house organs, publicly circulated and intended to be circulated in effect and substance, as follows: Then they detail the various—

JUROR HAYNES: A count, then, is just a subdivision under a particular?

THE COURT: Yes."

XX.

Said District Court erred in giving the following instructions to the Trial Jury:

"You will remember that the defendant asserted that he believed, himself, everything that was stated in the indictment—everything that was stated in all of the matters sent out."

XXI.

Said District Court erred in giving the following instructions to the Trial Jury:

"Now, with respect to these units, you will remember that some discussion was had of them. So far as I am advised, this system of selling in California is not pursued. The unit system or the trustestate, or what is known as the common law trust estate, is, in effect, a partnership; that is, you, the defendant—not a partnership as defined in the California law, but the party offering the trust estate announces that he has a certain property and he invites others to participate with him, not in buying stock in the corporation, but in buying units which give to the parties buying the units actual ownership in the properties then found. That is a legitimate system of business, in the state of Texas at least, and there is no reflection on anybody for adopting such a system. It, itself, does not give evidence of any dishonest motive. There are certain duties, however, which one engages, that are importatn to be considered.

There is evidence in this case tending to prove that the defendant, operating as a broker under the name of Gilbert Johnson & Company, entered into contracts with several syndicates or companies of which he was the promotor, organizer and dominant head, whereby Gilbert Johnson & Company undertook to sell the units or shates of these .syndicates or companies. There is also evidence tending to prove that in selling these units or shares to the public a considerable proportion of the purchase price paid by the public was absorbed by Gilbert Johnson & Company as commissions or expenses or otherwise, so that in many instances a comparatively small proportion of the amount thus paid by the public actually went into the treasury of the respective syndicates or companies and became available for the development purposes for which they were said to be organized. Further, it is the contention of the government in this case that in soliciting the public to purchase these shares or units the defendant failed to disclose that a large proportion of the money paid for the same would not go to the syndicates or companies, but would be absorbed in commissions and other charges by the said brokerage concern of Gilbert Johnson & Company.

Now, I charge you that the payment of an exorbitant and unreasonable commission, not warranted by the financial conditions or necessities of the occasion and undisclosed to the parties interested, is fraudulent if, in your judgment, they are grossly excessive and are not so disclosed.

And I further charge you that when the shares or units of such concerns as are involved in this case are selling for much more than their par value, it should not require the payment of large commissions to dispose of them. If it does, the selling price must be altogether artificial and the inference may be made by the jury either that the company is fraudulent if the commission is not excessive, or that the commission is fraudulent if the company is what it purports to be. I further charge you that the promotor of a corporation or other similar concern, such as these syndicates, stands in a relation of trust toward those who are invited to purchase the shares or units, and he must deal fairly with them and must faithfully disclose all facts which might influence them in deciding upon the judiciousness of the purchase.

If, therefore, you find from the evidence, beyond a reasonable doubt, that the defendant knowingly so manipulated the several contracts, or any of them, whereby Gilbert Johnson & Company were to sell these units or shares with a commission so grossly excessive as to convince you that they are fraudulent, and the amount of such commissions or deductions was not disclosed to the purchasers of such units or shares, such a finding by you would make it necessary to find the defendant guilty of devising the scheme to defraud described in the indictment, if, at the same time, you find beyond a reasonable doubt that he did so with the intent to defraud, as I have already defined it to you. And having so found, if you further find that he used the mails to carry the fraudulent scheme into effect, as alleged in the indictment, it will then be your duty to find him guilty as charged.

XXII.

Said District Court erred in giving the following instructions to the Trial Jury:

"It is essential only that it be shown that the scheme be formed with a fraudulent intent. It is necessary that the Government prove that the scheme or artifice employed by the defendant was of the kind charged in the indictment. It is not necessary that it be proved that the scheme and artifice included the making of all of the alleged false pretenses, representations and promises, but it is sufficient if any one or more of the same be proved to have been made, and that the same were designed to and would be reasonably effective in deceiving and defrauding persons with whom the defendant proposed to and did deal."

In connection with said charge the following colloquy occurred:

"MR. CANNON—I also take an exception to the Court's suggestion that it will be sufficient under the law to find any one of the elements of the alleged scheme as set out in the indictment would be sufficient; that is, if the Jury finds any one of those particulars exist, that that would be sufficient to sustain the charge laid in the indictment, so far as the devising of the scheme is concerned.

THE COURT: Well, there may be some confusion in that. That was qualified or followed by the statement that any one was sufficient to base a conviction on the count in the indictment relating to it."

XXIII.

Said District Court erred in giving the following instructions to the Trial Jury:

"If the defendant intended to convey a false impression for the purpose of securing money, that is determinative of the case, if you find that to be the case. If the defendant in this case attempted by his letters, by his circulars to give anything other than true and correct knowledge of the situation, that would be sufficient on which to base a judgment of fraudulent intent."

XXIV.

Said District Court erred in giving the following instructions to the Trial Jury:

"THE COURT: You are instructed, gentlemen, that these additional instructions are given you together with all the other instructions. I certainly think that you understand that intent must accompany everything. You understand that, of course; that is the general principal as to all crimes, and I am very sure the Jury understand that intent always must be proven in fact. The intent is the intentional—things having been intentionally done, are really the foundation of the case. There might be this to call to your attention, however; Certain of these Bulletins were sent out and the statements in them the defendant denied knowledge of. Defendant cannot deny knowledge of what was done by his employees. That is about the only room or occasion I could see for any particular question on intent, Mr. Arterberry.

MR. ARTERBERRY: One point, if your Honor please: You will recall that the defendant testified that he received certain information from the driller of the well in Desdemona when your Honor asked him on cross-examination about the " 'well being assured.' " The driller told him he was then in the pay sand and he had a well, and he made his representations based on that. Now, if the defendant in good faith and honestly made that representation based on that, he is entitled to the benefit of that.

THE COURT: Well, the defendant, of course, must have been justified from his knowledge of the situation. The fact that he believed it to be true, would not exonerate him unless he believed it on a sufficient foundation or evidence."

XXV.

Said District Court erred in delivering his charge as a whole to the Jury.

XXVI.

Said District Court erred in permitting this cause to go to the Jury for determination on an indictment such as that returned in this case, the Jury having had access to the said indictment and having used the said indictment upon their express request therefor during their deliberation on the verdict.

XXVII.

Said District Court erred in overruling and denying the Motion of the defendant for Arrest of Judgment.

The said Gilbert S. Johnson says that this Assignment of Errors has been prepared, filed and presented before the Bill of Exceptions in this case has been settled and prays leave to file Amended and Additional Assignment of Errors herein within 30 days after the settling, sealing and filing of the Bill of Exceptions herein.

WHEREFORE, the said defendant by reason of the errors aforesaid prays that judgment and sentence against and upon him may be reversed and held for naught.

.DATED this 15th day of December, 1930.

Gilbert S Johnson,
Defendant.

David H. Cannon
H L Arterberry
    Attorneys for Defendant.

[Endorsed]: Filed Dec 15 1930 R. S. Zimmerman, Clerk By W E Gridley Deputy Clerk

---

[TITLE OF COURT AND CAUSE.]

MOTION FOR ARREST OF JUDGMENT

Comes Gilbert S. Johnson and moves the Court to refrain from entering a judgment against him based upon the verdict entered in this case upon the following grounds:

1. That the said indictment does not, nor does any count or paragraph thereof, state facts sufficient to constitute a punishable offense, or any offense or crime against the laws, or against any law, or against the Constitution of the United States, and particularly said indictment does not, nor does any count or paragraph thereof, state facts sufficient to constitute a violation of Section 215 of the Federal Penal Code.

DATED this 15th day of December, 1930.

Gilbert S Johnson,
Defendant.

David H. Cannon
H L Arterberry
    Attorneys for Defendant.

[Endorsed]: Filed Dec 15 1930 R. S. Zimmerman, Clerk By W E Gridley Deputy Clerk

---

[TITLE OF COURT AND CAUSE.]

ORDER ALLOWING APPEAL

On reading the Petition of Gilbert S. Johnson for appeal, and upon consideration of the Assignment of Errors therewith,

IT IS ORDERED that the appeal as prayed for by the said Gilbert S. Johnson be and is hereby allowed.

IT IS FURTHER ORDERED that the Petitioner, Gilbert S. Johnson, be admitted to bail, pending the final determination of this appeal, in the sum of TEN THOUSAND (10,000) DOLLARS, a Cost Bond to be given by the said Petitioner in the sum of TWO HUNDRED FIFTY (250) DOLLARS.

DATED this 15th day of December, 1930.

Geo. Cosgrave

Judge

[Endorsed]: Filed Dec 15 1930 R. S. Zimmerman, Clerk By W E Gridley Deputy Clerk

---

[TITLE OF COURT AND CAUSE.]

COST BOND

KNOW ALL MEN BY THESE PRESENTS: That we Gilbert S. Johnson, as principal, and W. E. Connell and T. B. Yarbrough, County of Tarrant, State of Texas, as sureties, are held and firmly bound unto the United States of America in the just and full sum of

TWO HUNDRED FIFTY (250) DOLLARS for the payment of which well and truly to be made, we, and each of us, do hereby bind ourselves, our successors, personal representatives and assigns, jointly and severally, firmly by these presents.

Sealed with our seals and dated this 15th day of December, 1930.

The condition of the above and foregoing obligations is such that, whereas, lately at a session of the United States District Court for the Southern District of California, Central Division, in an action then pending in said Court at the City of Los Angeles, in said District, between the United States of America, as plaintiff, and Gilbert S. Johnson, as defendant, a judgment and sentence were rendered and pronounced by the District Court of the United States for the Southern District of California, Central Division, on the 15th day of December, 1930, upon a verdict against the said Gilbert S. Johnson, the principal herein, which judgment and sentence adjudged and sentenced the said Gilbert S. Johnson to be imprisoned in the United States Penitentiary for Four Years on the first count of the indictment in said action; and,

WHEREAS, the said Gilbert S. Johnson has filed his petition for and obtained an order allowing his appeal to reverse the judgment and sentence aforesaid, and citation therein has issued pursuant to law citing and admonishing the United States of America to appear at the United States Circuit Court of Appeals for the Ninth Circuit at San Francisco, California;

NOW, THEREFORE, if the said Gilbert S. Johnson, the principal herein, shall prosecute his appeal with effect and answer all costs, if he fails to make his said plea good, then the said obligation shall be null and void, otherwise to remain in full force and virtue.

GILBERT S. JOHNSON, Principal

W. E. CONNELL, Surety

T. B. YARBROUGH, Surety

STATE OF TEXAS)
) SS.
COUNTY OF TARRANT)

W. E. Connell and T. B. Yarbrough each being first duly sworn, according to law, each for himself and not one for the other, deposes and says:

That he is a surety in the above and foregoing Cost Bond in which one Gilbert S. Johnson is principal; that he is a freeholder of the State of Texas and is worth in excess of three hundred (300) dollars over and above all his just debts and liabilities exclusive of property exempt from execution.

W. E. CONNELL

T. B. YARBROUGH

Subscribed and sworn to before me this 15th day of December, 1930.

~~Clerk of the District Court of the United States.~~

(SEAL) LOIS NEWAM

United States Commissioner for the Northern District of Texas.

LN

Examined and recommended for approval as provided by rule 28.

DAVID H. CANNON
H. L. ARTERBERRY
Attorneys for Defendant and Appellant.

Approved as to form
S. W. McNABB
United States Attorney,
Attorney for Plaintiff and Appellee

The above and foregoing Cost Bond was acknowledged before me and approved on the day and year first therein written.

(SEAL) LOIS NEWAM

~~Clerk of the United States District Court for the~~........................~~District of Texas~~

United States Commissioner for the Northern District of Texas

LN

I hereby approve the foregoing bond.

Dated the 18th day of Dec. 1930

GEO. COSGRAVE
Judge.

[Endorsed]: Filed Dec. 18 1930 R. S. Zimmerman, Clerk By W. E. Gridley Deputy Clerk.

————

[TITLE OF COURT AND CAUSE.]

BOND PENDING DECISION UPON APPEAL

KNOW ALL MEN BY THESE PRESENTS: That we, Gilbert S. Johnson, as principal, and W. E. Connell and T. B. Yarbrough, County of Tarrant, State of Texas, ⁿ sureties, are held and firmly bound unto the United States of America in the just and full sum of TEN THOUSAND (10,000) DOLLARS for the payment of which well and truly to be made, we, and each of us, do hereby bind ourselves, our successors, personal representatives and assigns, jointly and severally, firmly by these presents.

Sealed with our seals and dated this 15th day of December, 1930.

WHEREAS, lately, to-wit, on the 15th day of December, 1930, at a term of the District Court of the United States in and for the Southern District of California, Central Division, in an action pending in said Court, between the United States of America, plaintiff, and Gilbert S. Johnson, defendant, a judgment and sentence was made, given, rendered and entered against the said Gilbert S. Johnson, in the above entitled action wherein he was convicted on count one of said indictment for a violation of Section 215 of the Penal Code of the United States; and,

WHEREAS, in said judgment and sentence so made, given, rendered and entered against the said Gilbert S. Johnson in said action, he was by said judgment sentenced to Four Years in the Federal Penitentiary.

The said Gilbert S. Johnson having obtained an appeal from the United States Circuit Court of Appeals from the Ninth Circuit to reverse said judgment and sentence, and a citation directed to the United States of America to be and appear in the United States Circuit Court of Appeals for the Ninth Circuit, at San Francisco, California, in pursuance to the terms and at the time fixed in said citation.

WHEREAS, the said Gilbert S. Johnson has been admitted to bail pending the decision upon said appeal in the sum of $10,000.

NOW, THEREFORE, the conditions of the above obligation are such that if the said Gilbert S. Johnson shall appear, either in person or by his attorney, in the United States Circuit Court of Appeals for the Ninth Circuit, on such day or days as may be appointed for the hearing of said cause in the said Court, and prosecute his appeal; and if the said Gilbert S. Johnson shall abide by and obey all orders made by the United States Circuit Court of Appeals, for the Ninth Circuit, in said cause; and if the said Gilbert S. Johnson shall surrender himself in execution of said judgment and sentence, if the said judgment and sentence be affirmed by the United States Circuit Court of Appeals, Ninth Circuit; and if the said Gilbert S. Johnson shall appear for trial in the District Court of the United States, in and for the Southern District of California, Central Division, on such day or days as may be appointed for the retrial by said District Court, and abide by and obey all orders made by said District Court, if the said judgment and sentence against him be reversed by the United States Circuit Court of Appeals for the Ninth Circuit, Then this obligation to be void, otherwise to remain in full force, virtue and effect.

GILBERT S. JOHNSON, Principal

W. E. CONNELL, Surety

T. B. YARBROUGH, Surety

STATF OF TEXAS,)
) SS.
COUNTY OF TARRANT)

W. E. Connell and T. B. Yarbrough each being first duly sworn, according to law, each for himself and not one for the other, deposes and says:

That he is a surety in the above and foregoing Bond Pending Decision upon Appeal in which one Gilbert S. Johnson is principal; that he is a freeholder of the State of Texas and is worth in excess of ten thousand (10,000) dollars over and above all his just debts and liabilities exclusive of property exempt from execution.

W. E. CONNELL
T. B. YARBROUGH

Subscribed and sworn to before me this 15th day of December, 1930.

....

~~Clerk~~ of the ~~District Court~~ of the ~~United States~~

(SEAL)   LOIS NEWAM
  United States Commissioner for the Northern
    District of Texas
LN

I am personally acquainted with both the foregoing sureties and know them to be worth many times the amount this bond. They are President and Vice President of the First National Bank of Fort Worth. 12/15/30

Norman A. Dodge
United States Attorney.

Examined and recommended for approval by rule 28.

H. L. ARTERBERRY
DAVID H. CANNON,
Attorneys for Defendant and Appellant.

Approved as to form

S. W. McNABB,

United States Attorney,

Attorney for Plaintiff and Appellee

The above and foregoing Bond Pending decision Upon Appeal was acknowledged before me and approved on the day and year first therein written.

(SEAL) LOIS NEWAM

~~Clerk of the United States District Court for the~~ ~~District of Texas~~

United States Commissioner for the Northern District of Texas.

LN

I hereby approve the foregoing bond.

Dated the 18th day of Dec. 1930.

GEO. COSGRAVE

Judge.

[Endorsed]: Filed Dec. 18, 1930 R. S. Zimmerman, Clerk, By W. E. Gridley, Deputy Clerk

———

[TITLE OF COURT AND CAUSE.]

STIPULATION

IT IS HEREBY STIPULATED by and between the parties hereto and their respective attorneys in the above entitled cause that the Clerk of the Court may, in preparing the certified transcript of the record, omit from the caption of all documents, except the Indictment, filed in said cause, the title of the court and cause and insert therein the words, "Title of Court and Cause".

IT IS FURT̶H̶ER STIPULATED that the Clerk of the Court may omit all words and figures upon the back of all documents in the record, except the filing mark thereof.

DATED this 31st day of March, 1931.

David H. Cannon

H. L. Arterberry

Attorneys for Defendant.

John S Pratt

Special Assistant to Attorney General

By P V Davis

P V Davis

Assistant to United States Attorney

Attorneys for Plaintiff

IT IS ORDERED.

Geo. Cosgrave

United States District Judge.

[Endorsed]: Filed Mar 31, 1931   R. S. Zimmerman, Clerk By F Betz Deputy Clerk

---

[TITLE OF COURT AND CAUSE.]

PRAECIPE

To the Clerk of Said Court:

SIR:

Please issue a certified transcript of the following matters and documents, including indorsements, in the above entitled cause:

1. Indictment,

3. Motion to Quash and Order thereon,

4. All stipulations and orders of court extending time for filing Bill of Exceptions and term,

5. Verdict,

6. Sentence and judgment,

7. Motion for new trial,

8. Order denying motion for new trial,

9. Motion for arrest of judgment,

10. Order denying motion in arrest of judgment,

11. Petition for appeal,

12. Assignment of Errors,

13. Order allowing appeal,

14. Citation on Appeal,

15. Bond on appeal,

16. Cost Bond,

17. Bill of Exceptions as approved and allowed by the Court,

18. Order approving and settling Bill of Exceptions,

19. Stipulations re eliminating title of court and cause in printing in record, and this praecipe.

Dated this 19th day of March, 1931.

> David H. Cannon
> H. L. Arterberry
> Attorneys for Defendant.

[Endorsed]: Filed Mar 31, 1931 R. S. Zimmerman, Clerk By F Betz, Deputy Clerk

[TITLE OF COUR. AND CAUSE.]

CLERK'S CERTIFICATE.

I, R. S. Zimmerman, clerk of the United States District Court for the Southern District of California, do hereby certify the foregoing volume containing 263 pages, numbered from 1 to 263 inclusive, to be the Transcript of Record on Appeal in the above entitled cause, as printed by the appellant, and presented to me for comparison and certification, and that the same has been compared and corrected by me and contains a full, true and correct copy of the citation, indictment, minute order of June 19, 1925, motion to quash indictment, points and authorities in support of motion to quash, minute order of Sept. 10, 1929, minute order of Nov. 15, 1929, ruling on notice to quash, minutes of the court, minute order of Dec. 5, 1930, sentence, verdict, bill of exceptions, orders extending time for filing bill of exceptions, orders extending time for filing proposed amendments to bill of exceptions, petition for appeal, assignment of errors, motion for arrest of judgment, order allowing appeal, cost bond, bond pending decision on appeal, stipulation re printing transcript of record and praecipe.

I DO FURTHER CERTIFY that the amount paid for printing the foregoing record on appeal is $ and that said amount has been paid the printer by the appellant herein and a receipted bill is herewith enclosed, also that the fees of the clerk for comparing, correcting and certifying the foregoing Record on Appeal amount to............ and that said amount has been paid me by the appellant herein.

IN TESTIMONY WHEREOF, I have hereunto set my hand and affixed the Seal of the District Court of the United States of America, in and for the Southern District of California, Central Division, this............ day of August in the year of Our Lord One Thousand Nine Hundred and Thirty-one, and of our Independence the One Hundred and Fifty-sixth.

R. S. ZIMMERMAN,

Clerk of the District Court of the United States of America, in and for the Southern District of California.

By

Deputy.

Gilbert S. Johnson,

Appellant,

vs.

United States of America,

Appellee.

BRIEF FOR APPELLANT.

H. L. ARTERBERRY,
Attorney for Appellant.

DAVID H. CANNON,
   of Los Angeles, California;
ATHEARN, CHANDLER & FARMER
   and
FRANK R. DEVLIN,
   of San Francisco, California;
McLEAN, SCOTT & SAYERS,
   of Fort Worth, Texas,
               Of Counsel.

FILED

SEP 25 1931

PAUL P. O'BRIEN,
               CLER

Parker, Stone & Baird Co., Law Printers, Los Angeles.

TOPICAL INDEX.

TABLE OF CASES AND AUTHORITIES CITED.

No. 6588.

IN THE

United States
Circuit Court of Appeals,

FOR THE NINTH CIRCUIT.

Gilbert S Johnson,

Appellant,

vs.

United States of America,

Appellee.

BRIEF FOR APPELLANT.

STATEMENT OF THE CASE.

This is an appeal to review the judgment and the sentence pronounced upon the appellant Gilbert S. Johnson by the District Court of the United States in the Southern District of California, Central Division.

The indictment was returned on June 19, 1925, against the appellant charging him in six counts with the violation of section 215 of the Criminal Code of the United States. The defendant resisted removal from Fort Worth, Texas, and he was finally ordered removed on the 19th day of December, 1928. Whereupon, the defendant made bond for his appearance in the United States District

Court, in and for the Southern District of California, Central Division. Before pleading to said indictment, the defendant through his counsel filed a motion to quash said indictment, which was on the 15th day of November, 1929, overruled by the Hon. Edward J. Henning, judge of said court, at said time. Thereafter, the defendant entered his plea of not guilty and the case proceeded to trial on November 11, 1930, after a jury had been duly impaneled and sworn to try the issues; the jury thereafter, to-wit, on December 4, 1930, returning a verdict of guilty on the first count of said indictment and not guilty on the other five counts [Tr. 163].

Motions for a new trial and in arrest of judgment filed on behalf of the appellant were overruled by the court.

Upon the verdict, the District Court rendered a judgment imposing a sentence on the first count of said indictment of four years imprisonment in the federal penitentiary at McNeil's Island [Tr. 162].

The Indictment.

Omitting the formal parts, the alleged scheme is attempted to be charged as follows:

That Gilbert S. Johnson, hereinafter referred to as the defendant, heretofore and prior to the several acts of using the United States mails hereinafter set out in this indictment, did devise and intend to devise, a certain scheme and artifice to defraud and to obtain money and property, by means of false and fraudulent pretenses, representations and promises from F. J. Rappe, H. W. Shafer, J. W. Barbee, E. F. Youngman, E. B. Boadway, J. T. Junell, May McCrail, Owen B. Jacoby, M. T. Clark,

W. H. Hemphill, Mrs. S. L. Wright and divers other persons throughout the United States of America, including the public generally, and whose names are too numerous to be set out herein and many of whom are to the grand jurors unknown, all of said persons being hereinafter referred to in this indictment as the persons to be defrauded. The said scheme and artifice was in substance and effect as follows, to-wit:

(1) That the said defendant would acquire or contract to acquire, large blocks of oil and gas leases in what is commonly known as wild-cat territory remote from existing oil and gas production, at nominal prices or through his agreements to drill a test well or wells, for oil and gas thereon.

(2) That the said defendant would then organize and control a succession of trust estates, corporations and concerns, among them being, Lewis Oil and Gas Company, Stephens Oil Syndicate, Texas Trojan Oil Company, Fernando Oil Company, Johnson Oil Company, Unit Production Syndicate, Banner Unit Syndicate, Runnels Oil Syndicate, Mexia-Terrace Oil Company, Corsicana-Mexia Oil Fields Syndicate, Mexia-Powell Oil Syndicate, Fortuna Petroleum Syndicate, Admiral Oil Company, Powell Petroleum Company, Gilbert Johnson and Company, Texas Oil and Stock Exchange, would prepare and cause to be prepared, Declarations of Trust creating each of said trust estates and articles of incorporation creating said corporations, and giving to himself full and complete control of the assets, operations and activities of said trust estates corporations and concerns.

(3)   It was further a part of said scheme and artifice, that the said defendant, after the organization of the respective trust estates, corporations and concerns, and after instituting a campaign for the sale of stock or units of beneficial interests therein, would assign certain oil and gas leases, previously acquired by himself as aforesaid, or portions of such leases, to such trust estates, at enormous and excessive prices and at unlawful and wrongful profit to himself, and would cause such trust estates, corporations and concerns to assume, carry out and complete the original drilling agreements through which such leases were obtained and to assume other obligations thereon, and would withhold and retain for himself, large portions of said leases, acquired as aforesaid, and would use and dispose of the same for his own benefit in fraud of the rights of the stockholders and unit-holders of said trust estates, corporations and concerns, and in fraud of the persons to be defrauded.

(4)   It was further part of said scheme and artifice that the said defendant would fix the amount of the capitalization of each of the said trust estates, corporations and concerns, in amounts ranging from one hundred thousand dollars to three million dollars, respectively, without regard to the actual value of the assets of such trust estates then owned or thereafter to be acquired, and greatly in excess thereof, and through the provisions of the respective Declarations of Trust, articles of incorporation and regulations, would authorize himself to increase such capitalization at his will and pleasure, and convenience, and without regard to the actual value of the

assets of such trust estates, then owned or thereafter to be acquired.

(5) It was further a part of said scheme and artifice that the defendant would sell and offer for sale, to the persons to be defrauded, the shares, units and stock of said several trust estates, corporations and concerns, by means of false and fraudulent pretenses, representations and promises, as hereinafter set forth, and would induce the said persons to be defrauded to pay their money to him, the said defendant, which said money he would thereupon, in large part, appropriate to his own use and benefit, and would embezzle and misappropriate the same.

(6) It was further a part of said scheme and artifice, that the said defendant, prior to, and before, the actual organization of some of the said trust estates and before such trust estates had acquired any assets whatsoever, would offer for sale and sell to the persons to be defrauded, stock or units of beneficial interests in such trust estates.

(7) It was further a part of said scheme and artifice, that the said defendant would organize, own and operate so-called brokerage companies, to-wit: Gilbert Johnson and Company and Texas Oil and Stock Exchange, as a medium through which to dispose of the stock or units of interest in the said trust estates and concerns, and as such brokerage concerns would fraudulently contract with himself as an officer and trustee of the respective trust estates and concerns, for the sale of the stock or units of interest of the said trust estates and concerns, and by and through such contracts appropriate to himself large portions of the money and property belonging to the said trust estates.

(8) It was further a part of said scheme and artifice, that the said defendant would, through his so-called brokerage companies, offer for sale and sell to the persons to be defrauded, stock or units of interest in the respective trust estates at gradually ascending prices ranging from slightly less than par value to greatly in excess of par value, through false and fraudulent misrepresentations as to the value of the lease holdings of the respective trust estates and corporations and concerns, the location of such leases as to oil producing or proven oil territory, the progress of development thereon, the assurance of gusher oil production through the drilling or development of the said leases and the unsual, enormous and unlimited profits to accrue to investors in the stocks or units of interest in the respective trust estates without regard to the actual facts or the real values of such stock or units of interest, it being intended wrongfully and fraudulently to lead the said persons to be defrauded to believe that the respective trust estates were growing financially stronger in the ratio represented by the increase in prices at which the stock or units of interest were being offered for sale.

(9) It was further a part of said scheme and artifice to defraud, that the said defendant would drill for oil, a well or wells, for many of the said trust estates, or cause the same to be drilled, upon some one or more of the leases assigned to each of the said trust estates, in a pretended search for oil or gas, and charge such trust estate such exhorbitant and excessive amounts for such drilling that the funds and assets of the said trust estate would be quickly exhausted and the trust estate become insolvent.

(10) It was further a part of said scheme and artifice to defraud, that the said defendant would use certain of the said trust estates, organized by him for that particular purpose, as merger companies, to-wit: the Johnson Oil Company and the Admiral Oil Company, to provide a burying ground for the trust estates previously organized by him and which under his management and control had become insolvent and so recorded and shown on the minute book of the insolvent company, and as a means whereby the persons to be defrauded, who were unit-holders or stockholders of said insolvent trust estates, could be induced to pay to him additional money and property as merger or exchange fees in exchanging their units or stock in said insolvent concerns for the units or stock of said merger companies and as a means of eliminating all such holders of units or stock of said insolvent companies as should refuse or fail to pay such merger or exchange fees.

(11) It was further a part of said scheme and artifice, that the said defendant would arrange mergers of said insolvent trust estates and would fraudulently and unlawfully assign or transfer title of all the remaining assets of such insolvent trust estates, if any, to the so-called merger companies, and then in a further effort to obtain money and property from the stockholders in the insolvent estates, and through and by the use of the United States mails, would notify such stockholders that upon surrender of the stock or units of interest in such insolvent trust estates and the payment to them of a specified exchange or merger fee, within a certain specified time arbitrarily

fixed by said defendant, stock or units of interest in the merger company would be issued to them in exchange.

(12)   It was further a part of said scheme and artifice, that in one of the trust estates, to-wit: the Johnson Oil Company, the said defendant, in order to stimulate the sale of its stock or units, would declare and advertise a fraudulent quarterly dividend payable at a future date to stockholders of record on an intervening date and after declaring such fraudulent dividend he would offer for sale and would sell to the persons to be defrauded, stock or units of interest in said Johnson Oil Company, which would participate in such dividend.

(13)   It was further a part of said scheme and artifice to defraud, that the said defendant would misappropriate, embezzle and convert to his own use and benefit, a part of the money and property obtained from the persons intended to be defrauded, the exact amount so misappropriated, embezzled and converted being to these grand jurors unknown.

(14)   It was further a part of said scheme and artifice to defraud, that the said defendant would make false and fraudulent representations, pretenses and promises to the said persons intended to be defrauded through and by means of divers letters, circular letters, pamphlets, newspapers, house organs, advertisements and publications, circulated and intended to be circulated by and through the United States mails, and in effect and substance as follows, to-wit:

(a)   To the effect following, the said representation being made about September 4, 1920, to-wit: That the

last offering of Lewis Oil and Gas stock at 85 cents was
then being made; that said stock would be absolutely withdrawn from the market on September 10, 1920; that,
therefore, this was the last opportunity to secure an interest in said company; that within 60 days or less it was
expected that three big wells on the Sloan tract would be
gushing forth big profits for the stockholders; that this
was but the beginning of the tremendous certain success
of the enterprise; that with the completion of these three
wells there was every probability that the earnings of the
Lewis Oil and Gas Company would be around $1,000,-
000.00 a year; whereas, in truth and in fact, as the defendant then and there well knew and intended, it was not
intended to withdraw the stock of the Lewis Oil and Gas
Company from the market on September 10, 1920, or on
any other date, as long as the persons to be defrauded
could be induced to purchase the same; that it was not
expected that the three wells on the Sloan tract would be
gushing forth big profits for the stockholders of said company, nor would the production from said wells be the
beginning of tremendous certain success of the enterprise,
nor would there be any probability or possibility of the
earnings of said company being $1,000,000.00 a year, for
the reason that the said defendant then intended that he
would by fraudulent devices, appropriate to his own use
and benefit, a large part of the income from said wells and
would divert to others of his promotional concerns, the
balance of said income so that the stockholders of the
Lewis Oil and Gas Company would receive little or no
part of the same.

(b) To the effect following, to-wit: That the defendant believed that the Stephens Oil Syndicate would be fully financed without the expense of a single dollar to the syndicate members, the entire financing cost to be borne by himself and that every dollar that the members had sent in would go into a drilling fund without deduction of a cent for commissions or expense to anyone; whereas, in truth and in fact, as the defendant then and there well knew and intended, it was at all times intended by said defendant that he would divert to himself in the name of Gilbert Johnson and Company, a large part of the proceeds of money received from the sale of the stock of said Stephens Oil Syndicate under the guise of a bonus and as commissions for the sale of said stock, so that only a portion of the money received from the members of said syndicate could or would go into a drilling fund for the operations of said syndicate.

(c) To the effect that Gilbert Johnson (meaning, thereby, the defendant), of Gilbert Johnson and Company, and president of the big, successful Johnson Oil Company, is president and general manager of the Fernando Oil Company, which in itself assures a competent administration of the affairs of the enterprise (meaning the said Fernando Oil Company), fair and square treatment for the stockholders, and an equitable distribution of all accruing profits; whereas, in truth and in fact, as the said defendant then and there well knew and intended, the Johnson Oil Company was not a big and successful oil company, but was a purely promotional stock selling enterprise, and that said defendant was not a successful or honest executive of any company, but was a promoter of many fraudulent enterprises and was a confidence man and swindler, and the fact that he was president and general manager of said Fernando Oil Company did not assure a competent administration of its affairs or a fair and square treatment of its stockholders, or an equitable distribution of all accruing profits, but in fact, gave assurance that there would be no distribution of money to stockholders, but that whatever profit accrued would be misappropriated and embezzled by said defendant.

(d) To the effect that after October 7, 1920, there would be no further offerings of Texas Trojan Oil Company stock at any price; whereas, in truth and in fact, as the defendant then and there well knew and intended, the said stock would not be withdrawn from the market and there would be further offerings of said stock as long as the persons to be defrauded could be induced to purchase the same, and said representation was made by the defendant for the purpose of inducing said persons to send their money to him, the said defendant, immediately and without delay, for the purchase of said stock, which said money would be, in large part, misappropriated and embezzled by the said defendant.

(e) That on March 19, 1921, the defendant made the following representations to the persons to be defrauded, to-wit:

"The Unit Production Syndicate has a total authorized capitalization of only $150,000.00, consisting of 3,000 units of the par value of $50.00 per unit. This No. 1 well will be rushed to completion at the earliest possible moment, and will, I am confident, be placed on production within 75 to 90 days of this date, possibly sooner. Judging from the production of the Guaranty gusher, and the other wells that have to date been brought in in this amazingly rich pool, it may be depended to come in with production of from 1,000 to 3,000 barrels of high gravity refining oil per day. A total of four wells will be drilled on this 40-acre lease, and the entire property is so thoroughly proven that every one of these four wells is practically certain to be a great gusher. From the facts already established, I believe that I am ultra conservative when I predict that this 40-acre lease of the Unit Production Syndicate will produce from 12,500 to 25,000 barrels of oil per acre, and "the reasonable probabilities greatly exceed even the higher figures. It is upon these figures that I base my estimate that I will be able to pay back to all unit-holders from $250.00 to $500.00 per unit, although it is easily possible for the profits to greatly exceed even the latter figure.

"The bringing in of the No. 1 well with a production of even 1,000 barrels of oil per day and there is every reason to believe that the well will come in with a flow of from 2,000 to 3,000 barrels of oil per day or more, will provide ample funds almost immediately for the payment of liberal dividends to all unit-holders of the Unit Production Syndicate, and also provide ample funds for the drilling of additional wells.

"Hence I am confident that within four to five months from this date the Unit Production Syndicate will begin the payment of big, regular dividends, and these units will, within a comparatively short time, pay profits of from $250.000 to $500.00 each, or in other words, from five to ten times the amount of the investment if units are bought now at the initial price of $50.00 each."

Whereas, in truth and in fact, as the said defendant then and there well knew and intended, there was no basis of fact for the prediction that any well on the property of said syndicate would come in with production of 1,000 to 3,000 barrels of high gravity refining oil per day; that it was not intended to drill four wells on said 40-acre lease; that said property was not thoroughly proven but was, in fact, purely wild-cat property; that there was no basis for the prediction that said 40-acre lease would produce from 12,500 to 25,000 barrels of oil per acre or of any amount remotely approximating said figures, or that said defendant would be able to pay back to the unit-holders from $250.00 to $500.00 per unit, or, in fact, any sum of money; that all the statements made by the defendant in regard to said syndicate and in regard to the prospective production and prospective profits to its unit-holders, were false, fraudulent, extravagant and grossly exaggerated, and were made for the purpose of inducing the persons to be defrauded to purchase said units and with the purpose on the part of the defendant to misappropriate and embezzle a large part of the money so received from the said persons.

(f) To the effect that the organization of the Banner Unit Syndicate had been effected along remarkably conservative lines; that at the time said representation was made, to-wit: on April 16, 1921, preparations had been made for drilling the first well on the syndicate's 100 acres and that 8 or 10 wells would be drilled on said land; that from facts already established regarding the richness of said land, the defendant estimated that the units of said syndicate, which were being offered at $50.00 each, would ultimately return profits of from $500.00 to $1,000.00 each; whereas, in truth and in fact, as the defendant then and there well knew, the said lease and property of said syndicate was not located in proven territory, nor were any facts established indicating a likelihood of finding oil in paying quantities thereon; that the defendant did not intend to drill 8 or 10 wells on said lease, and there was no foundation for the assertion that the units of said syndicate would return profits of $500.00 to $1,000.00 each or, in fact, any profit whatever.

(g) To the effect that, on May 1, 1921, the Marine Oil Syndicate owned 520 acres of the richest oil territory in Stephens county, Texas, including 320 acres located within 1,000 feet of the great Yeaman No. 1 gusher of the Johnson Oil Company; that the management of said syndicate pledged itself to immediately begin the drilling of two wells on the said land; whereas, in truth and in fact, as the defendant then and there well knew, the said syndicate had not been organized and owned no property at the time said representation was made; that the said Yeaman No. 1 well of the Johnson Oil Company was not a great well or a gusher well, but was only a gas well producing no oil, and that the management of said syndicate (to-wit: the defendant), would not drill two wells but would drill but one; that the 520 acres referred to were not in the part of Stephens county, Texas, where large production of oil was found, and was not the richest oil territory in said county, but was in disproven territory so far as production of oil was concerned.

(h) To the effect that the success of the Johnson Oil Company had been one of the sensations of the oil fields of Texas; that said company had only begun to grow and that each week, each month and each year would witness said enterprise becoming stronger and stronger, greater and greater, and more and more profitable to its thousands of stockholders; that the defendant was looking forward eagerly to the day when the said company would be a complete unit in the petroleum industry—producers, refiners, transporters and marketers—and that ultimately it would duplicate the gigantic success of the Texas Company and make for every stockholder who held even a fair sized block of the stock an independent fortune; whereas in truth and in fact, as the defendant then and there well knew, the Johnson Oil Company was not then or at any time, a sensational success, but was then experiencing great difficulty in raising money through sales of stock; that it did not at that time, or at any other time. have any prospect of becoming a great oil producing or profit earning institution or of becoming an organization of similar size and commercial importance as the Texas Company; that there was no basis for the profits held out as likely to accrue to investors in the stock of the Johnson Oil ompany, and that the false and fraudulent misrepresentations were made to deceive the persons to be defrauded, and to induce them to turn over money and property to the said defendant without receiving anything of value in return therefor, which said money would be, in large part, misappropriated and embezzled by said defendant.

(i)   To the effect that on January 6, 1922, Runnels Oil Syndicate had property holdings of 5,000 acres in one solid block on a clearly defined oil structure; that hundreds of producing oil wells were a possibility; that stupendous profits were possible and probable for unit-holders of said syndicate; that the defendant believed that well No. 1 of the said syndicate would prove a gusher and that these units, then obtainable at $30.00 per unit, would sell for at least $1,000.00 each; whereas, in truth and in fact, as the defendant then and there well knew, the properties of the said syndicate were purely wild-cat properties; were entirely unproven as oil or gas producing properties; had originally been acquired without cost other than an agreement to drill a test well for oil and gas thereon; were purely speculative; were at a great distance from oil producing fields; that there were no developments in the drilling of the well up to that time, or at any time, that justified or would form a reasonable basis for the defendant's expressed belief that the said well would be brought in as a gusher oil well or would produce oil or gas in any commercial quantities; that there was no basis in fact or in reason for his expressed belief that units of said syndicate would sell for $1,000.00 each upon the completion of said well; that said defendant had held said property with an uncompleted well from October 28, 1919, until July, 1921, as the property of the Lewis Oil & Gas Company, and of the Johnson Oil Company, without making any effort to complete the drilling of the well by those syndicates because of the improbability of finding oil or gas in commercial quantities therein, and that the said false and fraudulent misrepresentations were made by said defendant solely for the purpose of inducing the persons to be defrauded to purchase the units of said syndicate, which were then and thereafter of no value.

(j) To the effect that on April 21, 1922, all available units of the Corsicana-Mexia Oil Fields Syndicate had been subscribed, no more being offered at any price, and hence a large number of the clients of defendant and a great number of the readers of the Texas Oil Bulletin, being the advertisement and publication of defendant, had found it impossible to secure an interest in the Great Powell Structure; that, moved by an overwhelming desire to have every client of Gilbert Johnson and Company, and every reader of the Texas Oil Bulletin participate in the tremendous profits that the defendant was confident would be made by the bringing in of great gushers on the Powell structure, he had personally selected 500 acres of leases on the great Powell structure adjacent to and surrounding the three wells being drilled thereon, and had formed for the development of these leases the Mexia-Powell Oil Syndicate with a capitalization of $150,000.00, divided into 6,000 units of the par value of $25.00 per unit; that said announcement was first, last and only offering of units of Mexia-Powell Oil Syndicate units at $20.00 per unit; that the price of those units would rapidly advance and the bringing in of gusher production in the three wells then rapidly approaching the Woodbine gusher sand on the Powell structure might make them worth anywhere from $250.00 to $500.00 per unit during the few weeks then ensuing:

Thereby causing the persons intended to be defrauded to understand and believe that all the units of the Corsicana-Mexia Oil Fields Syndicate had been sold; that large numbers of readers of the Texas Oil Bulletin and others who were anxious to secure an interest in properties on the so-called Powell structure were unable to do so and that in order to give these persons such a chance the said defendant had organized the said Mexia-Powell Oil Syndicate purely and solely for the purpose of providing a means whereby these persons could secure an interest in the Powell structure; that 500 acres of leases had been selected for development by the said syndicate and that development upon adjacent leases might make the units of the said syndicate worth from $250.00 to $500.00 per unit within a few weeks:

Whereas, in truth and in fact, as the defendant then and there well knew, all the units of the Corsicana-Mexia Oil Fields Syndicate had not been sold, a large quantity were then available for sale, and would be, and were later offered for sale; that the Mexia-Powell Oil Syndicate had not been organized to provide means whereby those who were unable to secure an interest in the Powell structure through stockholdings in the Corsicana-Mexia Oil Fields Syndicate could secure such an interest, but had been organized on January 10, 1922, six days prior to the organization of the Corsicana-Mexia Oil Fields Syndicate, and efforts had continuously been made to sell its stock or units through a certain brokerage concern during all the intervening time and had proven unsuccessful, and the sale of the stock had been thrown back into the hands of the defendant; that all of the stock of the said Mexia-Powell Syndicate had been issued to the defendant for the said leases at the time the said syndicates were organized:

that this was not the first, last and only offering of units in the said syndicate, and that the defendant would, and did, make further offerings of the said units at $20.00 per share on subsequent dates, and that he would not, and did not, intend to develop the properties of the said syndicate, but would, and did, divert all the money and property of said syndicate to his own use and benefit, and that these false representations, pretenses and promises were knowingly and willfully made in an effort to induce the persons intended to be defrauded to turn over money and property to the said defendant in exchange for these worthless oil stocks and without giving anything of adequate value in return therefor.

(k)   That on September 22, 1922, the defendant made the following representation in a circular letter sent to the persons to be defrauded, to-wit:

"ABSOLUTELY LAST OFFERING OF UNITS OF FORTUNA PETROLEUM SYNDICATE AT TWENTY DOLLARS PER UNIT.

"For the purpose of providing funds to drill the No. 1 Halsell well of the Fortuna Petroleum Syndicate to the pay sand, we offer a limited allotment of these units of the par value of $25.00 per unit at the special price of $20.00 per unit, payable either all cash with order, or one-half cash with order, the balance in 30 days. Notice is hereby given, however, that all orders for units of the Fortuna Petroleum Syndicate at $20.00 per unit must be mailed to us not later than Saturday, September 30, after which this offer will be absolutely withdrawn from the market.

"The Fortuna properties are located in what has already been proven to be one of the richest oil zones in the world. These properties are located on one of the best defined oil structures in this entire zone, the Fortuna properties are of such an extent, aggregating 1,090 acres, that the bringing in of production in the No. 1 Halsell well will make them worth from $1,000,000.00 to $5,000,000.00. The capitalization of the Fortuna Petroleum Syndicate was extremely low, being only 4,000 units of the par value of $25.00 per unit, and the present offering is at the special price of $20.00 per unit.

"The No. 1 Halsell well is now actually under way, and drilling at a depth of about 500 feet by one of the most successful contractors in the business. The rapid completion of this well to the pay sand is absolutely assured. We believe therefore, that within a few weeks time every outstanding unit of Fortuna Petroleum Syndicate will be worth anywhere from $250.000 to $500.00 per unit or more."

Whereas, in truth and in fact, as the defendant then and there well knew, the said properties were not located in one of the richest proven oil zones in the world, but in purely wild-cat territory and remote from oil production; that the properties would not be worth from $1,000,000.00 to $5,000,000.00, but would be, and were, of a purely speculative value, and that no reasonable basis existed upon which a prediction could be made that every outstanding unit would be worth from $250.00 to $500.00 or more, that such statements were made by the said defendant solely for the purpose of deceiving the persons to be defrauded.

(1)   That the defendant, on December 1, 1922, made the following representations to the persons to be defrauded in a printed circular entitled "Progress Report No. 2," to-wit:

"IF YOU OWN STOCK OR UNITS OF JOHNSON OIL COMPANY, MARINE OIL SYNDICATE, MEXIA TERRACE OIL COMPANY, CORSICANA-MEXIA OIL FIELDS SYNDICATE, OR RUNNELS OIL SYNDICATE WHICH HAVE NOT YET BEEN FXCHANGED FOR STOCK OF THE ADMIRAL OIL COMPANY, THIS COMMUNICATION IS OF VITAL IMPORTANCE TO YOU.

"When the ADMIRAL OIL COMPANY was organized, every share of the stock was turned back into the treasury, with the exception of only 10,000 shares which was paid out for the lease holdings around which the Admiral Company was organized, and absolutely the only way that Admiral stock can be taken out of the treasury is through the surrender of stock or units of one of the above named enterprises which were absorbed and the payment in cash of the required consideration for such transfer, depending upon which security is surrendered.

"I know positively that the best interests of every individual stockholder have been served in bringing about the consolidation of these several companies into the Admiral Oil Company. Efficiency will be greatly increased, economies will be effected, and through the development of a large number of carefully selected properties large ultimate profits will be absolutely assured. . . . I am going to stay on the job day and night until we make of the Admiral Oil Company one of the giant independent oil projects of the Southwest.

"The Admiral Oil Company has before it a tremendously profitable future, we are confident, and if you own any of the securities which can be exchanged for Admiral stock at this time, do so without fail while the opportunity is still available."

Thereby the said defendant caused the persons to be defrauded, to understand and believe that the entire treasury stock of the Admiral Oil Company was outstanding, and that there would not be any stock for public sale; that the best interest of every stockholder in the various merged syndicates had been served by the bringing about of the merger into the Admiral Oil Company; that the merger would provide for more efficient management and economy of operation; that the development of the large number of properties obtained by the merger would, and did, assure the ultimate earning of large profits for stockholders of the Admiral Oil Company, and that by paying the merger or transfer fees they would participate in such profits; that Gilbert Johnson as president and manager of the Admiral Oil Company, would devote his entire attention to the affairs of the Admiral Oil Company until it became one of the giant independent oil projects of the Southwest; and that said company had in prospect a tremendously profitable future:

Whereas, in truth and in fact, as the defendant then and there well knew, the said defendant had previously increased the capitalization of the said Admiral Oil Company from $1,000,000.00 to $3,000,000.00, and would, and did, thereafter offer its stock for sale to the general public; that the best interests of the stockholders in the various syndicates merged by and into the Admiral Oil Company would not be served at all by the merger, but that in truth and in fact, the merging of these various insolvent syndicates by and into the Admiral Oil Company was simply another scheme and artifice by which the defendant could and would obtain additional money and property from the persons to be defrauded by and through the payment of the transfer or merger fees; that the consolidation or merger of the several syndicates into the Admiral Oil Company would not bring efficiency in management, or economy in operation as the management and operation of the said syndicates had been a joint and interchangeable operation, and the change of names would not affect inefficiency of the defendant in the operation and management of said Admiral Oil Company or of the merged syndicates; that the development upon the merged properties had already proven them worthless as oil producing properties and that there was little, if any, prospect of ultimate profits of any sort, and in truth and in fact, there never were any profits, and the whole enterprise was a failure, and the purchasers of its stock lost their entire investment, and that Gilbert Johnson, the said defendant, would not, and did not, devote his entire time to the making of the Admiral Oil Company into a giant independent oil project, but would devote his efforts towards making it a giant stock selling enterprise, and to the promotion of other fraudulent stock selling enterprises:

(m) To the effect that any money paid to the stockholders for shares of Johnson Oil Company went into the treasury of the company and had been used for drilling operations; that, although said company had met with some reverses in drilling, nevertheless an honest and

economical effort had been made to develop new production of oil, and that said company was then (July 21,
1922), continuing to make progress; whereas, in truth
and in fact, as the defendant then and there well knew,
all money received from the persons intended to be defrauded for stock of the Johnson Oil Company was not
used for drilling operations, but large sums were appropriated by the said defendant to his own use and benefit;
that no honest or economical effort had been made by the
defendant to develop new production; that the company
did not continue to make progress, but at that time was
on the verge of bankruptcy and did make a financial failure; that these statements were made by the defendant
for the purpose of deception and of inducing the persons
to be defrauded to part with their money and property
without receiving anything of value therefor.

(n)   That on August 30, 1924, the defendant made the
following representations to the persons to be defrauded,
in a circular letter sent by mail to said persons, to-wit:

"FORTUNE SMILES

THEN SMILES AGAIN

ON THOSE WHO GRASP THEIR GREAT OPPOR-
TUNITIES QUICKLY

"And before you right now is the kind of an offering that wins the smiles of fortunes.

"In the very limited offering of units of the Powell
Petroleum Company are embodied the features that
bring forth large and quick profits. Large acreage,
low capitalization and a rapid development campaign
have many times meant fortunes won.

"BUT! REMEMBER! In addition to these features,
the location for the first well of the Powell Petroleum

Company on their Greer lease has been made where they have actual, tangible assurance of bringing in a real gusher well. In addition to large acreage, low capitalization and a rapid development campaign you have actual assurance of production, without which these other features would be of little value.

"Many offers are made to participate in the drilling of wells. But! How many of these offers have any real assurance that the drilling of those wells will result in success? And right on this point investors can be assured hinges their opportunities of gaining financial independence with a modest investment. When the details of an offering are under consideration, let your most careful attention be directed at this feature. The first question to ask yourself is: "What assurance is there of actually securing production?

"In the offering of a small number of units of the Powell Petroleum Company can plainly be seen the assurance of an investment in these units resulting in splendid profits. In profits of 1000% in sixty days and greater profits with the further development of their properties. And to the investor who has enough energy and foresight to secure some of these units before they are all taken, just such profits should quickly accrue.

"The exact structures underlying the properties of the Powell Petroleum Company have been so well defined and the existence of a great pool of oil has been so amply assured through an expenditure of more than one hundred and fifty thousand dollars in drilling operations that the outcome of the Powell Petroleum Company Greer No. 1 well can hardly be other than a great woodbine gusher. Which should mean a profit on every dollar placed into this exceptional offer of 1000% in sixty days time and greater profits to follow.

"When an offering has even a fair chance of returning a profit of 1000% in sixty days time, with additional profits to follow, that offer is worthy of careful consideration. But—when in addition real assurance of realizing those profits and realizing them in so short a time is given, as it is in the limited offering of units in the Powell Petroleum Company, then that offer should be grasped quickly—before it has moved into the past."

Whereas, in truth and in fact, as the defendant then and there well knew, he had no actual or tangible assurance that the said well would be brought in a real gusher oil well or that it would produce oil in commercial quantities or at all, but in fact and in truth, he knew that the prospects of this well finding oil in any commercial quantity, or at all, had been disproven by the wells previously drilled by him on adjacent properties and which proved to be dry holes and not oil producers; that there was no basis in reason or in fact assuring the earnings of profits by the said company, and that there were no prospects of paying 1000 per cent in profits or any profits, to stockholders of the said company within sixty days or at any time, and in truth and in fact, the said well was completed as a dry hole, and no profits were ever earned by the said company; and that these false and fraudulent representations, pretenses and promises were purposely made to deceive the said persons to be defrauded and to induce them to pay their money to the said defendant without receiving anything of value in return therefor, which said money would be, by the defendant, misappropriated, embezzled and converted to his own use and benefit.

(o) And the Grand Jurors say and present that the defendant made many other false, inflammatory, exaggerated and gross misrepresentations, pretenses and promises, too numerous to mention or set forth herein, for the purpose of causing and inducing the persons to be defrauded to believe that they might make and would be safe in making safe and profitable investments in the shares, units and interests of the several corporations, trust estates and concerns hereinbefore mentioned, when in fact the said representations, pretenses and promises were and would be false and untrue and were and would be made by the defendant without any reasonable foundation to believe them to be true, and in fact were and would be known by the defendant to be false and untrue, and with the intent on the part of said defendant to appropriate to his own use and to embezzle and misappropriate a large part of the money to be paid and which was paid to him by the persons to be defrauded.

And the Grand Jurors aforesaid, upon their oaths aforesaid, do further present that the said defendant, on the 5th day of October, in the year nineteen hundred and twenty-two, at Los Angeles, California, in the Southern Division of the Southern District of California, and within the jurisdiction of this court, for the purpose of executing said scheme and artifice, unlawfully, willfully, knowingly and feloneously caused to be delivered by mail of the United States according to the direction thereon a certain letter * * * etc.

The succeeding five counts upon which the defendant was acquitted incorporate the same alleged scheme by reference.

ASSIGNMENT OF ERRORS 1 AND 2.

Motion to Quash Indictment.

The grounds relied upon in the motion to quash the indictment filed in this case are set forth in said motion which we herein set forth in full together with the points and authorities that were submitted therewith at said time:

To the Honorable Judge of Said Court:

Comes now the defendant, GILBERT S. JOHNSON, in the above entitled cause and moves the court to quash the indictment herein because said indictment, and each and every count thereof, is fatally and fundamentally defective and void upon its face for the following reasons, to-wit:

(1) Said indictment and each and every count thereof, fails to charge the crime against the laws of the United States pursuant to Section 215 of the Criminal Code.

(2) Said indictment, and each and every count thereof, fails to inform the defendant of the nature and cause of the accusation against him, in this, that said indictment charges only in general terms and this defendant will be unable to meet the charges of such a general nature.

(3) Because said indictment charges and attempts to charge other and different crimes and offenses not contemplated by Section 215 of the Criminal Code of the United States, which section contemplates only the misuse of the United States mail in furtherance of schemes to defraud, in this, that said indictment in paragraph 5 of page 3, solemnly charges the defendant with the crime of embezzlement, which said crime is not contemplated by Section 215 of the Criminal

Code. And again, in paragraph 13 of page 6 of said indictment, defendant is again charged and attempted to be charged with the crime of embezzlement.

(4) Because said indictment, and each and every count thereof, is founded upon malice, passion and prejudice, in this, that in paragraph (c) on page 8 of said indictment, the defendant is charged and attempted to be charged with being "a promoter of many fraudulent enterprises and was a confidence man and swindler," which said charges, are crimes and offenses not contemplated or cognizable by the laws or statutes of the United States, and particularly, Section 215 of the United States Criminal Code, and the same paragraph further charges and attempts to charge the crime of embezzlement.

(5) Because said indictment, and each and every count thereof, further charges and attempts to charge the defendant with the crime of embezzlement, in this, that said charge or attempted charge is · found in paragraph (d) of page 8 of said indictment. This same vice is found in paragraph (e) on page 9 of said indictment, and again the same charge is found in paragraph (h) on page 11 of said indictment.

(6) Because said indictment in paragraph (n) of page 19 again charges and attempts to charge the defendant with the crime of embezzlement and conversion, which said crimes and offenses, are not cognizable by Section 215 of the United States Criminal Code. The same vice is found in paragraph (o) on page 19 of said indictment.

(7) Because said other crimes charged and attempted to be charged, to-wit: the crimes of embezzlement and conversion, and also denominating the defendant as being "a promoter of many fraudulent enterprises," and further designating him as being

"a confidence man and swindler," tend to degrade the defendant and are highly prejudicial, and will prevent him from having a fair and an impartial trial under Section 215 of the Criminal Code, as guaranteed to him by the Constitution and laws of the United States.

WHEREFORE, defendant prays that this motion to quash be sustained and said indictment dismissed and that he be discharged.

(Signed)   McLEAN, SCOTT & SAYERS,
(Signed)   H. L. ARTERBERRY,
Attorneys for Defendant.

Points and Authorities in Support of the Motion to Quash.

An indictment must be so clear and exact in its language as to advise the accused and the court beyond doubt of the offense intended to be charged, *Rumley v. United States,* 293 Fed. 532 (C. C. A. 2).

In an indictment for use of mails in furtherance of a scheme to defraud, the particulars of the scheme are matters of substance and must be set forth with sufficient certainty to acquaint the defendant with the charge against him. *Savage v. United States,* 270 Fed. 14 (C. C. A. 8.)

In the case of *United States v. Howard,* Fed. Cas. No. 15, 403, Mr. Justice Story, in discussing the tests of surplusage and of material variance, used this language:

"The material parts which constitute the offense charged must be stated in the indictment, and that must be proved in evidence. But allegations not essential to such a purpose, which might be entirely omitted without affecting the charge against the defendant, and without detriment to the indictment:

are considered as mere surplusage, and may be disregarded in evidence. But no allegation, whether it be necessary or unnecessary, whether it be more or less particular, which is descriptive of the identity of that which is legally essential to the charge in the indictment, can ever be rejected as surplusage."

See also *Mathews v. United States,* 15 Fed. (2d) 139-143 (C. C. A. 8).

The case of *Naftzger v. United States,* 200 Fed. 494 (C. C. A. 8), holds that an unnecessary allegation which, however, was descriptive of the identity of something which was legally essential to the charge, could not be considered surplusage.

Kercheval v. United States, 12 Fed. (2d) 904-908, holds that conversion is not an element of crime under Section 215 of the Penal Code; see also *Nelson v. United States,* 16 Fed. (2d) 71-75 (C. C. A. 8).

In the very recent case of *Beck v. United States,* reported in the advance sheets of August 1st, 1929, 33 Fed. (2d) 107 (C. C. A. 8).

At page 109, among other things, the court says:

"There follows five printed pages of "representations," all of which, are alleged in the most general terms to be false and untrue. It is not alleged wherein they are false. It is true, as claimed by appellant, that there are many instances wherein order to comply with the constitutional requirements of certainty in the accusation, a pleader should not only allege the falsity of the misrepresentation, but "allege affirmatively in what the falsehood consisted." 25 C. J. 628. But the particular vice of this indictment reaches farther than that; the unfair part of it is that the defendant is charged with falsely representing many things which counsel for the government assure the court are not false at all."

In connection with the *Beck* case, *supra,* it is particularly interesting to note on page 110 thereof, in discussing the indictment in said case and what was generally referred to as the "shotgun" clause, and comparing same with paragraph (o) on page 19 of the indictment in this case, wherein the same vice is found in the present indictment that was condemned by the court in the *Beck* case and in this connection, we shall quote a part of the language of the court in the *Beck* case:

"The quoted "shotgun" clause is in such general terms that it is unfair to the defendants. It gives them no inkling of what facts may be concealed in the underbrush of glittering generality, and no opportunity to defend against them. The courts are properly lenient with regard to the form of an indictment which substantially advises the defendant of the charge; they are likewise critical of a charge which is that in form alone, and can serve no purpose save as a foundation for evidence that will catch the defendant off his guard. In the early history of civil pleading, plaintiffs used to allege certain acts of negligence and then quietly add "on account of the aforesaid and other negligent acts." Occasionally, it is still done; but not when the court's attention is directed thereto. The Constitution compels that the rule of criminal pleading should be at least as fair. A trial judge would be justified in sustaining a demurrer to an indictment with such Mother Hubbard allegations; or in treating it as surplusage. In this case, neither course was taken. The motion for a bill of particulars was asked and denied. While such a motion is generally within the sound discretion of the court, it should have been sustained."

In the case of *U. S. v. Cruikshank*, 91 U. S. 442, the Supreme Court laid down the following rule:

"It is an elementary principle of criminal pleading that when the definition of an offense, whether it be of common law or by statute, includes generic terms, it is not sufficient that the indictments which charge the offense be in the same generic terms as in the definition, but it must state the species; it must descend to particularities."

In the case of *U. S. v. Hess.* 31 L. Ed. 518, the Supreme Court said:

"The object of the indictment is: First, to furnish the accused with such a description of the charge against him as will enable him to make his defense and avail himself of a conviction or acquittal, for protection against a further prosecution for the same cause; and, second, to inform the court of the facts alleged so that it may decide whether they are sufficient in law to support a conviction if one should be had, for these facts are to be stated, not conclusions of law alone. A crime is made up of acts and intent, and these must be set forth in the indictment with reasonable particularity of time, place and circumstances."

In the case of *Brenner v. U. S.* 287 Fed. 640, opinion by the Circuit Court of Appeals, Second Circuit, Justice Manton speaking for the court, used this language:

"It is essential to the sufficiency of the indictment that it set forth the facts which the pleader claims constitute the alleged criminal breach, so distinctly as to advise the accused of the charge which he has to meet, and to give him a fair opportunity to prepare his defense so particularly as to avail himself of a conviction or acquittal in advance of another prosecution for the same offense, and so clearly that the court may be able to determine whether or not the facts as stated are sufficient to support a conviction. Fontana v. U. S., 262 Fed. 283. The indictment must charge the offense in more than the generic terms as in the definition. It must descend to particularities. U. S. v. Cruikshank, 92 U. S. 542, 23 L. Ed. 588. A crime, unless otherwise provided by statute, is made of acts and intent, and they must be set forth in the indictment with reasonable particularity as to time, place and circumstances. Such particularities are matters of substance and not of *form, and their omission is not aided or cured by a verdict."*

In *U. S. v. Hess,* 124 U. S. 483, 31 L. Ed. 516, it is said: "The essential requirements indeed or the particulars constituting the offense of devising a scheme to defraud are wanting. Such particulars are matters of substance and not of form, and their omission is not aided or cured by a verdict."

In the case of *U. S. v. Potter,* 56 Fed. 89-90, the Circuit Court of Appeals, speaking through Judge Putnam, used this language:

"In order to properly inform the accused of the 'nature and cause of the accusation,' within the meaning of the Constitution and of the rules of the common law, a little thought will make it plain, not only to the legal, but to all other educated minds, that not only must all the elements of the offense be stated in

the indictment, but that also they must be stated with
clearness and certainty, and with a sufficient degree
of particularity to identify the transaction to which
the indictment relates as to place, persons and things
and other details. The accused must receive sufficient
information to enable him to reasonably understand,
not only the nature of the offense, but the particular
act or acts touching which he must be prepared with
his proof; and when his liberty, and perhaps his life,
are at stake, he is not to be left so scantily informed
as to cause him to rest his defense upon the hypothesis
that he is charged with a certain act or series of acts,
with the hazard of being surprised by proofs on the
part of the prosecution of an entirely different act
or series of acts, at least so far as such surprise can
be avoided by reasonable particularity and fullness of
description of the alleged offense. These rules are
well expressed in U. S v. Cruikshank, 92 U. S. 542,
as follows:

'In criminal cases prosecuted under the laws of the
United States the accused has the constitutional right
to be informed of the nature and cause of the accusation.' Amendment 6 in U. S. v. Mills, 7 Pet. 142,
this was construed to mean that the indictment must
set forth the offense 'with clearness and all necessary
certainty to apprise the accused of the crime with
which he stands charged'; and in U. S. v. Cooke, 17
Wall. 174, that 'every ingredient of which the offense
is composed must be accurately and clearly alleged.'
It is an elementary principle of criminal pleading that
where the definition of an offense, whether it be at
common law or by statute, 'including generic terms,
it is not sufficient that the indictment shall charge
the offense in the same generic terms as in the definition; but it must state the species—it must descend
to particulars.' 1 Arch Cr. Pr. & Pl. 291. The ob-

ject of the indictment is, first, to furnish the accused with such a description of the charge against him as will enable him to make his defense, and avail himself of his conviction or acquittal for protection against a further prosecution for the same cause; and, second, to inform the court of the facts alleged, so that it may decide whether they are sufficient in law to support a conviction, if one should be had. For this, facts are to be stated, not conclusions of law alone. A crime is made up of acts and intent; and these must be set forth in the indictment with reasonable particularity of time, place and circumstances.' "

In the case of *Anderson v. U. S.,* 294 Fed. 597, opinion by the Circuit Court of Appeals, Second Circuit, the court held:

"The crime must be charged with precision and certainty, and every ingredient of which it is composed, must be accurately and clearly alleged. Evans v. U. S., 153 U. S. 584, 14 Sup. Ct. 934, 38 L. Ed. 830. To allege that what was done was unlawful is merely to state the conclusion of the pleader. Brenner v. U. S., *supra.* The facts supporting the legal conclusion must be alleged. To admit this essential fact is to render the indictment void."

In this connection see also *Goldberg v. U. S.,* 277 Fed. 215, opinion by the Circuit Court of Appeals, Eighth Circuit; *Reeder v. U. S.,* 262 Fed. 38, opinion by Elliott, District Judge, *certiorari* denied by Supreme Court, 64 L. Ed. 726.

The defect in the indictment for failure to charge the defendants with any criminal act distinctly and expressly, with precision and certainty, is not cured by the "whereas clauses" set forth in said indictment.

In the case of *Dalton v. U. S.,* 127 Fed. 547, the Circuit Court of Appeals, Seventh Circuit, had this very question under consideration. The court, speaking through Judge Jenkins, had this to say:

> "We then come to the 'whereas' clause, which is not an allegation of a scheme, but is a negation—a denial of the truth of preceding allegations. This word 'whereas' implies a recital, and, in general, cannot be used in the direct and positive averment of a fact. It is thus defined:
>
> (1) The thing being so that; considering that things are so; implying an admission of facts, something followed by a different statement, and sometimes by inference of something consequent. (2) While on the contrary; the fact or case really being that; when in fact.' (Century Dictionary.)
>
> The statement sought to be negatived by the 'whereas' clause should have been made positively in the indictment, the purpose of the 'whereas' clause being to set forth the real truth concerning the allegations supposed to have been theretofore averred. The difficulty here is that the allegations thus denied are not positively charged in the indictment to be part of the scheme to defraud. If it be a denial of anything averred, it is a denial of the allegations of the pleader with respect to the class of persons intended to be defrauded."

In the case of *Foster v. U. S.,* 253 Fed. 482, the Circuit Court of Appeals, Ninth Circuit, speaking through Judge Gilbert, used this language:

> "The plaintiffs in error had the constitutional right to be informed of the nature and cause of the accusation against them. To furnish them with that infor-

mation it was necessary to set forth in the indictment the particular facts and circumstances which rendered them guilty and to make specific that which the statute states in general."

Misconduct of Counsel in Drafting Indictment.

Counsel for the government may be guilty of misconduct just as prejudicial to the rights of a defendant as in making final argument to the jury in the case, by display of malice, hatred, contempt, ridicule or scorn, and making assertions and statements not based on truth or fact. Because in the latter case, defendant's counsel could make a proper objection and protect the rights of the defendant from such unwarranted abuse. While in the first instance, by heaping unwarranted abuse on a defendant under the guise of a solemn accusation by a grand jury in the form of an indictment; much greater harm and injury can result from attacks of that nature, than in the latter case. And it is these tactics to which we desire to direct the court's attention to the misconduct and evident unfairness of the drafter of this indictment, when he, knowingly and deliberately, inserted a lot of accusations which have no proper place in an indictment such as this. For instance, the indictment in the present case is literally honeycombed with charges and accusations against this defendant, charging that he *misappropriated, embezzled and converted* to his own use and benefit, large sums of money and property alleged to have been acquired by him in furtherance of the alleged scheme to defraud. This, in the face of all the courts saying that such allegations constitute no part or parcel of a mail fraud indictment. Not satisfied with these allegations, which are repeated in practically every paragraph of the alleged scheme to defraud, but the alleged scheme, and particularly paragraph (o) on page 19 of said indictment, contains what the court describes and condemns in the *Beck* case, as the "shotgun" clause.

Not satisfied with the wrongful allegations above referred to, but the pleader in this case so far forgets himself as to make charges against this defendant under the guise of a solemn charge of a Grand Jury of the United States, in charging this defendant with being "a confidence man and swindler," when the pleader knew, or by the slightest investigation, could have known, that this defendant has never been even as much as charged, much less, convicted of any offense against the laws of the United States, or of any state within the United States. This, in the face of the elementary principle that every man is presumed to be innocent until proven guilty.

We submit that all these unwarranted, unjustified, malicious, and slanderous statements, have only one purpose and effect, and that is to so prejudice this defendant before a jury upon the trial of said case, that he will be denied a fair and an impartial trial, as guaranteed to him by the laws and Constitution of the United States.

We further submit that such allegations cannot be treated as mere surplusage, as they are collateral to and a part of the main charge of the indictment. We, therefore, respectfully submit that the indictment in this case should be quashed and held for naught, and defendant be discharged. See

> *Beck v. United States,* 33 Fed. (2d) 107-113 (C. C. A. 8);
>
> *Latham v. United States,* 226 Fed. 420 (C. C. A. 5);
>
> *De Luca v. United States,* 298 Fed. 416;
>
> *United States v. Gradwell,* 227 Fed. 243;
>
> *Agnew v. United States,* 165 U. S. 36-45;
>
> *United States v. American Tobacco Co.,* 177 Fed. 774;
>
> *United States v. Nevin,* 199 Fed. 833;
>
> *McKinney v. United States,* 199 Fed. 29 (C. C. A. 7);

Which said motion to quash was overruled by the court and duly excepted to. [Tr. 57-59.] The assignment of errors [Tr. 235-253] relate (1) to the overruling of the motion to quash said indictment and to the introduction of any testimony in support of said indictment based on the grounds set out in said motion to quash and (2) for the failure and refusal·of the court to give certain requested instructions requested by the defendant, and (3) for errors committed by the court in giving certain instructions to the jury which were duly excepted to at said time.

ARGUMENT.

Misconduct of District Attorney.

The question presented in Assignments of Errors Nos. 1 and 2, so far as we have been able to find, is without precedent, and we will of necessity be compelled to argue from analogy.

We fully appreciate that courts are somewhat lenient in cases of claimed misconduct of prosecuting officers for things said or done in the heat of a hotly contested case, and especially so, when the matters complained of have been provoked perhaps by defense counsel, but the rule is entirely different when the matters complained of have been studiously and intentionally injected into a case.

For instance, we refer specifically to the charges made in the indictment in this case as follows:

In paragraph No. 5 of said indictment [Tr. pp. 5 and 6] this allegation is made: "and would embezzle and misappropriate the same," and again in paragraph No. 13 of the indictment [Tr. p. 9] "that the said defendant would misappropriate and embezzle and convert to his own use and benefit a part of the money and property obtained from the persons to be defrauded, the exact amount so misappropriated, embezzled and converted being to these Grand Jurors unknown," and again in Subdivision (c) of said indictment [Tr. p. 11] "that said defendant was not a successful or honest executive of any company, but was a promoter of many fraudulent enterprises and was a *confidence man and swindler.*"

We have taken excerpts from only a few of the paragraphs and subdivisions of said indictment, and upon a careful reading of the whole indictment this same vice appears in practically every paragraph and subdivision thereof. It therefore cannot be said that this vice was unintentional, but on the contrary, this scurrility and abuse is repeated again and again. For what purpose, and why? It seems to us quite apparent. Then as a final and parting shot, the pleader injects the famous subdivision (o) of said indictment [Tr. p. 27]. A similar indictment or an indictment containing similar language to the last mentioned subdivision (o) has been very aptly and appropriately described in the case of *Beck v. United States,* 33 Fed. (2d) 110, which refers to such a charge as the "shotgun clause" with its "Mother Hubbard" allegations.

As to the misconduct of counsel, we desire to quote from the *Beck* case, *supra,* at page 114, as follows:

"A trial in the United States court is a serious effort to ascertain the truth; atmosphere should not displace evidence; passion and prejudice are not aids in ascertaining the truth, and studied efforts to arouse them cannot be countenanced; the ascertainment of the truth, to the end that the law may be fearlessly enforced, without fear or favor, and that all men shall have a fair trial, is of greater value to society than a record for convictions.

The Supreme Court of the United States has very recently reversed a case because of improper argument by counsel. Although the case was one to which the government was not a party, the court spoke in strong language:

"But a trial in court is never, as respondents in their brief argue this one was, 'purely a private controversy * * * of no importance to the public.' The state, whose interest it is the duty of court and counsel alike to uphold, is concerned that every litigation be fairly and impartially conducted and that verdicts of juries be rendered only on the issues made by the pleadings and the evidence. The public interest requires that the court of its own motion, as is its power and duty, protect suitors in their right to a verdict, uninfluenced by the appeals of counsel to passion or prejudice. See Union Pac. Ry. Co. v. Field (C. C. A.) 137 F. 14, 15; Brown v. Swineford, 44 Wis. 282, 293 (28 Am. Rep. 582). Where such paramount considerations are involved, the failure of counsel to particularize an exception will not preclude this court from correcting the error."

The case of *Volkmor v. U. S.* 13 F. (2d) 594 (C. C. A. 6) holds that personal abuse of a defendant by counsel in argument, though the remarks were withdrawn, held error so egregious as to require reversal of a judgment of conviction, and among other things the court says at page 595: "This is not a case of inadvertence of statement, but of intentional abuse."

Compare *Warfield v. U. S.* 36 F. (2d) 903-904 (C. C. A. 5).

Indicting Citizens in Foreign Jurisdictions.

We shall refer to this phase of the case only for the purpose of showing unfairness from the inception of this case to its very end. We are willing to concede that the prosecuting officers of the government have the power and the right, legally, to indict in any jurisdiction, in cases such as this, wherever letters may have been delivered in furtherance of a scheme to defraud, but in this connection, we desire to call the court's attention to some rather illuminating cases whereby the Supreme Court of the United States, and inferior courts, condemn that practice as being unfair to a defendant, particularly the case of *Beavers v. Henkel,* 194 U. S. 73, 48 L. Ed. 886, the Supreme Court, speaking through Mr. Justice Brewer, uses this language:

> "It may be conceded that no such removal should be summarily and arbitrarily made. There are risks and burdens attending it which ought not to be needlessly cast upon any individual. These may not be serious in a removal from New York to Brooklyn, but might be if the removal was from San Francisco to New York. And statutory provisions must be interpreted in the light of all that may be done under them. We must never forget that in all controversies, civil or criminal, between the government and an individual, the latter is entitled to reasonable protection."

And again the Supreme Court passing on this same question of indicting citizens in distant states and jurisdictions from that of their domicile, wherein an indictment would lie, comdemned such practice in the case of *Hyde v. Shine,* 199 U. S. 62, 50 L. Ed. 94. The court, speaking through Mr. Justice Brown, used the following language:

> "But we do not wish to be understood as approving the practice of indicting citizens of distant states in the courts of this district, where an indictment will lie in the state of the domicile of such person, unless in exceptional cases, where the circumstances seem to demand that this course shall be taken. To

require a citizen to undertake a long journey across the continent to face his accusers, and to incur the expense of taking his witnesses, and of employing counsel in a distant city, involves a serious hardship to which he ought not be subjected if the case can be tried in a court of his own jurisdiction."

See also *Tinsley v. Treat,* 205 U. S. 689.

And again some rather illuminating language is used by Judge Anderson, now Circuit Judge of the Seventh Circuit, in the case of *United States v. Smith,* 173 F. 232; in refusing to remove a defendant who had been indicted in a foreign jurisdiction, among other things he said:

"To my mind, that man has read the history of our institutions to little purpose who does not look with grave apprehension upon the possibility of the success of a proceeding such as this. If the history of liberty means anything, if constitutional guaranties are worth anything, this proceeding must fail. If the prosecuting officers have the authority to select the tribunal, if there be more than one tribunal to select from, if the government has that power, and can drag citizens from distant cities to the capital of the nation, there to be tried, then, as Judge Cooley says, 'This is a strange result of a revolution where one of the grievances complained of was the assertion of the right to send parties abroad for trial.' "

No doubt this court is already aware that in the last session of the Sixty-ninth Congress in the Senate proceedings of June 30, 1926, pages 12,331 to 12,333, this very matter was the subject of considerable debate and discussion, so much so, that as an outgrowth of said discussion, a bill was introduced in both houses of Congress, namely, Senate Bill No. 5144 of January 8, 1927, and House Bill No. 16,256 of January 13, 1927, which proposed to amend Section 215 of the Criminal Code to prevent and prohibit the very practice complained of here and condemned by the Supreme Court.

As heretofore stated, that notwithstanding the condemnation of the courts in matters of this sort, they are compelled to order the removal of a defendant who has been thus indicted, but the point we make is, that when the prosecuting officers of the government see fit to put a defendant at such a disadvantage by dragging him half way across the continent to be tried before strangers in a strange land, they should at least be fair enough in presenting an indictment without the use of slanderous and scurrilous abuse being placed in said indictment such as is the case here. We respectfully insist that the unfairness in taking a man away from home to prosecute him, that the defendant is at least entitled to reasonable protection and a fair trial, which we insist has not been accorded here, either by the prosecuting officers or the trial judge.

We shall now take up the assignments of error relating to requested instructions which were refused and the assignments of error relating to the charge as given by the trial court and which were duly excepted to at the time.

Errors in Refusing Requested Instructions.

Errors Number III, IV, V, VI, VII, VIII, IX, X, XI, XII, XIII, XIV and XV.

All relate to the refusal of the court to charge the jury as requested by the defendant. [Tr. 236-242.]

We believe that the defendant was entitled to each and every one of the requests that have been listed in the Assignment of Errors III to XV inclusive.

Error No. V.

We desire to call particular attention to Assignment Number Five [Tr. 237] wherein the defendant requested the following instruction:

> "The defendant cannot be convicted unless you believe beyond all reasonable doubt that he made false representations with the intent to defraud. An incorrect statement, grossly misrepresenting facts, does not amount to fraud in law, unless the false representations were knowingly and wilfully made with fraudulent intent."

We believe that the defendant was clearly entitled to have that charge go to the jury and we base our opinion upon the following cases:

> *Slakoff v. U. S.* 8 F. (2d) 6 (C. C. A. 3);
> *Yusem v. U. S.* 8 F. (2d) 9 (C. C. A. 3);
> *Horn v. U. S.* 182 Fed. 721-737 (C. C. A. 8).

Error No. VI.

The defendant's requested instruction referred to herein as Error Number Six reads as follows:

> "It is common knowledge that most business enterprises are aided by advertisements passing through the mails and at every hand we see claims of capacity, performance and results which we know cannot stand cross-examination. Parties who have anything to sell have the habit of puffing their wares, and we are all familiar with the fact that it is a very prevalent thing

in the course of business to exaggerate the merits of goods people have to sell and within any proper, reasonable bounds, such a practice is not criminal. It must amount to a substantial deception."

The above request which we think the defendant was entitled to have given was based upon the case of *Harrison v. U. S.,* 200 Fed. 662-666 (C. C. A. 6).

Error No. VII.

The defendant's requested instruction referred to herein as Error Number Seven reads as follows:

"You are instructed that a man may be visionary in his plans and believe that they will succeed, and yet, in spite of their ultimate failure, be incapable of committing a conscious fraud. If you believe that the defendant in this case, really entertained the belief of the ultimate success of his projects, corresponding with his representations, he did not commit the offense charged and you should return a verdict of not guilty. The significant fact is the intent and purpose. The question presented to you in this case is not whether the business enterprises of the defendant, Gilbert S. Johnson, were practicable or not, if you believe from the evidence that the defendant entered, in good faith, into these business enterprises, believing that out of the monies received he could, by investment or otherwise, make enough to repay said investors according to his promises, he is not guilty, no matter how visionary might seem his plan or scheme."

The above requested instruction, we believe, the defendant was clearly entitled to have submitted to the jury, and for our authority we call the court's attention to the case of *Sandals v. U. S.* 213 Fed. 569 (C. C. A. 6).

Error No. XIV.

The defendant's requested instruction listed herein as Error Number Fourteen reads as follows:

"If upon a fair and impartial consideration, of all the evidence in the case, the jury finds that there are two reasonable theories supported by the testimony in the case, and that one of such theories is consistent with the theory that the defendant is guilty, as charged in some one or more or all of the counts in the indictment, and that the other of such theories is consistent with the innocence of the defendant, then it is the policy of the law, and the law makes it the duty of the jury to adopt that rule which is consistent with the innocence of the defendant and in such case to find the defendant not guilty."

Upon that proposition we desire to call the court's attention to the following authorities:

> *Union Pac. Coal Co. v. U. S.,* 173 Fed. 737-740 (C. C. A. 8);
> *People v. Ward,* 105 Cal. 335-341;
> *People v. Murray,* 41 Cal. 66-67;
> *Vernon v. U. S.,* 146 Fed. 123 (C. C. A. 8);
> *Isbell v. U. S.,* 227 Fed. 792 (C. C. A. 8);
> *Wright v. U. S.,* 227 Fed. 857 (C. C. A. 8);
> *Harrison v. U. S.,* 200 Fed. 664 (C. C. A. 6);
> *Hart v. U. S.,* 84 Fed. 804 (C. C. A. 3);
> *Weiner v. U. S.,* 282 Fed. 801 (C. C. A. 3);
> *Edwards v. U. S.,* 7 Fed. (2d) 360 (C. C. A. 8);
> *Ridenour v. U. S.,* 14 Fed. (2d) 892 (C. C. A. 3);
> *Haning v. U. S.,* 21 Fed. (2d) 509-510 (C. C. A. 8);
> *Van Gorder v. U. S.,* 21 Fed. (2d) 939-942 (C. C. A. 8);
> *Nosowitz v. U. S.,* 282 Fed. 575-578 (C. C. A. 2);
> *McLaughlin v. U. S.,* 26 Fed. (2d) 3 (C. C. A. 8).

Error No. XVI.

The defendant's instruction listed herein as Error Number XVI reads as follows:

"You are instructed that it is a matter of common knowledge that beginning in the year of 1921, the business of the country generally passed through a period of deflation and depression that brought loss and even ruin to business enterprises of supposed soundness and strength, and you are further instructed that from the evidence in this case, it appears that the price of oil in the State of Texas fell from a price of $3.50 per barrel to $1.00 per barrel and this is one of the reasons that the defendant ascribes to some of his misfortunes in the oil business, and if you so believe, you should give the defendant the benefit of such condition and take these facts into consideration with all the evidence in this case."

We believe that the defendant was entitled to the above requested instruction and base our reasons therefor upon the following authorities:

Corliss v. U. S., 7 F. (2d) 455 (C. C. A. 8);

Mandelbaum v. Goodyear Tire and Rubber Co., 6 F. (2d) 818 (C. C. A. 8).

We do not believe that these requested instructions were sufficiently covered in the court's general charge and, therefore, it was error to refuse these requests.

Errors in Court's Charge to the Jury.
Error No. XVII.

The 17th Assignment of Error is as follows:

Said District Court erred in giving the following instruction to the trial jury:

"You will remember that the defendant—apparently, he must have been a very young man—started in the town of Goldfield, promoting, according to his own admissions, promoting enterprises similar to this, and through the course of a good many years. he says that he has been selling stocks by means of the United States mails. He even condemns the government for interfering with his scheme, in some of the circulars, in which you will remember that he criticized the government and the postal authorities for interfering. He explained, I think, to some of the investors that except for the pernicious activity of the postal officials the enterprise would have continued.

"Now, no prejudice is to be entertained against one who does that, because the advertising of goods is legitimate. It is done all the time, and within certain limits a person has a right to what is known 'to puff his wares.' That is very true. The fact, however, that the defendant says he believed all these things that were stated, does not necessarily control you in your judgment. *You do not have to believe that if I am caught in the act of setting fire to a house and I say to the officer, 'Well, I did not intend to burn that house,' he does not have to believe that, and probably would not.*" [See page 243 of the Transcript for this assignment of error and see pages 211 and 212 of the Transcript wherein this language appears in the charge of the court.]

The defendant made the following exception to the charge:

"I except to the court's instruction with respect to the operations of the defendant with respect to his Goldfield operations as being similar to those charged in this indictment, it not being mentioned in the indictment." [Tr. p. 219.] "And I, furthermore, take exception to the court's comment on the facts and the analogy or the example which the court gave with respect to the commission of arson, or the burning of a building and particularly in that kind of a case the matter of intent of the defendant is not involved, and an example of that kind being prejudicial to the rights of the defendant, whereas, the matter of intent to defraud is the very crux of this case." [Tr. p. 222.]

This court is familiar with the rule that in cases involving fraud, or the intent with which an accused does an act, collateral facts and circumstances and his other acts of a kindred character, both prior and subsequent, *not too remote in time,* are admissible in evidence. See *Moffatt v. U. S.,* 232 Fed. 523-533 (C. C. A. 8). Compare the above with the language in the charge of the court [Tr. p. 211]:

> "You will remember that the defendant apparently —he must have been a very young man—started in the town of Goldfield, promoting, according to his own admissions, promoting enterprises similar to this, and through the course of a *good many years,* he says that he has been selling stocks by means of the United States mails."

Needless to say, that matter was gone into on cross-examination by counsel for the government over the objections of the defendant and exceptions to that portion of the charge is found at [Tr. p. 219].

Also, we call the court's attention to the case of *Sunderland v. U. S.,* 19 Fed. (2d) 202-214 (C. C. A. 8), relative to that portion of the charge in the illustration given about burning a house.

Error No. XVIII.

THE 18TH ASSIGNMENT OF ERROR IS AS FOLLOWS:

"There is evidence here that at one time he advertised that he had a certain lease and it would be the general understanding among oil people that all leases are subject to a royalty payment; that is the general understanding—and the court will take note of that—among oil men, so by saying that he owned a lease, that implies the owning of a lease subject to a royalty payment. That is all right. This defendant, however, did not say he owned only a one-half interest in it. Now, and, by the way, the defendant was to claim that certain explanations were made in some of his publications. So far, however, I have no recollection of any evidence of that fact, so it stands before you uncontradicted that he gave the customers to understand that he owned the lease, whereas, in fact, he owned only one-half of it. Now, that might be an oversight; it might have been unintentional. To my mind, that is not so very flagrant, but it is illustrative. *They say that 'straws tell which way the wind blows.' Now, it might be that the defendant did not consider that extremely important, but he was used to making reckless statements. That is an element that you may consider properly in this case, that there were extravagant statements made. Of course, there is no denying that.* For instance, I think it was yesterday afternoon, something was shown here where it was said that a big gusher was absolutely assured, a big gusher absolutely assured. *Now, it is difficult, gentlemen of the jury, to reconcile that with honest belief in anybody.* 'Assured' means, as we all know, 'sure,' 'that it was sure'; and it is significant, gentlemen, that every single one of these statements contains an invitation to buy stock; every single one without exception, so far as I remember, is an invitation to buy stock—not only an invitation, but an urgent invitation. *Well, now, the defendant might have been entirely innocent; he might have honestly believed that, but his honest belief is not sufficient unless the facts warranted him in expressing such belief, unless his information and facts warranted him.*

"The evidence in this case shows that from the very beginning this defendant pursued a consistent line of advertising, and I will not, I think, go too strong in calling it *extravagant advertising.* It is a little singular, gentlemen, that if he was honest in his belie. 'hat that continued."

The defendant made the following exception to the charge

"I take exception to the court's comment upon the facts in the case as being unfair and prejudicial to the defendant, and particularly to the court's comment with respect to the owning of a certain lease and the court's comments with respect to the failure of the defendant to show a correction of any such statement contained in the literature." [Tr. p. 222.) "And then I also except to the court's remarks with respect to the course of conduct of the operations of the defendant generally, and particularly with respect to his having made those reckless or extravagant statements as designated by the court over a course of five years." [Tr. p. 223.]]See pages 212 and *213* of Transcript] wherein this language appears in the charge of the court.

In this assignment of error we think the court's charge was very unfair and highly prejudicial to the defendant, wherein the court's opinion is substituted for that of the jury when it stated that "he was used to making reckless statements" and "that there were extravagant statements made. Of course, there is no denying that." And again, "Well, now, the defendant *might* have been entirely innocent; he *might* have honestly believed that, *but his honest belief is not sufficient* unless the facts warranted him in expressing such belief, unless his information and facts warranted him," and other similar language.

In our opinion such a charge is tantamount to telling the jury to find the defendant guilty. In cases such as this, wherein fraud is charged or attempted to be charged, the good faith or honest belief of a defendant is a complete defense. This is so elementary and fundamental that we feel that it would be an insult to this court's intelligence to burden the record with the citation of authorities.

Error No. XIX.

The 19th Assignment of Error is as follows:

"Juror H. Lewis Haynes: Your Honor, may I ask a question?

The Court: Yes, sir.

Juror Haynes: If it is proper, I would like to have you clarify to me the distinction between 'a particular' and 'a count,' which you refer to in that indictment.

The Court: A what?

Juror Haynes: A particular and a count, which you spoke of in the indictment; you refer to fourteen particulars and six counts, I believe. I do not understand the difference.

The Court: Well, I will go over that again. That was probably due to my confusion or inaccuracies in my statement. The indictment charges first, that he conceived and formed a plan to defraud; that Gilbert

Johnson did devise a scheme to defraud, and it was, in substance, as follows: Now. here follow fourteen particulars in which, according to the indictment and the position of the government, are constituted and made up the scheme to defraud. The instruction was that not all of those particulars constituting the scheme to defraud need to be proven; any of them relating to the letters that were sent would be sufficient. Then, in the last or fourteenth particular, that is divided up into, I think there are twenty-six letters in the alphabet—well, this runs up to L or runs up to O. That made sub-divisions of that fourteenth; that it was further a part of the scheme and artifice to defraud, that the defendant would make fraudulent. false pretenses and promises to the person intended to be defrauded, through and by means of divers circular letters, pamphlets, newspapers, and house organs, publicly circulated and intended to be circulated in effect and substance—

Juror Haynes: A count, then, is just a sub-division under a particular.

The Court: Yes." [Tr. pp. 246-247 for this assignment of error and see pages 214, 215 of the Transcript wherein this language appears in the charge of the court.]

The defendant made the following exception to the charge:

"I also take exception to the court's suggestion that it will be sufficient under the law to find any one of the elements of the alleged scheme as set out in the indictment would be sufficient; that is, if the jury finds any one of those particulars exist, that that would be sufficient to sustain the charge laid in the indictment, so far as the devising of the scheme is concerned.

The Court: Well, there may be some confusion in that. That was qualified or followed by the statement that any one was sufficient to base a conviction on the count in the indictment relating to it.

Mr. Cannon: I take an exception to that modified charge." [Tr. p. 220.]

In connection with this assignment of error, we invite the court's attention to the case of *Brown v. U. S.*, 146 Fed. 219 (C. C. A. 8) wherein the court at page 220 said:

"It follows that one must be convicted, if at all, on the scheme as alleged, and if the scheme as alleged is not substantially established by the proof he cannot be convicted."

Also the case of *Hendrey v. U. S.*, 233 Fed. 5 (C. C. A. 6) at page 18 the court says:

"We have often approved the practice of declining to give instructions which, though proper in themselves, would constitute mere repetitions, usually in less intelligible form, of subject-matter consecutively and logically treated in the general charge, but the respondents in a criminal case, no less than the parties in a civil case, are entitled of right to have clearly stated to the jury each distinct and important theory of defense, so that the jury may understand that theory and the essential rules applicable to it. We cannot avoid the conviction that the respondents' rights in these respects in this case were not sufficiently saved by the general charge."

Compare the language above quoted with the unintelligible and misleading charge here complained of.

Error No. XXI.

THE 21ST ASSIGNMENT OF ERROR IS AS FOLLOWS:

"Now, with respect to these units, you will remember that some discussion was had of them. So far as I am advised, this system of selling in California is not pursued. The unit system or the trust estate, or what is known as the common law trust estate, is, in effect, a partnership; that is, you, the defendant— not a partnership as defined in the California law, but the party offering the trust estate announces that he has a certain property and he invites others to participate with him, not in buying stock in the corporation, but in buying units which give to the parties buying the units actual ownership in the properties then found. That is a legitimate system of business, in the State of Texas at least, and there is no reflection on anybody for adopting such a system. It, itself, does not give evidence of any dishonest motive. There are certain duties, however, which one engages, that are important to be considered.

There is evidence in this case tending to prove that the defendant, operating as a broker under the name of Gilbert Johnson & Company, entered into contracts with several syndicates or companies of which he was the promoter, organizer and dominant head, whereby Gilbert Johnson & Company undertook to sell the units or shares of these syndicates or companies. There is also evidence tending to prove that in selling these units or shares to the public a considerable proportion of the purchase price paid by the public was absorbed by Gilbert Johnson & Company as commissions or expenses or otherwise, so that in many instances a comparatively small proportion of the amount thus paid by the public actually went into the treasury of the respective syndicates or companies and became available for the development purposes for which they were said to be organized. Further, it is the contention of the government in this case that in soliciting the public to purchase these shares or units the defendant failed to disclose that a large proportion of the money paid for the same would not go to the syndicates or companies, but would be absorbed in commissions and other charges by the said brokerage concern of Gilbert Johnson & Company.

Now, I charge you that the payment of an exorbitant and unreasonable commission, not warranted by the financial conditions or necessities of the occasion and undisclosed to the parties interested, is fraudulent if, in your judgment, they are grossly excessive and are not so disclosed.

And I further charge you that when the shares or units of such concerns as are involved in this case are selling for much more than their par value, it should not require the payment of large commissions to dispose of them. If it does, the selling price must be altogether artificial and the inference may be made by the jury either that the company is fraudulent if the commission is not excessive, or that the commission is fraudulent if the company is what it purports to be. I further charge you that the promoter of a corporation or other similar concern, such as these syndicates, stands in a relation of trust toward those who are invited to purchase the shares or units, and he must deal fairly with them and must faithfully disclose all facts which might influence them in deciding upon the judiciousness of the purchase.

If, therefore, you find from the evidence, beyond a reasonable doubt, that the defendant knowingly so manipulated the several contracts, or any of them, whereby Gilbert Johnson & Company were to sell these units or shares with a commission so grossly excessive as to convince you that they are fraudulent, and the amount of such commissions or deductions was not disclosed to the purchasers of such units or shares, such a finding by you would make it necessary to find the defendant guilty of devising the scheme to defraud described in the indictment, if, at the same time, you find beyond a reasonable doubt that he did so with the intent to defraud, as I have already defined it to you. And having so found, if you further find that he used the mails to carry the fraudulent scheme into effect, as alleged in the indictment, it will then be your duty to find him guilty as charged." [Tr. 247-250 for this assignment of error and see pages 205-208 of the Transcript wherein this language appears in the charge of the court.]

The defendant made the following exception to the charge:

"I also take exception to the court's instruction with respect to the trust estates, and particularly to the effect that the trust estates constituted a partnership, either under the law of this state or under the law of any other state."

"I also take exception to the court's instruction with respect to the duty devolving upon Mr. Johnson and upon the other trustees of these various syndicates, in the court's holding under the instructions, that there was any obligation on his part to disclose the full amount of the commission was, that he was receiving any commission or any profit from dealing with the particular syndicates themselves, in view of the fact that the declarations of trust themselves provided that he can so do."

"I except to the instructions of the court with respect to the nature of the declaration of trust, in view of the fact that it seems to me—"

Mr. Pratt: I object to the statement of counsel, in view of the fact that it is not the time and place for him—

The Court: Yes, just confine yourself to the exceptions.

Mr. Cannon: I am willing to make a blanket exception to the whole thing, except—

The Court: All right; then, make it.

Mr. Cannon: Except the fact, if the court please, the courts as I understand them, require me to particularize in what respect I object to the charges; and that is all I am attempting to do.

The Court: No, I do not agree with you, counsel, I think you protect your rights fully when you note the exception to that portion of the charge specified." [Tr. pp. 218-19.]

In Assignment Number 21, it occurs to us that court has erred by the use of the following language [Tr. p. 207]:

"Now, I charge you that the payment of an exorbitant and unreasonable commission, not warranted by the financial conditions or necessities of the occasion and undisclosed to the parties interested, is fraudulent, if, in your judgment, they are grossly excessive and are not so disclosed."

We believe that the above quoted portion of the court's charge falls within the condemnation pronounced in the case of *St. Clair v. U. S.*, 23 F. (2d) 76 (C. C. A. 9) at page 79, this court speaking through Judge Rudkin said:

"We will now consider the instruction given by the court to the effect that a scheme to take 50 per cent, or more of the purchase price of shares' of the treasury stock as commission and to turn over to the company only 50 per cent, or less of the purchase money, would be a scheme to defraud as a matter of law, unless the purpose to retain the commission was disclosed to the purchaser.

A corporation may lawfully pay a commission for procuring subscribers to, or for selling, its capital stock. Scott v. Abbott (C. C. A.) 160 F. 573; Royal Casualty Co. v. Puller, 194 Mo. App. 588, 186 S. W. 1099; Cranney v. McAlister, 35 Utah 550, 101 p. 985. If an apparently excessive commission is allowed, there may be room for a reasonable inference either that the corporation is engaged in a fraudulent enterprise, or that the agreement for the payment of the commission was fraudulently or improvidently made, but in either case the inference is one of fact and not of law. The stock of an established corporation, having a ready sale on the market, may be sold at a profit on a small commission, while stock of a purely speculative character, having no standing on the market, may only be sold through the greatest efforts, and upon a commission that might seem excessive. So an individual or a corporation may by force of circumstances be compelled to pay what might seem an exorbitant rate of interest, or to give what might seem a large bonus in order to raise money in a particular emergency, and yet the agreement to pay the interest or give the bonus may be prompted by honest motives and by sound business judgment. For these reasons, each case must depend on its own facts and circumstances. and the amount of the commission alone cannot be made the sole criterion of fraud."

Error No. XXII.

THE 22ND ASSIGNMENT OF ERROR IS AS FOLLOWS:

"It is essential only that it be shown that the scheme be formed with a fraudulent intent. It is necessary that the government prove that the scheme or artifice employed by the defendant was of the kind charged in the indictment. It is not necessary that it be proved that the scheme and artifice included the making of all of the alleged false pretenses, representations and promises, *but it is sufficient if any one or more of the same be proved to have been made,* and that the same were designed to and would be reasonably effective in deceiving and defrauding persons with whom the defendant proposed to and did deal."

In connection with said charge the following colloquy occurred:

"Mr. Cannon: I also take an exception to the court's suggestion that it will be sufficient under the law to find any one of the elements of the alleged scheme as set out in the indictment would be sufficient; that is, if the jury finds any one of those particulars exists, that that would be sufficient to sustain the charge laid in the indictment, so far as the devising of the scheme is concerned.

The Court: Well, there may be some confusion in that. That was qualified or followed by the statement that any one was sufficient to base a conviction on the count in the indictment relating to it." [See pages 250-251 of the Transcript for this assignment of error and see page 198 of the Transcript wherein this language appears in the charge of the court.]

The defendant made the following exception to the charge:

"I also take an exception to the court's suggestion that it will be sufficient under the law to find any one of the elements of the alleged scheme as set out in the indictment would be sufficient; that is, if the jury finds any one of those particulars exist, that that would be sufficient to sustain the charge laid in the indictment, so far as the devising of the scheme is concerned.

The Court: Well, there may be some confusion in that. That was qualified, or followed by the statement that any one was sufficient to base a conviction on the count in the indictment relating to it.

Mr. Cannon: I take an exception to that modified charge."

With reference to the 22nd assignment of error, we again call the court's attention to the fundamental principle of all criminal cases of this character, and that is, that the scheme must be proved *substantially* as charged. We believe the trial court fell far short of that rule in its charge here.

Assignment of Error XXIV.

THE 24TH ASSIGNMENT OF ERROR IS AS FOLLOWS:

"The Court: You are instructed, gentlemen, that these additional instructions are given you together with all the other instructions. I certainly think that you understand that intent must accompany everything. You understand that, of course; that is, the general principle as to all crimes, and I am very sure the jury understand that intent always must be proven in fact. The intent is the intentional—things having been intentionally done, are really the foundation of the case. There might be this to call to your attention, however; certain of these bulletins were sent out and the statements in them the defendant denied knowledge of. Defendant cannot deny knowledge of what was done by his employees. That is about the only room or occasion I could see for any particular question on intent, Mr. Arterberry.

Mr. Arterberry: One point, if Your Honor please: You will recall that the defendant testified that he received certain information from the driller of the well in Desdemona when Your Honor asked him on cross-examination about the 'well being assured.' The driller told him he was then in the pay sand and he had a well, and he made his representations based on that. Now, if the defendant in good faith and honestly made that representation based on that, he is entitled to the benefit of that.

The Court: Well, the defendant, of course, must have been justified from his knowledge of the situation. *The fact that he believed it to be true, would not exonerate him unless he believed it on a sufficient foundation or evidence."* [See pages 251-2 of Transcript for this assignment of error and see pages 226-227 of the Transcript wherein this language appears in the charge of the court.]

The 24th Assignment of Error is based upon additional charges given by the court to the jury after they had been deliberating for many hours and the jury was seeking further enlightenment. The entire colloquy is not listed in the assignment, as it should have been, but the entire matter is found on pages 224 to 227 of the Transcript, and we invite the court's careful consideration of the entire matter.

Again the court ignores the fundamental principle in all cases of this kind and character and sets at naught the

question of good faith and honest belief when the matter
is placed fairly and squarely before the court on that question when he says:

*"The fact that he believed it to be true, would not
exonerate him unless he believed it on a sufficient
foundation or evidence."* [Tr. 227.]

The above quoted portion of the court's charge, in our
opinion, is thoroughly unsound, as numerous cases hold
that a man may be the victim of his own self deception.
The Circuit Court of Appeals for the 6th Circuit in the
case of *Sandals v. U. S.*, 213 Fed. 569, at page 575 says:

"A man may be visionary in his plans and believe
that they will succeed, and yet, in spite of their ultimate failure be incapable of committing a conscious
fraud. Human credulity may include among its victims even the supposed imposter. If the men accused
in the instant case really entertained the conviction
throughout that the oil properties and the stock in
dispute possessed merits corresponding with their
representations, they did not commit the offense
charged."

Compare the above with the charge of the court in this
case. We believe that this court will be forced to the conclusion that the trial court clearly has invaded the province
of the jury and that this error is fundamental.

Errors Nos. XXV, XXVI and XXVII.

We believe these last three assignments of error have
already been covered by the argument and authorities heretofore made and cited, hence we shall not repeat same.

An Unfair Trial.

We shall summarize, to some extent, some of the matters heretofore discussed, touching upon the highlights in this case showing unfairness from the very beginning.

First: By dragging the defendant half way across the continent to try him instead of trying him in the state and district of his own domicile.

Second: By making such a scurrilous and abusive attack upon the defendant under the form and guise of an indictment.

Third: By the failure and refusal of the court to give the requested instructions of the defendant.

Fourth: By the court in its charge to the jury, erring in matters of law, and in a partisan one-sided charge, invading the province of the jury on questions of fact, and in effect instructing the jury to find the defendant guilty.

Argument.

We invite the court's attention in our argument to numerous cases to sustain our position on the question of a prejudicial charge given to the jury resulting in an unfair trial, and in this connection we call the court's attention to the case of *Sunderland v. U. S.,* 19 F. (2d) 202 (C. C. A. 8), where the Circuit Court of Appeals of the Eighth Circuit, at page 214, says:

> "It requires no argument to convince that this 'gold brick' illustration was unfortunate and prejudicial. This was finally conceded by the court, and the illustration withdrawn, but we entertain grave doubt whether the prejudice once created could be removed by mere withdrawal of the words. Rudd v. U. S., 173 Fed. 912 (C. C. A. 8)."

In the *Rudd* case, *supra,* we call the court's attention to the language found at page 914:

"As Chief Justice Fuller said in Starr v. U. S., 153 U. S. 614-626, 14 Sup. Ct. 919 38, L. Ed. 841, the influence of the trial judge on the jury is necessarily and properly of great weight, and his lightest word or intimation is received with deference and may be controlling. So positive and emphatic were the remarks of the court that it is not too much to say the jury may have believed a finding for the accused would have subjected them to ridicule. True, the court afterwards withdrew the language, and said that, 'It does not follow that a man is a fool or insane who believes the representations,' and that it was a question for the jury; but it is doubtful the damage was repaired, and when that is the case the just remedy is a new trial. A mere withdrawal of words, and a direction to the jury that the question is for them, is not always sufficient. The effect of what was said may remain."

Quoting further from the *Sunderland* case, *supra,* at page 216:

"While the judge in the federal courts 'may comment on the evidence and may express his opinion on the facts, provided he clearly leaves to the jury the decision of fact questions' (Weare v. U. S., 1 F. (2d) 617 (C. C. A. 8) (and cases cited), yet as was said in the same case, 'The instructions, however, should not be argumentative, the court cannot direct a verdict of guilty in criminal cases, even if the facts are undisputed. (Dillon v. U. S. (C. C. A.), 279 F. 639.) It should not be permitted to do indirectly what it cannot do directly and by its instructions to in effect argue the jury into a verdict of guilty.' See also, Parker v. U. S., 2 F. (2d) 710; Cook v. U. S. (C. C. A. 8), 18 F. (2d) 50.

We think the charge in the case at bar, taken as a whole, was clearly argumentative." * * *

"While the judge may and should direct and control the proceedings, and may exercise his right to comment on the evidence, yet he may not extend his activities so far as to become in effect either an assistant prosecutor or a thirteenth juror."

We think the court's charge in the *Sunderland* case, from which we have quoted, is similar in many respects to the charge in the case at bar, particularly the illustration drawn by the court in the *Sunderland* case regarding the 'gold brick' swindle with the trial court's charge in the case at bar, wherein the court uses this language:

"The fact, however, that the defendant says he believed all these things that were stated, does not necessarily control you in your judgment. You do not have to believe that if *I am caught in the act of setting fire to a house and I say to the officer, 'Well, I did not intend to burn that house,' he does not have to believe that, and probably would not."* [See pages 211 and 212 of the Transcript.]

And again, at page 213 of the Transcript, the court says:

"They say that 'Straws tell which way the wind blows,' now, it might be that the defendant did not consider that extremely important, but *he was used to making reckless statements. That is an element that you may consider properly in this case, that there were extravagant statements made. Of course, there is no denying that."*

And, again on page 213 of the Transcript:

"The evidence in this case shows that from the very beginning this defendant pursued a consistent line of advertising, *and I will not, I think, go too strong in calling it extravagant advertising. It is a little singular, gentlemen, that if he was honest in this belief, that that continued."*

And again, on this same page of the Transcript, we find this language:

"*Well, now, the defendant might have been entirely innocent; he might have honestly believed that, but his honest belief is not sufficient unless the facts warranted him in expressing such belief, unless his information and the facts warranted him."*

And, again, at page 227 of the Transcript:

"Well, the defendant, of course, must have been justified from his knowledge of the situation. *The fact that he believed it to be true would not exonerate him unless he believed it on a sufficient foundation or evidence."*

We have quoted several paragraphs from the court's charge in this case and we believe that from a reading of the whole charge and the exceptions taken thereto, together with the court's comments at the time the exceptions were made, shows that said charge was highly prejudicial and wholly unfair and this defendant did not receive at the hands of the court a fair or proper charge to which he was entitled.

On the question of an unfair charge, we respectfully call the court's attention to the dissenting opinion of the late lamented Judge Rudkin in the case of *Campbell v. U. S.,* 12 F. (2d) 873 (C. C. A. 9) at page 877, wherein this language is used:

"The charge to the jury was largely argumentative in form and favored the government throughout.

Inferences of fact were placed on the same footing as inferences of law, and no distinction whatever was made between implied fraud and actual fraud. In the end the verdict was made to turn upon the abstract legal right of the accused to pay commissions on sales of shares out of the proceeds of such sales, regardless of his belief or good faith in the premises. Indeed, no attempt was made on the oral argument to uphold the charge of the court, but the government pleaded for affirmance on the sole ground that the proof of guilt was so overwhelming that errors committed during the progress of the trial were not prejudicial. With such a contention I am unable to agree. A fair and impartial trial by jury is the constitutional right of every person accused of crime, whether guilty or innocent, and that constitutional guarantee is not satisfied by a partisan one-sided charge to the jury."

It is interesting to note that Judge Rudkin, in writing the opinion in the case of *St. Clair against the United States*, 23 F. (2d) 76 (C. C. A. 9) wherein this Honorable Court in an unanimous opinion in effect overruled and nullified the doctrine as announced in the *Campbell* case, and that the late Judge Gilbert who concurred in the majority opinion in the *Campbell* case, concurred in the opinion of the later *St. Clair* case.

In addition to the above authorities from which we have quoted on the question of an unfair trial, we call the court's attention to the following:

> *Rutherford v. U. S.,* 258 F. 855 (C. C. A. 2);
> *Connley v. U. S.,* 46 F. (2d) 53 (C. C. A. 9);
> *Adler v. U. S.,* 182 Fed. 464 (C. C. A. 5);
> *Glover v. U. S.,* 147 Fed. 426 (C. C. A. 8), 8 Ann. Cas. 1184;
> *People v. Mahoney,* 201 Cal. 618, 258 Pac. 607.

Conclusion.

We respectfully submit that we have clearly shown three main reasons, any one of which, not only justify, but, according to law, demand a reversal of this case, namely:

First: The failure of the trial court to sustain the motion to quash the indictment herein for the reasons set forth in said motion, based upon the points and authorities submitted therewith.

Second: The failure and refusal of the trial court to give each and every of the requested instructions of the defendant.

Third: Errors committed by the trial court in giving its instructions to the jury, and which said insructions given were argumentative, unintelligible, partisan and one-sided and highly prejudicial to the rights of the defendant. We anticipate that counsel for the Government in their brief when they attempt to defend and excuse the many matters herein complained of will attempt to seek refuge under the sheltering wing of section 269 of the Judicial Code, as amended (28 U. S. C. A. Sec. 391); we challenge them on that very question by quoting the language of the late Judge Rudkin of this court in the St. Clair case, 23 F. (2d) 76, at page 80:

> "The defendant in error contends, however, that the evidence of guilt as to the several plaintiffs in error was utterly overwhelming, and that, if any error was committed by the court, they were not prejudiced thereby. In support of this proposition, our attention is again directed to section 269 of the Judicial Code, as amended (28 U. S. C. A. 391, Comp. St. 1246), which provides:

'On the hearing of any appeal, certiorari, writ of error, or motion for a new trial, in any case, civil or criminal, the court shall give judgment after an examination of the entire record before the court, without regard to technical errors, defects, or exceptions which do not affect the substantial rights of the parties.'

That provision is not applicable here. As said by the Supreme Court in United States v. River Rouge Co., 269 U. S. 411, 421, 46 S. Ct. 144, 147 (70 L. Ed. 339):

'The present case is not controlled by the provision of section 269 of the Judicial Code, as amended by the Act of February 26, 1919 (28 U. S. C. A. 391; Comp. St. 1246), that in an appellate proceeding judgment shall be given after an examination of the entire record, "without regard to technical errors, defects, or exceptions which do not affect the substantial rights of the parties." We need not enter upon a discussion of the divergent views which have been expressed in various Circuits Courts of Appeals as to the effect of the act of 1919. It suffices to say that since the passage of this act, as well as before, an error which relates, not to merely formal or technical matters, but to the substantial rights of the parties—especially when embodied in the charge to a jury—is to be held a ground for reversal, unless it appears from the whole record that it was harmless and did not prejudice the rights of the complaining party.'

Only enough of the evidence has been brought to this court to present and explain the assignments of error, so that the government has not met the burden of showing that the error was harmless or without prejudice.

For error in the instruction, the judgment of the court below is reversed, and the case remanded for a new trial."

For the reasons herein set forth, we respectfully urge that the judgment of the lower court be reversed.

Respectfully submitted,

H. L. ARTERBERRY,
Attorney for Appellant.

DAVID H. CANNON,
of Los Angeles, California;

ATHEARN, CHANDLER & FARMER
and
FRANK R. DEVLIN,
of San Francisco, California;

McLEAN, SCOTT & SAYERS,
of Fort Worth, Texas,
Of Counsel.

/ 0

No. 6588

In the United States Circuit Court of Appeals for the Ninth Circuit

GILBERT JOHNSON, APPELLANT,

v.

UNITED STATES OF AMERICA

BRIEF FOR THE UNITED STATES

INDEX

In the United States Circuit Court of Appeals for the Ninth Circuit

---

No. 6588

GILBERT JOHNSON, APPELLANT

v.

UNITED STATES OF AMERICA

BRIEF FOR THE UNITED STATES

I

APPELLANT WAS NOT PREJUDICED BY THE USE IN THE INDICTMENT OF EXPRESSIONS COMPLAINED OF.

The chief assignment of error relied upon by appellant herein lies in the use of various expressions in the indictment; namely, the words "embezzle," "confidence man," and "swindler." It is urged that this tends, on the one hand, to degrade the defendant to his prejudice, and on the other, to charge him with the crime of embezzlement.

In describing a scheme to defraud in an indictment under Section 215, it is necessary to advise the defendant of the character of the scheme with such definiteness and precision that he properly can prepare his defense.

It is required in pleading the defendant's false representations to negative them with particularity. This is evidenced by the case cited by the appellant in his brief, namely, *Beck* v. *United States,* 33 F. (2d) 107, wherein the court says on page 109:

> It is true that * * * a pleader should not only allege the falsity of the misrepresentations, but allege affirmatively in what the falsity consisted.

It was proper and necessary to allege in connection with the description of the scheme to defraud that the money which defendant planned to obtain from the victims would be appropriated to his own use instead of being applied to the purposes which these representations described. Such intent as to appropriation was part of the scheme. Therefore, it was well pleaded. It is obvious that the term "embezzle" was used only in describing in particularity a portion of the scheme involved.

Appellant also insists that he has been gravely prejudiced by the use of the term "confidence man" and "swindler."

If this be true, then appellant might argue with equal logic and reason that he had been prejudiced by the very fact of being indicted.

However, the use of these terms is solely in connection with the falsity of the representation lettered (c) of the indictment, as follows:

> To the effect that Gilbert Johnson (meaning, thereby, the defendant), of Gilbert

Johnson and Company, and president of the big, successful Johnson Oil Company, is president and general manager of the Fernando Oil Company, which in itself assures a competent administration of the affairs of the enterprise (meaning the said Fernando Oil Company), fair and square treatment for the stockholders, and an equitable distribution of all accruing profits; whereas, in truth and in fact, as the said defendant then and there well knew and intended, the Johnson Oil Company was not a big and successful oil company, but was a purely promotional stock-selling enterprise, and that said defendant was not a successful or honest executive of any company, but was a promoter of many fraudulent enterprises and was a confidence man and swindler, and the fact that he was president and general manager of said Fernando Oil Company did not assure a competent administration of its affairs or a fair and square treatment of its stockholders, or an equitable distribution of all accruing profits, but in fact, gave assurance that there would be no distribution of money to stockholders, but that whatever profit accrued would be misappropriated and embezzled by said defendant.

A review of the foregoing makes it clear that an integral feature of the scheme to defraud was misrepresentation as to the character of the person who was handling the affairs of the company. The words complained of appear solely for the purpose of providing a negative to such misrepresentation, and alleging affirmatively in what the falsity consisted.

For instance, one engaged in a scheme to defraud might have as a dominant feature of such enterprise the representation, let us say, that a former President of the United States was actively handling the affairs of the company. If this representation were relied on, it might well prove the greatest feature of the scheme of misrepresentation. But a draftsman in preparing an indictment and charging that as part of the scheme to defraud, would not meet the requirements of ▄▄ pleading if he simply were to negative the assertion that the administrative officer was a former President of the United States. If it happened, in fact, that the officer really running the enterprise, was a notorious confidence man and swindler, there surely then would devolve upon the pleader the necessity of alleging affirmatively that fact in pleading the negative of the misrepresentation.

As a matter of fact the terms complained of—"confidence man" and "swindler"—might well be eliminated from the indictment, and an inspection of the contents of this pleading still reveals, without those words in fact being used, that he still was being charged with being a swindler and a confidence man.

Even the legal definition of the word "swindler" can claim close kinship, if not absolute identity, with one who is charged with violation of Section 215:

A swindler is one who secures or attempts to secure, a valuable right by some deceitful pretense or fraudulent representation. *Words and Phrases*, Second Series, Volume 4, page 821.

The *Standard Dictionary* defines "swindle" as follows:

To cheat and defraud grossly, or with deliberate artifice, and further defines the word "swindler" as:

One who swindles; a fraudulent schemer; cheat.

Webster defines the word as:

One who swindles or defrauds grossly, or one who makes a practice of defrauding others by imposition or deliberate artifice.

A "confidence man" is one who with intent to cheat and defraud obtains money from any other person by means of any trick or deception or false or fraudulent representation, or statement of pretense, or any other means, or instrument, or device commonly called the confidence game. *Words and Phrases,* First Series, page 883.

It is obvious, therefore, that the term "swindler" and "confidence man" are practically synonymous. The terms import a man who, by some device, gains the confidence of another, and by such means, defrauds him of his money or property. It is likewise clear that anyone who is guilty of devising a scheme to defraud and of carrying it, or attempting to carry it, into effect, is a confidence man and

a swindler. This is particularly true in the light
of the definition of fraud which the Supreme Court
of the United States has repeatedly made. *Ham-
merschmidt* v. *United States,* 265 U. S. 182, 188;
Fasulo v. *United States,* 272 U. S. 620, 627. In
both cases that Court defines the words "to defraud" and says they mean to cheat and that they
signify deprivation of something of value by trick,
deceit, chicane or overreaching.

The indictment in this case charges that the appellant, by various fraudulent devices, sought to
obtain the confidence of certain persons. Then
having obtained the good will of these persons, it
was part of the scheme to obtain their money under
the representation that it would be used for proper
and legitimate purposes, whereas it was the real
intention at all times to appropriate the money to
his own use in disregard of the rights of these
persons.

It seems somewhat absurb that because the terms
"swindler" and "confidence man" were used by the
draftsman the defendant should feel so aggrieved,
when as herein set forth, the whole document in its
description of the fraudulent enterprise carries the
unfailing implication that the words quoted are apt
and properly descriptive.

Also appellant in this case now stands convicted
of the scheme which in effect charged him with
being a confidence man and a swindler. It is rather
asking much of this court to reverse the judgment
of the lower court because the draftsman in the

indictment alleged certain facts which the jury apparently found to be true.

But this point must be considered also in connection with the charge of the court. The defendant apparently caused character testimony to be introduced in his behalf. Keeping in mind his assertion that he was gravely prejudiced by the use of the terms "swindler" and "confidence man" in the indictment, it is interesting to note what the court had to say of this appellant in the formal charge to the jury. (R. 209.)

You are instructed, gentlemen, that the good character of a person accused of a crime, when proven, for the traits involved in the charge—in this case, for honesty and integrity—is itself a fact in the case. It must be considered in connection with all the other facts and circumstances adduced in evidence on the trial, and if, after such consideration, the jury are not satisfied beyond a reasonable doubt of the defendant's guilt, you should acquit him. If, however, you are satisfied from all the evidence in the case, that the defendant is guilty, you are to convict him, notwithstanding proof of good character. In the Federal courts there is no presumption that the defendant is of good character. Neither is it presumed that he is of bad character.

Respecting the evidence introduced by the defendant of what is known as "character evidence" or evidence of "good character," particularly as to his honesty and fair dealing with his fellow men, and also as to his

veracity and truthfulness, you are instructed
that the law is: That good character, when
considered in connection with the other evidence in the case, may create a reasonable
doubt. The circumstances may be such that
an established reputation for good character,
if it is relevant to the issue (and is of especial value in cases like the one at bar, where
the element of intent to defraud is involved)
such evidence would alone create a reasonable doubt, although without the other evidence would be convincing.

Considering the foregoing this court is asked by
the appellant to indulge the bare presumption that
he had been prejudiced in the trial of his case by
the use of the terms "confidence man," "swindler,"
and "embezzle," whereas the record reveals that
appellant was granted a generous and precise
charge on the effect the jury was to accord the evidence of good character introduced in his behalf.
Then again the court in its charge to the jury was
most careful to point out the function of an indictment in a trial. His language is illuminating on
the proposition of whether the indictment or any
portion thereof could serve in any wise to prejudice
the appellant in his case (R. 196):

> By the finding of an indictment no pre-
> sumption whatsoever arises to indicate that
> a defendant is guilty, or that he has any con-
> nection with, or responsibility for, the act
> charged against him. A defendant is pre-
> sumed to be innocent at all stages of the
> proceeding until all of the evidence pre-

sented shows him to be guilty beyond a reasonable doubt. And this rule applies to every material element of the offense charged. Mere suspicion will not authorize a conviction. A reasonable doubt is such a doubt as you may have in your minds when, after fairly and impartially considering all of the evidence, you do not feel satisfied to a moral certainty of a defendant's guilt. In order that the evidence submitted shall afford proof beyond a reasonable doubt, it must be such as you would be willing to act upon in the most important and vital matters relating to your own affairs.

It is noteworthy that the appellant has failed to submit to this court in his brief any case whatsoever, Federal or State, which holds, even remotely, that the inclusion in an indictment of terms such as those complained of, is ground for reversal. It is true that appellant has cited many cases in support of these assignments of error, but there is none that appears upon even cursory inspection to have any applicability to the proposition at bar. Compare *Warfield* v. *United States,* 36 F. (2d) 903, in which similar expressions were addressed directly to the jury during argument of counsel.

II

THE INDICTMENT WAS SUFFICIENT TO ACQUAINT THE APPELLANT WITH THE CHARGE MADE AGAINST HIM.

The next point relied upon by the appellant consists of the contention that the indictment was not drawn with sufficient certainty to acquaint the defendant with the charge against him. An inspection of the indictment itself is the best reply to this claim of error. (R., 3–42.) The scheme to defraud is not the gist of the offense, and all that is required in describing it is thus stated in *Havener* v. *United States,* 49 F. (2d) 196, 198:

> The scheme need not be pleaded with all the certainty as to time, place, and circumstances required in charging the gist of the offense. *Brady* v. *United States, supra; Cochran* v. *United States, supra; Savage* v. *United States* (C. C. A. 8) 270 F. 14, 18; *Gardner* v. *United States* (C. C. A. 8) 230 F. 575; *McClendon* v. *United States* (C. C. A. 8) 229 F. 523, 525; *Brooks* v. *United States, supra; Chew* v. *United States* (C. C. A. 8) 9 F. (2d) 348, 351; *Mathews* v. *United States* (C. C. A. 8) 15 F. (2d) 139, 143.

Certiorari in the above case was refused by the Supreme Court of the United States on October 19, 1931.

If he desired further details he should have applied for a bill of particulars. *Martin* v. *United States,* 20 F. (2d) 785, 786; *Chew* v. *United States,* 9 F. (2d) 348, 353.

There is much discussion in this connection of the case of *Beck* v. *United States,* 33 F. (2d) 107 (C. C. A. 8). Reference is had to that portion of the opinion in the Beck case dealing with the so-called "shot gun" clause. The applicability of the

Beck case seems extremely doubtful when the indictment in the case at bar is read. That document appears to have been drawn, it is respectfully submitted, with a painstaking degree of precision. In any event, the indictment would seem to be good under Section 1025, R. S. (U. S. C., Title 18, Sec. 556).

III

THE APPELLANT WAS PROPERLY INDICTED IN THE SOUTHERN DISTRICT OF CALIFORNIA.

The next point raised in appellant's brief deals with his contention of alleged unfairness of the Government in indicting appellant in the State of California, rather than in the State of Texas.

Under Section 215 of the Criminal Code, knowingly to cause a letter to be delivered by mail in accordance with the direction thereon, for the purpose of executing a fraudulent scheme, is an offense separate from that of mailing a letter or causing it to be mailed for the same purpose; and where the letter is so delivered as directed, the person who caused the mailing, causes the delivery at the place of delivery, and may be prosecuted in that district, although he was not present there. The foregoing is the holding of the Supreme Court in *Salinger* v. *Loisel,* 265 U. S. 224, 233. In that case the Supreme Court passed on a proposition precisely in accord with the contention of appellant herein. It is submitted that the citation of further authority would be unnecessarily burdensome to the court.

IV

REQUESTS OF APPELLANT FOR SPECIFIC CHARGES TO
THE JURY WERE PROPERLY REFUSED.

The remaining assignments deal solely with alleged error on the part of the court in his charge
to the jury. The record does not contain a transcript of the testimony or any statement of the evidence. There are sundry references to the introduction of exhibits and to the appearance for examination and cross-examination of witnesses.
But what evidence was adduced either in behalf of
the Government or the appellant is not stated.
Therefore it would seem that in the main the questions relating to the charge are not available to the
appellant without the testimony being in the record
and subject to examination by the court to determine whether, on the whole, the charge meets the
requirements of the law. However, comparison of
the refused requests for instruction with the charge,
as given, demonstrates that portions of the requested charges which are to be considered by this
court as good law, were embodied in the general
charge of the court.

For instance the appellant lists as error the refusal of the court to grant the following instruction
(Appellant's Brief, p. 51):

> If upon a fair and impartial considera-
> tion, of all the evidence in the case, the jury
> finds that there are two reasonable theories

supported by the testimony in the case, and
that one of such theories is consistent with
the theory that the defendant is guilty, as
charged in some one or more or all of the
counts in the indictment, and that the other
of such theories is consistent with the innocence of the defendant, then it is the
policy of the law, and the law makes it the
duty of the jury to adopt that rule which is
consistent with the innocence of the defendant and in such case to find the defendant
not guilty.

However, with regard to the foregoing request
for instruction, the appellant overlooks the fact
that the charge substantially as requested was
given by the trial court (R. 203):

The defendant can not be convicted if all
the testimony is as fairly consistent with his
innocence as with his guilt; he can not be
convicted in the absence of an actual fraudulent intent, no matter how unsuccessful the
enterprise may have been or how inconsistent it may have been with sound judgment.

At pages 57, et cetera, of appellant's brief, error
is assigned to the following:

Juror HAYNES. A count, then, is just a
subdivision under a particular.
The COURT. Yes.

The brief, however, does not set forth the discussion between court and counsel which took place

immediately thereafter and would serve to qualify this seeming inaccuracy (R. 217):

> Mr. PRATT. I want to make this sugges-
> tion, if the Court please.
>
> The COURT. Yes, sir.
>
> Mr. PRATT. I am wondering if the juror
> who inquired as to the difference between
> a particular and a count has been confused,
> and may I state it?
>
> The COURT. Yes, you may.
>
> Mr. PRATT. That in this indictment, the
> defendant is charged with devising a scheme
> to defraud, and in several counts, namely,
> in six different counts, he is charged with
> causing the delivery of a specific letter to
> carry that scheme into effect. The scheme
> itself, as described in the indictment, has
> numerous features which the Court men-
> tioned as various particulars, but it is one
> scheme. Then he is charged with what is
> the gist of the offense, namely, the use of
> the mails, causing a letter to be delivered in
> furtherance of that scheme. That is the
> first count. And in the successive counts,
> the same scheme is adopted and separate
> letters in each count are described as hav-
> ing been caused to be delivered in further-
> ance of it. I make that suggestion to per-
> haps clarify it in the minds of the jury.
>
> The COURT. Yes, I think your suggestion
> is quite kindly, and I assume that the Jury
> understand that the indictment charges the
> scheme to defraud. It gives a great many
> particulars, as I explained to you, which con-
> stitute what the scheme was. That is all.

V

ATTENTION DIRECTED TO SECTION 269 OF THE JUDICIAL CODE

While not conceding that even harmless error is to be discovered in any portion of the record herein, appellee begs to call the attention of the court to Section 269 of the Judicial Code (U. S. C., Title 28, 391):

> On the hearing of any bill, certiorari, writ of error, or motion for a new trial, in any case, civil or criminal, the court shall give judgment after an examination of the entire record before the court, without regard to technical errors, defects or exceptions, which do not affect the substantial rights of the parties.

The appellant has not demonstrated on a consideration of the whole record that he has been denied any substantial right. *Rich* v. *United States,* 271 Fed. 566, 569–570·

CONCLUSION

We respectfully submit that the judgment of the lower court should be affirmed.

SAMUEL W. McNABB,
United States Attorney.

FRANK M. PARRISH,
Special Assistant to the Attorney General.

NEIL BURKINSHAW,
Special Assistant to the Attorney General.

JANUARY, 1932.

IN THE

United States
Circuit Court of Appeals,

FOR THE NINTH CIRCUIT.

Gilbert S. Johnson,

    Appellant,

   vs.

United States of America,

    Appellee.

PETITION FOR REHEARING.

H. L. ARTERBERRY,

  Attorney for Appellant.

FILED

JUN 21 1932

PAUL P. O'BRIEN,

CLERK

Parker, Stone & Baird Co., Law Printers, Los Angeles.

TOPICAL INDEX.

TABLE OF CASES AND AUTHORITIES CITED.

No. 6588.

Gilbert S. Johnson,

Appellant,

vs.

United States of America,

Appellee.

PETITION FOR REHEARING.

Appellant, Gilbert S. Johnson, respectfully petitions the above-entitled Honorable Court to grant appellant a rehearing in the above-entitled cause, and bases his application for a rehearing upon the following grounds, to-wit:

I.

The court erred in refusing to sustain the motion to quash the indictment filed in this case concerning which the court uses the following language in its opinion: "We cannot consider the motion to quash as the equivalent of a demurrer." (Page 2.)

In that connection we desire most respectfully to call the court's attention to the following authorities:

The case of *U. S. v. Oppenheimer,* 242 U. S. 85, 61 L. Ed. 161, holds that the designation given to a pleading by a defendant or by the court below cannot change its essential nature, and will disregard the misnomer and act upon the fact. The court saying:

> "The government brings this writ of error, treating the so-called motion to quash as a plea in bar, which in substance it was. (U. S. v. Barber, 219 U. S. 72.)"

In *U. S. v. Barber, supra,* the court says:

> "The claim that the pleas were not in bar, but merely in abatement, is, we think, equally untenable. The designation of the respective pleas as a plea in abatement did not change their essential nature."

Also the case of *U. S. v. Thompson,* 251 U. S. 407, 64 L. Ed. 341, the court says:

> "As it is settled that this question is to be determined, not by form, but by substance," (Citing U. S. v. Barber, *supra.*)

We believe that from the foregoing authorities this court should have treated the so-called motion to quash as the equivalent of a demurrer and, after so doing, to have then reversed the District Court for its failure to sustain said motion or demurrer for the reason stated therein.

II.

The court erred in refusing to consider the appellant's exceptions to the charge as given by the trial court because none of the evidence was set forth in the bill of exceptions (pages 4 and 5), for the following reasons:

(a)   That said instructions are fully set forth in the bill of exceptions, together with all exceptions thereto.

(b)   That said instructions are partisan, one-sided, and favored the government throughout.

(c.)   That said instructions invaded the province of the jury on questions of fact and, in effect, directed the jury to find the defendant guilty.

(d)   That prejudicial illustrations were given to the jury by the trial judge in its instructions.

(e)   That said instructions as given were clearly argumentative.

(f)   That said instructions excepted to were erroneous under every conceivable state of facts.

Argument and Authorities.

We recognize that "the settled rule is that where the record contains no part of the evidence that the judgment will not be disturbed on account of instructions alleged to be erroneous, *unless it appears that such instructions would have been erroneous under every conceivable state of facts.*"

> *Carpenter v. Ewing,* 76 Cal. 488, 18 Pac. 432;
> *Richmond Coal Company v. Commercial Assurance Company,* 169 Fed. 753 (C. C. A. 9).

Taking the above rule, can it not be said that the instructions complained of herein are "erroneous under every conceivable state of facts"? Particularly the following portions:

> "You do not have to believe that if I am caught in the act of setting fire to a house and I say to the

officer, 'Well, I did not intend to burn that house,'
he does not have to believe that, and probably would
not." [Tr. pp. 211 and 212.]

No good faith is involved in the illustration given,
whereas the question of good faith and honest belief is
involved in any condition or state of facts in a mail fraud
case.

>   *Sunderland v. U. S.,* 19 F. (2d) 202-214 (C. C.
>   A. 8).

Again at pages 212 and 213 of the transcript we find
this language:

>   "They say that 'straws tell which way the wind
>   blows'. Now, it might be that the defendant did
>   not consider that extremely important, but he was
>   used to making reckless statements. That is an
>   element that you may consider properly in this case,
>   that there were extravagant statements made; of
>   course, there is no denying that. For instance, I
>   think it was yesterday afternoon, something was
>   shown here where it was said that a big gusher was
>   absolutely assured, a big gusher absolutely assured.
>   Now, it is difficult, gentlemen of the jury, to reconcile
>   that with honest belief in anybody. 'Assured' means,
>   as we all know, 'sure,' 'that it was sure'; and it is
>   significant, gentlemen, that every single one of these
>   statements contains an invitation to buy stock; every
>   single one without exception, so far as I remember,
>   is an invitation to buy stock—not only an invitation,
>   but an urgent invitation. Well, now the defendant
>   might have been entirely innocent; he might have
>   honestly believed that, but his honest belief is not
>   sufficient unless the facts warranted him in express-
>   ing such belief, unless his information and facts
>   warranted him." "The evidence in this case shows
>   that from the very beginning this defendant pursued

a consistent line of advertising, and I will not, I think, go too strong in calling it extravagant advertising. It is a little singular, gentlemen, that if he was honest in his belief that that continued."

Under every conceivable state of facts that charge is erroneous, in our opinion. In speaking of extravagant statements, the court says: "Of course, there is no denying that," also when he says: "Now, it is difficult, gentlemen of the jury, to reconcile that with honest belief in anybody."

The above quote matter, coming from the trial judge in his charge to the jury, sets at naught defendant's plea of not guilty and the question of his good faith and honest belief.

Again the trial judge says: "Well, now, the defendant *might* have been entirely innocent; he *might* have honestly believed that, *but his honest belief is not sufficient unless the facts warranted him in expressing such belief. Unless his information and facts warranted him.*"

The trial court again ignores the fundamental principle in all cases of this kind and character on the question of the good faith and/or honest belief of the defendant. That charge is erroneous under every conceivable state of facts in a case of this kind. See *Sandals v. U. S.*, 213 Fed. 569-575 (C. C. A. 6), wherein that court says:

> "A man may be visionary in his plans and believe that they will succeed, and yet, in spite of their ultimate failure be incapable of committing a conscious fraud. Human credulity may include among its victims even the supposed imposter. If the men accused in the instant case really entertained the con-

viction throughout that the oil properties and the stock in dispute possessed merits corresponding with their representations, they did not commit the offense charged."

As was said by Chief Justice Fuller in *Starr v. U. S.*, 153 U. S. 614-626, 38 L. Ed. 841:

"The influence of the trial judge on the jury is necessarily and properly of great weight, and his lightest word or intimation is received with deference and may be controlling."

In the case of *Dolan v. U. S.*, 123 Fed. 54 (C. C. A. 9), the court says:

"An instruction that assumes the existence of a fact which should be left to the jury for ascertainment is erroneous."

In *Sunderland v. U. S.*, 19 F. (2d) 202-216 (C. C. A. 8), the court, in discussing how far judges may go in giving instructions to the jury, had this to say:

"It should not be permitted to do indirectly what it cannot do directly and by its instructions to in effect argue the jury into a verdict of guilty. * * * he may not extend his activities so far as to become in effect either an assistant prosecutor or a thirteenth juror."

In our opinion the court erred in invoking the provisions of section 269 of the Judicial Code, as amended, and quoting from the case of *Haywood v. U. S.*, 268 Fed. 795-798 (C. C. A. 7), which we believe to be contrary to the ruling of this Circuit in the case of *St. Clair v. U. S.*, 23 F. (2d) 76-80, and also, in our opinion, is contrary to the doctrine laid down by the Supreme Court in the case of *U. S. v. River Rouge Company,* 269 U. S. 411-421, 70 L. Ed. 339, in which this language was used:

"The present case is not controlled by the provision of section 269 of the Judicial Code, as amended by the Act of February 26, 1919 (28 U. S. C. A. 391; Comp. St. 1246), that in an appellate proceeding judgment shall be given after an examination of the entire record, 'without regard to technical errors, defects, or exceptions which do not affect the substantial rights of the parties.' We need not enter upon a discussion of the divergent views which have been expressed in various Circuit Courts of Appeals as to the effect of the Act of 1919. It suffices to say that since the passage of this act, as well as before, an error which relates, not to merely formal or technical matters, but to the substantial rights of the parties—*especially when embodied in the charge to a jury—is to be held a ground for reversal,* unless it appears from the whole record that it was harmless and did not prejudice the rights of the complaining party."

For the reasons hereinabove set forth we respectfully ask this court to grant the petition of the appellant for a rehearing in this case.

Respectfully submitted,

H. L. ARTERBERRY,
Attorney for Appellant.

I, H. L. Arterberry, one of the attorneys for appellant, do hereby certify that, in my judgment, the foregoing petition for rehearing is well founded and that the same is not interposed for delay.

H. L. ARTERBERRY.

United States
Circuit Court of Appeals
For the Ninth Circuit.

/ 2

SPOKANE, PORTLAND AND SEATTLE RAIL-
WAY COMPANY, a Corporation,

Appellant,

vs.

CHARLES A. COLE,

Appellee.

Transcript of Record.

**Upon Appeal from the United States District Court for
the District of Oregon.**

FILED

SEP 10 ...

PAUL P. O'BRIEN,
CLERK

Filmer Bros. Co. Print, 330 Jackson St., S. F., Cal.

United States
Circuit Court of Appeals
For the Ninth Circuit.

SPOKANE, PORTLAND AND SEATTLE RAIL-
WAY COMPANY, a Corporation,

Appellant,

vs.

CHARLES A. COLE,

Appellee.

Transcript of Record.

Upon Appeal from the United States District Court for
the District of Oregon.

Filmer Bros. Co. Print, 330 Jackson St., S. F., Cal.

INDEX TO THE PRINTED TRANSCRIPT OF RECORD.

[Clerk's Note: When deemed likely to be of an important nature, errors or doubtful matters appearing in the original certified record are printed literally in italic; and, likewise, cancelled matter appearing in the original certified record is printed and cancelled herein accordingly. When possible, an omission from the text is indicated by printing in italic the two words between which the omission seems to occur.]

Index.   Page

NAMES AND ADDRESSES OF ATTORNEYS OF RECORD.

Mr. CHARLES A. HART, Mr. FLETCHER ROCKWOOD, CAREY, HART, SPENCER and McCULLOCH, Yeon Building, Portland, Oregon,

    For the Appellant.

DAVIS & HARRIS, 507 Failing Building, Portland, Oregon,

    For the Appellee.

In the District Court of the United States for the District of Oregon.

No. L.–10,826.

CHARLES A. COLE,

                    Plaintiff,

vs.

SPOKANE, PORTLAND AND SEATTLE RAILWAY COMPANY, a Corporation,

                    Defendant.

CITATION ON APPEAL.

To Charles A. Cole, GREETING :

You are hereby cited and admonished to be and appear before the United States Circuit Court of Appeals for the Ninth Circuit, at San Francisco, California, within thirty (30) days from the date hereof, pursuant to a notice of appeal filed in the

Clerk's office of the District Court of the United States for the District of Oregon, wherein Spokane, Portland and Seattle Railway Company, a corporation, is appellant, and you are appellee, to show cause, if any there be, why the judgment in said cause should not be corrected and speedy justice *should be* done to the parties in that behalf.

Given under my hand at Portland, in said District, this 3d day of August, in the year of our Lord nineteen hundred thirty-one.

JOHN H. McNARY,

Judge. [1*]

District of Oregon,
County of Multnomah,—ss.

Due service of the within citation on appeal is hereby accepted in Multnomah County, Oregon, this 4th day of August, 1931, by receiving a copy thereof, duly certified to as such by Fletcher Rockwood, of attorneys for defendant.

DAVIS & HARRIS,

Attorneys for Plaintiff.

Filed Aug. 4, 1931. [2]

In the District Court of the United States for the District of Oregon.

July Term, 1929.

BE IT REMEMBERED, that on the 23d day of October, 1929, there was duly filed in the District

---

*Page-number appearing at the foot of page of original certified Transcript of Record.

Court of the United States for the District of Oregon, a complaint, in words and figures as follows, to wit: [3]

In the District Court of the United States for the District of Oregon.

No. L.–10,826.

CHARLES A. COLE,

Plaintiff,

vs.

SPOKANE, PORTLAND & SEATTLE RAILWAY COMPANY, a Corporation,

Defendant.

COMPLAINT.

Comes now the plaintiff, and for cause of action against said defendant complains and alleges as follows:

I.

That the defendant is a corporation duly organized and existing under and by virtue of the laws of the State of Washington and has duly complied with the laws of the State of Oregon entitling it to do business therein, and is engaged in the business of operating a railway system, a portion of which extends in a general easterly and westerly direction through portions of Skamania County, Washington.

II.

That plaintiff is a resident and inhabitant of the State of Oregon.

III.

That the plaintiff is the surviving father of Jacqueline A. Cole, who at the time she met her death, as hereinafter set forth, was a minor of the age of eight years.

IV.

That at all times hereinafter alleged there was in full force and effect in the State of Washington, the following [4] statute enacted by the Legislature of said State, the same being known as Section 184, Remington's Code, which said section is as follows:

> "A father or in case of the death or desertion of his family the mother, may maintain an action as plaintiff for the injury or death of a child, and a guardian for the injury or death of his ward."

V.

That at all times hereinafter alleged there was in full force and effect in the State of Washington the following statute enacted by the Legislature of said State, the same being Chapter 72 of the Session Laws of 1923 of the State of Washington, and entitled "An Act relating to the age of majority and amending sections 1572 and 10548 of Remington's Compiled Statutes," which said chapter reads as follows:

> "SECTION 1. That Section 1572 of Remington's Compiled Statutes be amended to read as follows:
>
> Section 1572. Guardians   herein   provided

for shall at all times be under the general direction and control of the Court making the appointment. For the purposes of this act, all persons shall be of full and legal age when they shall be twenty-one years old, and females shall be deemed of full and legal age at any age under twenty-one when with the consent of the parent or guardian, or the person under whose care or government they may be, they shall have been legally married.

SEC. 2. That Section 10548 of Remington's Compiled Statutes be amended to read as follows:

Section 10548. All persons shall be deemed and taken to be of full age for all purposes at the age of twenty-one years and upwards."

VI.

That approximately a half mile west of the City of Underwood in Skamania County, Washington, a road and thoroughfare leading to a Government Fish Hatchery and extending in a general northerly and southerly direction, crosses the defendant's right of way. [5]

VII.

That on or about the 30th day of August, 1928, the plaintiff's minor intestate was riding as a passenger in an automobile being operated in a northerly direction on said road and thoroughfare, when the same was violently run into and struck by a train being operated by the defendant in a westerly direction, and as a result thereof said intestate received injuries which resulted in her death.

VIII.

Plaintiff alleges that the defendant was then and there careless and negligent in the following particulars, to wit:

(a)   That the said defendant carelessly and negligently operated said train, in view of the character of the crossing and the conditions existing at the place of said collision, and in view of the fact that defendant failed to sound any warning or alarm of its approach, at a high, dangerous and reckless rate of speed, to wit: over forty miles per hour;

(b)   That said defendant carelessly and negligently failed to sound any warning or alarm in approaching said intersection to warn and advise travelers at said point;

(c)   That the said defendant carelessly and negligently maintained its right of way at and near said crossing in a dangerous condition, in that the defendant permitted unnecessary obstructions upon its right of way at or near said crossing so as to obstruct the view thereat, both of its servants approaching said crossing on a train and of persons upon said highway, in that the defendant allowed said right of way to become overgrown with bushes, weeds and grass so as to obstruct said view.   [6]

IX.

That at the time said minor intestate met her death, as heretofore alleged, she was an intelligent, industrious and healthy girl of the age of eight years and in full possession of all her faculties, and was the daughter of the plaintiff, and immediately prior to the time of her death was and had been living with and in the service and employment of this plaintiff, who was, and during her minority had she lived would have been, entitled to her earnings and the value of her services and earnings over and above the cost of providing her with the usual and customary necessities of life, which is and would have been of the value of Twenty-five Thousand ($25,000.00) Dollars, in which said sum plaintiff has been damaged.

WHEREFORE, plaintiff demands judgment against the defendant in the sum of Twenty-five Thousand ($25,000.00) Dollars, and for his costs and disbursements incurred herein.

DAVIS & HARRIS,
Attorneys for Plaintiff.

State of Oregon,
County of Multnomah,—ss.

I, Charles A. Cole, being first duly sworn, depose and say that I am the plaintiff in the above-entitled action; and that the foregoing complaint is true as I verily believe.

CHARLES A. COLE.

Subscribed and sworn to before me this 22d day of October, 1929.

[Seal]   F. C. HILLER,
          Notary Public for the State of Oregon.
My commission expires Jan. 21, 1931.

Filed October 23, 1929.   [7]

AND AFTERWARDS, to wit, on the 29th day of
October, 1929, there was duly filed in said court,
an answer, in words and figures as follows, to
wit: [8]

[Title of Court and Cause.]

ANSWER.

Defendant for answer to the complaint of the
plaintiff in the above-entitled case alleges:

I.

Admits the allegations of Paragraph I of the
complaint.

II.

Admits the allegations of Paragraph II of the
complaint.

III.

Admits the allegations of Paragraph III of the
complaint.

IV.

Admits the allegations of Paragraph IV of the
complaint.

V.

Admits the allegations of Paragraph V of the
complaint. [9]

VI.

Admits the allegations of Paragraph VI of the
complaint.

VII.

Admits that on or about August 30, 1928, the
said deceased daughter of plaintiff was riding as

a passenger in an automobile being operated in a northerly direction on a road and that at said time there was a collision between said automobile and a car being operated by the defendant on its track in a westerly direction, and that as a result thereof said deceased daughter received injuries which resulted in her death as alleged in Paragraph VII, but except as so admitted defendant denies the allegations of Paragraph VII of the complaint.

VIII.

Denies the allegations of Paragraph VIII of the complaint.

IX.

Defendant has no information relating to the facts alleged in Paragraph IX of the complaint and for this reason upon information and belief denies said allegations.

WHEREFORE, defendant demands that plaintiff take nothing by this action and that defendant have its costs and disbursements herein.

> CHARLES A. HART,
> FLETCHER ROCKWOOD,
> CAREY & KERR,
> Attorneys for Defendant. [10]

State of Oregon,
County of Multnomah,—ss.

I, Robert Crosbie, being first duly sworn, on oath depose and say: That I am the Secretary of Spokane, Portland and Seattle Railway Company, a corporation, defendant in the above-entitled action, that I have read the foregoing answer, know the contents thereof, and that the same is true as I verily believe.

ROBERT CROSBIE.

Subscribed and sworn to before me this 28th day of October, 1929.

[Seal] PHILIP CHIPMAN,
Notary Public for Oregon.

My commission expires: August 28, 1931.

District of Oregon,
County of Multnomah,—ss.

Due service of the within answer is hereby accepted in Multnomah County, Oregon, this 29th day of October, 1929, by receiving a copy thereof, duly certified to as such by Fletcher Rockwood of attorneys for defendant.

DAVIS & HARRIS,
Attorneys for Plaintiff.

Filed October 29, 1929. [11]

———

AND AFTERWARDS, to wit, on the 2d day of November, 1929, there was duly filed in said court a reply, in words and figures as follows, to wit: [12]

[Title of Court and Cause.]

REPLY.

Comes now the plaintiff and, in reply to defendant's answer, admits, denies and alleges, as follows:

I.

Denies each and every allegation, matter and thing contained in said answer, except as heretofore either expressly admitted, stated, qualified or explained in plaintiff's complaint.

WHEREFORE, plaintiff demands judgment as prayed for in his complaint.

DAVIS & HARRIS,
Attorneys for Plaintiff. [13]

State of Oregon,
County of Multnomah,—ss.

I, Charles A. Cole being first duly sworn, depose and say that I am the plaintiff in the above-entitled action; and that the foregoing reply is true as I verily believe.

CHARLES A. COLE.

Subscribed and sworn to before me this 29th day of October, 1929.

[Seal] F. C. HILLER,
Notary Public for the State of Oregon.
My commission expires Jan. 21, 1931.

Due service by copy admitted at Portland, Oregon, this 1st day of November, 1929.

FLETCHER ROCKWOOD,
Attorneys for Defendant.

Filed November 2, 1929. [14]

AND AFTERWARDS, to wit, on Wednesday, the
25th day of February, 1931, the same being the
78th judicial day of the regular November
Term of said court.—Present, the Honorable
JOHN H. McNARY, United States District
Judge, presiding,—the following proceedings
were had in said cause, to wit: [15]

[Title of Cause.]

MINUTES OF COURT—FEBRUARY 25, 1931—
JUDGMENT.

Now *at* this day comes the plaintiff by Mr. Paul
R. Harris and Mr. Donald K. Grant, of counsel,
and the defendant by Mr. Fletcher Rockwood, of
counsel. Whereupon the jurors impaneled herein
being present and answering to their names, the
further trial of this cause at the same time and
before the same jury as the cause of Charles A.
Cole vs. Spokane, Portland & Seattle Railway Company, No. L.-10,827, pursuant to the oral stipulation
of the parties hereto made and entered in open court
herein, is resumed. And the said jury having
heard the evidence adduced, the arguments of counsel, and the instruction of the court, retires in
charge of proper sworn officers, to consider of its
verdict. And thereafter said jury comes into court
and returns its verdict in words and figures as
follows, to wit:

"We, the Jury, duly empaneled and sworn,
in the above-entitled cause, find our verdict in

favor of the plaintiff and against the defendant and assess plaintiff's damages at Twenty-five Hundred ($2500) Dollars.

(Jacqueline A. Cole)

(8 years of age)

E. A. ROSS,

Foreman"

which verdict is received by the Court and ordered to be filed. Whereupon upon motion of plaintiff,—

IT IS ADJUDGED that plaintiff do have recover of and from said defendant the sum of $2,500.00, together with his costs and disbursements herein taxed at $31.50, and that execution issue therefor. [16]

———

AND AFTERWARDS, to wit, on the 25th day of February, 1931, there was duly filed in said court, a verdict, in words and figures as follows, to wit: [17]

[Title of Court and Cause.]

VERDICT.

We, the Jury, duly empaneled and sworn, in the above-entitled cause, find our verdict in favor of the plaintiff and against the defendant and assess plaintiff's damages at Twenty-five hundred ($2500.00) Dollars.   E. A. ROSS,

Foreman.

(Jacqueline A. Cole)

(8 years of age)

Filed February 25, 1931. [18]

AND AFTERWARDS, to wit, on the 2d day of March 1931, there was duly filed in said court, a motion for new trial and in *a* arrest of judgment, in words and figures as follows, to wit: [19]

In the District Court of the United States for the District of Oregon.

No. L.–10,826.

CHARLES A. COLE,

Plaintiff,

vs.

SPOKANE, PORTLAND AND SEATTLE RAILWAY COMPANY, a Corporation,

Defendant.

No. L.–10,827.

CHARLES A. COLE,

Plaintiff,

vs.

SPOKANE, PORTLAND AND SEATTLE RAILWAY COMPANY, a Corporation,

Defendant.

MOTION FOR NEW TRIAL AND IN ARREST OF JUDGMENT.

The defendant, Spokane, Portland and Seattle Railway Company, respectfully moves the court for a new trial in the above-entitled cases and in arrest of judgment upon the grounds that—

1. The damages awarded by the verdicts of the jury in each case are excessive and appear to have been given under the influence of passion and prejudice.

2. The court erred as a matter of law in declining to give defendant's requested instruction number IV reading as follows:

> "I instruct you that the evidence is insufficient to show any negligence on the part of the defendant in [20] the manner in which the crossing itself was maintained with respect to the view at the crossing of train operators along the highway and of automobile operators along the railroad. Consequently all allegations of negligence with respect to obstruction of view and the maintenance of the crossing itself are withdrawn from your consideration and you cannot base any recovery on any such allegations."

The foregoing motion is made upon the pleadings and files in this case, the proceedings in the trial including the minutes of the court, for the causes above specified, which are causes set forth in Section 2–802 Oregon Code, Annotated, 1930, being the same as Section 174 Oregon Laws, and in accordance with the rules of this court.

Dated March 2, 1931.

CHARLES A. HART,

FLETCHER ROCKWOOD,

CAREY, HART, SPENCER & McCULLOCH,

Attorneys for Defendant.

State of Oregon,
County of Multnomah,—ss.

Due service of the within motion is hereby accepted in Multnomah County, Oregon, this 2d day of March, 1931, be receiving a copy thereof, duly certified to as such by Fletcher Rockwood of attorneys for defendant.

DAVIS & HARRIS,
Attorneys for Plaintiff.

Filed March 2, 1931.   [21]

———

AND AFTERWARDS, to wit, on Monday, the 18th day of May, 1931, the same being the 60th judicial day of the regular March Term of said Court,—Present, the Honorable JOHN H. McNARY, United States District Judge, Presiding,—the following proceedings were had in said cause, to wit: [22]

[Title of Cause.]

MINUTES OF COURT—MAY 18, 1931—ORDER DENYING MOTION FOR NEW TRIAL.

This cause was heard by the Court upon the motion of the defendant for a new trial herein, and was argued by Mr. Paul R. Harris and Mr. Donald K. Grant, of counsel for plaintiff and by Mr. Fletcher Rockwood, of counsel for defendant. Upon consideration whereof,—

IT IS ORDERED that the said motion be and the same is hereby denied.   [23]

———

AND AFTERWARDS, to wit, on Monday, the 8th day of June, 1931, the same being the 77th judicial day of the regular March Term of said court,—Present, the Honorable JOHN H. McNARY, United States District Judge, presiding—the following proceedings were had in said cause, to wit: [24]

[Title of Court and Cause.]

MINUTES OF COURT —JUNE 8, 1931—ORDER EXTENDING TIME TO AND INCLUDING JULY 15, 1931, TO FILE BILL OF EXCEPTIONS.

Upon application of the defendant, and for good cause shown,—

IT IS HEREBY ORDERED that the time within which defendant may file and present its bill of exceptions herein is hereby extended to and including the 15th day of July, 1931.

Dated June 8, 1931.

JOHN H. McNARY,
Judge.

Filed June 8, 1931.   [25]

AND AFTERWARDS, to wit, on the 29th day
of July, 1931, there was duly filed in said court,
a bill of exceptions, in words and figures as
follows, to wit: [26]

[Title of Court and Cause.]

BILL OF EXCEPTIONS.

This cause came on for hearing before Honorable
John H. McNary and a jury, on the 19th day of
February, 1931, Messrs. Davis and Harris appear-
ing as attorneys for the plaintiff, and Messrs. Carey,
Hart, Spencer & McCulloch, and Mr. Fletcher
Rockwood, appearing as attorneys for the defend-
ant.

By stipulation of the parties, and on order of
the court this case was consolidated for trial with
the case of Charles A. Cole, plaintiff, vs. Spokane,
Portland and Seattle Railway Company, a corporation, defendant, No. L.–10,827. This case, Nos.
L.–10,826, arose out of the death of Jacqueline A.
Cole, a minor daughter of the plaintiff, and No.
L.–10,827 arose out of the death in the same accident of Leona J. Cole, another minor daughter
of the same plaintiff.

After hearing all of the evidence, the argument
of counsel and the charge of the Court, the jury
retired to consider the evidence and thereafter
returned a verdict in favor of the plaintiff in
this case, assessing his damages at $2,500.00 upon
which verdict judgment was thereafter on [27]

the 25th day of February, 1931, entered by the court against the defendant.

Thereafter and on the 2d day of March, 1931, the defendant served and filed its motion for a new trial and in arrest of judgment, upon the grounds that the damages awarded by the verdict of the jury were excessive and appeared to have been given under the influence of passion and prejudice, and that the trial court erred as a matter of law in declining to give defendant's requested instruction number IV, which is quoted in full hereinafter in this bill exceptions.

Thereafter and on the 20th day of April, 1931, the defendant's motion for a new trial and in arrest of judgment was argued orally to the court by counsel for both parties, and on the 18th day of May, 1931, the court made its order denying the said motion.

I.

At the trial the defendant requested the Court to instruct the jury as follows:

"IV.

I instruct you that the evidence is insufficient to show any negligence on the part of the defendant in the manner in which the crossing itself was maintained with respect to the view at the crossing of train operators along the highway and of automobile operators along the railroad. Consequently all allegations of negligence with respect to obstruction of view and the maintenance of the crossing itself are withdrawn from your consideration and you cannot base any recovery on any such allegations."

The court declined to give the requested instruction, and to the refusal of the court so to instruct the jury the [28] defendant duly excepted.

The evidence necessary to present clearly the questions of law involved in the ruling is as follows:

On the 30th day of August, 1928, Jacqueline A. Cole the daughter of the plaintiff, was killed in a collision between a gasoline propelled car operated by the defendant on its railroad, and a Ford touring automobile in which the decedent was a passenger, at a place approximately one-half mile west of the defendant's station at Underwood, Washington, where a roadway from the grounds of the United States Government fish hatchery leading to a county road crosses the railroad track and right of way of the defendant. The hatchery grounds are located on the southerly side of the defendant's right of way and the county road lies parallel to the right of way on the northerly side.

The crossing at which the accident occurred is a private crossing.

Witness Ray W. Hoffman, the Government employee in charge of the hatchery, a witness for the plaintiff testified:

"Q. You, yourself, built this road, you said?
A. It was partially built when I came. I completed it.
Q. That was about three years ago.

A. Yes.

Q. And the purpose the road was to furnish a means of getting to and from the fish hatchery? A. Yes.

Q. It is a private road, is it not?

A. I believe it is classed that way. [29]

Q. Well, you do know, do you not, that the crossing was built pursuant to a permit which was given by the railway company to the Bureau of Fisheries? A. Yes, sir.

Q. That is correct, is it not? A. Yes, sir.

* * * * * * * *

Q. The road ends right at the fish hatchery, does it? A. Yes, sir.

Q. It opens up in your yard, so to speak, at the fish hatchery building?

A. It does." (T. pp. 83, 84.)

Witness Hoffman further testified that he built the road from the hatchery grounds up to the railroad track, but that the railroad constructed the actual crossing, and has since maintained it. (T. pp. 79, 80.)

With respect to the use of the road the same witness testified:

"Q. Well, now, that road has been occupied there how long? Been used, I mean.

A. In the neighborhood of* three years.

(*The evidence of this witness at the trial was taken, by stipulation, reading into the record his testimony at the trial of the case of Cecile S. Cole vs. Spokane, Portland and

Seattle Railway Company, which was tried in this court in October, 1929.)

Q. Now, what would you say as to the number of people going up and down there?

A. Well, it depends on the season of the year. During the fishing season I would say there is about twenty cars a day cross over the crossing.

Q. What class of people come in there? Just explain that. [30]

A. It is ranchers, fishing men, movie men—practically all classes of people.

Q. When you say 'movie' men, what do you mean?

A. Cameramen coming in to take the pictures of the fish.

Q. Well, what would you say as to whether or not tourists and others coming there to look over the hatchery come in?

A. Yes, sir, they visit it often.

Q. This was in August. What would you say as to whether or not there were people coming in there frequently during that month?

A. Not so much right at that time of the year. Perhaps it would average two or three cars a day. That is outside cars.

COURT.—Outside cars?

A. Yes.

COURT.—There would be local cars, would there, that would use this road?

A. Speaking of outside cars, I mean the residents around Underwood there coming in; people that were not living at the hatchery.

Q. What would you say as to people that lived in there and worked there?

A. We crossed, probably, I would say, two or three trips a day out each car.

Q. And how many cars were there there?

A. There were three at the time." (T. pp. 80, 81.)

Mrs. Larson, a sister of Cecile S. Cole, the decedent's mother, was living at the hatchery grounds. Mr. Larson was then employed at the hatchery. (T. p. 33.) Just prior to the accident the decedent, with her mother, and her sisters and a brother had been visiting at the Larson home at the hatchery grounds. (T. p. 34.) Mrs. Larson with Mrs. Cole and their children were leaving the Larson home at the time of the accident to drive to the place where the Coles were then living at a point [31] to the north of the railroad. (T. pp. 47–49.) Mrs. Larson was driving the automobile and the decedent was a passenger in the back seat of the automobile at the time of the accident. (T. pp. 60, 62, 64, 65.)

Various witnesses gave testimony as to the state of the vegetation along the railroad right of way between the location of the crossing and the direction from which the railroad car approached.

Witness Hoffman for the plaintiff testified on this subject on direct examination as follows:

"Q. Now, at the time these women were hurt, will you tell this jury what was the condition of the brush and foliage at that point?

A. Along the edge here there was brush growing—well there was one that was cut down, that was at least six feet high; a maple I would judge that it was. And there was brush all along the edge of the cut, that hid the view.

COURT.—Was the brush on the right of way of the railroad?

A. Yes, sir.

Q. And when was that brush cut down?

A. The next morning after the accident.

Q. Who cut that down?

A. The section crew.

Q. Now, what would you say was the extent of the brush along on that point as to whether it was heavy, or not?

A. Well, in places it grew in bunches. In places it was quite heavy, and then there would not be any for a ways, and then there would be another bunch.

Q. How high would you say that brush grew?

A. The tallest was about six feet, around six feet. [32]

Q. And the cut was about how deep, did you say?

A. In the neighborhood of eight or ten feet.

Q. That is, down to the bed of the railroad track?   A. Yes.

Q. Well, at the time that brush was there, and the time these women were injured—you remember that very distinctly?

A. I certainly do.

Q. Well, now, what would you say then, as to whether or not that would obstruct the view a good deal worse than it did after they cut the brush down? A. Yes, it would.

Q. Would you estimate, then about how near they would get to the track before they could see a train?

A. Well, that would be a rather hard question to answer, Mr. Davis; probably around one hundred feet.

Q. Well, how far now—when you were back how far would you have to be from the track?

A. To see one hundred feet?

Q. Yes.

A. The driver, I imagine, would be about seventeen feet from the rail.

Q. And then the front of the car would be still nearer. Is that the way you estimate it?

A. Yes.

COURT.—You mean the driver would have to be seventeen feet?

A. Yes.

COURT.—Not the car?

A. Not the car, but the driver."

Mrs. Cole, the decedent's mother, who was a passenger in the front seat of the automobile, testified that the automobile stopped to allow her nephew, Elmer, to alight from the running-board of the automobile, where he had been riding. At that moment, she testified, the front end of the automobile was ten [33] to twelve feet from the railroad track. (T. pp. 50, 57, 58.) She testified further as follows:

"Q. There is one thing I neglected to ask you. At the time you stopped, when you were traveling up that road, about what distance would you say you could see towards Underwood, in that cut?

A. Well, I don't think you could see more than 150 feet, if you could see that far.

Q. What was there to prevent your vision, to prevent you from seeing?

A. There was quite a bit of brush on the cut there, which hung down. I don't know—there were trees, little trees, young willows, and there was quite a heavy brush there at the time.

Q. When you say hanging down, what do you mean?

A. They were leaning down towards the track from the top, leaning over like."

II.

The court denied the motion of the defendant for a new trial and in arrest of judgment, made on the ground, among others, that the damages awarded by the verdict of the jury were excessive and appeared to have been given under the influence of passion and prejudice. The evidence necessary to present clearly the questions of law involved in the ruling is as follows:

Jacqueline A. Cole, the decedent, was eight years of age at the time of her death. She would have been nine years of age on the 12th day of December, 1928 (T. p. 36). The accident occurred on August 30, 1928, so that at the date of her death she was eight years eight and one-half months old.

Witness Jessie Wilde, a teacher, testified that she had known Jacqueline "at least a year." The witness stated [34] "Well, I found her a very satisfactory child in every way. She was obedient and willing. She had a very fine attitude towards school, and her grades were especially good. I considered her above the average." (T. p. 29, 30.)

She was in the fourth grade in school. (T. p. 39.) She had always been in good health and was an energetic child. (Tr. p. 40.) The plaintiff, her father, testified that he had expected to send her through high school as he had done for the older daughter, so that Jacqueline would have been sixteen or seventeen years old when she finished school. (Tr. p. 41.)

The decedent's mother testified: "Well, she was considered rather a live wire. She never could keep quiet. She was always full of pep. At school the report cards showed she was an excellent student, and she had been skipped, one year. She was in the first half of the fourth year in school. The teachers were always sending home word that she was a very excellent student. She behaved very well at home. . . . She had never been sick in her life." (T. p. 55.)

Defendant tenders herein this its bill of exceptions to the action of the court in refusing to give the requested instructions and in denying defendant's motion for a new trial, as herein noted.

CHARLES A. HART,
FLETCHER ROCKWOOD,
CAREY, HART, SPENCER & McCULLOCH,
Attorneys for Defendant. [35]

[Title of Court and Cause.]

ORDER ALLOWING BILL OF EXCEPTIONS.

The defendant on July 13, 1931, and within the time allowed by the rules and orders of this court, delivered to the Clerk its bill of exceptions, and served a copy thereof on the attorneys for the plaintiff, and the court, having found that defendant's bill of exceptions is a true and correct statement of the facts therein referred to,—

NOW, THEREFORE, IT IS HEREBY ORDERED that the bill of exceptions presented by the defendant above referred to shall be allowed as the bill of exceptions in this case, and should be filed with the records in this case in the office of the Clerk of this court.

Dated July 29, 1931.

(Sgd.)   JOHN H. McNARY,
Judge.

Approved :

DAVIS & HARRIS,
Attorneys for Plaintiff.

Lodged in Clerk's office July 13, 1931. G. H. Marsh, Clerk. By F. L. Buck, Chief Deputy.

Filed July 29, 1931. G. H. Marsh, Clerk. By F. L. Buck, Chief Deputy. [36]

———

AND AFTERWARDS, to wit, on the 3d day of August, 1931 there was duly filed in said court, a petition for appeal, in words and figures as follows, to wit: [37]

[Title of Court and Cause.]

PETITION FOR APPEAL AND SUPERSEDEAS.

To the Honorable JOHN H. McNARY, District Judge, and One of the Judges of the Above-named Court:

Spokane, Portland and Seattle Railway Company, the defendant in the above-entitled case, considering itself aggrieved by the judgment entered herein on the 25th day of February, 1931, in favor of the plaintiff and against the defendant in the sum of Two Thousand Dollars ($2,000.00), hereby appeals to the United States Circuit Court of Appeals for the Ninth Circuit from said judgment and the whole thereof, for the reasons set forth in the assignment of errors which is served and filed herewith, and said defendant prays that this petition for said appeal may be allowed, and that a transcript of the record and of all proceedings upon which said judgment is based, duly authenticated, may be sent to the United States Circuit Court of Appeals for the Ninth Circuit, and defendant further prays that an order be made fixing the amount of security which the defendant shall give and furnish upon the allowance of said appeal, and that upon the giving of such security, all further proceedings in this court [38] shall be suspended and stayed until the determination of said appeal

by the United States Circuit Court of Appeals for
the Ninth Circuit.

CHARLES A. HART.

FLETCHER   ROCKWOOD,

CAREY, HART, SPENCER and McCUL-
LOCH,

Attorneys for Defendant.

State of Oregon,

County of Multnomah,—ss.

Due service of the within petition for appeal and
supersedeas is hereby accepted in Multnomah
County, Oregon, this 3d day of August, 1931, by
receiving a copy thereof, duly certified to as such
by Fletcher Rockwood of attorneys for defendant.

DAVIS & HARRIS,

Attorneys for Plaintiff.

Filed August 3, 1931.   [39]

———

AND AFTERWARDS, to wit, on the 3d day of
August, 1931, there was duly filed in said court,
an assignment of errors, in words and figures
as follows, to wit: [40]

[Title of Court and Cause.]

ASSIGNMENT OF ERRORS.

Now comes the defendant and files the following
assignment of errors upon which it will rely upon
the prosecution of its appeal in the above-entitled
cause from the judgment entered herein in favor of
the plaintiff and against the defendant on the 25th
day of February, 1931.

I.

The United States District Court in and for the District of Oregon erred in declining to give to the jury defendant's requested instruction Number IV, reading as follows:

"IV.

I instruct you that the evidence is insufficient to show any negligence on the part of the defendant in the manner in which the crossing itself was maintained with respect to the view at the crossing of train operators along the highway and of automobile operators along the railroad. Consequently all allegations of negligence with respect to obstruction of veiew and the maintenance of the crossing itself are withdrawn from your consideration and you cannot base any recovery on any such allegations."

[41]

II.

The United States District Court in and for the District of Oregon, erred in denying defendant's motion for a new trial made upon the ground, among others, that the damages awarded by the verdict of the jury were excessive and appeared to have been given under the influence of passion and prejudice.

WHEREFORE defendant prays that said judgment heretofore and on the 25th day of February, 1931, entered in this action against the defendant and in favor of the plaintiff, be reversed, and that said cause be remanded to the United States District

Court in and for the District of Oregon, for a new trial.

CHARLES A. HART,
FLETCHER ROCKWOOD,
CAREY, HART, SPENCER and McCUL-
LOCH,

Attorneys for Defendant.

State of Oregon,
County of Multnomah,—ss.

Due service of the within assignment of errors is hereby accepted in Multnomah County, Oregon, this 3d day of August, 1931, by receiving a copy thereof, duly certified to as such by Fletcher Rockwood of attorneys for defendant.

DAVIS & HARRIS,

Attorneys for Plaintiff.

Filed August 3, 1931. [42]

————

AND AFTERWARDS, to wit, on Monday, the 3d day of August, 1931, the same being the 24th judicial day of the regular July term of said court,—Present, the Honorable JOHN H. Mc-NARY, United States District Judge, presiding—the following proceedings were had in said cause, to wit: [43]

[Title of Court and Cause.]

MINUTES OF COURT—AUGUST 3, 1931—
ORDER ALLOWING APPEAL.

The above-named defendant, Spokane, Portland and Seattle Railway Company, having duly served

and filed herein its petition for appeal to the
United States Circuit Court of Appeals for the
Ninth Circuit, from the judgment entered herein
in favor of the plaintiff and against the defendant
on February 25, 1931, and having duly served and
filed its assignment of errors upon which it will
rely upon said appeal,—

IT IS ORDERED that the appeal be and is
hereby allowed to the United States Circuit Court
of Appeals for the Ninth Circuit from said judgment entered in this action in favor of the plaintiff
and against the defendant on February 25, 1931.

IT IS FURTHER ORDERED that the bond on
appeal herein has been fixed at the sum of $2,000.00,
the same to act as a supersedeas bond and is a
bond for costs and damages on appeal.

Dated August 3, 1931.

JOHN H. McNARY,
District Judge.

Filed August 3, 1931. [43½]

———

AND AFTERWARDS, to wit on the 3d day of
August, 1931, there was duly filed in said court,
an undertaking on appeal, in words and figures
as follows, to wit: [44]

[Title of Court and Cause.]

UNDERTAKING ON APPEAL.

KNOW ALL MEN BY THESE PRESENTS,
that the undersigned, Spokane, Portland and Seattle
Railway Company, of New York, a corporation, as

principal, and American Surety Company, a corporation organized and existing under the laws of the State of New York, having an office in Portland, Oregon, and being duly authorized to transact business pursuant to the Act of Congress of August 12, 1894, entitled "An act relative to recognizances, stipulations, bonds and undertakings, and to allow certain corporations to be accepted as surety therein," as surety, are held and firmly bound unto Charles A. Cole in the full and just sum of $3,000.00 to be paid to said Charles A. Cole, his executors, administrators or assigns, to which payment well and truly to be made, the undersigned bind themselves, their successors and assigns, jointly and firmly by these presents. Upon condition nevertheless that

WHEREAS, the above-named Spokane, Portland and Seattle Railway Company has appealed to the United States Circuit Court of Appeals for the Ninth Circuit, from a judgment in favor of the above-named plaintiff, Charles A. Cole, made and entered on [45] the 25th day of February, 1931, in the above-entitled action by the District Court of the United States for the District of Oregon, praying that said judgment be reversed.

NOW, THEREFORE, the condition of this obligation is such that if the above-named appellant shall prosecute its appeal to effect, and shall answer all damages and costs that may be awarded against it, if it fails to make its appeal good, then this obligation shall be void, otherwise the same shall remain in full force and effect.

IN WITNESS WHEREOF said principal and surety have executed this bond this 30th day of July, 1931.

> SPOKANE, PORTLAND AND SEATTLE
> RAILWAY COMPANY.
> By CHARLES A. HART,
> FLETCHER ROCKWOOD,
> CAREY, HART, SPENCER and McCUL-
> LOCH,
>
> > Its Attorneys.

AMERICAN SURETY COMPANY OF NEW YORK.

[Seal American Surety Company]

> By W. A. KING,
> Resident Vice-president.
> Attest: N. CODY,
> Resident Asst. Secretary.

The foregoing bond is hereby approved as to form, amount and sufficiency of surety.

Dated: August 3, 1931.

> JOHN H. McNARY,

Judge of the United States District Court, for the District of Oregon. [46]

State of Oregon,
County of Multnomah,—ss.

Due service of the within undertaking on appeal is hereby accepted in Multnomah County, Oregon, this —— day of July, 1931, by receiving a copy

thereof, duly certified to as such by Fletcher Rockwood of attorneys for defendant.

DAVIS & HARRIS,

Attorneys for Plaintiff.

Filed August 3, 1931. [47]

AND AFTERWARDS, to wit, on the 3d day of
August, 1931, there was duly filed in said court a
praecipe for transcript, in words and figures as
follows, to wit: [48]

[Title of Court and Cause.]

PRAECIPE FOR TRANSCRIPT OF RECORD ON APPEAL.

To G. H. Marsh, Clerk of the Above-entitled Court:

You will please make up the transcript on appeal
in the above-entitled case to be filed in the United
States Circuit Court of Appeals for the Ninth Circuit, and you will please include in such transcript
on appeal the following, and no other, papers and
exhibits, to wit:

1. Complaint.
2. Answer.
3. Reply.
4. Verdict.
5. Judgment.
6. Motion for a new trial and in arrest of judgment.
7. Order denying defendant's motion for a new
   trial and in arrest of judgment.
8. Bill of exceptions.

9. Order allowing bill of exceptions.

10. Petition for appeal and supersedeas.

11. Assignment of errors.

12. Order allowing appeal.

13. Undertaking on appeal.

14. Citation on appeal.

15. Copy of this praecipe, as served upon counsel.

Very respectfully yours,

CHARLES A. HART,

FLETCHER ROCKWOOD,

CAREY, HART, SPENCER and McCUL-
LOCH,

Attorneys for Defendant.   [49]

State of Oregon,
County of Multnomah,—ss.

Due service of the within praecipe for transcript is hereby accepted in Multnomah County, Oregon, this 3d day of August, 1931, by receiving a copy thereof, duly certified to as such by ————, of attorneys for ————.

DAVIS & HARRIS,

Attorneys for Plaintiff.

Filed August 3, 1931.   [50]

CERTIFICATE OF CLERK U. S. DISTRICT COURT TO TRANSCRIPT OF RECORD.

United States of America,
District of Oregon,—ss.

I, G. D. Marsh, Clerk of the District Court of the United States for the District of Oregon, do hereby certify that the foregoing pages, numbered from 3 to 50, inclusive, constitute the transcript of record upon the appeal in a cause in said court, No. 10,-826, in which Charles A. Cole, is plaintiff and appellee, and Spokane, Portland and Seattle Railway Company is defendant and appellant; that the said transcript has been prepared by me in accordance with the praecipe for transcript filed by said appellant, and is a full, true and complete transcript of the record and proceedings had in said Court in said cause, in accordance with the said praecipe, as the same appear of record and on file at my office and in my custody.

I further certify that the cost of the foregoing transcript is $7.50 and that the same has been paid by the said appellant.

IN TESTIMONY WHEREOF I have hereunto set my hand and affixed the seal of said court, at Portland, in said District, this 22d day of August, 1931.

[Seal]   G. H. MARSH,
                                    Clerk.   [51]

———

[Endorsed]: No. 6589. United States Circuit Court of Appeals for the Ninth Circuit. Spokane, Portland and Seattle Railway Company, a Corporation, Appellant, vs. Charles A. Cole, Appellee. Transcript of Record. Upon Appeal from the United States District Court for the District of Oregon.

Filed August 24, 1931.

PAUL P. O'BRIEN,

Clerk of the United States Circuit Court of Appeals
    for the Ninth Circuit.

In the United States Circuit Court of Appeals for the Ninth Circuit.

SPOKANE, PORTLAND AND SEATTLE RAIL-
WAY COMPANY, a Corporation,

Appellant,

vs.

CHARLES A. COLE,

Appellee.

SPOKANE, PORTLAND AND SEATTLE RAIL-
WAY COMPANY, a Corporation,

Appellant,

vs.

CHARLES A. COLE,

Appellee.

STIPULATION FOR CONSOLIDATION OF
CASES ON APPEAL.

It is hereby stipulated by the above-named parties, by and through their respective attorneys, as follows:

In each of the above cases the appellant named has appealed from a judgment in favor of the appellee and against appellant rendered by the District Court of the United States for the District of Oregon, each on February 25, 1931. The first of the above cases, numbered by the Clerk of said District Court as Number L.–10,826, is an action by the plaintiff as parent, for loss of services caused by the death of his minor daughter, Jacqueline A. Cole, alleged to have been caused by the negligence of the defendant, and the second of the above cases, numbered in the files of the Clerk of said District Court as L.–10,827, was an action by the same plaintiff as parent for loss of earnings caused by the death of his minor daughter, Leona J. Cole, alleged to have been caused by the negligence of the defendant. The two cases arose out of the same accident and were consolidated for trial in said District Court. By reason of the foregoing facts,—

IT IS STIPULATED that said cases may be consolidated for the purposes of appeal with a single printed transcript of record and consolidated for the purpose of preparation of briefs and oral argument, and that an order may be made by the Court giving effect to this stipulation.

CHARLES A. HART,

FLETCHER ROCKWOOD,

CAREY, HART, SPENCER & McCUL-
LOCH,

Attorneys for Appellant.

DAVIS & HARRIS,

Attorneys for Appellee.

So ordered.

CURTIS D. WILBUR,

United States Circuit Judge.

Dated: San Francisco, August 24, 1931.

[Endorsed]: Filed Aug. 27, 1931. Paul P. O'Brien, Clerk.

United States
Circuit Court of Appeals
For the Ninth Circuit. *13*

SPOKANE, PORTLAND AND SEATTLE RAIL-
WAY, COMPANY, a Corporation,

>Appellant,

vs.

CHARLES A. COLE,

>Appellee.

Transcript of Record.

**Upon Appeal from the United States District Court for
the District of Oregon.**

Filmer Bros. Co. Print, 330 Jackson St., S. F., Cal.

United States
Circuit Court of Appeals
For the Ninth Circuit.

———

SPOKANE, PORTLAND AND SEATTLE RAIL-
WAY, COMPANY, a Corporation,

Appellant,

vs.

CHARLES A. COLE,

Appellee.

———

Transcript of Record.

———

Upon Appeal from the United States District Court for
the District of Oregon.

———

Filmer Bros. Co. Print, 330 Jackson St., S. F., Cal.

INDEX TO THE PRINTED TRANSCRIPT OF RECORD.

[Clerk's Note: When deemed likely to be of an important nature, errors or doubtful matters appearing in the original certified record are printed literally in italic; and, likewise, cancelled matter appearing in the original certified record is printed and cancelled herein accordingly. When possible, an omission from the text is indicated by printing in italic the two words between which the omission seems to occur.]

NAMES AND ADDRESSES OF ATTORNEYS OF RECORD.

Mr. CHARLES A. HART, Mr. FLETCHER ROCKWOOD, CAREY, HART, SPENCER and McCULLOCH, Yeon Building, Portland, Oregon,

> For the Appellant.

DAVIS & HARRIS, 507 Failing Building, Portland, Oregon,

> For the Appellee.

In the District Court of the United States for the District of Oregon.

No. L.–10,827.

CHARLES A. COLE,

> Plaintiff,

vs.

SPOKANE, PORTLAND AND SEATTLE RAILWAY COMPANY, a Corporation,

> Defendant.

CITATION ON APPEAL.

To Charles A. Cole, GREETING:

You are hereby cited and admonished to be and appear before the United States Circuit Court of Appeals for the Ninth Circuit, at San Francisco, California, within thirty (30) days from the date hereof, pursuant to a notice of appeal filed in the Clerk's office of the District Court of the United

States for the District of Oregon, wherein Spokane, Portland and Seattle Railway Company, a corporation, is appellant, and you are appellee, to show cause, if any there be, why the judgment in said cause should not be corrected and speedy justice *should be* done to the parties in that behalf.

Given under my hand at Portland, in said District, this 3d day of August, 1931.

JOHN H. McNARY,
Judge.   [1*]

District of Oregon,
County of Multnomah,—ss.

Due service of the within citation on appeal is hereby accepted in Multnomah County, Oregon, this 4th day of August, 1931, by receiving a copy thereof, duly certified to as such by Fletcher Rockwood of attorneys for defendant.

DAVIS & HARRIS,
Attorney for Plaintiff.

[Endorsed]: Filed Aug. 4, 1931.   [2]

In the District Court of the United States for the District of Oregon.

July Term, 1929.

BE IT REMEMBERED, that on the 23d day of October, 1929, there was duly filed in the District Court of the United States for the District of Oregon, a complaint, in words and figures as follows, to wit: [3]

---

*Page-number appearing at the foot of page of original certified Transcript of Record.

In the District Court of the United States for the District of Oregon.

L.–10,827.

CHARLES A. COLE,

Plaintiff,

vs.

SPOKANE, PORTLAND & SEATTLE RAIL-WAY COMPANY, a Corporation,

Defendant.

COMPLAINT.

Comes now the plaintiff, and for cause of action against said defendant complains and alleges as follows:

I.

That the defendant is a corporation duly organized and existing under and by virtue of the laws of the State of Washington and has duly complied with the laws of the State of Oregon entitling it to do business therein, and is engaged in the business of operating a railway system, a portion of which extends in a general easterly and westerly direction through portions of Skamania County, Washington.

II.

That plaintiff is a resident and inhabitant of the State of Oregon.

III.

That the plaintiff is the surviving father of Leona J. Cole, who at the time she met her death, as here-

inafter set forth, was a minor of the age of eighteen
years.   [4]

IV.

That at all times hereinafter alleged there was in
full force and effect, in the State of Washington, the
following statute enacted by the Legislature of said
State, the same being known as Section 184, Remington's Code, which said section is as follows:

"A father or in case of the death or desertion
of his family the mother, may maintain an action as plaintiff for the injury or death of a
child, and a guardian for the injury or death of
his ward."

V.

That at all times hereinafter alleged there was in
full force and effect in the State of Washington the
following statute enacted by the Legislature of said
State, the same being Chapter 72 of the Session
Laws of 1923 of the State of Washington, and entitled "An act relating to the age of majority and
amending sections 1572 and 10548 of Remington's
Compiled Statutes," which said chapter reads as
follows:

"Section 1.   That Section 1572 of Reming
ton's Compiled Statutes be amended to read as
follows:

Section 1572.   Guardians herein provided
for shall at all times be under the general direction and control of the court making the appointment.   For the purposes of this act, all
persons shall be of full and legal age when they
shall be twenty-one years old, and females shall

be deemed of full and legal age at any age under twenty-one years when with the consent of the parent or guardian, or the person under whose care or government they may be they shall have been legally married.

Section 2. That Section 10548 of Remington's Compiled Statutes be amended to read as follows:

Section 10548. All persons shall be deemed and taken to be of full age for all purposes at the age of twenty-one years and upwards."

VI.

That approximately a half mile west of the City of Underwood in Skamania County, Washington, a road and thoroughfare leading to a Government Fish Hatchery and extending in a general [5] northerly and southerly direction, crosses the defendant's right of way.

VII.

That on or about the 30th day of August, 1928, the plaintiff's minor intestate was riding as a passenger in an automobile being operated in a northerly direction on said road and thoroughfare, when the same was violently run into and struck by a train being operated by the defendant in a westerly direction, and as a result thereof said intestate received injuries which resulted in her death.

VIII.

Plaintiff alleges that the defendant was then and there careless and negligent in the following particulars, to wit:

(a) That the said defendant carelessly and negligently operated said train, in view of the character of the crossing and the conditions existing at the place of said collision, and in view of the fact that defendant failed to sound any warning or alarm of its approach, at a high, dangerous and reckless rate of speed, to wit: over forty miles per hour.

(b) That said defendant carelessly and negligently failed to sound any warning or alarm in approaching said intersection to warn and advise travelers at said point;

(c) That the said defendant carelessly and negligently maintained its right of way at and near said crossing in a dangerous condition, in that the defendant permitted unneccessary obstructions upon its right of way at or near said crossing so as to obstruct the view thereat, both of its servants approaching said crossing on a train and of persons upon said highway, in that the defendant allowed said right of way to become overgrown with bushes, weeds and grass so as to obstruct said view. [6]

IX.

That at the time said minor intestate met her death, as heretofore alleged, she was an intelligent, industrious and healthy girl of the age of eighteen years and in full possession of her faculties, was unmarried, and was the daughter of the plaintiff, and immediately prior to the time of her death was and had been living with and in the service and employment of this plaintiff, who was, and during her minority had she lived would have been, entitled to her earnings and the value of her services and earnings over and above the cost of providing her with the usual and customary necessities of life, which is and would have been of the value of Ten Thousand ($10,000.00) Dollars, in which said sum plaintiff has been damaged.

WHEREFORE, plaintiff demands judgment against the defendant in the sum of Ten Thousand ($10,000.00) Dollars and for his costs and disbursements incurred herein.

DAVIS & HARRIS,
Attorneys for Plaintiff.   [7]

State of Oregon,
County of Multnomah,—ss.

I, Charles A. Cole, being first duly sworn, depose and say that I am the plaintiff in the above-entitled action; and that the foregoing complaint is true as I verily believe.

CHARLES A. COLE,

Subscribed and sworn to before me this 22d day of October, 1929.

[Seal]   F. C. HILLER,
Notary Public for the State of Oregon,
My commission expires Jan. 21, 1931.

Filed October 23, 1929.   [8]

———

AND AFTERWARDS, to wit, on the 29th day of October, 1929, there was duly filed in said court an answer, in words and figures as follows, to wit: [9]

[Title of Court and Cause.]

ANSWER.

Defendant for answer to the complaint of the plaintiff in the above-entitled case alleges:

I.

Admits the allegations of Paragraph I of the complaint.

II.

Admits the allegations of Paragraph II of the complaint.

III.

Admits the allegations of Paragraph III of the complaint.

IV.

Admits the allegations of Paragraph IV of the complaint.

V.

Admits the allegations of Paragraph V of the complaint.   [10]

VI.

Admits the allegations of Paragraph VI of the complaint.

VII.

Admits that on or about August 30, 1928, the said deceased daughter of plaintiff was riding as a passenger in an automobile being operated in a northerly direction on a road and that at said time there was a collision between said automobile and a car being operated by the defendant on its track in a westerly direction, and that as a result thereof said deceased daughter received injuries which resulted in her death as alleged in Paragraph VII, but except as so admitted defendant denies the allegations of Paragraph VII of the complaint.

VIII.

Denies the allegations of Paragraph VIII of the complaint.

IX.

Defendant has no information relating to the facts alleged in Paragraph IX of of the complaint and for this reason denies said allegations.

For a further and separate answer defendant alleges:

X.

That the plaintiff's daughter Leona J. Cole was contributorily negligent and that said contributory negligence was a proximate cause of the injuries to and the resulting death of said Leona J. Cole, and that said contributory negligence of the said Leona J. Cole consisted of failure to exercise proper or any precautions, in approaching said crossing as a passenger in said automobile, to observe the approach of trains upon said [11] railroad track or to warn the driver of said automobile of the approach of said car of the defendant which struck said automobile.

WHEREFORE, defendant demands that plaintiff take nothing by this action and that defendant have its costs and disbursements herein.

> CHARLES A. HART,
> FLETCHER ROCKWOOD,
> CAREY & KERR,
> Attorneys for Defendant [12]

State of Oregon,
County of Multnomah,—ss.

I, Robert Crosbie, being first duly sworn, on oath depose and say: That I am the Secretary of Spokane, Portland and Seattle Railway Company, a corporation, defendant in the above-entitled action, that I have read the foregoing answer, know the contents thereof, and that the same is true as I verily believe.

ROBERT CROSBIE.

Subscribed and sworn to before me this 28th day of October, 1929.

[Seal]   PHILIP CHIPMAN,
          Notary Public for Oregon.

My commission expires August 28, 1931.

District of Oregon,
County of Multnomah,—ss.

Due service of the within answer is hereby accepted in Multnomah County, Oregon, this 29th day of October, 1929, by receiving a copy thereof, duly certified to as such by Fletcher Rockwood of attorneys for defendant.

DAVIS & HARRIS,
Attorneys for Plaintiff.

Filed October 29, 1929.   [13]

————

AND AFTERWARDS, to wit, on the 2d day of November, 1929, there was duly filed in said court, a reply, in words and figures as follows, to wit:
[14]

[Title of Court and Cause.]

REPLY.

Comes now the plaintiff and, in reply to the defendant's answer, admits, denies and alleges, as follows:

I.

Denies each and every allegation, matter and thing contained in said answer, except as heretofore either expressly admitted, stated, qualified or explained in plaintiff's complaint.

Replying to defendant's further and separate answer plaintiff admits, denies and alleges:

I.

Denies each and every allegation, matter and thing contained in said further and separate answer, except as heretofore either expressly admitted, stated, qualified or explained in plaintiff's complaint.

WHEREFORE, plaintiff demands judgment as prayed for in his complaint.

DAVIS & HARRIS,
Attorneys for Plaintiff. [15]

State of Oregon,
County of Multnomah,—ss.

I, Charles A. Cole, being first duly sworn, depose and say that I am the plaintiff in the above-entitled action; and that the foregoing reply is true as I verily believe.

CHARLES A. COLE.

Subscribed and sworn to before me this 29th day of October, 1929.

[Seal]   F. C. HILLER,
          Notary Public for the State of Oregon.
My commission expires Jan. 21, 1931.

Due service by copy admitted at Portland, Oregon, this 1st day of Nov., 1929.

                    FLETCHER ROCKWOOD,
                        Attorneys for Defendant.

Filed November 2, 1929.   [16]

———

AND AFTERWARDS, to wit, on Wednesday, the 25th day of February, 1931, the same being the 78th judicial day of the regular November term of said court—Present, the Honorable JOHN H. McNARY, United States District Judge, Presiding—the following proceedings were had in said cause, to wit: [17]

[Title of Cause.]

MINUTES OF COURT—FEBRUARY 25, 1931— VERDICT.

Now *at* this day comes the plaintiff by Mr. Paul R. Harris and Mr. Donald K. Grant, of counsel, and the defendant by Mr. Fletcher Rockwood, of counsel. Whereupon the jurors impaneled herein being present and answering to their names, the further trial of this cause at the same time and before the same jury as the cause of Charles A. Cole vs. Spokane, Portland & Seattle Railway Company, No.

L.-10,826, pursuant to the oral stipulation of the parties hereto made and entered in open court herein, is resumed. And the said jury having heard the evidence adduced, the arguments of counsel, and the instructions of the court, retires in charge of proper sworn officers, to consider of its verdict. And thereafter said jury comes into court and returns its verdict in words and figures as follows, to wit:

"We, the Jury, duly empaneled and sworn, in the above-entitled cause, find our verdict in favor of the plaintiff and against the defendant and assess plaintiff's damages at Two Thousand ($2000.00) Dollars.

E. A. ROSS,
Foreman."

(Leona J. Cole)
(18 years of age)

which verdict is received by the court and ordered to be filed. Whereupon upon motion of plaintiff,—

IT IS ADJUDGED that plaintiff do have and recover of and from said defendant the sum of $2,000.00, together with his costs and disbursements herein taxed at $20.00, and that execution issue therefor. [18]

———

AND AFTERWARDS, to wit, on the 25th day of February, 1931, there was duly filed in said court a verdict, in words and figures as follows, to wit: [19]

[Title of Court and Cause.]

VERDICT.

We, the jury, duly empaneled and sworn, in the above-entitled cause, find our verdict in favor of the plaintiff and against the defendant and assess plaintiff's damages at Two Thousand ($2,000.00) Dollars.

E. A. ROSS,
Foreman.

(Leona J. Cole)

(18 years of age)

Filed February 25, 1931.   [20]

———

AND AFTERWARDS, to wit, on the 2d day of March, 1931, there was duly filed in said court a motion for new trial and in arrest of judgment, in words and figures as follows, to wit: [21]

In the District Court of the United States for the District of Oregon.

No. L.–10,826.

CHARLES A. COLE,

Plaintiff,

vs.

SPOKANE, PORTLAND AND SEATTLE RAILWAY COMPANY, a Corporation,

Defendant.

No. L.–10,827.

CHARLES A. COLE,

Plaintiff,

vs.

SPOKANE, PORTLAND AND SEATTLE RAIL-
WAY COMPANY, a Corporation,

Defendant.

MOTION FOR NEW TRIAL AND IN ARREST OF JUDGMENT.

The defendant, Spokane, Portland and Seattle
Railway Company, respectfully moves the court for
a new trial in the above-entitled cases and in arrest
of judgment upon the grounds that—

1. The damages awarded by the verdicts of the
jury in each case are excessive and appear to have
been given under the influence of passion and
prejudice.

2. The court erred as a matter of law in declining to give defendant's requested instruction number IV reading as follows:

"I instruct you that the evidence is insufficient to show any negligence on the part of the
defendant in [22] the manner in which the
crossing itself was maintained with respect to
the view at the crossing of train operators along
the highway and of automobile operators along
the railroad. Consequently all allegations of
negligence with respect to obstruction of view
and the maintenance of the crossing itself are

withdrawn from your consideration and you cannot base any recovery on any such allegations.''

The foregoing motion is made upon the pleadings and files in this case, the proceedings in the trial including the minutes of the court, for the causes above specified, which are causes set forth in Section 2–802, Oregon Code, Annotated, 1930, being the same as Section 174, Oregon Laws, and in accordance with the rules of this court.

Dated March 2, 1931.

CHARLES A. HART,

FLETCHER ROCKWOOD,

CARY, HART, SPENCER & McCULLOCH,

Attorneys for Defendant.

State of Oregon,

County of Multnomah,—ss.

Due service of the within motion is hereby accepted in Multnomah County, Oregon, this 2d day of March, 1931, by receiving a copy thereof, duly certified to as such by Fletcher Rockwood of attorneys for defendant.

DAVIS & HARRIS,

Attorneys for Plaintiff.

Filed March 2, 1931.   [23]

AND AFTERWARDS, to wit, on Monday, the 18th day of May, 1931, the same being the 60th judicial day of the regular March term of said court—Present, the Honorable JOHN H. McNARY, United States District Judge, Presiding—the following proceedings were had in said cause, to wit: [24]

[Title of Cause.]

MINUTES OF COURT—MAY 18, 1931—ORDER DENYING MOTION FOR NEW TRIAL.

This cause was heard by the Court upon the motion of the defendant for a new trial herein, and was argued by Mr. Paul R. Harris and Mr. Donald K. Grant, of counsel for plaintiff and by Mr. Fletcher Rockwood, of counsel for defendant. Upon consideration whereof,—

IT IS ORDERED that the said motion be and the same is hereby denied. [25]

———

AND AFTERWARDS, to wit, on Monday, the 8th day of June, 1931, the same being the 77th judicial day of the regular March term of said court—Present, the Honorable JOHN H. McNARY, United States District Judge, Presiding—the following proceedings were had in said cause, to wit: [26]

[Title of Court and Cause.]

MINUTES OF COURT—MAY 8, 1931—ORDER EXTENDING TIME TO AND INCLUDING JULY 15, 1931, TO FILE BILL OF EXCEPTIONS.

Upon application of the defendant, and for good cause shown, it is hereby

ORDERED that the time within which defendant may file and present its bill of exceptions herein is hereby extended to and including the 15th day of July, 1931.

Dated June 8, 1931.

JOHN H. McNARY,

Judge.

Filed June 8, 1931.   [27]

AND AFTERWARDS, to wit, on the 29th day of July, 1931, there was duly filed in said court, a bill of exceptions in words and figures as follows, to wit: [28]

[Title of Court and Cause.]

BILL OF EXCEPTIONS.

This cause came on for hearing before the Honorable John H. McNary and a jury, on the 19th day of February, 1931, Messrs. Davis and Harris appearing as attorneys for the plaintiff, and Messrs. Carey, Hart, Spencer and McCulloch, and Mr.

Fletcher Rockwood, appearing as attorneys for the defendant.

By stipulation of the parties, and on order of the court this case was consolidated for trial with the case of Charles A. Cole, Plaintiff, vs. Spokane, Portland and Seattle Railway Company, a Corporation, Defendant, No. L.–10,826. This case, No. L.–10,827, arose out of the death of Leona J. Cole, a minor daughter of the plaintiff, and No. L.–10,826 arose out of the death in the same accident of Jacqueline A. Cole, another minor daughter of the same plaintiff.

After hearing all of the evidence, the argument of counsel and the charge of the court, the jury retired to consider the evidence and thereafter returned a verdict in favor of the plaintiff, in this case, assessing his damages at $2,000.00, upon which verdict judgment was thereafter on [29] the 25th day of February, 1931, entered by the court against the defendant.

Thereafter, on the 2d day of March, 1931, the defendant served and filed its motion for a new trial and in arrest of judgment, upon the grounds that the damages awarded by the verdict of the jury were excessive and appeared to have been given under the influence of passion and prejudice, and that the trial court erred as a matter of law in declining to give defendant's requested instruction number IV, which is quoted in full hereinafter in this bill of exceptions.

Thereafter, on the 20th day of April, 1931, the defendant's motion for a new trial and in arrest of judgment was argued orally to the court by counsel for both parties, and on the 18th day of May, 1931, the court made its order denying the said motion.

I.

At the trial the defendant requested the court to instruct the jury as follows:

"IV.

I instruct you that the evidence is insufficient to show any negligence on the part of the defendant in the manner in which the crossing itself was maintained with respect to the view at the crossing of train operators along the highway and of automobile operators along the railroad. Consequently all allegations of negligence with respect to obstruction of view and the maintenance of the crossing itself are withdrawn from your consideration and you cannot base any recovery on any such allegations."

The court declined to give the requested instruction, and to the refusal of the court so to instruct the jury the   [30]   defendant duly excepted.

The evidence necessary to present clearly the questions of law involved in the ruling is as follows:

On the 30th day of August, 1928, Leona J. Cole, the daughter of the plaintiff, was killed in a collission between a gasoline propelled car operated by the defendant on its railroad, and a Ford touring automobile in which the decedent was a passenger, at a place approximately one-half mile west of the defendant's station at Underwood, Washington, where a roadway from the grounds of the United States Government fish hatchery leading to a county road crosses the railroad track and right of way of the defendant. The hatchery grounds are located on the southerly side of the defendant's right of way and the county road lies parallel to the right of way on the northerly side.

The crossing at which the accident occurred is a private crossing. Witness Ray W. Hoffman, the Government employee in charge of the hatchery, a witness for the plaintiff, testified:

"Q. You, yourself, built this road, you said?

A. It was partially built when I came. I completed it.

Q. That was about three years ago?

A. Yes.

Q. And the purpose of the road was to furnish a means of getting to and from the fish hatchery? A. Yes.

Q. It is a private road, is it not?

A. I believe it is classed that way. [31]

Q. Well, you do know, do you not, that the crossing was built pursuant to a permit which was given by the railway company to the Bureau of Fisheries? A. Yes, sir.

Q. That is correct, is it not? A. Yes, sir.

* * * * * * * *

The road ends right at the fish hatchery, does it? A. Yes, sir.

Q. It opens up in your yard, so to speak, at the fish hatchery building?

A. It does." (T. pp. 83, 84.)

Witness Hoffman further testified that he built the road from the hatchery grounds up to the railroad track, but that the railroad constructed the actual crossing, and has since maintained it. (T. pp. 79, 80.)

With respect to the use of the road the same witness testified:

"Q. Well, now, that road has been occupied there how long? Been used, I mean.

A. In the neighborhood of* three years.

(*The evidence of this witness at the trial was taken, by stipulation, by reading into the record his testimony at the trial of the case of Cecile S. Cole vs. Spokane, Portland and Seattle Railway Company, which was tried in this court in October, 1929.)

Q. Now, what would you say as to the number of people going up and down there?

A. Well, it depends on the season of the year. During the fishing season I would say there is about twenty cars a day cross over the crossing. [32]

Q. What class of people come in there? Just explain that.

A. It is ranchers, fishing men, movie men— practically all classes of people.

Q. When you say 'movie' men, what do you mean?

A. Cameramen coming in to take pictures of the fish.

Q. Well, what would you say as to whether or not tourists and others coming there to look over the hatchery come in?

A. Yes, sir, they visit it often.

Q. This was in August. What would you say as to whether or not there were people coming in there frequently during that month?

A. Not so much right at that time of the year. Perhaps it would average two or three cars a day. That is outside cars.

COURT.—Outside cars?

A. Yes.

COURT.—There would be local cars, would there, that would use this road?

A. Speaking of outside cars, I mean the residents around Underwood there coming in; people that were not living at the hatchery.

Q. What would you say as to people that lived in there and worked there?

A. We crossed, probably, I would say, two or three trips a day out each car.

Q. And how many cars were there there?

A. There were three at the time.'' (T. pp. 80, 81.)

Mrs. Larson, a sister of Cecile S. Cole, the decedent's mother, was living at the hatchery grounds. Mr. Larson was then employed at the hatchery. (T. p. 33.) Just prior to the accident the decedent, with her mother, and her sisters and a brother had been visiting at the Larson home at the hatchery grounds. (T. p. 34.) Mrs. Larson with Mrs. Cole and their children were leaving the Larson home at the time [33] of the accident to drive to the place where the Coles were then living at a point to the north of the railroad. (T. pp. 47–49.) Mrs.

Larson was driving the automobile and the decedent was a passenger in the back seat of the automobile at the time of the accident. (T. pp. 60, 62, 64, 65.)

Various witnesses gave testimony as to the state of the vegetation along the railroad right of way between the location of the crossing and the direction from which the railroad car approached.

Witness Hoffman for the plaintiff testified on this subject on direct examination as follows:

"Q. Now, at the time these women were hurt, will you tell this jury what was the condition of the brush and foliage at that point?

A. Along the edge here there was brush growing—well there was one that was cut down, that was at least six feet high; a maple I would judge that it was. And there was brush all along the edge of the cut, that hid the view.

COURT.—Was the brush on the right of way of the railroad?

A. Yes, sir.

Q. And when was that brush cut down?

A. The next morning after the accident.

Q. Who cut that down?

A. The section crew.

Q. Now, what would you say was the extent of the brush along on that point as to whether it was heavy, or not?

A. Well, in places it grew in bunches. In places it was quite heavy, and then there would not be any for a ways, and then there would be another bunch. [34]

Q. How high would you say that brush grew?

A. The tallest was about six feet, around six feet.

Q. And the cut was about how deep, did you say?

A. In the neighborhood of eight or ten feet.

Q. That is, down to the bed of the railroad track?   A. Yes.

Q. Well, at the time that brush was there, and the time these women were injured—you remember that very distinctly?

A. I certainly do.

Q. Well, now, what would you say then, as to whether or not that would obstruct the view a good deal worse than it did after they cut the brush down?   A. Yes, it would.

Q. Would you estimate, then, about how near they would get to the track before they could see a train?

Well, that would be a rather hard question to answer, Mr. Davis; probably around one hundred feet.

Q. Well, how far now—when you were back how far would you have to be from the track?

A. To see one hundred feet?

Q. Yes.

A. The driver, I imagine, would be about seventeen feet from the rail.

Q. And then the front of the car would be still nearer. Is that the way you estimate it?

A. Yes.

COURT.—You mean the driver would have to be seventeen feet?

A. Yes.

COURT.—Not the car?

A. Not the car, but the driver.''

Mrs. Cole, the decedent's mother, who was a [35] passenger in the front seat of the automobile, testified that the automobile stopped to allow her nephew, Elmer, to alight from the running-board of the automobile, where he had been riding. At that moment, she testified, the front end of the automobile was ten to twelve feet from the railroad track. (T. pp. 50, 57, 58.) She testified further as follows:

"Q. There is one thing I neglected to ask you. At the time you stopped, when you were travelling up that road, about what distance would you say you could see towards Underwood, in that cut?

A. Well, I don't think you could see more than 150 feet, if you could see that far.

Q. What was there there to prevent your vision, to prevent you from seeing?

A. There was quite a bit of brush on the cut there, which hung down. I don't know—there were trees, little trees, young willows, and there was quite a heavy brush there at the time.

Q. When you say hanging down, what do you mean?

A. They were leaning down towards the track from the top, leaning over like.''

II.

The court denied the motion of the defendant for a new trial and in arrest of judgment, made on the ground, among others, that the damages awarded by the verdict of the jury were excessive and appeared to have been given under the influence of passion and prejudice. The evidence necessary to present clearly the question of law involved in the ruling is as follows:

Leona J. Cole, the decedent, was 18 years of age at the time of her death. She would have become 19 years of age on the 16th of October, 1928. (T. p. 36.) The [36] accident occurred on August 30, 1928, so that at the date of her death she was 18 years 10½ months old.

Witness Lewis testified that she was "very intelligent, very pleasant" and "very industrious." (T. p. 26.)

She had always been in good health. (T. p. 37.) She finished grammar school at the age of twelve years, and attended the high school for three and one-half years. (T. p. 37.) She had done housework for a family named Nash. (T. p. 38.) She had worked in fall seasons packing apples at Underwood for which she was paid $3.50 per day (T. p. 56) during a season from in August to December 1st (T. p. 32), and just a few days prior to her death she had gone to Underwood for such work during the coming fall season. (T. p. 32.)

She had been employed by a Mrs. Simmons who testified as follows:

"A. Well, she worked off and on, different times and then she worked for me about six months.

Q. What kind of work did she do for you?

A. Well, just general housework and taking care of the children.

Q. Well, now, what would you say about her as to being industrious and efficient in her work?

A. She did her work very well.

Q. And she worked for you six months at one time, and then worked for you off and on, did she?   A. Yes.

Q. Well, what did you pay her for her services?

A. I paid her ten dollars a week.'' (T. p. 28.)

She assisted with the work at home, doing housework [37] and assisting in the care of the younger children. (T. p. 56.)

Whatever earnings she received from outside sources she turned over to her parents for use as a part of the family income in the support of the household. (T. p. 41, 56.) Her living expenses were then paid by her parents. (T. p. 41, 56.) Her clothes were not expensive because her mother made over for the children clothes given to her. (T. p. 38, 56.) As testified by her mother, ''Usually all we had to buy was their shoes and stocking—something like that. Once in a while I would get them something new. And we lived very plain.'' (T. p. 56.)

Defendant tenders herein this its bill of exceptions to the action of the Court in refusing to give the requested instruction and in denying defendant's motion for a new trial, as herein noted.

CHARLES A. HART,
FLETCHER ROCKWOOD,
CAREY, HART, SPENCER & McCUL-
LOCH,
Attorneys for Defendant. [38]

[Title of Court and Cause.]

ORDER ALLOWING BILL OF EXCEPTIONS.

The defendant on July 13, 1931, and within the time allowed by the rules and orders of this court, delivered to the Clerk its bill of exceptions, and served a copy thereof on the attorneys for the plaintiff, and the court, having found that defendant's bill of exceptions is a true and correct statement of the facts therein referred to,—

NOW, THEREFORE, IT IS HEREBY ORDERED that the bill of exceptions presented by the defendant above referred to shall be allowed as the bill of exceptions in this case, and should be filed with the records in this case in the office of the Clerk of this court.

Dated July 29, 1931.

(Sgd.)   JOHN H. McNARY,
Judge.

Approved.

DAVIS & HARRIS,
Attorneys for Plaintiff.

Lodged in Clerk's Office July 13, 1931. G. H. Marsh, Clerk. By F. L. Buck, Chief Deputy. Filed July 29, 1931. G. H. Marsh, Clerk. By F. L. Buck, Chief Deputy.   [39]

———

AND AFTERWARDS, to wit, on the 3d day of August, 1931, there was duly filed in said court a petition for appeal, in words and figures as follows, to wit: [40]

[Title of Court and Cause.]

PETITION FOR APPEAL AND SUPERSEDEAS.

To The Honorable JOHN H. McNARY, District Judge, and One of the Judges of the Above-named Court:

Spokane, Portland and Seattle Railway Company, the defendant in the above-entitled case, considering itself aggrieved by the judgment entered herein on the 25th day of February, 1931, in favor of the plaintiff and against the defendant in the sum of Two Thousand Dollars ($2,000.00), hereby appeals to the United States Circuit Court of Appeals for the Ninth Circuit from said judgment and the whole thereof, for the reasons set forth in the assignment of errors which is served and filed herewith, and said defendant prays that this petition for said appeal may be allowed, and that a transcript of the record and of all proceedings upon which said judgment is based, duly authenticated, may be sent to the United States Circuit Court of Appeals for the Ninth Circuit, and defendant further prays that an order be made fixing the amount of security which the defendant shall give and furnish upon the allowance of said appeal, and that upon the giving of such security, all further proceedings in [41]   this court shall be suspended and stayed until the determination of said appeal by the United

States Circuit Court of Appeals for the Ninth Circuit.

CHARLES A. HART,
FLETCHER ROCKWOOD,
CAREY, HART, SPENCER and McCUL-
LOCH,

Attorneys for Defendant.

District of Oregon,
County of Multnomah, —ss.

Due service of the within petition for appeal is hereby accepted in Multnomah County, Oregon, this 3d day of August, 1931, by receiving a copy thereof, duly certified to as such by Fletcher Rockwood, of attorneys for defendant.

DAVIS & HARRIS,
Attorneys for Plaintiff.

Filed August 3, 1931. [42]

———

AND AFTERWARDS, to wit, on the 3d day of August, 1931, there was duly filed in said court, an assignment of errors, in words and figures as follows, to wit: [43]

[Title of Court and Cause.]

ASSIGNMENT OF ERRORS.

Now comes the defendant and files the following assignment of errors upon which it will rely upon the prosecution of its appeal in the above-entitled cause from the judgment entered herein in favor of the plaintiff and against the defendant on the 25th day of February, 1931.

I.

The United States District Court in and for the District of Oregon erred in declining to give to the jury defendant's requested instruction Number IV, reading as follows:

"IV.

I instruct you that the evidence is insufficient to show any negligence on the part of the defendant in the manner in which the crossing itself was maintained with respect to the view at the crossing of train operators along the highway and of automobile operators along the railroad. Consequently all allegations of negligence with respect to obstruction of view and the maintenance of the crossing itself are withdrawn from your consideration and you cannot base any recovery on any such allegations." [44]

II.

The United States District Court in and for the District of Oregon, erred in denying defendant's motion for a new trial made upon the ground, among others, that the damages awarded by the verdict of the jury were excessive and appeared to have been given under the influence of passion and prejudice.

WHEREFORE, defendant prays that said judgment heretofore and on the 25th day of February, 1931, entered in this action against the defendant and in favor of the plaintiff, be reversed, and that said cause be remanded to the United States District Court in and for the District of Oregon, for a new trial.

CHARLES A. HART,

FLETCHER ROCKWOOD,

CAREY, HART, SPENCER & McCUL-
LOCH,

Attorneys for Defendant.

State of Oregon,

County of Multnomah,—ss.

Due service of the within assignment of errors is hereby accepted in Multnomah County, Oregon, this 3d day of August, 1931, by receiving a copy thereof, duly certified to as such by Fletcher Rockwood of attorneys for defendant.

DAVIS & HARRIS,

Attorneys for Plaintiff.

Filed August 3, 1931.   [45]

———

AND AFTERWARDS, to wit, on Monday, the 3d day of August, 1931, the same being the 24th judicial day of the regular July term of said court—Present, the Honorable JOHN H. Mc-NARY, United States District Judge, Presiding—the following proceedings were had in said cause, to wit: [46]

[Title of Court and Cause.]

ORDER ALLOWING APPEAL.

The above-named defendant, Spokane, Portland and Seattle Railway Company, having duly served and filed herein its petition for appeal to the United States Circuit Court of Appeals for the Ninth Circuit, from the judgment entered herein in favor of the plaintiff and against the defendant on February 25, 1931, and having duly served and filed its assignment of errors upon which it will rely upon said appeal,—

IT IS ORDERED that the appeal be and is hereby allowed to the United States Circuit Court of Appeals for the Ninth Circuit from said judgment entered in this action in favor of the plaintiff and against the defendant on February 25, 1931.

IT IS FURTHER ORDERED that the bond on appeal herein has been fixed at the sum of $2,000.00, the same to act as a supersedeas bond and is a bond for costs and damages on appeal.

Dated August 3, 1931.

JOHN H. McNARY,
District Judge.

Filed August 3, 1931. [47]

———

AND AFTERWARDS, to wit, on the 3d day of August, 1931, there was duly filed in said court a bond on appeal, in words and figures as follows, to wit: [48]

[Title of Court and Cause.]

UNDERTAKING ON APPEAL.

KNOW ALL MEN BY THESE PRESENTS, that the undersigned, Spokane, Portland and Seattle Railway Company a corporation, as principal, and American Surety Company of New York, a corporation organized and existing under the laws of the state of New York, having an office in Portland, Oregon, and being duly authorized to transact business pursuant to the Act of Congress of August 12, 1894, entitled "An act relative to recognizances, stipulations, bonds and undertakings, and to allow certain corporations to be accepted as surety therein," as surety, are held and firmly bound unto Charles A. Cole in the full and just sum of $2,500.00 to be paid to said Charles A. Cole, his executors, administrators or assigns, to which payment well and truly to be made, the undersigned bind themselves, their successors and assigns, jointly and firmly by these presents. Upon condition nevertheless that

WHEREAS the above-named Spokane, Portland and Seattle Railway Company has appealed to the United States Circuit Court of Appeals for the Ninth Circuit, from a judgment in favor of the above-named plaintiff, Charles A. Cole, made and entered on the 25th day of February, 1931, in the above-entitled action [49] by the District Court of the United States for the District of Oregon, praying that said judgment be reversed.

NOW, THEREFORE, the condition of this obligation is such that if the above-named appellant shall prosecute its appeal to effect, and shall answer all damages and costs that may be awarded against it, if it fails to make its appeal good, then this obligation shall be void; otherwise the same shall remain in full force and effect.

IN WITNESS WHEREOF said principal and surety have executed this bond this 30th day of July, 1931.

> SPOKANE, PORTLAND AND SEATTLE RAILWAY COMPANY.
> > By CHARLES A. HART,
> > FLETCHER ROCKWOOD,
> CAREY, HART, SPENCER and McCULLOCH,
> > > > Its Attorneys.
> AMERICAN SURETY COMPANY, OF NEW YORK.
> > By W. A. KING,
> > Resident Vice-president.
> > Attest: N. CODY,
> > Resident Assistant Secretary.

[Seal American Surety Company]

The foregoing bond is hereby approved as to form, amount and sufficiency of surety.

Dated August 3, 1931.

> JOHN H. McNARY,

Judge of the United States District Court, for the District of Oregon.

District of Oregon,
County of Multnomah,—ss.

Due service of the within undertaking on appeal is hereby accepted in Multnomah County, Oregon, this 3d day of August, 1931, by receiving a copy thereof, duly certified to as such by Fletcher Rockwood of attorneys for defendant.

DAVIS & HARRIS,
Attorneys for Plaintiff.

Filed August 3, 1931. [50]

———

AND AFTERWARDS, to wit, on the 3d day of August, 1931, there was duly filed in said court, a praecipe for transcript, in words and figures as follows, to wit: [51]

[Title of Court and Cause.]

PRAECIPE FOR TRANSCRIPT OF RECORD ON APPEAL.

To G. H. Marsh, Clerk of the Above-entitled Court:

You will please make up the transcript on appeal in the above-entitled case to be filed in the United States Circuit Court of Appeals for the Ninth Circuit, and you will please include in such transcript on appeal the following, and no other, papers and exhibits, to wit:

1. Complaint.
2. Answer.
3. Reply.

4. Verdict.
5. Judgment.
6. Motion for a new trial and in arrest of judgment.
7. Order denying defendant's motion for a new trial and in arrest of judgment.
8. Bill of exceptions.
9. Order allowing bill of exceptions.
10. Petition for appeal and supersedeas.
11. Assignment of errors.
12. Order allowing appeal.
13. Undertaking on appeal.
14. Citation on appeal.
15. Copy of this praecipe as served upon counsel.

Very respectfully yours,

CHARLES A. HART,

FLETCHER ROCKWOOD,

CAREY, HART, SPENCER and McCULLOCH,

Attorneys for Defendant and Appellant, Spokane, Portland and Seattle Railway Company. [52]

State of Oregon,

County of Multnomah,—ss.

Due service of the within praecipe for transcript is hereby accepted in Multnomah County, Oregon, this 3d day of August, 1931, by receiving a copy thereof, duly certified to as such by ————, of attorneys for ————.

DAVIS & HARRIS,

Attorneys for Plaintiff.

Filed August 3, 1931. [53]

CERTIFICATE OF CLERK U. S. DISTRICT COURT TO TRANSCRIPT OF RECORD.

United States of America,

District of Oregon,—ss.

I, G. H. Marsh, Clerk of the District Court of the United States for the District of Oregon, do hereby certify that the foregoing pages, numbered from 3 to 53, inclusive, constitute the transcript of record upon the appeal in a cause in said court, No 10,827, in which Charles A. Cole is plaintiff and appellee, and Spokane, Portland and Seattle Railway Company is defendant and appellant; that the said transcript has been prepared by me in accordance with the praecipe for transcript filed by said appellant and is a full, true and complete transcript of the record and proceedings had in said court in said cause, in accordance with the said praecipe, as the same appear of record and on file at my office and in my custody.

I further certify that the cost of the foregoing transcript is $7.75 and that the same has been paid by the said appellant.

IN TESTIMONY WHEREOF I have hereunto set my hand and affixed the seal of said court, at Portland, in said District, this 22d day of August, 1931.

[Seal]   G. H. MARSH,

Clerk. [54]

[Endorsed]: No. 6590. United States Circuit Court of Appeals for the Ninth Circuit. Spokane, Portland and Seattle Railway Company, a Corporation, Appellant, vs. Charles A. Cole, Appellee. Transcript of Record. Upon Appeal from the United States District Court for the District of Oregon.

Filed August 24, 1931.

PAUL P. O'BRIEN,

Clerk of the United States Circuit Court of Appeals for the Ninth Circuit.

No. 6589
No. 6590

In the

United States Circuit Court of Appeals

For the Ninth Circuit /4

Spokane, Portland and Seattle Railway Company
a Corporation
Appellant

vs.

Charles A. Cole
Appellee

(TWO CASES)

Upon Appeal from the District Court of the United
States for the District of Oregon

Brief of Appellant

Charles A. Hart
Fletcher Rockwood
Carey, Hart, Spencer & McCulloch
1410 Yeon Building, Portland, Oregon
Attorneys for Appellant

FILED

OCT 12 1931

PAUL P. O'BRIEN,
CLERI

CONTENTS

AUTHORITIES CITED

No. 6589
No. 6590

In the
United States Circuit Court of Appeals
For the Ninth Circuit

SPOKANE, PORTLAND AND SEATTLE RAILWAY COMPANY
a Corporation
Appellant

vs.

CHARLES A. COLE
Appellee

(TWO CASES)

Upon Appeal from the District Court of the United
States for the District of Oregon

Brief of Appellant

STATEMENT OF THE CASES

These two actions were brought by plaintiff, the
father (respondent here), against defendant (appellant here), to recover damages for the loss of
services on account of the death of his two minor
daughters occurring at a private railroad crossing
near Underwood, Washington. The cases were con-

solidated for trial and judgments in both were recovered by plaintiff.

The private crossing where the accident occurred ran from the property of the United States Bureau of Fisheries lying south of defendant's right of way, over its railroad tracks to a point of connection with the county road lying north of and parallel with the right of way. This private crossing had been constructed by the Bureau of Fisheries over defendant's railroad track and right of way under a license granted by defendant. At the time of the accident plaintiff's two daughters were riding over this private crossing in an automobile driven by their aunt, Mrs. Larson, who lived on the Bureau of Fisheries' property south of the right of way. The collision occurred between her automobile and defendant's car, resulting in the death of plaintiff's daughters.

These cases arose from the same accident as was involved in *Spokane, Portland and Seattle Railway Company v. Cecile S. Cole,* 40 Fed. (2nd) 172, decided by this court on April 30, 1930; but the issues involved in this appeal are not the same as those presented in that case. There the only charges of negligence were the alleged failure of the defendant to give warning of the approach of defendant's car and the alleged excessive speed. In the two present cases a third charge of negligence is made with respect to permitting vegetation to grow on the right of way interfering with the view of the driver at the crossing.

In the first of these present cases, No. 6589, the daughter, Jacqueline A. Cole, was eight years old at the time of her death, and there was a verdict for $2500.00. In case No. 6590, the daughter, Leona J. Cole, was just under nineteen years of age, and there was a verdict of $2000.00.

During the trial defendant requested the court to withdraw from the jury the charge of negligence to the effect that defendant had permitted vegetation to grow upon its right of way, which request was denied. Defendant also moved for a new trial upon the ground that the court erred in refusing to withdraw from the jury the charge of negligence as to vegetation at the crossing, and upon the further ground that the verdict in each case was excessive, which motion was denied and defendant brings this appeal.

The questions presented under the specifications of error are: (1) Did the defendant owe any duty to these decedents to take affirmative steps to cut vegetation in order to make the private crossing safe for their use, so that the jury might find that defendant was negligent in failing to cut the vegetation, and (2) were the verdicts so excessive as to show that they were given under the influence of passion and prejudice.

SPECIFICATIONS OF ERROR

1. The District Court erred in declining to give to the jury defendant's requested instruction Number IV, reading as follows:

> "I instruct you that the evidence is insufficient to show any negligence on the part of the defendant in the manner in which the crossing itself was maintained with respect to the view at the crossing of train operators along the highway and of automobile operators along the railroad. Consequently, all allegations of negligence with respect to obstruction of view and the maintenance of the crossing itself are withdrawn from your consideration and you cannot base any recovery on any such allegations."

(R. No. 6589, pp. 19, 20; R. No. 6590, p. 20).

2. In No. 6589 the District Court erred in denying the defendant's motion for a new trial, made upon the ground, among others, that the damages awarded by the verdict of the jury were excessive and appeared to have been given under the influence of passion and prejudice. (R. p. 31).

3. In No. 6590 the District Court erred in denying the defendant's motion for a new trial, made upon the ground, among others, that the damages awarded by the verdict of the jury were excessive and appeared to have been given under the influence of passion and prejudice. (R. p. 32).

ARGUMENT

I.

It was error to refuse to withdraw from the jury the charge relating to the condition of the premises.

The first specification of error relates to the refusal of the court to withdraw from the jury the charge of negligence as to the condition of the crossing. The complaints charge, among other things, the negligent maintenance of the crossing in that defendant permitted the right of way to be overgrown with vegetation so as to obstruct the view of one driving over the crossing. (R. No. 6589, p. 6; R. No. 6590, pp. 5, 6). The defendant requested an instruction, which was refused, withdrawing such third charge from the jury.

The crossing at which the accident occurred is about half a mile west of Underwood, Washington. It is a private crossing, constructed under a permit from the defendant to the United States Bureau of Fisheries, in order to furnish a means of access from the county road on the north of and parallel to the track, and running to the fish hatchery grounds, which lie on the southerly side of and adjacent to the right of way. The private crossing was constructed by government employes and terminates at the hatchery. (R. pp. 20, 21).*

*References, unless otherwise noted, are to pages in the Transcript of Record in No. 6589. The bills of exceptions in the two cases are identical insofar as they relate to the first specification of error.

During the fishing season the crossing is used by visitors to the hatchery to the extent of about twenty cars a day, but during other seasons it is used almost exclusively by those who work and live at the hatchery. (R. pp. 22, 23). It is used only by persons who for reasons of business or pleasure have occasion to go to the hatchery.

Mr. Larson, an uncle of the two decedents, was an employe at the hatchery, and his wife and family lived on the hatchery grounds. Decedents, with their mother, Cecile S. Cole, had been visiting at the Larson home. Mrs. Larson and Mrs. Cole, with their children, including the decedents, were leaving the hatchery grounds at the time of the accident. (R. p. 23).

There was evidence that vegetation grew on the railroad right of way which interfered with the view of the track from the crossing. (R. pp. 23-26). But the undisputed evidence showed that the relation between the defendant and each of the two decedents was that of licensor and licensee, so that there was no duty resting on the defendant to maintain its premises free from vegetation and consequently there was no evidence upon which the jury could predicate a finding that the defendant was negligent in the particular respect charged.

The duties and obligations of the owner of land with respect to the condition of the premises vary, depending upon the relationship between the owner and the person injured. To the trespasser the owner owes no duty whatever except to refrain from wilful or wanton injury after the presence of the trespasser is discovered; with respect to the condition of the premises the owner owes no duty to a trespasser other than to refrain from setting traps. *United Zinc & Chemical Co. v. Britt,* 258 U. S. 268; 42 S. Ct. 299. To the licensee the owner owes a positive duty to refrain from *active* negligence when the presence of the licensee is known or may reasonably be anticipated. But there is no duty to make the premises safe; the licensee takes the premises as he finds them subject to all risks. The owner is not responsible for mere *passive* conduct. (See authorities cited, post.) To the invitee the owner owes the higher duty, to make the premises reasonably safe. Inaction,—the failure to take steps to make the premises reasonably safe,—may be the basis of liability to an invitee. *Bennett v. Railroad Company,* 102 U. S. 577.

A person using a private crossing over a railroad right of way is a mere licensee.

The true test to determine whether one on the land of another is a licensee or an invitee is found in the language in *Bennett v. Railroad Company, supra,* wherein Mr. Justice Harlan said:

> "It is sometimes difficult to determine whether the circumstances make a case of invitation, in the technical sense of that word, as

used in a large number of adjudged cases, or only a case of mere licensee. 'The principle,' says Mr. Campbell, in his treatise on Negligence, 'appears to be that invitation is inferred where there is a common interest or mutual advantage, while a license is inferred where the object is the mere pleasure or benefit of the person using it'."

In *Jonosky v. Northern Pacific Railway Company,* 57 Mont. 63; 187 Pac. 1014, the court said:

"Passing to a consideration of the duty owed to a licensee, however, we enter a veritable maze of conflicting and contradictory decisions. Much of the confusion arises from the failure of the courts to distinguish between a license and an invitation, and particularly between an implied license and an implied invitation. The distinction is not merely one of descriptive phraseology, but has its foundation in sound common sense. *An invitation is inferred where there is a common interest or mutual advantage, while a license is implied where the object is the mere pleasure, convenience, or benefit of the person enjoying the privilege.* (Citing cases). (Italics ours).

See also *Midland Valley R. Co. v. Littlejohn,* 44 Okla. 8, 143 Pac. 1; *L. E. Meyers' Co. v. Logue's Adm'r.,* 212 Ky. 802, 280 S. W. 107; *Lange v. St. Johns Lumber Co.,* 115 Ore. 337, 237 Pac. 696; *Watson v. Manitou & Pikes Peak Ry. Co.,* 41 Colo. 138, 92 Pac. 17, *Gasch v. Rounds,* 93 Wash. 317, 160 Pac. 962; *Coburn v. Village of Swanton,* 95 Vt. 320, 115 Atl. 153; *Bush v. Weed Lumber Co.,* 63 Cal. App. 426, 218 Pac. 618.

An application of the rule established by the authorities to the facts as we have summarized them

establishes that the decedents were mere licensees.
The private crossing was constructed solely for the
"pleasure, convenience or benefit" of the limited
number of people who had occasion to go to the
hatchery. There was no "common interest" between the decedents and the defendant; the use
of the crossing by the decedents did not redound to
the "mutual advantage" of the decedents and the
defendant. They were licensees rather than in-
vitees.

The case of *Felton v. Aubrey,* 74 Fed. 350, decided by a court including the late Chief Justice
Taft, and the late Justice Lurton, is the leading authority on the duty of a railroad with respect to
persons at permissive crossings. The court in that
case said:

> "If the evidence shows that the public had
> for a long period of time, customarily and con-
> stantly, openly and notoriously, crossed a rail-
> way track at a place *not a public highway,* with
> the knowledge and acquiescence of the company,
> a *license or permission* by the company to all
> persons to cross the track at that point may be
> presumed." (Italics ours).

In *Conn v. Pennsylvania R. Co.,* 288 Pa. 494, 136
Atl. 779, the court says:

> "A permissive way *is a license* to pass over
> the property of another; it may be either ex-
> press or implied, . . . " (Italics ours).

In *Pennsylvania R. Co. v. Breeden,* 140 Atl. 82
(Md.), the accident occurred at a crossing by a pri-

vate lane leading from a highway to a residential community. The court held that the plaintiff was a mere licensee, quoting with approval Elliott on Roads and Streets (2nd Ed.) Sec. 1019, as follows:

> " 'Unless the company has done something to allure or invite travelers to cross, or has in some manner treated it as a public crossing, we are inclined to think the better rule is that they are, *at the most, mere licensees* to whom no duty of active vigilance is ordinarily due. Mere permission or passive acquiescence under ordinary circumstances does not constitute an invitation'." (Italics ours).

And see, to the same effect, *Sypher v. Director General,* 243 Mass. 568, 137 N. E. 916; *Chesapeake & Ohio Ry. Co. v. Hunter's Admr.,* 170 Ky. 4, 185 S. W. 140; *Atlantic Coast Line R. Co. v. Carter,* 214 Ala. 252, 107 So. 218; *Johnson v. C. M. & St. P. Ry. Co.,* 96 Minn. 316, 104 N. W. 961; *Pomponio v. N. Y. N. H. & H. R. Co.,* 66 Conn. 528, 34 Atl. 491.

The owner of land is under no duty to make the premises safe for a licensee. His only duty is to refrain from affirmative acts of negligence when the presence of the licensee is known or may reasonably be anticipated.

The rule as to the duty which a landowner owes to a licensee with respect to the condition of the premises is stated in 45 Corpus Juris 798, as follows:

"A mere licensee takes the property on which he enters as he finds it, enjoys the license subject to its concomitant perils, and assumes all the ordinary risks incident to the condition of the property and the manner of the conduct of the owner's business thereon. *Accordingly, the owner or person in charge of property is ordinarily under no duty to make or keep the property in a safe condition for the use of licensees; . . .* " (Italics ours).

This rule is universally accepted. *Smith v. Day,* 100 Fed. 244 (9th C. C. A.) ; *Rhode v. Duff,* 208 Fed. 115 (8th C. C. A.) ; *Branan v. Wimsatt,* 298 Fed. 833 (D. C. C. A.) ; *Peebles v. Exchange Building Co.,* 15 Fed. (2nd) 335 (6th C. C. A.).

The specification of negligence which we are now considering consists merely of a charge that the defendant allowed its premises to be in an unsafe condition. By the failure to cut vegetation the view of travelers on the private lane was somewhat obscured. That constituted a mere condition of the premises and unless there is some duty on railroad owners, which is not imposed on property owners generally, there was no basis for submission of this charge to the jury.

There is no exception to the general rule as it relates to the condition of railroad premises. In *Northern Pacific Railway Company v. Curtz,* 196 Fed. 367, this court held that a boy who was in a box car sweeping loose grain, with the knowledge and acquiescence of the railway company, was a licensee. The plaintiff was permitted to recover for negligence consisting of a sudden movement of the car without warning to the plaintiff. This court said:

> "The occupant or owner of premises who invites, either expressly or impliedly, others to come upon them, owes to them the duty of using reasonable and ordinary diligence to the end that they be not necessarily or unreasonably exposed to danger; . . . *This doctrine has often been applied to cases where a railroad company permits the public to cross its tracks between given points,* and it is universally held that, where for a considerable period persons have been accustomed so to cross a railroad track, the employes of the company in charge of its trains are required to take notice of that fact, and to use reasonable precautions to prevent injury to persons whose presence there should be anticipated."

The basis of the rule applied in the Curtz case is found in the last clause of the quotation, "persons whose presence should be anticipated." When a landowner knows of or may reasonably anticipate the presence of a licensee, it is then his duty to refrain from active, affirmative negligent acts which may result in injury. But he is not required to prepare his premises in advance in anticipation of the coming of the licensee. The rule is clearly stated in *John P. Pettyjohn & Sons v. Basham,* 126 Va. 72, 100 S. E. 813, wherein the court said:

> "In the case of licensees, the occupant is charged with knowledge of the use of his prem-

ises by the licensee, *and, while not chargeable with the duty of prevision or preparation for the safety of the licensee,* he is chargeable with the duty of lookout, with such equipment as he then has in use to avoid injury to him at the time and place where the presence of the licensee may be reasonably expected." (Italics ours).

The best exposition on the subject of the duties of an owner of land is found in *Felton v. Aubrey, supra,* the decision of Judge (later Justice) Lurton. That case is the first of those cited by this court in support of the language which we have quoted from *Northern Pacific Railway Company v. Curtz, supra.* The doctrine taught in *Felton v. Aubrey* is that though a landowner may be under the duty of anticipating the presence of and keeping a lookout for a licensee, so that the owner may be liable for *affirmative conduct,* he cannot be held for mere *passive conduct.* In that case a boy was struck by a train at a place which the public had long used as a crossing, with the knowledge and acquiescence of the company. The evidence tended to show that the train was operated without any warnings to those who might be using the crossing. In making the distinction between the consequences of active and passive conduct under such circumstances, the court said:

"It seems to us that many of the American cases which we have cited fail to draw the proper distinction between the liability of an owner of premises to persons who sustain injuries as a

result *of the mere condition of the premises* and
those who come to harm by reason *of subsequent
conduct of the licensor, inconsistent with the
safety of persons permitted to go upon his premises,* and whom he was bound to anticipate might
avail themselves of his license. This distinction
seems to be sharply emphasized in the case of
Corby v. Hill [4 C. B. (N. S.) 556], and is a
distinction which should not be overlooked. If
there be any substantial difference between the
legal consequence of permitting another to use
one's premises and inviting or inducing such
use, the distinction lies in the *difference between active and the merely passive conduct of
such a proprietor.* It may be entirely consistent
with sound morals and proper regard for the
rights of others that the owner of premises
should not be held liable to one who goes upon
another's premises for his own uses, and sustains some injury by reason of the unfitness of
the premises for such uses, not subsequently
brought about by the active interference of the
owner. If such person goes there by mere suf-
ferance or naked license, it would seem reasonable that he should pick his way, and accept the
grace, subject to the risks which pertain to the
situation. But, on the other hand, if, with
knowledge that such person will avail himself
of the license, the owner actively change the situation by digging a pitfall, or opening a ditch,
or obstructing dangerously the premises which
he has reason to believe will be traversed by his
licensee, sound morals would seem to demand
that he should give reasonable warning of the
danger to be encountered. *This distinction seems
to be more marked in cases where the evidence
establishes in the public a permission or license
to cross a railway at a given place or locality.*

If the company has so long acquiesced in the continuous and open use of a particular place as a crossing as to justify the inference that it acquiesces in that use, it would seem to follow that it was *bound to anticipate the presence of such licensees* upon its track at the place where such crossing had been long permitted. In such a case it would not be consistent with due regard to human life, and to the rights of others, to say that such licensees are mere trespassers, or that the duty of the acquiescing company was no greater than if they were mere trespassers. Nonliability to trespassers is predicated upon the right of the company to a clear track, upon which it is not bound to anticipate the presence of trespassers. It therefore comes under no duty to a trespasser until his presence and danger are observed. But if it has permitted the public for a long period of time to habitually and openly cross its track at a particular place, or use the track as a pathway between particular localities, it cannot say that it was not bound to anticipate the presence of such persons on its track and was therefore not under obligation to operate its trains with any regard to the safety of those there by its license. *This distinction between liability for the passive and active negligence* of the owner of premises to licensees is recognized very clearly by the court of appeals of New York. Barry v. Railroad Co., 92 N. Y. 290; Byrne v. Railroad Co., 104 N. Y. 363, 10 N. E. 539.'' (Italics ours).

In *Northern Pacific Railway Company v. Curtz, supra,* the negligence was active, the bumping of one car against another; and this court held that the railway company was liable to the licensee whose presence should have been anticipated. So in the other cases cited in the Curtz case. In *Garner v. Trumbull,* 94 Fed. 321, the court in the Eighth Circuit held the company liable for the affirmative act of operating a train without a lookout for those whose presence should have been anticipated. Likewise in *Thompson v. Northern Pacific Railway Company,* 93 Fed. 384, this court held the defendant liable for the affirmative act of operating without signals. And in *Northern Pacific Railway Company v. Baxter,* 187 Fed. 787, this court held the defendant liable for injury resulting from the affirmative act of performing a "flying switch."

On the other hand where the conduct of the defendant was merely passive, the defendants were excused in *Branan v. Wimsatt, supra,* and *Peebles v. Exchange Building Company, supra.* In the *Branan* case (Court of Appeals, District of Columbia), the negligence alleged related to the manner in which lumber was piled on the defendant's premises. In the *Peebles* case (Sixth Circuit, C. C. A.) the alleged negligence was the failure to light a stairway. In each case the court held that the defendant was not responsible for injuries to a licensee resulting from an unsafe condition of the premises.

Today, in large measure because of the clear exposition by Judge Lurton in *Felton v. Aubrey, supra,* the distinction between liability to licensees for active as distinguished from passive conduct is almost universally recognized by American courts.

In 49 A. L. R., at page 778, there is an extensive annotation on the subject.

A failure to cut weeds at a private crossing is, at most, non-feasance. It is only passive conduct and is not negligence at all; it is merely a circumstance as to the condition of the premises. For that the railroad company is not responsible to a licensee who may choose to use the crossing.

The rule of non-liability to a licensee for non-feasance, for the condition of the premises, applies to private railroad crossings just as it does to any other real property. This was clearly stated in *Felton v. Aubrey, supra.* The rule of non-liability for injuries to licensees at private crossings, resulting from the condition of the premises, has been directly applied in the cases from the jurisdictions where the courts have had occasion to consider the subject. In *Johnson v. C. M. & St. P. Ry. Co., supra,* the court held that the defendant was not liable for an injury to a licensee resulting from a defective condition of a farm crossing. In *Pomponio v. N. Y. N. H. & H. R. Co., supra,* in speaking of injuries sustained at a private crossing, the court said:

> "A licensee must take the premises as he finds them, and the owner is not, as to him, bound to use care and diligence to keep the premises safe, while he does owe such a duty to one using his premises upon invitation."

In *Atlantic Coast Line Co. v. Carter, supra,* the court said:

"But, notwithstanding any consideration that may be thought to have been imported into the case by the presence of weeds and bushes on the right of way, *the crossing was, at best, for plaintiff's intestate, a private crossing, he was a mere licensee, he took the crossing as he found it,* and the duty the defendant owed him was that stated by the authorities heretofore cited. There are cases holding—properly, no doubt—that the fact that weeds and bushes are allowed by a railroad company to grow upon its right of way so as to obstruct a view of the track at the crossing of a public highway may be considered in determining the question of negligence in the operation of trains at such crossing, but not as actionable negligence *per se. Corley v. Railway,* 133 P. 555, 90 Kan. 70, Ann. Cas. 1915B, 764; *Cowles v. Railroad,* 66 A. 1020, 80 Conn. 48, 12 L. R. A. (N. S.) 1067, 10 Ann. Cas. 481, and cases cited in the notes. But that rule is applied, not indiscriminately to all crossings, but to the crossings of public highways." (Italics ours).

And see *Sypher v. Director General, supra; Bryant v. Missouri Pacific Ry. Co.,* 181 Mo. App. 189, 168 S. W. 228; *New Orleans Great Northern R. Co. v. McGowan,* 71 So. 317 (Miss.); *Atchison, Topeka & Santa Fe Ry. Co. v. Parsons,* 42 Ill. App. 93.

The error in the submission to the jury of the charge relating to the mere condition of the crossing requires a reversal of the judgments.

II.

The Verdicts Were Excessive

The second and third specifications assert error in the refusal of the District Court to grant a new trial upon the ground that the verdict in each case was excessive. The second specification relates to the recovery of $2,500 in No. 6589, involving the death of Jacqueline A. Cole. The third specification is similar except that it relates to the recovery of $2000 in No. 6590, involving the death of Leona J. Cole.

The actions were brought under the provisions of the statutes of Washington, the state in which the action arose. Section 184, Remington's Compiled Statutes, upon which each of the actions is based (R. p. 4) provides:

> "A father, or in case of the death or desertion of his family, the mother may maintain an action as plaintiff for the injury or death of a child, and a guardian for the injury or death of his ward."

By the terms of the Washington statutes a child attains majority at the age of twenty-one years. (R. p. 5).

Since the right of a parent to recover for the loss of services of which he has been deprived by reason of the death of a minor child is statutory, we must look to the decisions of the Washington courts to determine the extent of the right.

In addition to Section 184, quoted above, there are other Washington statutes relating to actions for death by wrongful act as follows:

Section 183:

"When the death of a person is caused by the wrongful act, neglect or default of another his personal representative may maintain an action for damages against the person causing the death; and although the death shall have been caused under such circumstances as amount, in law, to a felony."

Section 183-1:

". . . If there be no wife or husband or child or children, such action (under Section 183) may be maintained for the benefit of the parents, sisters or minor brothers, *who may be dependent upon the deceased person for support,* and who are resident within the United States at the time of his death. In every such action the jury may give such damages as, under all circumstances of the case may to them seem just." (Italics ours).

Section 194:

"No action for a personal injury to any person occasioning his death shall abate, nor shall such right of action determine, by reason of such death, if he have a wife or child living, or leaving no wife, or issue, if he have dependent upon him for support and resident within the United States at the time of his death, parents, sisters or minor brothers; but such action may be prosecuted, or commenced and prosecuted, in favor of such wife, or in favor of the wife and children, or if no wife, in favor of such child or children, or if no wife or child or children, then in favor of his parents, sisters, or minor brothers *who may be dependent upon him for support,* and resident in the United States at the time of his death." (Italics ours).

These statutes were construed in *Machek v. City of Seattle,* 118 Wash. 42, 203 Pac. 25. In that case the administrator of the estate of a minor brought an action to recover $35,000. The action was prosecuted for the benefit of the father and mother, dependent upon the minor decedent for support. In distinguishing the various rights, the court said:

"Taking the exact situation which is presented by the complaint in this case, involving the death of a minor leaving no husband or child or children, but only dependent parents, we have this result, that the *administrator could maintain an action* for the benefit of the parents to recover the amount that would have been contributed by the deceased to their support; this amount *not* being limited to what would have been furnished during decedent's minority only. Or, *in the alternative,* the parents themselves, whether dependent or not, could maintain an action in their own name for the loss of services of the minor, *from the time the loss was occasioned until such time as the minor would have arrived at majority. And in addition to either one of the foregoing actions,* under either sections 183 or 184, the administrator could maintain an action, under section 194, in favor of the dependent parents for the damages suffered by the deceased from the time of the injury until death. This action is entirely independent of actions under either section 183 or section 184, and could be concurrently maintained with

actions under either one of those sections."
(Italics ours).

A condition necessary to the existence of the right of an administrator under either Section 183 or Section 194 is dependency of the beneficiaries upon the decedent. In neither of the present cases was there any allegation that the plaintiff, the father, was dependent on the decedent for support. He sues in his individual capacity as he is permitted to do by Section 184. Consequently the right to recover is limited to the "loss of services of the minor, from the time the loss is occasioned until such time as the minor would have arrived at majority." The Washington rule as to measure of damages in such an action was stated in the early case of *Hedrick v. Ilwaco Ry. & Nav. Co.,* 4 Wash. 400, 30 Pac. 714, wherein the court said:

> "The measure of damages in such cases is the value of the child's services from the time of the injury until he would have attained the age of majority, *taken in connection with his prospects in life, less the cost of his support and maintenance."* (Italics ours).

We must inquire, then, whether the two verdicts were so clearly in excess of the probable future value of the services of these two minors, up to the time each would have attained majority, considering their "prospects in life," with the deductions for the cost of support.

Inasmuch as most of the evidence as to earnings was introduced in case No. 6590, we will reverse the order of the second and third specifications of error and will discuss case No. 6590 first.

The Verdict in No. 6590, Leona J. Cole

Leona J. Cole, the decedent, was 18 years 10½ months old at the time of her death, so that, had she lived, she would have attained her majority in 2 years 1½ months. She was intelligent, industrious and in good health. She completed grammar school at the age of 12, and attended high school for three and a half years. Her prior earnings had included wages for packing apples for three-month periods each fall. For this she received $3.50 a day. Other than that she had performed general housework at intervals for a wage of $10 a week. (R. pp. 27, 28).* Her earnings were turned over to her parents, who paid her living expenses. Her clothes were not expensive; many were made by her mother. The family lived modestly. (R. p. 28).

Her actual earning power at the time of her death can be calculated within very narrow limits.

---

*In this portion of the brief, relating to damages in the Leona J. Cole case, the references are to pages in the Transcript of Record in No. 6590.

Earnings from packing apples—$3.50 per day for 3 months each fall (assuming 25 working days each month, or 75 working days per season)..$262.50

Intermittent employment at general housework at $10 per week (assuming constant employment for periods when not engaged in packing apples)... 390.00

Total annual earnings............................$652.50

At $652.50 per year, her earnings for 2 years 1½ months would have been $1386. From this total the cost of her living—her food, shelter and clothing—must be deducted. If we assume the cost of her support and maintenance at as little as $10 a month the cost for 2 years 1½ months would have been $255. On that basis the net loss to her father occasioned by her death is only $1131. That is a maximum figure because we have assumed constant employment during those periods when she was not packing apples, whereas the evidence shows only intermittent employment. Likewise we have used a figure of $10 per month for expense which would be insufficient to sustain life.

The verdict of $2000 is nearly double this maximum figure sustained by the evidence. Courts are loath to set aside a verdict of a jury as excessive. Particularly do appellate courts hesitate to declare a verdict excessive when the trial court has declined to grant a new trial upon that ground. Nevertheless when there is a complete absence of any showing to support an award, it is the duty of the appellate court to see that an injustice is not perpetrated.

When the interval from the date of death to the date that the minor would have attained her majority is short, the probable amount of future earnings can be determined within narrow limits; it is a matter susceptible of direct proof. There is little room for the exercise of discretion by the jury; and to permit a jury to ignore the evidence is to give to it a discretion which it does not possess. The only conclusion possible under these facts is that the verdict was excessive. This court should correct the error by reversing No. 6590 and ordering a new trial.

The Verdict in No. 6589, Jacqueline A. Cole

Jacqueline A. Cole was 8 years 8½ months old at the date of her death. She was in the fourth grade in school. Her school work was above average. The plaintiff, her father, intended that she should go through high school. She was active and her health was good. (R. pp. 26-27).

With 4½ years of grammar school and 4 years of high school ahead of her she would have been between 17 and 18 years of age before she could begin to earn steadily. Her contribution from earnings to her father could not, at most, have exceeded a period of 4 years before she reached majority. Her father at most has been deprived only of earnings for 4 years less the cost of her support for 12 years 3½ months.

· If we assume a future earning power equal to that of her older sister, Leona, as hereinbefore discussed, her total earnings for 4 years would have been $2610. The cost of her maintenance and education, at the same low rate of $10 a month, would have amounted to $1475. Her net earnings, of which the father has been deprived would not have been over $1135.

With that evidence before it, the jury awarded $2500, in No. 6589. In the case of a young child the probable future earnings cannot be determined with as much certainty as in the case of a child nearly 21 years old. We recognize that the jurors in the exercise of their best judgment could not fix the damages as exactly as in the case of an older child. Nevertheless, when the recovery is over 100 per cent greater than an amount computed on the basis of the only figures given in the testimony of the witnesses, it must be apparent that the jury has gone far beyond the limits of any evidence in the case.

We urge that the trial court committed error in submitting to the jury the charge of negligence with reference to vegetation obstructing the view at the crossing, because no duty was owed to the decedents in that respect. We further submit that the verdicts in both cases go beyond any evidence of earnings and were excessive. These errors were prejudicial, and because of them the cases should be reversed.

Respectfully submitted,

CHARLES A. HART,

FLETCHER ROCKWOOD,

CAREY, HART, SPENCER & McCULLOCH,

Attorneys for Appellant.

No. 6589
No. 6590

In the United States
Circuit Court of Appeals
For the Ninth Circuit

SPOKANE, PORTLAND AND SEATTLE
RAILWAY COMPANY, a corporation,

Appellant,

vs.

CHARLES A. COLE,

Appellee.

(TWO CASES)

BRIEF OF APPELLEE.

**Upon Appeal from the District Court of the United
States for the District of Oregon.**

DAVIS & HARRIS and
DONALD K. GRANT,
Attorneys for Appellee.
Failing Building, Portland, Oregon.

INDEX TO AUTHORITIES.

INDEX TO AUTHORITIES.

Page

No. 6589
No. 6590

In the United States
Circuit Court of Appeals
For the Ninth Circuit

SPOKANE, PORTLAND AND SEATTLE

RAILWAY COMPANY, a corporation,

Appellant,

vs.

CHARLES A. COLE,

Appellee.

(TWO CASES)

BRIEF OF APPELLEE.

Upon Appeal from the District Court of the United States for the District of Oregon.

STATEMENT OF THE CASES.

These two actions, which were consolidated, both in the trial court and in this court, were brought by plaintiff, the father of two minor girls of the ages of eighteen and eight years, to recover damages for the loss of services on account of the death of said minor daughters, as a result of a collision between an automobile in which they were riding and a gasoline motor car operated by the defendant along its main line near Underwood, Washington.

These cases arose from the same accident which was involved in the case of *Spokane, Portland and Seattle Railway Company vs. Cecile S. Cole*, 40 *Fed.* (*2nd*) 172, decided by this Court on April 30, 1930, and in which case this Court affirmed a judgment recovered against the defendant Railway Company by the mother of plaintiff's decedents.

In the instant case the complaint contained the following allegations not found in the *Cecile S. Cole* case:

> "(c) That the said defendant carelessly and negligently maintained its right of way at and near said crossing in a dangerous condition, in that the defendant permitted unnecessary obstructions upon its right of way at or near said crossing so as to obstruct the view thereat, both of its servants approaching said crossing on a train and of persons upon said highway, in that the defendant allowed said right of way to become overgrown with bushes, weeds and grass so as to obstruct said view."

The first error assigned by the defendant is the failure of the trial court to give the following instruction:

> "I instruct you that the evidence is insufficient to show any negligence on the part of the defendant in the manner in which the crossing itself was maintained with respect to the view at the crossing

of train operators along the highway and of automobile operators along the railroad. **Consequently, all allegations of negligence with respect to obstruction of view and the maintenance of the crossing itself are withdrawn from your consideration** and you cannot base any recovery on any such allegations."

ARGUMENT.

In connection with appellant's assignment of error number one, it is submitted that this Court will not be compelled to go beyond a preliminary consideration in determining that it was not error to fail to give the requested instruction above set forth. ' In this connection it is not necessary to cite authority for the proposition that, if an instruction is subject to criticism or is erroneous in any particular, it is not error to fail to give the same. We will endeavor to demonstrate to the Court that the requested instruction now under consideration is erroneous in certain particulars and that, under the rule contended for, it was not error to fail to give the same.

From an inspection of Paragraph VIII of the complaint (Tr. 6), the Court will ascertain that there were allegations to the effect that the motor car operated by the defendant was traveling at an excessive rate of speed, and that the defendant failed to sound any warning or alarm of its approach. That there was evidence sufficient to support said allegations is

settled by this Court in the *Cecile S. Cole* case supra
and is not questioned in any way by the defendant
upon this appeal. Therefore, waiving for the purposes ,of this immediate discussion the question as
to wh'ether or not there existed a duty upon the part
of the defendant relative to the obstructions which
it permitted to exist upon its right of way, it is
clear from a review of the authorities that the presence
of said obstructions was a material circumstance to
be considered by the jury in connection with the care
required by |the defendant in the operation of its
trains at the point of the accident and that the above
instruction which would have ,**entirely removed** these
allegations relative to said obstructions **from the consideration of the jury** was entirely too broad and erroneous. In other words, this requested instruction,
which we are now reviewing, conclusively and entirely
eliminates the allegations of obstruction from the case
for all purposes when, at the |very least, said allega-
tions and evidence in support thereof were relevant
to be considered by the jury in conjunction with plaintiff's allegations of negligent speed and failure to give
a warning. In support of our contention that the
allegations with respect to the obstruction of view
and the maintenance of the crossing at the very least
were pertinent circumstances to be considered by the
jury in connection with the manner in which the defendant operated its motor car, we cite the following
from 22 *R. C. L.* 995, *Railroads*:

> "The rule obtaining in other jurisdictions is
> that the presence of unnecessary obstructions on
> the right of way, which may obscure the view, does

not in itself establish negligence on the part of the company nor constitute an independent ground of recovery. **The fact of the existence of such obstructions may be considered, however, upon the question of the degree of care and vigilance which the company is bound to exercise in the running and management of its trains, and in giving warning of their approach.** And the same rule applies where the obstructions to view are necessary in the legitimate conduct of the business."
(Emphasis ours).

We also refer the Court to the following statement found in 3 *Elliott on Railroads, Page* 531, *Section* 1656:

"Where a crossing is unusually dangerous because the track is curved or the view obstructed, or because of its peculiar construction or situation, it is the duty of the company to exercise such care and take such precautions as the dangerous nature of the crossing requires. Its duty to travelers upon the highway is to exercise reasonable care under the circumstances, and reasonable care in such cases may require it to exercise precautions not demanded in ordinary cases. This rule is especially applicable when the company itself causes the obstruction, as, for instance, where it has allowed weeds and trees to grow up on its right of way, or has piled up wood, or left cars in such a place that they obstruct the view."

In this connection, in the *Cecile S. Cole case supra*, and in the case of *Southern Pacific Company vs. Stephens,* 24 *Fed.* (2d) 182, this Court has held that speed may not of itself be found negligent by the jury except in view of the fact that warning or alarm was not sounded of the approach of a train. The contention here made is not different in principle, to wit: that the operation of the train in question, both with respect to speed and failure to sound a warning or alarm of the approach, should be considered in the light of the existence of obstructions present upon the right of way of the defendant. It is, therefore, submitted that the requested instruction now being reviewed is erroneous in that it is too broad, because it removes all allegations with respect to the obstruction of view and the maintenance of the crossing from the consideration of the jury, when under the authorities above set forth, these were material circumstances to be considered upon the questions we have above referred to. We consequently believe that this instruction requested by the defendant is erroneous in the particulars we have above set forth and that it was not error to fail to give the same.

In support of the argument advanced by the defendant that plaintiff's decedents were licensees and that the defendant owed them no duty with respect to the obstructions which it permitted to exist upon its right of way, the defendant has cited decisions from outside circuits and certain state decisions. Although the particular question involved, as far as we are able to ascertain, has never been before this Court for determination, this Court has firmly adhered to the legal proposition that a railroad company owes the duty to a licensee to exercise reasonable care for his safety.

Northern Pacific Railway Co. v. Curtz, 196 *Fed.*
367, 368-369 (*C.C.A.* 9);
Northern Pacific Railway Co. v. Chervenak,
203 *Fed.* 884-885 (*C.C.A.* 9).

However, the appellant contends that this Court
should not follow its prior decisions relative to the
duty owing a licensee because the negligence now under consideration pertains to the condition of the
crossing rather than to the operation of its trains. In
support of this contention the appellant has cited
certain cases wherein courts have held that there was
no obligation upon a railroad company to remove
obstructions from its crossings, among them being:

Johnson v. C.M. & St. P. Ry. Co., 96 *Minn.* 316,
104 *N.W.* 961;
Atlantic Coast Line R. Co. v. Carter, 214 *Ala.*
218 (*should be* 252), 107 *So.* 218.

However, it is submitted that these decisions and
similar ones cited by the appellant are distinguishable
because these were private crossings usually enclosed
by fences and limited to the use of farmers whose
property was adjacent to the railroad, and such limitation of use was known to the injured persons in most
instances. However, in the instant case, the crossing was both built and maintained by the defendant
itself (Tr. 21) and, connecting with a county road,
was open to all members of the general public who
had occasion to use the same. No signs were placed
upon the right of way that permission to use the
crossing was merely a matter of license revocable at
any time. Defendant failed to introduce any written
documents purporting merely to give a license to the

Bureau of Fisheries, but relied merely upon the oral testimony of the witness Hoffman to the effect that he believed the road was classed as a private road. It may be here stated that, to all intents and purposes, the road appeared to those using it the same as any public highway and that, if there were any limitations upon its use, they were secret and unknown to plaintiff's decedents and to others using the crossing which was maintained by the defendant. **Insofar as the general public was induced to believe,** if the road was a private road, it was private merely because of some secret agreement, and there was nothing in the way of signs, bars, gates or other means to inform and advise the general public that it was a private road. It is submitted that, under the facts and circumstances, existent in the instant case, and particularly the conduct of the defendant in building and maintaining a crossing, and the free use of the crossing by members of the public, under the best reasoned and by what we believe to be the weight of authority, the use of the highway by the plaintiff's decedents partook of the nature of an invitation rather than that of a bare license, and that consequently the defendant company was under obligation to use ordinary care to keep the crossing free from danger. We freely concede that, where a railway company does no more than to suffer or permit a person to cross the tracks or to use the tracks, the rule of invitation does not apply. However, in the light of the record in the instant case, it is submitted that the rule applicable is the one announced in 3 *Elliott on Railroads* 497-499:

"If, however, the traveler uses a place as a cross-

ing by invitation of the company, it must use ordinary care to prevent injury to him, as, where
the company **constructs a grade crossing and holds
it out to the public as a suitable place to cross.**
Where by fencing off a foot way over its tracks it
induces the public to so use it, by building to the
track plank bridges for foot passengers, or by constructing gates in the railroad fence for the use of
pedestrians who habitually cross the track, it thereby **holds out the place as proper for them to use.**
Such invitation as imposes on the company the
duty of ordinary care is implied, where **by some act
or designation of the company persons are led to
believe that a way was intended to be used by
travelers or others having lawful occasion to go
that way, and the company is under obligation to
use ordinary care to keep it free from danger.**
There is much conflict of authority as to
what constitutes such a general use of a place as
a crossing or such recognition of the right to use
such a place as will impose upon the company the
duty of observing the precaution required at public
crossings, but we think the doctrine we have expressed is the **true one supported by the best reasoned cases and by the recognized principles of
law.**"

(Emphasis ours.)

One of the very cases cited by the appellant at page
twenty of its brief, to wit: *Bryant v. Missouri Pacific
Railway Company,* 181 *Mo. App.* 194, recognizes the
rule here contended for. In that case, the plaintiff, a
farm laborer, sued to recover for injuries while moving a hay bailer over a private farm railroad crossing.
As a result of the condition of the crossing plaintiff
was injured. It was held in that case that the Court
committed error in not allowing the plaintiff to prove
that by use the crossing had been open to the public

and consequently the plaintiff in using it was entitled to a reasonably safe crossing. The Court held as follows, at page 194:

> "If the company had been **recognizing the farm crossing as a public crossing and the public had been using it as such,** the company **owed the public the duty of maintaining it in a reasonably safe condition,** but as to a farm crossing not so used, the company would owe no duty to maintain it in repair to anyone but the owner of the farm, his family and servants." (Emphasis ours).

The instant case comes squarely within the rule above announced in view of the fact that the crossing in question had been recognized by the defendant as a public crossing and the public had been using it as such. And here we emphasize a very important matter which we request the Court to bear in mind in connection with the above and following citations, to wit: That, at the very most, the defendant was only entitled to have the matter submitted as a jury question as to whether or not the plaintiff was using the crossing under the invitation or inducement of the defendant within the rule above announced which would require the defendant to exercise reasonable care in its maintenance, rather than as a bare licensee, which fact under some of the authorities would not entitle the plaintiff's decedents to any degree of care on the part of the defendant relative to the maintenance of the crossing. In other words, the force and effect of the requested instruction now under consideration is to have the Court **positively declare, as a matter of law, the exact status of the plaintiff,** when under the authorities above cited and to be cited, and under the record in the instant cause, relative to the crossing and its use it is submitted that, at the very least, this Court is not in a position to declare, **as a matter of law,** that the status of plaintiff's decedents was such that the defendant owed no duty to them relative to the condition of the crossing. If there is room for the suggestion that different inferences might be drawn as to the rights of the plaintiff's decedents and the duties of the defendant, that matter should have been submitted to the jury under proper instructions, and in the light of the instant record, no court would be justified in declaring as a matter of law as the rejected instruction would require that the defendant owed no duty to the plaintiff in connection with the specification of negligence now under consideration.

In other words, the sole question before the court is whether or not it was error to fail to give defendant's requested instruction now being reviewed. There is no question involved here as to whether or not the jury might under proper instructions have decided, **as a matter of fact,** that the crossing was not one held out or treated as a public crossing, or one where the defendant by its conduct did not invite a public use thereof. However, the defendant by its requested instruction now asks this court to declare, **as a matter of law,** irrespective of the record and the decisions, that the status of plaintiff's decedents was such that the defendant owed them absolutely no duty with respect to the condition of the crossing.

In support of the proposition we are here contending for, that is that the plaintiff's decedents were using the crossing as a matter of invitation, we refer the Court to the case of *Murphy v. Boston Ry. Co.,* 133 *Mass.* 121, 124-125. The facts in this case were that the injury occurred at a private crossing which had been maintained by the defendant. The plaintiff was a pupil at a public school and had occasion to cross the tracks on the way to school. The Court held that since there was evidence from which the jury could find that the defendant held out the crossing as a suitable place for foot passengers to cross, that the plaintiff may be said to have attempted to cross by inducement or invitation of the defendant, and the recovery was upheld.

Also see the following cases:

> *Hanks v. Boston & Albany Ry. Co.,* 147 *Mass.* 495, 498-499. 18 *N. E.* 218.
> *Pomponio v. N. Y. Ry. Co.* 66 *Conn.* 528, 540.

In the recent Federal case of *St. Louis-San Francisco Ry. Co. v. Ready,* 15 *Fed.* (2d) 370, the declaration alleged that the crossing was put in and maintained by the defendant railway company. The evidence showed that, although the crossing was not a public crossing, it had been established and kept up by the defendant, and that the custom had been observed of giving warnings of approach (in this case, the evidence of the defendant's motorman was that he always blew the whistle at this crossing). The evidence failed to show that the crossing was frequently used. In affirming the case, Judge Bryan of the Circuit Court of Appeals for the Fifth Circuit held as follows:

> "The sole question is whether defendant owed
> any duty to a person using the railroad crossing.
> Ready was not a trespasser or licensee, but an in-
> vitee. He had a right to be where he was, and it
> was the duty of the railroad company to give
> reasonable notice and warning of the approach of
> its train. Evidence of the frequency of use of a
> private crossing put in by others than the railroad
> company affected is material to show that such
> railroad company had notice and acquiesced in the
> use; but **where, as here, a railroad company itself
> establishes the crossing, it has notice and know-
> ledge of existing conditions, and is bound to use
> reasonable care to keep from injuring any persons,**
> whether few or many, who may have occasion to
> use such crossing. Walker v. Alabama, etc. R. Co.,
> 194 Ala. 360, 70 So. 125; Shearman & Redfield on
> Negligence, §464."

(Emphasis ours).

It will be noted in all the cases we have referred
to that the courts lay greater stress on the **conduct**
of the railway companies in constructing and maintaining crossings and the manner in which the same
are **held out to the public** than to the unknown and
secret arrangements made between the railway company and third parties. We submit that this distinction is a just and reasonable one.

Although applied to a different state of facts, we
submit that the observation of this Court in the case
of *Northern Pacific Ry. Co. v. Curtz,* 196 *Fed.* 367,
369, is pertinent and should be controling in the instant controversy:

> "The occupant or owner of premises who in-

vites, either expressly or impliedly, others to come upon them, owes to them the duty of using reasonable and ordinary diligence to the end that they be not necessarily or unreasonably exposed to danger; and an implied invitation to another to enter upon or occupy premises arises from the **conduct of the parties,** and from the owner's **knowledge,** actual or imputed, that the general use of his premises has given rise to the belief on the part of the users thereof that he consents thereto."   (Emphasis ours).

Counsel for appellant, at page twelve of their brief, quote from Elliott on Roads and Streets, (2nd Ed.) Section 1019, emphasizing the same as follows:

"Unless the company has done something to allure or invite travelers to cross, or has in some manner treated it as a public crossing, we are inclined to think the better rule is that they are, **at the most, mere licensees** to whom no duty of active vigilance is ordinarily due. Mere permission or passive acquiescense under ordinary circumstances does not constitute an invitation."

We concur in the soundness of this citation. However, we change the emphasis to the following:

"Unless the company has done something to allure or invite travelers to cross, **or has in some manner treated it as a public crossing,** we are inclined to think the better rule is that they are, at the most, mere licensees to whom no duty of active vigilance is ordinarily due. Mere permission or passive acquiescence under ordinary circumstances does not constitute an invitation."

In the case of *Johnson v. C. M. & St. P. Ry. Co.,* 96 *Minn.* 316, which is cited and relied upon by the defendant, the railway company had constructed a private farm crossing, and it was held that, since the crossing was constructed only for the use and benefit of the owner of the farm, "there is no question but that the company was under obligation to keep and maintain it in good condition for use * * * * *" In the Johnson case there was no indication that the crossing was for the use of the general public because it was fenced and led only to the farm mentioned. Therefore, there was no duty owing to the general public because the defendant by its conduct had not led the general public to believe that the crossing was for its use.

Defendant also relies upon the case of *Atlantic Coast Line Co. v. Carter*, 214 *Ala.* 252. That this case is not in point is clear from the following statement of the court, at page 254:

> "But the evidence fairly construed affords no reasonable basis for the inference of an invitation to the general public to cross at that place (a plantation crossing). The defendant did nothing to hold the crossing out to the public as a suitable place to cross; on the contrary, its contract with the land owner definitely excluded the idea of public right."

Furthermore, the case was decided upon a line of reasoning contrary to every decision of the Ninth Circuit of Appeals, namely: that the only duty owing to a licensee is to refrain from injuring him after becoming aware of his presence.

Appellant at pages twelve and thirteen of its brief quotes 45 *Corpus Juris* 798 to the effect that a mere licensee assumes all the risks incident to not only the condition of the property by the **manner of the conduct of the owner's business thereon.** This has never been the law in this circuit.

> *Northern Pacific Railway Co. v. Curtz* 196
> *Fed.* 367, 368-369 (*C.C.A.* 9):
> *Northern Pacific Railway Co. v. Chervenak,*
> 203 *Fed.* 884-885 (*C.C.A.* 9).

Upholding the general rule we are contending for are the following cases :

> *Connell v. Electric Ry. Co.,* 131 *Ia.* 622,
> 626; 109 *N. W.* 177.
> *St. Louis Railway Company v. Dooly,* 92
> *S. W.* 789; 77 *Ark.* 561.
> *St. Louis Railway Co. v. Simons,* 76 *N.E.*
> 883 (*Ind.*)

The courts have held that negligence may consist in allowing obstructions upon the right of way, of a railroad such as was disclosed by the record in this case.

> *St. Louis-San Francisco Ry. Co. v. Simmons,*
> 242 *Pac.* (*Okla.*) 151, 152;
> *Corley v. Atchison, T. & S. F. Ry. Co.,* 133 *Pac.*
> (*Kan.*) 555, 556;
> *Burzio v. Joplin & P. Ry. Co.,* 171 *Pac.* (*Kan.*)
> 351, 353-354.

No question is raised by the defendant, if the duty existed to maintain the crossing, that there was not sufficient evidence of negligence relative to the obstructions which the defendant permitted to exist upon its right of way. In fact, the defendant itself recognized that the obstructions were of a dangerous character because the **very day following the occurrence of the accident the section crew of the defendant removed the obstructions complained of** (Tr. 24).

To summarize, it is submitted that the refusal to give the requested instruction under discussion was not error for the following reasons:

1. That the instruction was erroneous in that it was too broad and removed from the consideration of the jury allegations that at all events were relevant in connection with other charges of negligence;

2. That, under the weight of and the best reasoned authorities, plaintiff's status was that of an invitee because the conduct of the defendant in constructing and maintaining the crossing, together with other facts heretofore pointed out, rendered the plaintiffs' use of the crossing one of invitation;

3. That at the very least this Court would not be in a position to declare, as a matter of law, as the requested instruction would require, that the status of plaintiff's decedents was such that the defendant owed them no duty insofar as the condition of the crossing was concerned, it being at the very least a question of fact which should have been submitted to the jury under proper instructions, as to the status of the plaintiff's decedents and the corelative duty and obligation of the defendant.

ANSWER TO ASSIGNMENTS OF ERROR II AND III.

Under these assignments of error, the defendant complains of the ruling of the Trial Court denying its motion for a new trial on the ground that the amounts of the verdicts were excessive, and appeared to have been given under the influence of passion and prejudice.

ARGUMENT.

The rule is well established in the Federal Courts that the denial of a motion for a new trial is discretionary with the Trial Court and will not be reviewed upon appeal.

The United States Supreme Court has so held in *Pittsburgh, Cincinnati and St. Louis Railway Company v. Heck, 26 L. Ed. (U.S.) 58*, where Chief Justice Waite states the rule as follows:

> "We have uniformly held that, as a motion for new trial in the Courts of the United States is addressed to the discretion of the court that tried the cause, the action of that court in granting or refusing to grant such a motion cannot be assigned for error here."

Likewise it has been held in other circuits that the denial of the motion for a new trial on the ground of the excessiveness of the verdict is not reviewable upon repeal. In such instances the denial of the motion for a new trial is discretionary, and therefore not reviewable. In this connection we refer the Court to *Chesapeake O. Ry. Co. v. Proffitt,* 218 *Fed.* 23, 28, where the rule is thus stated:

> "(2) It is further insisted that the court erred in denying a motion to set aside the verdict, based upon the ground that it was excessive. In the case of North Pacific R. R. Co. v. Charless, 51 Fed. 562, 2 C.C.A. 380, syllabus 7, is in the following language:
>
> **'The correction of an excessive verdict is a question for the trial court on a motion for a new trial, the granting or refusing of which will not be reviewed by the federal appellate courts.'**
>
> The cases of Erie R. R. Co. v. Winter, 143 U. S. 61, 12 Sup. Ct. 356, 36 L. Ed. 71, and of Fitch v. Huff, 218 Fed. 17, 134 C.C.A. 31, decided at this term of the court, and the cases cited therein, are to the same effect."

To the same effect is *Yellow Cab Co. v. Earle,* 275 *Fed.* 928 (*C.C.A.* 8) (*certiorari denied in* 42 *Sup. Ct.* 317):

> (1) The second, third, and fourth specifications are that the court erred in denying the motion of the defendant to set aside the verdict and grant a new trial (a) on the ground that it was not justified by the evidence; (b) on the ground that it was contrary to law; and (c) on the ground that the damages were excessive and appeared to have been given under the influence of passion and prejudice. But as the denial of a motion to set aside a verdict and grant a new trial on either of these grounds is discretionary with the trial court, and not reviewable on a writ of error in a federal appellate court, these specifications are futile. Chicago, M. & St. P. Ry. v. Heil, 154 Fed. 626, 629, 83 C.C.A. 400."

This Court has likewise held that motions for a new trial are not reviewable upon appeal.

In *American Trading Co. v. North Alaska Salmon
Co. (9th Circuit)*, 248 *Fed.* 665, in which certiorari
was denied, in 38 *Sup. Ct.* 581, 247 *U.S.* 518, 62 *L. Ed.*
1245, Judge Gilbert stated as follows, at page 670 of
the decision:

> "(6) It is suggested that the court below erred
> in not setting aside the verdict and ordering a new
> trial. **It is well settled that in the United States
> courts the refusal of the trial judge to set aside a
> verdict or grant a new trial is not subject to re-**
> view. In Great Northern Ry. Co. v. McLaughlin, 70
> Fed. 669, 17 C.C.A. 330, we held that a court of er-
> ror cannot review evidence to determine the cor-
> rectness of a verdict, saying:
>
> 'The relief from such mistakes if any are made,
> is to be sought in applications to the trial court
> for a new trial.'
>
> ——and citing Mills v. Smith, 8 Wall 32, 19 L. Ed.
> 346, where the court said:
>
> 'This court have no right to order a new trial
> because they may believe that the jury may have
> erred in their verdict on the facts. If the court
> below have given proper instructions on the ques-
> tions of law, and submitted the facts to the jury,
> there is no further remedy in this court for any sup-
> posed mistake of the jury.'
>
> We find no error. The judgment is affirmed."
> (Emphasis ours).

In the recent Ninth Circuit case of *First National
Bank of San Rafael v. Philippine Refining Corporation,* 51 *Fed. (2d)* 218, *decided July* 13, 1931, the
question of the sufficiency of the evidence to support
a judgment was not raised during the trial but by
motions made after trial. Judge Wilbur stated on
page 221.

"It is fundamental that the exercise of the discretion of the trial court is not subject to review on appeal, so that the ruling of the trial court in denying or granting such a motion made after a judgment cannot be reviewed."

Thus the rule is conclusively established under the above authorities that a motion for a new trial is discretionary with the Trial Court, and the denial of the same cannot be considered upon an appeal. In this connection we desire to call to the Court's attention that the denial of defendant's motion for a new trial is the only way in which the defendant has attempted to bring to this Court for review the alleged excessiveness of the verdicts, and since this matter is not properly one for review, it is submitted there is nothing for this Court to pass upon as far as these two assignments of error are concerned.

However, even if the alleged excessiveness of the verdicts were properly before this Court for review, under well established principles of law the verdicts in the instant causes could not be considered as excessive.

The instant cases are based upon the statutes of the State of Washington giving right of action to the surviving parent in the event of the injury or death of his minor children. Therefore, the decisions of the Supreme Court of the State of Washington interpreting these statutes are controling in the instant controversies. We will, therefore, demonstrate that, under the Washington decisions, the verdicts in the cases now before this Court could in no event be considered as excessive. Under Specification of Error Number II, it is asserted that the allowance of the sum of $2500 for the loss of services of Jacqueline A. Cole, the eight year old daughter of the plaintiff, was excessive and indicated passion or prejudice on the part of the jury. That such a contention is untenable is settled by the Supreme Court of Washington in the case of *Sasse v. Hale Morton Taxi & Auto Co. et al*, 139 *Wash.* 356, 246 *Pac.* 940. In this case a father recovered the sum of $3833.50 in addition to $575 actual expenses connected with the death of his nine year old daughter. The Supreme Court held as follows, at page 361:

> "There is not nor can there be any fixed standard by which damages in cases of this sort can be ascertained and allowed, in the absence of legislative expression. In 1906 in the case of Abby v. Wood, 43 Wash. 379, 86 P. 558, a verdict for $2,-160.20 was approved for the wrongful death of a child one year of age. In 1916, in the case of Kranzusch v. Trustee Co., 93 Wash. 629, 161 P. 492, a verdict for $3,576 was held not to be excessive for the wrongful death of a son four years of age, in the absence of an affirmative showing of passion or prejudice. In the present case the evidence shows that the deceased child was of robust health and that, 'as understood by everybody, her intelligence and capacity generally was above that of the average child of her age.' **There is in the case no affirmative showing of passion or prejudice. It cannot be inferred from the amount of the verdict.** Sherrill v. Olympic Ice Cream Co., 135 Wash. 99, 237 P. 14."   (Emphasis ours).

The case of *Atkeson v. Jackson Estate, 72 Wash.* 233, 240-241, 130 *Pac.* 102, 105, deals with the necessity for actual proof of earnings or future earning capacity in cases such as the one now before the Court. In this action the minor daughter of well-to-do parents was killed, and it was the contention of the defendants that plaintiff was entitled only to nominal damages since, because of the parents' financial status, the daughter during her minority would probably be a financial detriment to her parents rather than an asset. In sustaining a substantical verdict in favor of the plaintiff, the Court held as follows:

"It is argued that, since a girl in this state reaches the age of majority at her eighteenth birthday, and since statistics show that the average age of girls who graduate from the high schools in the state of Washington is in excess of 18 years, it is idle to say that a girl so graduating prior to that age has an earning capacity in excess of her cost of maintenance; that every father, who has reared a girl to that age and given her an education equivalent to that of graduation from the state high school, knows that the cost of her maintenance must, of necessity, exceed her earning capacity; and that any different claim is pure fiction.

But this reasoning does not seem to us to be controlling. It may be that, had the daughter reached her majority, and had the respondents maintained their present financial condition and carried out their expectations concerning her, the expense of her care, nurture, and education would have exceeded her earnings on their behalf. But, since adversity and misfortune are sometimes the accompaniments of life, as well as prosperity and success, there is another side to the picture. It is possible that the respondents may lose the property they have accumulated, and at the same time their health and ability to earn money. If such a misfortune should befall them, might it not be said that the daughter's earnings, had she lived, would have greatly exceeded her cost of maintenance? And who shall say that such a misfortune may not befall them? And if the probability exists, why may not a recovery be based thereon? There is, of course, no certain measure of damages in cases of this character; but, notwithstanding this difficulty, the great weight of authority is that a substantial recovery may be had.

* * * * * * * *

(5) On another principle, also, there can be a substantial recovery in this case. Where the child killed is of tender years, proof of special pecuniary damages is not necessary to maintain the action or warrant a recovery for more than nomial damages."

The cases heretofore cited are just as applicable in answer to appellant's Specification of Error No. III, which complains of the excessiveness of the verdict of $2000.00 for loss of services of plaintiff's eighteen year old daughter. Furthermore, we desire to point out to the Court a factor which has apparently been overlooked by the defendant, that is that the measure of damages is the value of the child's services from the time of death until she would have attained the age of majority (twenty-one years), less the cost of her support and maintenance. This measure, although necessarily a pecuniary one, does not mean the jury is limited to a consideration of what the child would have earned if put to **outside** labor. In this connection, under a similar state of facts, the Missouri court held, in *Lindstrom v. Peper,* 203 *Mo. App.* 278, 291, as follows:

> " 'The probable money value of the child's services,' however, is not solely tested by what he might earn if put to outside labor."

Counsel for appellant have endeavored to demonstrate by mathematics that the verdicts in the instant cases are excessive, but in this connection they failed to take into consideration the value of the child's services to the home and the possible fact that the child might have secured other employment during the remainder of her period of minority. During the apple picking season, the eighteen year old daughter was employed at the rate of $3.50 per day. The jury had the right to take into consideration the fact that the value of her services would be the same whether working at home or at some outside occupation. Under such circumstances it is clear that a verdict of $2000.00 could in no event be held to be excessive.

It is submitted that not only are the instant verdicts not excessive, but on the contrary we believe they are very moderate.

We submit this case to the Court with the firm conviction that no reversible error is present in the record and that the judgments appealed from should be affirmed.

Respectfully submitted,

DAVIS & HARRIS and
DONALD K. GRANT,
Attorneys for Appellee.

United States
Circuit Court of Appeals
For the Ninth Circuit. /6

LI BING SUN,

Appellant,

vs.

JOHN D. NAGLE, as Commissioner of Immigration, Port of San Francisco,

Appellee.

Transcript of Record.

Upon Appeal from the United States District Court for the Northern District of California, Southern Division.

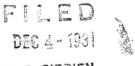

Filmer Bros Co. Print, 330 Jackson St., S. F., Cal.

United States
Circuit Court of Appeals

For the Ninth Circuit.

LI BING SUN,

Appellant,

vs.

JOHN D. NAGLE, as Commissioner of Immigration, Port of San Francisco,

Appellee.

Transcript of Record.

Upon Appeal from the United States District Court for the Northern District of California, Southern Division.

Filmer Bros Co. Print, 330 Jackson St., S. F., Cal.

INDEX TO THE PRINTED TRANSCRIPT OF RECORD.

NAMES AND ADDRESSES OF ATTORNEYS OF RECORD.

For Petitioner and Appellant:
STEPHEN M. WHITE, Esq., 576 Sacramento St., San Francisco, California.

For Respondent and Appellee:
UNITED STATES ATTORNEY, San Francisco, Cal.

In the Southern Division of the United States District Court, in and for the Northern District of California, Second Division.

No. 20,506–S.

In the Matter of LI BING SUN on Habeas Corpus. No. 29841/3–9; ex SS. "PRESIDENT CLEVELAND," November 26, 1930.

PETITION FOR WRIT OF HABEAS CORPUS.

To the Honorable, the Southern Division of the United States District Court, for the Northern District of California:

The petition of Li Bing Jing respectfully shows:

I.

That his brother, Li Bing Sun, hereinafter referred to as the detained, is 26 years old, that he is a person of Chinese descent, that he was born in China and that he has always been a subject of China.

II.

That the detained was first admitted to the United States on February 16, 1920, by the United States Immigration authorities for the Port of San Francisco, California, under the status of a minor son of a Chinese merchant, and that, thereafter, he made the following trips to China: departed on November 27, 1926, and returned on October 20, 1927; departed on November 22, 1929, and returned on November 26, 1930.

III.

That incident to the detained's departure from the United States on November 22, 1929, he applied to the United States Immigration authorities for the Port of San Francisco, for a so-called [1*] laborer's return certificate, Form 432, which certificate was issued to him by the said immigration authorities as the result of evidence produced by the detained showing that he was a Chinese person, who was lawfully domiciled in the United States and who had property therein to the amount of $1,000.00, the property consisting of money in the amount of $1,000.00 on deposit with the American Trust Company, No. 464 California Street, San Francisco, California.

IV.

That, incident to his return to the United States on November 26, 1930, the detained presented to the United States Immigration authorities for the Port of San Francisco, as evidence of his right to admission, the so-called laborer's return certificate,

---

*Page-number appearing at the foot of page of original certified Transcript of Record.

which had been issued to him prior to his departure from the United States on November 22, 1929, as aforesaid, but that the said immigration authorities, through a Board of Special Inquiry, while admitting that the said certificate was regularly and properly issued and that the detained was the proper holder thereof, nevertheless, refused to admit the detained to the United States upon the said certificate, for the reason that the detained was absent from the United States for more than one (1) year, to wit: one (1) year and four (4) days, having departed from the United States on November 22, 1929, and having returned on November 26, 1930, and that his failure to present another and further certificate issued by the American Consul in China showing that his absence of more than one year was necessitated by sickness or other cause of disability beyond his control; that the detained was thereupon excluded from admision to the United States by a Board of Special Inquiry and ordered deported to China; that an appeal was taken to the Secretary of Labor with the result that the decision of the Board of Special Inquiry was affirmed.

V.

That the detained is now in the custody of John D. Nagle, Commissioner of Immigration for the Port of San Francisco, at the [2] United States Immigration station at Angel Island, State and Northern District of California, Southern Division thereof, and that the said John D. Nagle, acting under the orders of the Secretary of Labor, has given notice of his intention to deport the detained

away from and out of the United States to China
on the first available steamer and, unless this Court
intervenes, the detained will be deported on the SS.
"President Madison," which sails from the Port
of San Francisco on the 13th day of February, 1931.

VI.

That your petitioner alleges that the Board of
Special Inquiry and the Secretary of Labor, and
each of them, in excluding the detained from admission to the United States and in ordering his deportation to China, and the said John D. Nagle, in
holding him in custody so that his deportation may
be effected, are unlawfully imprisoning, confining
and restraining the detained of his liberty in each
of the following particulars, to wit:

A. That the so-called laborer's return certificate,
Form 432, upon which the detained departed from
the United States for China on November 22, 1929,
and which he presented to the said immigration authorities, as evidence of his right to admission, upon
his return to the United States on November 26,
1930, was issued to the detained by the United States
Immigration authorities for the Port of San Francisco, under and by virtue of the Act of Congress of
September 13, 1888 (25 Stat. L. 476, 477), providing as follows:

"Sec. 5. That from and after the passage of
this act, no Chinese laborer in the United States
shall be permitted, after having left, to return
thereto, except under the conditions stated in
the following sections.

Sec. 6. That no Chinese laborer within the purview of the preceding section shall be permitted to return to the United States unless he has a lawful wife, child, or parent in the United States, or property therein of the value of one thousand dollars, or debts of like amount due him and pending settlement.

*   *   *   *   *   *   *   [3]

If the right to return be claimed on the ground of property or of debts, it must appear that the property *in bona fide* and not colorably acquired for the purpose of evading this act, or that the debts are unascertained and unsettled and not promissory notes or other similar acknowledgments of ascertained liability.

Sec. 7. That a Chinese person claiming the right to be permitted to leave the United States and return thereto on any of the grounds stated in the foregoing section, shall apply to the Chinese inspector in charge of the district from which he wishes to depart at least a month prior to the time of his departure, and shall make on oath before the said inspector a full statement descriptive of his family, or property, or debts, as the case may be, and shall furnish to said inspector such proofs of the facts entitling him to return as shall be required by the rules and regulations prescribed from time to time by the Secretary of Labor, and for any false swearing in relation thereto he shall incur the penalties of perjury.

*   *   *   *   *   *   *

And if the said inspector, after hearing the

proofs and investigating all the circumstances of the case, shall decide to issue a certificate of return, he shall at such time and place as he may designate, sign and give to the person applying a certificate containing the number of the description last aforesaid, which shall be the sole evidence given to such person of his right to return.

* * * * * * *

The right to return under the said certificate shall be limited to one year; but it may be extended for an additional period, not to exceed a year, in cases where, by reason of sickness or other cause of disability beyond his control, the holder thereof shall be rendered unable sooner to return, which facts shall be fully reported to and investigated by the consular representative of the United States at the port or place from which such laborer departs for the United States, and certified by such representative of the United States to the satisfaction of the Chinese inspector in charge at the port where such Chinese person shall seek to land in the United States, such certificate to be delivered by said representative to the master of the vessel on which he departs for the United States.

And no Chinese laborer shall be permitted to reenter the United States without producing to the proper officer in charge at the port of such entry the return certificate herein required. A Chinese laborer possessing a certificate under this section shall be admitted to the

United States only at the port from which he departed therefrom, and no Chinese person, except Chinese diplomatic or consular [4] officers, and their attendants, shall be permitted to enter the United States except at the ports of San Francisco, Portland, Oregon, Boston, New York, New Orleans, Port Townsend, or such other ports as may be designated by the Secretary of Labor.

Sec. 8. That the Secretary of Labor shall be, and he hereby is, authorized and expowered to make and prescribe, and from time to time to change and amend such rules and regulations, not in conflict with this act, as he may deem necessary and proper to conveniently secure to such Chinese persons as are provided for in articles second and third of the said treaty between the United States and the Empire of China, the rights therein mentioned, and such as shall also protect the United States against the coming and transit of persons not entitled to the benefit of the provisions of said articles.''

That, by virtue of the power vested in the Secretary of Labor under Section 8 of the Act of Congress of September 13, 1888, *supra,* the Secretary of Labor promulgated rules and regulations governing the issuance of so-called laborers' return certificates, which rules and regulations were in full force and effect at the time of the issuance to the detained of his laborer's return certificate; that the said rules and regulations provide as follows:

RULE 12. LABORER'S RETURN CERTIFI-
CATE, WHO ENTITLED TO.

"The laborer's return certificate provided by section 7 of the act of September 13, 1888, shall be issued only to such Chinese persons as have been duly registered under the provisions of the act of May 5, 1892, or the act of November 3, 1893, and present a certificate issued thereunder, or such as have established before a court of competent jurisdiction the lawfulness of their residence in the United States and presented a certified copy of the court's decision, or such as otherwise establish before the immigration official to whom application for the return certificate is made that they are lawfully within the United States."

RULE 14. EXTENSION OF TIME LIMIT OF RETURN CERTIFICATES.

'Whenever a Chinese laborer holding a return certificate is detained by his sickness or by other disability beyond his control for a time in excess of one year after the date of his departure from the United States, the facts shall be fully reported to and investigated by the consular representative of the United States at the port or place from which such laborer [5] departs for the United States, and such consular representative shall certify, to the satisfaction of the officer in charge at the port of return, which must be the port from which such laborer departed, that he has fully investigated the statements of such laborer and believes that he was unavoidably detained for the time specified and for the reason stated, such certificate to be delivered by such consular representative to the master of the vessel on which the Chinese laborer departs for the United States, and by the master delivered to the officer in charge at the port of return.''

That your petitioner alleges that under Section 7 of the Act of Congress of September 13, 1888, and Rules XII and XIV, *supra,* of the Secretary of Labor, the validity of the so-called laborer's return certificate issued to the detained and the right of the detained to return to the United States and to be admitted thereto upon said certificate could not, as a matter of law, be affected by the absence of the detained from the United States for a period of more than one (1) year and less than two (2) years, provided (1) that he was unable to return to the United States within one year by reason of sickness or other cause of disability beyond his control and (2) that the facts pertaining to the sickness or other cause of disability were made known to the American Consular representative at Hongkong, China, the port at which the detained departed for the United States and that the said Consular representative, after an investigation, reported and certified the facts to the satisfaction of the Commissioner of Immigration for the Port of San Francisco, the port from which the detained departed from the United States; that, in this connection, your petitioner alleges that the detained, for a period of several months previous to his embarkation at Hongkong, China, for the United States, was suffering from boils on his feet and that on August 14, 1930, and, again, on September 20, 1930, he reported his condition to the American Consul at Hongkong, on each of which occasions he applied to the said Consul for the issuance of a certificate showing that his condition was such as to [6] prevent him from returning to the United States within one year from the date of his departure therefrom, but that the said Consul failed and neglected to investigate the facts pertaining to the detained's sickness and/or to fully report and certify the facts thereof and/or to issue a certificate disclosing whether or not the detained's sickness was such as to prevent him from returning to the United States within one year from the date of his departure therefrom; that the Board of Special Inquiry and the Secretary of Labor, decided that the detained was not prevented from returning to the United States within one year from the date of his departure therefrom by reason of sickness or other cause of disability beyond his control without the certificate of the American Consul at Hongkong, China, or of any consular representative, disclosing the facts pertaining to the detained's sickness and/or a full and complete report by said Consul or of any consular representative as to the facts pertaining to the detained's sickness; that the said American Consul at Hongkong, China, in failing and neglecting to fully investigate, report and certify the facts pertaining to the detained's sickness, omitted to perform his duty as required by law, and the Board of Special Inquiry and the Secretary of Labor, in denying the detained admission to the United States, without a full investigation, report and certificate by said American Consul or his representative as to facts pertaining to the detained's sickness, acted without jurisdiction and in excess of the authority and power committed to them by the statute in such cases made and provided for and rules and regulations promulgated in pursuance thereof, that they have thereby acted arbitrarily and unfair and have denied the detained the full and fair hearing to which he was and is entitled.

B. That your petitioner alleges that the evidence adduced before the Board of Special Inquiry, which evidence was before the Secretary of Labor, discloses that the detained for several months [7] prior to his departure at Hongkong, China, for the United States, was suffering from boils on his feet, on account of which he was unable to travel, and that his condition continued until about October 7, 1930, and that thereafter he was placed under observation by the United States Public Health Service at Hongkong, China, for a period of 14 days for the purpose of ascertaining whether or not he was afflicted with cerebro-spinal meningitis and that during this period he was required by said Service to be vaccinated; that he was not discharged from observation and treatment by the United States Public Health Service until October 21, 1930, and that thereafter, to wit, on November 4, 1930,

he sailed on the first available steamer leaving
Hongkong, China, for the United States; that, by
virtue of the facts aforesaid the detained was unable
to sooner return to the United States and that his
return on November 26, 1930, and not prior thereto
was due to no fault of his but was caused by sickness or other cause of disability beyond his control;
that the facts, aforesaid, pertaining to the detained's delay in China were known to the American
Consul of Hongkong, but that the said Consul
failed and neglected to investigate, report and
certify said facts as required by law; that there
was no certificate of said Consul, as to the facts
pertaining to the delay of the detained in China,
before the Board of Special Inquiry and the Secretary of Labor, or either of them, and no evidence
of any kind or character showing that the delay
of the detained in China and his failure to return
to the United States within one year from the date
of his departure therefrom were not caused by
sickness or other disability beyond his control; that
the said Board of Special Inquiry and the Secretary of Labor, in denying the detained admission
to the United States without evidence of any kind
or character showing that the detained's delay in
China and his failure to return to the United States
within one year from the date of his departure
therefrom, were not caused by [8] sickness or
other cause of disability beyond his control, have
acted without jurisdiction and in excess of the
power and authority committed to them by the
statute in such cases made and provided for and have

thereby acted arbitrarily and unfair and have denied the detained the full and fair hearing to which he was and is entitled.

VII.

That your petitioner has filed herewith, as Exhibit "A," testimony adduced before the Board of Special Inquiry and a copy of the findings and decision of the Board of Special Inquiry and hereby makes the said testimony and decision a part of this petition with the same force and effect as if set forth in full herein.

VIII.

That the said detained is in detention, as aforesaid, and for said reason is unable to verify this said petition upon his own behalf and for said reason petition is verified by your petitioner, but for and as the act of the said detained, and upon his behalf.

WHEREFORE, your petitioner prays that a writ of habeas corpus be issued and directed to John D. Nagle, Commissioner of Immigration for the Port of San Francisco, California, commanding and directing him to hold the body of your petitioner's brother, the detained, within the jurisdiction of this Court, at a time and place to be specified in this order, together with the time and cause of his detention, so that the same may be inquired into to the end that said detained may be restored to his liberty and go hence without day.

Dated at San Francisco, California, February 11th, 1931.

STEPHEN M. WHITE,
Attorney for Petitioner.   [9]

United States of America,
State of California,
City and County of San Francisco,—ss.

Li Bing Jing, being first duly sworn, deposes and states as follows: That he is the petitioner named in the foregoing petition; that the petition has been read and explained to him and he knows the contents thereof; that the same is true of his own knowledge, except those matters stated therein on information and belief and, as to those matters, he believes it to be true.

LI BING JING.

Subscribed and sworn to before me this 10th day of February, 1931.

. [Seal]   STEPHEN M. WHITE,
Notary Public in and for the City and County of San Francisco, State of California.

[Endorsed]: Filed Feb. 11, 1931.   [10]

EXHIBIT "A."

(Testimony Adduced Before Board of Special Inquiry and Findings and Decision of Board of Special Inquiry.)

HEADING FOR TESTIMONY.

U. S. DEPARTMENT OF LABOR

IMMIGRATION SERVICE.

B.S.I. No. 4.

Manifest No. 29841/3–9.

November 29, 1930.

In the Matter of LI BING SUN, Laborer 432 O. T.

C. M. WURM, Chairman.

R. J. McGRATH, Member.

H. M. DOWNIE, Member.

APPLICANT sworn and admonished that if at any time he fails to understand the Interpreter to immediately so state. Advised of perjury.

Q. What are all your names?

A. LI BING SUN, LI FAT YIM, no other.

Q. You are advised your right to admission to this country will be to-day considered by this board. No witnesses are present. The regulations under which this hearing is being conducted permit you to have a friend or relative present during the hearings to be conducted but such relative or friend cannot be your attorney nor the representative of any immigrant aid or other similar society; he must actually be a relative or friend of yours. Do you wish to use this right?

A. No, I waive my right.

Q. You are also informed that the burden of proof rests upon you to show you are not subject to exclusion under any provisions of the Immigration laws.   A. I understand.

NOTE: Applicant present upon arrival original Form 432, numbered 12017/38212, showing departure from San Francisco Nov. 22, 1929.

APPLICANT answers manifest questions as follows: I am 26 years old, born KS. 32–3–3 (March 27, 1906) at the Hong Woo Village, SND; male of the Chinese *reac*; my residence for the past five years was San Francisco until my departure for China in Nov. 1929, since when I have been living in the HONG WOO VILLAGE; I have been married once only; I was married CR. 15–12–21 (Jan. 24, 1927) to HOM SHEE, who is about 23 years old, has natural feet and is now living at HONG WOO VILLAGE; I have one son, no daughters, his name is [11] LI KEN HONG, 4 years old, born CR. 16–12–2 (Dec. 25, 1927), now living with my wife in HONG WOO VILLAGE; my wife is an expectant mother; my occupation is that of a cook; I can speak, read and write Chinese only; my parents are LI PUN or LI CHUNG FON, my father, now living in Stockton, and CHIN SHEE, my mother, about 54 years old, now at HONG WOO VILLAGE, SND; I am destined to San Francisco where I expect to resume my occupation as cook; I intend to remain in this country permanently; I have never been arrested or supported by charity neither myself nor parents have ever been treated for insanity; I have never been excluded and deported or arrested and deported; I do not believe in polygamy or anarchy; I have $1000 in American currency on deposit in the bank, and the pass-book is with the CHUN FOOK COMPANY in San Francisco, at 1041 Grant Ave., in the care of LI OAK LOY.

Q. Did you live in the HONG WOO VILLAGE CONTINUOUSLY after reaching China until you departed for this country? A. Yes.

Q. What occupation did you follow while you were last in China?

A. I had no occupation during that period.

Q. How many visits have you made to China as a laborer on Form 432? A. Two.

Q. Did you know prior to leaving on both of those two visits that you must return to the U. S. within one year from the date of your departure?

A. Yes.

Q. What caused you to return to the U. S. after a year from date of departure?

A. I was suffering from boils on my feet and on account of that I had to postpone my return to the U. S. I expected to return on the "Press. Grant" but I thought that being 4 days overtime would not cause any difficulty in my landing.

Q. When did the "Pres. Grant" leave Hongkong?

A. About the 30th day of the 8th month, this year, Chinese reckoning (Oct. 21, 1930).

Q. When did you cease having trouble from boils?

A. About the 16th day of the 8th month (Oct. 7, 1930).

Q. Then you deliberately delayed your return to the U. S. until the "Pres. Cleveland" sailed. Is that right?

A. I was detained for about 2 weeks in Hongkong on visits to the doctor for examination.

Q. Do you mean the U. S. Public Health doctor?
A. Yes.

Q. Have you any papers showing this to be a fact?

A. (Present certificate of L. C. Stewart, Medical Officer, U. S. P. H. S. certifying that LI BING SUN, sailing to-day for San Francisco from Hongkong on the "Pres. Cleveland" has not been in contact during the last 14 days with anyone suffering from cerebro-spinal meningitis; also vaccination certificate and inspection card of U. S. P. H. S., Hongkong, showing LI BING SUN, who departed Nov. 4, 1930, on "Pres. Cleveland" was vaccinated Oct. 18, 1930, and reported Oct 20, and Oct. 21. This card bears applicant's photograph. Same are retained on file.)

Q. Was there an epidemic of spinal meningitis in Hongkong during the time you were there?
A. No.

Q. When you were in Hongkong did you *go the* American Consulate?   A. Yes.

Q. Do you remember the date when you first went there?

A. It was before I went to the U. S. Public

Health Service. It was about the 29th day of the 8th month (Oct. 20). [12]

Q. You knew then that you could not return here on the "Pres. Grant," did you not? A. Yes.

Q. Why did you not get an overtime certificate from the Consul?

A. I attempted to secure an overtime certificate but the American Consul refused to issue it to me. He did not state any reasons for refusing to do so. Chairman to other Board Members.

Q. Do you wish to question the applicant?

Member McGRATH: No.

Member DOWNIE: No.

(Chairman to Applicant.)

Q. Have you understood the interpreter?

A. Yes. (Thru Mrs. D. K. Chang).

Signed.

PERSONAL DESCRIPTION: Male of the Chinese race; 5' 6"; pinmole outer corner left eye.

I hereby certify to the correctness of the above transcript.

DOWNIE, Steno.

SUMMARY.

This applicant first arrived in this country Dec. 29, 1919, admitted Feb. 16, 1920, as the son of a merchant. He has made one visit, other than the present one, to China, departing on Form 432 Nov. 27, 1926, and returning Oct. 20, 1927. He departed on his last trip to China, from which he is now returning on Form 432, Nov. 22, 1929, returning here Nov. 26, 1930, thus having been absent

from the United States one year and four days.
From the above it will be seen that he has had,
prior to last departure, nine years and nine months
residence in the United States.

Statement was taken by this board from the ap-
plicant and it will be noted therein that the reason
he was delayed in China and prevented from re-
turning within the year was on account of boils.
He further stated that he had attempted to obtain
overtime certificate from the American Consul at
Hongkong, but was refused. It will be noted on
the reverse side of the Form 432 presented by this
Chinese the following notations: "8/14/30 Ext.
Req. RMJ"; and "American Consulate General
Oct. 20, 1930, Hongkong Sailing Oct. 23, 1930. O. K.
RMJ."

As he was granted Form 432 prior to departure
on property, money in the bank, deposited with the
American Trust Co., 464 California St., San Francisco, Account No. 2919. which passbook, so applicant states, is now in the hands of one LI OAK
LOY, who can be located at the CHUN FOOK CO.,
1041 Grant Ave., San Francisco, I believe that before final action is taken in this case that the matter
of this property being in the bank should be investigated, and I make a motion to defer for that purpose.

Member McGRATH: I second the motion.
Member DOWNIE: I concur.   [13]

HEADING FOR TESTIMONY.

U. S. Department of Labor,
Immigration Service.

B. S. I. No. A.

Manifest No. 29841/3–9.   Dec. 3, 1930.   Pg. 4.

In the Matter of LI BING SUN, Laborer 432 Ot.

C. M. WURM, Chairman.

R. J. McGRATH, Member.

H. M. DOWNIE, Member.

By CHAIRMAN: Supplementing previous deferring decision of this board of Nov. 29, 1930.

Investigation since then conducted discloses that the basis of the applicant for Form 432, namely, deposit of $1000 in the applicant's name carried by the American Trust Co., 464 California St., San Francisco, remains the same as when this applicant proceeded from the United States.

As stated in the first paragraph of the board's previous summary of November 29th, the applicant has remained away from the United States over the statutory period of one year; he is not in possession of an overtime consular certificate as provided for in the Act of Sept. 13, 1888, nor does it appear that he was rendered unable sooner to return to this country through sickness or other causes of disability beyond his control. The said act further states: "And no Chinese laborer shall be permitted to reenter the United States without producing to the proper officer in charge at such port of entry the return certificate herein required." The applicant was employed as a cook before proceeding to China on November 22, 1929, hence he is a laborer.

I move that the applicant be excluded on the ground that he is a Chinese laborer not in possession of a *balid* laborer's return certificate, nor in possession of an overtime consular certificate, nor does the evidence [14] reasonably establish that his return to the United States at this time was delayed by sickness or other cause of disability beyond his control, and for the further reason that the burden of proof has not been sustained as required by Section 23 of the Act of 1924.

Member McGRATH: I second the motion.

Member DOWNIE: I concur. [15]

SUMMARY.

This applicant first arrived in this country Dec. 29, 1919, admitted Feb. 16, 1920, as the son of a merchant. He has made one visit, other than the present one, to China, departing on Form 432 Nov. 27, 1926, and returning Oct. 20, 1927. He departed on his last trip to China, from which he is now returning, on Form 432, Nov. 22, 1929, returning here Nov. 26, 1930, thus having been absent from the United States one year and four days. From the above it will be seen that he has had, prior to last departure, nine years and nine months residence in the United States.

Statement was taken by this Board from the applicant and it will be noted therein that the reason he was delayed in China and prevented from returning within the year was on account of boils.

He further stated that he had attempted to obtain overtime certificate from the American Consul at Hongkong, but was refused. It will be noted on the reverse side of the Form 432 presented by this Chinese the following notations: "8/14/30 Ext req. RMJ"; and "American Consulate General Oct. 20, 1930 Hongkong Sailing Oct. 23, 1930 O. K. RMJ."

As he was granted Form 432 prior to departure on property, money in the bank, deposited with the American Trust Co., 464 California St., San Francisco, Account No. 2919, which passbook, so applicant states, is now in the hands of one LI OAK LOY, who can be located at the CHUN FOOK CO., 1041 Grant Ave., San Francisco, I believe that before final action is taken in this case that the matter of this property being in the bank should be investigated, and I make a motion to defer for that purpose.

By Member McGRATH: I second the motion.

Member DOWNIE: I concur. [16]

29841/3–9.

By CHAIRMAN.—Supplementing previous deferring decision of this board of Nov. 29, 1930:

Investigation since then conducted discloses that the basis of the applicant for Form 432, namely, deposit of $1000 in the applicant's name carried by the American Trust Co., 464 California St., San Francisco, remains the same as when this applicant proceeded from the United States.

As stated in the first paragraph of the board's previous summary of November 29th, the applicant has remained away from the United States over the statutory period ofn one year; he is not in possession of an overtime consular certificate as provided for in the Act of Sept. 13, 1888, nor does it appear that he was rendered unable sooner to return to this country through sickness or other cause of disability beyond his control. The said act further states: "And no Chinese laborer shall be permitted to reenter the United States without producing to the proper officer in charge at such port of entry the return certificate herein required." The applicant was employed as a cook before proceeding to China on November 22, 1929, hence he is a laborer.

I move that the applicant be excluded on the ground that he is a Chinese laborer not in possession of a valid laborer's return certificate, nor in possession of an overtime consular certificate, or does the evidence reasonably establish that his return to the United States at this time was delayed by sickness or other cause of disability beyond his control, and for the further reason that the burden of proof has not been sustained as required by Section 23 of the Act of 1924.

Member McGRANT: I SECOND THE MOTION.

Member DOWNIE: I CONCUR.

[Endorsed]: Filed Feb. 11, 1931. [17]

[Title of Court and Cause.]

ORDER TO SHOW CAUSE.

Good cause appearing therefor, and upon reading the verified petition on file herein—

IT IS HEREBY ORDERED that John D. Nagle, Commissioner of Immigration for the Port of San Francisco, appear before this court on the 2d day of March, 1931, at the hour of 10 o'clock A. M. of said day, to show cause, if any he has, why a writ of habeas corpus should not be issued herein, as prayed for, and that a copy of this order be served upon the said Commissioner, and a copy of the petition and said order be served upon the United States Attorney for this District, his representative herein.

AND IT IS FURTHER ORDERED that the said John D. Nagle, Commissioner of Immigration, as aforesaid, or whoever, acting under the orders of the said Commissioner, or the Secretary of Labor, shall have the custody of the said Li Bing Sun, or the Master of any steamer upon which he may have been placed for deportation by the said Commissioner, are hereby ordered and directed to retain the said Li Bing Sun, within the custody of the said Commissioner of Immigration, and within the jurisdiction of this Court until its further order herein.

Dated at San Francisco, California, February 11th, 1931.

FRANK H. KERRIGAN,
United States District Judge.

[Endorsed]: Filed Feb. 11, 1931. [18]

[Title of Court and Cause.]

APPEARANCE OF RESPONDENT.

Now comes respondent through its undersigned attorney and in return to the order to show cause herein, files herewith as Respondent's *Excerpts* "A" to "D," inclusive, the original Immigration records of the proceedings before the Bureau of Immigration and the Secretary of Labor relative to the above-named person, Li Bing Sun.

GEO. J. HATFIELD,
United States Attorney,
(Attorney for Respondent).

[Endorsed]: Filed May 4, 1931, 2:44 P. M. [19]

District Court of the United States, Northern District of California, Southern Division.

At a stated term of the Southern Division of the United States District Court for the Northern District of California, held at the courtroom thereof, in the City and County of San Francisco, on Monday, the 4th day of May, in the year of our Lord one thousand nine hundred and thirty-one. Present: The Honorable A. F. ST. SURE, District Judge.

No. 20,506.

In the Matter of LI BING SUN, on Habeas Corpus.

MINUTES OF COURT—MAY 4, 1931—ORDER
SUBMITTING APPLICATION FOR WRIT
OF HABEAS CORPUS.

The application for a writ of habeas corpus (by
order to show cause) came on this day to be heard.
S. M. White, Esq., appearing as attorney for
petitioner, and H. A. van der Zee, Esq., Asst. U. S.
Atty., appearing as attorney for respondent. Mr.
van der Zee introduced and filed the record of the
Bureau of Immigration and the appearance of the
respondent. After hearing the attorneys, IT IS
ORDERED that the application for a writ of habeas corpus be submitted upon the filing of briefs in
5 and 3 days. [20]

[Title of Court and Cause.]

ORDER DENYING AND DISMISSING AP-
PLICATION FOR WRIT OF HABEAS
CORPUS, ETC.

This matter having been heard on the application
for a writ of habeas corpus (by order to show
cause), and having been argued and submitted,—

IT IS ORDERED, after a full consideration, that
the application for a writ of habeas corpus be and
the same is hereby DENIED; that the petition be
and the same is hereby DISMISSED; that the

order to show cause be, and the same is hereby DIS-
CHARGED; and that the applicant be deported by
the United States Immigration Authorities at San
Francisco, California.

Dated: August 11, 1931.

A. F. ST. SURE,

U. S. District Judge.

[Endorsed]: Filed Aug. 11, 1931, 3:02 **P. M.**
[21]

[Title of Court and Cause.]

NOTICE OF APPEAL.

To the Clerk of the Above-entitled Court, to JOHN
D. NAGLE, Commissioner of Immigration,
and to GEORGE J. HATFIELD, Esq., United
States Attorney, His Attorney:

You and each of you will please take notice that
Li Bing Jing, the petitioner in the above-entitled
matter, hereby appeals to the United States Circuit
Court of Appeals for the Ninth Circuit, from the order and judgment rendered, made and entered
herein on August 11, 1931, denying the petition for
a writ of habeas corpus filed herein.

Dated this 19th day of August, 1931.

STEPHEN M. WHITE,

Attorney for Appellant.   [22]

[Title of Court and Cause.]

PETITION FOR APPEAL.

Comes now Li Bing Jing, the petitioner in the above-entitled matter, through his attorney, Stephen M. White, Esq., and respectfully shows:

That on the 11th day of August, 1931, the above-entitled court made and entered its order denying the petition for a writ of habeas corpus, as prayed for, on file herein, in which said order in the above-entitled cause certain errors were made to the prejudice of the appellant herein, all of which will more fully appear from the assignment of errors filed herewith.

WHEREFORE, the appellant prays that an appeal may be granted in his behalf to the Circuit Court of Appeals of the United States for the Ninth Circuit thereof, for the correction of the errors as complained of, and further, that a transcript of the record, proceedings and papers in the above-entitled cause, as shown by the praecipe, duly authenticated, may be sent and transmitted to the said United States Circuit Court of Appeals for the Ninth Circuit thereof, and further, that the said appellant be held within the jurisdiction of this court during the pendency of the appeal herein, so that he may be produced in execution of whatever judgment may be finally entered herein.

Dated at San Francisco, California, August 19th, 1931.

STEPHEN M. WHITE,
Attorney for Appellant.　[23]

———

[Title of Court and Cause.]

ASSIGNMENT OF ERRORS.

Now comes the appellant, Li Bing Sun, through his attorney, Stephen M. White, Esq., and sets forth the errors he claims the above-entitled court committed in denying his petition for a writ of habeas corpus, as follows:

I.

That the court erred in not granting the writ of habeas corpus and discharging the appellant, Li Bing Sun, from the custody and control of John D. Nagle, Commissioner of Immigration at the Port of San Francisco.

II.

That the court erred in not holding that it had jurisdiction to issue the writ of habeas corpus as prayed for in the petition on file herein.

III.

That the court erred in not holding that the allegations set forth in the petition for a writ of habeas corpus were sufficient in law to justify the granting and issuing of a writ of habeas corpus.　[24]

IV.

That the court erred in holding that the evidence

adduced before the immigration authorities, was sufficient, in law, to justify the conclusion of the immigration authorities that the appellant was not entitled to admission to the United States.

V.

That the court erred in not holding that the evidence adduced before the immigration authorities was not sufficient, in law, to justify the conclusion of the immigration authorities that the appellant was not entitled to admission to the United States.

VI.

That the court erred in holding that the immigration authorities had jurisdiction to determine that the appellant was not entitled to admission to the United States for the reason that he was not in possession of a valid laborer's return certificate or an overtime certificate as provided for by the Act of Congress of September 13, 1888 (25 Stat. L. 476, 477).

VII.

That the court erred in not holding that the immigration authorities were without jurisdiction to determine that the appellant was not entitled to admission to the United States for the reason that he was not in possession of a valid laborer's return certificate or an overtime certificate as provided for by the Act of Congress of September 13, 1888 (25 Stat. L. 476, 477).

VIII.

That the court erred in holding that the immigration authorities did not act arbitrarily in denying the appellant admission to the United States for the reason that he was not in possession of a valid laborer's return certificate or an overtime certificate as provided for by the Act of Congress of September 13, 1888 (25 Stat. L. 476, 477. [25]

IX.

That the court erred in not holding that the immigration authorities acted arbitrarily in denying the appellant admission to the United States for the reason that he was not in possession of a valid laborer's return certificate or an overtime certificate as provided for by the Act of Congress of September 13, 1888 (25 Stat. L. 476, 477).

X.

That the court erred in holding that there was substantial evidence adduced before the immigration authorities to justify the conclusion of the immigration authorities that the appellant's absence from the United States for a period of more than one year was not unavoidable and that he was not entitled to any equitable relief for failing to produce an overtime certificate, as provided for by the Act of Congress of September 13, 1888 (25 Stat. L. 476, 477), showing that his absence from the United States for a period of more than one year was unavoidable.

XI.

That the court erred in not holding that there was no substantial evidence adduced before the immigration authorities to justify the conclusion of the immigration authorities that the appellant's absence from the United States for a period of more than one year was not unavoidable and that he was not entitled to any equitable relief for failing to produce an overtime certificate, as provided for by the Act of Congress of September 13, 1888 (25 Stat. L. 476, 477), showing that his absence from the United States for a period of more than one year was unavoidable.

XII.

That the court erred in holding that the appellant was accorded a full and fair hearing before the immigration authorities. [26]

XIII.

That the court erred in not holding that the appellant was not accorded a full and fair hearing before the immigration authorities.

WHEREFORE, appellant prays that the said order and judgment of the United States District Court for the Northern District of California made, given and entered herein in the office of the Clerk of said court on the 11th day of August, 1931, denying the petition for a writ of habeas corpus, be reversed and that he be restored to his liberty and go hence without day.

Dated at San Francisco, California, August 19, 1931.

STEPHEN M. WHITE.
Attorney for Appellant.

[Endorsed]: Filed Aug. 19, 1931. [27]

[Title of Court and Cause.]

ORDER ALLOWING APPEAL.

It appearing to the above-entitled court that Li Bing Jing, the petitioner herein, has this day filed and presented to the above court his petition praying for an order of this court allowing an appeal to the United States Circuit Court of Appeals for the Ninth Circuit from the judgment and order of this court denying a writ of habeas corpus herein and dismissing his petition for said writ, and good cause appearing therefor,—

IT IS HEREBY ORDERED that an appeal be and the same is hereby allowed as prayed for herein; and

IT IS HEREBY FURTHER ORDERED that the Clerk of the above-entitled court make and prepare a transcript of all the papers, proceedings and records in the above-entitled matter and transmit the same to the United States Circuit Court of Appeals for the Ninth Circuit within the time allowed by law; and

IT IS FURTHER ORDERED that the execution of the warrant of deportation of said Li Bing Sun, be and the same is hereby stayed pending this appeal and that the said Li Bing Sun, be not removed from the jurisdiction of this court pending this appeal.

Dated at San Francisco, California, August 19th, 1931.

A. F. ST. SURE,
United States District Judge.

[Endorsed]: Filed Aug. 19, 1931. [28]

[Title of Court and Cause.]

ORDER TRANSMITTING ORIGINAL EXHIBITS.

Good cause appearing therefor, IT IS HEREBY ORDERED that the Immigration Records filed as exhibits herein, may be transmitted by the Clerk of the above-entitled court to and filed with the Clerk of the United States Circuit Court of Appeals for the Ninth Circuit to be taken as a part of the record on appeal in the above-entitled cause with the same force and effect as if embodied in the transcript of record and so certified by the Clerk of this court.

Dated at San Francisco, California, this 19th, day of August, 1931.

A. F. ST. SURE,
United States District Judge.

[Endorsed]: Filed Aug. 19, 1931. [29]

[Title of Court and Cause.]

PRAECIPE FOR TRANSCRIPT OF RECORD.

To the Clerk of Said Court:

Sir: Please issue for transcript on appeal the following papers, to wit:

1. Petition for writ of habeas corpus.
2. Order to show cause.
3. Exhibit "A" (testimony adduced before Board of Special Inquiry and findings and decision of Board of Special Inquiry).
4. Minute order respecting introduction of original immigration records.
5. Order denying petition for writ of habeas corpus.
6. Notice of appeal.
7. Petition for appeal.
8. Assignment of errors.
9. Order allowing appeal.
10. Citation on appeal.
11. Order transmitting original immigration records.
12. Praecipe.
13. Appearance of respondent.

STEPHEN M. WHITE,
Attorney for Appellant.

[Endorsed]: Filed Aug. 19, 1931.   [30]

[Title of Court.]

CERTIFICATE OF CLERK U. S. DISTRICT COURT TO TRANSCRIPT OF RECORD.

I, Walter B. Maling, Clerk of the United States District Court, for the Northern District of California, do hereby certify that the foregoing —— pages, numbered from 1 to ——, inclusive, contain a full, true, and correct transcript of the records and proceedings in the matter of Li Bing Sun, on habeas corpus, No. 20506–S, as the same now remain on file and of record in my office.

I further certify that the cost of preparing and certifying the foregoing transcript of record on appeal is the sum of Thirteen Dollars and 15/100, and that the said amount has been paid to me by the attorney for the appellant herein.

IN WITNESS WHEREOF, I have hereunto set my hand and affixed the seal of said District Court, this 24th day of August, A. D. 1931.

[Seal]   WALTER B. MALING,

Clerk.

By C. M. Taylor,

Deputy Clerk. [31]

[Title of Court and Cause.]

CITATION ON APPEAL.

United States of America,—ss.

The President of the United States, to JOHN D. NAGLE, Commissioner of Immigration, Port of San Francisco, and GEORGE J. HATFIELD, United States Attorney, GREETING:

You are hereby cited and admonished to be and appear at a United States Circuit Court of Appeals for the Ninth Circuit, to be holden at the City of San Francisco, State of California, within 30 days from the date hereof, pursuant to an order allowing an appeal, of record in the Clerk's office of the United States District Court for the Northern District of California, wherein Li Bing Sun, is appellant and you are appellee, to show cause, if any, why the decree rendered against the said appellant, as in the said order allowing appeal mentioned, should not be corrected and why speedy justice should not be done to the parties in that behalf.

WITNESS, the Honorable A. F. ST. SURE, United States District Judge for the Southern Division of the Northern District of California, this 19th day of August, 1931.

A. F. ST. SURE,
United States District Judge. [32]

Due service and receipt of a copy of the within citation on appeal is hereby admitted this 19th day of August, 1931.

GEORGE J. HATFIELD,
United States Attorney,

By ————————————,
Asst. U. S. Attorney,
Attorneys for Respondent.

[Endorsed]: Filed Aug. 19, 1931, 4:09 P. M. [33]

————

[Endorsed]: No. 6593. United States Circuit Court of Appeals for the Ninth Circuit. Li Bing Sun, Appellant, vs. John D. Nagle, as Commissioner of Immigration, Port of San Francisco, Appellee. Transcript of Record. Upon Appeal from the United States District Court for the Northern District of California, Southern Division.

Filed August 26, 1931.

PAUL P. O'BRIEN,
Clerk of the United States Circuit Court of Appeals for the Ninth Circuit.

No. 6593

United States Circuit Court of Appeals

For the Ninth Circuit

LI BING SUN,

Appellant,

vs.

JOHN D. NAGLE, as Commissioner of Immigration for the Port of San Francisco,

Appellee.

BRIEF FOR APPELLANT.

STEPHEN M. WHITE,
576 Sacramento Street, San Francisco,
Attorney for Appellant.

FILED

JAN 20 1932

PAUL P. O'BRIEN,
CLERK

PERNAU-WALSH PRINTING CO., SAN FRANCISCO

Subject Index

Table of Authorities Cited

No. 6593

United States Circuit Court of Appeals
For the Ninth Circuit

Li Bing Sun,

Appellant,

vs.

John D. Nagle, as Commissioner of Immigration for the Port of San Francisco,

Appellee.

BRIEF FOR APPELLANT.

STATEMENT OF THE CASE.

This appeal is taken from an order of the District Court for the Northern District of California, Southern Division, denying a petition for a writ of habeas corpus. (Tr. of R., pp. 27-28.)

The appellant, Li Bing Sun, a male Chinese alien, aged 26 years, first arrived in the United States on December 29, 1919, and was admitted on February 16, 1920, by the immigration authorities, under the status of a minor son of a Chinese merchant. *(Cheung Sum Shee v. Nagle,* 268 U. S. 336, 69 L. Ed. 985; *U. S. v. Gue Lim,* 176 U. S. 459, 44 L. Ed. 544.) Following his admission, he made two trips to China, as follows: departed on November 27, 1926, and returned on October 20, 1927; departed on November 22, 1929, and returned on November 26, 1930. Prior to his departure on each of his trips, he secured from the immigration authorities a so-called laborer's return certificate, designated as Form 432, which was issued in each instance upon proof that he had property in the United States to the amount of, at least, one thousand ($1,000.00) dollars. (Tr. of R., p. 22 et seq.) He was admitted upon his return from his first trip in 1927 without question, but, upon his return from his second trip in 1930, it was decided by a Board of Special Inquiry, which had been convened at the port, that he was not entitled to admission and, upon appeal to the Secretary of Labor, the decision of the Board of Special Inquiry was affirmed. Having been ordered deported and held in custody by the appellee for deportation, proceedings in habeas corpus were instituted and, from the order of the Court below denying the petition for a writ of habeas corpus, this appeal comes.

The original immigration records were made a part of the appellee's return to an order to show cause in the Court below (Tr. of R., p. 26) and these records have been transmitted to this Court as part of the record on appeal. (Tr. of R., p. 35.)

REASONS FOR EXCLUSION.

The reasons for the exclusion of the appellant from admission to the United States, incident to his return to the United States on November 26, 1930, from his second trip to China, have been specified, as follows:

1.   That he was not prevented from returning to the United States within one year from the date of his departure therefrom by reason of sickness or other disability beyond his control.

2.   That he was not in possession of a so-called overtime certificate issued by an American Consular representative abroad showing that his failure to return to the United States within one year from the date of his departure therefrom was caused by sickness or other disability beyond his control.

In urging the foregoing reasons, the Secretary of Labor wrote, as follows:

"This case comes before the Board of Review of appeal from a decision of a Board of Special Inquiry at San Francisco denying admission as a returning laborer.

Attorney George W. Hott has filed a brief. Attorneys White and White at the port.

The record shows that after investigation the alien was issued a laborer's return certificate with which he departed from the port of San Francisco on November 22, 1929. Returning he arrived at San Francisco on November 26, 1930, four days over a year after his departure and without the overtime certificate which the law requires.

Asked why he did not return within the year, the applicant says he was suffering from boils on account of which he had to postpone his return. From communication of the American Consulate General at Hongkong, however, it appears that

the alien was physically examined at the Hongkong Consulate on August 14, 1930, by a Public
Health Surgeon and certified as able to return to
the United States. He himself testified that about
October 7, 1930, he had recovered from his boil
affliction. His United States Public Health Service Vaccination and Inspection Card shows that
he was vaccinated on October 13, 1930, and reported on October 20, 1930, and again on October
21, 1930. Thus it appears that he had fully recovered from whatever may have been his physical disability in time for him to reach San
Francisco well within the year after his departure
from that port.

Asked why he did not present an overtime certificate, the alien stated that he had attempted to
secure an overtime certificate but 'the American
Consulate refused to issue it to him.' The State
Department was requested to ascertain from the
American Consulate General at Hongkong whether he had in fact refused an overtime certificate
applied for by this alien. From the Consul's reply it appears that the alien did not go to the
Consulate at all after the time had expired within
which he could have reached an American port
within the year. What the American Consul did
refuse if anything was not an overtime certificate
applied for when such application would be proper but an assurance that a (favorable) overtime
certificate would be issued after the expiration of
the year, this refusal being apparently in view of
the fact that as stated above a physical examination of the alien showed him to be able to travel.
This action at the Consulate was taken on August
14, 1930, when the alien had plenty of time to

reach San Francisco before the expiration of the year.

The Consul further states that on September 20, 1930, the alien applied by mail for an extension and was informed of the requirement of evidence of disability for the issuance of a (favorable) overtime certificate. The Consul adds 'No further record. Apparently (the alien) secured approval of his form for passage arriving in United States before November 22, 1930, and later changed (his) plans without reference this Consulate General.' However, it appears that the alien did go to the Consulate on October 20, 1930, for his Form 432 certificate bears the stamp 'American Consulate General, Hongkong, October 20, 1930,' and the written notation 'Sailing October 23, 1930, O. K. pnj' apparently the initials of Vice Consul Perry N. Jester. The significance of this 'O. K.' is obviously that this applicant gave his sailing date October 23, 1930, or as in his testimony he has said that he intended to sail on the 'President Grant' which was due to leave Hongkong October 23, 1930, which ship would have brought him to San Francisco within the year making his return satisfactory.

The real reason and the only reason for the alien's failure to arrive at San Francisco within the year after his departure from that port appears to be in his statement 'I expected to return on the President Grant but I thought that being four days overtime would not cause any difficulty in my landing,' i. e., in his case the law would not be enforced.

In the opinion of the Board of Review, the evidence does not establish that the alien was

prevented from returning to the United States
by a cause beyond his control, or that he was
refused a return certificate applied for at the
proper time for such application, or that he is in
any way exempted from the exclusion required
by the Act of September 13, 1888, of a Chinese
laborer who has not the overtime certificate required in that Act.

It is recommended that the appeal be dismissed.

Howard S. Eby,
Acting Chairman, Sec'y. and Comm.
Genl's. Board of Review.

EJW/ws

So Ordered:

P. F. Snyder,
Assistant to the Secretary."

(Immigration Records, Ex. "A," pp. 30-29.)

ISSUES IN THE CASE.

In behalf of the appellant, we contend, as follows::

1. That the finding of the immigration authorities that the appellant was not prevented
from returning to the United States within one
year from the date of his departure therefrom is
without substantial evidentiary support and is,
therefore, arbitrary.

2. That the appellant should not suffer the
penalty of deportation for failure to present an
overtime certificate issued by an American Consular representative abroad disclosing the facts
pertaining to his disability, by which he claims
to have been prevented from returning to the

United States within one year from the date of his departure therefrom, inasmuch as the facts show that he made application for such a certificate, but that the said Consular representative omitted to issue the document.

3. The appellant's right to admission to the United States was not necessarily prohibited through his failure to present a certificate of facts or overtime certificate issued by an American Consular representative.

ARGUMENT.

THE APPELLANT'S RIGHT TO ABSENT HIMSELF FROM THE UNITED STATES FOR A PERIOD OF, AT LEAST, ONE YEAR AND FOR AN ADDITIONAL PERIOD OF ONE YEAR UNDER CONDITIONS PRESCRIBED BY STATUTE.

The Act of Congress of September 13, 1888 (8 U. S. C. A., Sections 275, 276 and 277; 25 Stat. L. 476, 477), provides as follows:

"Sec. 5. That from and after the passage of this act, no Chinese laborer in the United States shall be permitted, after having left, to return thereto, except under the conditions stated in the following sections.

Sec. 6. That no Chinese laborer within the purview of the preceding section shall be permitted to return to the United States unless he has a lawful wife, child, or parent in the United states, or property therein of the value of one thousand dollars, or debts of like amount due him and pending settlement. * * *"

Sec. 7. That a Chinese person claiming the right to be permitted to leave the United States and return thereto on any of the grounds stated in the foregoing section, shall apply to the Chinese inspector in charge of the district from which he wishes to depart at least a month prior to the time of his departure, and shall make on oath before the said inspector a full statement descriptive of his family, or property, or debts, as the case may be, and shall furnish to said inspector such proof of the facts entitling him to return as shall be required by the rules and regulations prescribed from time to time by the Secretary of Labor, and for any false swearing in relation thereto he shall incur the penalties of perjury.

He shall also permit the Chinese inspector in charge to take a full description of his person, which description the inspector shall retain and mark with a number.

And if the said inspector, after hearing the proofs and investigating all the circumstances of the case, shall decide to issue a certificate of return, he shall at such time and place as he may designate, sign and give to the person applying a certificate containing the number of the description last aforesaid, which shall be the sole evidence given to such person of his right to return. * * *.

The right to return under the said certificate shall be limited to one year; but it may be extended for an additional period not to exceed a year, in cases where, by reason of sickness or other cause of disability beyond his control, the holder thereof shall be rendered unable sooner to return, which facts shall be fully reported to and investigated by the consular representative of the United States at the port or place from which such laborer departs for the United States, and certified by such representative of the United States to the satisfaction of the Chinese inspector in charge at the port where such Chinese shall seek to land in the United States, such certificate to be delivered by said representative to the master of the vessel on which he departs for the United States. * * *."

The statute, therefore, provides that an alien Chinese, who has a wife, child or parent in the United States or property therein in the amount of one thousand ($1,000.00) dollars, is entitled to a return certificate, which is commonly called a laborer's return certificate and which entitles him to go abroad for a period of one year and to absent himself from the United States for an additional period of one year, providing that, "by reason of sickness or other cause of disability beyond his control," he is unable to return to the United States within the original period of one year. The statute further provides that, in the event that the alien Chinese finds that on account of sickness or other disability beyond his control he is unable to return to the United States within the original period of one year, he shall report the facts pertaining to the disability to an American Consular representative, who shall investigate the facts and certify the same to the satisfaction of the immigration authorities at the port where the alien Chinese shall seek to enter the United States.

THE APPELLANT'S ABSENCE FROM THE UNITED STATES FOR
A PERIOD OF MORE THAN ONE YEAR WAS DUE TO A
DISABILITY BEYOND HIS CONTROL AND A CONTRARY
FINDING BY THE IMMIGRATION AUTHORITIES WAS
ARBITRARY.

As the facts show, the appellant departed from the
United States for China on November 22, 1929, and
returned on November 26th, 1930, a period of one year
and four days having, therefore, elapsed between the
date of his departure and the date of his return. As
it must be conceded, in view of the clear language of
the statute, that he had the right, under his laborer's
return certificate, which he secured prior to his departure, to absent himself from the United States for,
at least, one year, the question arises:

"Was his entry upon his return necessarily
prohibited by virtue of the fact that he was absent from the United States for a period of four
days beyond the one year period prescribed by
his laborer's return certificate?"

Obviously, the question should be answered in the
negative, as the statute explicitly states:

"The right to return under the said certificate
(laborer's return certificate) shall be limited to
one year; *but it may be extended for an additional period not to exceed a year, in cases where,
by reason of sickness or other cause of disability
beyond his control, the holder thereof shall be
rendered unable sooner to return,* * * *." .

Here, therefore, a preliminary inquiry should be made
into the cause of the appellant's absence for a period
of four days beyond the one year period prescribed

by his laborer's return certificate to ascertain whether or not this absence was due to "sickness or other cause of disability beyond his control."

The only evidence adduced before the Board of Special Inquiry, in respect to the cause of the appellant's absence from the United States, and particularly, in respect to his failure to return within one year from the date of his departure therefrom, consists in the testimony of the appellant, himself, and in certain documents which the appellant presented during the course of his examination. We take the liberty to quote the appellant's testimony, as follows:

"Q. Did you live in the Hong Woo village continuously after reaching China until you departed for this country?

A. Yes.

Q. What occupation did you follow while you were last in China?

A. I had no occupation during that period.

Q. How many visits have you made to China as a laborer on Form 432?

A. Two.

Q. Did you know prior to leaving on both of those two visits that you must return to the U. S. within one year from the date of your departure?

A. Yes.

Q. What caused you to return to the U. S. after a year from date of departure?

A. I was suffering from boils on my feet and on account of that I had to postpone my return to the U. S. I expected to return on the Pres. Grant but I thought that being 4 days overtime would not cause any difficulty in my landing.

Q. When did the Pres. Grant leave Hong-kong?

A. About the 30th. day of the 8th. month, this year, Chinese reckoning (October 21, 1930).

Q. When did you cease having trouble from boils?

A. About the 16th. day of the 8th. month (October 7, 1930).

Q. Then you deliberately delayed your return to the U. S. until the Pres. Cleveland sailed. Is that right?

A. I was detained for about 2 weeks in Hongkong on visits to the doctor for examination.

Q. Do you mean the U. S. Public Health doctor?

A. Yes.

Q. Have you any papers showing this to be a fact?

A. (Present certificate of L. C. Stewart, Medical Officer, U. S. P. H. S. certifying that Li Bing Sun, sailing today for San Francisco from Hongkong on the Pres. Cleveland has not been in contact during the last 14 days with anyone suffering from cerebro-spinal meningitis; also vaccination certificate and inspection card of U. S. P. H. S., Hongkong, showing Li Bing Sun, who departed Nov. 4, 1930, on Pres. Cleveland was vaccinated Oct. 18, 1930, and reported Oct. 20, and Oct. 21. This card bears applicant's photograph. Same are retained on file.)

Q. Was there an epidemic of spinal meningitis in Hongkong during the time you were there?

A. No.

Q. When you were in Hongkong did you go *to the American Consulate?*

A. Yes.

Q. Do you remember the date when you first went there?

A. It was before I went to the U. S. Public Health Service. It was about the 29th. day of the 8th. month (Oct. 20).

Q. You knew then that you could not return here on the Pres. Grant, did you not?

A. Yes.

Q. Why did you not get an overtime certificate from the Consul?

A. I attempted to secure an overtime certificate but the American Consul refused to issue it to me. He did not state any reasons for refusing to do so."

(Immigration Record, Ex. "A," pp. 4-5.)

The certificate of L. C. Stewart, Medical Officer, United States Public Health Service at Hongkong, China, to which reference has been made in the appellant's testimony, and which was introduced in evidence, reads as follows:

"This is to certify that Li Bing Sun bearer of passport No. .... sailing to-day for San Francisco per SS President Cleveland has complied with the provisions contained in Executive Order of June 21, 1929, and as far as can be ascertained he has not been in contact during the last fourteen days with anyone suffering from cerebro-spinal meningitis.

L. C. Stewart,
Medical Officer, United States Public
Health Service."

(Immigration Record, Ex. "B," p. 2.)

Thus, according to his testimony, the appellant, during the latter part of his stay in China had been suffering from boils on his feet, by reason of which condition he was unable to travel, that this condition existed until on or about October 7, 1930, and that he was thereafter detained at Hongkong, China, by a doctor of the United States Public Health Service for a period of fourteen days for physical examination. The documentary evidence, which has been heretofore mentioned, corroborates the appellant's testimony in respect to his detention and examination at Hongkong by the United States Public Health Service, the certificate of this service showing, as heretofore indicated, that the appellant had been under examination for a period of fourteen days, immediately prior to embarking for the United States, to determine whether or not he had been in contact with cerebro-spinal meningitis. The examination was evidently necessary and required under an Executive (Presidential) Order, as disclosed by the certificate, supra, of the United States Public Health Service, and, in passing. it may be said that this Executive Order extended to all aliens, who were about to embark for the United States, requiring them to be examined by the United States Public Health Service and to be held under observation for a period of fourteen days in order to make certain that they had not been afflicted with cerebro-spinal meningitis or been in contact with any person, who was afflicted, the purpose being manifestly to prevent the carrying of the disease to the United States. It further appears from the appellant's testimony that there was a vessel, the SS "President Grant," sailing from Hongkong for the United States on October 21, 1930 (not October 23, 1930, as stated by the Secretary of Labor in his decision, supra), that the appellant did not take passage on this vessel, but waited for the next vessel, the SS "President Cleveland," which sailed from Hongkong on November 4, 1930, and arrived at San Francisco on November 26, 1930, or four days beyond the one year period prescribed by his laborer's return certificate.

We do not particularly rely upon the fact that the appellant has been suffering from boils, as a direct cause for his failure to return to the United States within one year from the date of his departure therefrom, inasmuch as he testified that this condition had cleared on or about October 7, 1930, and it may, therefore, be considered that he thereafter had ample time to reach the United States within the one year period, provided no circumstance intervened to delay his return. There is no question, however, as to the appellant being required to conform to the Executive Order requiring all aliens, who are about to embark for the United States to submit to medical observation and examination for a period of fourteen days, immediately prior to embarking for the United States, and this requirement, we contend, was the proximate and direct cause of his delay in returning to the United States. Manifestly, in the event that he had not been required to submit to examination and observation for a period of fourteen days, he would have been able to sail for the United States fourteen days prior to the time that he actually did and, therefore. instead of arriving in the United States four days after the expiration of the one year period prescribed by his return certificate, he would have arrived ten days prior thereto, or, in other words, instead of sailing from Hongkong on November 4, 1930, on the SS "President Cleveland" and arriving at San Francisco on November 26, 1930, he would have been able to sail on October 21, 1930, on the SS "President Grant," which admittedly (decision of Secretary of Labor, supra), arrived at San Francisco well in advance of November 22, 1930, the date of the expiration of the one year period. To, again, quote from the certificate, supra, of the United States Public Health Service:

> "This is to certify that Li Bing Sun * * * sailing today for San Francisco per SS President Cleveland has complied with the provisions contained in Executive Order of June 21, 1929, and as far as can be ascertained he has not been in contact during the last fourteen days with anyone suffering from cerebro-spinal meningitis.
> *   *   *."

Inasmuch as the SS "President Cleveland" sailed from Hongkong on November 4, 1930 (see vaccination and inspection card, Immigration Record, Ex. "B," p. 3), it is accurately established that his detention by the United States Public Health Service began on October 20, 1930, and, therefore, inasmuch as this detention continued for fourteen days, it was not only impossible for him to sail on the SS "President Grant" on October 21, 1930, but it was, also, impossible for him to sail sooner than November 4, 1930, the date upon which he actually did take passage.

Clearly, therefore, if the facts establish, as we submit they do, that the appellant's delay in returning to the United States of four days beyond the one year period prescribed by his laborer's return certificate, was due to the action of the United States Public Health Service at Hongkong in detaining him for examination and observation for a period of fourteen days, immediately prior to his embarkation for the United States, or from October 20, 1930, to November 4, 1930, it will necessarily follow that his delay was by reason of a disability beyond his control. He was powerless to interfere with the action and requirements of the United States Public Health Service or to escape detention by this Service.

The Secretary of Labor has concluded that the appellant had no substantial reason for absenting himself from the United States for a period of four days beyond the one year period prescribed by his laborer's return certificate and that his delay in returning was simply the result of a desire to remain longer in China, in the expectation that the law would not be enforced against him. The Secretary of Labor stated:

> "The real reason and the only reason for the alien's failure to arrive at San Francisco within the year after his departure from that port appears to be in his statement 'I expected to return on the President Grant but I thought that being four days overtime would not cause any difficulty in my landing,' i. e., in his case the law would not be enforced."

The Secretary, however, ignores and omits to quote a very pertinent part of the appellant's testimony, as follows:

"Q. Then you deliberately delayed your return to the U. S. until the Pres. Cleveland sailed. Is that right?

A. I was detained for about 2 weeks in Hongkong on visits to the doctor for examination.

Q. Do you mean the U. S. Public Health doctor?

A. Yes."

(See appellant's testimony, Immigration Record, Ex. "A," p. 4.)

No doubt, as he testified, the appellant intended to return on the SS "President Grant," which sailed from Hongkong on October 21, 1930, and which, admittedly, reached the United States prior to November 22, 1930, the date of the expiration of the one year period prescribed by his laborer's return certificate. However, owing to circumstances, over which he had no control and which we have already discussed, he was prevented from carrying out his intention. He evidently considered that these circumstances justified his delay in returning and, therefore, being impressed with the righteousness of his cause, he would naturally and properly state that he expected to experience no difficulty in securing admission. Viewed in the light of the entire record, which shows that there were circumstances justifying the appellant's delay in returning to the United States, we submit that no sinister motive should be imputed to the appellant merely because he expected to gain admission.

THE APPELLANT SHOULD NOT BE PENALIZED AND DE-
PORTED FOR FAILURE TO PRESENT AN OVERTIME CER-
TIFICATE ISSUED BY AN AMERICAN CONSULAR OFFICER,
WHERE THE FACTS ESTABLISH THAT HE MADE APPLI-
CATION FOR THE CERTIFICATE, BUT THAT THE CONSU-
LAR OFFICER WRONGFULLY FAILED TO ISSUE THE SAME.

The Secretary of Labor further contends that the
appellant was not entitled to admission for the reason
that he did not present a so-called overtime certificate
issued by the American Consul at Hongkong showing
that his delay of four days, in returning to the United
States, was caused by sickness or other disability beyond his control. It is conceded that the appellant
did not present the certificate mentioned. In this connection, however, we urge that he should not be
penalized and deported for not presenting the certificate, inasmuch as the facts establish that he made
application for the document, but that the Consular
Officer, in neglect of the duty imposed upon him by
law, failed to issue it.

The appellant testified as follows:

"Q. When you were in Hongkong did you go
to the American Consulate?

A. Yes.

Q. Do you remember the date when you first
went there?

A. It was before I went to the United States
Public Health Service. It was about the 29th.
day of the 8th. month (October 20).

Q. You knew then that you could not return
here on the SS President Grant, did you not?

A. Yes.

Q. Why did you not get an overtime certificate from the Consul?

A. I attempted to secure an overtime certificate but the American Consul refused to issue it to me. He did not state any reasons for refusing to do so.''

(Immigration Record, Ex. ''A,'' pp. 4-5.)

A reference to the documentary evidence of record corrobates the appellant's testimony, at least, to the extent that he went to the American Consulate at Hongkong on October 20, 1930, which is the date upon which his detention, for a period of fourteen days, by the United States Public Health Service began. The laborer's return certificate, upon which the appellant departed from the United States on November 22, 1929, was placed in evidence (Immigration Record, Ex. ''B''), and on the reverse side of this certificate there appears a notation, as follows:

''American Consulate General October 20, 1930, Hongkong—Sailing October 23, 1930, O. K. p. n. j.''

The Secretary of Labor, in his decision, supra, has commented upon the foregoing notation, as follows:

''* * *. However, it appears that the alien did go to the Consulate on October 20, 1930, for his Form 432 certificate bears the stamp 'American Consulate General, Hongkong, October 20, 1930,' and the written notation 'Sailing October 23, 1930, O. K. pnj,' apparently the initials of Vice Consul Perry N. Jester. * * *.''

Taking, therefore, the direct testimony of the appellant, together with the notation of the Consular officer appearing on the laborer's return certificate, we submit that it must be conceded that there was undisputed evidence establishing his claim that he appeared at the American Consulate at Hongkong on October 20, 1930, and made application to this Consulate for a so-called overtime certificate.

The applicable statute, namely, the Act of September 13, 1888, 25 Stat. L. 476, 477, supra, provides, in part, as follows:

> "The right to return under the said certificate (laborer's return certificate), shall be limited to one year; but it may be extended for an additional period not to exceed a year, in cases where, by reason of sickness or other cause of disability beyond his control, the holder thereof shall be rendered unable sooner to return, which facts shall be fully reported to and investigated by the consular representative of the United States at the port or place from which such laborer departs for the United States, and certified by such representative of the United States to the satisfaction of the Chinese inspector in charge at the port where such Chinese shall seek to enter the United States, such certificate to be delivered by said representative to the master of the vessel on which he departs for the United States. * * * ".

Clearly, therefore, the *duty* is imposed upon a Consular officer to investigate the facts pertaining to the cause of delay, in returning to the United States within one year from the date of departure therefrom, of a Chinese alien, who is in possession of a laborer's return certificate, and to certify the facts pertaining to the delay to the satisfaction of the immigration officer in charge at the port where the alien seeks to

enter the United States. The certificate of facts of
the Consular officer has been called an overtime certificate, which, however, is a misnomer, in that the
Consular officer has no power whatever to issue a
certificate granting or denying the alien an extension
of his stay away from the United States, but his
power is limited wholly to an investigation and certification of the facts pertaining to the delay, the decision
as to whether or not the facts, as certified by the Consular officer, are true or constitute grounds sufficient
to have justified the alien in remaining away from the
United States for more than one year being a matter
for determination by the immigration officer at the
port of intended arrival.

> *Nagle v. Wong Bing Jung,* 22 Fed. (2d) 20, C.
> C. A. 9th;
> *Nagle v. Toy Young Quen,* 22 Fed. (2d) 18, C.
> C. A. 9th.

In respect to the *duty* of a Consular officer to investigate and certify the facts pertaining to the cause
of delay, Judge Neterer, in *Ex Parte Woo Show How,*
17 Fed. (2d) 652, at page 653, D. C., said:

> "That the vice consul erred in denying the over-
> time certificate is concluded by the direction of
> the Department of State to the consul general in
> its instructions to direct the issuance of the cer-
> tificate. The delay in returning was not caused
> by any intent on the part of the applicant to not
> return, but because of inability to travel by reason
> of ulcers, or boils, on his leg. *It was the duty of
> the vice consul, first, to investigate the facts of
> disability; second, to certify his findings to the*

satisfaction of the collector of customs at the port of entry, and deliver a copy to the master of the ship. The delay was not the fault of the applicant. The prompt discharge of official duty by the vice consul would have permitted entry within the limitation fixed by statute. The applicant may not be made to suffer because of the error of the vice consul, but be held accountable only for his own contract. Such clearly must be the intent of the statute, and so concluding, it is apparent applicant was denied a fair trial."

Ex Parte Yee Gee, 17 Fed. (2d) 653, D. C.

The appellant, of course, had no means by which to compel the Consular officer to perform the duty imposed upon him by statute and to, therefore, issue him a certificate of facts or so-called overtime certificate, as the result of his application of October 20, 1930, for such a document. The appellant, by making the application, complied with all the requirements of the law; the Consular officer, in failing to investigate the application and to certify the facts, as the result of his investigation, did not comply with any part of the law.

"Equity will consider that as done which ought to have been done," and it may, therefore, be deemed that the Consular officer issued to the appellant a certificate of facts or so-called overtime certificate, as the result of his application of October 20, 1930, for such a document.

In *Ex Parte Yee Gee,* 17 Fed. (2d) 653, at pages 655, 656 and 657, D. C., Judge St. Sure said:

"That part of the opinion appearing to be determinative of any facts on which the Board of Inquiry excluded, is expressed thus: 'This is probably true' (of the statements of detained for reasons for delay); and 'it is plain that equity is in favor of the admission of this Chinese as the only reason why he did not return within the two-year period * * * is a mistake on the part of a consular officer.' We may eliminate 'the reasons for extension being considered insufficient' from the Board of Inquiry summary on the appeal for this reason, and arrive again at the action of the consuls. Muccio's statement that the consulate was not satisfied with applicant's reasons for delay is that of a different vice consul, after instruction by the State Department following complaint of failure to exercise proper powers, and abuse and excess of authority by a different vice consul, Hawkins, in arbitrary refusal to grant a certificate, and is necessarily based on such arbitrary and mistaken refusal. Hawkins' refusal is not a certificate of facts required; Muccio's cannot be, and there was therefore practically nothing but the bare return certificate, coupled with the date of physical arrival at San Francisco beyond the time caused only by the mistake of the first vice consul acting, and in no wise the result of any neglect or failure of the applicant.

In the case of Woo Show How, W. D. Wash., No. 11175, 17 F. (2d) 652, Jan. 17, 1927, Judge Neterer said of a similar situation:

'The prompt discharge of official duty by the vice consul would have permitted entry within the limitation fixed by statute. The applicant may not be made to suffer because of the error of the vice consul, but be held accountable only for his own conduct. Such clearly must be the intent of the statute, and, so concluding, it is apparent that applicant was denied a fair trial.'

With this I agree. *On the record as stated I also consider that though there is no estoppel against the government by reason of acts of its officers, the equity in the case will consider that as done which should have been done, and will therefore consider that the time of entry is within the time limit because actually prevented by recognized and corrected mistake or abuse of power by an officer not of the branch having actual authority to exclude. * * *.*

The expiration of the time limit, under the circumstances here, where the applicant has made every effort to secure his document on which to take passage, and where he was actually on an American ship bound for his return port before the expiration of the time limit, becomes of little consequence, and should be deemed to date back to March, when he was prevented from sailing."

Ex Parte Woo Show How, supra;

In Re Spinella, 3 Fed. (2d) 196, D. C.;

Ex Parte Seid Soo Hong, 23 Fed. (2d) 847, **D. C.**

It is apparently conceded, at least not denied, by the Secretary of Labor, that the appellant applied to the American Consulate at Hongkong on October 20, 1930, for an overtime certificate. However, he states that the appellant "did not go to the Consulate at all after the time expired within which he could have reached an American port within the year." Evidently, he means that the application of October 20, 1930, to the Consulate, for a certificate of facts or overtime certificate was premature, or, in other words, it is virtually contended that inasmuch as twenty-four days are consumed in making the voyage from Hongkong to the United States, the appellant should have deferred his application until, at least, twenty-four days prior to November 22, 1930, the date of the expiration of the one year period prescribed by his laborer's return certificate. There is no authority for such a contention. Clearly, the statute contemplates the filing of the application at such time when the alien finds it impossible for him to return to the United States within the one year and, hence, on October 20, 1930, when the appellant found that he could not return within the one year period by reason of the fact of his detention for a period of fourteen days, commencing on October 20, 1930, by the United States Public Health Service, he acted within his rights by filing his application and as any prudent person would act.

The Secretary of Labor not only entirely ignores the appellant's detention by the United States Public Health Service for a period of fourteen days, immediately prior to his embarkation for the United States, as a ground for his delay in returning to the United States within the period of one year, but, also, ignores the fact that the appellant fully complied with the law by filing with the American Consul on October 20, 1930, his application for a Consular certificate of facts and that the Consul complied with no part of law in refusing to issue the certificate. Apparently, he places his adverse decision wholly upon the grounds that the appellant had previously applied for overtime certificates on August 14, 1930, and on September 20, 1930, on the ground of physical disability, to-wit: boils on his feet, that the application of August 14, 1930, was denied, because the appellant was medically examined and found able to travel, and that the application of September 20, 1930, was never completed through the fault of the appellant in failing to produce a medical certificate requested by the Consul. In support of his adverse decision, he does not rely upon any evidence adduced before the Board of Special Inquiry, but entirely upon a communication received from the American Consul at Hongkong after the Board of Special Inquiry had rendered its decision and while the case was pending on appeal. This communication is dated January 15, 1931, and the appellant was denied admission by a Board of Special Inquiry on December 3, 1930. (Immigration Record, Ex. "A," pp. 8-9.) The communication reads as follows:

"Li Bing Sun applied personally August 14, 1930, for assurance of favorable action on overtime certificate, after expiration one year, was examined by the U. S. Public Health Officer this office and certified able to return to the United States, was advised to return to San Francisco before November 22. On September 20th he applied by mail for extension and was informed of provisions of law concerning issuance of overtime certificates and the necessity of submitting proof of disability beyond control, in his case a medical certificate. No further record apparently received approval of his form for passage arriving United States before November 22 and later changed plans without reference this Consulate General.''

(Immigration Record, Ex. ''A,'' p. 26.)

The communication, not having been produced at the hearing before the Board of Special Inquiry, by reason of which the appellant was not confronted with it, the Secretary of Labor acted unfairly in utilizing it as evidence. Speaking of the ''indispensable requisites of a fair hearing,'' the Circuit Court for the Eighth Circuit in *Whitfield v. Hanges,* 222 Fed. 745, at page 749, said:

> ''Indispensable requisites of a fair hearing according to these fundamental principles are that the course of proceeding shall be appropriate to the case and just to the party affected; that the accused shall be notified of the nature of the charge against him in time to meet it; that he shall have such an opportunity to be heard that he may, if he chooses, cross-examine the witnesses against him; *that he may have time and opportunity, after all the evidence against him is produced and known to him, to produce evidence and witnesses to refute it; that the decision shall be governed by and based upon the evidence at the hearing, and that only; and that the decision shall not be without substantial evidence taken at the hearing to support it.''*

> *Chin Quong Mew ex rel. Chin Bark Keung v. Tillinghast,* 30 Fed. (2d) 684, C. C. A. 1st;

> *Kwock Jan Fat v. White,* 253 U. S. 454, 457-458, 40 Sup. Ct. 566, 567, 64 L. Ed. 1010.

In any event, the communication is immaterial, in that the information contained therein pertains only to the applications of August 14, 1930, and September 20, 1930, and not to the application of October 20, 1930, involving the proximate and direct cause of the appellant's delay through his detention by the United States Public Health Service. It is true that the communication indicates that the Consulate had no record of the appellant after September 20, 1930, but, nevertheless, the conclusion is not thereby justified that the appellant did not appear at the Consulate and make application for a certificate of facts or overtime certificate on October 20, 1930, not only on account of the direct testimony of the appellant that he did appear, but, also, on account of the notation of the Consular officer, himself, appearing on the reverse side of the appellant's return certificate (Immigration Record, Ex. "B"), and showing the appellant's appearance at the Consulate on the date mentioned.

Furthermore, as heretofore observed, the Secretary of Labor admits that the appellant did appear at the American Consulate on October 20, 1930, and, in connection with this appearance, he states:

"* * * However, it appears that the alien did go to the Consulate on October 20, 1930, for his Form 432 certificate bears the stamp 'American Consulate General, Hongkong, October 20, 1930,' and the written notation 'Sailing October 23, 1930, O. K. pnj,' apparently the initials of Vice Consul Perry N. Jester. The significance of this 'O. K.' is obviously that this applicant gave his sailing date October 23, 1930, or as in his testimony he has said that he intended to sail on the 'President Grant' which was due to leave Hongkong October 23, 1930, which ship would have brought him to San Francisco within the year making his return satisfactory.''

Of course, the action of the Consular officer in giving the appellant an ''O. K.'' to sail on October 23, 1930, was an empty gesture, because he had no authority whatever to limit or extend the appellant's stay abroad or determine when the appellant should depart for the United States, but his power, as we have heretofore contended, was limited entirely to the issuance of a certificate of facts, the decision as to the sufficiency of the certificate and the right of the appellant to return and to be admitted to the United States being matters for determination by the immigration authorities. The statement of the Secretary of Labor that the appellant testified that he ''intended to sail on the SS. 'President Grant,' *which was due to leave Hongkong on October 23, 1930,*'' is not correct. He testified that the SS. ''President Grant'' sailed from Hongkong on October 21, 1930 (Immigation Record, Ex. ''A,'' p. 4), and his testimony is undisputed by any evidence. Therefore, the Consular officer's ''O. K.'' for the appellant to sail on October 23, 1930, was absolutely ineffectual, there being no vessel sailing on that date, and, furthermore, there was no vessel sailing thereafter until November 4, 1930, the date upon which the appellant actually did take passage for the United States. In any event, the ''O. K.'' given by the Consular officer to the appellant was certainly not the certificate of facts to which the appellant was entitled and which, admittedly, he never received.

THE APPELLANT'S RIGHT TO ADMISSION TO THE UNITED STATES WAS NOT NECESSARILY PROHIBITED THROUGH HIS FAILURE TO PRESENT A CERTIFICATE OF FACTS OR OVERTIME CERTIFICATE ISSUED BY AN AMERICAN CONSULAR OFFICER.

Moreover, we submit that the presentation by the appellant of a certificate of facts or so-called overtime certificate issued by a Consular officer was not absolutely essential to his admission. The applicable statute, namely, the Act of September 13, 1888, 25 Stat. L. 476, 477, supra, explicitly provides that the holder of a laborer's return certificate, when he absents himself from the United States for a period of more than one year, shall report the facts pertaining to the cause of his absence to a Consular officer, who shall investigate the facts and *certify the same to the satisfaction of the immigration authorities.* In deciding, however, as we have heretofore urged, whether or not the holder of the laborer's return certificate was unavoidably delayed, the immigration authorities are not bound by the Consular certificate of facts, but they are at liberty to decide the question upon such testimony as may be adduced before them or upon any substantial evidence that may be presented, and this is, in effect, the view taken by this Court in its decisions in *Nagle v. Wong Bing Jung,* 22 Fed. (2d) 20, supra, and in *Nagle v. Toy Young Quen,* 22 Fed. (2d) 18, supra, in each of which cases it was held that the immigration authorities were not bound by a statement of facts contained in a Consular certificate, but that they were free to decide whether or not the holder of a laborer's return certificate was unavoidably detained upon the testimony of the holder, as given before the immigration authorities.

If the immigration authorities are free to decide the question as to whether or not the holder of a laborer's return certificate was unavoidably delayed, upon the testimony as adduced before them and irrespective of the facts certified by the Consular officer, it must follow that the Consular certificate of facts is without binding or legal effect, that it is, at most, evidentiary in character and that its purpose is merely to serve as a guide for the immigration authorities in their determination of the case. In this situation, we submit that it was immaterial to the right of the appellant to enter the United States whether or not he had a Consular certificate of facts or overtime certificate, as long the immigration authorities had before them all the evidence showing and establishing the only fact, which was essential to his admission and which the Consular certificate would have showed, if issued, the fact being, as heretofore stated, his detention by the United States Public Health Service at Hongkong for a period of fourteen (14) days immediately prior to his embarkation for the United States.

In speaking of an immigration document, which was evidentiary in character, the Court in *U. S. ex rel. Patti v. Curran*, 22 Fed. (2d) 314, at page 317, said:

"Their permits under the immigration laws had
no effect, except to furnish evidence in convenient
form that they were returning from the temporary visit abroad. When the permits expired, it
is true they were deprived of validity; *but, since
their only effect was evidentiary, invalidity became utterly immaterial, upon the production 'of
testimony establishing the only fact of which the
permits, if they had been valid, would have been
evidence. * * *.*"

In *U. S. ex rel. Gentile v. Day,* 25 Fed. (2d) 717,
C. C. A. 2nd, the Court, at page 719, said:

"All we have here is the question whether an
alien loses his exemption from the quota for one
reason merely because upon his arrival he gets an
exemption for another. It is quite true that, if
he had presented his present ground originally,
the board of injury might have rejected it, but by
hypothesis that rejection would have been wrong
and should have been corrected on appeal. There
is no reason to assume that the opportunities for
examination at that time were better than before
the inspector, or that the government was prejudiced by the delay in its opportunity to ascertain
the facts. *The exemption is granted by the statute and is independent of the procedure for its
determination; it should not be forfeited unless
the alien's conduct has so clogged it that he 'ought
not to assert it thereafter.* We cannot see that
this is such a case."

The power having been vested by statute in the immigration authorities to accept or reject the Consular
certificate of facts, the provision in respect to ob-

taining such a document must be held to be directory, rather than mandatory. In *French v. Edwards,* 20 L. Ed. 702, at p. 703, the Supreme Court said:

"There are, undoubtedly, many statutory requisitions intended for the guide of officers in the conduct of business devolved upon them, which do not limit their power or render its exercise in disregard of the requisitions ineffectual. Such, generally, are regulations designed to secure order, system and dispatch in proceedings, and by a disregard of which the rights of parties interested cannot be injuriously affected. Provisions of this character are not usually regarded as mandatory unless accompanied by negative words importing that the acts required shall not be done in any other manner or time than that prescribed. * * *."

CONCLUSION.

We respectfully submit that the testimony of the appellant and the documentary evidence of record established that the appellant's delay in returning to the United States of four days beyond the one year period prescribed by his laborer's return certificate was proximately and directly caused by his detention by the United States Public Health Service at Hongkong for a period of fourteen days, immediately prior to his departure for the United States, a matter over which he had manifestly no control. The immigration authorities had not a particle of evidence before them to justify the conclusion that the appellant was not delayed in the manner mentioned and, furthermore, these authorities entirely ignored his detention by the United State Public Health Service, as an unavoidable circumstance causing his delay in returning to the United States. In this situation, it will follow that the decision of the immigration authorities to the effect that the appellant was not unavoidably delayed is arbitrary and unfair.

In *Johnson v. Tertzag,* 2 Fed. (2d) 40, at p. 41, C. C. A. 1st, the Court said:

"The case is, on the facts, radically different from United States v. Commissioner (C. C. A.), 288 F. 756, relied upon by the government, where it appears (see page 758) that neither the alien 'nor the intended husband, in the testimony before the board, had a word to say as to religious persecution in Roumania.' This alien disclosed all essential facts before the board, making a plain case of fleeing from religious persecution.

It is as much the duty of the immigration officials to admit aliens exempted from the general policy of exclusion as it is to exclude those falling within the excluded classes. Administrative officials may not ignore essential parts of the statutes they are administering."

The decision of the immigration authorities must be after a hearing in good faith, however summary, *Chin Yow v. U. S.,* 208 U. S. 8, 12, 52 L. Ed. 369, and it must find adequate support in the evidence.

Zakonaite v. Wolf, 226 U. S. 272, 274, 57 L. Ed. 218;

Kwock Jan Fat v. White, 253 U. S. 454, 457-458, 64 L. Ed. 1010.

Furthermore, the appellant should not be penalized and deported for failure to produce a Consular certificate of facts or overtime certificate, disclosing the grounds for his delay in returning to the United States. The record establishes that the appellant made application for the certificate mentioned on October 20, 1930, but that the Consular officer failed to issue the same. By making the application, the appellant complied with the law; in failing to issue the certificate, the Consular officer complied with no part of the law. "Equity will consider that as done which ought to have been done," and it may, therefore, be deemed that the appellant was in possession of the proper Consular certificate.

> *Ex Parte Yee Gee,* 17 Fed. (2d) 653, supra;
>
> *Ex Parte Woo Show How,* 17 Fed. (2d), 652, supra;
>
> *In Re Spinella,* 3 Fed. (2d) 196, supra;
>
> *Ex Parte Seid Soo Hong,* 23 Fed. (2d) 847, supra.

Moreover, a Consular certificate of facts or overtime certificate is purely evidentiary in character, in that it has no binding effect upon the immigration authorities, who are free to decide the alien's application for admission upon evidence adduced before them and irrespective of the facts disclosed by the Consular certificate.

> *Nagle v. Wong Bing Jung,* supra;
>
> *Nagle v. Toy Young Quen,* supra.

Being evidentiary in character, it was immaterial to the right of the appellant to enter the United States whether or not he had a Consular certificate of facts or overtime certificate, as long as the immigration authorities had before them all the evidence showing and establishing the only fact, which was essential to his admission and which the Consular certificate would have showed, if issued, the fact being his detention by the United States Public Health Service at Hongkong for a period of fourteen days immediately prior to his embarkation for the United States.

U. S. ex rel. Patti v. Curran, supra;

U. S. ex rel. Gentile v. Day, supra.

The power having been vested by statute in the immigration authorities to accept or reject the Consular certificate of facts, the provision in respect to obtaining such a document must be held to be directory, rather than mandatory.

French v. Edwards, supra.

It is respectfully asked that the order of the Court below denying the petition for a writ of habeas corpus be reversed with direction to issue the writ as prayed for.

Dated, San Francisco,
    January 18, 1932.

Respectfully submitted,
STEPHEN M. WHITE,
    Attorney for Appellant.

No. 6593

IN THE

United States Circuit Court of Appeals

For the Ninth Circuit

1 8

LI BING SUN,

Appellant,

vs.

JOHN D. NAGLE, as Commissioner of
Immigration for the Port of
San Francisco,

Appellee.

BRIEF FOR APPELLEE:

GEO. J. HATFIELD,
United States Attorney,
I. M. PECKHAM and
HERMAN A. VAN DER ZEE,
Asst. United States Attorneys,
Attorneys for Appellee.

Parker Printing Company, 545 Sansome Street, San Francisco

Subject Index

Table of Authorities

No. 6593

United States Circuit Court of Appeals

For the Ninth Circuit

Li Bing Sun,

Appellant,

vs.

John D. Nagle, as Commissioner of
Immigration for the Port of
San Francisco,

Appellee.

BRIEF FOR APPELLEE.

STATEMENT OF THE CASE.

This appeal is from an order of the District Court
for the Southern Division of the Northern District of
California, denying appellant's petition for a writ of
habeas corpus (Tr. pp. 27 and 28).

FACTS OF THE CASE.

Appellant is a male Chinese, 26 years of age. He
left the United States for China on November 22,
1929 after having obtained a Laborer's Return Certi-

ficate (Respondent's Exhibit B, p. 1). He returned to the United States aboard the SS. "President Cleveland", which arrived at San Francisco on November 26, 1930, one year and four days after his departure. He was thereupon excluded by a Board of Special Inquiry which found that the right to return under the certificate was limited by statute to one year, and that appellant had not brought himself within the exception allowed by the statute for two reasons:

First. Because he had not satisfactorily established that he was rendered unable sooner to return by sickness or other cause of disability beyond his control.

Second. Because he presented no certificate of a United States consular representative certifying the facts of any alleged disability. (Tr. pp. 19 to 22, inclusive.)

The board's decision was affirmed by the Secretary of Labor on appeal (Resp. Exhibit A, pp. 30, 29).

THE STATUTE.

Section 5 of the Chinese Exclusion Act of September 13, 1888 as amended and extended (8 U. S. C. A., Sec. 275) provides that:

"No Chinese laborer in the United States shall be permitted, after having left, to return thereto, except under the conditions stated in the following sections."

Section 6 of said Act (8 U. S. C. A., Sec. 276) limits the privilege of return to laborers who have certain kin or certain property in the United States.

Section 7 (8 U. S. C. A., Sec. 277) provides that a Chinese person claiming the right to leave and return shall procure a return certificate prior to departure and that:

> "No Chinese laborer shall be permitted to re-enter the United States without producing to the proper officer in charge at the port of such entry the return certificate herein required."

That section provides further, as follows:

> "The right to return under the said certificate shall be limited to one year; but it may be extended for an additional period, not to exceed a year, in cases where, by reason of sickness or other cause of disability beyond his control, the holder thereof shall be rendered unable sooner to return, which facts shall be fully reported to and investigated by the consular representative of the United States at the port or place from which such laborer departs for the United States, and certified by such representative of the United States to the satisfaction of the Chinese inspector in charge at the port where such Chinese person shall seek to land in the United States * * *"

The validity of the certificate, therefore, is limited to one year, and it may be extended only when two conditions concur:

(1) The applicant must have been rendered unable to return within the year by sickness or other cause of disability beyond his control, and

(2) The facts of the alleged disability must have been fully reported to and investigated by a consular representative of the United States and certified by said representative to the satisfaction of the immigration officials.

THE ISSUES.

Appellee contends that the order of the Court below denying the petition for writ should be affirmed, for two distinct reasons:

(1) The decision of the administrative tribunals that appellant was not rendered unable to return within the year by sickness or other cause of disability beyond his control is final.

(2) Appellant failed in any event to bring himself within the statutory exception because he did not report the facts of the alleged disability to a consular representative for his investigation and certification.

ARGUMENT.

1. THE DECISION OF THE ADMINISTRATIVE TRIBUNALS THAT THE APPLICANT HAD NOT ESTABLISHED THAT HE WAS RENDERED UNABLE TO RETURN WITHIN THE YEAR BY SICKNESS OR OTHER CAUSE OF DISABILITY BEYOND HIS CONTROL IS FINAL.

It is to be noted that by express terms of the statute the right to return is limited to one year but *"may"* be extended not to exceed an additional year. This power to extend the time may be exercised only when sickness or other disability beyond the applicant's control has rendered him unable sooner to return, and only when the facts of such disability are certified "to the *satisfaction* of" the immigration officials.

It is obvious, therefore, that the power to extend the time for reentry is discretionary with the immigration officials, and is only to be exercised when they are satisfied that the delay was caused by such a disability as is mentioned in the statute. Necessarily their discretion could not be interfered with on habeas corpus.

> " * * * in such a case, as in all others, in which a statute gives a discretionary power to an officer, to be exercised by him upon his own opinion of certain facts, he is made the sole and exclusive judge of the existence of those facts, and no other tribunal, unless expressly authorized by law to do so, is at liberty to re-examine or controvert the sufficiency of the evidence on which he acted."
>
> *Nishimura Ekiu v. U. S.,* 142 U. S. 651, at 660.
> *Lem Moon Sing v. U. S.,* 158 U. S. 538, at 544.

On principle, it would seem that the inquiry into the facts need proceed no further than this. However, we shall touch upon the evidence on the issue of fact passed upon by the executive officers.

Section 23 of the Immigration Act approved May 26, 1924 (8 U. S. C. A., Sec. 221) provides

"Whenever any alien attempts to enter the United States the burden of proof shall be upon such alien to establish that he is not subject to exclusion under any provision of the Immigration laws."

The most recent expression of the United States Supreme Court is contained in the opinion of Mr. Justice Holmes in

U. S. ex rel. Polymeris et al. v. Trudell, 52 S. Ct. 143, decided January 4, 1932,

wherein the relators were seeking to return without a visa after a temporary visit abroad and the statute there involved prohibited reentry without such a visa, except under such conditions as may be prescribed by regulations of the Secretary of Labor. In that case Mr. Justice Holmes said:

"The relators have no right to enter the United States unless it has been given to them by the United States. The burden of proof is upon them to show that they have the right. Immigration Act of 1924, Sec. 23, 43 Stat. 165 (U. S. Code, Tit. 8, Sec. 221, 8 U. S. C. A., Sec. 221) * * * The relators must show not only that they ought to be admitted, but that the United States by the only voice authorized to express its will has said so."

The statutes likewise expressly provide that the decision of the Board of Special Inquiry and of the Secretary of Labor "shall be final".

8 U. S. C. A., Secs. 153, 174.

In

United States v. Ju Toy, 198 U. S. 253, at 262,

the Supreme Court said:

"It is established, as we have said, that the Act purports to make the decision of the Department final, *whatever the ground on which the right to enter the country is claimed*—as well when it is citizenship as when it is domicil and the belonging to a class excepted from the Exclusion Acts. *United States v. Sing Tuck,* 194 U. S. 161, 167; *Lem Moon Sing v. United States,* 158 U. S. 538, 546, 547."

In

Chin Yow v. United States, 208 U. S. 8,

the Supreme Court said:

"If the petitioner was not denied a fair opportunity to *produce* the evidence that he desired, or a fair though summary hearing, the case can proceed no farther. *Those facts are the foundation of the jurisdiction of the District Court, if it has any jurisdiction at all.* It must not be supposed that the mere allegation of the facts opens the merits of the case, *whether those facts are proved or not.* And, by way of caution, we may add that jurisdiction would not be established simply by proving that the Commissioner and the Department of Commerce and Labor did not accept certain sworn statements as true, *even though no contrary or impeaching testimony was adduced.*"

And in conclusion the Supreme Court said:

"But unless and until it is proved to the satisfaction of the Judge that a hearing properly socalled was denied, the merits of the case are not open, and, we may add, the denial of a hearing cannot be established by proving that the decision was wrong."

In

Tisi v. Tod, 264 U. S. 131,

the Supreme Court said:

"We do not discuss the evidence; because the correctness of the judgment of the lower court *is not to be determined by inquiring whether the conclusion drawn by the Secretary of Labor from the evidence was correct* or by deciding whether the evidence was such that, if introduced in a court of law, it would be held legally sufficient to prove the fact found."

In the recent case of

Louie Lung Gooey v. Nagle, 49 Fed. (2d) 1016,

the Court said:

"We cannot too often repeat that in immigration cases of this character brought before us for review, the question is not whether we, with the same facts before us originally, might have found differently from the Board; rather is it a question of determining simply whether or not the hearing was conducted with due regard to those rights of the applicant that are embraced in the

phrase 'due process of law.' *Tang Tung v. Edsel,*
223 U. S. 673. Even if we were firmly convinced
that the Board's decision was wrong, if it were
shown that they had not acted arbitrarily but had
reached their conclusions after a fair consideration of all the facts presented, we should have no
recourse.''

With these fundamental principles in mind, we proceed to analyze the facts as disclosed by the evidence
before the immigration authorities.

Appellant, as we have stated, departed from the
United States on November 22, 1929. The report of
the American Consul General at Hongkong (Respondent's Ex. A, p. 26) is as follows:

"Li Bing Sun applied personally August 14,
1930, for assurance of favorable action on overtime certificate after expiration one year, was
examined by the United States Public Health
Officer this office and certified able to return to
the United States, was advised to return to San
Francisco before November 22nd. On September
20th he applied by mail for extension and was informed of provisions of law concerning issuance
of overtime certificates and the necessity for submitting proof of disability beyond control, in his
case a medical certificate. No further record.
Apparently secured approval of his form for
passage arriving United States before November
22nd and later changed plans without reference
this Consulate General.''

The last sentence of that cablegram is borne out by the endorsement on the reverse of appellant's return certificate showing that he appeared at the Consulate General at Hongkong on October 20, 1930, and that his form was indorsed for passage by a vessel sailing on *October 23, 1930* (see reverse of certificate—Respondent's Ex. B, p. 1).

The record shows, therefore, that on August 14, 1930, while he still had more than four months left to return to the United States within the year, appellant applied for assurance that at the expiration of the year he would be granted a favorable overtime certificate, and that he was then examined and *found to be able to return* to the United States and was then advised to return before the year expired.

It is also shown that a month later he applied to the Consulate by mail for an extension and was requested to "fully report the facts," as required by the statute, by furnishing a medical certificate showing said facts. It is shown that appellant ignored this request to supply the facts of the alleged disability.

It is shown further that a month later, viz., on October 20, 1930, appellant appeared at the Consulate and obtained an endorsement allowing him to book passage on a vessel sailing on *October 23, 1930 without* any *suggestion* of *disability*. He did not, however, proceed to the United States on October 23d, but, as we shall show, elected to remain over for a later sailing.

Upon arrival at San Francisco appellant testified before the Board of Special Inquiry as follows:

"Q. How many visits have you made to China as a laborer on Form 432?

A. Two.

Q. Did you know prior to leaving on both of those two visits that you must return to the U. S. within one year from the date of your departure?

A. Yes.

Q. What caused you to return to the U. S. after a year from date of departure?

A. I was suffering from boils on my feet and on account of that I had to postpone my return to the U. S. I expected to return on the 'Pres. Grant' *but I thought that being four days overtime would not cause any difficulty in my landing.*

Q. When did the 'Pres. Grant' leave Hongkong?

A. About the 30th day of the 8th month, this year, Chinese reckoning (October 21, 1930).

Q. When did you cease having trouble from boils?

A. About the 16th day of the 8th month, (October 7, 1930).

Q. Then you deliberately delayed your return to the U. S. until the 'Pres. Cleveland' sailed. Is that right?

A. I was detained for about two weeks in Hongkong on visits to the doctor for examination.

Q. Do you mean the U. S. Public Health doctor?

A. Yes. * * *

Q. When you were in Hongkong did you go to the American Consulate?

A. Yes.

Q. Do you remember the date when you first went there?

A. It was before I went to the U. S. Public Health Service. It was about the 29th day of the 8th month. (October 20th)

Q. You knew then that you could not return here on the 'Pres. Grant', did you not?

A. Yes.

Q. Why did you not get an overtime certificate from the Consul?

A. `I attempted to secure an overtime certificate but the American Consul refused to issue it to me. He did not state any reasons for refusing to do so.'' (Tr. pp. 17 to 19, incl.)

In his examination, therefore, appellant at first attributed his failure to return within the time allowed to the fact that he was suffering from boils.

This particular claim, as appellant now tacitly concedes in his brief, is without substance. Appellant was examined on August 14th in China and was found to be able to return to the United States then. On September 20th he requested a certificate of disability from the American Consul but ignored the Consul's request that he furnish a report of the facts in the form of a medical certificate. If such a disability existed, appellant was required under the act to report the facts fully to the American Consul for his investigation and certification. He was requested to do this by sending a medical certificate, and this he did not do.

Appellant's second version is that "I expected to return on the President Grant but thought that being four days overdue would not cause any difficulty in my landing". We shall advert to this statement later.

Appellant argues that he would have returned on a vessel leaving Hongkong about October 21st or October 23rd but that he was delayed two weeks by quarantine restrictions.

We might remark here that "a quarantine is not 'actus Dei' but an ordinary incident of travel by sea, to be contemplated by one undertaking a voyage" (21 Opn. Atty. Genl. at p. 576).

In any event it is not shown that appellant could not have returned by the vessel sailing from Hongkong on October 23, 1930, which would have brought him here well within the year.

Appellant in his brief assumes that this sailing was on October 21st. The endorsement of the Consul, however, on the reverse of the laborer's return certificate (Respondent's Exhibit B, p. 1) shows that he was scheduled to sail on October 23, 1930. His own testimony merely is that the sailing was *"about"* October 21st. It may be taken as established, therefore, that the sailing was on October 23rd, since the notation of the Consul was made at Hongkong only three days before said sailing, and it may be assumed that said notation was in accordance with the facts as then disclosed to the Consul.

Appellant states that he expected to return by that sailing. The notation of the Consul shows that the Consul was informed that such was appellant's intention. Remember, in all this transaction, there is no suggestion of disability. Appellant, however, says that he thought that being four days over time would not cause any difficulty in his landing. The Secretary of Labor was of the opinion that this was the real reason for his failure to return within the year, and that appellant elected to remain over one sailing in sanguine assumption that as to him the limitation of the statute would not be enforced (Respondent's Exhibit A, p. 29).

Appellant's argument now is that he ran afoul of a quarantine regulation which held him at Hongkong for about two weeks longer than he had expected.

This argument is not supported by the record. The inspection card of the United States Public Health Service at Hongkong (Respondent's Exhibit B, p. 3) shows that appellant was vaccinated on October 18, 1930 and appeared for inspection only on that date and on October 20th and October 21st. There is nothing in the record showing that he appeared for inspection or was required to appear for inspection at any time between October 21st and the date when he actually sailed, two weeks later.

There is in the record a certificate of the United States Public Health Service, issued on November 4th, 1930, the day appellant actually sailed for the United

States, certifying that appellant had complied with the provisions of executive order of June 21, 1929, "and as far as can be ascertained he has not been in contact during the last 14 days with anyone suffering from cerebro-spinal meningitis" (Respondent's Exhibit B, p. 2). From this appellant would have us assume that the executive order mentioned required appellant's detention for 14 days and that he was so detained for 14 days prior to November 4th and hence was unable to sail on the vessel departing about October 21st or October 23rd.

This assumption is likewise without basis in the record. While appellant stated that he was detained for about two weeks on visits to the doctor for examination, the inspection card shows that the only visits he made were on October 18th, October 20th and October 21st. The certificate that as far as could be ascertained the passenger had not been in contact, during the 14 days previous to sailing, with anyone suffering from cerebro-spinal meningitis does not state that the passenger was detained during these 14 days or required to report for inspection during those 14 days.

As a matter of fact, the executive order of June 21, 1929, No. 5143, promulgated by President Hoover under authority of Section 7 of the Act of February 15, 1893, regarding quarantine powers, merely directed that no person might come from any port in China, except under such conditions as the Secretary of the Treasury might prescribe.

. The regulations of the Secretary of the Treasury which were in force at the time appellant embarked from Hongkong were those issued on November 6, 1929, the pertinent portion of which is as follows:

"1. Persons shall be permitted to embark for United States ports only * * * under the immediate supervision of a medical officer of the United States Public Health Service, who shall assure himself that such persons are free from signs or symptoms of meningitis.

"2. Persons *known* or *suspected* by the medical officer to have resided within 14 days in premises in which meningitis then existed or otherwise having had direct contact with cases of meningitis, shall not be permitted to embark."

The regulations, therefore, do not require detention for 14 days nor inspection for 14 days, but merely prohibit the embarkation of persons *known* or *suspected* to have been in contact with the disease within 14 days. The inspection card in the record shows that appellant appeared for inspection only on October 18, October 20th and October 21st.

So far as the record shows there was absolutely nothing to prevent appellant from sailing on October 23, 1930. The inspection card shows that his inspection was completed on October 21st. Furthermore, as stated above, quarantine restrictions are necessary incidents of ocean travel and should be contemplated by the passenger.

Certainly appellant showed nothing which prevented him from sailing even earlier than October 23rd. His alleged sickness up to October 7th does not appear to have furnished any such reason, because on August 14th he was able to return, and on September 20th he claimed to be disabled from returning but declined to furnish the facts of the alleged disability by filing a medical certificate.

In view of the conflicting and unsatisfactory character of the showing offered by appellant as to why he did not return within the year, we submit that there was certainly nothing arbitrary in the refusal of the executive authorities to exercise their discretion in his favor by finding that he was rendered unable to return within the year by a disability beyond his control.

This Court has passed upon similar facts in two cases.

In

Nagle v. Toy Young Quen, 22 F. (2d) 18,

the appellee obtained a certification of the facts from the Consul on the claim that his delay beyond the year was caused by illness of his mother, resulting in his marriage being delayed. On arrival at San Francisco he testified that he was delayed by illness of his mother and that he had to remain in China to care for her. The Department was not satisfied that his delay was actually due to the illness of his mother, as he claimed. This Court said:

"As the reasons given by petitioner for delay in returning were found by the Immigration officials to be insufficient in fact, and as their conclusion is in harmony with the statute cited, the demurrer was well taken and should have been sustained."

In

Nagle v. Won Bing Jung, (C. C. A. 9) 22 F. (2d) 20,

the appellee obtained a certification of facts from the Consul and the file also contained a statement from the American Consul that the appellee had applied for a certification alleging that he had been afflicted with hernia but that a medical examination disclosed no sign of such an affliction. Before a board of special inquiry the appellee stated that he was delayed by unsettled conditions in China, making travel connections impossible. This Court said:

"In the light of the contradictory statements made by petitioner the court will not disturb the well-supported finding of the examining authorities."

In the case at bar there is a similar situation. The appellant's original claim of disability by illness was found, on examination by the medical officer on August 14, 1920, to be unfounded. In his second attempt to obtain assurances of an extension, likewise based on alleged physical disability, he did not comply with the Consul's request to furnish a medical certificate showing the facts. He now claims that quarantine restrictions kept him beyond the year. His testimony, however, would tend to indicate that he intentionally remained in China until too late for him to return within the year.

Certainly there is nothing surprising in the fact that the executive authorities were not satisfied of the existence of such a disability as the statute contemplates, upon this state of the record.

In

Tulsidas et al. v. Insular Collector of Customs,
262 U. S. 258 at 266,

the Supreme Court said:

"It was for them to establish their exemption from the prohibition of the law, for them to satisfy the Insular officials charged with the administration of the law. If they left their exemption in doubt and dispute, they cannot complain of a decision against it."

In the same case the Supreme Court made the following significant statement:

"It would seem, therefore, as if something more is necessary to justify review than the basis of a dispute. The law is in administration of a policy which, while it confers a privilege, is concerned to preserve it from abuse and, therefore, has appointed officers to determine the conditions of it, and speedily determine them, *and on practical considerations, not to subject them to litigious controversies, and disputable, if not financial, distinctions."*

Where the facts are so disputable as they are in the present case, and where the showing as to the alleged disability is so unsatisfactory and incomplete, we submit that there are no grounds for interference with the executive decision that appellant had not brought himself within the exception authorized by the statute to be made.

---

2. APPELLANT FAILED TO BRING HIMSELF WITHIN THE STATUTORY EXCEPTION, BECAUSE HE DID NOT REPORT THE FACTS OF THE ALLEGED DISABILITY TO A CONSULAR REPRESENTATIVE FOR HIS INVESTIGATION AND CERTIFICATION.

As we have pointed out above, the statute permits extension of the time for return under a laborer's return certificate only where certain disabilities exist, and in such cases the statute expressly provides further that the

> "facts *shall* be fully reported to and investigated by the consular representative of the United States * * * and certified * * * to the satisfaction of the Chinese Inspector in charge * * * ."

It is obvious that the purpose of this requirement is to insure proper investigation of the facts in China, where investigation would be productive of result. This statutory mode has obviously been prescribed to insure against false claims being made upon arrival in the United States which could not be so effectively investigated or combatted here.

It is contended in appellant's brief that the absence of a consular certificate of the facts in this case is due to no omission of appellant, but to a dereliction of the Consul.

In this contention appellant points to his statement, "I attempted to secure an overtime certificate but the American Consul refused to issue it to me" (Tr. p. 19).

Consuls are public officers, as to whom the maxim *"omnia praesumitus rite facta"* applies, especially in the exercise of quasi-judicial functions.

Nowhere in the record is there a scintilla of evidence that it was ever claimed before the Consul or reported to him that appellant was being held for fourteen days by the Public Health Officers. The endorsement of the Consul on the reverse of the laborer's return certificate expressly shows that on appellant's last appearance before the American Consul on October 20, 1930, the Consul was led to believe that appellant was sailing from Hongkong on October 23, 1930, the Consul having noted that information upon the certificate, with no suggestion of any claim of disability. This also is in accordance with appellant's first explanation of the reason for his delay beyond the year, viz., that he expected to return on the steamer "President Grant", but thought that being four days overtime would not cause any difficulty in his landing (Tr. p. 17). He gambled and lost! His statement later in the examination, that he was detained for about two weeks on visits to the doctor for examination, is obviously an afterthought. As we have heretofore pointed out, the record does not bear out the claim that he was actually prevented from sailing in time to arrive in the United States within the year by any quarantine regulation or inspection.

Nowhere in his testimony did appellant state that he had reported the facts of this alleged delay to the Consul. The brief merely assumes that he made such a report, and further assumes in the face of the presumption of *rite facta,* that the Consul was derelict in his duty, and failed to investigate or certify facts reported to him. Certainly, every presumption of official regularity is opposed to any such inference, particularly in the absence of evidence not only that appellant was actually prevented from sailing sooner by restrictions imposed upon him by the public health officers, but also that he ever reported such alleged impediment to the Consul.

Appellant attempts to dispose of the Consul's notation on the reverse of the return certificate dated October 20, 1930, that the holder was sailing on October 23, 1930, by a statement that the Consul had no authority to limit or extend the appellant's stay abroad. But the significance and purpose of that endorsement, as appellant is doubtless well aware, is that the travel documents of aliens in the Orient are endorsed by the American Consul to permit them to book passage for the United States without question. As indicated by the endorsement and by the Consul's cablegram, on October 20th appellant called at the Consulate and obtained approval of his form to sail on October 23rd. Whatever occurred to cause a change in that arrangement, it is obvious that appellant never thereafter returned to the Consulate nor informed the Consul of any contemplated or necessary change.

The authorities cited by appellant are not in point.

The cases of

Nagle v. Wong Bing Jung,

and

Nagle v. Toy Young Quen, supra,

we have already discussed. In those cases there was a Consular certificate of the facts of the alleged disability, but the Immigration authorities found that the appellees had not established that the delay beyond the year was caused by a disability beyond their control, and this Court held that the determination of the Immigration authorities on that point could not be interfered with.

In the case of

Ex parte Woo Show How, 17 Fed. (2d) 652,

which appellant cites, the applicant likewise presented a certificate of facts by the Consul and the Board found, "the applicant has exhibited scars on one of his legs that indicate healed sores, and his claim of disability may be true." Hence in that case questions of the existence of the disability, and of absence of a Consular certificate of the facts, were not involved. The applicant in that case was excluded because he did not arrive until after the second year had expired, the statute limiting extensions to not more than a year. The facts were, however, that the applicant had reported the facts to the Consul in time to permit him to return well within the second year, but instead of making an investigation and certification of the facts, favorable or unfavorable, the Consul refused to certify the facts at all. Subsequently the superior officers of the Consul in the Department of State at Washington instructed the Consul that his action was erroneous, and that he should certify the facts. Were it not for the admittedly erroneous omission of the Consul in that case, the applicant would have arrived within the time allowed for the extension to which he was admittedly entitled.

The case of

Ex parte Yee Gee, 17 Fed. (2d) 653,

involved virtually the same situation. There, the applicant presented an overtime certificate of the Consul, and the Department of Labor found that his claim of delay due to illness and disrupted communications "is probably true", but that due to a mistake of the Consular Officer in refusing to furnish a certificate of the facts until advised some months later by the Department of State that such refusal was erroneous and that he should certify the facts, the applicant did not arrive in the United States until after the period of a year for which a certificate might be extended had expired.

In each of those cases, therefore, it was conceded that so far as the alleged disability was concerned, the applicants were entitled to an extension. In each of those cases, likewise, the applicants had fully reported the facts of the alleged disability to the Consul. There was no dispute about either of those points. The applicants in those cases, although entitled to the extension of one year, and although they had obtained Consular certifications of the facts entitling them to such extension, were prevented from returning within the period for which the extension might be granted by an admittedly erroneous stand of the Consular Officer which resulted in the withholding of the proper Consular action until the period for extension had expired.

It is obvious that the doctrine of these cases is in nowise applicable to the facts of the case at bar. It will be noted that the opinion in the *Yee Gee case* was written by the same District Judge who decided the case at bar in the Court below.

In the case at bar, not only has appellant failed to satisfy the officers of the existence of any disability preventing his return within the year, but the record shows that he did not report the facts of the alleged disability, upon which he *now* relies, to the Consular Officer and made no attempt to have such facts investigated or certified by the Consul.

Appellant objects to the action of the Secretary of Labor in considering the report made by the Consul relative to the Consul's record of this case. It will be observed, however, that upon receipt of this communication from the Consul, appellant's Washington attorney was advised of it, and was allowed ten days within which to review it (Respondent's Exhibit "A", page 28). Thereafter, appellant's Washington attorney filed an additional brief on January 30, 1931, stating that he had examined the communication from the American Consul, and stating further:

> "This communication appears to fully confirm the applicant's testimony on this point." (Respondent's Exhibit "A", page 24.)

Appellant's attorney made no objection to the consideration of the Consul's communication. He made no request for any continuance or opportunity to furnish any additional evidence after he had examined that communication.

From this it is immediately obvious that there was no unfairness here.

In

Kamiyama v. Carr, 44 Fed. (2d) 503, at 505,

this Court said:

> "Where an alien is represented by an attorney before the Immigration Authorities, it is clear

·that the very least that can be required of such
a party so represented is that he should object
in such proceedings to the unfairness of which he
later complains to the Court in habeas corpus proceedings.''

The Court also said in that case:

"It is sufficient, however, to say that after this
recommendation was made, appellant argued the
case before the Board of Review, without any
objection to the recommendation in that regard
and without making any contention that the statement of the inspector should not be considered
by the Board of Review.''

See, also:

Soo Hoo Hung et al. v. Nagle (C. C. A. 9), 3
Fed. (2d) 267, at 268.

In the cases cited at page 28 of Appellant's Brief,
evidence was considered without the knowledge of the
alien or his attorney, and neither the alien nor his
attorney was given any opportunity to meet it.

The ultimate contention of appellant is that it is
immaterial whether or not he reported the facts of
the alleged disability to a Consular Officer.

Such a contention is directly in the teeth of the
statutory provision that the facts *shall* be fully reported to and investigated by the Consular Officer.
If his contention be correct, there is no need for that
requirement in the statute because no applicant need
report the facts of the alleged disability to the Consul.

Any applicant might disregard that provision in the statute entirely, and proceed to the United States for a determination of his right to enter without making any report to the Consul.

While we are not here concerned with the wisdom of the statutory requirement, the necessity for some such procedure is well exemplified in the present case, wherein an effort to ascertain here just what the facts are relative to the delay occurring in China, is attended with such difficulty and doubt.

Appellant cites:

U. S. ex rel. Patti v. Curran, 22 Fed. (2d) 314.

However, the documents in that case were permits issued under Section 10 of the Immigration Act of 1924 (8 U. S. C. A. Sec. 210), and the statute relative thereto expressly states that the permit shall have no effect except to show that the holder is returning from a temporary visit abroad, and that the permit shall not be construed as the exclusive means of establishing that fact. Furthermore, no alien is *required* to obtain such a permit, but any alien "may make application" for such a permit.

In the case of

U. S. ex rel. Gentile v. Day, 25 Fed. (2d) 717,

which appellant cites, the quota Act of 1921 (42 Stat. 5, 540) was involved. That statute exempted from the quota restrictions aliens of certain professions. The applicant in that case was admitted for a temporary visit in exemption of the quota, but it later turned out that at the time of his entry he was of an exempt class, because he was an artist. The Court merely held that the fact of his having temporarily entered as a visitor did not alter the fact that on his arrival he was entitled to permanent entry as an artist.

We can see no conceivable analogy between those cases and the case at bar.

CONCLUSION.

The extension of a laborer's return certificate is, by express terms of the statute, only to be allowed in the discretion of the Immigration Officials when they are satisfied that the delay was caused by disability beyond the applicant's control. As a condition precedent to such extension, it is required that the facts of the alleged disability be fully reported to the Consul abroad for his investigation and certification. Appellant failed to show satisfactorily that he was delayed by such a disability. His ultimate reliance is on an alleged delay by certain quarantine restrictions. We have shown that this claim is not borne out by the record. In any event, a quarantine restriction is an ordinary incident of ocean travel, which should be contemplated by a passenger. Furthermore, there is no evidence whatever that appellant ever reported any such alleged disability to the Consul, and the record shows that no such report was made.

We submit that the order of the Court below was correct and should be affirmed.

Respectfully submitted,

GEO. J. HATFIELD,
United States Attorney,

I. M. PECKHAM and

HERMAN A. VAN DER ZEE,
Asst. United States Attorneys,
Attorneys for Appellee.

No. 6593

IN THE

9

United States Circuit Court of Appeals

For the Ninth Circuit

LI BING SUN,

Appellant,

vs.

JOHN D. NAGLE, as Commissioner of Immigration for the Port of San Francisco,

Appellee.

APPELLANT'S PETITION FOR A REHEARING.

STEPHEN M. WHITE,
576 Sacramento Street, San Francisco,
*Attorney for Appellant
and Petitioner.*

PERNAU-WALSH PRINTING CO., SAN FRANCISCO

No. 6593

LI BING SUN,

Appellant,

VS.

JOHN D. NAGLE, as Commissioner of Immigration for the Port of San Francisco,

Appellee.

APPELLANT'S PETITION FOR A REHEARING.

To the Honorable Curtis D. Wilbur, Presiding Judge, and to the Associate Judges of the United States Circuit Court of Appeals for the Ninth Circuit:

The appellant respectfully petitions this Honorable Court for a rehearing of the above-entitled cause.

Briefly, the facts are: The appellant, a male Chinese, was first admitted to the United States by the immigration authorities on February 16, 1920. On November 22, 1929, he departed from the United States for China on a laborer's Return Certificate, which was issued by the immigration authorities upon proof that he had property in the United States to the amount of $1,000.00. In accordance with the terms of his return certificate, the appellant was required to return to the United States within one year from the date of his departure, unless by reason of sickness or other disability beyond his control he was unable to return within one year. Returning to the United States from this trip, he departed from China on November 4, 1930, or eighteen days *prior* to the expiration of the one year period, and arrived in the United States on November 26, 1930, or four (4) days *after* the expiration of the one year period. He was excluded and ordered deported by the immigration authorities on the ground that he did not present an overtime certificate issued by an American Consular officer abroad showing that his absence from the United States for a period of four (4) days beyond the one (1) year period prescribed by his laborer's return certificate was caused by sickness or other disability beyond his control, although the appellant claimed that he had applied for such a certificate to an American Consular officer prior to his departure from China, but that this officer refused to issue the same.

As we interpret the rule laid down in the opinion filed, a Chinese alien, who has departed from the United States on a Laborer's Return Certificate, which has been issued under Section Six (6) of the Act of Congress of September 13, 1888 (8 U. S. C. A. Sec. 275), but who is unable to return to the United States within one year from the date of his departure therefrom by reason of sickness or other disability beyond his control, is entitled, as a matter of right, to obtain from the American Consular officer abroad an overtime certificate, *providing the application therefor is made after a year from the date of the alien's departure from the United States.* The pertinent part of the Court's opinion is as follows:

"The instant case is distinguished from the cases of Ex parte Yee Gee, 17 Fed. (2d) 653, and Ex parte Woo Show How, 17 Fed. (2d) 652. Therein the petitioners applied for overtime certificates after a year from their departure from the United States had expired. The district courts held, and rightly we think, that the consuls should have issued the certificates and left the final decision to the immigration authorities in the United States. Here the appellant applied for an overtime certificate before the time legally allowed him had expired and we think the consul acted correctly in refusing to issue a certificate, or rather in refusing to issue a certificate, or rather in refusing to issue what would have been assurance of favorable action on an overtime certificate."

Thus, in the case at bar, the Court held that the application for an overtime certificate, being made *prior* to the expiration of the one year period from the date of his departure from the United States, was premature and that, therefore, there was no duty imposed upon the American Consular officer to issue such a document.

We do not question the correctness of the rule laid down and, in fact, we now freely concede that it is the only rule possible under the applicable statute, which provides, in part, as follows:

"The right to return under the said certificate (Laborer's Return Certificate) shall be limited to one year; but it may be extended for an additional period, not to exceed a year, in cases where, by reason of sickness or other cause of disability beyond his control, the holder thereof shall be rendered unable sooner to return, which facts shall be fully reported to and investigated by the consular representative of the United States at the port or place from which such laborer departs for the United States, * * *."

(8 *U. S. C. A.* Sec. 277.)

Manifestly, a different ruling would permit a laborer to apply for an overtime certificate at a time far in advance and would require the consular officer to investigate the facts of his alleged disability and to certify whether or not the same *rendered* the laborer unable to return within the one year period, although the one year period might not expire for several months.

However, we earnestly believe that the adoption of the rule requires an interpretation of the statute in respect to reckoning the time allowed for the laborer's return to the United States. In other words, does the word "return," as used in the statute, mean that the laborer must actually be in the United States within one year from the date of his departure therefrom or does it mean only that he shall be bound for the United States at the expiration of the one year period?

Webster defines the word "return" as "to turn back; to go or come again to the same place." Hence, in the one instance, a "return" may be said to be made at the point of the journey where one turns back or is homeward bound; in the other instance, a "return" may be said to be made at the point where the journey actually commenced or originated. However, entirely aside from the adequacy of, at least, one of its accepted definitions, we respectfully submit that the rule adopted, as to the time when an application may be made to an American consular officer for an overtime certificate, fully impels the conclusion that the word "return" shall be construed with respect to the time when the laborer is bound for the United States, rather than in respect to the time when he actually enters the United States.

In the case of *Ex parte Yee Gee,* 17 Fed. (2d) 653, which has been expressly approved by this Honorable Court in the case at bar, it was expressly held that the expiration of the time limit of the laborer's return certificate became of little consequence where the facts showed that the laborer was actually bound for the United States *before* the expiration of the time limit. Quoting from the case cited, at page 657:

"* * * The expiration of the time limit, under the circumstances here, applicant has made every effort to secure his document on which to take passage, and where he was actually on an American ship bound for his return port before the expiration of the time limit, becomes of little consequence, * * *."

The consular overtime certificate is obviously intended not only as a benefit to the laborer to lessen the burden of proof placed upon him to establish his disability, but, also, as a guide and protection to the immigration authorities against fraudulent claims of disability. However, if a laborer be absolutely unable to travel at a time when it would ordinarily be possible for him to reach the United States within the one year period, but able to travel before the expiration of the time limit, although too late to reach the United States, we submit that unjust and absurd results will follow in the event that the word "return" be construed to mean the time of his actual arrival in the United States; if he commence his homeward journey at the time when he is able to travel, as he ordinarily and reasonably would be expected and required to do, he will not be able to enter, at least, his ability to establish his right of entry will be seriously handicapped, because of the lack of a certificate, which it was impossible for him to obtain; yet, if he merely linger abroad from the time when he is able to travel until the expiration of the one year period, he will be in a position to obtain the certificate. It does not seem reasonable that Congress contemplated to discriminate in favor of one who lingers abroad, when he is able to travel, in order to obtain the consular certificate, over one who endeavors to shorten his absence from the United States as much as possible by commencing his homeward journey as soon as he is able to travel.

If, however, the word "return" be construed to mean the time when the laborer turns back to or is bound for the United States, there will be no such unfair or unreasonable discrimination as suggested. The laborer, who commences his journey as soon as he is able to travel and who is actually *bound* for the United States at the expiration of the one year period prescribed by his return certificate, will need no consular overtime certificate, because he has returned within the time limit. As a result, the laborer, who lingers abroad from the time that he is able to travel until the expiration of the one year period, for no reason at all, except to obtain the consular overtime certificate, will be entirely eliminated from the picture, and, thus, full effect will be given to the intention of Congress that a laborer's absence from the United States shall not be unduly prolonged.

In *Stockyards Loan Company v. Nichols,* 245 Fed. 511, C. C. A. 8th, at page 516, it is said:

> "In order to ascertain the intention of the Legislature * * *, the court may look to each part of the statute, to other statutes upon the same or related subjects, to the old law upon the subject, to the evils and mischiefs to be remedied, and to the natural or absurd consequences of any particular interpretation. (Cases cited.)"

> *Church of the Holy Trinity v. U. S.,* 143 U. S. 457, 12 Sup. Ct. 511, 36 L. Ed. 226;
>
> *Lau Ow Bew v. U. S.,* 144 U. S. 47, 12 Sup. Ct. 517, 36 L. Ed. 340;
>
> *U. S. v. Gue Lim,* 176 U. S. 459, 20 Sup. Ct. 415, 44 L. Ed. 544.

In the case of *In re Ah Quan,* 21 Fed. 182, the Court said:

> "The act imposes a duty and obligation on the government, through the Collector, correlative and precedent to the obligation imposed upon the Chinese laborer to produce the prescribed certificate, and the obligation of the latter to produce the certificate necessarily arises subsequently to, and is dependent upon, the performance of the

correlative and precedent duty and obligation on
the part of the government to furnish it. To hold
that Congress intended to require the performance of the dependent obligation on the part of
the Chinese laborer until the government has discharged its correlative and precedent duty and
obligation upon which his obligation rests, imposed by the act, by furnishing the certificate and
thereby rendering it possible for him to produce
it, would be to attribute to Congress a deliberate
intent to enact a palpable and glaring absurdity,
thereby violating one of the most venerable
canons of statutory construction, that a statute
must not be so construed as to lead to an absurd
conclusion. We must conclude, therefore, that it
was not intended to require the production of the
certificate by those who departed from the
country before it was possible to obtain it. And
that Congress did not intend to exclude such
Chinese laborers as were in this country at the
time mentioned is clearly manifest, because it
has said so in express terms in the provision of
section 3, 'that the two foregoing sections (excluding Chinese laborers) shall not apply to
Chinese laborers who were in the United States
on the seventeenth day of November, 1880,' etc.
It is clear, from the necessities of the case, that
this section is only applicable to those who departed after the act, and who had the opportunity
to procure the certificate. To hold otherwise
would be to render this clause, making the impossible certificate the only evidence as to those
who had departed before the passage of the act,
absolutely inconsistent with the clause of section
3 referred to, that the preceding sections 'shall
not apply to Chinese laborers who were in the

United States' at the designated period, and render that provision wholly nugatory, as well as to violate the treaty which the act professes to execute and not to abrogate. The different provisions of the statute must be so construed, if possible, that they can stand together, and not so as to nullify each other."

Chew Heong v. U. S., 112 U. S. 536, 5 Sup. Ct. 255, 28 L. Ed. 770;

In re Low Yam Chow, 13 Fed. 605;

In re Chin Ah On, 18 Fed. 506;

In re Leong Yick Dew, 19 Fed. 490.

We, therefore, respectfully submit that as long as it is impossible for a Chinese laborer to obtain a consular overtime certificate until the one year period prescribed by his return certificate has expired, it is proper and necessary, in order to be consistent and to avoid unjust and unreasonable consequences, to reckon the time allowed for his return under the return certificate with respect to the time when he is actually bound for the United States, rather than with respect to the time of his actual arrival or entry in the United States.

It is established, in fact, expressly conceded, that the appellant departed from China on his homeward journey to the United States on November 4, 1930, or eighteen days prior to the expiration of the one year period prescribed by his return certificate. As long as he was, therefore, bound for the United States at the expiration of the time limit, it will follow that his return was made within the time limit.

The Court is at liberty to draw its own conclusions from the established facts. In *Weedin v. Mon Him,* 4 Fed. (2d) 533, at page 534, C. C. A. 9th, it is said:

"* * *. In disposing of the question of the appellee's right to enter the United States we are not confined to a consideration of the grounds on which he was excluded by the local authorities; we may properly advert to other ground on which as matter of law that conclusion would follow."

We respectfully ask that the petition for a rehearing be granted.

Dated, San Francisco,
April 23, 1932.

STEPHEN M. WHITE,
*Attorney for Appellant
and Petitioner.*

CERTIFICATE OF COUNSEL.

I hereby certify that I am counsel for appellant and petitioner in the above entitled cause and that in my judgment the foregoing petition for a rehearing is well founded in point of law as well as in fact and that said petition for a rehearing is not interposed for delay.

Dated, San Francisco,
April 23, 1932.

STEPHEN M. WHITE,
*Counsel for Appellant
and Petitioner.*

United States
Circuit Court of Appeals
For the Ninth Circuit.

2 s

PUGET SOUND NAVIGATION COMPANY,
a Corporation,

Appellant,

vs.

HANS NELSON,

Appellee.

Transcript of Record.

Upon Appeal from the United States District Court for
the Western District of Washington,
Northern Division.

FILED
OCT - 7 1931

PAUL P. O'BRIEN,
CLERK

Filmer Bros Co. Print, 330 Jackson St., S. F., Cal.

United States
Circuit Court of Appeals
For the Ninth Circuit.

PUGET SOUND NAVIGATION COMPANY,
a Corporation,

Appellant,

vs.

HANS NELSON,

Appellee.

Transcript of Record.

Upon Appeal from the United States District Court for the Western District of Washington, Northern Division.

Filmer Bros Co. Print, 330 Jackson St., S. F., Cal.

INDEX TO THE PRINTED TRANSCRIPT OF RECORD.

[Clerk's Note: When deemed likely to be of an important nature, errors or doubtful matters appearing in the original certified record are printed literally in italic; and, likewise, cancelled matter appearing in the original certified record is printed and cancelled herein accordingly. When possible, an omission from the text is indicated by printing in italic the two words between which the omission seems to occur.]

Index.   Page

Index. Page

NAMES AND ADDRESSES OF COUNSEL.

Messrs. BRONSON, JONES & BRONSON, Attorneys for Appellant,

    614 Colman Building, Seattle, Washington.

Mr. WINTER S. MARTIN and Mr. ARTHUR COLLETT, Jr., Attorneys for Appellee,

    2014 Smith Tower, Seattle, Washington.

In the Superior Court of the State of Washington for King County.

No. 20,246.

No. 219,944.

HANS NELSON,

                        Plaintiff,

vs.

PUGET SOUND NAVIGATION COMPANY, a Corporation,

                        Defendant.

COMPLAINT.

Plaintiff for cause of action against defendant complains and alleges:

I.

That defendant is a Nevada corporation which [1*] now is and during all times herein mentioned was doing business within this State with its office

---

*Page-number appearing at the foot of page of original certified Transcript of Record.

and principal place of business at Seattle in the county of King. That it maintains an office for the transaction of business at said Seattle and was engaged in the transaction of business in and maintained an office for that purpose in said King County at the time the cause of action herein pleaded arose.

II.

That the gas screw "Magna" was an undocumented vessel of the United States, which on and prior to December 5th, 1927, was and had been numbered "M–1157" by the Collector of Customs at Seattle, Washington, pursuant to the Act of June 17th, 1918, which said number had been duly recorded by the said collector. That said "Magna" was about 34 feet over-all, 4 tons burden, equipped with one mast and trunk cabin, and was at the time of the collision hereinafter complained of fully equipped as a trolling vessel. That plaintiff herein on said 5th day of December, 1927, was, and for a long time prior thereto had been the sole owner of all of said vessel.

III.

That the steam ferry "Olympic" hereinafter referred to is a merchant vessel of the United States which at the time of the collision hereinafter referred to was owned, controlled and operated by the [2] defendant as a ferry on the run between Seattle and Port Townsend, Washington.

IV.

That on said 5th day of December, 1927, at about five o'clock in the afternoon of said day, the said

"Magna," while en route from Salmon Bay in the Ballard district of Seattle, across Puget Sound, and while steering a course about west northwest, was overtaken, run down and sunk by said "Olympic," which was then and there traveling upon a northerly and overtaking course, while en route from Seattle to Port Townsend.

V.

That the said "Magna" then and there foundered and became a total loss. That the collision and loss of the "Magna" was caused solely by the gross negligence and fault of the master and officers of the said "Olympic" in this:

That at the time of the collision it was still daylight, the weather clear and there was sufficient light to see clearly a small vessel like the "Magna" at a distance of about a half mile.

That the "Magna" was making about five knots and the "Olympic" about 15 knots at the time of and immediately prior to the collision.

That the "Olympic" was pursuing an overtaking course which would place her upon the "Magna's" port beam and quarter.

1. That the master and officers of the "Olympic" were grossly negligent and at fault for not [3] then and there keeping and posting a proper and efficient lookout as required by law and the "Inland Rules."

2. That the master and officers of the "Olympic" failed to sound or give any whistle, blast or other warning due by the "Inland Rules," and

"Pilot Rules" on the part of a vessel overtaking and attempting to pass another vessel.

3. That the master and officers of the said "Olympic" then and there violated Article 24 of the "Inland Rules" in that the "Olympic" did not keep out of the way of the "Magna," the said "Olympic" then and there being an overtaking vessel.

4. That the master and officers of the "Olympic" failed to keep and post a lookout in the fore part of the ship on the main-deck, when a proper and efficient lookout would and could have seen the said "Magna" in ample time to have reported the "Magna" to those in command of the "Olympic" whereby the collision could have been avoided.

5. That the "Olympic" then and there failed to slacken her speed, stop and reverse as required by Article 23 of the "Inland Rules," when she approached and overtook the "Magna," said "Olympic" then and there being an overtaking vessel.

6. That the master and officers of the "Olympic" then and there violated Article 29 of the "Inland Rules" in that they and each of them, all and singular, failed to keep such a lookout, and failed [4] to maintain such a speed as common prudence and good navigation required when they and each of them, knew or in the exercise of due care should have known the "Olympic," being then and there off the entrance to Salmon Bay in the Ballard District where at all times of day or night small vessels which are going into or leaving Salmon Bay

may be encountered. That large numbers of vessels of the "Magna" type commonly resort to Salmon Bay for anchorage or wharfage.

VI.

That at the time and immediately prior to the time when she foundered and became a total loss, said "Magna" was of the reasonable value in the sum of $4,200.00. That there was equipment and personal property on board at said time which became a total loss of a value of $636.20, an itemized list of which is hereto attached and made a part hereof.

VII.

That the master and officers of the "Olympic" were, at and prior to the collision, in charge of the operation and navigation of said vessel for and on behalf of defendant while in its employ and while the said vessel was being used and employed in the defendant's service for defendant's profit and advantage.

That the plaintiff for a further and second cause of action alleges as follows:

I.

That plaintiff hereby incorporated by reference [5] Paragraphs I, II, III, IV, V, VI, and VII of his first cause of action herein, and makes the same a part of this second cause of action as if set out in full herein.

II.

That when the above-mentioned collision occurred the impact of the colliding vessel was such that the "Magna" immediately filled with water and sank, and the plaintiff was thrown into the waters of Puget Sound and narrowly escaped drowning. That plaintiff went completely under water twice before he was finally rescued by the crew of the "Olympic."

III.

That the master, officers and members of the crew of said "Olympic," were incompetent and inexperienced in handling and manning the lifeboats and life-saving apparatus of said vessel. That thru the incompetency, inexperience and negligence of the master, officers and crew of said "Olympic," undue delay was caused in effecting the rescue of plaintiff from the waters of Puget Sound. That approximately one-half hour was consumed in said rescue. That during his struggle in the water, before being finally rescued, plaintiff was forced to swallow a large quantity of salt water which resulted in gastritis, causing plaintiff great pain and suffering, and which still causes him a great pain and suffering which will continue for a long time in the future as he verily believes.

That when said collision occurred, plaintiff was [6] thrown violently against the engine of his vessel. That as a result thereof, his right leg was cut, bruised and made sore and lame. That it was still sore and lame. That said cut, bruised and lame condition of his said leg caused plaintiff great pain and suffering and will continue to cause him great pain and suffering in the future as he verily believes.

WHEREFORE, plaintiff demands judgment against the defendant as follows, viz.:

1. For his FIRST CAUSE OF ACTION herein in the sum of $4,836.20.

2. For his SECOND CAUSE OF ACTION herein, in the sum of $2,500.00.

3. For his fees, costs and disbursements herein, and for such other and further relief as to the Court may seem just and equitable in the premises.

WINTER S. MARTIN,

ARTHUR COLLETT, Jr.,

Attorneys for Plaintiff.

LIST OF PLAINTIFF'S PERSONAL PROPERTY ON BOARD "MAGNA."

200 gals. gasoline at 18¢ *$30.00*

8 gals. lubricating oil at 90¢ 7.20

Weather glass 13.00

Compass 15.00

Charts 30.00

Binoculars 15.00

Automobile tools 15.00

Cooking utensils, dishes, etc. 30.00

[7]

500 lbs. lead at 17¢ 85.00

5½ doz. spoons at $9.00 .... 49.50

1 doz. hooks 5.00

Lines (fish) 25.00

1 dress suit 60.00

1 overcoat 35.00

1 pr. shoes 8.00

1 dress shirt 2.00

1 cap 3.00
2 blankets 10.00
1 suit oil clothes 5.00
1 pr. rubber boots 7.50
Money (Cash) 125.00
Gun 20.00
Watch 35.00

Total......$636.20.

State of Washington,
County of King,—ss.

Winter S. Martin, being first duly sworn, upon his oath deposes and says: That he is attorney for the plaintiff in the above cause and makes this verification for and upon his behalf for the reason that Hans Nelson, plaintiff in the above-entitled cause, is not now within King County, Washington, that is to say, said Nelson is in the territory of Alaska. That affiant has read the foregoing complaint, knows the contents thereof and the same is true as he verily believes.

WINTER S. MARTIN. [8]

Subscribed and sworn to before me this 14th day of May, 1929.

KENNETH DURHAM,
Notary Public in and for the State of Washington,
Residing at Seattle.

Filed in County Clerk's Office King County, Wash., May 15, 1929. Abe N. Olson, Clerk. By A. L. Lawrence, Deputy.

[Endorsed]: Filed Jul. 1929. Ed. M. Lakin, Clerk. By S. Cook, Deputy.

In the District Court of the United States for the Western District of Washington, Northern Division.

No. 20,246.

HANS NELSON,

Plaintiff,

vs.

PUGET SOUND NAVIGATION COMPANY, a Corporation,

Defendant.

ANSWER.

Comes now the defendant, Puget Sound Navigation Company, a corporation, and without waiving its demurrer herein to the amended complaint of plaintiff, but still insisting upon the same, in answer to said amended complaint admits, denies and alleges as follows: [9]

I.

Answering paragraph I, defendant admits the same.

II.

Answering paragraph II, defendant has not sufficient knowledge or information to form a belief as to the truth or falsity thereof, and therefore denies the same, and each and every allegation, matter and thing in said paragraph contained.

III.

Answering paragraph III, defendant admits the same.

IV.

Answering paragraph IV, defendant admits that on the 5th day of December, 1927, at a point adjacent to West Point, Puget Sound, the steamship "Olympic" came into collision with the gas screw "Magna," and, except as herein expressly admitted, defendant denies each and every allegation, matter and thing in said paragraph contained.

V.

Answering paragraph V, defendant admits that within one hour after said collision, said gas screw "Magna" foundered and became a total loss.

Further answering said paragraph, defendant denies that the said collision and the loss of said "Magna" was caused, or contributed to in any manner, respect or circumstance, by any negligence and/or fault of the master and/or officers of the said "Olympic," and further denies that at the [10] time of said collision, it was still daylight and/or that the weather was clear, and/or that there was sufficient light to see clearly, or at all, a small vessel like the "Magna" at a distance of a half a mile, or any other distance other than that hereinafter expressly admitted.

Further answering said paragraph, defendant denies that at the time of the collision the "Olympic" was making 15 knots per hour, but admits that prior to said collision the said vessel was making about 15 knots per hour; admits that the "Magna" was making about 5 knots per hour at the time of said collision, and admits that the "Olympic" was pursuing an overtaking course on a bearing of approximately 2 or 3 points on the "Magna's" port quarter.

Answering subparagraphs 1, 2, 3, 4, 5 and 6 of said paragraph V, defendant denies the same, and each and every allegation, matter and thing in said subparagraphs contained.

VI.

Answering paragraph VI, defendant denies each and every allegation, matter and thing in said paragraph contained, especially denying that at the time of the loss of said "Magna" she was of the reasonable value of $4,200.00, or any other sum or amount whatsoever, or at all, defendant being without knowledge or information as to the amount or extent of the value of said vessel. Further answering said paragraph, defendant is without sufficient knowledge or information to form a belief [11] as to the amount or value of any personal property on board said vessel, if any, and therefore denies that there was on board said vessel personal property of the value of $636.20, or any other sum or amount whatsoever, or at all, which became a total loss, or a loss in any respect or amount whatsoever, or at all.

VII.

Defendant admits paragraph VII of said amended complaint.

Answering the alleged second cause of action in said amended complaint of plaintiff herein, defendant admits, denies, and alleges as follows:

I.

Answering paragraph I of said alleged second cause of action, defendant reiterates and hereby incorporates, by reference, paragraphs I, II, III, IV, V, VI and VII of its foregoing answer herein, and makes the same a part of its answer to plaintiff's alleged second cause of action as fully as though again herein set forth in words and figures in full.

II.

Answering paragraph II, defendant denies each and every allegation, matter and thing in said paragraph contained.

III.

Answering paragraph III, defendant denies each and every allegation, matter and thing in said paragraph contained, especially denying that plaintiff was or has been damaged in the further sum [12] of $2,500.00, or any other sum of amount whatsoever, or at all.

Further answering plaintiff's alleged first and second causes of action, and, by way of a first, separate and affirmative defense to each thereof, defendant alleges as follows:

I.

That at the time of the collision alleged in the complaint herein, the sky was overcast, it was dark, or nearly so, sunset having occurred on said day at 4:17 o'clock P. M., a strong northwest wind was blowing against an ebb tide, causing a rough, choppy sea, with waves cresting over; that under such conditions small boats, or floating objects, of

35 feet or under, without lights, were visible for a distance of less than 100 feet from the bow of the steamship "Olympic," which was, at 5:19 o'clock P. M. of said day, proceeding down sound on a northerly course between West Point and Point No Point, on the inland waters of Puget Sound.

II.

That at about 5:19 o'clock P. M., on said 5th day of December, 1927, the SS. "Olympic," then bound on a voyage from Seattle to Port Townsend, was proceeding on her regular course from West Point to Point No Point, and had reached a position of approximately 3 miles NNW. of West Point light, when a small boat, later identified as the gas screw "Magna," was observed close aboard directly ahead and less than 100 feet [13] distant from the SS. "Olympic," said "Magna," when so first discernible from the "Olympic," being under the bow of the latter vessel, and proceeding on a course of 2 to 3 points to the westward of that being taken by the "Olympic."

III.

That at said time and place the said gas screw "Magna" carried no light of any character showing abaft her beam and visible to those in charge of the navigation of the "Olympic"; that said "Magna" was not visible or discernible until actually seen by the officers and crew of "Olympic" at which time said vessels were in the jaws of collision, and the resultant collision, damage and loss was then inevitable, notwithstanding which all steps were taken and all things done by those having in charge the navigation of the said "Olympic" tending to avoid said collision and to minimize and lessen the damage and loss resulting therefrom.

IV.

That at the time of and prior to the said collision all proper lights, as required by law, were carried, shown and burning brightly on said "Olympic," and the navigation of said vessel was then in charge of a full watch complement of licensed officers and crew, who were diligently and carefully attending to their duties in the navigation of said vessel in all respects; that the aforesaid collision and loss, damage and injury resulting therefrom was due solely and proximately to the gross negligence [14] and carelessness of the plaintiff herein, said gross negligence and carelessness being, viz.:

1. That said gas screw "Magna" was not rigged for, and did not carry or show a white or any other light visible abaft the beam, as required by Section (f) of Inland Pilot Rule No. 2, and subsection (b) of Section 3 of an Act of Congress, approved June 9, 1910, entitled "An Act to Amend Laws for Preventing Collision of Vessels and to Regulate Equipment of Certain Motor Boats on the Navigable Waters of the United States."

2. For some time prior to and at the time of the collision between said vessels, the plaintiff was the only *peron* on board the "Magna" and left the wheel of said vessel and had gone below deck leaving said vessel under way and proceeding at random with no lookout being kept for, and no atten-

tion paid to, the approach of proximity of other
vessels, including the "Olympic," notwithstanding
that plaintiff well knew that said "Magna" was
then and there in waters frequented by a large
number of vessels and in the mian channel path of
all vessels proceeding up and down the Sound.

Further answering plaintiff's alleged second cause
of action, and by way of a second, separate and affirmative defense thereto, the defendant alleges as
follows:

I.

The defendant hereby reiterates and incorporates
by reference paragraphs I to IV of the first affirmative defense herein, and makes the same a part of
this second affirmative defense, in all respects as
[15]   though herein again set forth in full in words
and figures.

II.

That in addition to the acts of negligence and
carelessness on behalf of plaintiff, set forth in the
preceding paragraphs of this answer, all loss, damage or injury, if any, which plaintiff may have suffered, as alleged in his alleged second cause of action, was further proximately caused and contributed to by the sole negligence of the plaintiff in
the following respects:

1.   That following the collision between said vessels, plaintiff negligently and carelessly failed and
neglected to stop the engine of the said "Magna"
and allowed said vessel to proceed under power
from the scene of the collision and approximately
at right angles to the course of the "Olympic" until
the engine of said "Magna" was stopped by the

rise of water in said vessel, thereby rendering difficult, and causing delay and additional time to be expended in the maneuvering of the SS. "Olympic" to reach the spot where said "Magna" finally foundered and sank; and

2.   That plaintiff negligently and carelessly, voluntarily and unnecessarily jumped overboard from said "Magna" prior to the arrival of rescue and prior to the sinking of said "Magna"; and

3.   That plaintiff negligently and carelessly failed and neglected to have on board or use either life-preservers or life-belts or buoyant cushions or ring-buoys, or other device as required by Section 5 of the Act of Congress approved June 9, 1910, entitled [16] "An Act to Amend Laws for Preventing Collision of Vessels and to Regulate Equipment of Certain Motor Boats on the Navigable Waters of the United States."

WHEREFORE, having fully answered, defendant prays that plaintiff's complaint and that the alleged first and second causes of action therein may be dismissed and that defendant do have and recover of and from the plaintiff herein its costs and disbursements to be taxed.

BRONSON, JONES & BRONSON,
Attorneys for Defendant.

Office and P. O. Address:
614 Colman Bldg.,
Seattle, Washington.

United States of America,
Western District of Washington,
Northern Division.

Ira Bronson, being first duly sworn, on oath deposes and says: That he is the president of Puget Sound Navigation Company, a corporation defendant in the above-entitled action and that he makes this verification for and on behalf of said defendant; that he has read the above and foregoing answer, knows the contents thereof, and that the same is true, except as to the matters therein stated to be alleged on information and belie*ve,* and as to those matters he believes it to be true.

IRA BRONSON.   [17]

Subscribed and sworn to before me this 19th day of September, 1929.

[Seal]   R. E. BRONSON,

Notary Public in and for the State of Washington,
Residing at Seattle.

Copy rec'd this 20th day Sept., 1929.

W. S. MARTIN,
Atty. for Pltff.
By M. S.

[Endorsed]: Filed Sep. 20, 1929.

[Title of Court and Cause.]

REPLY.

Comes now the plaintiff, Hans Nelson, and for his

reply to the affirmative matter contained in defendant's answer herein, admits, denies and alleges as follows, to wit:

Replying to defendant's first affirmative defense contained in said answer, plaintiff admits, denies and alleges as follows, to wit:

I.

Replying to Paragraph I of said affirmative defense, plaintiff denies the same, and denies each and every allegation therein contained.

II.

Replying to Paragraph *I* of said affirmative defense, plaintiff denies the same, and denies each and every allegation therein contained.   [18]

III.

Replying to Paragraph III of said affirmative defense, plaintiff denies the same, and denies each and every allegation therein contained.

IV.

Replying to Paragraph IV of said affirmative defense, plaintiff denies the same, and denies each and every allegation therein contained, except that plaintiff admits that "for some time prior to and at the time of the collision between said vessels, the plaintiff was the only person on board the "Magna."

Replying to defendants' second affirmative defense contained in said answer, plaintiff admits, denies and alleges as follows, to wit:

I.

Replying to Paragraph I of said affirmative defense, the plaintiff hereby reiterates and incorporates by reference paragraphs I to IV of the reply to the first affirmative defense herein, and makes the same a part of this reply in all respects as though herein again set forth in full in words and figures.

II.

Replying to Paragraph II of said affirmative defense, the plaintiff hereby denies the same, and denies each and every allegation therein contained.

WHEREFORE, having fully replied, plaintiff prays that defendant's answer and the alleged first and second affirmative defenses therein contained may be dismissed, and that plaintiff have and recover [19] from defendant as prayed for in his complaint herein.

WINTER S. MARTIN,
ARTHUR COLLETT, Jr.,
Attorneys for Plaintiff.

United States of America,
Western District of Washington,
Northern Division.

Hans Nelson, being first duly sworn, upon his oath says: That he is the plaintiff in the above-entitled cause; that he has read the above and foregoing reply, knows the contents thereof, and that the same is true, except as to the matters therein stated to be alleged on information and belief, and as to those matters he believes it to be true.

HANS NELSON.

Subscribed and sworn to before me this 9th day of October, 1929.

[Seal]   ARTHUR COLLETT, Jr.,

Notary Public in and for the State of Washington,
    Residing at Seattle.

Service of a copy hereof admitted this 9 day of October, 1929.

BRONSON, JONES & BRONSON,
                Attorneys for Defendant.

[Endorsed]: Filed Oct. 9, 1929.   [20]

[Title of Cause and Court.]

MINUTES OF COURT—MAY 5, 1931—ORDER DENYING MOTION FOR DIRECTED VERDICT.

Counsel for defendant moves for a directed verdict on the ground of insufficient evidence. The motion is denied.

[Title of Cause and Court.]

MINUTES OF COURT—MAY 6, 1931—ORDER DENYING RENEWED MOTION FOR DIRECTED VERDICT.

* * * Counsel for the defendant renews motion for a directed verdict and the same is denied.
* * * [21]

[Title of Court and Cause.]

VERDICT.

We, the jury in the above-entitled cause, find for the plaintiff, and fix the amount of his recovery in the sum of Two Thousand Two Hundred & Fifty Dollars ($2,250.00) on the first cause of action, and in the sum of Two Hundred and Fifty Dollars ($250.00) on the second cause of action.

J. HEPWORTH, (Signed)
Foreman.

[Endorsed]: Filed May 8, 1931.

Journal 19, Pg. 275.   [22]

United States District Court for the Western District of Washington, Northern Division.

No. 20,245.

HANS NELSON,

Plaintiff,

vs.

PUGET SOUND NAVIGATION COMPANY, a Corporation,

Defendant.

JUDGMENT.

The above-entitled cause having been tried to a jury in the above-entitled court on the 5th and 6th days of May, 1931, before Hon. George A. Bourquin, United States District Judge, and the jury having returned a verdict for Twenty-two Hundred and Fifty Dollars ($2,250.00) on plaintiff's first cause of action, and Two Hundred and Fifty Dollars ($250.00) on plaintiff's second cause of action, now, upon motion of the plaintiff for judgment on the verdict,—

IT IS ADJUDGED AND DECREED that plaintiff have and recover Twenty-five Hundred Dollars ($2500.00), less the sum of Three Hundred Twelve and 5/100 Dollars ($312.05), costs duly awarded and entered in favor of defendant in the United States Circuit Court of Appeals and the Supreme Court of the United States, or the sum of Twenty-one Hundred Eighty-seven & 95/100 Dollars ($2187.95), together with plaintiff's costs to be taxed by the Clerk and that execution may issue for said sum of Twenty-one Hundred Eighty-seven & 95/100 Dollars ($2187.95), plus the amount of plaintiff's costs, as finally taxed herein. Defendant's exception is hereby noted and allowed.

Done in open court this 11 day of May, 1931.

GEORGE M. BOURQUIN,
United States District Judge.

At law is power to offset judgments on motion. Orally moved here and granted.

BOURQUIN, J.   [23]

[Endorsed]: Filed May 11, 1931.

J. & D. 7, Pg. 36.   [24]

[Title of Court and Cause.]

PROPOSED BILL OF EXCEPTIONS.

Comes now the defendant and herewith files and submits the following proposed bill of exceptions for settlement and certification.

BRONSON, JONES & BRONSON,
Attorneys for Defendant. [25]

————

[Title of Court and Cause.]

BILL OF EXCEPTIONS.

BE IT REMEMBERED that heretofore, to wit, on Tuesday, the 5th day of May, 1931, at the hour of ten o'clock in the forenoon, the above-entitled cause came regularly on for trial before the Honorable George M. Bourquin, and a jury duly and regularly impaneled and sworn to try the same;

The plaintiff appearing in person and by Winter S. Martin, Esq. (Martin & Collett), his attorney and counsel.

The defendant appearing by Robert E. Bronson, Esq. (Bronson, Jones & Bronson), its attorneys and counsel.

WHEREUPON the following proceedings were had and testimony given, to wit:

(Opening statements to the jury by counsel for the respective parties.)

Thereupon the following testimony was introduced on behalf of the plaintiff:

TESTIMONY OF R. G. GUERIN, FOR PLAINTIFF.

R. G. GUERIN, called as a witness on behalf of plaintiff, being first duly sworn, testified as follows:

Direct Examination.

My name is R. G. Guerin. I am a resident of Seattle, and one of the court reporters who reported the previous trial of this case. I recall taking the testimony of a witness, Mrs. Hattie Schuman, in the former trial. She testified as [26] follows, as transcribed by me in my notes:

On direct examination by Mr. MARTIN: My name is Hattie Schuman. I live at Port Townsend, and lived there in December, 1927. My husband is here in court with me. On December 5th I went on board the steam ferry "Olympic." The boat left at 4:30. My husband was with me. We were eating lunch. It wasn't dark. That was around about five o'clock. I couldn't say. I had no timepiece. I was eating lunch when I heard a terrible bumping of the boat. For a little while we didn't pay much attention to it. My thought was that the boat had struck a log. We sat there quite a while and then saw a commotion on the boat. We all jumped up and ran to the windows. Then it was getting dark, but I still saw the boat. When I jumped up I went right to about the center of the boat and had an outlook on the sinking boat. I looked out the window and stayed near the window. They had all the windows open and

(Testimony of R. G. Guerin.)

everybody was looking out. I looked right out the
window and saw the boat sinking. It as still a
little light and I could see the boat. The boat
was maybe 150 yards away. I saw a light on the
boat. I saw the light as the boat sank out of sight.
The light was still burning. I saw just one man
that was drowning. He as screaming for help,
telling us that he was drowning. That is all I
know about it. I saw the man just at first, but
it grew dark quickly. I didn't see him any more.
I could just hear him calling for help. It was
about fifteen minutes between the time when I
felt the crash and when I went to the window and
looked out. At the time I felt the bump it was
just light enough outside to know that it was growing dusk, but it wasn't dark. It seemed a long
time from the time I saw the man in the water
until he was brought to the ship, maybe half an
hour. [27]

On cross-examination by Mr. BRONSON: When
I first saw him the vessel was 150 yards away,
because the "Olympic" had backed, that left that
boat that far away from him. I should judge about
as far as a city block. I saw no illumination, only
the light on the boat. I didn't see any light shining
down on the boat. It was very dark when the
boat sank. I lost sight of the man when the boat
sank. I never lost sight of the light. The boat
had sunk out of sight we could still see the light.
I couldn't tell how long it was after I first saw the
boat until she sank. We were greatly excited.

(Testimony of Emil F. Schuman.)

It was fully half an hour I should judge. When we were eating dinner the electric lights were on in the dining saloon. The lights were all on in the cabin.

TESTIMONY OF EMIL F. SCHUMAN, FOR PLAINTIFF.

EMIL F. SCHUMAN, called as a witness on behalf of plaintiff, being first duly sworn, testified as follows:

Direct Examination.

My name is Emil F. Schuman. I have lived at Port Townsend since 1914. I was a passenger on the steamer "Olympic" on December 5, 1927. Mrs. Schuman, my wife, was with me. She is not living now. She passed away July 12th of last year. She is the lady whose testimony was just given by the court reporter. I left Seattle at 4:30 P. M. on the "Olympic." There was later a collision between the "Olympic" and a fishing vessel. We started out on schedule time as usual and when we got down there where the spar buoy is, down there by the West Point lighthouse, we sat down to eat with some ladies, and they had lunch, and it was not more than a few minutes longer when we struck something I thought. My wife ate lunch at the lunch-counter aft on the main deck. I was eating down about amidship on the main deck [28] in the passenger's room. As soon as we struck I didn't know what had happened. I rushed over to the window and I could not see anything,

(Testimony of Emil F. Schuman.)

so I rushed right upstairs because there is no veranda around the "Olympic," and I saw that we had struck a boat. I was then on the upper deck.

(At this point, three photographs were offered and admitted in evidence as Plaintiff's Exhibits 1, 2 and 3.)

(Upon examining the photographs the witness stated that he took a position behind the first lifeboat shown on Exhibit 2, on the port side.)

It did not take me over a minute to get to that point after I felt the bump. At that time it was getting dusk. It was then perhaps close to five o'clock. An object of any size I could see quite aways, say a thousand feet. At that time I would not have needed any artificial light to have seen an object 1,000 feet away on the water. It was quite a ways past the fishing boat. When I got up there I noticed the starboard light and the white light in front. The starboard light was green. At that time the "Olympic" backed up and it was getting quite dark fast, and I could see the man on board that boat. We backed up far enough and I could see where the port side of this fishing boat was stove in as far as the water-line. I could see a big hole there. I could see the crushed outside boards. That was in the stern. I should say the "Olympic" passed the "Magna" a couple of blocks before she stopped. Then the "Olympic" backed up and tried to rescue the man. I cannot say whether she went directly astern or made a circle and turned and came back. The "Magna"

(Testimony of Emil F. Schuman.)

was astern of us. We later backed up a little beyond the "Magna."

Thereupon the following proceedings were had:

Q. Now, as you passed the "Magna," after you stopped, or as you backed up, did you observe any other light? [29]   A. I did.

Mr. BRONSON.—Just a minute. I object to that as immaterial, your Honor.

The COURT.—Overruled.

The WITNESS.—I did.

Mr. BRONSON.—Exception.

Q. What lights, if any, did you see?

A. I saw a white light —

Mr. BRONSON.—(Interrupting.) Just a minute. I object again, your Honor. May I state the grounds of my objection, please?

The COURT.—Surely.

Mr. BRONSON.—This witness is not testifying to any time prior to this collision. He is testifying to what he saw after he came on deck, after the collision, and what lights might appear on the vessels before they had passed each other and swung out into different positions is a matter of speculation.

The COURT.—That is no speculation at all.

Mr. BRONSON.—Well, it is a speculation, your Honor, as to what lights were showing before this accident.

The COURT.—That might be open to question, of course, but this was so near after the event that it is at least permissible to go to the jury, and

(Testimony of Emil F. Schuman.)
the jury will understand the whole situation. Objection overruled.

Mr. BRONSON.—We ask for an exception.

The COURT.—Exception allowed.

Thereupon the witness continued his testimony as follows: I saw a white light. Do you want me to state where I saw that light. It was a white light in the center of the door [30] where you go down into the engine-room or cabin, whatever it may be, and I do not know whether there was another light in the cabin or not, and the cabin was quite lit up and I could see Mr.—what is his name, the skipper. The door was open. The light was hanging right in the center where you step down into the engine-room. At that time I could see the stern of the vessel and deck of the vessel aft of the light. That is the time when I observed when the collision occurred. Somehow or other the boat shifted around a little to the left so that she was at a four or five degree angle from the "Olympic," and I could see the crushed side. There was nothing on the stern of the boat which interfered with my vision of the light. It was a white light. It looked like an electric light. It was a little over a hundred feet, I guess, away when I saw the light. It was getting dusk then. I could not observe the light closely. The white light appeared approximately four feet above the "Magna's" main deck. I did not see more than one white light at any time when we were passing the "Magna," either the first or second time. I saw a white light and the green light on the starboard

(Testimony of Emil F. Schuman.)

at the same time, but do not remember seeing the red light. Then, after seeing those lights, I saw the light in the door.

Thereupon the following proceedings took place:

Q. Now, when you first went on deck, could you have seen the "Magna," I think you said a thousand feet away—could you have seen this vessel without any light on?

Mr. BRONSON.—I object to that as speculative and calling for a conclusion of the witness.

The COURT.—Well, it goes to a situation with respect to which it is impossible otherwise to explain to the jury how good the light was on the water. I think that he may answer. [31]

Mr. BRONSON.—Exception.

The COURT.—If he formed any judgment. The objection is overruled.

Mr. BRONSON.—Exception.

A. Yes, sir.

The COURT.—Now, again, are you fixing any distance on the vessel?

Q. Would you estimate the distance when you first went on deck—the distance away that you could see the "Magna" without any artificial light on it?

Mr. BRONSON.—Same objection, your Honor.

The COURT.—Overruled.

Mr. BRONSON.—Exception.

A. Two small city blocks.

Q. Can you estimate in feet what that would be?

A. Approximately four hundred feet.

Q. Do you mean, now, when you actually did

(Testimony of Emil F. Schuman.)

see it, or the distance you could have seen it?
Mr. Collett has called my attention to that difference.

Mr. BRONSON.—Same objection.

The COURT.—Same ruling. Do you understand the question?

Mr. BRONSON.—Exception.

The WITNESS.—No, sir.

The COURT.—When you say "approximately
400 feet," is that the distance that it was when you
came on deck, or is that the distance you estimate
that you could have seen it without lights?

A. No, that was the distance that I could see it
without any light, easy.

A. And how far do you think it was away from
you when you came on deck and first saw the
"Magna"? [32]

A. When I first saw the "Magna"?

Q. Yes.   A. Not over a block.

Mr. MARTIN.—That is all.

Mr. BRONSON.—If the Court please, at this
time I move that all the witness' testimony with
reference to lights which he observed after the
collision between these vessels be stricken from
the record, and the jury instructed to disregard
it, as wholly immaterial to any issue in this case.

The COURT.—Not necessarily. I think it is a
matter that can be shown to the jury, under proper
instructions later. You understand, Gentlemen
of the Jury, the vital issue in this case is in respect
to the light at the time of the collision. This witness is speaking about lights after the collision,

(Testimony of Emil F. Schuman.)

and the court allows it to go in, to you, but you will be controlled in your instructions as to what weight or what importance it bears on the case. The motion will be denied.

Mr. BRONSON.—Exception.

The COURT.—Yes.

Mr. BRONSON.—I also ask that the testimony of the witness with respect to how far he could have seen the light be stricken as not predicated upon any facts in this case, and also on the ground that it is speculative and remote, and pure guess-work on the part of the witness.

The COURT.—The matter of light at that time, the jury has heard the witness' statement of the conditions, and his judgment, and they will give it just as much weight as they think it is entitled to and no more. The motion is denied.

Mr. BRONSON.—Exception. [33]

The COURT.—Proceed with your cross-examination.

Cross-examination.

On cross-examination the witness further testified:

When I proceeded from the interior of the vessel, I went up the stairway of the left-hand side and I first looked over the port side and saw the "Magna" a little over one hundred feet away. Our boat was still moving. The "Magna" was heading toward Port Townsend. She was not moving that I know of. She seemed to be dead in the water. I did not see any sign of life about

(Testimony of Emil F. Schuman.)

the vessel at that time, or until we had backed up
and got astern of the "Magna." I then saw Mr.
Hans Nelson when the boat was sinking very fast
and he shouted, "For God's sake, help me, I am
drowning!" The boat was then about 150 feet
away, northwest from where we were, astern of
our vessel. I did not see any other objects anywhere around there. At that time it was getting
quite dusk. When I said that I could have seen
objects in the water. I did not see any. I did not
say I did see the "Magna" a thousand feet away.
The fartherest away I saw her was a couple of city
blocks, something around four hundred feet. When
we backed up alongside the "Magna" there was
illumination inside of her cabin. I don't know
how many boats the "Magna" had. I didn't look
to see. She didn't have any mast that I know of.
I could not observe the small mast nohow at the
time that we got there, it was so dark. The shape
of her house was just the same as any other fishing
boat's house. Just a small cabin on her, the cabin
and engine-room combined, I presume. The doorway leading down into the engine-room was
right in back. It was aft of the cabin leading
down into the engine-room. That is the door that
I say is open when I looked down there. Something leading down into the ship. [34] That is
where I saw this light. The "Magna" had a pilot-
house that sat up on top of the rest of the boat.
Aft the pilot-house she had a cabin and a pilot-house
combined, a trunk cabin.

TESTIMONY OF OSCAR W. DAM, FOR PLAINTIFF.

OSCAR W. DAM, called as a witness on behalf of plaintiff, having been first duly sworn, testified as follows:

My name is Oscar W. Dam. I am a Deputy Collector of Customs in this district. I am custodian of the records of vessels as well as the vessels merely numbered under the customs law. The M.1557 is what is called an undocumented vessel. We had assigned that customs identification number. Her tonnage is 4.73 net. It is not large enough to be documented.

(Whereupon the witness identified exhibits 4, 5 and 6 as admeasurement and certificate cards relating to the "Magna," which were admitted in evidence). The vessel's length is 33 feet, beam 8 feet. That was the record that existed on December 5, 1927.

TESTIMONY OF PETER J. CARLSON, FOR PLAINTIFF.

PETER J. CARLSON called as a witness on behalf of plaintiff, being first duly sworn, testified as follows:

My name is Peter J. Carlson. I am a resident of Tacoma. I am a fisherman and boat builder, and was so engaged in 1926 and 1927. I have built boats for more than twenty years. I built the "Magna" in 1926. (The balance of this wit-

(Testimony of Peter Garvey.)
ness' testimony relates to valuations not involved
in the appeal.)

TESTIMONY OF PETER GARVEY, FOR PLAINTIFF.

PETER GARVEY called as a witness on behalf
of plaintiff, being first duly sworn, testified as follows :

My name is Peter Garvey. I live in Everett,
Washington. I am engaged in painting boats. I
am employed by the Puget Sound [35] Navigation Company. I was employed by them on December 5, 1927. On that day I was a deck-hand on
the "Olympic." On that day the boat left the
Colman Dock at 4:30. I went on lookout. I recall
the collision with the fishing boat. For three or
four minutes before the collision I was fixing curtains on the windows. The windows shown on
Plaintiff's Exhibit 2. The curtains are made of
canvass. They are already attached to the house.
You just pull a little string and they drop down.
There are hooks underneath with eyes in them and
you hook them with them. I as doing that at the
time of the collision and had been possibly for
three or four minutes. On lookout I stand in the
bow of the vessel. I imagine the windows are about
forty feet from the bow. My back was forward
and I was facing aft. I was using my hands to
fasten the curtains.

Cross-examination.

On cross-examination the witness further testi-

(Testimony of Peter Garvey.)

fied: As we came around West Point there was a spray coming over the bow of the "Olympic." If you were standing in the bow of the ship the wind itself would affect your eyes so that you could not really see anything. If you were back where I was standing, where I was putting those curtains down, you know, not exactly back that far, but you would have to be back quite aways to keep the wind out of your eyes and the spraying of the water. It was blowing fresh at the time and some spray was coming over the bow. I would normally stand under those conditions forward of the stairway, about twenty feet from the bow, about ten feet from the windows. I put the curtains down. They were not down when I went on watch. I put them down just before we had the collision. Before that I had been on lookout. I had been looking ahead. I had seen West Point light. [36]

TESTIMONY OF HANS NELSON, FOR PLAIN-
TIFF.

HANS NELSON, the plaintiff, called as witness in his own behalf, having been first duly sworn, testified as follows:

My name is Hans Nelson. I am the plaintiff in this case. I live at Poulsbo, and I am a fisher-man, and have been since I was twelve years old. In 1927 I owned the "Magna." After January, 1927, I was the sole owner until she was lost. (Witness here testifies as to construction and value of

(Testimony of Hans Nelson.)

the boat.) On December 5, 1927, I left the Standard Oil Dock at Salmon Bay at 4:30 in the afternoon, and went out of the locks. When I got outside it was blowing westerly, a good breeze, westerly wind, and I got out and by the light and took a course west by west, going across the sound, and I was standing steering and watching the boat, and I never knew anything before there was something hitting me. It was daylight at the time I left the locks and when I got out there to the lights I put a light in the lantern and put up the lights on the boat. I put up the two side lights and the masthead light and the stern light. The masthead light was a bright light in the front of the pilot-house. It shows three points around the vessel. It shows a little bit abaft the beam. It was an electric light. It was located on the bow on top of the pilot-house on the front end of the pilot-house and facing forward. The side lights were the usual green and red lights. They were on the back end of the pilot-house with a screen on each side. In addition, I had one light hanging in the back of the pilot-house, right in the door of the pilot-house, two inches inside of the door. The pilot-house is five feet above the main deck. The pilot-house is located forward on top of the trunk cabin. The trunk cabin extends twelve inches above the main deck, and the pilot-house [37] is five feet high. The after side of the pilot-house would be about the forward half of the boat. The door

(Testimony of Hans Nelson.)

of the pilot-house opens aft on the starboard side of the pilot-house. Looking forward you step right from the main deck through this door into the pilot-house. There is a bulkhead there on the cabin. There is a foot and a half from the decking where you step over going to the pilot-house, so the door of the pilot-house is five feet high from that there. The light is right in the middle of the door, a six-volt electric light connected with the light system on the engine. The bulb was the same as Plaintiff's Exhibit 7, which was thereupon admitted in evidence. The light was hanging on an extension cord two inches inside of the door. It was a solid door open at the time of the collision, and all the time, The light was lighted at the time of the collision. It had been right from the time *the time* that I lighted the lights at Ballard. The side lights were lighted when I left Ballard. The cabin light was not lighted when I left Ballard. When I got out to the light in Ballard then the light was burning. I put the light on about 100 feet from shore. I had the lights burning after that, including the light in the door. There was nothing aft of the light. That light can show all over the after part of the boat.

Thereupon the following proceedings were had:

Q. Could anybody see that light suspended in the door of your vessel—in that open door, approaching from the stern?

(Testimony of Hans Nelson.)

Mr. BRONSON.—I object to that as calling for a conclusion.

A. Yes.

The COURT.—Overruled.

Mr. BRONSON.—Exception.

Q. Hans, did you ever have occasion to be away from your own vessel at night-time, either on the shore or on another vessel, [38] when you could see that light suspended in the doorway of your cabin?

Mr. BRONSON.—I object to that as immaterial, your Honor.

Mr. MARTIN.—It bears upon the—

The COURT.—(Interrupting.) Overruled.

Mr. BRONSON.—Exception.

Q. Go ahead. Did you? A. Yes, sir.

Q. How far could you see that light when the light was on and when it was hanging in the doorway, suspended as it was at the time of the collision?

Mr. BRONSON.—I object to that.

The COURT.—Overruled.

Mr. BRONSON.—Exception.

A. Half a mile away.

Q. Have you actually seen that light half a mile away?

Mr. BRONSON.—I object to that.

The COURT.—Overruled.

Mr. BRONSON.—Exception.

A. Yes, I have been on shore many times, and I have had that light burning, and I have seen it. I seen that light on my own boat.

(Testimony of Hans Nelson.)

The witness further testified as follows: At the time of the collision it was just in the twilight. It was not dark and it was not regular daylight, I estimate, because the collision occurred around five o'clock and my watch stopped at 5:15, and I figured that it was around fifteen minutes that I was there. During that time I was on the boat first. At the time the ferry struck me I fell down [39] between the engine and the tanks, and I got up from there and I was hanging with one hand on the steering-wheel and the other hand on the front, and they broke the rudder chain so that the boat was turning around and I got up and went out on the deck and I seen that the ferry-boat was up to the window. I never knew what struck me in the first place until I saw that boat and then he was backing up. He was about a quarter of a mile away. (Witness here testified as to personal injuries not involved in appeal.) I went overboard after I seen that the boat was filling up fast, that it was mostly sinking, and I was afraid that I would go down with the boat, and I took a hatch and threw it overboard and I jumped for that away from the boat. The "Magna" sank. I could see easily a half a mile on the water. I saw a towboat that was coming towing logs. I had an open window in the pilot-house. I saw the towboat coming in, and he had not had any light on at that time. I seen him first and that was before the ferry struck me. I saw the towboat through the window about a half a mile away, about eight minutes before the collision.

(Testimony of Hans Nelson.)

Thereupon the following proceedings were had:

Q. How far could you see any vessel ahead of you, a vessel of the size of the "Magna"?

Mr. BRONSON.—I object to that as speculative and calling for a conclusion.

The COURT.—Overruled.

Mr. BRONSON.—Exception.

A. You could see a vessel like the "Magna" a quarter of a mile away, easy, at the time of that collision.

The witness further testified: It was a full moon. The moon was not yet up. It was [40] not dark enough to see the moon at the time of the collision, and the moon came up a little afterwards. After I got aboard the ferry then the moon was up. At the time of the collision the sky was clear. The wind was westerly blowing a good breeze, westerly wind. There was a heavy sea and the tide was going up with the wind, and that makes kind of big swells. My boat was about in the middle of the sound, about three quarters of a mile north of West Point, northwest of West Point.

Thereupon the following proceedings took place.

Mr. MARTIN.—If your Honor please, I have a little picture here, your Honor—a photograph of a vessel not the "Magna," but one I would like to introduce for the purpose of illustration.

Cross-examination.

On cross-examination the witness further testified:

(Testimony of Hans Nelson.)

It was 4:30 when I left at the locks. It was daylight then. The sun was not shining but it was daylight yet. The sun wasn't shining because it was just going back of the mountains. About 4:45 I got through the locks and the sun was just going down behind the mountains then. That was about 4:40, and the sun was just going behind the mountains. The sky was clear to the west, no clouds, and no moon in sight. At that time I was just outside the railroad bridge. (Witness marked cross on chart at point indicated. Defendant's Exhibit 11.) I was heading for Suquamish. That is shown on the chart. At 4:40 I was still in the entrance of the canal. My vessel made about 5½ miles an hour. The collision occcured about 5 o'clock. I didn't look at the watch. The last time I looked at the watch was when I left Ballard at 4:30. I never again looked at any watch or clock. I was judging that it was about 5 o'clock. My watch [41] stopped at 5:15. From 4:30 on I simply estimate the time. About four minutes after I saw this tug about half a mile away the tug's lights went on. I wasn't up to the tug at that time. The tug was away out from me. It came from Richmond Beach that way, and I went further across. I went further away from the tug rather than closer to it. When my boat was built it had three navigation lights on it, two side lights and one bow light, and the light behind on the boat. At that time there were four lights. Those lights were two side lights, one head

(Testimony of Hans Nelson.)

light and one mast light. The mast light is the light you use when you have the mast on the boat. I had no mast on the boat. I testified before the Local Inspectors and I testified before at this trial that I had a pole mast at the after end of the vessel, and that I had taken it off. I testified that I had taken it off the boat, but it was not at that time. It had a mast on before I went to Ballard, aft of the pilot-house, and that had a light on top of it, a light that showed all around the horizon. We had the light on the mast at the time we had the mast up. It shown all around the horizon. I took this mast out of the boat before I went to Ballard. I didn't have it on when the collision occurred, and I didn't have it on when I went out from Ballard, and the mast and light were missing at the time I came out in the Sound on the evening of the collision. I had another light on the boat that I normally carry, a six-volt light, a white light, and it would shine aft of the beam of the boat and aft. That showed from the stern of the vessel.

(The COURT.—I think you are both confused. You are talking about what he calls the bow light and he thinks you are talking about the light on the pole.)

I had five lights up. I had a green, a red and a white. Those are the bow running lights. You could not see [42] those lights from the stern. You are not supposed to see them on the stern.

(Testimony of Hans Nelson.)

They are screened so that they do not show that way. The light that had been on the boat mast was not there but there was a light behind in place of that. I had a light in the cabin too, and them lights were showing, and there was a light back in the pilot-house in the door of the pilot-house, and that showed all that part of the boat. I never went outside of the wheel-house after I left Ballard. After the collision I went out, but up to that time I had been inside navigating the vessel. I did not have time to look astern of the ship to see what was coming in that direction. I never looked at all. I don't have to look back. I was looking to the windward. That was the only way I had to look. I was not wrong coming up into the wind. I had the right of way. If a vessel overtook me there he had to give me a warning. I had a six-volt light system, a 6–8 volt Robertson dynamo, 10 watts, that was running with the engine. We had batteries when the engines stopped. One battery will burn five of those lights without a dynamo. The light that was hanging on a suspension cord was right in the pilot-house with me. The pilot-house is 5x4. I could see out of this room with a light on there to navigate the vessel. I could see what I could see in the light. It was not dark. At the time of the collision you could see without lights. The light in the little room would not bother my eyes. I was standing steering when the ferry hit. My vessel was on its course running with the

(Testimony of Hans Nelson.)

engine. I was headed west northwest. I wasn't
rolling much in the sea. There was a little spray
once in a while, and that was all there was. The
wind was coming from the west northwest. I was
heading into the wind. The swell was more northerly so it was going a little more on its [43] side.
At the time the ferry struck me I was heading for
Indianola. I was then about half a mile from
West Point in the direction of north northwest.
(Witness then indicated with a circle the point
where collision took place on chart, Defendant's
Exhibit 11.) We were then a little over a mile
from the blinker. I cannot say how long I had
been running. I should judge I had been out from
Ballard about half an hour. There were no clouds
in the sky. I cannot say whether the moon was
shining. I could not see the moon. I could not see
any sign of the moon, but I saw the moon later when
I was in the water. And after my vessel was hit it
broke the rudder chain and I proceeded at random.
It was hanging on the ferry and it broke the
door of the pilot-house at the time that it was
hanging on the ferry. I jumped overboard before
my boat sank. It was pretty nearly sunk. I was
just hanging onto the cabin and the pilot-house.
I have two life-rings on the boat. They were on
top of the pilot-house. They were fastened. We
had to have them fastened when we were out
fishing. We never used them life-preservers and
I took the first thing that I could see that I could

(Testimony of Hans Nelson.)

throw overboard. There was a big hatch on top
of the place where the fish is put in and I threw
it overboard and I put my hand on that and it
held me up, but when I got in the tide it was not
strong enough to hold me up so I went down twice
with that. My life-preservers were lashed down
in the pilot-house so I could not pick up one of them
and jump overboard with it.

Redirect Examination.

On redirect examination the witness testified as
follows:

The hull of my boat was exactly the same as the
hull of the boat in the photograph. It was a double
ended vessel [44] like that and it had the same
pilot-house. It is arranged the same way and here
is the mast and the pole. Everything is all there
on that picture, though that picture doesn't show
aft as it does on my boat. I mean that I did not
have any mast or pole. The same deck arrangement. The back part of the pilot-house on the
"Magna" was all straight. There was no overhang
on it. (Thereupon the photograph was admitted
in evidence as Plaintiff's Exhibit 8.) The "Olympic" cut in clear to the keel. There was a water
tank back there and it shoved that water tank
straight up through the hatch. There is the trolling
hatch where we stand when we fish and it cut
across that hatch clear into the keel, and through
that tank and the planks and the side opened up
so that all the water went in there.

(Testimony of Hans Nelson.)

Recross-examination.

On recross-examination the witness further testified:

My vessel did not have trolling masts. There was a smokestack on the forecastle. The trunk cabin on the boat was forward of the wheel-house.

Redirect Examination.

On redirect examination the witness testified as follows:

I have been around the Sound and in and around the Locks at West Point about twelve years. At that point there is all the traffic that goes from Seattle in and out.

Recross-examination.

On recross-examination the witness further testified:

All the ships pass West Point that go to Seattle. The place where the "Magna" was at the time of the collision was the path where the ships go in and out of Seattle, and I was crossing that path. [45]

(At this point an extract from the Weather Bureau records was introduced in evidence as Plaintiff's Exhibit 9.)

Thereupon the following proceedings took place: The COURT.—Go to the defense.

Mr. BRONSON.—If your Honor please, I would like to make a motion.

The COURT.—Very well, proceed.

Mr. BRONSON.—We at this time move the court for a directed verdict.

The COURT.—Are you resting your case at this time?

Mr. BRONSON.—I beg your pardon?

The COURT.—Are you resting your case?

Mr. BRONSON.—No, I am not resting my case. I am challenging the sufficiency of the evidence plaintiff has produced to justify a verdict in favor of the plaintiff under any circumstance.

The COURT.—Proceed.

Mr. BRONSON.—The plaintiff in this case has admitted that he did not have the lights required by the law. He has admitted that it was after sunset. He has admitted that he was—

The COURT.—(Interrupting.) What was sunset that day?

Mr. BRONSON.—I beg your pardon?

The COURT.—When did the sun set that day? There is no evidence about that.

Mr. BRONSON.—He testified that the sun set at the Ballard Bridge just as he was coming out under the railroad bridge. He said that it was 4:40.

The COURT.—He said that it was going behind the mountains.

Mr. BRONSON.—Yes. [46]

The COURT.—Is that sun setting when it goes behind the mountains? I doubt it.

Mr. BRONSON.—That is his own evidence, that the sun had set.

The COURT.—I know, but how is sunset and sunrise measured under the law?

Mr. BRONSON.—Under the law, sunset is measured by when the sun's upper rim disappears upon a water level horizon.

The COURT.—The law requires a light after sunset. Now, what does that mean? Proceed with your motion. I asked you what evidence there was of sunset, but if there is none in the record, I suppose it can be judically noted that it is fixed by the table.

Mr. BRONSON.—That is the basis of my motion, your Honor, that under the law, it being admitted that he was proceeding with lights that did not come up to the prescribed lights prescribed by statute, he is guilty of negligence as a matter of law, and the burden is upon him to prove that his failure to carry the proper lights could not have been one of the causes of the collision.

Now, there certainly is no evidence in this case whatsoever from which any reasonable person would assume that the absence to have this light, which the law requires and the light which this witness admitted that his vessel had been equipped with originally, was not one of the causes of the collision.

Since this is an action at law and not an Admiralty proceeding, contributory negligence is a complete bar, irrespective of any action or failure of per-

(Testimony of William Seatter.)

formance on the part of the defendant, and I think at this time there is [47] not anything left for determination by anyone other than whether, as a matter of law, this plaintiff was guilty of contributory negligence.

The COURT.—I am of the opinion that as the case now stands, it ought to go to the jury. The Court would be justified in referring it to the jury. The motion will be denied.

Mr. BRONSON.—Exception.

The COURT.—Call your witness.

Thereupon the following proceedings took place:

TESTIMONY OF WILLIAM SEATTER, FOR DEFENDANT.

WILLIAM SEATTER, called as a witness on behalf of defendant, being first duly sworn, was examined and testified as follows:

My name is William Seatter. I live at Kingston. I am employed by the Puget Sound Navigation Company and was so employed on the 5th day of December, 1927. I was on the steamer "Olympic" as a watchman. I remember the day of the collision with the "Magna," and I was on the "Olympic" that day. The boat left Seattle at 4:30; that is her scheduled time. The lights were burning at the time. I always look at them when we left. It is part of my duty. After leaving the Colman Dock at 4:30 in the afternoon the whether was choppy. There was quite a wind from

(Testimony of William Seatter.)

the northwest. I went out and looked at the side lights, the head light and the stern light. At five o'clock I took the wheel. The vessel was at West Point. That was the time I was supposed to go on watch. My duties at the wheel are to steer. The captain was in the pilot-house. His name is Louis Van Bogaert. He was looking out of the window. The wheel is right in front of the window. It is directly back of the window. [48] I stood at the wheel facing forward. There is a window in front of me as I stand, about two or three feet. I was standing on the starboard side of the cabin. He was on the port side, almost right dead ahead of me on the port side. He was looking out of the front windows. The windows were open. At West Point the sea was quite choppy. The seas was from the northwest and the wind was coming from that direction. At that time it was quite dark. I could not see the hills and the shore on the sides of the Sound as we went along. I did not see any light ahead of us at all. I could not see a quarter of a mile to make out waves or anything on the water. The waves had little white caps on. We had proceeded I should say nineteen or twenty minutes, something like that, after leaving West Point before anything happened. I don't know what happened. I was at the wheel at the time and something happened. I don't know what it was. I did not see anything ahead at all. I looked out of the window ahead at times. If there had been any light ahead I should have seen

(Testimony of William Seatter.)

it. I looked out when we struck this object and I did not see any lights at all. The first time that I saw the sign of an object was about 5:18 or 5:20. I didn't see any boat. I didn't see anything of a boat after the collision. There is a searchlight on top of the pilot-house in the "Olympic." I didn't have anything to do with the searchlight.

Cross-examination.

On cross-examination the witness further testified:

The pilot-house of the "Olympic" is so designed as to permit a person to stand behind it and look forward out of the window. There is room for a person to pass in front of the wheel between the windows and the wheel, about two feet and a half, something like that. The captain was standing looking out [49] of the window a little on the port side, looking out of the window. I was steering the boat by compass. Once in a while I can take a look out of the window. The compass bowl is arranged so that I can look right down at it. I always do look out of the window. They had a look-out on the bow of the ship. The master was occupying one of the windows and I could not see out of that one. I was looking out about a minute before the collision. I didn't say anything before the impact and I did not see anything after the impact. I knew that we had gotten in collision with some object but I didn't know what it was. I testified before the Local Steamboat Inspectors

(Testimony of William Seatter.)

on December 6, 1927. I there testified that I did not see any lights on the fishing boat before the collision. The first knowledge I had of the collision was when I saw an object ahead which proved to be the fishing boat. I didn't know whether it was a boat or not. I knew it was an object. The weather was clear. I didn't see any moon. It was dusk. It was that state between light and dark that you could see an object out of the water out ahead of you if you were looking. If there was a vessel ahead of you you could see her 1,000 feet ahead and you could see that vessel without any artificial lights before the collision. I would not say that it was light enough to see an object out there without an artificial light because I know it was quite dark. I know that.

Redirect Examination.

It was pretty dark at that time. I was not able to see the headlands, that is, the land on either side of the Sound.

TESTIMONY OF PETER GARVEY, FOR DEFENDANT (RECALLED).

PETER GARVEY, a witness recalled on behalf of the defendant, being previously sworn, testified as follows: [50]

I testified that about three or four minutes before the collision I was fastening some curtains on the cabin windows. Prior to that time I was look-

(Testimony of Peter Garvey.)

ing out, walking back and forth on the bow. I did not see any lights ahead at all. I could see the light on West Point, and I could see the light on Apple Cove Point. I could not see any other lights in the neighborhood ahead at all. That was just before I started to fasten the curtains. I had not seen any sign of the vessel without lights ahead at all.

Cross-examination.

On cross-examination the witness further testified:

I was lookout before I started to put up the curtain. I was engaged in putting up the curtain for about three or four minutes. It doesn't take that long to put the curtains up because you just pull a little string and they flop down and you just hook them onto the bottom of the window. I had my back to the bow while fixing the curtain. Before that I was on lookout looking back and forth on the bow. It took me possibly four or five minutes to fix the curtains, to the best of my knowledge, and during those four or five minutes I was not giving attention to looking out. It was dark at that time,—well dusk or whatever you want to call it. It was dusk or dark. When I said dusk before the local Steamboat Inspectors I meant dark. It was not light enough to see the hull of this little vessel off on the water without the aid of artificial lights. I remember talking to you and another gentleman on the Colman Dock before the

(Testimony of Peter Garvey.)

other trial. You and Mr. Redpath talked to me about the case at the time I was subpoenaed. I did not say to you or Mr. Redpath that it was light enough to see the hull of the "Magna" a half a mile away on the water in answer to any questions. I absolutely made no such statements. I said nothing of the kind. I did not say, [51] "sure I could" in answer to any question by you as "then it was not necessary to have a light on the hull because you could see it so clearly half a mile away." I never said that you could see very plainly out on the water from the "Olympic," or anything of the kind, or words to that effect.

Redirect Examination.

On redirect examination the witness further testified:

Things which counsel has asked me as being statements that I made were absolutely not true. I never said nothing of the kind.

At this point court was adjourned until ten o'clock of the morning of the following day, May 6, 1931.

Upon court convening, the following proceedings were had:

TESTIMONY OF WILLIAM J. MALONEY, FOR DEFENDANT.

WILLIAM J. MALONEY, called as a witness on behalf of the defendant, having been first duly sworn, testified as follows:

(Testimony of William J. Maloney.)

My name is William J. Maloney, address 404 Colman Building. I am a marine surveyor. I am a master mariner, master of ocean vessels, steamer and sail, and have a pilot's license for all ports of the United States. I have a master's and pilot's license since 1905. I have had experience in navigation of vessels. I surveyed the "Magna" at one time and I am familiar with her. As to the effect of having a naked white light in the wheel-house on a small vessel such as that vessel had and endeavoring to operate that vessel after sundown, I doubt very much if you could see anything with a light in the pilot-house. I really do not think you could see out very good with a light in the pilot-house of any description. [52]

TESTIMONY OF WILLIAM SEATTER, FOR DEFENDANT (RECALLED).

WILLIAM SEATTER, recalled as a witness by the defendant, testified as follows:

I testified yesterday but I don't remember anything about the searchlight. I have had an illness affecting my mind since the date of the last trial. I am subject to epileptic fits and I know that that has had affect upon my memory. I did not talk to you before I came up to testify this time. I don't remember whether I testified at the former trial that I operated a searchlight after the collision between the vessels. Sometimes I remember good and sometimes I do not. I don't re-

(Testimony of William Seatter.)

member now whether or not that I testified at the former trial that I operated a searchlight after the collision. I first told you about these spells that I have had yesterday after court adjourned.

Thereafter the following proceedings occurred:

Mr. BRONSON.—If the Court please, I would like the record to show that we have been taken by surprise by this witness.

The WITNESS.—I have got witnesses to that effect, that I have always been subject to fits.

Mr. BRONSON.—That witness has testified almost directly opposite to his testimony at the preceding trial, and he has been called as a witness by the defendant in this case, and I desire to show, if your Honor please, the sudden change which has occurred in his testimony.

The COURT.—Well, the other testimony is not before the jury at all.

Mr. BRONSON.—That is precisely what I wish to show, your Honor.

The COURT.—He says that he remembers at times, and that he does not remember at other times, and that is before [53] the jury, and that is all you are entitled to. Proceed with anything further that you have with this witness.

Q. I would like to ask you if you did not testify as follows at the former trial: ''Were you able to see the headlands on either side of the Sound after passing the Point?'' And your answer: ''No, sir.'' A. No, sir; I was not.

Mr. MARTIN.—Just a moment. I object to that.

The COURT.—If this is not for the purpose of refreshing his recollection so that he may testify now but merely an indirect way of getting his former testimony into the record, as it looks now, the objection is good and it will be sustained.

Mr. BRONSON.—If the Court please, I desire to make a showing at this time that we have been taken by surprise by this witness, and his testimony here is obviously not testimony with reference to the facts, and I think we are entitled to show that the witness testified entirely different than he testified here—testified entirely different at a former trial, and that this is without any fair warning or notice to us.

The COURT.—If you can show me any authority for your position, I might consider your motion more seriously. You want to show what, now?

Mr. BRONSON.—This witness has testified that he has had a failure of memory.

The COURT.—Very well.

Mr. BRONSON.—And I am asking him if he did not testify in a certain way. In other words, I am impeaching my own witness. That is what I am doing, and I think under all the authorities, we are entitled to do that where a witness [54] takes an attorney by surprise and testifies differently than the attorney has reasonable grounds to believe that he will testify. Your Honor heard the witness testify before—

(Testimony of William Seatter.)

The COURT. — (Interrupting.) It is not within my memory. I have heard *thousand* of cases here, and you could not expect me to remember what the witness said before.

Mr. BRONSON.—We have the record in the former hearing right here, certified by your Honor, and I think we are entitled to show that this man's testimony now is almost diametrically opposed to what it was at the former trial. Having been taken by surprise; I think we are entitled to show that.

Mr. MARTIN.—Let me ask this question. How long have you been suffering, Mr. Seatter, from this ailment that you speak of?

The WITNESS.—All my life.

Mr. MARTIN.—And your condition to-day is in nowise different from what your condition was when you testified at the former trial?

The WITNESS.—Some days it is, and some days it is not. Some days I remember good, and some days I do not remember at all. I may be sitting here now, and in a second I might be off.

Mr. MARTIN.—In view of that, I renew my objection on the ground that it is not competent testimony.

The COURT.—Do you ever remember things that do not happen, or think that you remember them? How about that?

The WITNESS.—I do not know how that would be, I am sure.

(Testimony of Harry John Whaley.)

The COURT.—Well, we will let it go until this afternoon. [55] We will not finish this case anyway before that time. You can show me some authorities by that time, I presume, Counsel, and then you can call him again.

Mr. BRONSON.—Very well. You step down, Mr. Seatter. However, I want you to remain in attendance on the court please, Mr. Seatter.

TESTIMONY OF HARRY JOHN WHALEY, FOR DEFENDANT.

HARRY JOHN WHALEY, called as a witness on behalf of defendant, being first duly sworn, testified as follows:

My name is Harry John Whaley. I live at 9233–39th Ave. South, Seattle, Washington. I am a master mariner. I have held a master's license, first class, on Puget Sound since December 12, 1929. Prior to that I held a first class mate of lakes, bays and sounds and second class pilot of Puget Sound and adjacent waters. I have held such a license for seven years. At the present time I am in the wholesale fuel business for myself. In 1927, December, I was employed by the Puget Sound Navigation Company as first mate on the "Olympic" and was aboard that vessel when she left Seattle the afternoon of December 5, as first officer. The vessel left Seattle, as I remember, at 4:31 or 4:32. The regular schedule is 4:30, but it takes a minute or a minute and a half to get away.

(Testimony of Harry John Whaley.)

When the master of the vessel gave the let go whistle I gave orders for the line to be cast loose and I walked to the stern of the vessel and stood there while he was backing out, so that no traffic would come across us and when he put her on the course I relieved the skipper so that he could go down and have his supper. The weather at that time was kind of heavy and very cloudy, so that it was slightly dim. The lights were on the vessel at the time. The vessel proceeded on her course to Port Townsend. The first [56] change that I put her on was at Four Mile Rock. I relieved the captain. He gave me the course and I repeated it back to him, and then he went down to eat. I took charge of the vessel until he returned. I was then in the pilot-house. With me was the quartermaster. As I remember the vessel arrived off West Point about 5:01 or 5:02. At that time there was a very strong northwest wind and overhanging heavy clouds which cut off the headlands so that they could not be seen. It was dark. The only light which was visible was the Shilshole auto light. That is what is called the blinker light. I remained in charge of the navigation of the vessel up to Four Mile Rock. I then stepped back into my room and washed up, and then walked out around the pilot-house. I always went down the forward stairs as a rule, and the skipper was just changing the course at West Point. (Witness indicates position of Four Mile Rock and West Point on chart. Defendant's Exhibit 11.) The

(Testimony of Harry John Whaley.)

blinker light is right at the entrance to the Lake
Washington ship canal, that is where you come in
and start to go up to the Locks. I don't know
anything about the collision until the shipper had
blown the signal calling the crew to the boats. He
blew the regular boat whistle, three blasts of the
whistle. I was down in the lunch-counter eating
I left my meal and came right up to the boat deck.
I didn't see anything. I went and took my station,—that is No. 2 of the port side. I saw no sign
of any vessel in the vicinity of the "Olympic" at
that time. The "Olympic" was backing. When I
was setting down eating my dinner the first thing
I heard was the ringing of the telegraph, which
you can hear pretty much all over the "Olympic,"
and the first thing I knew I felt a strong vibration
and the skipper gave the call to go to the stations,
and the boat was backing up pretty hard at [57]
that time. You can tell that by the vibration. I
didn't see anything of this small boat until I was
talking to the skipper. I spoke to him and asked
him if he had hit anything, and he said he didn't
know for sure yet. Just then we happened to
turn around and I saw a dark object on the water.
I could not make it out until finally somebody came
out of the cabin. Then I could see him on the
deck. This object was about seventy-five feet from
the stern of the "Olympic." The "Olympic" was
then backing up. She was coming back. I did
not see any lights on this boat until his boat had
turned around. The captain gave orders to lower

(Testimony of Harry John Whaley.)

the boat and when he gave orders to lower the boat, my attention was attracted from that then until she was launched. After we lowered the boat and started the crew off I saw the boat again. It was about fifty feet from the boat that they had the searchlight on the man who was in the water. I did not see the man when he got into the water. It was then dark. You could not see anything without a searchlight. The searchlight had been played on the boat. That was how I happened to see him come out of his cabin, was through the searchlight. The searchlight was on the pilot-house of the "Olympic." The sky was cloudy. I did not see any sign of a moonlight on the water. The wind was strong from the northwest. The sea was rolling pretty heavy,—enough to fetch spray over the bow of the "Olympic." The visibility was a very short distance. I saw this man after he was picked up. I helped him in the boat when they came to the ship. I raised the boat and helped to put him in the skipper's room. The skipper gave me orders to undress him and give him some of his clothes to put on. I carried those orders out. I did not see any sign of injury on him. I asked the gentlemen if he was hurt or bruised in any way and he [58]   said he was not. I talked to him about the accident. I asked him, "Gee, it's a wonder that you could not see the 'Olympic' coming," and he said, "Well, I looked around and I could not see anything, or hear, and I went down to oil or fix my light generator," or

(Testimony of Harry John Whaley.)

something to that effect. I don't recall exactly what was said, and he told me that when we hit him that he fell over on the engine. I asked him where his range light was, and he said, "Well, my mast,"—I forget just exactly whether he said it was broken and he left it in Ballard to fix or what, but he said that he had left his mast behind. Then I think he said something about money being in his clothes that had been taken down to the boiler-room, and I sent one of the boys down to get the money and to return it. I was the one who took his watch out of his pocket. I took that out of his pants myself and gave it to Roy Neal to take to the master. This man had no appearance of any physical injuries to be seen when he was changing his clothes. To my experience a white light in the wheel-house to navigate with is an impossibility. The light blinds you. It blinds you so that it is just as if you do not shut off the little dash light on your car when driving at night. It is just the same thing with having a white light burning in the wheel-house. It is strictly against the law, and is never permitted in the pilot-house of a vessel.

Cross-examination.

On cross-examination the witness further testified:

I was in the wheel-house from the time we got clear of the dock until we got to Four Mile Rock. That would be a matter of eighteen or nineteen minutes. As I came out of my room and started below

(Testimony of Harry John Whaley.)

at West Point, I stopped and particularly looked at the condition of the sky. It is always the nature of seafaring [59] men when we come out of our room to look at the weather conditions. It was more cloudy then then at 4:30. I distinctly remember that the cloudiness had increased. The sky was overcast. I couldn't see any stars at all. I did not see any moon at all. It was just dark. Practically just as dark as night. The light had disappeared because the sun had set at 4:17. It was absolutely dark at five o'clock. That is my recollection. It was darker then than it was at eleven o'clock. I was on deck two or three minutes at the pilot-house before going below, and the next thing I knew about the affair was the telegraph bells and vibration of the vessel when going astern. The first thing I saw of anything on the water was after I had talked to the skipper and turned to go back to my station. My station is only about ten or fifteen feet from the pilot-house. When I turned around and the searchlight played on the boat I first saw this object. I could not see anything until the searchlight was put in use. I remember testifying at the former trial that I went and reported to the captain and that it was dark, and there was a strong northwest wind blowing about a twenty or twenty-two mile gale. I remember stating that I didn't see any floating object in the vicinity until I happened to turn and I noticed a dark object going past our stern, and I just stated in my testimony when I was talking to Mr. Bronson that

(Testimony of Harry John Whaley.)

I had seen a dark object but I didn't know what it was until they had played a searchlight on it. I said that I didn't see any lights on it until the boat had turned around. I meant the little fishing boat. I then saw a red light. I should judge that we never got more than six or seven hundred feet from the "Magna." It was dark when I left the wheelhouse at Four Mile Rock,—not quite as dark as it was when we were called to the boat, or when I came out of the wheel-house. We ordinarily [60] put the curtains down on the main deck when the lights are turned on in the forward cabin. But the lights are not always turned on the forward part of the cabin until it commences to get dark. The purpose of putting the curtains down is so the light won't show out ahead and thus interfere with the navigation of the vessel. The curtains are not put up until it commences to get dark and the lights are turned on.

TESTIMONY OF LAWRENCE C. FISHER, FOR DEFENDANT.

LAWRENCE C. FISHER, called as a witness on behalf of defendant, having been first duly sworn, testified as follows:

My name is Lawrence C. Fisher. I live in Seattle. I am a Meteorologist of the United States Weather Bureau of Seattle. The office of the Bureau is in the Hoge Building, and that is where our observations are taken for this port. I have

(Testimony of Lawrence C. Fisher.)

brought the records of the United States Weather Bureau here at your request. On December 5, 1927, the sun set at 4:17 P. M. I mean by that, the upper rim disappeared beneath the ideal horizon,—the sea level horizon. The upper rim is the upper edge of the sun, and the upper edge of the sun had disappeared below the water level horizon at 4:17 between the hours of four and five. Wind velocities of twenty miles were actually recorded; between five and six, seventeen miles; between six and seven, ten miles. The records show that the sun went down behind these clouds. The sun was obscure. The prevailing direction of the wind for the hour from four to five was from the northwest. This being December 5th, it is my opinion that the sun would set to the south of true west. On that day civil twilight would continue for thirty-five minutes. One way of defining civil twilight is that it is the length of time after sunset, in this case [61] until the upper rim of the sun was six degrees below the horizon. That is the period of time during which ordinary outdoor occupations are regarded as possible. At the end of the period of civil twilight one would get out of the period of practical twilight. The end of civil twilight on December 5th was 4:52. Regular telegraph observations started at twenty minutes to five, and at that time on that evening the state of the sky was regarded as clear. There were a few cumulus clouds observed from the Hoge Building roof. Our records do not show the condition of the sky nine or ten miles northwest of the city. There

(Testimony of Lawrence C. Fisher.)

is nothing to show the actual distribution of the clouds. It was recorded as full. The end of civil twilight is always taken at ideal conditions, that is at water level horizon and cloudless sky. If the sun set behind clouds that would shorten the period of civil twilight. It would also affect the degree of darkness which would come on at the end of the twilight. Our records show that the sun setting behind a solid bank of clouds was obscured. The clouds, of course, were in the west. According to the definition of civil twilight it is more or less dependent upon the cloudiness of the sky after sunset, and the period of practical twilight is dependent upon the clearness of the sky. The sun setting behind clouds will advance the time of the end of civil twilight.

Cross-examination.

On cross-examination the witness further testified: I would not say that the condition of cloudiness in the western sky was observed from the roof of the Hoge Building. It may have been taken from one of the windows. It is one of the duties of the observers to take note of the sunset and sunrise. The kind of clouds at sunset for that day is not recorded. [62] The kind of clouds at the observation taken immediately before five o'clock was cumulus clouds. Cumulus clouds are thick clouds. At twenty minutes to five there were still a few clouds. I would suppose that the dark clouds behind which the sun is recorded to have set would have been on the western horizon. There is nothing to show the

(Testimony of Lawrence C. Fisher.)

distribution of the other clouds. The sum total of the clouds was less than one-half of one-tenth of the sky. So far as the surface conditions are concerned the storm condition of the afternoon was quieting down. I don't think that it always follows that the sky condition clears with the wind dying down The moon on December 5th rose at 2:47 P. M. That is the upper rim of the moon just reached an assumed ideal horizon. The moon was approaching the full. Two days later the moon was full. My recollection is that that was on the 8th. My certificate confirms that. Ordinarily, it takes about seven days for the moon to pass from one phase to the next phase, and there are four phases. This would be the second quarter. At the first quarter it is half a moon. The jury understands what is meant by a full moon. This is just halfway between the first quarter and the full moon. At five o'clock on December 5th, the moon would be roughly sixty degrees from the zenith. That would be about one-third of the way from the horizon to the zenith. I have no records and would not care to express an opinion whether the moon was showing over the waters of Elliott Bay at five o'clock. Astronomical twilight continues from the time that the upper rim of the sun disappears below the horizon until the center of the sun is eighteen degrees below the horizon. That is one hour and fifty-one minutes. It is possible that there would be still some light in the west. The end of astronomical twilight ends the light of day, and from then on there is only the

(Testimony of Lawrence C. Fisher.)

astral light in [63] the sky. Astronomically that is correct. The end of civil twilight occurs when the center of the sun is six degrees below the horizon. To a certain extent that is an arbitraty period. That is fixed at thirty-five minutes at Seattle. The only statement that I can add is that between the time that the sun is four degrees below the horizon and six degrees, the statement is given by authorities that the light fades very rapidly.

Redirect Examination.

On redirect examination the witness testified as follows:

Civil twilight is something that has been set up to apply to practical occupations of mankind in the world, and astronomical twilight is something pertaining to instruments and the last physical speck of light in the heaven for scientific purposes.

TESTIMONY OF DONALD S. AMES, FOR DEFENDANT.

DONALD S. AMES, called as a witness on behalf of defendant, having been first duly sworn, testified as follows:

My name is Donald S. Ames. I live in Seattle. I am United States Local Inspector of Steam and Motor Vessels. I hold a license as navigating officer, master of steam, sail and motor, any ocean. I have held such license forty years. I am one of the local inspectors in this district. As such, my duties

(Testimony of Donald S. Ames.)

are the inspecting of all vessels under steam or motor power, with the exception of motor boats under sixty-five feet in length, and also with examining all candidates and granting licenses to those successfully applying for licenses in the deck department and engineer officers. One of my duties is to enforce the local rules and the International rules of navigation as promulgated by the Secretary of Commerce. [64]

Thereafter the following proceedings were had:

Q. How long have you been doing that work?

The COURT.—I will tell your witness to vacate the stand if you do not bring him to the point that you want to ask him about. I told you that his qualifications are sufficiently established. Come to what is material in this case.

Mr. BRONSON.—I want to bring him back to the date of this accident.

The COURT.—He has had a license for forty years. He has told us. Proceed.

Q. I wish you would tell, Captain, what the requirements for a vessel 33 feet in length were on December 5, 1927?

Mr. MARTIN.—I object to that. The laws speaks for itself.

The COURT.—Sustained.

Mr. BRONSON.—Exception.

Q. Captain, handing you Defendant's Exhibit 10 for identification, I will ask you whether or not that is an official publication issued by the Secretary of

(Testimony of Donald S. Ames.)

Commerce, and in effect on the 5th day of December, 1927 (handing document to witness).

A. Yes, sir.

Q. Is that correct?   A. Yes, sir.

Mr. BRONSON.—I offer this in evidence, if the Court please.

The COURT.—Admit it.

(Whereupon regulation of motor boats, issued by the Department of Commerce was admitted in evidence as Defendant's Exhibit 10.) [65]

Mr. BRONSON.—That is all.

The COURT.—Well, if you have anything material, present it to the jury right now so that they can know what it all means.

Mr. BRONSON.—I will read Exhibit No. 10 to the jury.

"Be it enacted by the Senate and House of Representatives of the United States of America in Congress assembled, that the words 'motor boat' where used in this Act shall include every vessel propelled by machinery and not more than sixty-five feet in length except tugboats and towboats propelled by steam. The length shall be measured—"

The COURT.—(Interrupting.) The jury does not care to hear the whole law. What is there in these rules that you call particularly to the attention of this jury?

Mr. BRONSON.—"That motor boats subject to the provisions of this Act shall be divided into classes as follows:

"Class One. Less than twenty-six feet in length.

(Testimony of Donald S. Ames.)

Class two. Twenty-six feet or over and less than forty feet in length.

Class three. Forty feet or over and not more than sixty-five feet in length.

Sec. 3. That every motor boat in all weathers from sunset to sunrise shall carry the following lights, and during such time no other lights which may be mistaken for those prescribed shall be exhibited.

(a) Every motor boat of class one shall carry the following lights:

First. A white light aft to show all around the horizon.''

I will omit that and go to classes two and three.

''(b) Every motor boat of classes two and three shall [66] carry the following lights:

First. A bright white light in the forepart of the vessel as near the stem as practicable, so constructed as to show an unbroken light over an arc of the horizon of twenty points of the compass, so fixed as to throw the light ten points on each side of the vessel, namely, from right ahead to two points abaft the beam on either side. The glass or lens shall be of not less than the following dimensions:''

I will omit that.

''Second. A white light aft to show all around the horizon.''

That pursuant to the provisions of that law, the Secretary of Commerce promulgated certain rules and regulations with reference to those lights, Section 8 of which is as follows:

(Testimony of Louis Van Bogaert.)

"The aft light should be higher and so placed as to form a range with the forward light, and should be clear of house awnings and other obstructions."

The COURT.—Call your next witness.

TESTIMONY OF LOUIS VAN BOGAERT, FOR DEFENDANT.

LOUIS VAN BOGAERT, called as a witness on behalf of defendant, having been first duly sworn, testified as follows:

My name is Louis Van Bogaert. I am a master mariner, employed by the Puget Sound Navigation Company and was so employed on the 5th day of December, 1927, as the master of the steamer "Olympic." The vessel left Seattle that day at 4:32 o'clock. I have a clock in the pilot-house and navigate according to the same. At 4:32 of that day it was getting dusk. It was dusk. We had our lights on. The vessel proceeded to Four Mile Rock. From Seattle to Four Mile Rock I was not in charge but after passing Four Mile Rock I took charge of the vessel. [67] We passed West Point light at 5:01. There was a strong northwest wind blowing, and it was getting dark at the time, and it was cloudy. The sea was very rough. The tide was ebbing, running out against the wind. There were quite a few white caps and quite a spray running. It was very dark. You could see light but you could not see anything else. It was overcast and cloudy. You could see the highlands but you could

(Testimony of Louis Van Bogaert.)

not see the shorelands on either side. After rounding West Point I was standing on the starboard side in the wheel-house, looking out, not through a window. The window was down. I remained there until I saw an object ahead of me about four miles northwest of West Point. I saw a dark object about one hundred feet ahead of us. I could not make out what it was. I *though* it would be a dolphin adrift or something like that. At that time it would not seem to have any motion in the water. As we struck the object I saw it was a boat. I did not see any light on this object until after we struck it. I saw a red light on the port side after it swung around under the port bow. I saw no other lights ahead of me after I came around West Point, except Point Monroe. (Witness indicates Point Monroe on chart, Defendant's Exhibit 11.) I had run nineteen minutes from West Point when I came into collision with this object. The vessel's speed was 13.8 miles per hour or 12 knots. The vessel was on her regular course. From West Point we were proceeding for President Point. I was laying a course for President Point, and from there to Apple Tree and on to No Point, and up to Port Townsend. (Witness then lays off course of "Olympic" on chart by line marked "C–D," and also lays off course on chart indicating course of a vessel proceeding from Lake Washington Canal to Suquamish as "A–B," Defendant's Exhibit 11.) My vessel was pursuing the [68] course of "C–D." When we came into collision with this object we were not in the line

(Testimony of Louis Van Bogaert.)

of intersection of a course of a vessel proceeding from Shilshole Bay or the entrance of the Lake Washington ship canal to Suquamish. We were at least two miles past that point. We struck this object in the water at 5:20. We had the clock right there and when anything happened we take the time right away because it is very important to record the time. Between the time when I first saw this object and the time when we struck it I reversed the engine. I could tell that the engine was put astern by the vibration. That was about one hundred feet from this object. Mr. Seatter, the quartermaster was in the wheel-house with me. I was not quite able to stop the vessel before striking the object but the headway was checked considerably. We struck this object on the port quarter. We got real close to it. I could see it was a boat and I hit her on the port quarter. Both were going the same way and approximately in the same direction when we hit. He was proceeding on the starboard bow, just about ahead. He was heading the same way that we were going. He was going right into the sea. When the small boat had moved away it swung on our port side and it went away one hundred feet, and I put a searchlight on it as soon as it got by our guard. I could not see him at first, and then he got away from us and the quartermaster, Seatter, kept the searchlight on the boat all the time. Then, when the boat got away one hundred and fifty feet or two hundred feet a man came out on the deck and hollered something to me, and I could not make out

(Testimony of Louis Van Bogaert.)

what he was hollering, and then he threw a piece of board about two feet square into the water and jumped after that, and his boat was still having motion ahead when he jumped. The "Olympic" was stopped and I ordered a lifeboat to go over to [69] rescue this man. It was about five minutes until he was picked up. He was brought aboard and given first aid in my room. His boat had not actually swung when he was picked up. I cannot say how far away his boat was then because we kept the searchlight on the man all the time, but the rays of the searchlight showed on the boat and the boat had not sunk yet when we picked him up. The man's watch and money were given to me and they were returned to him that evening, after the man was dried. I took care of the pocketbook and dried it. The only thing I asked Mr. Nelson was why he did not have the proper lights up, and he told me that he did not have his range light. Range light and stern light are the same thing. He said that the mast had been repaired and taken down in some manner and he had not had time to put up this mast. He was figuring on putting it up the next morning over in Poulsbo, and I said to him, "You should have put up some kind of light." And he said he tried to put up some kind of light off the dolphin of Ballard but it was too rough to put up a light and I asked him if he had seen us at any time, and he said "No" that he did not see us approaching. He did not say what dolphin it was where he tried to put up the mast. This conversation took place in

(Testimony of Louis Van Bogaert.)

my room on the way to Port Townsend. At the
point of collision it was very cloudy. Quite a heavy
sea was running there because we had quite a time
to maneuver around. I could not see unlighted objects in the water that evening. About all that I
could do was to see about one hundred feet ahead.
And I was looking right ahead at the time. The
visibility was bad. There was no precipitation.
There were a few clouds overhead. This was about
ten miles north of the Colman Dock. It would be
seven or eight miles on a direct line. This man
made no complaint to me about being injured. But
we had   [70]   a lot of trouble to keep the man on
our ship. As soon as we hoisted him up on deck he
wanted to jump out and we had quite a lot of trouble
keeping him in. In fact, before the lifeboat was
hoisted on deck he jumped out before it was brought
on board the deck.

(At this point Defendant's Exhibit 11, being a
chart, was admitted in evidence.)

Cross-examination.

On cross-examination the witness testified as follows:

When we left Seattle I would not call it dark.
It was dusk. We had to turn our lights on at four
o'clock that day at the Colman Dock. The cabin
lights were on at that time. Plaintiff's Exhibit 2
is a good picture of the "Olympic." I should judge
it is about twenty-five feet from the bow to the front
windows of the cabin. The saloon deck, or outside

(Testimony of Louis Van Bogaert.)

deck, is about fifteen feet above the water. The saloon deck, or passenger deck, as we call it. The next deck is eight feet higher. That is the boat deck. The floor of the pilot-house is about four feet above the boat deck. That would be approximately twenty-seven feet above the water. I did not sound any whistle signal. I am not supposed to give any blasts of the signal unless I know what to do. I did not put my wheel from one side to the other. This object might have been a long dolphin with piles sticking out and I could not do that for fear of running into that. You see, they have old dolphins in some of these ferry slips on the Sound, and they break loose, and the piles will hang out behind the dolphin, and if you should swing your ship on those submerged parts, your propeller would be broken. I immediately stopped and reversed. We never stopped. We just put her in reverse. I did not give a blast of the signal then because I could not make out [71] what the object was. The curtains on the cabin windows are generally put down at Seattle when we leave the dock. They were dropped down at Seattle but they were not fastened on that night. I heard the testimony of Mr. Garvey, that he was fastening the curtains then because I told him to fasten the curtains, to fasten them good. I gave him that order about 5:15. I was then in the pilot-house. I had a helmsman in the pilot-house with me. Garvey had been on lookout. I gave him an order to fasten the curtains because they generally flop around when the wind is hitting them. Sometimes the curtains are fas-

(Testimony of Louis Van Bogaert.)

tened when they are put down and sometimes they
are not. If we have no wind we do not fasten them.
We just drop them down because there is a big iron
pipe that holds them down. I ordered him to leave
the lookout and go fasten the curtains. His station as lookout is not in the eyes of the vessel because he could not walk across the bow. His place
of lookout was forward of the windows on the bow.
I don't know whether he was fastening the curtains
for four or five minutes. I did not time him on
that. I know the distinction between the weather
being overcast and cloudy and being clear. I testified before the local inspectors that the weather
was clear, but that is as regards fog and snow. The
Local Steamboat Inspector's question had reference
as to whether there was fog or snow. I haven't
changed my testimony at all. If you would ask me
if it was foggy and smoky I would answer that it
was clear, but there was no clouds in the sky mentioned at all at the investigation before the inspectors. The question was asked me before the inspectors, "What was the condition of the weather
before the collision," and I answered "a strong
northwest wind and ebb tide," and "was it clear"
was asked me, and I answered "Yes, sir, it was
clear." That was with respect to fog and snow,
[72] because Captain Ames was wanting to know
whether I was running full speed or not, and I
told him that I was. I would not say that they
asked me directly about fog and snow, but that was
what we had reference to in the Inspector's Office,
as to the condition of the weather, and it had not

(Testimony of Louis Van Bogaert.)

any reference at all as to what the sky was overhead. What I wish to convey is that it was cloudy but that there was no fog or snow. We were an overtaking vessel. There was nobody on lookout at the time except Mr. Garvey. I did not observe the moon.

Redirect Examination.

On redirect examination the witness testified as follows: It is my testimony to-day that it was clear, and also was overcast, clear but cloudy. What we had reference to when we spoke of clear weather is with regard to fog or snow. If anybody comes into the pilot-house and asks you "how was the night last night," you would say, "Why, it was clear last night," but it refers to fog, rain or snow. It would mean that the visibility would be clear so far as seeing ahead was concerned. It is my recollection that it was clear at the time. I know that the curtains were down in the cabin windows before we got to West Point. I saw them in Seattle. They were down before we backed out. They have an iron bar, a weight on the bottom of them to hold them down. My instructions to the lookout before the collision were just to fasten them at the bottom to keep them from hitting against the house on account of the wind that was blowing. From my position in the pilot-house I had a clear and unobstructed view ahead, a very good view.

At this point court was adjourned until 1:30 of the same day, at which time the following proceedings took place: [73]

(Testimony of Louis Van Bogaert.)

Recross-examination of LOUIS VAN BOGAERT.

I would say the ship had between forty and fifty passengers. I do not have an actual count.

Redirect Examination.

I do not keep a list of the passengers. I have no records of the passengers. We just take the tickets at the plank and that is all.

TESTIMONY OF WILLIAM SEATTER, FOR DEFENDANT (RECALLED).

WILLIAM SEATTER, witness called on behalf of the defendant, recalled, and testified as follows:

Q. I will ask you if you did not testify as follows, Mr. Seatter, at the former trial:

"Now, just describe the maneuvers the 'Olympic' made after this gas boat had pulled off the left-hand side, as you say? A. Well, the captain gave orders to put a searchlight on this object, which I did, and I held it on there all the time. Q. Where was the searchlight? A. Right upon the pilot-house. Q. Was it inside or outside? A. The switch is inside the pilot-house and the searchlight is outside. Q. How is it controlled—from the inside or the outside? A. From the inside. Q. The control of the searchlight is inside and the search-light is outside? A. Yes, sir. The captain turned the light on, and I operated it. Q. He turned it on? A. Yes, sir. Q. What did you have to do with the searchlight? A. You have got to turn it up and down and work it so as to show on this object

(Testimony of William Seatter.)

that we hit. Q. Was the vessel stopped when you had the searchlight turned on? A. Yes, sir. Q. Could you then see this little boat without a searchlight? A. No, sir. Q. Were you able to see where it was? A. No, sir; I could not see it without the searchlight. Q. Were you able to find it [74] with the searchlight? A. Yes, sir. Q. Where was it with reference to your ship? A. Well, it was—I cannot say exactly how far it was away. Q. Was it astern of you or on your port beam, or where? A. On the port beam, sir.''

I will ask you whether or not you testified in that fashion at the former hearing, Mr. Seatter?

A. Well, it seems to me that I did, but under the condition that I am in, now, I don't remember whether I operated the searchlight or not.

Q. You don't remember now whether you did or not? A. I don't remember now.

The COURT.—He did so testify, whether he remembers it now or not, and you have read it to the jury, and that is all there is to that. You can now ask him how he accounts for the difference between his testimony at that time and now.

Mr. BRONSON.—He says he does not remember now.

The COURT.—He says that he does not remember what he testified to at the former trial. You have read to him what he testified to from a written document, and now you are going to put yourself to the trouble of denying it.

Mr. BRONSON.—That is not my purpose at all. I would like to have the witness step down and call

(Testimony of William Seatter.)

Mr. Lescher, the Court Reporter who reported that case.

The COURT.—The Court will not permit you to do that. The Court has told you that you have the evidence settled in the bill of exceptions. Suppose the stenographer denies it?

Mr. BRONSON.—Well, if the stenographer denies it, why that is the fact.

The COURT.—Well, it is in the settled bill of exceptions. What more do you want than that? You have got [75] it in the bill of exceptions.

Mr. BRONSON.—At this time we offer the bill of exceptions in evidence.

The COURT.—Oh, no. You can proceed as I told you. You have stated to the jury what he did testify at the former trial. Now, you can ask him if he can explain it. He testifies one way here and he has testified in another way at the former trial, and how is the jury going to know which way it is?

Q. Can you explain why you testify one way now and testified another way at a former trial?

A. No, sir; I cannot.

Q. You cannot explain it?

A. Not in the condition that I am in.

Q. Do you know whether or not you did testify one way at the former trial and—

A. (Interrupting.) Well, if I testified only a few days afterwards, I can remember for a few days, but two or three years afterwards, I cannot remember.

Q. You have no recollection of having testified in the manner that I have just indicated in reading these questions and answers to you?

(Testimony of William Seatter.)

A. Well, it seems to me that I did.

Q. Well, do you know whether or not those are facts that you states there—whether those are the facts?

A. Yes, sir; those are facts that I stated there. Of course, take it for two years—

Cross-examination.

Thereupon, upon cross-examination the further proceedings were had: [76]

Q. As you have said this morning, you have been in that condition all your life?   A. Yes, sir.

Q. You memory is no better now than it was on the day that you testified in this court formerly?

A. Sometimes I feel all right, and other times I do not.

Q. As a matter of fact, you do not remember anything for more than two or three days, do you?

A. Well, sometimes for a week or ten days, but when it comes to two or three years, then I do not remember.

Q. You have difficulty in remembering anything after a week or ten days, don't you?

A. Yes, sir, and sometimes not that long, and sometimes it may be longer than that.

Mr. MARTIN.—That is all.

The COURT.—Just a moment. The other trial was when?

Mr. BRONSON.—Two years after the accident, approximately?

Mr. MARTIN.—Yes, your Honor.

(Testimony of William Seatter.)

The COURT.—And this is a year and a half since then?

Mr. MARTIN.—Yes, sir.

The COURT.—Now, you are trying to tell us the truth as near as you can?

The WITNESS.—Yes, sir.

The COURT.—Now, you have told us of your affliction and it does appear in the record of the former trial that you operated the searchlight, and at this time you say that you did not operate the searchlight, or that you do not remember. Now, are you able to tell us from your recollection which one of those statements is the truth, or are you still at sea about it? [77]

The WITNESS.—Well, I recollect that I did. It is coming back to me.

Thereupon the defendant rested its case.

TESTIMONY OF LYDIA KNAAK, FOR PLAINTIFF (IN REBUTTAL).

Thereupon, in rebuttal, LYDIA KNAAK, produced as a witness on behalf of plaintiff, having been first duly sworn, testified as follows:

I am a stenographer employed as a reporter for the steamboat inspectors of this port. On December 6, 1927, I took a shorthand account of the interrogation of the officers of the steamship "Olympic."

Thereupon the following proceeds were had:

Q. "What was the condition of the weather at the time of the collision?

(Testimony of Lydia Knaak.)

A. Strong northwest wind and ebb tide." Did he make that answer?

A. (Interrupting.) I cannot remember it offhand. I can verify it by looking at my notes.

Q. Please verify it. This is preliminary to what follows. It is the third or fourth question from the beginning of his examination.

The COURT.—As a matter of fact, I do not know what the witness denied, or even what you are talking about. I do not know whether the witness denied it or not.

Mr. MARTIN.—Yes, your Honor. I do not mean to contradict your Honor, but—

The COURT.—(Interrupting.) He said, "Yes, I so testified, but I had in mind the absence of fog and snow."

Mr. MARTIN.—He said that that was in the question: that they put that question to him.

The WITNESS: The question is, "What was the condition of the weather at the time of the collision," and the answer is "strong northwest wind and ebb tide." [78]

Q. And then this next question, "Was it clear?" And his answer, "Yes, it was clear."

A. Yes, sir.

Q. Do you find in any of those questions any reference to fog or snow?

A. Not in either one of those.

Q. Will you look and see, in connection with that examination, going on a few more questions, whether there was any such reference—

Mr. BRONSON.—(Interrupting.) I do not

(Testimony of Lydia Knaak.)

think that this is a contradiction of anything, your Honor. The witness testified that he did so testify.

The COURT.—That is true, but the question is, was anything said about fog and snow right then which might have some bearing as to the inferences intended by the questions with respect to the weather. Do you find anything of that sort there?

The WITNESS.—That is all that was said about the weather.

Mr. MARTIN.—That is all.

Mr. BRONSON.—No questions.

TESTIMONY OF HANS NELSON, IN HIS OWN BEHALF (RECALLED IN REBUTTAL).

HANS NELSON, the plaintiff, recalled as a witness in his own behalf, testified as follows:

After the collision I was taken aboard the "Olympic." They took my money to the captain's room I had some conversation with the captain and the mate. I never stated to them that I was not injured. I did not say that just before the collision I was having any trouble with the engine or lighting system. I did not tell them that I did not have any light aft, for the [79] reason that I thought that I would put one up at the buoy, and it was too rough and I couldn't put up the light aft. No such conversation took place. After the collision no searchlight from the "Olympic" was played on either myself or my boat.

(Testimony of Hans Nelson.)

Thereupon, in response to questions put to him by the Court, the witness testified as follows:

I had a light in the bow, six feet above the water, and I had a light aft just above the same, or five feet above the water. I put that on all the lights when I left the Locks at Ballard that day. I put all the lights up that day. The light was hanging on the sill, right up in the door. Hanging on the sill there is a cross-beam across the door frame. It was hanging on the extension cord from the battery. There was a hook up there that we use to hang the light on, on that hook all the time, and that light with a bulb hanging down came about two inches from the beam. The cord was six feet from the battery. The bulb was just hanging under the hook.

Thereafter, in response to question by counsel for plaintiff, plaintiff further testified:

My watch stopped at 5:15. It was full of water. It was all rusted up when I got home. That is the same watch I was claiming damages for. It did not go down with the vessel. The light was two inches below the sill to which it was hanging. Two inches on the inside. If it had been moved out two inches it would be right in the same as the pilot-house. The door was open and the light was lighted.

Cross-examination.

On cross-examination the witness testified as follows:

Q. You stated in answer to a question by the

(Testimony of Hans Nelson.)

Court what light you had aft. You did not have any light in the after part of the ship, did you? [80]

The COURT.—In the cabin, of course.

Q. Both lights were in the forward part of the ship, that is *t*hat I am getting at—at the wheel-house?

A. I never had any light in the wheel-house. I had it in the door of the wheel-house. It was not in the wheel-house.

Q. Both lights were up where the wheel-house is, of the vessel? A. No.

Recross-examination.

On recross-examination the witness testified as follows:

I had the window open in the pilot-house on the lee side, the second window from aft. There are five windows in the house, and the second window from aft was open. I had a light in the forecastle of the boat. The light in the pilot-house and the one down below in the forecastle did not bother me to see ahead of the vessel. The door is three feet wide. The light was in the middle of the door.

TESTIMONY OF HARRY S. REDPATH, FOR PLAINTIFF (IN REBUTTAL).

HARRY S. REDPATH, called as a witness on behalf of plaintiff, in rebuttal, having been first duly sworn, testified as follows:

My name is Harry S. Redpath. I live in Seattle,

(Testimony of Harry S. Redpath.)
and I am associated with the counsel for plaintiff in
the practice of law in the Colman Building. Two
or three days before the former trial I went down
with Mr. Martin to the Colman Dock and we inter-
viewed Mr. Garvey, the witness previously called
here. He said that you could see the "Magna"
without the aid of artificial light when the "Olympic" backed away; that the "Olympic" backed
away about half a mile, and that you could see her
about a half a mile out in the water without an artificial light. [81]

Thereupon the testimony was closed.

Thereupon Mr. Bronson, attorney for the defendant moved the Court to instruct the jury to return
a verdict for defendant, which motion was by the
Court denied, and an exception claimed.

Thereupon the following proceedings were had:

Mr. BRONSON.—If the Court please, at this
time I wish to renew the motion which I made at
the close of the plaintiff's case, for the reasons there
stated, and also for the reasons stated in the trial
brief which has been submitted.

The COURT.—The motion will be denied. The
case will go to the jury.

Mr. BRONSON.—Note an exception.

Thereupon the Court proceeded to instruct the
jury as follows:

INSTRUCTIONS OF THE COURT TO THE JURY.

The COURT.—Well, Ladies and Gentlemen of the
Jury, you have heard the evidence, and the argu-

ments, and now it is for the Court to deliver to you
the instructions. That is mainly to make you acquainted with the law that applies to the case, and
in the light of which you determine the facts. Remember, you take the law from the Court, but what
witnesses to believe, how far, and what weight to
give to their testimony, and to the circumstances
that surround the whole case, that is esclusively
your function. Jurors are brought into court to determine questions of fact in the light of the law as
the court gives it. This case as the Court commented
once or twice during the trial, is after all, fairly
simple. It resolves itself into one or two plain,
distinct questions, and there is not a great deal of
law involved so far as is necessary to give it to the
jury. As a matter [82] of fact, the Court agrees
with the statement of counsel for the defense in his
argument that if the plaintiff had that light in the
doorway of his boat, lit long enough before the collision so that it could have been seen by a proper
lookout on the "Olympic," they would have avoided
him, and the collision would have never occurred.
And if the plaintiff had it there, as he says that he
did, and which the defendant denies, there is no
reason why he should not recover in this action.

Before we come to any more of the law, I am
simply stating that I agree with counsel's position,
and I think the plaintiff does now, too. That is
all I can see in this case. You must remember
this, that the plaintiff must prove his case by a
greater weight of the evidence. The burden is on
him throughout to prove that he had that light
there, lit there for the length of time that I have

stated to you, and to prove that it was a good and sufficient light to serve its purpose, and to prove the amount of his damages. The burden is on him to prove all those things before he can recover. So you see that in this case, there is mainly involved the credibility of witnesses where there is a direct conflict between the witnesses for the plaintiff and the witnesses for the defendant.

You are to determine which witnesses to believe; what weight to give to their testimony, and the weight to be given to circumstances in the case.

You determine the credibility of witnesses in court just as you determine the credibility of people with whom you deal in your daily life. I have no doubt that you all take some pride in your knowledge of human nature; and in your experience in bargaining or talking with other people, that you are able to penetrate whether they are dealing fairly and squarely, and telling [83] the truth, or not, instead of letting them put something over on you. And in just the same way as you determine the truth of those with whom you deal or converse in daily life, you determine the truthfulness of those you hear on the witness-stand. You take into consideration their appearance; their demeanor; their disposition; whether they seem to be endeavoring to lay before you a plain, unvarnished tale of what occurred, giving you the whole truth of it, no more and no less; or whether they are inclined to exaggerate or to depreciate events or circumstances, and whether their statements are reasonable or not; whether they conform to common experience—your experience—and whether the witnesses are interested in the case. Of course, that is very important in this case. The plaintiff is vitally interested of course. He has lost his boat and suffered losses in connection with it that run up into a considerable amount of money for anyone, and we can assume that if the plaintiff is a fisherman, it is rather a large sum of money.

On the other hand, the defendant's witnesses are interested—some of them. The captain of the boat is certainly interested because it is assumed that he was on watch at the time, and he is held responsible for due care and attention to his boat.

The captain says that he took the bow lookout away from him post of duty to attend to the curtains on the windows. So you can see that he is interested. If the captain is not expert or skillful or careful, he may lose his rating as a captain, and not be able to operate vessels as a captain thereafter.

There there were two or three other witnesses that testified on behalf of the company, and they are still in the employ of the company. Remember, there is no rule of law that a person interested in a case as the plaintiff is, or the witnesses [84] interested in a case as the captain, mate and others of the defendant's witnesses are, will by reason of that fact testify falsely. There is no rule of law that so provides, but the rule of law is this, that you will remember the interest of the parties and of the witnesses, and you will determine whether that self-interest of theirs, taking note of the extent of from the truth in their endeavor to deceive you and it, has caused them in any particular to deviate procure something that they are not entitled to, or to resist something that they ought to pay.

You must remember that if witnesses conflict, it is for you to determine who is telling the truth. Witnesses sometimes conflict with each other on the same side of the case. It may be due to a mistake, or to faulty recollection. No man's recollection is perfect—or otherwise. So you must take that all into consideration.

Remember in starting out in this case, too, that it is not enough that there was a collision and the plaintiff has suffered serious loss, to entitle him to a verdict. We all understand that, but it is good to remember.

The plaintiff bases his right to recover in this action on the fact that the collision was due, as he alleges, to the negligence and fault of the defendant, and the defendant alone, and the defendant resists on the theory, as it alleges, that it was not negligent and at fault at all, but that the plaintiff himself is the guilty person, by reason of not conforming to the rules with respect to his lights.

Nor are you to be moved by sympathy for the plaintiff because of his loss, or by sympathy for any party. And certainly you are not to be moved by prejudice. Sympathy and prejudice are both enemies of justice, because they affect your ability to [85] judge honestly and justly. If you are moved by sympathy or prejudice, you are moved by your emotions, rather than by your reasoning. So dismiss all sympathy and prejudice from the case.

You are not entitled to consider that the plaintiff may be poor. There is no evidence here, in his station of life, which would seem to spell very much wealth; nor are you to be moved by the fact that the defendant is a corporation and may be wealthy, because justice does not take note of those conditions. It provides compensation for one injured, as in this case, not because he has lost something; not because the defendant may be able to pay, but, if at all, because he was injured by the fault of the defendant. A jury, or any of us, are entitled to go down into our own pockets out of sympathy, to assist anybody, but neither you nor I are entitled to go down into the pockets of the defendant simply because the plaintiff has lost something, unless you can form an honest judgment that the defendant is at fault, as will be a little later explained to you.

Now, Lady and Gentlemen of the Jury, what is involved in this case is nothing more nor less than the law of the road at sea. Ships running on the ocean have their lanes to travel—their roads to travel, and laws are provided to govern their maneuvers and their safety, and that is what is involved here. Among those laws is one which requires that every vessel shall carry certain lights. We will deal with that first. And, I might say, that law is as binding on the plaintiff as upon the defendant, if those lights are at fault.

The law with respect to the plaintiff's boat requires that it shall be equipped as follows, "From sunset to sunrise,"—that means from the ideal or astronomical sunset, when *the* the sun goes below water level or the plain surface where you can see it going down—"From sunset to sunrise," a boat like the [86] plaintiff's must have a bright, white light in the front of the ship, as near the stem as practicable, so constructed as to throw its light forward and on the sides until the range of vision is two points, in compass vernacular, abaft the beam. That is, back of the middle of the ship. Most of you know what the nautical terms are better than I do. I may get them mixed up, myself. We are not interested in that light. Well, I will not say so, either, because the defendant insists—it maintains that the plaintiff had no light at all except a red light that showed after the collision when the boat turned. Anyhow, that is part of the lights. He must have this front light—this bow light. He must then have a white light aft. That is supposed to be beyond the middle of the ship— the beam of the ship, towards the stern—which will show all around the horizon. The stern light, mind you, will only show in front, and on each side, but this light in the rear—the aft light—must show all around the horizon. Then on the starboard side, he must have a green light, which shows a certain distance on each side forward, and towards the rear as the boat proceeds, and on the port side, he must have a red light, showing likewise on the sides. You can see that those four lights, if lit, are an invaluable index to the course of the ship, and other ships seeing them, can govern their courses accordingly. If the ship, other than the one on which the lights are, would see the two white lights, it would also see one of the side lights that was there, and it would know at once which way that boat was going, and which side was turned towards it. Or if it would see but one white light—Counsel, these red lights and green lights show forward, do they not?

Mr. MARTIN.—Yes.

Mr. BRONSON.—They show forward and to the side. [87]

The COURT.—These side lights show forward, so that if the party on the other boat would see one white light and two side lights, he would know at once that that boat was coming towards him. But if he would see nothing but one white light, then he would know inevitably that that ship was ahead of him—if he saw the rear light— and that he was pursuing the same course, and that is the object of the lights, so that other vessels may know how that vessel is maneuvering, and so that they can manoeuver accordingly.

Now, the law is further that the following vessel, in the situation of the "Olympic" here, has to look out for and see that it does not overtake and collide with the vessel ahead of it, providing that that vessel is carrying the proper lights, and their lights are visible. The following vessel, as the "Olympic" in this case, is responsible that it does not overtake and collide with the vessel ahead that has the proper lights.

The vessel following, as the "Olympic" in this case, has the right to assume that any vessel has proper lights, but that does not absolve it, of course, from looking out. It must be watching for it. It is not enough to have lights. It must have a lookout, so that it can see that *is* is there.

Now, in this case, the "Olympic" had no lookout

to comply with the law. The law says that the lookout must be placed at the best available point, to see what he is looking for, and in the bow of the vessel or as near thereto as is practicable. He must give his undivided duty to looking out and seeing what is in the lanes of traffic. He must be there as a lookout and not for any other purpose. Of course, the evidence is this case is that the lookout was fixing curtains for four or five minutes before the collision. He was not lookout at all within the law. [88]

Up in the pilot-house of the "Olympic"—the defendant's vessel, was the captain, according to the testimony, and the helmsman Seattor. You have heard Seattor's testimony, and I, too, do not think that there is much confidence to be placed in any part of his testimony. The question is whether it is very material. His testimony is that he cannot remember; that he may remember one time and not another, and he was hard put to it before he could remember as to what he testified at the other trial, and it comes back to him now that there was a searchlight that was played on the other boat. I do not think that that is very material, except that it might show the darkness at the time. Furthermore, he thinks that he looked out shortly before the collision, and he did not see the boat.

The captain was there, and his duty was to navigate the vessel and see that it was kept on its course, as he outlined it, but he is not a satisfactory lookout to come within the provisions of the law requiring a lookout to be kept, as I have defined it to you. And, again, that is the attitude of counsel for the plaintiff, when he says there is only one question in this case, and I agree with him, whether the aft light on this vessel of the fisherman was there.

Now, you have heard the testimony of the plaintiff. He tells you that he had started out from a point at the mouth of the canal, I think, and was proceeding in his motor-boat north, northwest. That he left at a certain time; that he had his lights on. That it was not dark yet, but he had taken down some time before his aft light—his mast light and that his aft light, or light that he calls his aft light, was a light that hung in the cabin door of the pilot-house; that it hung by a cord, he said, two inches below the top of the door frame, a door I think about three feet wide he said; that it was open, and he was in [89]   there navigating his vessel north, northwest, the same course as the defendant's vessel was going when it overtook him. He testified that he had placed those lights on some little time before—that he had put them all up that day—these four lights. He does not testify that he never had them on before, but he says that he put them on at the time that he started out. This was a 6-watt light that he testified that he had.

Mr. MARTIN.—A 6-volt light.

The COURT.—What is that?

Mr. MARTIN.—A 6-volt light.

The COURT.—A 6-volt light?

Mr. MARTIN.—Yes.

The COURT.—And he says that it was lit, as were his other lights, when he started out and all the time thereafter. This light, as he was in the pilot-house directing his vessel, would be behind him.

Argument is made by the defendant against the probability and reasonableness of that light being lit, because it would interfere with the navigation of the vessel, it says, and you are cited to the fact that if you have your dash lights unscreened so that they throw their rays upon your face, you find it difficult to navigate your auto. Perhaps all of you are familiar with the situation when you are in a lighted room, looking out into a dark night —the effect of that. That is for you to consider. The argument is legitimate, and it is for you to give such weight to it, in determining the truthfulness of the plaintiff that he had that light lit, as in your judgment you think it is entitled.

The plaintiff was not obliged to keep any lookout behind him, because if he had his lights lit, he was entitled to presume that any vessel following him would take note of him [90] and would comply with the law and not run him down.

The defendant's witnesses tell you that they did not see any such light. I think only one witness for the defendant has testified to being on the lookout at that particular time, and that is the captain— Captain Van Bogaert, I think his name is. He says that he was looking forward just before the collision; that he saw a dark object on the water which turned out to be this boat; that he saw it about 100 feet distant, but it had no lights visible at all on it, and only after it had collided with him and there had been some backing, and the plaintiff's boat was turned around, did he see a light, and that was a red light on plaintiff's boat and no other. Whaley also testified to that.

On the other hand, there are two witnesses for the plaintiff who testified to seeing the light shortly after the collision occurred. Mrs. Schuman, now deceased, whose testimony was read to you, testified that she was eating when she felt the vibration of the reversing; that she sat still for quite a while, and hearing more commotion, she went to the window and saw a boat and say a light on top of the vessel. She does not say whether that was a light in the cabin door, or at the bow of the vessel. She said she saw it on top of the vessel. That was her testimony, and Mr. Schuman testified that he came out some time after the collision—you remember the time—of course the intervals, perhaps, were not very long, any of them—and that after the "Olympic" had backed so that it was in the rear of plaintiff's boat, he saw this white light burning in the cabin door. The defendant's witnesses say that there was no light except the red light when the plaintiff was turned around.

Now, Lady and Gentlemen of the Jury, the law is, with respect to this light, that if it is not in the place and the kind of a light which the law requires it to be, if a collision [91] occurs, it imposes the burden upon the plaintiff to satisfy you that the light differing from the light established by law could not have been any part of the cause of the collision. That it did not contribute to the collision. That burden is on the plaintiff. If that was his aft light, and there is no reason why it could not have been, even though it was not across the dividing line in the middle of the ship—between the bow and the stern—if that was his aft light, and it was the only aft light that he had, if it was not so placed that it could be seen all around the horizon. It could be seen from behind, but it could not be seen from either side, because it was within the frame two inches, and, of course, it could not be seen from the front. But you must remember, too, that the law is a practical thing, and it does not require any useless thing. If that light served the purpose of an aft light to a following vessel, it was altogether immaterial whether it would show from the sides or show from ahead, so far as that vessel is concerned, but provided it was sufficient to serve the purpose of an aft light for the following vessel, and could not at all have misled it or have contributed to the collision which happened. I myself cannot reason out, and I think counsel has taken that attitude—I cannot reason out why, if that light was there, lit, and no obstruction in plaintiff's rear, and plaintiff testifies that there was none—I cannot understand why it would not serve just as well for the following vessel as if it could be seen from either side and ahead. If you can, why that is your privilege, for you to finally determine this. So it comes right down to that question—the attitude taken by the plaintiff's counsel in his argument, and the court takes it as a matter of law.

You have two questions to decide in this case, outside of the damage, and you must decide them both in the affirmative [92] before you can find for the plaintiff. First, it is proven by the greater weight of the evidence that Nelson's light in his cabin door was where he testified that it was; that

it was of the kind that he testified it was, and lit
sufficiently long before the collision so that it could
have been seen by the defendant's lookout, had he
been exercising his function properly and in time
so that the collision might have been avoided. If
you answer that that is proven by the greater weight
of the evidence, then you proceed to the next question. If you do not find that the greater weight
of the evidence proves that in Nelson's favor, that
ends the case. Of course, if he did not have that
light lit, and lit sufficiently long so that a watchful lookout on the defendant's vessel could have
seen it in time to avoid him; why he has no right
to any recovery here, because he was negligent.
In that case, he violated the law, and I do not
care whether it was five o'clock or five-twenty, or
whether it was more or less dark, it is inevitable
that the absence of his light, if it was absent, would
have contributed something to the collision that
followed. He is out of the case and out of court
right there, unless you find by the greater weight
of the evidence that his light was there, as he tells
you, with that degree of sufficiency—a 6-volt light—
and lit long enough to have been seen and avoided
by the defendant's vessel, had it a watchful lookout at the time.

If, however, you find that in favor of the plaintiff, then the next question is, in its position there
in the door, if you find it was there and lit—not
visible ahead and not visible on the sides—did it
have anything to do with or is it clear to you that
it contributed nothing to the collision that followed?
Here is a vessel coming from behind—the defend-

ant's vessel. If that light had been visible on the sides and [93] ahead, would it have better enabled the defendant's vessel aft to avoid him and to see him and avoid him? I do not think so, and counsel's attitude for the plaintiff in his argument likewise was the same. That is common sense. If the light was there, and visible from the defendant's vessel, had it a watchful lookout, as counsel said fairly in his argument, if it was there long enough, it would have enabled the defendant to avoid the collision.

So, if you answer those two questions in the affirmative, proven by the greater weight of the evidence, favorable to the plaintiff, then there is only one more question, and that is, how much was the damage? And that brings you to a consideration of the value of the boat at that time; of its fittings and accessories and supplies on board, and what was its reasonable market value at that time. That would be the amount that you would award to him in any event.

Then he has another cause of action for his personal damages which he alleges were inflicted upon him by the collision, scratching his leg. He says that the collision threw him down against his engine, and scratched his leg, and that he was laid up for some time afterward, and he says that he feels sick now on that account. You have heard his testimony. The defendant disputes it. The employees of the defendant company say that he was not injured at all and that he told them so on board the boat. They say that he did, and he testifies that he did not, and they say that he is entitled to nothing. But if you find that he has been injured by the fault of the defendant as I have heretofore defined it to you—if you answer the two questions that I first put to you in favor of the plaintiff, then he is at least [94] entitled to something for having his personal rights invaded by being thrown into the water. The defendant argues that he jumped in, but you must remember that the plaintiff was confronted at that time by an emergency, and if he was put into that condition and situation by the fault of the defendant, then the fact that he may not have acted with the best judgment does not relieve the defendant from compensating him for any injury that he may have suffered. When one person puts another person in a place of imminent peril, that other person is not bound to exercise the best judgment to get away. His judgment may be poor, and in consequence he may be more injured, but still the party putting him in that situation is liable to him later.

That is the case before you. It simmers down to this, Lady and Gentlemen of the Jury, that taking into consideration all of the evidence in the case, both for the plaintiff and the defendant, and the circumstances, if you find by the greater weight of the evidence that the plaintiff had, as he testified to you, a light in the door of his pilot-house, facing the rear, of 6-volt size, as he tells you, and burning long enough before the collision so that a watchful lookout on defendant's vessel could have seen it, and so could have avoided the collision, he is entitled to recover. If you do not find that by the greater weight of the evidence, he is not entitled to recover.

When you retire to the jury-room, you will select one of your number as foreman, and you will proceed to your verdict. It takes twelve to agree on a verdict. Any exceptions?

Mr. MARTIN.—May I suggest that I have such a doubt in my own mind, that I do not want any reference that I may have made as to the official log to be considered by the jury, and I will ask your Honor to so instruct. [95]

The COURT.—Well, Lady and Gentlemen of the Jury, counsel, whether he is right or wrong about the law, he says now that he wants you instructed not to consider anything about that log. Forget all about it. Dismiss all that from your mind. Do not attach any weight because of its absence against this defendant. So remember that. So dismiss that entirely from your mind—everything that has been said to you about the log. Are there any exceptions for the defendant?

Mr. BRONSON.—I wish to note an exception to the failure of the court to give each one of the requested instructions which we have submitted in writing, and I also wish to except to the instructions which were given as I have taken them down the best I could as your Honor gave them to the jury.

The COURT.—Well, what are they, Counsel?

Mr. BRONSON.—I wish to except to your Honor's instruction as follows, referring to this light in the pilot-house, that if he had it there, as he claims, there is no reason why he should not recover.

Again, I wish to except to the instruction given that the defendant relies on the contention that it was not negligent at all. That is not our contention, your Honor.

The COURT.—Well, just state it. If I am in error, I will correct it.

Mr. BRONSON.—Our contention is that whether or not there was negligence on the part of the defendant, or defendant's lookout, if there was any negligence—that coupled with any negligence on the part of the plaintiff is sufficient to find in defendant's favor.

The COURT.—I told that to the jury. That is true. I thought I made that plain to the jury by stating that the whole question depended upon whether or not he had his light lit. [96] If the plaintiff did not have his light there, as he testified, lit as I have stated it to you—there was not any negligence on the part of the defendant, as a matter of fact, because if the plaintiff was negligent by not having that light, why his negligence did undoubtedly contribute to the collision, and the defendant would not be liable then at all. But the defendant's attitude is that even if it were guilty of some negligence at the time, the plaintiff was also negligent, and hence he is not entitled to recover. That question, then, comes to the question of light. If the light was not there, of course the plaintiff was negligent even though the defendant was negligent, if the plaintiff was negligent, too, why the defendant is entitled to a verdict.

Mr. BRONSON.—So that I may be fair with the court and make my position clear, my objection does not go alone to whether he had such a light there but whether or not it was visible and whether or not it could be seen. We are not relying on the fact whether he had the light or did not have it, but the question which I think should be submitted to the jury is whether or not he had the light which the law requires, and that the court, in instructing the jury—

The COURT.—(Interrupting.) I will tell them right now that he did not. I told them so, that he did not have the light that the law requires. The law requires a light that is visible all around the horizon. Proceed.

Mr. BRONSON.—I will limit myself to the specific instruction, that the defendant claims that he had no light. That is what you instructed them.

The COURT.—What is that?

Mr. BRONSON.—You instructed them that the defendant claimed that he had no light. That is not our contention. We do not deny that he had the side lights and the light showing forward, [97]

The COURT.—That does not cut any figure in the case. The defendant does not contend that he did not have his bow light and side lights. They are not disputing but what he had the side lights and the bow light.

Mr. BRONSON.—I think that we are entitled to except also, your Honor, to the instruction with reference to the corroboration by the Schumans. As pointed out, the Schumans did not profess to see any light on the vessel before the collision, and lights visible after the accident have no bearing as to what was on the vessel of the plaintiff before the accident.

The COURT.—I told the jury that. Nobody, of course, professed to have seen the situation as it was at the moment of the accident, or to know just what it was, except the plaintiff himself and the captain of the "Olympic," who says that he was on lookout at that moment. The Schumans came up several minutes after the accident occurred. Of course, a light lit then is not proof that it was lit before, because it might well be that the plaintiff could have turned his lights on after the collision, but a thing happening so recently after the collision as the Schumans coming up and seeing the light, it has to be given as much weight as in your judgment you think it is entitled to upon the point, was the light lit when the collision occurred?

Mr. MARTIN.—May I ask your Honor, in view of your Honor's instructions touching that point, and the emphasis laid upon it, that your Honor instruct the jury as to the rule between the positive and negative testimony, namely—

The COURT.—(Interrupting.) Let counsel conclude taking his exceptions.

Mr. MARTIN.—May I renew that after counsel finishes?

The COURT.—Yes.

Mr. BRONSON.—I wish to further except, your Honor, to the [98] instruction which you have, in language as accurately as I could take it down, as follows, "If you take that as a light, referring to the light in the pilot-house, there is no reason why you should not take that to be an aft light."

The COURT.—Yes. I mean in its place, forward by the beam, as it apparently was, it served every purpose of an aft light which the law requires and names as an aft light. Your exceptions are noted, of course, as you make them.

Mr. BRONSON.—Your Honor instructed also that it was immaterial if the light could not have been seen from either side. I think that is one of the primary issues in this case.

The COURT.—It is immaterial if it could not be seen on either side, if that fact did not contribute at all to the collision that followed.

Mr. BRONSON.—The point I make is that these vessels were on courses which did not coincide, and according to the testimony of the plaintiff, the other vessel was on his quarter, so that he was looking out from behind and at the side also.

The COURT.—The captain testified that they were on the same course.

Mr. BRONSON.—He said that they appeared to be headed the same way when they were in the jaws of collision.

The COURT.—The jury will remember. As I told you, Lady and Gentlemen of the Jury, if the fact that this light would not show to the side, contributed at all—unless you are satisfied that .it did not contribute to the injury, why, of course, the plaintiff is entitled to recover.

Mr. BRONSON.—Your Honor has said that there were two questions to decide, which your Honor later extended to three. That is, first, is it proven by the greater weight that the light was where plaintiff says it was. The burden is upon the plaintiff, [99] and it goes further than that. He just prove that the failure to have the omitted light was not one of the causes of the accident. That burden is on the plaintiff, and that proof must be forthcoming. The second point your Honor made was, in its position did it do anything to contribute to the accident. I do not know what you meant by that, but I do not believe that that fulfills the requirements.

The COURT.—The Court was taking, and it supposed that it was justified in taking, your statement in your argument to the jury. In other words, if you are not maintaining the argument that you made to the jury, let the jury know it right now.

Mr. BRONSON.—Your Honor—

The COURT.—(Interrupting.) I will read that much to answer your exception. The instruction asked by the defendant, and handed up before the argument, is this, "Under the facts in this case, the failure of the 'Magna' to carry the prescribed white light aft to show all around the horizon, is a fault sufficient to fix the plaintiff with at least contributing fault for the collision between the vessels and consequent loss and damage, if any, suffered by the plaintiff, requiring you to return a verdict for the defendant, unless you shall find that the failure to carry a white light aft to show all around the horizon, by the 'Magna,' could not have been one of the causes of the collision by this defendant vessel following from behind."

Mr. BRONSON.—Just one more, your Honor, and that is with reference to the second cause of action. Your Honor will recall that there are two causes of action, and that whether or not there was negligence on either party at the time of this collision, there is still a second question as to the negligence of either or both parties following—pertaining to the second cause of action—that is the immersion in the water overboard. [100]

The COURT.—I do not get you at all.

Mr. BRONSON.—We have passed the point of collision. After that, there is still the second cause of action involved, namely, the jumping overboard; the failure to carry the life-saving equipment prescribed by law, and the negligence or lack of negligence on the part of plaintiff in jumping overboard. That affects the second cause of action where it would not the first cause of action.

The COURT.—Very well.

Mr. MARTIN.—Your Honor—

The COURT.—(Interrupting.) What is it, now?

Mr. MARTIN.—I do not think there is any dispute in the maritime law with respect to this proposition. The court has said many times that it frequently happens that there is positive testimony that lights were burning, and testimony on the other hand that they did not see the lights, and the rule is that negative testimony is not entitled to the weight of positive testimony. In this case the positive testimony is that there was a lighted light, and that is entitled therefore to the greater weight.

The COURT.—That is a question for the jury. That is something for the jury to consider in weighing the evidence. You know, Lady and Gentlemen of the Jury, that persons do not see the same thing at the same time in the same way. For instance, two people go downtown and look at a show-window, and in describing later, what they saw in that show-window, one may state, and state honestly, things that were not there at all.

Now, the law says that where two persons testify to a situation at the same time, the one who testifies positively that it was thus and so—"I saw it"— is entitled to more weight than one who says, "No, it was not that way. I didn't [101] see it."

That is the point that counsel wants to make, and it is for you to say whether it applies in this case. The plaintiff says, "I had the light there," and the captain says, "He did not have the light there, because I did not see it." Of course, that involves whether he saw it or he did not see it because it was not there.

Mr. MARTIN.—Would your Honor permit me to take an exception to your Honor's instructions—

The COURT.—(Interrupting.) You require no permission. You can take as many exceptions as you dictate into the record.

Mr. MARTIN.—I have this in mind, your Honor—

The COURT.—(Interrupting.) Take your exceptions and be through with them.

Mr. MARTIN.—I except to the instructions as given, for the reason that the matter of divided damages and the question of fault, mutual and sole, was not mentioned in the court's instructions. The court has tried the case as one at common law with respect to contributory negligence, which is a bar to the action at common law. We take this position with respect to this, that maritime law applies in its entirety, and there should be an instruction to that feature.

The COURT.—I quite agree with you, but the Circuit Court of Appeal has said otherwise, and that is why we are having this trial.

Mr. BRONSON.—I would like to make this further exception with reference to negative and positive testimony. Negative and positive testimony have no application in this case. The testimony on behalf of the defendant is not that there was not any light in any particular place, but that it was not visible. Now, there was not any negative testimony on that. There was [102] positive testimony.

The COURT.—Lady and Gentlemen of the Jury, I will give you the pleadings in this case. You do not need to read the pleadings if you do not want to. The matter is clear enough before you as to what the question involved is. You can read them if you want to. When you retire to your juryroom, you may proceed upon your verdict. It takes twelve to decide this case.

Mr. BRONSON.—There is a rule in this state that the pleadings will not go to the jury.

The COURT.—This is the first time that I have ever heard of that.

Mr. COLLETT.—Will your Honor call attention to the jury which is the first cause of action and which is the second cause of action? You mention them in the proposed forms of verdict.

The COURT.—The first cause of action relates to the boat and its accessories; the second cause of action relates to the personal injuries claimed by the plaintiff. You may now retire.

VERDICT.

Thereafter, on the 7th day of May, 1931, at the hour of one o'clock in the afternoon, the jury returned a verdict finding for the plaintiff on his first cause of action for the sum of Twenty-two hundred fifty ($2250.00) Dollars, and on his second cause of action in the sum of Two Hundred Fifty ($250.00) Dollars.

JUDGMENT.

Thereafter, on the 11th day of May, 1931, the following judgment was signed and entered:

The above-entitled cause having been tried to a jury in the above-entitled court on the 5th and 6th days of May, 1931, before Hon. George A. Bourquin, United States District [103] Judge, and the jury having returned a verdict for Twenty-two Hundred and Fifty Dollars ($2,250.00) on plaintiff's first cause of action, and Two Hundred and Fifty Dollars ($250.00) on plaintiff's second cause of action, now, upon motion of the plaintiff for judgment on the verdict,—

IT IS ADJUDGED AND DECREED that plaintiff have and recover Twenty-five Hundred Dollars ($2,500.00), less the sum of Three Hundred

Twelve and 5/100 Dollars ($312.05), costs duly awarded and entered in favor of defendant in the United States Circuit Court of Appeals and the Supreme Court of the United States, or the sum of Twenty-one Hundred Eighty-seven and 95/100 ($2,187.95), together with plaintiff's costs to be taxed by the Clerk, and that execution may issue for said sum of Twenty-one Hundred Eighty-seven and 95/100 Dollars ($2,187.95), plus the amount of plaintiff's costs, as finally taxed herein. Defendant's exception is hereby noted and allowed.

Done in open court this 11th day of May, 1931.

(Sgd.) GEORGE M. BOURQUIN,
United States District Judge.

Respectfully submitted,
BRONSON, JONES & BRONSON,
Attorneys for Defendant.

Copy of within proposed bill of exceptions received this 9th day of June, 1931.

MARTIN & COLLETT,
Attys. for Plaintiff.

[Lodged]: Jun. 9, 1931. [104]

CERTIFICATE OF JUDGE TO BILL OF EXCEPTIONS.

The foregoing bill of exceptions, amended, to which this certificate is attached, is hereby certified, settled and allowed as true, full and complete, and made a part of the record for appeal.

This 22 day of June, 1931.

BOURQUIN,
U. S. District Judge.

[Endorsed]: Filed Jun. 23, 1931. [105]

———

[Title of Court and Cause.]

PLAINTIFF'S PROPOSED AMENDMENTS TO DEFENDANT'S BILL OF EXCEPTIONS.

Plaintiff now proposes the following amendments to the defendant's bill of exceptions filed in the above cause, to wit:

That after and following line 24, page 78, of the defendant's proposed bill of exceptions, which is at the conclusion of the statement as to the verdict rendered in the above cause, the following proceedings should be noted and set forth in said bill of exceptions, to wit:

That the plaintiff prepared a form of judgment upon the verdict, and duly served the same upon defendant's attorneys on the 8th day of May, 1931, which judgment proposed by the plaintiff was in the terms as follows, to wit:

No. 20,246.

"HANS NELSON,

Plaintiff,

vs.

PUGET SOUND NAVIGATION COMPANY,
a Corporation,

Defendant.

JUDGMENT.

The above-entitled cause having been tried to a jury in the above-entitled court on the 5th and 6th days of May, 1931, before the Honorable George M. Bourquin, United States District Judge, and the jury having returned a verdict for $2250.00 on plaintiff's first cause of action, and $250.00 on plaintiff's second cause of action; now, upon motion of plaintiff for judgment on the verdict,—

IT IS ADJUDGED AND DECREED that plaintiff have and recover $2500.00, of and from defendant, together with his costs to be taxed by the Clerk, and execution to issue thereon for the full amount of said judgment and costs.

Done in open court this —— day of May, 1931.

—————————————,

United States District Judge.

Copy received this 8th day of May, 1931.

BRONSON, JONES & BRONSON,

Attorneys for Defendant."

That thereafter, on the 11th day of May, 1931, Harry S. Redpath, Esquire, of plaintiff's counsel, moved the entry of the [106] said judgment as proposed by plaintiff; that Mr. Robert S. Bronson, of defendant's counsel, moved the entry of the judgment as proposed by himself on behalf of defendant, which the court subsequently entered as the judgment in this cause, which is set forth on pages 78 and 79 of defendant's proposed bill of exceptions. That in resisting the entry of defendant's proposed form of judgment and in urging the court to enter the judgment proposed by plaintiff, Mr. Redpath took the position that the judgment in favor of the defendant for its costs in the Circuit Court of Appeals in the sum of Three Hundred Twelve Dollars and Five Cents ($312.05) was a judgment wholly apart from the proposed judgment against the defendant for Twenty-five Hundred Dollars ($2500.00), upon the verdict. That no set-off had been pleaded in this cause, and that defendant could not legally have its judgment for costs set-off as indicated in the form of the judgment proposed by the defendant.

Thereupon the Court took the matter under advisement and subsequently entered judgment in the form and manner as proposed by the defendant for the sum of Twenty-one Hundred Eighty-seven Dollars and Ninety-five Cents (2187.95), together with plaintiff's costs to be taxed, instead of entering judgment for Twenty-five Hundred Dollars ($2500.00) as proposed by the plaintiff.

In signing the said judgment, the Court appended thereto on the face of the judgment beneath his signature the following opinion or memorandum, to wit:

"At law is power to offset judgments on motion. Orally moved here and granted." Signed Bourquin, J."

Plaintiff desires the record thus made to show that the set-off contained in the judgment as entered was upon the motion of the defendant, resisted and opposed by the plaintiff.

We respectfully submit the foregoing this 18th day of June, 1931.

WINTER S. MARTIN,
MARTIN & COLLETT,
Attorneys for Plaintiff. [107]

Copy of the foregoing proposed amendment to defts. bill of exceptions recd. and acknowledged this 18 day of June, 1931.

BRONSON, JONES & BRONSON,
Attorneys for Deft.

[Endorsed]: Filed Jun. 18, 1931.

Allowed June 22, 1931.

BOURQUIN, J. (Signed)

[Endorsed]: Filed Jun. 23, 1931. [108]

———

[Title of Court and Cause.]

PETITION FOR ALLOWANCE OF APPEAL.

To the Honorable GEORGE M. BOURQUIN, Under Special Assignment Judge of the Above-entitled Court:

Comes now the Puget Sound Navigation Company, a corporation, defendant, in the above-entitled preceeding, and respectfully petitions and prays the court for an order allowing the taking and prosecution to conclusion of an appeal in the above-entitled matter to the Honorable Circuit Court of Appeals of the United States, for the Ninth Circuit, from that certain judgment heretofore entered on the 11th day of May, 1931, and from each and every part thereof.

And said defendant further prays that a citation on appeal may issue according to the custom and practice of this Honorable Court, and that a transcript of record, together with bill of exceptions and other proceedings in said cause, may be prepared by the Clerk of the above-entitled court and transmitted to said Circuit Court of Appeals, all in accordance with the usual custom and practice of this Honorable Court and the law and rules in such cases made and provided, and

Said defendant further petitions and prays that this Court fix and determine the amount of cost and supersedeas bond to be forthwith submitted for approval and filed by defendant in order to perfect said appeal and effect a stay and supersedeas of said judgment.

Dated at Seattle, Washington, this 3d day of August, 1931.

BRONSON, JONES & BRONSON,
Attorneys for Defendant.

Received copy of foregoing petition for allowance this 5th day of August, 1931.

WINTER S. MARTIN.

GVC.

[Endorsed]: Filed Aug. 5, 1931. [109]

[Title of Court and Cause.]

ORDER ALLOWING APPEAL AND FIXING AMOUNT OF COST AND SUPERSEDEAS BOND.

Upon the petition of the Puget Sound Navigation Company, a corporation, defendant in the above-entitled proceeding,—

IT IS HEREBY ORDERED that an appeal, pursuant to law and the rules of court may be, and the same is hereby allowed defendant, Puget Sound Navigation Company, from that certain judgment heretofore entered in this cause on the 11th day of May, 1931, to the Honorable United States Circuit Court of Appeals, for the Ninth Circuit; and

IT IS FURTHER ORDERED that the amount of cost and supersedeas bond to be forthwith filed, sufficient as to form, security and amount, be and the same is hereby fixed in the sum of Twenty-five Hundred ($2500.00) Dollars, and

IT IS FURTHER ORDERED that citation on appeal, pursuant to law and usual practice of the above-entitled court, may thereupon issue, and said appeal proceed as in other cases.

This 8th day of August, 1931.

BOURQUIN,

U. S. District Judge, by Special Assignment Trial Judge of the Above-entitled Court.

[Endorsed]: Filed Aug. 10, 1931.   [110]

[Title of Court and Cause.]

ASSIGNMENT OF ERRORS.

Comes now Puget Sound Navigation Company, a corporation, defendant in the above proceedings, and hereby assigns as errors in the proceedings and trial of said cause, and in the rulings, orders, opinions and judgments of the above-entitled court to the manifest prejudice of the defendant, the following:

I.

The Court erred in permitting the witness, Emil Schuman, to testify as to lights observed following the collision, and as to the visibility of the M. S. "Magna" following the collision and after substantial change of bearing and positions of the two vessels, and in denying defendant's motion to strike out such testimony. (Bill of Exceptions, pages 5 to 8.)

II.

The Court erred in permitting the plaintiff, over objection, to answer the following question:

"Could anybody see that light suspended in the door of your vessel—in that open door approaching from the stern?"

(Bill of Exceptions, page 13.)

III.

The Court erred in permitting the plaintiff, over objection, to answer the following question:

"Hans, did you ever have occasion to be away from your own vessel at night-time, either on the shore or on another [111] vessel, when you could see that light suspended in the doorway of your cabin?"

(Bill of Exceptions, pages 13 and 14.)

IV.

The Court erred in permitting the plaintiff, over objection, to answer the following question:

"How far could you see that light when the light was on and when it was hanging in the doorway, suspended as it was at the time of the collision?"

(Bill of exceptions, page 14.)

V.

The Court erred in permitting the plaintiff, over objection, to answer the following question:

"Have you actually seen that light half a mile away?"

(Bill of Exceptions, page 14.)

VI.

The Court erred in permitting the plaintiff, over objection, to answer the following question:

"How far could you see any vessel ahead of you, a vessel the size of the "Magna?"
(Bill of Exceptions, page 15.)

VII.

The Court erred in overruling defendant's challenge to the sufficiency of plaintiff's evidence and the motion for nonsuit and directed verdict at the close of plaintiff's case, it then being conclusively established by the admissions of plaintiff that plaintiff had violated Article II of the Inland Pilot's Rules, promulgated by the Steamboat Inspection Service of the Department of Commerce, and also the provisions of Chapters 513, 514 and 515 of the Act of June 9th, 1910, U. S. C. A., Title 46, in that said plaintiff admittedly failed to carry, show or display upon his [112] vessel the white range light aft, elevated and unobscured, and showing around the horizon as required by said rules and said act, there being no evidence then adduced proving, tending to prove, or from which the jury were entitled to infer that such violation of the rule and statute by the plaintiff could not have been one of the causes proximately contributing to the collision and the loss, damage, injury and destruction for which plaintiff seeks recovery in said cause, and it further conclusively appearing from admissions of plaintiff with reference to plaintiff's alleged second cause of action, that plaintiff was negligent and careless in voluntarily and unnecessarily jumping overboard from his vessel and further negligent as a matter of law in failing, omitting and neglecting to have and carry on said vessel, in the manner prescribed, the life saving equipment required by the Act of June 9th, 1910, U. S. C. A., Title 46, Section 515.

(Bill of Exceptions, pages 21–23.)

VIII.

The Court erred in denying defendant's motion for a directed verdict interposed at the close of all of the evidence of said cause, it then appearing, in addition to the matters set forth in the preceding assignment, number VII, by direct, positive and uncontradicted evidence that no range light or other light on plaintiff's vessel was actually visible at any time prior to the collision, in the direction of the approach of defendant's vessel, and it then being positively proven and established by uncontradicted evidence that the absence of such range light and the invisibility of any light on plaintiff's vessel, as prescribed by said rule and said aforementioned statute, was a proximate cause contributing to, if not the sole cause of the collision between the said vessels and all the loss, damage, injury or destruction for which plaintiff seeks recovery in said cause, and that the absence of such light constituted negligence of the plaintiff [113] as a matter of law, sufficient to preclude plaintiff from any right of recovery in said cause.

(Bill of Exceptions, pages 21–23.)

IX.

The court erred in failing and refusing to give the following instruction to the jury, as requested by the defendant in writing:

"Plaintiff admits, in this case, that his vessel was not equipped with a range light. I instruct you that defendant's motor-boat, being less than forty (40) feet and more than twenty-six (26) feet, is classified, under the law, as a motor-boat of the second class. You are instructed that, under the law, every motor-boat, in all weathers from sunset to sunrise, shall carry the following lights, and during such time no other lights which may be mistaken for those prescribed shall be exhibited; every motor-boat of class 2 shall carry the following lights:

First: A bright white light in the fore part of the vessel as near the stem as practicable, so constructed as to show an unbroken light over an arc of the horizon of twenty points of the compass, so fixed as to throw the light ten points on each side of the vessel, namely, from right ahead to two points abaft the beam on either side.

Second: A white light aft to show all around the horizon.

Third: On the starboard side, a green light so constructed as to show unbroken light over an arc of the horizon of ten points of the compass, so fixed as to throw the light from right ahead to two points abaft the beam on the starboard side. On the port side, a red light so constructed as to show an unbroken light over an arc of the horizon of ten points of the compass, so fixed as to throw the light from the right ahead to two points abaft the beam on the port side.

I further instruct you that since it is admitted by both parties that the defendant's steamer, 'The Olympic,' was an overtaking vessel, she was approaching the 'Magna' from an angle of more than two points abaft the beam, and so as to be out of view of the white light in the forepart of the 'Magna,' and the red and green colored lights, if those lights were burning and placed according to law.

Under these admitted facts and the law, which I have mentioned, the admitted failure of the 'Magna' to carry the prescribed white light aft to show all around the horizon is a fault sufficient to fix plaintiff with at least contributing fault for the collision between the vessels and the consequent loss and damage, if any, suffered by the plaintiff, requiring you to return a verdict for the defendant unless you shall find that the failure to carry such white light aft to show all around the horizon, by the 'Magna,' could not have been one of the causes of the collision.''

The ''Pennsylvania,'' 19 Wallace, 125.

Belden vs. Chase, 150 U. S. 674.

The ''Martello,'' 153 U. S. 64.

The ''Britannia,'' 153 U. S. 130.

X.

The court erred in failing and refusing to give the following [114] instruction to the jury, as requested by the defendant in writing:

''You are further instructed that if you should find that the plaintiff was guilty of negligence as claimed by the defendant, and that such negligence might possibly have contributed to the collision, then the plaintiff cannot recover, and it will be your duty to return a verdict for the defendant, notwithstanding that you may also find that the defendant's officers or agents were also guilty of some act of negligence likewise contributing to the disaster.''

XI.

The court erred in failing and refusing to give the following instruction to the jury, as requested by the defendant in writing:

"You are further instructed that the lights required by law must be carried by all vessels after sundown, and that it is no legally sufficient excuse that some other light is carried in lieu of those prescribed by law for, under the law, no other lights than those actually prescribed shall be exhibited which may be mistaken by another vessel for the prescribed lights. There can be no substitution for the requirements of the law, and you are instructed that under the law plaintiff was required to carry at the time of the collision between the two vessels involved in this case a white light aft to show all around the horizon, placed at a higher elevation than the white light showing forward, and so placed as to form a range with the forward light, and to be clear of house awnings and all other obstructions so as to be actually visible to a vessel approaching from the direction of the defendant's vessel, and the plaintiff's admitted failure to carry and show such a light renders the plaintiff guilty of negligence, as a matter of law, sufficient to bar him from any recovery, in this case, unless the plaintiff shall prove that his admitted failure in this respect could not have been one of the causes which contributed to the collision, and in the absence of such proof it will be your duty to return a verdict for the defendant.

Act of June 9, 1910, Chap. 268, par. 1, 2, 3 and 8.

36 Stats. 462, Title 46, U. S. C. A., Secs. 511, 512, 513 and 518.

Department Circular No. 236, 12th Ed., issued by Secretary of Commerce regulating motor-boats, under date of May 1, 1928.

The 'Breakwater,' 155 U. S. 252.

The 'Delaware,' 161 U. S. 459.

The 'Luckenbach,' 50 Fed. 129.

The 'Straits of Dover,' 120 Fed. 900.

Belden vs. Chase, 150 U. S. 674.''

XII.

The court erred in failing and refusing to give the following instruction to the jury, as requested by the defendant in writing:

"You are instructed that all persons navigating vessels are entitled to assume and to place reasonable reliance upon the assumption that persons navigating other vessels will obey the law as to lights required to be carried on such other vessels, and that the defendant was not guilty of negligence if those in charge of the

navigation of defendant's vessel failed to anticipate or to guard against the absence of proper
lights upon the plaintiff's vessel, or to act otherwise than a reasonably careful [115] or prudent person or persons would have acted under
similar circumstances.

Belden vs. Chase, 150 U. S. 674, 699, 37
L. Ed. 1218.

The Oregon vs. Rocca, 59 U. S. 18, Howard
570, 15 L. Ed. 515.''

XIII.

The court erred in failing and refusing to give
the following instruction to the jury, as requested
by the defendant in writing:

"You are instructed that under the law, plaintiff was required to carry on board his vessel
either life-preservers or life-belts, or buoyant
cushions or other device sufficient to sustain him
afloat and so placed as to be readily accessible
Plaintiff admits that the life-preservers which
were carried on board his vessel, were not so
placed as to be readily *assessable,* and you are
instructed that such failure on the part of plaintiff renders him guilty of contributory negligence
as a matter of law, barring him from any right
to recover for injury or damage alleged to have
been sustained as a result of his immersion
in the water, unless you shall find that plaintiff's
failure in this respect was not a contributing
cause to any injury or damage which plaintiff

may have suffered or sustained by reason of such immersion, if you shall find that plaintiff suffered any damage at all from such immersion, but in no event shall you allow any recovery to plaintiff for any such injury or damage unless you shall first find that plaintiff's failure to carry the after white light prescribed by law could not have been one of the causes of the collision between said vessels.

Act of June 9, 1910, Chap. 268, par. 5.

36 Stat. 463.

Act of March 4, 1913, Chap. 141, Par. 1.

37 Stat. 736.

Title 45, U. S. C. A., Sec. 515.

Belden vs. Chase, 150 U. S. 674, 699; 37 L. Ed. 1218.''

XIV.

The court erred in giving the following instruction to the jury:

''As a matter of fact, the court agrees with the statement of counsel for the defense in his argument that if the plaintiff had that light in the doorway of his boat, lit long enough before the collision so that it could have been seen by a proper lookout on the 'Olympic,' they would have avoided him, and the collision would have never occurred. And if the plaintiff had it there, as he says that he did, and which the defendant denies, there is no reason why he should not recover in this action.

Before we come to any more of the law, I
am simply stating that I agree with counsel's
position, and I think the plaintiff does now,
too. That is all I can see in this case. You
must remember this, that the plaintiff must
prove his case by a greater weight of the evidence. The burden is on him throughout to
prove that he had that light there, lit there
for the length of time that I have stated to you,
and prove that it was a good and sufficient
light to serve its purpose, and to prove the
amount of his damages. The burden is on him
to prove all those things before he can recover.
So you see that in this case, there   [116]   is
mainly involved the credibility of witnesses
where there is a direct conflict between the witnesses for the plaintiff and the witnesses for
the defendant."

(Bill of Exceptions, pages 57 and 58.)

XV.

The court erred in giving the following instruction to the jury:

"The plaintiff bas*i*s his right to recover in
this action on the fact that the collision was due,
as he alleges, to the negligence and fault of the
defendant, and the defendant alone, and the
defendant resists on the theory, as it alleges,
that it was not negligent and at fault at all,
but that the plaintiff himself is the guilty per-

son, by reason of not conforming to the rules with respect to his lights."

(Bill of Exceptions, page 60.)

XVI.

The court erred in giving the following instruction to the jury:

"The Captain was there, and his duty was to navigate the vessel and see that it was kept on its course, as he outlined it, but he is not a satisfactory lookout to come within the provisions of the law requiring a lookout to be kept, as I have defined it to you. And, again, that is the attitude of counsel for the plaintiff, when he says there is only one question in this case, and I agree with him, whether the aft light on this vessel of the fisherman was there."

(Bill of Exceptions, page 64.)

XVII.

The court erred in giving the following instruction to the jury:

"Now, you have heard the testimony of the plaintiff. He told you * * * he was in there navigating his vessel north, northwest, the same course as the defendant's vessel was going when it overtook him."

(Bill of Exceptions, pages 64 and 65.)

XVIII.

The court erred in giving the following instruction to the [117] jury:

"The plaintiff was not obliged to keep any lookout behind him, because if he had his lights lit, he was entitled to presume that any vessel following him would take note of him and would comply with the law and not run him down."

(Bill of Exceptions, pages 65 and 66.)

XIX.

The court erred in giving the following instruction to the   [117]   jury:

"On the other hand, there are two witnesses for the plaintiff who testified to seeing the light shortly after the collision occurred. Mrs. Schuman, now deceased, whose testimony was read to you, testified that she was eating when she felt the vibration of the reversing; that she sat still for quite a while, and hearing more commotion, she went to the window and saw a boat and saw a light on top of the vessel. She does not say whether that was a light in the cabin door, or at the bow of the vessel. She said she saw it on top of the vessel. That was her testimony, and Mr. Schuman testified that he came out some time after the collision— you remember the time—of course the intervals, perhaps, were not very long, any of them —and that after the 'Olympic' had backed so that it was in the rear of plaintiff's boat, he saw this white light burning in the cabin door."

(Bill of Exceptions, page 66.)

XX.

The court erred in giving the following instruction to the jury:

"If that was his aft light, and there is no reason why it could not have been, even though it was not across the dividing line in the middle of the ship—between the bow and the stern —if that was his aft light, and it was the only aft light that he had, if it was not so placed that it would be seen all around the horizon, It could be seen from behind, but it could not be seen from either side, because it was within the frame two inches, and, of course, it could not be seen from the front. But you must remember, too, that the law is a practical thing, and it does not require any useless thing. If that light served the purpose of an aft light to a following vessel, it was altogether immaterial whether it would show from the sides or show from ahead, so as far as that vessel is concerned, but provided it was sufficient to serve the purpose of an aft light for the following vessel, and could not at all have misled it or have contributed to the collision which happened. I myself cannot reason out, and I think counsel has taken that attitude—I cannot reason out why, if that light was there, lit, and no obstruction in plaintiff's rear, and plaintiff testifies that there was none—I cannot understand why it would not serve just as well for the following vessel as if it could be seen

from either side and ahead. If you can, why
that is your privilege, for you to finally determine this. So it comes right down to that
question—the attitude taken by the plaintiff's
counsel in his argument, and the court takes
it as a matter of law.''

(Bill of Exceptions, page 67.)

XXI.

The court erred in giving the following instruction to the jury:

"You have two questions to decide in this
case, outside of the damage, and you must decide them both in the affirmative before you can
find for the plaintiff. First, it is proven by
the greater weight of the evidence that Nelson's light in [118] his cabin door was where
he testified that it was; that it was of the kind
that he testified it was, and lit sufficiently long
before the collision so that it could have been
seen by the defendant's lookout, had he been
exercising his function properly and in time
so that the collision might have been avoided.
If you answer that that is proven by the greater
weight of the evidence, then you proceed to the
next question. If you do not find that the
greater weight of the evidence proves that in
Nelson's favor, that ends the case. Of course,
if he did not have that light lit, and lit sufficiently long so that a watchful lookout on the
defendant's vessel could have seen it in time
to avoid him, why he has no right to any re-

covery here, because he was negligent. In that case, he violated the law, and I do not care whether it was five o'clock or five-twenty, **or** whether it was more or less dark, it is inevitable that the absence of his light, if it was absent, would have contributed something to the collision that followed. He is out of the case and out of court right there, unless you find by the greater weight of the evidence that his light was there, as he tells you, with that degree of sufficiency—a 6-volt light—and lit long enough to have been seen and avoided by the defendant's vessel, had it a watchful lookout at the time.

If, however, you find that in favor of the plaintiff, then the next question is, in its position there in the door, if you find it was there and lit—not visible ahead and not visible on the sides—did it have anything to do with or is it clear to you that it contributed nothing to the collision that followed. Here is a vessel coming from behind—the defendant's vessel. If that light had been visible on the sides and ahead, would it have better enabled the defendant's vessel aft to avoid him and to see him and avoid him? I do not think so, and counsel's attitude for the plaintiff in his argument likewise was the same. That is common sense. If the light was there, and visible from the defendant's vessel, had it a watchful lookout, as counsel said fairly in his argument,

if it was there long enough, it would have enabled the defendant to avoid the collision.

So, if you answer those two questions in the
affirmative, proven by the greater weight of the
evidence, favorable to the plaintiff, then there
is only one more question, and that is, how much
was the damage?"

(Bill of Exceptions, pages 67, 68, 69.)

XXII.

The court erred in giving the following instruction to the jury:

"But if you find that he has been injured
by the fault of the defendant as I have heretofore defined it to you—if you answer the two
questions that I first put to you in favor of
the plaintiff, then he is at least entitled to
something for having his personal rights invaded by being thrown into the water."

(Bill of Exceptions, pages 69 and 70.)

XXIII.

The court erred in giving the following instruction to the jury: [119]

"That is the case before you. It simmers
down to this, Lady and Gentlemen of the Jury,
that taking into consideration all of the evidence in the case, both for the plaintiff and
the defendant, and the circumstances, if you
find by the greater weight of the evidence that
the plaintiff had, as he testified to you, a light
in the door of his pilot-house, facing the rear,

of 6-volt size, as he tells you, and burning long
enough before the collision so that a watchful
lookout on defendant's vessel could have seen
it, and so could have avoided the collision, he is
entitled to recover."

(Bill of Exceptions, page 70.)

XXIV.

The court erred in giving the following instruction to the jury:

"Now, the law says that where two persons
testify to a situation at the same time, the one
who testifies positively that it was thus and so—
'I saw it'—is entitled to more weight than one
who says, 'No, it was not that way.' 'I didn't
see it.'

That is the point that counsel wants to make,
and it is for you to say whether it applies in
this case. The plaintiff says, 'I had the light
there,' and the captain says, 'He did not have
the light there, because I did not see it.' Of
course, that involves whether he saw it or he
did not see it because it was not there."

(Bill of Exceptions, pages 76 and 77.)

XXV.

The court erred in entering judgment in favor
of plaintiff on each cause of action and in entering
any judgment in favor of plaintiff whatsoever.

Respectfully submitted,

BRONSON, JONES & BRONSON,

Attorneys for Defendant.

Received copy of foregoing assignment of errors this 5th day of August, 1931.

WINTER S. MARTIN,

GVC.

[Endorsed]: Filed Aug. 5, 1931.   [120]

[Title of Court and Cause.]

SUPERSEDEAS AND COST BOND ON APPEAL.

KNOW ALL MEN BY THESE PRESENTS: That said Puget Sound Navigation Company, a corporation, as principal, and Columbia Casualty Company, a corporation organized anl existing under and by virtue of the laws of the State of New York and duly authorized to transact business within the State of Washington, as surety, are held and firmly bound unto Hans Nelson, the plaintiff in the above-entitled case, in the just and full sum of Twenty-five Hundred Dollars ($2500.00), for which sum well and truly to be paid we bind ourselves, our and each of our heirs, executors, administrators, successors and assigns jointly and severally, firmly by these presents.

Sealed with our seals and dated this 11th day of August, 1931.

The condition of this obligation is such, that,

WHEREAS, lately in the term of the District Court of the United States for the Western District of Washington, Northern Division, and on, to wit, the 11th day of May, 1931, in the suit pending in said court between the said Hans Nelson, as plaintiff, and the above-named Puget Sound Navigation Company, as defendant, a final judgment was rendered against the said Puget Sound Navigation Company, a corporation, for the sum of Twenty-five Hundred Dollars ($2500.00), together with costs, and the said defendant has served and filed, in accordance with law, a notice of appeal from such judgment to the United States Circuit Court of Appeals for the Ninth Circuit, and has obtained a citation thereon, directed to the said Hans Nelson, citing him to be and appear before the said United States Circuit Court of Appeals for the Ninth Circuit, to be held in San Francisco, in the State of California, according to law, within forty (40) days from the date thereof. [121]

Now, if the said Puget Sound Navigation Company, a corporation, principal above named, shall prosecute its appeal to effect, and pay and satisfy all damages and costs that may be awarded against it, in the event of its failure to make good it plea upon such appeal, then this obligation to be void; otherwise to be and remain in full force and effect.

  PUGET SOUND NAVIGATION COMPANY.
  By BRONSON, JONES & BRONSON,
  (Signed).
           Its Attorneys.
 COLUMBIA CASUALTY COMPANY.
[Seal] By ELSIE LEDGERWOOD, (Signed)
         Attorney-in-fact.

Approved.

BOURQUIN, (Signed)

Judge.

[Endorsed]: Filed Aug. 20, 1931.   [122]

[Title of Court and Cause.]

PRAECIPE FOR TRANSCRIPT OF RECORD.

To the Clerk of the Above-entitled Court:

Kindly prepare record on appeal in the above-entitled matter to the United States Circuit Court of Appeals for the Ninth Circuit, consisting of the following, all, other than the complaint, answer and reply, pertaining to the second trial of the above-entitled court:

1. Complaint.
2. Answer.
3. Reply.
4. Verdict.
5. Judgment.
6. Defendant's motion for nonsuit and dismissal.
7. Defendant's motion for directed verdict.
8. Bill of exceptions, as amended, together with court's certificate.
9. Petition for allowance of appeal.
10. Order allowing appeal and fixing appeal and supersedeas bond.
11. Appeal and supersedeas bond.
12. Assignment of errors.
13. Citation on appeal.
14. Plaintiff's original Exhibits, 1, 2, 3, 8 and 9.

15. Defendant's Exhibits 10 and 11.
16. This praecipe.

BRONSON, JONES & BRONSON,
Attorneys for Defendant.

Received copy of foregoing praecipe for transcript of record this 20th day of August, 1931.

WINTER S. MARTIN,
By Miss CLARK.

[Endorsed]: Filed Aug. 21, 1931. [123]

[Title of Court and Cause.]

STIPULATION AND ORDER RE TRANSMISSION OF ORIGINAL EXHIBITS.

IT IS HEREBY STIPULATED by and between the parties hereto through their respective attorneys undersigned, that the following original exhibits may be forwarded with the transcript on appeal to the Clerk of the United States Circuit Court of Appeals in San Francisco, to be used as part of the record in the appeal of the above-entitled proceeding: Exhibits I, II, III, VIII, IX and XI.

Dated at Seattle, Washington, this 26th day of August, 1931.

MARTIN and COLLETT, (Signed)
Attorneys for Plaintiff.
BRONSON, JONES & BRONSON,
Attorneys for Defendant.

ORDER.

Pursuant to the above and foregoing stipulation, IT IS HEREBY ORDERED that the Clerk of the above-entitled court transmit to the Clerk of the United States Circuit Court of Appeals at San Francisco, as part of the record on appeal, the following original exhibits admitted in evidence in the trial of the above-entitled exhibits proceeding, viz.: Exhibits I, II, III, VIII, IX, X and XI.

Done in open court this 27th day of August, 1931.

JEREMIAH NETERER, (Signed)

U. S. District Judge.

[Endorsed]: Filed Aug. 27, 1931. [124]

[Title of Court and Cause.]

CERTIFICATE OF CLERK U. S. DISTRICT COURT TO TRANSCRIPT OF RECORD.

United States of America,

Western District of Washington,—ss.

I, Ed. M. Lakin, Clerk of the United States District Court for the Western District of Washington, do hereby certify this typewritten transcript of record, consisting of pages numbered from 1 to 122, inclusive, to be a full, true and correct and complete copy of so much of the record, papers and other proceedings in the above and foregoing entitled cause, as is required by praecipe of counsel, filed and shown herein, as the same remain of record and on file in the office of the Clerk of said District Court, and that the same constitute the record on appeal herein from the judgment of the said United States District Court for the Western District of Washington to the United States Circuit Court of Appeals for the Ninth Circuit.

I further certify that the following is a full, true and correct statement of all expenses, costs, fees and charges incurred in my office by or on behalf of the appellant herein, for making record, certificate or return to the United States Circuit Court of Appeals for the Ninth Circuit in the above-entitled cause, to wit:

Clerk's fees (Act Feb. 11, 1925) for making
    record, certificate or return 365 folios
    at 15¢ $54.75
Appeal fee (Section 5 of Act) 5.00
Certificate of Clerk to original exhibits,
    with seal .... .50
Certificate of Clerk to Transcript of Record
    ord with seal .... .50
                  Total $60.75

[125]

I hereby certify that the above cost for preparing and certifying record, amounting to $60.75, has been paid to me by attorneys for the appellant.

I further certify that I herewith transmit the original citation issued in the above-entitled cause.

IN WITNESS WHEREOF I have hereunto set my hand and affixed the official seal of said court, at Seattle, in said District, this 24th day of August, 1931.

[Seal]   ED. M. LAKIN,

Clerk of the United States District Court for the
    Western District of Washington.

By E. W. Pettit,
    Deputy.   [126]

[Title of Court and Cause.]

CITATION ON APPEAL.

The President of the United States to the Above-
    named Plaintiff, Hans Nelson, and to Winter
    S. Martin and Arthur Collett, Jr., His Attor-
    neys, GREETING:

YOU ARE HEREBY CITED AND ADMON-
ISHED to be and appear in the United States Circuit Court of Appeals for the Ninth Circuit, to be
held in the City of San Francisco, in the State of
California, within forty days from the date of this
writ, pursuant to an appeal filed in the office of the
Clerk of the District Court of the United States
for the Western District of Washington, Northern
Division, wherein Hans Nelson is plaintiff and the
Puget Sound Navigation Company, a corporation,
is defendant, to show cause, if any there be, why
the judgment in such appeal mentioned should not

be corrected and speedy justice should not be done in that behalf.

[Seal] BOURQUIN,

Judge.

Copy of above citation received and due service of the same is hereby acknowledged this —— day of June, 1931.

————————————————,

Attorneys for Plaintiff.

[Endorsed]: Filed Aug. 10, 1931. [127]

———

[Endorsed]: No. 6600. United States Circuit Court of Appeals for the Ninth Circuit. Puget Sound Navigation Company, a Corporation, Appellant, vs. Hans Nelson, Appellee. Transcript of Record. Upon Appeal from the United States District Court for the Western District of Washington, Northern Division.

Filed September 2, 1931.

PAUL P. O'BRIEN,

Clerk of the United States Circuit Court of Appeals for the Ninth Circuit.

No. 6600

UNITED STATES
CIRCUIT COURT OF APPEALS

FOR THE NINTH CIRCUIT

PUGET SOUND NAVIGATION COMPANY,
  a corporation,

Appellant,

vs.

HANS NELSON,

Appellee.

UPON APPEAL FROM A JUDGMENT OF THE
UNITED STATES DISTRICT COURT FOR THE
WESTERN DISTRICT OF WASHINGTON,
NORTHERN DIVISION

HONORABLE GEORGE M. BOURQUIN, *Judge*

Brief of Appellant

FILED

FEB 29 1932

PAUL P. O'BRIEN,

H. B. JONES   CLERK

ROBERT E. BRONSON
Attorneys for Appellant.

Office and Post Office Address:
  614-620 Colman Building,
  Seattle, Washington.

SUBJECT INDEX

TABLE OF CASES

DECISIONS—

UNITED STATES CIRCUIT COURT OF APPEALS

FOR THE NINTH CIRCUIT

PUGET SOUND NAVIGATION COMPANY,
a corporation,

Appellant,

vs.

HANS NELSON,

Appellee.

UPON APPEAL FROM A JUDGMENT OF THE UNITED STATES DISTRICT COURT FOR THE WESTERN DISTRICT OF WASHINGTON, NORTHERN DIVISION

HONORABLE GEORGE M. BOURQUIN, *Judge*

Brief of Appellant

STATEMENT OF THE CASE

This is an appeal from a judgment of the United States District Court for the Western District of Washington, Northern Division, which was entered upon May 11th, 1931, by Honorable George M. Bourquin, Judge, in an action at law before the court sitting with a jury, in a cause instituted by the appellee to recover damages for loss of property and alleged personal injury.

This case has previously been before this court on appeal, cause No. 6099, decision reported 41 Fed. 2d 356, 1930 A.M.C. 1386.

Appellee sets forth two causes of action, one for the loss of property, consisting of a small power fish boat, including certain equipment and personal effects, and the second for alleged personal injuries claimed to have been sustained by appellee resulting from a collision between said fish boat and the steam ferry Olympic. The fish boat Magna was owned and being operated by the appellee at the time of the collision, appellee being the only person aboard the fish boat.

The steam ferry Olympic was owned and operated by the appellant as a common carrier for hire, its navigation being in control of its master, officers and crew, servants and employees of appellant.

The collision took place on the inland waters of Puget Sound, State of Washington, on the main channel course of vessels proceeding down sound to the north from Seattle, and at a distance several miles in a general northerly direction from West Point.

Appellant's vessel, the Olympic, was enroute from Seattle to Port Townsend, and having rounded West Point was proceeding down the main channel course approximately NNW½W magnetic. The Magna was proceeding from the entrance to the Lake Washington Ship Canal, at Ballard, diagonally across the course of vessels bound down Sound on the main channel course, and was heading west northwest magnetic (see chart, defendant's exhibit 11 on which course of Olympic is shown as line CD and course of fish boat Magna shown as line AB.)

The collision occurred, according to the pilot house clock of the Olympic at 5:20 P.M., and according to the estimates of the appellee at about 5:00 P.M., on the 5th day of December, 1927, the bow of the Olympic striking the port quarter of the Magna, with the result that the Magna shortly thereafter filled and sank.

In his first cause of action, appellee sought recovery of damages in the amount of $4,836.20, for the loss of his vessel, and personal property thereon, and in his second cause of action, damages in the amount of $2,500.00 for personal injuries alleged to have been sustained and to have resulted from said collision, and the subsequent jumping overboard of the appellee. (Tr. p. 5-7.)

The jury returned a verdict for plaintiff in the amount of $2,250.00 on his first caust of action and in the amount of $250.00 on his second cause of action. (Tr. p. 21.)

The trial occurred on the 5th and 6th days of May, 1931, and on May 11th, 1931, judgment in appellee's favor upon the verdict of the jury was entered by the court. (Tr. p. 21.)

At the close of appellee's case, appellant moved for non-suit and directed verdict (Tr. p. 20 and 48), which motion was by the court denied over exception of appellant. (Tr. p. 50.)

At the close of all of the evidence appellant renewed its motion for a directed verdict. (Tr. p. 20 and 91.) This motion was by the court denied over exception of appellant. (Tr. p. 20 and 91.)

At the close of the evidence appellant filed certain requested instructions which will hereafter be more fully identified and discussed, but the court declined to submit these instructions to the jury.

The evidence may perhaps be considered as divided into two separate parts, as far as periods of time are concerned, using the actual occurrence of the collision as the dividing line, in view of the particular issues which are submitted on this appeal, for neither the appellee nor any witnesses who testified in his behalf saw the appellant's vessel until after the collision, and none of appellee's witnesses, other than himself, saw his own vessel until after the collision. Certain of the witnesses for the appellant saw the appellee's vessel just prior to the collision and also, of course, observed both vessels thereafter, and in discussing this case hereafter in the argument, this circumstance as to the evidence which was produced, becomes very material, as will subsequently appear.

Those of the facts which appear from the evidence without direct contradiction and which are material to this appeal are substantially the following:

THE FACTS

On December 5th, 1927, the appellee set out alone in his gas boat, the Magna, a vessel 33 feet in length, from the Ballard locks entrance to the Lake Washington Ship Canal, Seattle, Washington, for Suquamish on the opposite side of Puget Sound, after sunset, which occurred on said day at 4:17 o'clock P.M. (See Exhibit 9.)

Previous to the day in question, appellee's boat had been equipped with an after range light on top of a pole mast in the after part of the boat, but, prior to the day of the collision, this mast and light had been removed by the appellee and not replaced, and appellee was proceeding at the time of the collision admittedly without his after mast or any light on the after part of his boat. (Tr. p. 42-43.)

The appellee, with his boat, left the Standard Oil Dock inside the Government Locks on the day in question at 4:30 o'clock P.M., proceeded through the locks, being still inside the entrance of the canal at 4:40 o'clock, his vessel making about 5½ miles an hour.

The appellee testified that at 4:40 he got through the locks and the sun was just going down behind the mountains then. (Tr. p. 42.) He further testified that at the time, the wind was westerly, blowing a good breeze, and that there was a heavy sea, and that the tide was going up with the wind, making big swells (Tr. p. 41); that appellee set out upon the course of West Northwest; that the wind was coming from west northwest and that he was heading into the wind, but the swell was more northerly. (Tr. p. 45.)

The appellee further testified that after he left the locks, and that when he got out by the blinker at the entrance to the Canal, he put up the two side lights and the mast head light on his vessel; that the mast head light was a bright light in front of the pilot house, being an electric light on the bow on top of the pilot house showing forward; that the side lights were the usual green and red lights which were on the after end of the pilot house with a screen on each side; that in addition to said lights he had one light hanging two inches inside the door of the pilot house, the door being on the starboard side of the pilot house, opening aft (Tr. p. 37); that the door of the pilot house was a solid door and that it was open at the time of the collision, and at all times thereafter; that the pilot house was on the forward part of the boat; that all of said lights were burning in the positions stated from about 4:40 onward until after the collision (Tr. p. 38); and that he never went outside of the wheel house after first leaving the Standard Oil Dock, until after the collision. (Tr. p. 44.)

Appellee testified that he had no warning of the collision and did not see the appellant's vessel until after the vessels came together, and that at all times prior to the collision he was inside the pilot house looking ahead and navigating his boat, and never looked astern to see what was coming from that direction.

The foregoing is all of the direct material evidence introduced on behalf of appellee until after the time of the collision, and, with the exception of certain evidence, the introduction of which by the court, is claimed as error in this appeal, and which will hereafter be discussed, was all of the evidence affecting the question of negligence on the part of the appellee at the time appellee rested his direct case.

The evidence as to appellant's vessel by appellant's witnesses was as follows:

The steamer Olympic, a passenger and vehicle ferry, of considerable size, the appearance of which is shown in plaintiff's exhibits 1, 2 and 3, was enroute from Seattle to Port Townsend, having left Seattle at 4:31 or 4:32 o'clock in the afternoon; the Olympic had all of her lights on, both navigation lights and lights in her cabins, when leaving Seattle. The vessel was in charge of the first officer, Harry John Whaley, from Seattle to Four Mile Rock, and at Four Mile Rock the master took over the navigation and remained in the pilot house with the quartermaster, who was steering the vessel at all times thereafter. The Olympic passed abeam of West Point Light at 5:01 P.M., according to the pilot house clock. There was a strong northwest wind blowing, and the sea was rough; the tide was ebbing, running out against the wind, and there were quite a few white caps and spray upon the water. (Tr. p. 74.) After rounding West Point, the master of the Olympic was standing on the starboard side of the pilot house looking out through an open window ahead. About four miles northwest of West Point the master saw a dark object almost directly ahead of his vessel, but was not able to make out what it was. He thought it was a drifting dolphin or something of that character, which did not seem to have any motion in the water. The Olympic was making 13.8 miles, or 12 knots per hour on her regular course, until this object was sighted between 100 and 200 feet ahead of the Olympic, at which time the engines of the Olympic were put full speed astern. The master saw no light on this object, which proved to be the appellee's boat, until after it was struck by the Olympic and swung around under the Olympic's port bow. The Olympic had been running 19 minutes on her course from West Point, and the collision occurred, according to the pilot house clock of the Olympic, at 5:20 P.M. The master could tell that the engines were reversed promptly from the resulting vibration to the ship, but its headway could not be checked in time to avoid the collision, but it was checked considerably. (Tr. p. 75-76.)

The quartermaster on the Olympic, William Seatter, was called as a witness on behalf of appellant and testified as to events up to the point of collision, and substantially corroborated the master of the Olympic up to that point. It then appeared that his testimony as to certain occurrences after the collision substantially differed from testimony which he had

given at the former trial, and it developed that he had
suffered from epileptic fits since the first trial, which
affected his memory. The appellant, being taken by
surprise, was therefore obliged to impeach this witness (Tr. pp. 56-60), and his testimony was in effect
repudiated for all purposes.

For four or five minutes prior to the collision, the
lookout on the Olympic, who was stationed at the
foot of the stairway or ladder leading from the main
deck to the boat deck forward (see plaintiff's exhibits
1, 2 and 3), was securing some heavy curtains on the
passenger cabin windows forward, which were used to
screen cabin lights from showing forward, and which
had blown loose in the wind. He was doing this work
at the direction of the master, and did not see the appellee's vessel until after the collision. The foregoing
facts are without direct contradiction and with the
exception of the question of visibility, are all of the
material facts bearing upon the actual occurrence of
the collision itself.

As to the visibility, appellee admitted that the sun
was setting behind the mountains at about 4:40 P. M.
(Tr. p. 42.) Mr. Lawrence Fisher, government meteorologist of the Seattle Weather Bureau, testified that
on the day of the collision the sun set below a water
level horizon at 4:17 P. M.; that on that day under

ideal conditions, civil twilight would continue there-after for a period of 35 minutes, or until 4:52 P. M. He defined civil twilight as that period after sunset during which ordinary outdoor occupations are regarded as possible under ideal or cloudless conditions of the sky and a water-level horizon. The master, mate and lookout of the appellant's vessel testified that, at 4:32, when that vessel left Seattle, it was getting dusk, the master and lookout testified that upon reaching West Point light it was dark, with clouds banking mountains on the western horizon, and that only the high lands were visible, the water being dark, and that the collision occurred one hour and three minutes after the time of scientific sunset.

The appellee testified that at the time of the collision he could see easily one half mile on the water; that upon coming out of the canal he saw a tug on his starboard hand, off to the northward about one half mile away.

All witnesses agree that the moon was not visible prior to the collision, but the meteorologist, Mr. Fisher, testified that the moon was in the eastern quarter of the sky at the time, there being a few cumulous clouds observed from the Seattle Station some miles to the south of the point of collision at about 20 minutes before five, and that his records did not show the conditions of the sky nine or ten miles northwest of the city, though his records showed that the sun set behind a solid bank of clouds in the West and was obscured on setting; that the period of practical twilight is dependent on the clearness of the sky and that the sun setting behind clouds will advance the time of the end of civil twilight.

SUMMARY OF MATERIAL IMPORTANT FACTS

1. The appellant's vessel Olympic was showing all lights prescribed by law.

2. The Olympic's lookout was not looking ahead for four or five minutes prior to the collision.

3. No lights on the Magna were visible to those in charge of the navigation of the Olympic until after the Magna swung about, following the collision, and the Magna herself was not seen, except as a dark outline in the water, practically ahead and one or two hundred feet distant from the Olympic before the collision.

4. The collision occurred one hour and three minutes after the sun had set beneath an ideal or water level horizon but scientific observation has it first descending behind a solid bank of clouds and the Olympic Mountains on the western horizon.

5. After the dark outline of the Magna became visible, everything possible within the judgment of the master of the Olympic was done to avoid the collision.

6. The appellee had removed the mast and range light prescribed by law from his vessel, but claimed to have an electric light hung inside the doorway of his pilot house on the starboard side aft thereof, with the door open.

7. Appellee never went outside the pilot house to observe whether this light was visible from any portion of the stern of his vessel, and there is no testimony *that this light was visible* to a vessel approaching from the port quarter, as was the Olympic, or from any other point *until after the collision.*

ARGUMENT

It is regrettable that appellant has been obliged to assign so many specific errors, but an examination of these assignments (Tr., pp. 124 to 141), will disclose that they all bear vitally upon one principal point, with the exception of the 13th and 22nd, and that is upon the primary question of the negligence or contributory negligence of the appellee in bringing about the collision, barring any right of recovery. The 13th and 22nd bear upon the primary question of appellee's negligence, or contributory negligence effecting his alleged personal injuries suffered *after* the collision in the water.

The appellee's vessel was 33 feet in length (Tr. p. 34). By law a motor vessel of this size, between sunset and sunrise, is required to carry a white range light in the after part of the vessel, showing all around the horizon. The Act of June 9th, 1910, U. S. C. A., Title 46, Section 511, provides in part as follows:

"The words 'motor boat' where used in this chapter shall include every vessel propelled by machinery and not more than sixty-five feet in length except tugboats and towbats propelled by steam. The length shall be measured from end to end over the deck, excluding sheer. * * * * * *."

Sec. 512 of the same title provides as follows:

"Motor boats subject to the provisions of this chapter shall be divided into classes as follows:

Class 1. Less than twenty-six feet in length.

Class 2. *Twenty-six feet or over and less than forty feet in length.*

Class 3. Forty feet or over and not more than sixty-five feet in length."

Sec. 513 of the same title provides as follows:

"Every motor boat in all weathers from sunset to sunrise shall carry the following lights, and during such time no other lights which may be mistaken for those prescribed shall be exhibited. * * * * * * *

(b) Every motor boat of classes 2 and 3 shall carry the following lights:

First. A bright white light in the fore part of the vessel as near the stem as practicable, so constructed as to show an unbroken light over an arc of the horizon of twenty points of the compass, so fixed as to throw the light ten points on each side of the vessel, namely, from right ahead to two points abaft the beam on either side. * * * * * * * *

Second. *A white light aft to show all around the horizon.*

Third. On the starboard side a green light so constructed as to show an unbroken light over an arc of the horizon of ten points of the compass, so fixed as to throw the light from right ahead to two points abaft the beam on the starboard side. On the port side a red light so constructed as to show an unbroken light over an arc of the horizon of ten points of the compass, so fixed as to throw the light from right ahead to two points abaft the beam on the port side." (Italics ours.)

Appellee had admittedly removed this light and the mast upon which it was placed, from his vessel, and had no light in the after part of his ship at all, the only lights which he carried being the white so-called mast head light, the red port light and the starboard green light which were on his wheel house, and which were properly screened so as not to be apparent to a vessel approaching from the quarter, as was the Olympic, and a light inside the pilot house, all of these lights being in the forward part of the boat.

The appellee was therefore guilty of negligence as a matter of law, for failure to carry the prescribed range light aft, *or any range light aft,* and this negligence was of such a character as to bar appellee from any recovery in this case, unless appellee proved that his failure to so carry a range light *could not have been* a contributing cause of the collision. As stated by Justice Rudkin in the former appeal, *Puget Sound Navigation Company vs. Nelson,* 41 Fed. 2d 356, 1930 A. M. C. 1386, which has now become the law in this case:

> "On the foregoing facts the jury would be warranted in finding that both vessels were at fault, the Olympic for failure to keep a proper lookout, and the Magna for failure to display a proper signal; and in admiralty the rule is well settled that a vessel committing a breach of statutory duty must not only show that probably her fault did not contribute to the disaster, but that it could not have done so. *Belden v. Chase,* 150 U. S. 674, 699, 14 S. Ctfl 264, 269, 37 L. Ed. 1218. And, while this action was tried in the common law side of the court, the rights and liabilities of the parties are measured by the admiralty law, and not by common-law standards. *Chelantis v. Luckenbach S. S. Co.,* 247 U. S. 372, 38 S. Ct. 501, 62 L. Ed. 1171."

See also *The Pennsylvania,* 19 Wall. 125; *The Martello,* 153 U. S. 64; *The Britannia,* 153 U. S. 130.

The undisputed facts in this case are that no light whatsoever was visible on the Magna to anyone on board the Olympic prior to the collision, that the master of the Olympic saw the Magna as a dark outline after the vessels got into the jaws of collision but saw no sign of any light. There is likewise no testimony in this case that any light was visible on the Magna prior to the collision, from any point outside of the wheel house of the Magna, when viewed from the after part of that vessel. It is the efforts which the appellee made to fill in this fatal gap and deficiency in his case by improper testimony, which we will hereinafter point out, which makes pertinent and necessary the first, second, third, fourth, fifth and sixth assignments of error. And, no evidence being in this case which would possibly justify anyone, finding that this statutory breach of duty by the appellee could not have contributed to the collision, made necessary the granting of a directed verdict at the close of appellee's case, and this forms the basis of appellant's assignment of errors number seven and twenty-five. The action of the trial court in repeatedly instructing the jury contrary to the foregoing law, upon such evidence, and mis-stating the evidence itself, has made pertinent and necessary appellant's assignment of errors IX, X, XI, XII, XIV, XV, XVI, XVII, XVIII, XIX, XX, XXIII and XXIV.

The case is thus reduced down to an elementary basis for argument in this form, viz: there being no proper evidence in the case from which the jury could possibly be warranted in finding that the failure of the appellee to carry a visible white light in the after part of his boat as a range light, could not have contributed to the collision, the court committed errors in ruling upon evidence which the appellee put forward in an effort to fill in this deficiency of his case, being rulings covered by assignments of error I, II, III, IV, V and VI, and these errors seem to us logically grouped and discussed as one specification of error.

Next, upon the competent and proper evidence in the case, the court committed error in failing to hold appellee guilty of negligence barring recovery as a matter of law, by reason of his admitted failure to carry any visible light in the after part of his vessel, as required by law, and in thereupon denying appellant's motion for directed verdict at the close of appellee's case, assignment of error number VII, and the renewal of this motion, assignment of error number VIII, which we believe to be properly combined as a second general specification of error.

Next, upon the proper evidence in the case, and the law of this case as laid down by this court upon the former appeal, the court erred in refusing to give the specific instructions requested by appellant, covered by assignments of error IX, X, XI, XII and XIII, and these errors, we believe, are properly grouped for discussion and argument under a third general specification of error.

Next, the court erred in a series of erroneous instructions which were repeated and intermingled, repeatedly instructing the jury as a matter of law that the appellee's light, which he claimed to have had within the wheel house, was a sufficient and proper light as a substitute for an after range light, and that the only question to be decided by the jury was whether or not such light was there and lit before the collision, which was in effect a directed verdict in favor of appellee, for no other person than appellee was in a position to have any knowledge as to whether such light was where it was claimed to be. In fact, no other witness testified concerning the same, and hence appellee's testimony that he had such a light was wholly undisputed, though the testimony of the case was, without contradiction, that no such light was visible to anyone other than appellee within his own wheelhouse. We believe that this series of related erroneous instructions should properly be grouped under a fifth specification of error, covering assignments of error numbers XIV, XV, XVI, XVII, XVIII, XIX, XX, XXI, XXII and XXIII.

The court made another separate and distinct error in instructing the jury with respect to the question of positive and negative evidence, which was not supported by the facts of this case, being assignment of error number XXIV, and this assignment forms a basis of a sixth specification of error.

Assignment of error number XXV, relating to the entry of judgment in favor of the appellee, goes to the whole case, and will, of course, be covered by the beforementioned specifications of error.

SPECIFICATIONS OF ERROR

SPECIFICATION NUMBER I: The court erred in admitting in evidence and submitting to the jury the testimony of Emil Schuman, witness for appellee, as to the visibility of the light in the cabin or pilot house after the collision, as testimony bearing upon the collision itself. (Assignment of error number I, Tr. p. 124.)

SPECIFICATION NUMBER II: The court erred in admitting and submitting to the jury testimony of appellee as to the visibility of other lights in his pilot house at times prior to the day of the collision, and his speculation upon the visibility of the light in the pilot house at the time of the collision. (Assignments of error numbers II, III, IV, V and VI, Tr. pp. 124-125.)

SPECIFICATION NUMBER III: The court erred in denying appellant's motion for directed verdict at the close of appellee's case (assignment of error number VII, Tr. p. 126), and in denying appellant's motion for directed verdict at the close of all of the evidence. (Assignment of error number VIII, Tr. p. 127.)

SPECIFICATION NUMBER IV: The court erred in refusing to give the specific instructions to the jury requested by appellant, and covered by written requested instructions. (Assignments of error, numbers IX, X, XI, XII and XIII, Tr. pp. 127-132.)

SPECIFICATION NUMBER V: The court erred in giving the specific instructions covered by assignments of error numbers XIV, XV, XVI, XVII, XVIII, XIX, XX, XXI, XXII and XXIII, being the following:

"As a matter of fact, the court agrees with the statement of counsel for the defense in his argument that if the plaintiff had that light in the doorway of his boat, lit long enough before the collision so that it could have been seen by a proper lookout on the 'Olympic,' they would have avoided him, and the collision would have never occurred. And if the plaintiff had it there, as he says that he did, and which the defendant denies, there is no reason why he should not recover in this action.

"Before we come to any more of the law, I am simply stating that I agree with counsel's position, and I think the plaintiff does now, too. That is all I can see in this case. You must remember this, that the plaintiff must prove his case by a greater weight of the evidence. The burden is on him throughout to prove that he had that light there, lit there for the length of time that I have stated to you, and prove that it was a good and sufficient light to serve its purpose, and to prove the amount of his damages. The burden is on him to prove all those things before he can recover. So you see that in this case, there [116] is mainly involved the credibility of witnesses where there is a direct conflict between the witnesses for the plaintiff and the witnesses for the defendant."

"The plaintiff basis his right to recover in this action on the fact that the collision was due, as he alleges, to the negligence and fault of the defendant, and the defendant alone, and the defendant resists on the theory, as it alleges, that it was not negligent and at fault at all, but that the plaintiff himself is the guilty person, by reason of not conforming to the rules with respect to his lights."

"The Captain was there, and his duty was to navigate the vessel and see that it was kept on its course, as he outlined it, but he is not a satisfactory lookout to come within the provisions of the law requiring a lookout to be kept, as I have defined it to you. And, again, that is the attitude of counsel for the plaintiff, when he says there is only one question in this case, and I agree with him, whether the aft light on this vessel of the fisherman was there."

"Now, you have heard the testimony of the plaintiff. He told you * * * he was in there navigating his vessel north, northwest, the same course as the defendant's vessel was going when it overtook him."

"The plaintiff was not obliged to keep any lookout behind him, because if he had his lights lit, he was entitled to presume that any vessel following him would take note of him and would comply with the law and not run him down."

"On the other hand, there are two witnesses for the plaintiff who testified to seeing the light shortly after the collision occurred. Mrs. Schuman, now deceased, whose testimony was read to you, testified that she was eating when she felt the vibration of the reversing; that she sat still for quite a while, and hearing more commotion, she went to the window and saw a boat and saw a light on top of the vessel. She does not say whether that was a light in the cabin door, or at the bow of the vessel. She said she saw it on top of the vessel. That was her testimony, and Mr. Schuman testified that he came out some time after the collision—you remember the time—of course the intervals, perhaps, were not very long, any of them—and that after the 'Olympic' had backed so that it was in the rear of plaintiff's boat, he saw this white light burning in the cabin door."

"If that was his aft light, and there is no reason why it could not have been, even though it was not across the dividing line in the middle of the ship—between the bow and the stern—if that was his aft light, and it was the only aft

light that he had, if it was not so placed that it
would be seen all around the horizon, it could be
seen from behind, but it could not be seen from
either side, because it was within the frame two
inches, and, of course, it could not be seen from
the front. But you must remember, too, that the
law is a practical thing, and it does not require
any useless thing. If that light served the purpose of an aft light to a following vessel, it was
altogether immaterial whether it would show from
the sides or show from ahead, so far as that
vessel is concerned, but provided it was sufficient
to serve the purpose of an aft light for the following vessel, and could not at all have misled it
or have contributed to the collision which happened. I myself cannot reason out, and I think
counsel has taken that attitude—I cannot reason
out why, if that light was there, lit, and no obstruction in plaintiff's rear, and plaintiff testifies
that there was none—I cannot understand why it
would not serve just as well for the following
vessel as if it could be seen from either side and
ahead. If you can, why that is your privilege, for
you to finally determine this. So it comes right
down to that question—the attitude taken by the
plaintiff's counsel in his argument, and the court
takes it as a matter of law.''

"You have two questions to decide in this
case, outside of the damage, and you must decide
them both in the affirmative before you can find
for the plaintiff. First, it is proven by the greater
weight of the evidence that Nelson's light in
[118] his cabin door was where he testified that
it was; that it was of the kind that he testified it
was, and lit sufficiently long before the collision
so that it could have been seen by the defendant's
lookout, had he been exercising his function prop-

erly and in time so that the collision might have
been avoided. If you answer that that is proven
by the greater weight of the evidence, then you
proceed to the next question. If you do not find
that the greater weight of the evidence proves
that in Nelson's favor, that ends the case. Of
course, if he did not have that light lit, and lit
sufficiently long so that a watchful lookout on the
defendant's vessel could have seen it in time to
avoid him, why he has no right to any recovery
here, because he was negligent. In that case, he
violated the law, and I do not care whether it was
five o'clock or five-twenty, or whether it was more
or less dark, it is inevitable that the absence of
his light, if it was absent, would have contributed
something to the collision that followed. He is out
of the case and out of court right there, unless
you find by the greater weight of the evidence
that his light was there, as he tells you, with that
degree of sufficiency—a 6-volt light—and lit long
enough to have been seen and avoided by the defendant's vessel, had it a watchful lookout at the
time.

If, however, you find that in favor of the
plaintiff, then the next question is, in its position
there in the door, if you find it was there and lit—
not visible ahead and not visible on the sides—did
it have anything to do with or is it clear to you
that it contributed nothing to the collision that
followed. Here is a vessel coming from behind—
the defendant's vessel. If that light had been visible
on the sides and ahead, would it have better enabled the defendant's vessel aft to avoid him and
to see him and avoid him? I do not think so, and
counsel's attitude for the plaintiff in his argument likewise was the same. That is common
sense. If the light was there, and visible from the
defendant's vessel, had it a watchful lookout, as

counsel said fairly in his argument, if it was there long enough, it would have enabled the defendant to avoid the collision.

"So, if you answer those two questions in the affirmative, proven by the greater weight of the evidence, favorable to the plaintiff, then there is only one more question, and that is, how much was the damage?"

"But if you find that he has been injured by the fault of the defendant as I have heretofore defined it to you—if you answer the two questions that I first put to you in favor of the plaintiff, then he is at least entitled to something for having his personal rights invaded by being thrown into the water."

"That is the case before you. It simmers down to this, Lady and Gentlemen of the Jury, that taking into consideration all of the evidence in the case, both for the plaintiff and the defendant, and the circumstances, if you find by the greater weight of the evidence that the plaintiff had, as he testified to you, a light in the door of his pilot-house, facing the rear, of 6-volt size, as he tells you, and burning long enough before the collision so that a watchful lookout on defendant's vessel could have seen it, and so could have avoided the collision, he is entitled to recover."

SPECIFICATION NUMBER VI: The court erred in instructing the jury as follows:

"Now, the law says that where two persons testify to a situation at the same time, the one who testifies positively that it was thus and so— 'I saw it'—is entitled to more weight than one who says, 'No, it was not that way.' 'I didn't see it.'

"That is the point that counsel wants to make, and it is for you to say whether it applies in this case. The plaintiff says, 'I had the light there,' and the captain says. 'He did not have the light there, because I did not see it.' Of course, that involves whether he saw it or he did not see it because it was not there." (Assignment of error number XXIV, Tr. p. 141.)

ARGUMENT ON SPECIFICATION NUMBER I

The witness Emil Schuman, saw nothing of the appellee's boat and admittedly made no effort to do so, until after the collision, when the appellant's vessel had backed up into proximity with it, and when both vessels were swinging about in varying positions, and his testimony as to the visibility of a light in the wheel house of the appellee's boat at such a time could not possibly have any relavency or materiality in this case, and should not have been submitted to the jury, as being any proof as to the visibility or lack of visibility of any light upon the appellee's vessel, prior to the collision, when they are upon different and fixed courses, and had a definite and fixed bearing, one from the other. This testimony was, however, submitted to the jury as evidence of the fact that the light which appellee claimed to have had in his pilot house was visible prior to the collision, as note particularly the court's instruction under assignment of error number XIX (Tr. p. 136), which will hereafter be discussed.

This was unquestionably clear and prejudicial error, since this testimony was submitted in an effort to prove that appellee's failure to carry a range light aft on his vessel could not have been one of the causes of the collision.

ARGUMENT ON SPECIFICATION NUMBER II.

It was equally clear and equally prejudicial error for the court to permit the appellee himself to answer the following question in the affirmative: "Could anybody see that light suspended in the door of your vessel—in that open door approaching from the stern?" The admission of such testimony is pure speculation and guess work, since appellee admitted that he was never outside of his wheel house after lighting his lights and suspending the light mentioned inside his pilot house door. As appears from the transcript he stated: "I never went outside of the wheelhouse after I left Ballard. After the collision I went out, but up to that time I had been inside navigating the vessel. I did not have time to look astern of the ship to see what was coming in that direction. I never looked at all. I don't have to look back. I was looking to the windward; that was the only way I had to look." (Tr. p. 44.)

There was, therefore, no excuse or justification whatsoever for permitting the witness to testify and submitting to the jury the appellee's guess that anybody could have seen the light suspended in the door of his vessel, approaching from the stern, and even less for submitting this to the jury as evidence that such a light could have been seen by anyone approaching on the port quarter of the appellee's boat, and this was clearly improper and prejudicial, being submitted in an effort to prove that appellee's failure to carry any after light could not have been a cause of the collision.

The court committed error of the same character in permitting the appellee to answer the following questions, which all stand upon the same footing:

"Hans, did you ever have occasion to be away from your own vessel at night-time, either on the shore or on another vessel, when you could see that light suspended in the doorway of your cabin?" (Assignment of error number III, Tr. p. 125.)

"How far could you see that light when the light was on and when it was hanging in the doorway, suspended as it was at the time of the collision?" (Assignment of error, No. IV, Tr. p. 125.)

"Have you actually seen that light half a mile away?" (Assignment of error Number V, Tr. p. 125.)

"How far could you see any vessel ahead of you, a vessel the size of the Magna?" (Assignment of error number VI, Tr. p. 126.)

The appellee answer the first two questions "Yes," the third question, "half a mile away," the fourth question "Yes, I have been on shore many times, and I have had that light burning and I have seen it. I seen that light on my own boat" (Tr. p. 39), and the last question the witness answered: "You could see a vessel like the Magna a quarter of a mile away, easily, at the time of that collision." (Tr. p. 41.)

The foregoing is all of the evidence offered or submitted upon the entire case tending in any way to establish that the failure of the appellee to carry a visible light aft in his vessel as required by statute, could not be one of the direct contributing causes of the collision, and all of this evidence was clearly improper in every sense of the word, leaving this case with no testimony or evidence which anyone was entitled to consider proving, or in any manner tending to prove that the failure of the appellee to carry such a light could not be one of the contributing causes of the collision, since the positive testimony of the appellant's master, Van Bogaert, was that he was looking directly ahead for 19 minutes prior to the collision, and that no light was visible upon the appellee's boat at any time prior to the collision, nor was the boat itself visible as an unidentifiable object, until the collision was unavoidable.

ARGUMENT ON SPECFICATION NUMBER III.

This is an action at law before a jury, and contributory negligence on the part of the appellee is sufficient to constitute a complete bar to any recovery in this case.

As stated by Judge Rudkin of this court upon the former appeal (supra):

> "The appellee contends further that contributory fault or negligence on the part of a plaintiff is no bar to a recovery in an action of this kind. The settled rule is otherwise. In *Belden v. Chase, supra,* the court said:

> 'The doctrine in admiralty of an equal division of damages in the case of a collision between two vessels, when both are in fault contributing to the collision, has long prevailed in England and this country. The *Max Morris,* 137 U. S. 1, 11 S. Ct. 29, 34 L. Ed. 586. But at common law the general rule is that, if both vessels are culpable in respect of faults operating directly and immediately to produce the collision, neither can recover damages for injuries so caused. *Atlee v. Packet Co.,* 21 Wall, 389, 22 L. Ed. 619.

> 'In order to maintain his action, the plaintiff was obliged to establish the negligence of the defendant, and that such negligence was the sole cause of the injury, or, in other words, he could not recover, though defendant were negligent, if

it appeared that his own negligence directly contributed to the result complained of'.''

This collision occurred on the 5th day of December, one hour and three minutes after the sun had set
below the ocean level behind a bank of clouds and a
mountain range.

The appellee claims it was not dark. Witnesses for
the appellant testified that it was dark. The undisputed testimony of the meteorological expert was that
under ideal conditions of sky and horizon, the end of
civil twilight had occurred thirty minutes prior, and
we submit that no reasonable mind could believe that
there was not sufficient absence of natural light to
make the absence of an artificial light on a vessel a
contributing cause to a collision of this character. It
is also admitted that no moon was visible at the time
and the duty therefore devolved upon appellee to
prove as a condition precedent to the avoidance of a
directed verdict at the close of his case, that he *prove*
that his failure to carry the light prescribed by law
after sunset *could not have been one of the causes of
the collision.* With the exception of the improper testimony discussed under the foregoing specification of
error, there is not a scintilla or iota of evidence in the
entire record touching this burden of proof.

Even after the admission of the above mentioned improper testimony, the testimony itself does not constitute any competent proof as to what was or was not visible to those on board the Olympic at any time prior to the collision, and lights which became visible after the vessels had changed their position and swung about in different directions is, of course, no evidence bearing upon the collision in any manner. We conclude, therefore, that it was the duty of the trial court to have granted appellant's motion for a directed verdict at the close of appellee's case, and that this duty became even more imperative, if such a thing were possible, at the close of all of the testimony, when there had been submitted the positive testimony of the master of the Olympic, as a result of his own continued observations through an open window, that no light was visible.

It was for the court as a matter of law to say whether the light which appellee claims he had in the wheelhouse, was sufficient to comply with the law, and unless proof had been produced from which a reasonable mind might conclude that this violation of the law by appellee could not have contributed to the collision, it was likewise the duty of the trial court to have directed a verdict for appellant, irrespective of any fault upon the part of appellant, because of its lookout momentarily attending to the fastening of the curtains.

ARGUMENT ON SPECIFICATION NUMBER IV

Under the undisputed facts of this case, the instructions requested by the appellant were correct and proper, and under the law should have been given to the jury.

It will be noted that there is no dispute as to the course of the two vessels. The Magna was steering a course of West northwest (Tr. p. 45), whereas the course of the Olympic as appears from appellant's Exhibit 11, line CD was approximately north northwest, half west, so that 3½ points (or by matter of simple calculation, each point being 11 degrees and 15 minutes), 38 degrees, 22 minutes 30 seconds, or approximately 38½ degrees separated the course of these two vessels, and the Olympic was overtaking the Magna a little less than broad or 45 degrees on the Magna's port quarter, a position which put her out of range of all proper navigation lights of the Magna, except the after range light, if one had been carried, since neither the masthead light nor either of the colored sidelights is visible more than two points abaft the beam. (Title 46, U.S.C.A., section 513.)

The first portion of appellant's first requested instruction (assignment of error number IX, Tr. p. 128), was a statement of the law itself. The next to the last paragraph is a necessary conclusion of law drawn from such statute and the last paragraph of the requested instruction is simply a statement of the law as to contributory negligence, all of which this court on the prior appeal held to be a proper instruction, and the refusal of the trial court to give which, was held to be reversable error.

See also:
> The "*Pennsylvania*," 19 Wall. 125;
> *Belden v. Chase*, 150 U. S. 674;
> The "*Martello*," 153 U. S. 64;
> The "*Britannia*," 153 U. S. 130.

The second instruction requested by appellant (assignment of error number X, Tr. p. 129), is an alternative re-statement of the last paragraph of the preceding requested instruction.

The third requested instruction (assignment of error number XI, Tr. p. 130) is an instruction covering the enlargement upon section 513, Title 46 U.S. C.A., as promulgated by the Secretary of Commerce (Defendant's Exhibit 10), pursuant to authority vested in him by Title 46 U.S.C.A., section 518, requiring the after white light prescribed by section 513, to be "placed at a higher elevation than the white light showing forward and so placed as to form a range with the forward light, and to be clear of house awnings and other obstructions," so as to be actually *visible* to a vessel approaching from the direction of appellant's vessel, and being part of the law applicable to the features of this case, appellant was entitled to have such instruction given to the jury.

> Act of June 9, 1910, Chapter 268, paragraph 1, 2, 3, and 8;
>
> 36 Stats. 462;
>
> Department Circular Number 236, 12th edition, issued by Secretary of Commerce, regulating motor boats under date of May first, 1928 (Defendant's Exhibit 10);
>
> The *"Breakwater,"* 155 U. S. 252;
>
> The *"Delaware,"* 161 U. S. 459;
>
> The *"Luckenbach,"* 50 Fed. 129;
>
> The *"Straits of Dover,"* 120 Fed. 900;
>
> Belden v. Chase, 150 U. S. 674.

The court further erred in refusing to instruct the jury as requested in assignment of error number XII. (Tr. p. 131.) This instruction bears upon the question of any negligence upon the part of the appellant's vessel Olympic, and was as follows:

> "You are instructed that all persons navigating vessels are entitled to assume and to place

reasonable reliance upon the assumption that persons navigating other vessels will obey the law as to lights required to be carried on such other vessels, and that the defendant was not guilty of negligence if those in charge of the navigation of defendant's vessel failed to anticipate or to guard against the absence of proper lights upon the plaintiff's vessel, or to act otherwise than a reasonable careful (115) or prudent person or persons would have acted under similar circumstances.

> *Belden v. Chase*, 150 U. S. 674, 699, 37 L. Ed. 1218;
>
> *The Oregon v. Rocca*, 59 U. S. 18, Howard 570, 15 L. Ed. 515.''

The master of the Olympic had been running 14 or 15 minutes beyond West Point, and seeing no lights or anything indicating a vessel in his proximity ahead of him, we believe was entitled to assume that no vessel was ahead of him, violating the law by failing to carry the prescribed lights, and that he was entitled to rely upon this assumption to the extent of directing the lookout, who was almost directly below him, owing to the character of the weather and the taking of spray over the Olympic's bow, to fasten down curtains, which had commenced to blow loose, and that therefore the Olympic was not negligent in any respect.

The law clearly gives the master of the Olympic the right to assume that other vessels will be navigated according to law and to place reasonable reliance upon that assumption. And if the court had so instructed the jury, the jury might properly have found that the Olympic was not guilty of any negligence, and so have returned a verdict for the appellant, notwithstanding all of the other errors in the record, and the failure of the court to give this instruction was therefore prejudicial error.

> *Belden v. Chase, supra;*
>
> *The Oregon v. Rocca,* 59 U. S. 18, Howard 570, 15 L. Ed. 515.

The statutory law required the appelee to carry life preservers, life belts, buoyant cushions or other devices sufficient to sustain him afloat, and so placed as to be readily accessable.

> Title 46 U.S.C.A., section 515.

Appellee admitted that the only life saving equipment which he carried on his boat were some life preservers lashed down on the top of his pilot house where he could not get at them, and he therefore jumped overboard without this protection, and at the same time seeks damages against the appellant for personal injuries claimed to have been sustained due to swallowing water while immersed. His failure to carry the prescribed life saving equipment was contributory negligence as a matter of law on this phase of the question, and the appellant was entitled to have the jury properly instructed thereon. The court refused to so instruct the jury and entirely ignored this element of the case, to the prejudice of appellant.

ARGUMENT ON SPECIFICATION NUMBER V

Notwithstanding the decision of this court upon the prior appeal, the trial court consistently refused, in instructing the jury, to determine the insufficiency of the light which appellee claimed to have carried, in lieu of the range light prescribed by law, and told the jury repeatedly that the only question before it was whether or not the appellee had the light which he claimed to have had in his pilot house, lit and in place a sufficient length of time to have permitted it to be seen. The court instructed the jury, as a matter of law, that the light which the appellee claims to have had *was* legally sufficient. His instructions on this point are covered by assignments of errors numbers XIV, XV, XVI, XVIII, XX, XXI, XXII, and XXIII. (Tr. p. 133-140.)

The vital error of these instructions is made apparent by the following condensed extracts which are quoted literally and which run through the assignments last above noted, viz.:

"As a matter of fact, the court agrees with the statement of counsel for the defense in his argument that if the plaintiff had that light in the doorway of his boat, lit long enough before the collision so that it could have been seen by a proper lookout on the Olympic, they would have avoided him, and the collision would have never occurred. *And if the plaintiff had it there, as he says that he did, and which the defendant denies, there is no reason why he should not recover in this action.* * * * That is all l can see in this case. * * * The burden is on him throughout to prove that he had that light there, lit there for the length of time that I have stated to you, and prove that it was a good and sufficient light to serve its purpose, and to prove the amount of his damages. * * * And, again, that is the attitude of counsel for the plaintiff, when he says there is only one question in this case, *and I agree with him, whether the aft light* on this vessel of the fisherman *was there.* * * * The plaintiff was not obliged to keep any lookout behind him, because *if he had his lights lit, he was entitled to presume that any vessel following him would take note of him and would comply with the law and not run him down.* * * * If that was his aft light, *and there is no reason why it could not have been seen,* even though it was not across the dividing line in the middle of the ship—between the bow and the stern—if that was his aft light, and it was the only aft light that he had, if it was not so placed that it would be seen all around the horizon, it could be seen from behind, but it could not be seen from either side, because it was within the frame two inches, and, of course, it could not be seen from the front. *But you must remember, too, that the law is a practical thing, and it does not require any useless thing.* If that light served the purpose

of an aft light to a following vessel, it was altogether immaterial whether it would show from the
sides or show from ahead, so as far as that vessel
is concerned, but provided it was sufficient to
serve the purpose of an aft light for the following
vessel, and could not at all have misled it or have
contributed to the collision which happened. * * *
So it comes right down to that question—the attitude taken by the plaintiff's counsel in his argument, *and the court takes it as a matter of law.*
* * * You have two questions to decide in this
case, outside of the damage, and you must decide
them both in the affirmative before you can find
for the plaintiff. First, it is proven by the greater
weight of the evidence that Nelson's light in his
cabin door *was where he testified that it was;* that
it was of the kind that he testified it was, *and lit
sufficiently long before the collision so that it
could have been seen by the defendant's lookout,*
had he been exercising his function properly and
in time so that the collision might have been avoided. * * * Of course, if he did not have that light
lit, and lit sufficiently long so that a watchful
lookout on the defendant's vessel could have seen
it in time to avoid him, why he has no right to any
recovery here, because he was negligent. *In that
case, he violated the law,* and I do not care
whether it was five o'clock or five-twenty, or
whether it was more or less dark, it is inevitable
that the absence of his light, if it was absent,
would have contributed something to the collision
that followed. He is out of the case and out of
court right there, *unless you find* by the greater
weight of the evidence *that his light was there,* as
he tells you, with that degree of sufficiency—a
6-volt light—*and lit long enough to have been seen
and avoided by the defendant's vessel,* had it a
watchful lookout at the time. * * * *If that light*

had been visible on the sides and ahead, *would it have better enabled the defendant's vessel aft to avoid him and to see him and avoid him? I do not think so,* and counsel's attitude for the plaintiff in his argument likewise was the same. *That is common sense.* * * * *So, if you answer those two questions in the affirmative,* proven by the greater weight of the evidence, favorable to the plaintiff, *then there is only one more question, and that is, how much was the damage?* * * * That is the case before you. It simmers down to this, Lady and Gentlemen of the Jury, that taking into consideration all of the evidence in the case, both for the plaintiff and the defendant, and the circumstances, *if you find* by the greater weight of the evidence *that the plaintiff, as he testified to you, a light in the door of his pilot house,* facing the rear, of 6-volt size, as he tells you, *and burning long enough before the collision so that a watchful lookout on defendant's vessel could have seen it,* and so could have avoided the collision, *he is entitled to recover."* (Italics ours.)

This is precisely the same series of instructions which the trial court gave in the first trial, and which this court on the former appeal held to be reversable error.

The late Judge Rudkin, in deciding the first appeal, held as follosw:

"The appellant requested an instruction in conformity with the foregoing rule in admiralty, but the request was refused. On the contrary, the court instructed the jury in effect, that, *if the appellee had a proper and sufficient light aft which could be seen at a sufficient distance by a vigilant lookout on the overtaking vessel, he was entitled to recover.* In other words, *the court ignored the mandatory requirement of the statute in reference to the light aft, leaving the question of its sufficiency entirely to the jury, and imposed upon the appellant the burden not only of proving a breach of statutory duty on the part of the appellee, but also that such breach contributed to the disaster.* The requested instruction was in accordance with the admiralty rule, *and the instruction given ignored the statute and was contrary to the admiralty rule.* For these errors, the judgment must be reversed." (Italics ours.)

The error of the trial court in the case now on appeal is identical with that of the first case, with the single exception, that, whereas he formerly merely ignored the statutory law, in the instance case, he again completely ignores that law, and further ignores the law of this case as laid down by this court in the former appeal.

There might as well be no law as to lights, if the law is to be completely ignored, and the jury, without any evidence and only speculation and guess work to rely upon, is to be instructed that some other light inside of a vessel's structure is all that is required to be carried in order to entitle a vessel owner to recover, and to absolve him from contributory negligence.

Chief Justice Fuller, in the case of *Belden v. Chase, supra,* states the rule as follows:

"and it is the settled rule in this court that when a vessel has committed a positive breach of statute, she must show not only that probably her fault did not contribute to the disaster, but that it could have done so. The *Pennsylvania v. Troop,* 86 U. S., 19 Wall. 125, 136; 22 L. Ed. 148, 151; *Richelieu & O. Nav. Co. v. Boston Marine Ins. Co.,* 136 U. S. 408, 422; 34 L. Ed. 398, 403. * * * Masters are bound to obey the rules and entitled to rely on the assumption that they will be obeyed, and should not be encouraged to treat the exceptions as subjects of solicitude rather than the rules. *The Oregon v. Rocca,* 59 U. S. 18 Howard 570; 15 L. Ed. 515."

The Martello, 153 U. S. 64;

The Britannia, 153 U. S. 130;

Lie, etc. v. San Francisco & Portland S. S. Co., 243 U. S. 291;

The Fanny M. Carvill, 2 Asp. M. C. (N. S.) 565;

The Duke of Buccleuch, 7 Asp. M. C. (N. S.) 68;

The Corinthian, 11 Asp. M. C. (N. S.) 264;

The Beryl, 9 Prob. Div. 137;

The Voorwartz—The Khedive, L. R. 5, App. Cas. 876.

In the *Straits of Dover,* 120 Fed. 900, 903-905, it was held:

"The obligation imposed to obey these rules is imperative, and those violating them, except under circumstances contemplated by the rules, must bear the consequences if damages ensue. * * * Citing *The Breakwater,* 155 U. S. 252; *The Dela-*

ware, 161 U. S. 459; *The Luckenbach,* 50 Fed. 129, *The Chittagong,* App. Cas. 597. * * * * * Every consideration requires that these rules should be strictly observed by those for the government of whose conduct they were prescribed, and any departure therefrom should not be lightly overlooked or passed by. To do so would destroy the symmetry of the whole, and would place questions affecting the navigation of ships, now well settled and certain, in utter chaos and confusion."

These rules and the duty of strict compliance with them applies equally to vessels both large and small.

The Bellingham, 138 Fed. 619.

Under the law, the only light which should have been exhibited on the "Magna," visible to those upon the "Olympic," was a white light aft showing all around the horizon, and placed higher than the foremast light and free from all obstructions, and the admitted failure to carry this light cannot possibly be construed as other than one of the major causes, if not the sole cause of the collision.

The imperative nature of the requirements of the rules as to the maintenance of proper lights has been often stated by the courts.

The head note to the case of *The Royal Arch,* 22 Fed. 457, 458, is as follows:

"The Royal Arch was improperly navigated, in that she did not have her regulation side lights, and especially her green light, properly and brightly burning, and for that reason she was the sole culpable cause of the collision. It was her duty to keep her course, as she did, on seeing the red light of the Nellie Floyd. *It was the duty of the Nellie Ford to avoid the Royal Arch, but she was relieved from such duty by the failure of the Royal Arch to exhibit any light which those on the Nellie Floyd could see before the collision;* and their ignorance of the course of the Royal Arch, until it was too late for the Nellie Floyd to do anything to avoid the collision, was excusable, and was produced by such fault of the Royal Arch." (Italics ours.)

In the case of *The Mary Lord*, 26 Fed. 862, 866, it was held:

"The want of a red light was primarily the whole cause of the collision. The other vessel was deceived and misled by this failure to show that light. * * * The fault, then, being wholly on the part of the vessel libelled, there must be a decree accordingly."

In the case of *The Komuk*, 120 Fed. 841, at 842, it is held:

"A more serious charge against the Komuk and the Griggs is, that the latter did not display lights according to Rule 11 of the Pilot Rules. * * * The Griggs concededly did not comply with this rule but only exhibited one light, which was placed on her cabin. * * * In the absence of proper lights, it was incumbent upon the Komuk and the Griggs to show that the neglect to comply with the rule did not contribute to the collision. This they have failed to do and they must bear a part of the loss.''

In the case of *The Narragansett,* 11 Fed. 918, a case involving a schooner, which has the right of way over all power craft, when it obeys the rules, the court held:

"The libel alleges that the schooner was 'duly lighted'; that her green and red lights were 'brightly burning'; that she 'had all proper, sufficient, and lawful lights set and burning, as aforesaid.' The burden is on her to show this, and she has not done so.''

In the case of *The Amboy,* 22 Fed. 555, the court observed:

"The purpose of lights is to be seen. If they do not fulfill that office to ordinary observation, the vessel must be held in fault; * * *

In the case of *The Mary Morgan,* 28 Fed. 333, the court held:

"The Pierrepont's side lights were up and burning, but they were in bad condition, the lanterns being incrusted with smoke. * * *''

"Upon these facts I am of opinion that the Pierrepont was in fault in not having her lights in proper condition * * *.''

W. H. LaBoyteaux, in his *"The Rules of the Road at Sea,"* 1920 Ed., observes, p. 13:

"Special attention should be given to insure that all lights are placed in their proper locations *in strict compliance with the rules,* and that they are not obscured by deck houses, deck cargo, sails, smoke from the galley, or other obstructions or causes." (Italics ours.)

Again in the case of the *Vesper,* 9 Fed. 569, involving a schooner having the right of way over the power vessel, which ran her down, if she complied with the rules as to lights, it was held:

"But had the red light been continuously hidden by the jib, as claimed, that would not improve the libellant's case. The Vesper can only be charged for some fault of her own. *Her duty to keep out of the way of the schooner was conditioned upon her having notice of the situation and course of the John Jay by proper and visible lights.* The rules of navigation require that these lights shall be 'so constructed as to show a uniform and unbroken light over an arc of the horizon of 10 points of the compass, and so fixed as to throw the light from right ahead to two points abaft the beam,' on either side, * * * If either light is so obscured that a steamer is misled and deceived as to the course of the sailing vessel, and a collision ensues in consequence, it is manifestly no fault of the steamer; and if the sailing vessel suffer damage, it must be set down to her own fault or misfortune, as the case may be." (Italics ours.)

In the case of *The Johanne Auguste,* 21 Fed. 134, the court held:

"It is impossible, and it is unnecessary, to determine in what particular way, or from what cause, the red light of the Fontenaye was obscured. I am satisfied it was obscure'd. Had it been seen when it ought to have been seen, I cannot doubt that the Johanne Auguste, by porting earlier that she did, might have escaped the collision, and would have done so. The Fontenaye must be held responsible for any obscuration of her light, especially when placed in the extreme after-part of the ship, where there is such increased danger of obstruction * * *."

In the case of *The Virginian,* 235 Fed. 98, it was held:

"* * * * * she was at fault, in that she was not equipped with proper side lights, that the lights were not ordinarily bright, and were not visible at as great a distance as they should have been, and that they were so placed or so obstructed by the deck load or otherwise that they were not discernible from all points ahead."

Again in the case of *Clendinin v. The Steamship Alhambra,* 4 Fed. 86, which involved a schooner and a power vessel, the schooner, ordinarily the privileged vessel, was held at fault for improper lights. The court said:

"This testimony from the respective vessels in regard to the course of the schooner, and the lights she displayed, apparently so contradicting, can, I think, be reconciled by reference to the fact, stated by the master of the schooner in the most positive manner, that the side lights of the schooner were placed so that when he stood at the stem he could see both the red and green light at the same time without moving his head. * * * But this explanation convicts the schooner of fault for carrying lights so arranged as to mislead an approaching vessel in regard to the course she was pursuing.''

LaBoyteaux, in *The Rules of the Road at Sea, supra,* p. 15, observes:

"Upon the master rests the responsibility of seeing that the proper lights are carried, correctly placed and kept burning brightly. The fact that improper lights are carried under the instructions of a compulsory pilot will not relieve the master from responsibility or the vessel from liability therefor.

"It is significant that not only do the rules begin with prescribing lights and signals to be carried, but they end with the caution in Article 29:

" 'Nothing in these rules shall exonerate any vessel * * * from the consequences of any neglect to carry lights or signals * * *.'

"The most rigid adherence to these rules in their minutest detail is required by the courts, and any deviation will inevitably involve the offending vessel in fault for a resulting collision.

"As was said by the Circuit Court in *The Titan,* 23 Fed. 413, 416:

" 'The rule requiring lights may as well be disregarded altogether as to be partially complied with, and in a way which fails to be of any real service in indicating to another vessel the position and course of the one carrying them'.'' (Italics ours.)

The real matter of importance is that it was the failure of the Magna to carry the prescribed range light, which brought the vessels into a position of extremis, resulting in the collision.

In the case of *The Genevieve,* 96 Fed. 859, it was held:

"The cause for such collisions as this must generally be sought for at a time prior to the few moments immediately preceding the impact. After the vessels are in close proximity either or both, in the stress of sudden danger, may adopt an unwise and imprudent course. The question is, who is to blame for bringing the vessels into a position where cool calculation is impossible."

In the case of *The Transfer No.* 10, 137 Fed. 666, it was held:

"And the question in this case, as in all collision cases, is not what the colliding vessels do when they get down close to each other, but what was the maneuver which they adopted and what was the maneuver which it was their duty to adopt, under the rules of the road when they were still far enough apart to adopt those maneuvers deliberately and safely."

The Frank P. Lee, 30 Fed. 277:

The court said, at page 279:

"She was, however, guilty of fault in failing to display a torch or white light, in coming up to the wind, in the respondent's front, and virtually stopping in her track; as required by statute.

It is impossible to say that such a light would not have tended to avoid the collision. The Assessor thinks it would and his conclusion is reasonable. It is sufficient, however, that it might possibly have done so. *The Pennsylvania,* 12 Fed. Rep. 916, *The Evcelsior,* Id. 203; *The Hercules,* 17 Fed. Rep. 606.''

The Roman, 14 Fed. 61.

The court said, at page 63:

''If the schooner had performed its duty by exhibiting the prescribed light, presumably it would have escaped injury. The burden is upon it to show that the cause was the misconduct or negligence of somebody else; *and it must be borne upon no uncertain proof or doubtful conclusions.* We cannot relieve it of the full consequences of its own deriliction by transferring them partly to another, whose culpability is problematical.''

The Florence P. Hall, 14 Fed. 408.

The court said, at page 416:

''Where as in this case, the defense of inevitable accident is raised, and the pleadings make a direct issue upon the question whether the weather was such that the lights of the libellant's vessel could be seen in time to enable the claimant's vessel, by due nautical skill, to keep out of the way, the burden of proof is upon the libellants to show, not only that the lights were set and burning, but also that the weather was such that they *could be seen* at a sufficient distance to avoid the collision. * * * In case of a collision on a dark night, these necessary conditions include proof, not merely that the libellant's vessel had proper lights set and burning, but also that such lights

were visible at a distance sufficient to enable the
other vessel, by due nautical skill, to keep out of
the way. Otherwise no negligence can be inferred.''

The Act of June 9, 1910, makes it definitely unlawful for any substitute or makeshift light in the
cabin or wheel-house to be carried in lieu of the prescribed light. Sec. 3 of that Act provides:

"Sec. 3: Every motor boat in all weathers
from sunset to sunrise shall carry the following
lights, *and during such time no other lights which
may be mistaken for those prescribed shall be
exhibited.*" (Italics ours.)

Under the admitted facts of this case, therefore,
and the settled and unvarying law applicable to such
facts, and the admitted failure of the plaintiff to
carry the prescribed or any range light, the plaintiff
must be charged with at least contributory negligence,
and the instructions to which exceptions were taken
are fundamentally erroneous.

It was stated by Chief Justice Fuller in *Belden v.
Chase, supra,* as follows:

"The rules laid down * * * as thus authorized
have the force of statutory enactment, and their
construction * * * as well as that of the rules
under section 4233, is for the court, whose duty it
is to apply them as a matter of law upon the facts
of a given case. They are not mere prudential
regulations, but binding enactments, obligatory

from the time that the necessity for precaution begins, and continuing so long as the means and opportunity to avoid the danger remains. *Peters v. The Dexter*, 90 U. S. 23 Wallace 29. Obviously they must be rigorously enforced in order to attain the object for which they were framed which could not be secured if the masters of vessels were permitted to indulge their discretion in respect of obeying or departing from them.''

ARGUMENT ON SPECIFICATION NUMBER VI

There remains only one further error to be considered. The testimony in this case was by the appellee that he had a light inside the door of his pilot house. No witness produced by the appellant was able to say that this was not so. He may have had a dozen lights inside his vessel, which would be wholly immaterial to this case.

The witness for the appellant testified that no light was visible from the Olympic. No witness contradicted this testimony. There, therefore, was present no situation where one witness testified that he saw something and another witness testified that he did not see the same thing, which is necessary to bring into play the rule of positive and negative testimony. The court therefore erred in giving any instruction with reference to positive and negative testimony, and the instruction which he did give upon the subject is erroneous, even upon that subjejct. He instructed the jury as follows:

> "Now, the law says that where two persons testify to a situation at the same time, the one who testifies positively that it was thus and so—'I saw it'—is entitled to more weight than one who says, 'No, it was not that way.' 'I didn't see it.'
>
> "That is the point that counsel wants to make, and it is for you to say whether it applies in this case. The plaintiff says, 'I had the light there,' and the captain says, 'He did not have the light there, because I did not see it.' Of course, that involves whether he saw it or he did not see it because it was not there."

The instruction is patently bad upon its face and in addition to every other objectionable feature the court leaves the applicability of the instruction to the jury, whereas the law requires him to decide and to instruct the jury accordingly.

WHEREFORE, it is respectfully submitted that appelant, by the foregoing manifest errors of the trial court, has been deprived of a fair and proper trial, and the judgment of the lower court should be reversed.

Respectfully submitted,

H. B. JONES,

ROBERT BRONSON,

Attorneys for Appellant.

No. 6600

UNITED STATES
CIRCUIT COURT OF APPEALS

NINTH CIRCUIT

PUGET SOUND NAVIGATION COMPANY,
a corporation,

Appellant,

vs.

HANS NELSON,

Appellee.

UPON APPEAL FROM A JUDGMENT OF THE
UNITED STATES DISTRICT COURT FOR THE
WESTERN DISTRICT OF WASHINGTON,
NORTHERN DIVISION

HONORABLE GEORGE M. BOURQUIN, *Judge*

Brief of Appellee

WINTER S. MARTIN,
ARTHUR COLLETT, Jr.,
HARRY S. REDPATH,
Attorneys for Appellee.

Office and Post Office Address:
605 Colman Building, Seattle, Washington.

MARTIN & DICKSON, PRINTERS, SEATTLE

FILED

MAR 25 1932

SUBJECT INDEX

TABLE OF CASES

Page

UNITED STATES
CIRCUIT COURT OF APPEALS

NINTH CIRCUIT

PUGET SOUND NAVIGATION COMPANY,
a corporation,

Appellant,

vs.

HANS NELSON,

Appellee.

UPON APPEAL FROM A JUDGMENT OF THE
UNITED STATES DISTRICT COURT FOR THE
WESTERN DISTRICT OF WASHINGTON,
NORTHERN DIVISION

HONORABLE GEORGE M. BOURQUIN, *Judge*

Brief of Appellee

STATEMENT OF THE CASE

The opening statement of appellant does not adequately or accurately present the essential facts necessary to an understanding of this appeal. The sufficiency of the court's instructions in this case, and the verdict of the jury, cannot be fully appreciated or understood without a more detailed statement touching the kind and character of the "Magna's" stern light and the actual condition of natural light or darkness which prevailed at the time of the collision. It will be borne in mind in this case that at all times prior to this collision, the "Olympic" was an overtaking vessel which, under Inland Rules 23 and 24, was required to keep out of the way of the "Magna." It will, likewise, be understood that the vessel which is ahead of the other and is being overtaken, owes no duty under the law to keep a lookout astern.

THE MAGNA'S STERN LIGHT

The "Magna," of course, was required to have and maintain a stern light which would be visible to an overtaking vessel. It is admitted, in this case, that the "Magna," did not have a stern light which was sufficient to meet the technical requirements of the Motor Boat Act. The stern light on the "Magna" did not show all around the horizon, as provided by said Act. This stern light was a six volt, white, incandescent electric light, attached to the sill of the after-door of the pilot-house, suspended at a height of five feet above the "Magna's" main deck aft in the open doorway, in such manner as to show and be clearly visible from any angle aft of the beam of said vessel on each side. This light was burning brightly from the time the "Magna" left Ballard until she sank after the collision. It was fully exposed to view from an overtaking vessel, with nothing on the after deck of the "Magna" to obstruct its view of this light. It is admitted in this case that the "Olympic" was overtaking the "Magna" on about the same course. There was not over two points difference. (Tr. 76.)

Insofar as an overtaking vessel is concerned, this light served the same purpose as the light prescribed by the Rules to warn the overtaking vessel of her presence ahead, and the mere fact that this stern light did not show ahead or forward of her beam could not possibly have made any difference in this case.

Captain Nelson, master and owner of the "Magna" who was operating and navigating his vessel alone, testified as to the location, power, kind, color and visibility of his stern light as above indicated.

In addition to the testimony given by Mr. Nelson concerning the location and place of his afterlight, and that it was within the range of vision of vessels approaching from astern, Mr. Emil F. Schuman, of Port Townsend, Washington, a passenger on the "Olympic" when the collision occurred, gave independent and disinterested testimony as to the white stern light of the "Magna." Mr. Schuman was in the cabin with his wife when the impact of collision took place. He rushed to the "Olympic's" upper deck and saw the "Magna." He observed her masthead and side lights and after the "Olympic" had backed away from the "Magna" saw her stern light in the open door way of the after-cabin door. He positively identified this white electric light as the light Captain Nelson said was lighted and suspended from the upper sill of the door.

At page 27, Tr., Mr. Emil F. Schuman testified for the plaintiff, as follows:

"When I got up there (referring to the upper deck of the "Olympic") I noticed the starboard light and the white light in front. The starboard light was green. At that time the "Olympic" backed up and it was getting quite dark fast, and I could see the man on board that boat."

At page 28, Tr., Mr. Schuman was asked.

"Q. Now, as you passed the "Magna," after you stopped, or as you backed up, did you observe any other light?

A. I did."

Mr. Bronson objected to this question, his objection was overruled, and he took exception. Mr. Schuman was then asked:

"Q. What lights, if any, did you see?

A. I saw a white light—"

Over Mr. Bronson's further objections and exceptions, the witness continued to give his testimony. He said in substance:

"I saw a white light. Do you want me to state where I saw that light? It was a white light in the center of the door where you go down into the engine-room or cabin, whatever it may be, and I do not know whether there was another light in the cabin or not, and the cabin was quite lit up and I could see Mr.—what is his name, the skipper. The door was open. The light was hanging right in the center where you step down into the engine-room. At that time I could see the stern of the vessel and deck of the vessel aft of the light. That is the time when I observed when the collision occurred. Somehow or other the boat shifted around a little to the left so that she was at a four or five degree angle from the "Olympic," and I could see the crushed side. There was nothing on the stern of the boat which interfered with my vision of the light. It was a white light. It looked like an electric light. It was a little over a hundred feet, I guess, away when I saw the light. It was getting dusk then. I could not observe the light closely.

The white light appeared approximately four feet above the "Magna's" main deck. I did not see more than one white light at any time when we were passing the "Magna," either the first or second time. I saw a white light and the green light on the starboard at the same time, but do not remember seeing the red light. Then, after seeing those lights, I saw the light in the door."

From the above testimony, it sufficiently appears from positive evidence, that the "Magna's stern light was burning and was visible as claimed by Captain Nelson. We shall argue that this testimony comes within the *res gestae* rule as to what was seen and observed at the time the collision occurred and was clearly admissible as such.

We now call attention to the statement of appellant at page 5, of its brief, as follows:

"* * * Appellee was proceeding at the time of the collision admittedly *without his after mast or any light on the after part of his boat.*"

This statement is grossly inaccurate, for the truth respecting the kind of light, its position, et cetera, appears in the record (Tr., pp. 42-43).

The only testimony in the record offered by appellant, with respect to this light is wholly negative. Appellant's master, who was on watch in the pilot-house, did not see this light. Appellant's lookout, at the time of the collision, and for four or five minutes prior thereto, was engaged in putting up the night shades, or curtains, over the windows of the saloon and passenger quarters in the fore part of the "Olympic," on her main deck, in order to keep the lights of the social hall and saloon, or observation room, from shining out forward, and thus obscuring the vision of those on watch in the pilot-house directly above the passenger quarters. Peter Garvey, the only man on lookout, was standing about forty feet from the stem of the "Olympic," facing aft, engaged in his work, and could not from his position see the "Magna."

The "Olympic" is a large vessel which has a freeboard of approximately fifteen feet above water level in the forward part of the vessel. Photographs of the "Olympic" were introduced in evidence. Plaintiff's (Appellant's) Exhibit 2, will give a very fair view of the height of the "Olympic's" pilot-house above the water, thus showing that the Pilot was looking out ahead from a place where he could not get the best view ahead. He was not standing forward in the eyes of the ship while attending to his navigation.

THE CONDITION OF NATURAL LIGHT

It was still light enough at the time of collision and for such a sufficient time before the collision, even though after sunset, for those on the "Olympic" to see an object out on the water ahead of them very clearly and for such a distance as to enable the "Olympic's" pilot and lookout to see the "Magna" very clearly if they had been attending to their duties.

At page 53, Tr., in the cross-examination of William Seatter, helmsman on the "Olympic," the following appears:

"* * * The weather was clear. I didn't see any moon. It was dusk. It was that state between light and dark that you could see an object out of the water out ahead of you if you were looking. If there was a vessel ahead of you you could see her 1,000 feet ahead and you could see that vessel without any artificial lights before the collision."

It appears from the testimony of Mr. and Mrs. Emil F. Schuman, that it was still quite light during the two or three minutes before the collision when the "Olympic" was rapidly overtaking and about to collide with the "Magna."

Mr. and Mrs. Schuman were passengers on the "Olympic" bound from Seattle to Port Townsend. At the time of the collision they were in the cabin, and in a position to observe the condition of light and darkness.

Mrs. Schuman testified at the first trial of the case. In the interim before the second trial, Mrs. Schuman died. Her testimony given at the first trial was offered in evidence and read by Mr. R. G. Guerin, Court Reporter, at the second trial.

Mr. Schuman was with his wife in the dining room when the collision occurred and he testified that he rushed right upstairs and went upon the upper deck. We quote from the record at page 27 (Tr.):

"It did not take me over a minute to get to that point after I felt the bump. At that time it was getting dusk. It was then perhaps close to five o'clock. An object of any size I could see quite aways, say a thousand feet. At that time I would not have needed any artificial light to have seen an object 1,000 feet away on the water. * * * We backed up far enough and I could see where the port side of this fishing boat was stove in as far as the water-line. I could see a big hole there. I could see the crushed outside boards. That was in the stern."

At Tr. p. 40, Hans Nelson, appellee, said:

"At the time of the collision it was just in the twilight. It was not dark and it was not regular daylight, * * *. * * * I could see easily a half a mile on the water. I saw a towboat that was coming towing logs. I had an open window in the pilot-house. I saw the towboat coming in, and he had not had any light on at that time. I seen him first and that was before the ferry struck me. I saw the towboat through the window about a half mile away, about eight minutes before the collision."

At Tr. p. 41, he was asked:

"Q. How far could you see any vessel ahead of you, a vessel of the size of the 'Magna'?"

Mr. Bronson objected, his objection was overruled and exceptions noted.

The witness answered:

"A. You could see a vessel like the 'Magna' a quarter of a mile away, easy, at the time of that collision."

The witness further testified:

> "It was full moon. * * * It was not dark
> enough to see the moon at the time of the colli-
> sion, * * *. At the time of the collision the sky
> was clear."

In cross-examination, at page 44, Tr., Captain Nelson said he could see out of his pilot-house with a
light on there to navigate the vessel. He said: "I could
see what I could see in the light. It was not dark. At
the time of the collision you could see without lights.
The light in the little room would not bother my
eyes."

There was introduced in evidence on behalf of
appellee, plaintiff's Exhibit 8, which was a photograph of a boat, similar in size, design, deck and
pilot-house arrangement from which we have a very
good general picture of the deck arrangements, place
of the after-light and relative size of the two vessels.

The only testimony offered by the "Olympic"
owners respecting the "Magna's" stern light at the
time of collision, and for a time before collision when
collision could have been avoided if the "Olympic"
had taken proper steps to keep out of her way, was
given by the master and the wheelsman, who were in
the pilot-house navigating and steering the vessel during said period when risk of collision existed. They

testified that they did not see any stern light or any other light on the "Magna." Their place of observation was against a favorable view.

As to the condition of natural light, the master testified that the sky was overcast, and that it was quite dark. The Weather Bureau records contradicted him. Seatter, "Olympic's" helmsman, said it was clear and light enough to see without artificial light. Garvey, lookout, said it was dark when the collision occurred, but was impeached by Mr. Harry S. Redpath to the contrary.

At page 54, during the cross-examination of Garvey, who was supposed to be on lookout on the "Olympic," the following testimony was given:

> "I had my back to the bow while fixing the curtains. Before that I was on lookout looking back and forth on the bow. *It took me possibly four or five minutes to fix the curtains, to the best of my knowledge,* and during those four or five minutes I was not giving attention to looking out. It was dark at that time,—well, dusk or whatever you want to call it. It was dusk or dark. When I said dusk before the local Steamboat Inspectors I meant dark. It was not light enough to see the hull of this little vessel off on the water without the aid of artificial lights."

Peter Garvey's attention was then called to a conversation which he had with Mr. Martin and Mr. Redpath the day before the case was first tried in the District Court. He admitted having had a conversation with Messrs. Martin and Redpath, but denied he had made any contrary statements. At pages 90 and 91 Tr., Mr. Harry Redpath, associated with appellee's attorneys in the trial of the cause, gave the following testimony:

> "My name is Harry S. Redpath. I live in Seattle, and I am associated with the counsel for plaintiff in the practice of law in the Colman Building. Two or three days before the former trial I went down with Mr. Martin to the Colman Dock and we interviewed Mr. Garvey, the witness previously called here. He said that you could see the 'Magna' without the aid of artificial light when the 'Olympic' backed away; that the 'Olympic' backed away about half a mile, and that you could see her about a half a mile out in the water without an artificial light."

It thus appears as a statement of fact that the master of the vessel was in the pilot-house at the time attending to the navigation of his ship. That the helmsman was in the pilot-house attending to his duty in steering the ship, and that the ship was actually without a lookout. The master while testifying said: "There was nobody on lookout at the time except Mr. Garvey."

APPELLANT'S WAIVER OF RIGHT TO AP-PEAL—APPELLEE'S MOTION TO DISMISS THE APPEAL

The appellant recovered judgment against appellee in the sum of $312.05, for its costs of appeal when the mandate of this cause on the former appeal was entered in the District Court.

After the plaintiff, Hans Nelson had prevailed at the second trial, the jury having returned a verdict for $2500.00, in his favor, the appellant procured the Trial Court to set off the amount of its judgment for costs in the District Court in the first trial (costs of appeal on reversal), against the appellant's verdict and to enter judgment thereon for $2187.95 in the instant case.

Appellant had not theretofore pleaded counterclaim or set-off and the issue of set-off was not raised in the case until the entry of final judgment. The trial court in entering judgment for the lesser amount thereby, at the instance of the appellant, recognized the validity of the $2500.00 verdict.

The record shows that appellee tendered a proposed judgment on the verdict in the sum of $2500.00. Appellant (defendant) proposed a form of judgment for $2187.95, thus paying the older judgment in its favor for $312.05. Appellee tendered as an amendment to the bill of exceptions, his proposed judgment for $2500.00, which amendment was duly allowed. (See Tr., pages 117 to 121, inclusive.) The court included the proposed amendment with the recital as to what took place respecting the allowance of the set-off, and certified the amendment as part of the bill.

From the foregoing recital, the record clearly shows the effort which appellee made to retain and have judgment for the amount of his verdict.

Before answering appellant's brief we urge this question of waiver, which we think concludes the case.

Appellant had a valid subsisting judgment for $312.05, against appellee as the result of the reversal on the first appeal to this Court. It had at its command the right to levy on appellee's property. But it elected to set this judgment off against the larger sum found by the jury on the trial to be due the appellee. If the larger judgment should be collected against appellant it was to its advantage to set-off the smaller judgment and thus reduce the amount of the greater judgment it had to pay. Whether properly so or not the court did set off the smaller against the larger. The test of this question is, — what became of the smaller judgment? It was not assigned, transferred or in any manner kept alive. On the contrary it was merged and its own individual character as a judgment expunged and cancelled as against an identical sum which was also destroyed and cancelled in the larger judgment. A judgment in appellant's favor for $312.05, was thus cancelled, paid and wiped out. A similar amount was deducted from appellee's verdict of $2500.00. Appellant in claiming and taking credit for $312.05, for the cancellation and satisfaction of its own judgment thereby paid $312.05 toward a definite indivisible and entire obligation of $2500.00. It thereby recognized the validity of Mr. Nelson's (appellee's) verdict upon which a judgment should issue in a like sum and satisfied its own claim against Nelson in that sum.

Appellee's judgment could never be $2500.00, on the verdict in his favor, but only $2187.95, and the $312.05 judgment could not again come to life and be operative and have the qualities of a valid judgment, for it no longer existed. Could appellant now revive its judgment and pursue its remedy of levy and execution sale against Mr. Nelson's property if a new trial should be held and a jury should return a verdict against the appellee? Could it be heard to say that its judgment had come to life again? This seems to answer the question in our favor. If the verdict was valid and sufficient to permit a valid set-off to the extent of $312.05, it must be held valid for all purposes, for it could not be divided or apportioned. If valid for a set-off it must be valid for all purposes. Hence, an estoppel was established. See *Kansas City, etc. R. Co., vs. Murray,* 57 Kan. 697, 47 Pac. 835, from which we quote the following:

"DOSTER, C. J. This is the second time this case has been brought to this court by the plaintiff in error. In both instances the proceeding was based upon a judgment for damages for bodily injuries. Upon the hearing of the first case the judgment was reversed, and a new trial ordered. *Railroad Co. vs. Murray,* 55 Kan. 336, 40 Pac. 646. The order of reversal included a judgment against the defendant in error and in favor of the plaintiff in error for $54.40, the costs of this court. * * * Upon a second trial of the case a verdict was again returned against plaintiff in error (defendant below), and after the overruling of its motion for a new trial, and the rendition against it of the judgment which is now in question, it moved the court below for an offset against such judgment of the judgment for costs which it had formerly recovered in this court against the plaintiff, now defendant in error. To this the defendant in error consented. The credit or offset was thereupon allowed, and the judgment satisfied *pro tanto.* The defendant in error now moves for a dismissal of the case from this court upon the ground that such demand for credit on the judgment, the allowance of the same, and the consequent partial satisfaction of such judgment, was such a recognition of its validity and justice as to constitute a waiver of the right to prosecute error therefrom. The plaintiff in error contends against this motion, because, as it says, the rule of estoppel applies only in cases where the complaining party has accepted some benefit under the judgment against him, and constituting a part of the same; that, inasmuch as the judgment it asked to offset, and for which it received credit on the judgment below, was in no wise connected therewith, but evidenced a right counter to such judgment, and not a right under the same, it should not be held to have waived its right to prosecute error ffrom the unpaid residue; and it also contends that, in the event of a reversal of the case in this court, the judgment complained of would be vacated, and, per consequence, the order to offset and partial satisfaction, which would fully restore to the parties their former rights; and, furthermore, that the defendant in error, having consented to the offset and partial satisfaction, should not now be heard to urge that which he agreed to as a reason for denying the claim of error. *None of these reasons in resistance to the motion to dismiss appear sound.* If the motion for offset and partial satisfaction and the order allowing the same, would of themselves constitute a waiver of the errors complained of, their effect could not be neutralized by the plaintiff's consent thereto. So far as the compensation *pro tanto* of one judgment by the other is concerned, the law required the same, and the plaintiff was compelled to submit thereto, whether he consented or not. His consent to the order of offset and satisfaction is no estoppel upon his right to urge a dismissal of the case, because the law imposed the obligation upon him without his consent. *Turner vs. Crawford,* 14 Kan. 499; *Read vs. Jeffries,* 16 Kan. 534; *Herman vs. Miller,* 17 Kan. 328. It may be granted that the effect of a reversal of the case by this court would be to vacate the judgment complained of, and to restore the other one to its condition as a valid subsisting claim; but the question does not relate to the effect of its reversal as an erroneous or unjust judgment, but to the effect of its recognition by plaintiff in error as a just and valid judgment. It may also be admitted that to ask and obtain the credit or the offset against the judgment was not the acceptance of a benefit under such judgment, and which formed a constituent part of the same. *It was, however, an admission of its validity and justice, an acceptance of the same as right and proper, an abandonment of further contest over the dispute.* No one can make payment upon a demand against him, entire and indivisible in character as this judgment, without being taken to admit it as a just and indisputable claim. Upon no other ground can the doctrine of waiver by voluntary payment be rested. The credit or offset was, in legal contemplation, a payment on the judgment, as much so as if it had been made in money. It was the parting by the plaintiff with a thing of value, and its application towards the satisfaction of a legal demand. The fact, if it be such, that the plaintiff below (the defendant in error here), was and is insolvent, as suggested by counsel, does not alter the legal rule. We cannot frame an issue in this case to determine the charge of insolvency. Except in cases where that can be properly done, the law will esteem the judgment as valuable.

* * * No one in a legal controversy can be heard to say to his adversary: 'Your judgment against me is erroneous and unjust, and my purpose is to demonstrate such to be the case to the appellate courts; but nevertheless I will pay off a portion of it'; or will be heard to say: 'I demand that you accept from me, as a credit on your er-

roneous and unjust judgment, what you owe me
in respect of another account.' * * * In the case at
bar the sum of $54.40, the portion of the plain-
tiff's judgment which the defendant demanded
should be satisfied by the offset of its claim to that
amount, was in controversy. The defendant denied throughout the trial that it owed that sum,
or any sum whatever. The sum was in inseparable
portion of the entire judgment; and a recognition
of the validity and binding force of that portion
of such judgment cannot in law be regarded otherwise than as a recognition of the validity and
binding force of the whole. Whosover litigates a
claim, and, being defeated, pays the judgment, or
surrenders the subject-matter of the controversy,
waives his right to prosecute error therefrom.
State vs. Conkling, 54 Kan. 108, 37 Pac. 992; *Fen-
lon v. Goodwin,* 35 Kan. 123, 10 Pac. 553. It is no
answer to say that in these cases the entire judgment was paid, or the whole subject of controversy surrendered. There is no difference in principle between paying all or a part, or surrender-
ing all or a part, of a legally entire and indivisible
thing. * * *

We are quite clear the petition in error should
be dismissed, and it is so ordered.''

In the case of *In re Minot Auto Co., Inc.,* 298 Fed.
853, C. C. A. 8 Cir. (1924), the Circuit Court of Appeals say:

"Counsel for the respondent maintain that the
petitioner, having received and retained the full
amount awarded to it by the order of the referee,
has waived its right to have the order in question
reviewed. The rule is well settled that one cannot
accept a benefit under a judgment, and then ap-

peal from it, when the effect of the appeal may be to annul the judgment, unless his right to the benefit is absolute, and cannot be affected by the reversal of the judgment. *Embry vs. Palmer,* 107 U. S. 3, 8, 2 Sup. Ct. 25, 27 L. Ed. 346; *Gilfillan vs. McKee,* 159 U. S. 303, 311, 16 Sup. Ct. 6, 40 L. Ed. 161; *Albright vs. Oyster* (C. C. A. 8) 60 Fed. 644, 9 C. C. A. 173; *Worthington vs. Beeman* (C. C. A. 7) 91 Fed. 232, 33 C. C. A. 475; *Chase vs. Driver* (C. C. A. 8) 92 Fed. 780, 34 C. C. A. 668; *In re Letson* (C. C. A. 8) 157 Fed. 78, 84 C. C. A. 582; *Carson Lumber Co. vs. St. Louis & F. R. Co.* (C. C. A. 8) 209 Fed. 191, 126 C. C. A. 139; *Peck vs. Richter* (C. C. A. 8) 217 Fed. 880, 133 C. C. A. 590.''

See, also, *Carson Lumber Co. vs. St. Louis & S. F. R. Co.,* 209 Fed. 191, at 193, (C. C. A. 8):

"It is undoubtedly the general rule that a party who obtains the benefit of an order or judgment, and accepts the benefit or receives the advantage, shall be afterwards precluded from asking that the order or judgment be reviewed."

In the case of *Albright et al vs. Oyster, et al,* (C. C. A. 8, 1894), 60 Fed. 644, we quote from the syllabus the following:

"APPEAL—RIGHT TO APPEAL—ESTOPPEL.

Parties who, pursuant to the provisions of a decree, demand and receive a conveyance of lands from a trustee, are thereby estopped from appealing from the decree; for they cannot accept its benefits, and at the same time have a review in respect to its burdens."

The Velma L. Hamlin (C. C. A., 4th, 1930), 40 Fed.
(2) 852, 855:

"" * * For, except in the case where a judgment or decree represents an uncontroverted part of a demand, the ordinary rule is that one who accepts payment thereof will not be heard to question its correctness by appeal. 3 *C. J.* 681; 2 *R. C. L.* 63; Notes 45 *Am. St. Rep.* 271, and cases cited; *Ann. Cas.* 1914 C., 301."

West vs. Broadwell (Ore. 1928) 265 Pac. 783:

"A defeated litigant cannot accept a part of the benefits of the judgment and appeal from the remainder. He cannot accept and acquiesce in a part of the judgment and appeal from the remainder. This was expressly held to apply to costs and disbursements in *Moore vs. Floyd,* 4 Ore. 260, 261. This case was decided in 1872, and this court has adhered consistently to that principle ever since."

Winsor vs. Schaeffer (Mo. App.) 34 S. W. (2) 989:

"One cannot accept of, or acquiesce in judgment, and at same time appeal therefrom."

Nat'l. Bank of Summers of Hinton vs. Barton (W. Va.) 155 S. E. 907:

"Party may not appeal from decree under which he enjoys benefits inconsistent with appeal."

2 Cyc. 656:

"An act on the part of a defendant by which he impliedly recognizes the validity of a judgment against him operates as a waiver of his right to appeal therefrom, or to bring error to reverse it."

Smith vs. Smith (Okla. 1925), 236, Pac. 578 at 580-1:

"Can a man thus blow hot and cold at the same time? Can he question the correctness and validity of a judgment for one purpose while asserting its validity and binding force for another purpose? The case of the *City of Lawton vs. Ayres,* 40 Okla. 524, 139 P. 963, appears to be directly in point and decisive of the question presented by this motion to dismiss. In that case Ayres had recovered judgment against the City of Lawton, from which judgment the City of Lawton prosecuted proceedings in error to this court. On the motion to dismiss the appeal it appeared that subsequent to the rendition of the judgment against it the city of Lawton commenced proceedings for the purpose of funding certain warrant and judgment indebtedness, and among the judgments listed in said proceeding as an outstanding indebtedness against the city was the Ayres judgment. Justice Kane, in passing upon the motion to dismiss, said:

'The contention of the movant is that this proceeding constitutes a recognition on the part of the city of the validity of the judgment rendered against it, and a waiver of its right to appeal therefrom or to bring error to reverse it; we think this position is well taken. The rule is "that any act on the part of the defendant by which he impliedly recognized the validity of a judgment against him operates as a waiver to appeal therefrom, or to bring error to reverse it." 2 *Cyc.* 656. It is difficult to conceive a more solemn recognition by a municipality of the validity of a judgment rendered against it than is involved in a proceeding to find the same, under our statute.' "

State vs. Masse (S. C. Kan. 1913), 132 Pac. 1182:

> *Held*: Payment of costs bar to appeal. "The rule rests upon the recognition of the judgment as valid. *R. R. Co. vs. Murray*, 57 Kan. 697, 47 Pac. 835; 12 Cyc. 807, 808. This recognition is shown *by partial, as well as by full*, compliance. A judgment in such a case could not be valid, as to costs and invalid as to fine and imprisonment."

Party accepting benefits of part of judgment waives right of appeal as to unfavorable part thereof.

> *Pickering Lbr. Co. vs. Harris* (Okla.) 283 P. 563, 140 Okla. 303;
>
> *McLachlan vs. McLachlan,* (Cal. App.) 276 P. 627.

Acceptance of attorney fee in action to set aside former judgment construing will was waiver of right to appeal.

> *Fadely vs. Fadely* (Kan.) 276 P. 826, 128 Kan. 287.

Appellant's affidavit showing settlement of judgment appealed from, insofar as it related to costs, *held*, to require dismissal of appeal.

> *West vs. Broadwell* (Oregon) 265 P. 783, 124 Ore. 652.

3 *Corpus Juris* 669, Section 542:

> "As a general rule any act on the part of a party by which he expressly or impliedly recognizes the validity of a judgment, order, or decree against him *operates as a waiver of his right to appeal therefrom* or to bring error to reverse it."

The case of *Kansas City, etc. R. Co. vs. Murray,* 47 Pac. 835, has been cited with approval in the following cases:

> *Fidelity & Deposit Co. of Md. vs. Kepley* (Kan. 1903) 71 Pac. 819;
>
> *Seaverns vs. State* (Kan. 1907), 93 Pac. 164;
>
> *Elevert vs. Marley* (Ore. 1909) 99 Pac. 888;
>
> *State vs. Masse* (Kan. 1913) 132 Pac. 1183;
>
> *Smith vs. Smith* (Okla. 1925) 236 Pac. 581.

Kansas City, etc. Ry. vs. Murray, supra, is exactly and squarely in point on identical facts. There as here the appellant had set off a judgment for costs on a former appeal. The setoff was against a total and indivisible greater sum.

On the foregoing authorities and the record in this case, appellee moves to dismiss the appeal.

REPLY TO APPELLANT'S ARGUMENT ON SPECIFICATIONS OF ERROR
SPECIFICATION NO. I.

As its first specification of error, appellant contends that the court erred in admitting in evidence the testimony of Emil F. Schuman as to the visibility of the light in the cabin or pilot-house of the "Magna," immediately after the collision. Clearly appellant's position with respect to this testimony is unfounded, as said testimony is unquestionably admissible upon several grounds.

Captain Nelson, owner and master of the "Magna," described the arrangement, position and brilliancy of this stern light, and testified that there were no obstructions on the after part of the "Magna" to prevent an overtaking vessel from seeing this light if maintaining any lookout.

Emil F. Schuman, a passenger on board the "Olympic" at the time of the collision, testified that, as soon as the "Olympic" struck the "Magna," he *rushed* over to the window of the lower cabin where he was having lunch but could not see anything, so he *rushed* right upstairs to the upper deck, which did not take over a minute after the impact of collision. (Tr. 26, 27.) At the time he reached the upper deck, the "Olympic" was backing up, passing the "Magna" a couple of blocks before she stopped. The witness was then asked what, if any, lights of the "Magna" he observed from the deck of the "Olympic" as the latter vessel passed the "Magna" after backing up. Mr. Schuman testified as follows (Tr. 29, 30):

> "I saw a white light. Do you want me to state where I saw that light? It was a white light in the center of the door where you go down into the engine-room or cabin, whatever it may be, and I do not know whether there was another light in

the cabin or not, and the cabin was quite lit up and I could see Mr.—what is his name, the skipper. The door was open. The light was hanging right in the center where you step down into the engine-room. At that time I could see the stern of the vessel and deck of the vessel aft of the light. That is the time when I observed when the collision occurred. Somehow or other the boat shifted around a little to the left so that she was at a four or five degree angle from the "Olympic," and I could see the crushed side. *There was nothing on the stern of the boat which interfered with my vision of the light.* It was a white light. It looked like an electric light. It was a little over a hundred feet, I guess, away when I saw the light. It was getting dusk then. I could not observe the light closely. The white light appeared approximately four feet above the "Magna's" main deck. I did not see more than one white light at any time when we were passing the "Magna," either the first or second time. I saw a white light and the green light on the starboard at the same time, but do not remember seeing the red light. Then, after seeing those lights, I saw the light in the door.''

Unquestionably, this testimony was admissible upon the following grounds and for the following reasons:

(1). These observations, having taken place immediately (about one minute) after the impact of collision, are part of the *res gestae.*

"Facts as well as declarations may form parts of the *res gestae,* and be admissible for that reason, * * *." (10 R. C. L. 982, Sec. 164.)

(2). This testimony surely corroborates Captain Nelson relative to the existence of said stern light; the location thereof in the door-way of the pilot-house, facing aft; the brilliancy thereof; and the fact that there were no obstructions on the after deck of the "Magna."

(3). Irrespective of its corroborative value, this testimony clearly establishes the facts set forth in the last preceding paragraph.

If it appears that the physical condition afterwards is the same as at the time of the accident its condition after the accident may always be shown. This court has recognized this rule in numerous cases.

See: *Alaska S. S. Co. vs. Katzeek,* 16 Fed. (2d) 210, where Judge Gilbert said, at page 211:

> "This is not a case where evidence of a similar accident was introduced to prove the negligence of the defendant in the particular act declared upon. *Here the purpose of the evidence was to show that immediately after the accident the conditions had not changed and that the tackle used by the defendant was defective.* By the decided weight of authority evidence of similar accidents may be adduced, when it is given only to illustrate a physical fact before or after the occurrence which is under investigation and the conditions of that occurrence." Citing numerous cases.

See, also, *O'Brien vs. Las Vegas & T. R. Co.*, 242
Fed. 850, where Judge Gilbert in speaking for this
Court at page 852 says:

> "Where, in an action for personal injuries,
> the condition of machinery, appliances, or places
> for work, as they appeared within a reasonable
> time after the accident, warrants an inference as
> to the conditions existing at the time of the acci-
> dent, such condition may be given in evidence."

Citing 26 *Cyc.*, 1427, and many other cases.

SPECIFICATION II.

Next, appellant specifies error upon the court's
admitting testimony of the appellee as to the visibility
of the stern light of the "Magna," at times prior to
the day of the collision (appellant's Brief, pp. 28-31).

Counsel for appellant, in his argument upon this
specification of error, seems to us to take a decidedly
inconsistent and ridiculous position, viz: That the
burden is upon the appellee to prove that his failure
to have a stern light on his vessel exactly as prescribed
by the Rules *could not* have contributed to the collision; yet that the appellee should be precluded from
introducing any testimony tending to prove such issue. (Appellant's Brief, p. 30.)

After the appellee had testified as to the location
of the six volt electric light hanging in the doorway

of the after part of the pilothouse, about five feet above the main deck, showing aft, with the said door open at and prior to the collision, he was asked if this light was visible to one approaching from the stern. To this question he answered "Yes." He then testified that he had had occasion before the collision to be away from this vessel at night-time when he could see this light suspended in the doorway of the cabin of the "Magna;" that he had been on shore many times, and had seen that light burning half a mile away. (Tr. 39.)

This testimony is clearly admissible as competent proof upon one of the most important issues of the case, to-wit: Could this light have been seen by the officers of the "Olympic?" If Hans Nelson could see this very same light a half a mile away, surely Peter Garvey, the lookout of the "Olympic" could have seen it in time to have avoided this collision if he had been attending to his duties as lookout instead of fixing the curtains of the forward cabin with his back turned to the bow of the "Olympic" for four or five minutes immediately prior to the collision. According to the testimony of Van Bogaert, master of the "Olympic," no one else except Peter Garvey was on lookout. (Tr. 81.)

The only testimony given by Van Bogaert, master of the "Olympic," concerning the stern light of the "Magna" was that he *did not see it,* and not that "no light was visible upon the appellee's boat at any time prior to the collision," as counsel for appellant would have the court believe from his brief. (p. 30.) The law is too well settled for argument that the master in the pilot-house in charge of the navigation of his vessel, or the wheelsman steering the vessel, are not sufficient lookouts. It is not their duty. They were stationed in the pilot-house, the floor of which was about 27 feet above the water, and about 25 feet from the bow of the vessel. The place for the lookout, as set forth in innumerable decisions, is in the "eyes of the ship" as close to the water as possible. The courts, also, hold that testimony of the watch officers in the pilot-house that they did "not see the lights" of a vessel they are overtaking, is not proof that the lights were not burning. This is entirely consistent with the positive testimony of witnesses from the other vessel that their running lights *were burning.* See *The Buenos Aires* (C.C.A. 2, 1924), 5 Fed. (2d) 425, and cases therein cited. The positive testimony of those on the overtaken vessel that their lights were burning, being in a position to see the lights and know their condition, will not be lightly rejected because other persons, whose duty it was to have seen them, either failed to observe, or happened not to see them. Negative evidence of this character cannot be accepted to outweigh positive evidence. The failure to observe a light cannot be said to disprove its existence.

See: *The Buenos Aires* (C.C.A-2), 5 Fed. (2d) 425, 430;

The Fin MacCool (C.C.A.-2), 147 Fed. 123;

Horn vs. Baltimore & Ohio R. Co. (C.C.A.-6), 54 Fed. 301;

Rhodes vs. U. S. (C.C.A.-8), 79 Fed. 740;

Stitt vs. Huidekoper, 17 Wall. 393, 21 L. Ed. 644.

SPECIFICATION NO. III.

For this specification, appellant assigns error upon the court's denial of appellant's motions for a directed verdict. (Appellant's Brief, p. 21.) In his argument on this specification of error, counsel's only basis for his contention is that the appellee was guilty of contributory negligence as a matter of law. (Appellant's Brief, p. 31.)

Appellant lays great stress on the fact that because the stern light of the "Magna" was not visible all around the horizon that the case should have been taken from the jury on the motion for non-suit.

Breach of statutory duty is not important if the breach did not and could not have contributed to the collision. The mere failure to show all around the horizon could not possibly have affected a vessel coming up from astern almost dead aft. The failure of this light to show forward of the beam and to shed its rays in the forward hemisphere of the vessel, viz., from the beam on one side, around forward through the arc of the half circle to the beam on the other side, could not possibly have helped the overtaking vessel. We call the court's attention to the navigation lights which are required by the International Rules, for an ocean going vessel. The stern light shall only show through 135 degrees, from 2 points abaft the beam on one side, around the stern to a place 2 points abaft the beam on the other side. The ocean going vessel is not required to have a range light, the function of which is to have two white lights at the mast heads so that when vessels are on meeting or are travelling upon crossing courses the range of the lights as they open and close will more accurately show the exact course of the approaching vessels. The range light serves no purpose when a vessel is overtaking another from aft or nearly aft on the same course. On these facts, assuming that Captain Nelson was telling the truth about his stern light, it is idle to say that because this particular stern light did not shed its rays outward from the fore part of the "Magna" so as to have been seen by a vessel approaching the "Magna" on a meeting or crossing course, that such failure could possibly have affected the "Olympic" coming up astern.

Appellant's argument supporting his third specification wholly disregarded the matter of the natural light of day. The "Magna" was in plain view out on the water ahead of the "Olympic." If they saw what Emil F. Schuman and his wife easily observed, viz., the hull of the "Magna" out on the water several hundred feet away from the "Olympic" at a time after the collision, the jury, believing them, could easily have found that the presence or absence of a light on board the "Magna" had nothing at all to do with seeing the "Magna" if those on board had been attending to their duties. We know the lookout on the "Olympic" was not attending to his duty. We know the wheelsman could not have done his duty steering the vessel if he had spent his time trying to do what the lookout, Garvey, was employed to do. And the master's failure to see the "Magna" in the twilight could easily have been explained by the fact that he was engaged in checking his courses or attending to his navigation and did not see what he readily could and should have seen.

Counsel for appellant cites at great length from this court's previous decision in this case, which is undoubtedly the rule of law herein. In its previous decision, this court, following *Belden vs. Chase,* held that contributory negligence is a complete defense. Counsel's argument upon this specification may very well have been a fitting argument to have been presented to the jury. In fact, it is the *very argument* Mr. Bronson did make to the jury. But the jury, by their verdict, refused to accept Mr. Bronson's statements as to the facts of the case. He is now attempting to place the same argument before this court in an extreme effort to so cloud the issues in such a manner as to have the court accept his version of the case, irrespective of the testimony adduced by the appellees.

We contend that there was ample evidence to support the verdict of the jury, and for that reason appellant's motions for a directed verdict should have been overruled.

We shall not burden the court with restating the evidence in support of appellee's cause of action, but only refer to the same as set forth at some length at the opening of this brief. We respectfully submit that, from this testimony, it amply appears not only that for all practical purposes the stern light of the "Magna" was sufficient; but, also, that the natural light of day was such that the "Magna" would have easily been seen by the officers and lookout of the "Olympic" if they had been attentive to looking out.

SPECIFICATION NO. IV.

Appellant assigns error upon the court's refusal to give the specific instructions requested by it. (Appellant's brief, pp. 34-39.)

Appellant's first requested instruction, for the failure to give which error is now assigned, merely sets forth the prescribed lights, and then closes with the instruction that the failure of the "Magna" to carry the stern light as prescribed by the Act was a fault sufficient to fix plaintiff (appellee) with at least contributory fault for the collision, requiring the jury to return a verdict for the defendant unless the jury should find that the failure to carry such white light aft to show all around the horizon, by the "Magna," *could not have* been one of the causes of the collision.

The trial court did instruct the jury very fully and accurately regarding the prescribed lights for the "Magna." (Tr. 96-98.) *In this instruction, the court put particular emphasis upon the white light aft to show all around the horizon.* (Tr. 97.)

At Tr. 102, the court very clearly and emphatically instructed the jury as follows:

> "Now, Lady and Gentlemen of the Jury, the law is, with respect to this light, that if it is not in the place and the kind of a light which the law requires it to be, if a collision occurs, it imposes the burden upon the plaintiff to satisfy you that the light differing from the light established by law could not have been any part of the cause of the collision."

Again at Tr. 112, *the court read to the jury, word for word, the written instruction prepared and requested by Mr. Bronson regarding contributory negligence as being a complete bar:*

> "Under the facts in this case, the failure of the 'Magna' to carry the prescribed white light aft to show all around the horizon, is a fault sufficient to fix the plaintiff with at least contributing fault for the collision between the vessels and consequent loss and damage, if any, suffered by the plaintiff, requiring you to return a verdict for the defendant, unless you shall find that the failure to carry a white light aft to show all around the horizon, by the 'Magna', could not have been one of the causes of the collision by this defendant vessel following from behind."

We submit that these instructions meet every requirement of the previous decision of this court upon this phase of the case.

Regarding appellant's requested instruction that the officers of the "Olympic" had a right to assume that no vessel was ahead, we submit that this general matter was properly submitted to the jury under instructions relating to burden of proof. The specific instruction requested is obviously incorrect in that the proof of all of the witnesses testifying upon the subject was that the "Olympic" had no lookout whatsoever for a period of four or five minutes before the collision. The master of the "Olympic" very frankly admitted that the only one on lookout was Peter Garvey, who was engaged with his back turned to the bow of the "Olympic" fixing curtains for four or five minutes immediately preceding the collision. To have given the instruction requested (appellant's brief, pp. 36-37) would have been equivalent to putting the court's "stamp of approval" upon a ferry boat such as the "Olympic" travelling in congested waters without any lookout whatsoever. Such would have been, in effect, to have overruled every decision upon the subject of competent and attentive lookouts.

SPECIFICATION NO. V.

As its fifth specification, appellant assigns error upon the instructions as given by the court. (Appellant's brief, pp. 39-54.)

Since the instructions should be construed in their entirety, it seems grossly unfair that Mr. Bronson, for the appellant, should omit in his brief the correct instructions upon the phase of the case to which he is most strenuously objecting and assigning error, viz: The effect of appellee's failure to carry a stern light, as prescribed by the Rules, to show all around the horizon.

In replying to counsel's argument on specification No. IV, we set forth the court's instructions upon this issue of the case, in which he advises the jury, in no uncertain terms, that in order to find for the plaintiff (appellee) they must find that the failure of the plaintiff to carry the prescribed range light not only *did not* but *could not* have contributed to the collision.

Mr. Bronson, at the conclusion of the court's charge to the jury, took an exception to the court's failure to fully instruct the jury upon this issue of the case, whereupon the court immediately corrected any misstatement or omission relative to the effect of contributory negligence by reading to the jury the identical instruction prepared and requested by Mr. Bronson as follows (Tr. 112):

"Under the facts in this case, the failure of the 'Magna' to carry the prescribed white light aft to show all around the horizon, is a fault suffi-

> cient to fix the plaintiff with at least contributing
> fault for the collision between the vessels and con-
> sequent loss and damage, if any, suffered by the
> plaintiff, requiring you to return a verdict for
> the defendant, unless you shall find that the fail-
> ure to carry a white light aft to show all around
> the horizon, by the 'Magna,' could not have been
> one of the causes of the collision by this defen-
> dant vessel following from behind.''

We do not find it necessary to take issue with Mr.
Bronson concerning the numerous cases cited in his
brief upon this point, as we are governed by the previous decision of this court upon the former appeal of
this case. And we respectfully submit that the instructions given by the court meet every requirement of
said decision. The court, upon the second trial, placed
the burden squarely upon the shoulders of appellee
(plaintiff) to prove that his failure to carry the prescribed range light not only *did not* but *could not* have
contributed to the collision.

In order that there may be no doubt concerning
the law relative to the court's power to correct his instructions, we call attention to the recent case of *An-
thony O'Boyle vs. Northwestern Fire & Marine Ins.
Co.* (C.C.A.-2), 1931 A.M.C. 1385, where it was held
that in an action on a policy of marine insurance,
where the court erroneously charges the jury in regard to the burden of proof, but subsequently, and

before the jury had finished its deliberations, corrected the charge and properly instructed them, such previous error is cured and the defendant has no complain upon appeal.

The cases cited by appellant merely serve as a digest upon the matter, not inconsistent with said previous decision of this court. This being a trial at law before a jury (as distinguished from the admiralty cases cited by appellant), the question as to whether the failure of appellee (plaintiff) to provide the "Magna" with the prescribed stern light *could have contributed to the collision* is a matter to be presented to the jury under proper instructions, which, we submit, was done in this case.

SPECIFICATION NO. VI.

Finally, counsel for appellant assigns error upon the instruction given by the court pertaining to "negative vs. positive" testimony. (Appellant's brief, pp. 54-55.)

In this case, Hans Nelson, the appellee, testified *positively* that his stern light was burning brightly at the time of the collision, and had been burning brightly since leaving Ballard. He testified *positively* regarding the location of this light, its brilliancy, and the visibility thereof from an overtaking vessel. Emil

F. Schuman testified *positively* that he saw this light from the deck of the "Olympic" *immediately* after the collision. As against this *positive* testimony regarding this stern light, we have the *negative* testimony of the master and wheelsman of the "Olympic" that they *did not see this stern light.*

In view of this testimony, the court very properly instructed the jury that positive testimony of this nature is entitled to more weight generally than negative testimony that a witness "did not see it." The court further instructed the jury that it was for them to say whether this rule of law was applicable in this case.

The law is too well settled to admit argument that "positive evidence that lights were burning brightly *will* ordinarily outweigh negative testimony that lights were not seen.

See: *"Annie"-"Commonwealth,"* (D. Alaska), 1928
A.M.C. 1114;

"Annie"-Commonwealth," (C.C.A.-9), 1930 A.
M.C. 38, 36 Fed. (2d) 581;

"Gillen"-"Van Dyck," (D.C.-E.D.-N.Y.) 1929
A.M.C. 1358;

"Lakewood"-"Mohegan," (C.C.A.-2) 1928 A.
M.C. 1759;

"Columbia F. C., (C.C.A.-4) 1928 A.M.C. 1211,
26 Fed. (2d) 583;

"Hendrick Hudson"-"Juliette," (D.C.-E.D.-N.
Y.) 1928 A.M.C. 428;

"Socony No. 14"-"Worthington" (E.D.-N.Y.)
1928 A.M.C. 1361;

"The Buenos Aires" (C.C.A.-2-1924), 5 Fed.
(2d) 425;

"The Fin MacCool," (C.C.A.-2, 1906) 147 Fed.
123;

"Skanstad"-"Lake Charles," 1929, A.M.C. 148.

In the case of *"The Buenos Aires," supra,* the Circuit Court of Appeals for the Second Circuit, in quoting from *"The Fin MacCool," supra,* holds as follows:
(5 Fed. (2d) at p. 430.)

"We again call attention to what this court
said in *The Fin MacCool,* 147 F. 123, 77 C.C.A.
349, where we remarked as follows:

'The case is one for the application of the rule
of evidence that positive evidence is ordinarily
to prevail over strictly negative evidence, and
that when one or more witnesses testify that they
saw an object or heard a signal upon a given occasion, their testimony is to prevail over that of
a same number of witnesses, of equal candor, who
testify that they did not see or heard it. There
is, in such cases, no necessary conflict of evidence as to the fact in question. The observation
of the fact by some of the witnesses may be entirely consistent with the failure of the others to
observe it, or their forgetfulness of its occurrence. *Horn vs. Balt. & Ohio R. Co.,* 54 F. 301, 4
C.C.A. 346, 351; *Rhodes vs. U. S.,* 79 F. 740, 21 L.

Ed. 644, 25 C.C.A. 186; *Stitt vs. Huidekoper,* 17 Wall. 393. Of course, in each case the opportunities of observation, and the interest prompting the witnesses to attentive observation are to be considered; and the rule referred to is not inexorable, but is to be applied with due regard to the circumstances of the particular case. The whole subject is excellently treated in 17 Cyc. pp. 801-803, where all the authorities are collected'.''

In *"Annie" - "Commonwealth"* (Booth Fisheries Co, vs. Hans Danielson) *supra,* this court remarked as follows (1930 A.M.C. 38, at 39):

"The two witnesses on board the Annie at the time of the collision testified that her lights were burning brightly. Three witnesses on board the Commonwealth testified that they saw no lights. The former testimony was positive and the latter negative in its character. The testimony was taken largely in open court, and the finding of the court, based on conflicting testimony, if there was such conflict, should not be disturbed. And if the lights on the Annie were burning brightly as found by the court, it follows almost as a matter of course that the Commonwealth did not maintain a sufficient lookout, or that the lookout did not attend properly to his duties. *New York,* 175 U. S. 187, 204.''

In conclusion, it is respectfully submitted that the appellant has been accorded a fair and proper trial in this case. It is further submitted that there is ample testimony in the record to support the verdict of the jury, and that the instructions given by the court were in entire accordance with the previous decision of the court upon the former appeal. It is therefore earnestly urged that this appeal be dismissed.

Respectfully submitted,

WINTER S. MARTIN

ARTHUR COLLETT, JR.

HARRY S. REDPATH

Attorneys for Appellee.